assessment of young children

Libby G. Cohen
University of Southern Maine

Loraine J. Spenciner
University of Maine at Farmington

Longman
New York & London

Assessment of Young Children

Longman, 10 Bank Street, White Plains, N.Y. 10606

Associated companies:
Longman Group Ltd., London
Longman Cheshire Pty., Melbourne
Longman Paul Pty., Auckland
Copp Clark Pitman, Toronto

This book is dedicated to the children and families
from whom we have learned so much
and to our students and colleagues
who continue to help us refine our ideas.

Acquisitions editor: Stuart B. Miller
Sponsoring editor: Naomi Silverman
Production editor: Linda W. Witzling
Cover design: Judy Forster
Cover illustration: Rita Langlois
Production supervisor: Richard Bretan

Library of Congress Cataloging-in-Publication Data

Cohen, Libby G.
    Assessment of young children / Libby G. Cohen, Loraine J.
Spenciner.
       p. cm.
    Includes bibliographical references.
    ISBN 0-8013-0965-4
    1. Psychological tests for children. 2. Child development–
Testing. 3. Behavioral assessment of children. 4. Educational
tests and measurements. I. Spenciner, Loraine J. II. Title.
BF722.C64   1993
153.9′4′00083—dc20   92-35208
                                         CIP

3 4 5 6 7 8 9 10-MA-989796

Contents

CHAPTER 14   INTERPRETING AND REPORTING ASSESSMENT INFORMATION   463

Preface

Assessment of young children is an integral part of intervention. Our primary goal in writing this book was to provide a clearly written, well-organized introductory guide to the assessment of infants, toddlers, and young children from birth to eight years of age. This book will provide the reader with a basic understanding of the assessment process, assist in helping to develop assessment skills, and show how the results of assessment are linked to planning for instruction.

RECENT DEVELOPMENTS

This book, which reflects recent changes in the field of early intervention, includes up-to-date material on legislation relating to early intervention and assessment. Other chapters address the technical aspects of tests and the assessment of general development, adaptive development, cognition, and achievement. Individual tests are discussed in depth, and we hope that the book will also serve as a reference to professionals. Separate chapters are included on the following topics:

- The family's role in the assessment process
- Observing young children in their environments
- Assessing play
- Using alternative assessment instruments
- Program evaluation
- Report writing

We have tried to be sensitive to issues of cultural and linguistic diversity. We have included numerous examples, figures, and tables that help to explain and elaborate on the material that is discussed. The use of assessment information is illustrated through case studies.

ORGANIZATION

Each chapter begins with a set of goals. We hope that the reader will be well on the way to meeting these goals by the end of the chapter. Key terms are introduced and defined before they are used in the chapter. Each chapter concludes with a section called "Preferred Practices" in which we summarize key points from the chapter and highlight best professional practices. Finally, at the end of each chapter, we offer a group of questions for reflection.

SUPPLEMENTARY MATERIAL

An Instructor's Manual includes chapter outlines, transparency masters, class activities, discussion questions, and a test bank.

ACKNOWLEDGMENTS

We extend our grateful appreciation to the many people who helped and supported us in the development of this book. We are especially grateful to Sharon Rosenkoetter from the Associated College of Central Kansas, who provided an insightful and comprehensive review of the manuscript. Other manuscript reviewers were

Carolyn Cooper, Eastern Illinois University

Merith Cosden, University of California, Santa Barbara

Ann Cairns Federlein, University of Northern Iowa

Susan Hupp, University of Minnesota

Barbara Lowenthal, Northeastern Illinois University

We are deeply grateful for the helpful advice of Toni Rees in developing the chapter on specialized testing and to Bob Atkinson for sharing his work on life stories. We appreciate the help of Harvey Berman and Peter Macpherson of the Spurwink School.

Thank you to the many publishers and agencies who granted us permission to reproduce their materials. We extend our deepest thanks to Nancy Lightbody for her generous and invaluable help. Grateful thanks to Jane Blais, Julie Gillies, Catherine Landry, Julie Mennella, Becky Neidetcher, and Shelia Nurse for their assistance with the development of this book. To our students Wendy Deming, Brenda Drapeau, Catherine Hall, Kim Labbe, Sissy Newenham, Jane Scanlon, and Mary Zutautas, many thanks for reviewing an early draft. A very special thank you is extended to Pearl Wuthrich for her patience, support, and good humor. And, thanks to Dale Blanchard for his support. We deeply appreciate the help and assistance of the editorial and production staff at Longman—thank you to Linda Witzling, Stuart Miller, Deborah L. Moore, and Brenda Griffing.

Finally, we are especially grateful to our families, Les, Seth, Jay, Amy, Dave, Dina, and Ruth—we couldn't have completed this book without your support.

COVER ARTIST

Rita Langlois is a self-taught artist who works primarily in watercolor and ink. Her art comes from her imagination and she enjoys painting people and houses.

Rita's work is in numerous private and public collections and has been featured in several galleries and museums. Rita lives in Brunswick, Maine, and is part of SPINDLEWORKS, an artists' cooperative where her talent and dedication are encouraged and supported.

CHAPTER 1

A Window on Assessment

CHAPTER OBJECTIVES

A new child will be joining an early education program soon. During an initial meeting with the family, one of the parents shares several concerns she has about her child's development with the staff. What procedures should be followed now? How can a child's needs be determined? Could the child benefit from special services? How is eligibility determined for early intervention and for special education and related services? What are some approaches for measuring the child's progress? Early childhood teachers and other practitioners face many questions like these.

The purposes of this chapter are to provide a rationale for assessing children with disabilities and children at risk for disabilities and to introduce you to the steps in the assessment process. The chapter begins by providing an overview of federal legislation related to the assessment of young children. We will examine some of the differences in legislation that applies to children from birth through the age of two years, from three to five years, and from five to eight years. This information will provide the reader with an understanding of the public laws and their effect on children and their families.

Upon completing this chapter, you should be able to:

Describe the general requirements for assessment as mandated by federal legislation.

Provide a rationale for the participation of families in the assessment process.

Describe the different steps and purposes of the assessment process.

Describe the different teaming approaches to assessment: multidisciplinary, interdisciplinary, and transdisciplinary.

Differentiate among the various models of assessment: direct, indirect, and arena assessment.

Understand the general considerations involved in assessing young children.

Discuss some of the issues related to assessing children who come from diverse cultures.

Understand issues of confidentiality and family rights.

CASE STUDY: A WINDOW ON ASSESSMENT

September 15 will be forever etched in my memory. That day was the beginning. . . . My new job. As a teacher (and home visitor!) who would be working with 7 to 12 children in their homes and at school, I wondered about the different needs the children coming into the program might have. The program director had explained that, although most of the children were developing typically, some concerns had been raised about three of the children, and vision or hearing impairments were suspected for two.

The first day at work included a home visit with the family of one of the children who would be coming into our early childhood program. On my way to their home, I tried to recapture some of the enthusiasm I'd felt when I first read the job description: "Teacher of young children with training and experience in working with children with disabilities wanted for innovative program. Travel required."

The child's name was Scott. Walking up the steps to his house, I clutched my bag of assorted toys. This initial visit would allow me to observe Scott in his natural environment, a beginning in our assessment process. Scott's mother was waiting at the door. Our conversation that morning covered Scott's developmental history, including several hospital stays, and outlined the family's daily routines.

Scott was three years old with bright blue eyes and a devilish grin. His language was limited to a few words, which I had difficulty understanding. Scott's mother was looking forward to registering him at our neighborhood preschool program next week, but she was also anxious about letting him attend. During this first visit she began to share some of her concerns for Scott. Did I think that he should be talking by now? Would he get along with the other children? What activities would he do? I began to wonder if we should arrange an early childhood team meeting to make some plans.

. . . and so began my acquaintance with Scott and his family. Over that year, my visits to the home provided opportunities to gather family members' comments and suggestions and to discuss Scott's progress at home and school. In addition, Scott's parents were able to provide important feedback to the program staff during our program evaluation in the spring.

WORKING WITH CHILDREN AND THEIR FAMILIES

Infants, Toddlers, and Preschoolers

Young children who can benefit from special services are identified much earlier today than ever before. Infants as well as toddlers and their families are able to receive early intervention services because their needs are identified early. In fact, many infants with or at risk for disability are identified before leaving the hospital, while others are identified during the first year of life.

In the past, preschoolers with or at risk for disability would not have received services. Today these children may be initially identified through community screening clinics. Further assessment may indicate that they are eligible for special services within a variety of regular early childhood programs, without waiting until they reach school age.

Children Ages Five through Eight

Many school-based programs are placing less emphasis on traditional teacher-centered academics while including more developmental activities that allow children to learn through exploration and manipulation of materials. Other programming options include nongraded classrooms, designed to include children who are six, seven, or eight years old. Learning activities involve children of different ages working and playing together.

In these various settings, children with special needs are supported within the regular classroom through teaching teams that include both regular and special educators, as well as therapists, specialists, or consultants.

Key Terms

Free Appropriate Public Education (FAPE). PL 101–476 (reauthorization of PL 94–142 and PL 99–457) specifies that each child with a disability between the ages of three and twenty-one must have an opportunity to attend public school and to receive services that address the individual unique needs at no cost to the family.

Child Find. One of the provisions of PL 101–476 (reauthorization of PL 94–142), Child Find is a series of activities that increase public awareness by providing information about screening and intervention.

Due Process. Another provision of PL 101–476 (reauthorization of PL 94–142). This is a procedure followed during assessment and throughout the delivery of services. Due process ensures that the rights of children and their families are not violated.

Least Restrictive Environment (LRE). PL 101–476 (reauthorization of PL 94–142) specifies that children and youth with disabilities be educated to the maximum extent appropriate with children who are nondisabled, while also meeting the child's needs for special and related services. In addition, PL 101–476 specifies that to maximize opportunities for interaction with nondisabled peers, nonacademic and extracurricular services and activities be offered.

Early Childhood Team. A team includes parents, the family service coordinator, and other practitioners from various disciplines who assess and implement early childhood intervention services.

Individualized Family Service Plan (IFSP). PL 101–476 mandates that all young children (birth through two years) and their families have an IFSP. Children aged three to five years may receive services provided by an IFSP or an IEP. An IFSP is a written document that specifies the plan for early intervention services and is guided by the family's concerns, priorities, and resources.

Individualized Education Program (IEP). PL 101–476 mandates that all children and youth (aged three to twenty-one years) who require special education services have a written education plan called an IEP. (Children aged three to five may have an IFSP if state policy allows and if the parents concur.)

IMPACT OF FEDERAL LEGISLATION ON ASSESSMENT PRACTICES

To ensure that children with special needs and their families receive the appropriate services, their needs and concerns are identified through the assessment process. Many of the procedures used in assessment practices today are mandated by federal legislation. In the following section, we examine the federal legislation (Table 1.1) in relation to assessment issues.

Locating Young Children with or At Risk for Disabilities

The Early Periodic Screening, Diagnosis, and Treatment Program. One of the first efforts to locate young children who are disabled or at risk began in 1967 with the Early Periodic Screening, Diagnosis, and Treatment (EPSDT) Program. This nationwide program, which was created as part of Medicaid and the Maternal and Child Health Program, focuses on children from birth through age five whose families meet certain income requirements. The EPSDT Program attempts to locate and overcome medical and developmental difficulties through regular screenings and assessments of children. The program also refers children for medical care and provides treatment if needed.

PL 94–142, The Education for All Handicapped Children Act.   This public law guaranteed the right of *all* school-aged children to a free appropriate public education and defined the criteria according to which children ages 5 to 21 could be eligible for special education and related services. In addition, this law set forth requirements that all children from birth through 21 years of age who might have a disability be identified and evaluated. This process is known as *Child Find.*

Federal Legislation and Early Intervention Services for Infants, Toddlers, and Families

In 1986 PL 99–457 was passed to encourage states to institute early intervention services for infants, toddlers, and families and to develop guidelines for statewide systems. Within a few years, all 50 states had agreed to participate. PL 99–457 defined the areas of eligibility for infants and toddlers and also included an option for states that choose to serve very young children (from birth through age two) who are *at risk* of having a substantial developmental delay.

Federal legislation passed in 1991 (PL 102–119) further defined the provision of early intervention services and areas of eligibility. The following list indicates the areas of eligibility for these very young children.

TABLE 1.1 Highlights of federal legislation and the assessment process

Date	Legislation	Description
1967	Early Periodic Screening, Diagnosis, and Treatment Program	The Early Periodic Screening, Diagnosis, and Treatment Program focuses on identifying health problems and developmental disabilities in preschool children whose families meet certain income requirements.
1974	PL 93–380 Family Educational Rights and Privacy Act (FERPA)	The Family Educational Rights and Privacy Act prevents educational agencies from releasing student information without written consent from the child's parents.
1975	PL 94–142 The Education for All Handicapped Children Act	The Education for All Handicapped Children Act (later amended in 1990 by PL 101–476, known as the Individuals with Disabilities Education Act) defines eligibility criteria according to which school-aged children with disabilities may receive special education or related services. In addition, this public law requires that all children from birth through twenty-one years of age who may have a disability be identified and evaluated.
1986	PL 99–457 The Education of the Handicapped Act Amendments	The Education of the Handicapped Act Amendments (later included in PL 101–476) mandate the same provision of services to preschool-age children (ages three to five years). The law now requires that families be involved at all levels of identification, assessment, and intervention. In addition, these amendments provide incentives for states to provide interdisciplinary early intervention services to infants and toddlers.
1990	PL 101–476 Individuals with Disabilities Education Act (IDEA)	The Individuals with Disabilities Education Act (the reauthorization of PL 94–142 and PL 99–457) further defines eligibility criteria for persons with disabilities, aged three to twenty-one years, to receive special educational or related services. The language of this law emphasizes "people first, then the disability."
1991	PL 102–119 Individuals with Disabilities Education Act Amendments	The amendments to the Individuals with Disabilities Education Act allow noncategorical definitions for eligibility for children aged three to five years under the term "developmental delay," according to a state's discretion. This law also permits local educational agencies to use Individualized Family Service Plans (IFSPs) in lieu of Individualized Education Programs (IEPs) for children aged three to five years if consistent with state policy and with concurrence of the parents.

Areas of Development in which Infants and Toddlers (from birth through two years) with Disabilities May Receive Services

- Cognitive development
- Physical development (including vision and hearing)
- Communication development
- Social and emotional development
- Adaptive development (self-help skills)
- Diagnosed physical or mental condition that is highly likely to result in developmental delay (Education of the Handicapped Act Amendments, 1986, Sec. 672[1]; Individuals with Disabilities Education Act Amendments, 1991, Sec. 12[a])

The types of service outlined by federal legislation for eligible children include a wide variety of options depending on the child and the family's needs. These services include but are not limited to (Education of the Handicapped Act Amendments 1986, Sec. 672):

- Medical services for diagnosis and evaluation
- Early identification, screening, and assessment services
- Special instruction
- Speech pathology and audiology
- Occupational or physical therapy
- Family training, counseling, and home visits
- Nursing services
- Nutritional services
- Psychological services
- Case coordination

Later, PL 102–119 added the following services (Individuals with Disabilities Act Amendments, 1991, Sec. 12[b]):

- Vision services, including orientation and mobility specialists
- Assistive technology devices and services
- Transportation and related costs
- Family therapists
- Pediatricians and other physicians

The Early Childhood Team.   The early childhood team includes the child's parents or guardian, the family service coordinator, and other representatives of a variety of disciplines (occupational therapy, physical therapy, social work, speech and language pathology, etc.), depending on the needs of the child and family. Team members work together in assessing the needs of the child. Information regarding the needs of the family should be gathered only with permission of the family. After the initial assessment has been completed, the team meets to plan the early intervention services and to write a plan for providing services and assessing progress. This plan is called the Individualized Family Service Plan (IFSP). All children (birth through two years of age) who receive early intervention services are required to have an IFSP. Older children (ages three to five years) may have an IFSP rather than an IEP as long as (1) the IFSP is consistent with state policy and (2) the parents concur (*Federal Register,* 1992, p. 44796).

The Individualized Family Service Plan.   The Individualized Family Service Plan (IFSP) is a document developed by the early childhood team and based on assessment information. This plan for each infant or toddler and the family should include (Education of the Handicapped Act Amendments, 1986, Sec. 677[d]; Individuals with Disabilities Education Act Amendments, 1991, Sec. 14[c]):

1. A statement of the child's present level of development: physical, cognitive, communication, social, emotional, and adaptive (self-help skills), based on acceptable objective criteria.
2. An optional statement of the family's concerns, resources, and priorities related to enhancing their child's development. As noted earlier, this information, called *family-directed assessment,* is gathered only with parental permission.
3. A statement of the major outcomes expected to be achieved for the child and family, and the criteria, procedures, and timelines used to document progress.
4. A statement of specific early intervention services necessary to meet the needs of the child and family, including the frequency, the intensity, and the method of delivering services.
5. A statement of the natural environments in which early intervention services will be provided.
6. The projected dates for the beginning of services and the anticipated duration.
7. The name of the family service coordinator who will be responsible for the implementation of the plan and coordination with other agencies and persons.
8. The date for periodic review of the IFSP (at 6-month intervals or more frequently when appropriate) and the date for reevaluation (at 12 months or more frequently when appropriate).
9. The steps to be taken supporting the transition of the toddler to preschool or into other appropriate placement(s) if the child is no longer eligible for intervention services. (Practitioners should note that in some states the eligibility criteria for toddlers and for preschoolers differ. These important considerations in implementing the transition between service systems and their implications for children and families are discussed later in this chapter.)
10. The contents of the plan will be fully explained to the parents or guardian, who must give written consent prior to provision of services described in the plan. If consent is not provided with respect to a particular early intervention service, then early intervention services to which consent is given will be provided.

Team members should be aware that assessment of each child (including the needs identified by the family) must be completed within 45 calendar days from the time the child is referred to the team. The law also provides that the team, with the consent of the parents, may begin early intervention services before the assessment has been completed if an interim IFSP is written (Education of the Handicapped Act Amendments, 1986, p. 12).

CASE STUDY: TWIN GIRLS BETHANY AND BELINDA, AGE TWO

Setting: The Southwest Community Parent Child Center provides home-based intervention for families who are income eligible. The center is part of the national Parent and Child Center Program, which focuses on parents and children from birth to three years and works collaboratively with the Southwest Community Head Start Program.

Bethany and Belinda A. and their mother participate in the Southwest Community Parent Child Center. The home visitor comes to see Bethany and Belinda every Monday and encourages the twins (and their mother) in activities that promote language development and social skills. The twins' mother looks forward to these visits because she can talk freely about her concerns and feel that someone is listening. On Wednesdays, the girls attend a center-based program for play and socialization. Both girls have been exhibiting aggressive behavior in the home as well as at the center, and the home visitor and center staff have observed the girls hit and push other children frequently in play activities. On some days they are destructive to materials in the center.

Ms. A. works a night shift to support the family. At this point, the mother is feeling overwhelmed. The parent, with the assistance and support of the home visitor, made a referral to the community early childhood team. She hoped that the team could develop some suggestions for help in managing the girls' behavior in the home. She also hoped that the girls' language skills could be assessed. A convenient meeting was scheduled, and the Head Start educational coordinator discussed parental rights and procedures for determining eligibility for early intervention services.

The early childhood team meeting was attended by Ms. A., the speech and language pathologist, the Head Start home visitor, the Head Start educational coordinator and special needs assistant, and the PCC early intervention specialist. The team discussed the girls separately. Several members of the team shared their observations about Bethany's current level of language development. Other members suggested immediate ways of addressing the mother's concerns regarding behavior problems at home and at the center. Team members agreed to begin by having Bethany's vision and hearing screened to ensure that the behavioral outbursts were not due to a sensory problem (such as intermittent otitis media).

At the next team meeting, vision and hearing results were discussed. Bethany had passed both tests, so the team decided to gather additional information regarding the behavioral outbursts. The early intervention specialist offered to do several observations of the girls at home as well as at the center. The team also decided that Bethany should receive a speech and language assessment.

When all the information had been gathered, the team met again. Ms. A. indicated that she would like some additional help with behavior management strategies. The team members also agreed that Bethany should increase her use of verbal language. The intervention services that would help achieve these outcomes were included as part of the written plan for assisting this family, the Individualized Family Service Plan (Figure 1.1). The team decided to meet again in three months, or sooner if needed.

In PL 99–457, the beginning of family-focused legislation, the individual needs of the child are viewed within the context of the family. Services are designed to build on family strengths and resources and to empower the family to support and enhance the development of the child.

What does "family-focused" mean to practitioners? Working within this context means addressing a family's identified needs. For example, one family may make feeding needs of the child a priority for early intervention services. Family members may request assistance on procedures to improve liquid intake as well as information about a local parent support group for high-risk infants. The early childhood team would identify these needs in the IFSP and would include an outcome statement such as, "Mary and James (Mr. and Mrs. Sanders) will receive help with feeding techniques so that Baby Jo will begin to take liquids and grow stronger." One of the activities described to meet this outcome might be: "Joanie Turio, public health nurse, will come to their home twice a week to work with Mr. and Mrs. Sanders on feeding."

Families are not just recipients of information provided by other team members; they are providers of and active participants in the assessment process, as well. PL 99–457 created new awareness and support for the role of the family in the care and education of a young child with a disability. Information that a family has gathered and observed about the child is of critical importance to the assessment process. In fact, families are likely to have information about the child's developmental progress that would not be readily obtained in direct observation by a professional or by more formal testing (Cunningham & Davis, 1985). Family members know about the child's typical functioning at home and in the community, and they have information about interaction with siblings, neighborhood children, and grandparents. This information is critical in understanding the child's strengths and needs. In addition to providing valuable data, the family can confirm or modify the information obtained by other team members during the assessment process.

The emphasis on the active role of families in early intervention has encouraged the search for new terminology. Bennett, Lingerfelt, and Nelson (1990) suggest that the *S* in IFSP might stand for *Support,* to better reflect the emphasis on enabling and assisting families.

There is a growing recognition of the importance of continued emphasis on the strengths, needs, and resources of the *family* even as children and families move from infant and toddler services to services for the preschool child. Some states specify that IFSPs be used not only for infants and toddlers but for preschoolers as well. Yet, even when state law does not specify, best practices suggest writing an IFSP for preschool children rather than an IEP.

FIGURE 1.1 Sample pages of a fictitious IFSP

SOUTHWEST COMMUNITY HEAD START PARENT CHILD CENTER

INDIVIDUALIZED FAMILY SERVICE PLAN (IFSP)

Child's name: Bethany Ansy   Medicaid #: 0462 0000

Date of birth: March 15, 1991   Gender: F

Father's name: Jeremy Ansy   Phone: —

Address: unknown

Mother's name: Andrea Ansy   Phone: 691-2492

Address: 30 Westerly Rd.   Farmington, ME

Child lives with: Mother

Referral date: September 15, 1993   Review date: March 15, 1994

Disability: Communication

Family Service Coordinator: Sandra Tephani

Team Participants:

Andrea Ansy – mother

Sandra Tephani – home visitor

John Wull – speech & language pathologist

Jerry Wimber – Head Start Educational Coordinator

Jill Dunn – early intervention specialist

Parent signature: Andrea Ansy

Date: 10/15/93

Child: Bethany Ansy

Child/family strengths:

Bethany has continued to show growth since she and her family have participated in PCC. Bethany is becoming more independent. Her attendance at PCC has been good.

Child/family needs and concerns:

Bethany's language development. Bethany has some behavioral difficulties and Mrs. Ansy would like some assistance.

Assessment reports:

Speech and language informal assessment. Bethany uses a combination of sign and verbalization.

INDIVIDUALIZED FAMILY SERVICE PLAN

Date: October 15, 1993

Child: Bethany A.   Area: Communication

Present level of functioning	Outcomes	Strategy/ Materials	Date begin	Date changed/ achieved	Review date/ Comments
Bethany uses many gestures and some single words to communicate	For Bethany to increase her use of language	Provide consultation to PCC staff on an on-going basis - 30 minutes weekly	10/30/93		1/30/94 consultation with speech and language pathologist
		Encourage language in small group activities during PCC socialization	10/1/93		1/30/94

*part of Bethany's IFSP

INDIVIDUALIZED FAMILY SERVICE PLAN

Date: October 15, 1993

Family members: Mrs. Ansy, Bethany & Belinda   Area: Social/emotional

Present level of functioning	Outcomes	Strategy/ Materials	Date begin	Date changed/ achieved	Review date/ Comments
Mrs. A. would like to know how to help Bethany during emotional outbursts	To link Mrs. A. with practitioners and other parents so that she can gain ideas	Identify a behavioral consultant	10/30/93		Mrs. T. will assist parent in finding a consultant
		Share information about parent group meetings	10/30/93		Ms. D. will assist

Federal Legislation and Eligibility for Services
for Preschoolers and School-Age Children

PL 101–476, the Individuals with Disabilities Education Act (IDEA), specifies that services be available for children and youth aged three through twenty-one. This law reauthorized the provisions in the early legislation, PL 94–142 and PL 99–457.

One of the main principles of services to children and youth with disabilities is the guarantee to the right of a *free, appropriate public education* (FAPE). Children and youth may be supported in their education program by receiving special education and/or related services if their disability adversely affects their educational performance and if these special services would allow them to benefit from the education program. The following list describes the areas of eligibility according to PL 101–476 (*Federal Register,* 1992, Sec. 300.7).

Children Who Are Eligible for Special Education and Related Services

Autism: A child with autism has a developmental disability that significantly affects verbal and nonverbal communication and social interaction, typically observed before age three, and adversely affects the child's educational performance. (If a child manifests characteristics of autism after the age of three, the child can still be eligible for services under this definition if these criteria are satisfied.) Other characteristics often associated with autism include engagement in repetitive activities and stereotyped movements, resistance to change in the environment or during daily routines, and unusual responses to sensory experiences. The term does not apply if a child's educational performance is adversely affected primarily as a result of a serious emotional disturbance.

Deaf–blindness: A child with deaf–blindness exhibits concomitant visual and hearing impairments, which together cause such severe communication and other developmental and educational problems that the child cannot be accommodated in special education programs solely for children with deafness or children with blindness.

Deafness: A child who is deaf has a hearing loss so severe that with or without amplification the child is unable to process language through hearing. The condition adversely affects the child's educational performance.

Hearing impairment: A child has a hearing impairment, whether permanent or fluctuating, that adversely affects the child's educational performance but is not included under the definition of deafness.

Mental retardation: A child with mental retardation is significantly below average in intellectual functioning; concurrent deficits in adaptive behavior are manifested during the developmental period.

Multiple disabilities: A child has multiple disabilities (such as mental retardation–blindness or mental retardation–orthopedic impairment), the combination of which causes educational problems so severe that they cannot be accommodated in special education programs solely for one of the impairments. This term does not include deaf–blindness.

Orthopedic impairment: A child has a severe orthopedic impairment that adversely affects educational performance. The term includes impairments caused by congenital anomaly (e.g., clubfoot, absence of some member, etc.), impairments caused by disease (e.g., poliomyelitis, bone tuberculosis, etc.), and impairments from other causes (e.g., cerebral palsy, amputations, and fractures or burns that cause contractures).

Other health impairment: A child with a health impairment shows limited strength, vitality, or alertness because of chronic or acute health problems such as heart condition, tuberculosis, rheumatic fever, nephritis, asthma, sickle cell anemia, hemophilia, epilepsy, lead poisoning, leukemia, or diabetes that adversely affect educational performance.

Serious emotional disturbance: A child with a serious emotional disturbance exhibits one or more of the following characteristics over a long period of time and to a marked degree that adversely affects the child's educational performance:

1. An inability to learn that cannot be explained by intellectual, sensory, or health factors;
2. an inability to build or maintain satisfactory interpersonal relationships with peers and teachers;
3. inappropriate types of behavior or feelings under normal circumstances;
4. a general pervasive mood of unhappiness or depression;
5. a tendency to develop physical symptoms or fears associated with personal or school problems.

The term includes schizophrenia. The term does not apply to children who are socially maladjusted, unless it is determined that they have a serious emotional disturbance.

Specific learning disability: A child with a specific learning disability exhibits a disorder in one or more of the basic psychological processes involved in understanding or using spoken or written language, which may manifest itself in an imperfect ability to listen, think, speak, read, write, spell, or to do mathematic calculations. The term includes such conditions as perceptual disabilities, brain injury, minimal brain dysfunction, dyslexia, and developmental aphasia. The term does not apply to children who have learning problems that are primarily the result of visual, hearing, or motor disabilities; of mental retardation; of emotional disturbance; or of environmental, cultural, or economic disadvantage.

Speech or language impairment: A child with a speech or language impairment has a communication disorder such as stuttering or impaired articulation, a language impairment, or a voice impairment that adversely affects educational performance.

Traumatic brain injury: A child has a traumatic injury to the brain, caused by an external physical force, that has resulted in total or partial functional disability or psychosocial impairment, or both, adversely affecting the child's educational performance. The term applies to open or closed head injuries resulting in impairments in one or more areas, such as cognition; language; memory; attention; reasoning; abstract thinking; judgment; problem solving; sensory, perceptual, and motor abilities; psychosocial behavior; physical functions; information processing; and speech. The term does not apply to brain injuries that are congenital or degenerative, or to brain injuries induced by birth trauma.

Visual impairment including blindness: A child has an impairment in vision that, even with correction, adversely affects the child's educational performance. The term includes both partial sight and blindness.

Children with disabilities, including children in public or private institutions or other care facilities, should be educated with children who are nondisabled. The removal of children with disabilities from the regular educational environment should occur only when the nature or severity of the disability is such that even with aids and special or related services education cannot be achieved satisfactorily (*Federal Register,* 1992, Sec. 300.550).

Related services include special transportation or developmental, corrective, and other supportive services that assist the child to benefit from special education.

Related Services that Assist the Child to Benefit from Special Education

Transportation and specialized equipment (such as special or adapted buses, lifts, and ramps)

Speech pathology and audiology

Psychological services

Physical and occupational therapy

Recreation, including assessment of leisure function and therapeutic recreation

Early identification and assessment of disabilities in children

Counseling services, including rehabilitation counseling

Medical services for diagnostic or evaluation purposes

School health services

Social work services in schools

Parent counseling and training (*Federal Register,* 1992, Sec. 300.16)

IDEA specifies that services be available for children and youth from ages three through twenty-one. States may vary slightly in the upper age range of youth who are served. In addition, some states have chosen to use slightly different terminology; for example, seven states use the term "communication disorder" rather than "speech–language impaired" (Salvia & Ysseldyke, 1991, pp. 8–9).

Key Components of IDEA Relating to Assessment

IDEA includes several key components relating to assessment:

1. Child Find.   Child Find is an identification process for locating children in need of services. All children

. . . who have disabilities, regardless of the severity of their disability, and who are in need of special education and related services, are identified, located, and evaluated. . . . The local education agency is responsible for ensuring that all children with disabilities within its jurisdiction are identified, located, and evaluated, including children in all public and private agencies and institutions within that jurisdiction. (*Federal Register,* 1992, Sec. 300.220)

As part of Child Find activities, public schools may sponsor screening clinics and state personnel work to establish a network of individuals who come in contact with young children and their families and to provide information to these professionals regarding coordination of other statewide efforts. Other Child Find activities might include the development of posters, flyers, and brochures to create awareness of typical and atypical development. These flyers are distributed to various PTA and other parent groups, pediatricians' offices, hospitals, and so on. Many different practitioners, such as public health professionals, Head Start staff, and family child care providers, also participate in Child Find activities by helping to alert parents to the availability of screening services in their community.

2. Due Process.   Due process is a specific procedural guarantee of the rights of parents and children (*Federal Register,* 1992, Sects. 300.500, 300.502–515, 300.530–534). The procedure entails the following conditions:

> Parents must provide consent for their child to participate in any assessment including a preplacement evaluation.
>
> Parents have a right to review all records with respect to the "identification, evaluation, and educational placement" of their child.
>
> Parents may obtain an independent evaluation of their child by a qualified examiner who is not employed by the public agency, and that public agency must either pay for the evaluation or ensure that the evaluation is provided at no cost to the parent.

Due process also makes available a procedure that parents, schools, or agencies can follow when an agreement cannot be reached regarding services. When disagreements occur, parents have a right to an impartial hearing conducted by a hearing officer. A hearing can be requested by either a parent or a school district.

3. Multidisciplinary Teams.   Assessment procedures must be conducted by a team of trained professionals who represent different disciplines such as early intervention, early childhood special education, occupational therapy, physical therapy, and speech and language pathology. When a child with a disability is being evaluated for the first time, a member of the evaluation team or someone who is knowledgeable about the assessment procedures used with the child and the results of the assessment must be present at the team meeting (*Federal Register,* 1992, Sec. 300.344).

4. General Requirements of Assessment.   Assessment procedures must be fair and equitable for all children and youth. It is required (*Federal Register,* 1992, Sec. 300.532) that:

The test be administered in the child's native language or other mode of communication.

The test be validated for the purpose that it is being used.

The test be administered by trained personnel in conformance with instructions from the test producer.

Assessment be not merely an intelligence quotient but additional information about educational need.

The assessment of children with impaired sensory, manual, or speaking skills be completed with tests selected and administered to accurately reflect the child's aptitude or achievement level (or other factor), rather than reflecting the child's impaired sensory, manual, or speaking skills (except where these skills are the factors being measured).

No single test be used to determine an appropriate education program.

The child be assessed in all areas related to the suspected disability including, where appropriate, health, vision, hearing, social and emotional status, general intelligence, academic performance, communicative status, and motor abilities.

The assessment be made by a multidisciplinary team including at least one team member with knowledge in the suspected area of disability.

5. Individualized Education Program. Each child or youth who receives services must have an IEP. This written document is based on a comprehensive assessment and is developed by the multidisciplinary team, which includes the parents. The IEP must include specific assessment information including (*Federal Register,* 1992, Sec. 300.533, Sec. 300.346):

Names of tests and other sources of information used to develop the IEP

The child's current level of educational performance

Annual goals as well as short-term instructional objectives

A statement regarding the specific special education and related services to be provided and the extent to which the child will be able to participate in the regular education program

The projected dates for the beginning of services and the anticipated length of services

Information as to how the child's progress will be assessed and when the assessment will occur

A full reevaluation of a child's needs must be completed at least every three years. In working with children ages three to five, remember that services may be provided by an IFSP, as we described earlier.

6. Least Restrictive Environment. In writing the IEP, the multidisciplinary team must consider the setting that would maximize opportunities for the child to interact with children without disabilities, in conformity with the provisions of IDEA.

Additional Components of IDEA for Practitioners Working with Young Children

IDEA includes a number of other important components. This legislation recognizes the importance of thinking and speaking of persons first, rather than emphasizing a disability. Thus, we say "a child with cerebral palsy" or "a child who has a developmental delay" rather than referring to the disability first.

The change in the use of terms also reflects the preference for the use of "disabilities" over the terminology of "handicaps." Many people feel that *disability* describes a difficulty in thinking, moving, learning, seeing, or hearing. The difficulty becomes a "handicap" only when the environment or the society creates a barrier for the individual who experiences that difficulty. Thus, one may have a disability in moving, but the physical disability is not a handicap unless, for example, the individual encounters an environment lacking in enlarged doorways, ramps, or other means of physical access.

In addition to changing terminology, IDEA addresses the importance of assistive technology devices and services. Assistive technology includes any equipment "used to increase, maintain or improve the functional capabilities of children with disabilities" (*Federal Register,* 1992, Sec. 300.5). Assistive devices including equipment or adapted materials should be considered when addressing learning and development needs. Team members work together in assessing a child's needs for assistive devices. As a result of the assessment, team members might recommend the use of a corner chair to improve seating position for a child with physical needs or the use of an augmentative communication device that incorporates a speech synthesizer for a child with communication needs. Assistive devices provide increased opportunities in inclusive environments as well as in changed perceptions of the child by the family and the community.

Recognizing the Special Needs of Children from Ages Three to Five

One of the first challenges to teachers and other professionals who work with preschool children is to determine which children should receive special services. Yet, many practitioners have voiced concerns over (1) the potential detrimental effects of labeling a child at a young age, (2) the lack of adequate assessment tools for preschool children, and (3) some of the disability categories used with school-age children (see pages 12–14), which may not be appropriate for determining eligibility for preschool children. Several of these categories address learning and behavior needs typically observed in academic settings. A term was needed to allow for flexibility to address the differences in development.

Developmental delay is a noncategorical term that is used with infants and toddlers in order that they may be identified and receive early intervention services without being labeled for a specific disability. The term may be used with preschoolers (children aged three to five) in order that they may receive educational and related services without being labeled for a specific disability category. PL 102–119 allows states to choose whether or not to use this term for preschoolers; thus, practitioners should check with their state department of education to determine specific state practices.

A developmental delay is a delay in one or more of the following:

- Physical development [which includes fine and gross motor]
- Cognitive development
- Communication development
- Social or emotional development, or
- Adaptive development (*Federal Register,* 1992, Sec. 300.7)

Although young children vary greatly in their rate of development, this term was designed to reflect a *significant* delay in development. The term refers to:

> a condition which represents a significant delay in the process of develop-
> ment. It does not refer to a condition in which a child is slightly or momen-
> tarily lagging in development. The presence of developmental delay is an
> indication that the process of development is significantly affected and that
> without special intervention, it is likely that educational performance at
> school age will be affected. (McLean, Smith, McCormick, Schakel, &
> McEvoy, 1991, p. 2)

PL 102–119 allowed states to develop different criteria for serving preschool children under the term *developmental delay* than criteria used for infants and toddlers being served under this term. McLean et al. (1991) recommended that the criteria for determining a delay be documented (1) by performance on a stan-dardized development assessment instrument, to be reported by representing the child's score in terms of standard deviations below the mean, (2) by a specific assessment of one of the developmental domains, or (3) through observation.

Issues in Transitions

Transition planning is critical. In many states, the eligibility criteria are different for preschoolers and for very young children and their families who receive early inter-vention services. As the child and family move from infant–toddler services to preschool services, careful planning must occur. Will the child be eligible for special education services? If not, would the family like assistance in locating other appro-priate services?

For children who are eligible, each state has developed a method for ensuring the transition process from infant–toddler services to preschool service. The 1991 amendments to the Individuals with Disabilities Education Act (Sec. 613[a][15]) require states to develop procedures to ensure a smooth transition by means of developing an IFSP (or IEP) and having it implemented by the child's third birthday. The 1991 amendments also allowed, at each state's discretion, to provide two-year-old children with disabilities who will reach age three during the school year with preschool services, regardless of whether the child received infant–toddler services (Sec. 619[B][iii]). Members of early childhood teams must be knowledgeable about the policy and procedures of their state.

Practitioners have also expressed concerns about difficulties that may arise for children and their families when the children leave preschool services. For example, preschool children who receive services under the eligibility category of "develop-mental delay" may move into school-age programs in which there is no developmentally delayed category. One of the common concerns that parents and preschool practitioners express is, "Will children who receive preschool services because of a 'developmental delay' continue to be eligible for services in public school?" McLean et al. (1991) suggest:

> Clearly, there are some categories of handicapping conditions that are relatively easy to identify and for which relatively concrete and objective criteria exist at all ages. The expressed concerns about transition to categorical labels at age six usually center on the less readily identifiable categories of Mental Retardation, Specific Learning Disabilities, and Emotional Disturbance. By age six, however, with data documenting a child's functioning and progress in an "educational" setting, it is no more difficult (and perhaps less difficult because of the accumulated knowledge of the child's individual strengths and needs) to assign these categorical labels than it is to categorize a newly identified primary-aged child. (p. 5)

One of the most common areas of need for children entering school programs is in the area of speech and language. The following case study illustrates how a six-year-old boy with language needs came to receive special education services and support in his regular education program.

CASE STUDY: MICAH, AGE SIX

Micah V. and his family moved to a new city shortly before the beginning of September. On the first day of school, Mrs. V. accompanied Micah to Norman Street Elementary School and enrolled him in first grade. Mr. Tonnerly, Micah's first grade teacher, began to have questions about Micah's development almost immediately. He observed that Micah was very quiet and usually indicated what he wanted by pointing and gesturing. Other children seemed to have difficulty in understanding Micah, and Mr. Tonnerly found that he, too, often could not understand what the boy said. As the first week drew to a close, Micah's teacher realized that in addition to difficulties in being understood by his classmates and teacher, Micah rarely used phrases of more than two or three words.

Mr. Tonnerly spoke to Micah's mother, who reported that her son enjoyed school, but she had also wondered whether he should be talking more. She indicated that a doctor had told her that Micah would talk "when he was ready." Mr. Tonnerly explained that he would like to involve the school's preassessment team. This team of three teachers, including the special education consultant, would be making some observations in the classroom and would have some suggestions regarding the classroom setup, teaching strategies, and Micah's work. The team would try to assist Micah and his teacher without going through the formal IEP team meetings and without defining eligibility for special education services.

The preassessment team suggested several modifications to the room arrangement and offered some teaching ideas to Mr. Tonnerly; however, Micah continued to have difficulty in expressive language. Micah's mother indicated that she would be willing to come to a meeting to discuss Micah's needs, and Mr. Tonnerly filled out a referral form, which was forwarded to the IEP team. Mr.

and Mrs. V. were invited to the team meeting and were provided with a copy of parents' rights.

The team meeting was attended by Mrs. V., the first grade teacher, the school principal, a special educator, the school nurse, and a speech and language pathologist. During the meeting, Mrs. V. indicated that Micah had missed the preschool screening clinic, which was held the week after they had moved. The team agreed that Micah's hearing should be tested by an audiologist and that the speech and language pathologist should assess the child's receptive and expressive language. The special educator was asked to complete an assessment of cognitive and developmental skills.

When the testing had been completed, the team reconvened and discussed the results of the assessment. The audiological report indicated that Micah did not have a hearing loss. The special educator had found Micah's motor and cognitive development to be within the range typical of children his age. Results of the language assessment, however, showed that although Micah's understanding of language was average for a child of his age, his ability to express himself was substantially below that of other six-year-olds. The team decided that based on the language assessment, Micah needed to increase his expressive language skills. Together the team members wrote Micah's individualized education program (see Figure 1.2).

In summary, we have seen the impact of federal legislation on the assessment process and on services to young children. In 1986 PL 99–457 marked the beginning of legislation that focuses on educational and related services to preschool-age children and requires that family members be involved at all levels of the assessment process. This legislation also marked the beginning steps in encouraging states to plan interdisciplinary early intervention services to infants, toddlers, and families. In 1990 PL 101–476 reauthorized the earlier legislation and made provisions for noncategorical definitions for eligibility for children three to five years old. Future federal legislation may continue to help in refining services and procedures. Next, we will take a closer look at the assessment process.

Key Terms

Assessment. A global term for observing, gathering, and/or recording information for the purpose of decision making. Assessment consists of screening, determining eligibility, program planning, monitoring individual progress, and program evaluation.

Screening. The purpose is to identify children who may be disabled or at risk for delay or disability and to make a referral for further assessment (*Step 1*). Screening typically involves testing large numbers of children, usually in a short amount of time.

Determining Eligibility. The purpose is to determine whether a child meets federal and state eligibility criteria for services (*Step 2*). This assessment involves professionals from various disciplines who have received specific training on assessment approaches and on specialized instruments. Special educators and early intervention specialists may be involved in cognitive, readiness, adaptive development, or academic assessments.

Planning the Program. The purpose is to determine the child's current level of functioning (*Step 3*). This information, which is critical in the planning of an appropriate program, must be included in the development of the Individualized Family Service Plan (IFSP) or

INDIVIDUAL EDUCATION PROGRAM

Name: _Micah Valez_

Date of Birth: _6/25/87_

School/Grade: _Norman St. Ele School – grade 1_

Exceptionality: _Speech/language impairment_

Date of Meeting: _10/20/93_

Triennial Review Date: _10/20/96_

Projected Date of Graduation: _____
(beginning at age 15)

Present Level of Educational Performance	Observed or Measurable Constraints on Performance
Micah demonstrates good understanding of language (receptive skills) but is functioning substantially below age level in expressive language	_Micah uses two and three word phrases – but most communication is by gesture. Micah performed as well as or better than 21% (score of the 21st percentile) on PPVT–R_

Special Education Service to be Provided	Supportive Service to be Provided	Staff Positions Responsible	Amount of Each Service Required	Date of Initiation	Date of Termination (not to exceed 12 months)
Special education teacher will support Micah in the classroom		_Ms. Johnson_	_3× ea. week 120 minutes each_	_10/26/93_	_6/15/94_
	Speech/language pathologist will support Micah in the classroom	_Mr. Kane_	_2× ea. week 20 minutes each_	_10/27/93_	_6/15/94_

Extent of participation in regular education program   _Full participation_

Description of any necessary special education transportation   _None_

Description of any necessary adaptations of state and local graduation requirements (beginning at age 15)   _Not applicable_

(continued)

FIGURE 1.2 Sample pages of Micah's IEP

SOURCE: Maine State Department of Education, Division of Special Education, State House Station #23, Augusta, ME. Reprinted by permission.

FIGURE 1.2 (continued)

Name: _Micah Valez_

ANNUAL EDUCATIONAL GOAL

Micah will increase his use of language skills during classroom activities by the end of the school year

Staff position responsible: _Mr. Kane (with assistance from Ms. Johnson and Mr. Tonnerly)_

SHORT-TERM OBJECTIVES

Conditions (Given...)	Behavior (the student will...)	Means (as measured by...)	Schedule of Measurement (by...)
1. _During routine classroom activities_	_Micah will use words to request (make his request known)_	_by observation_	_90% of the time_
2. _During small group activities_	_Micah will use words to share ideas and discoveries_	_by observation_	_90% of the time_
3.			
4.			

Individualized Education Program (IEP). Assessment of the child's environment is also an important aspect of this step.

Monitoring Individual Progress. The purpose is to assess the child's progress (*Step 4*). Practitioners who work directly with the child review the child's work, accomplishments, and achievements regularly.

Evaluating the Program. The purpose is to assess the effectiveness of the program (*Step 5*). This step allows the team members to change or modify the program if needed.

STEPS IN THE ASSESSMENT PROCESS

Assessment is a global term for observing, gathering, and/or recording information. Based on the information obtained, members of the team make decisions regarding early intervention, special education, related services, and referral to other community services. In many communities, children under the age of six come to the assessment process as a result of Child Find. These activities alert parents to the importance of early identification and intervention and to the availability of screening programs.

Step 1: Screening

The first step in the assessment process is called *screening*. A screening procedure is used to determine which children in a large population may fall outside normal ranges of development. Comprehensive screening includes several components: parental input regarding any special concerns; medical history (often given through parental report or completed by a parent using a checklist); vision and hearing tests; and the use of commercial screening instruments and observation reports in the examination of areas of general development, abilities, and skills. Screening measures of school-age children may include some academic areas. Screening instruments are generally inexpensive and are designed to be completed in 30 minutes or less. (See Chapter 5 for a complete discussion of specific screening instruments.)

Screening procedures differ depending on the age of the population of children. Infants and toddlers may be screened in the home by an early intervention specialist. Many communities conduct screening clinics several times a year as part of the Child Find system. These clinics may be open to infants, toddlers, and preschoolers. Children about to enter public school may be screened before starting kindergarten, while school-age children who enroll in a new school may be screened by a special educator. Classroom teachers may "screen" a child's work and performance in the classroom and make a referral on that basis. Thus, as a result of the screening process, children suspected of having a disability will be referred for additional assessment to determine whether they are eligible for services; other children will not need to be referred for additional follow-up based on the screening.

Caveat.   The purpose of screening is to find from the larger group of children who are screened a subgroup of children who may have a disability or be at risk for disability. To identify the children who truly are part of this subgroup, the community needs a screening tool that yields an accurate assessment. If the screening instrument is not accurate, some children who do not belong in the subgroup will be referred for more in-depth assessment, and children who do belong will not be identified.

Consumers need to become familiar with the characteristics of good screening instruments as a basis for developing skills in evaluating new screening tools. Although some instruments have more sources of error than others, no test is error free. Most screening teams prefer to err in the direction of overidentifying children.

Step 2: Determining Eligibility

The second step is to determine whether a child does in fact have a disability as defined by the categorical definitions in PL 101–476 (see pages 12–14) or by the term *developmental delay* and thus is eligible to receive services. Note that the term developmental delay is used with infants and toddlers, and, at a state's discretion, with preschoolers. The term is not used with school-age children.

A child who is suspected of having a specific disability may undergo several types of assessment to determine the nature and extent of the problem. For example, a child who is nonverbal may undergo a cross-disciplinary evaluation. The child may be seen by an audiologist, to determine the extent, if any, of a hearing loss; a speech and language pathologist, an early intervention specialist or special educator, to determine communication needs and adaptive skill development; and a psychologist, to determine social–emotional development. All these professionals may work together to view and analyze the child's behavior jointly, with each contributing expertise from one discipline.

Generally, evaluators who conduct these assessments have received specific training in the administration and interpretation of specialized instruments. Chapter 12 presents a detailed description of specialized instruments and their interpretation. As specified in the federal legislation, assessment for the purposes of eligibility must be conducted by a multidisciplinary team.

This step is often referred to as "diagnosis." The results of this assessment may determine the exact nature of the disability, such as "a moderate hearing loss." Yet, often an exact diagnosis of the disability cannot be made, especially with young children. If this is the case, a general statement such as "general developmental delay" is recorded.

Determining a child's eligibility for services depends, in part, on the age of the child. Practitioners who work with an infant or toddler will need to know the eligibility criteria their state has developed for very young children as well as whether the state provides services to these children.

Infants and Toddlers.   Some states provide both assessment and services to infants and toddlers; other states provide funding for assessment but not for services. Still other states may *permit* services for infants and toddlers, without *mandating* their availability for all children.

States that do serve very young children (birth through two years) base eligibility for services on their respective definitions of delay in one or more areas of development (see page 6). Some states have also chosen to provide services to children from birth through age two who are defined as *at risk* for development delay. Eligibility for services under this category is defined by the individual state's definition of "at risk for developmental delay."

Preschoolers, Ages Three to Five. All states provide services to eligible pre-schoolers between the ages of three and five. Children are eligible for services if they have a disability or show a developmental delay.

School-Age Children. All states provide services to eligible children based on the categories listed on pages 12–14.

Caveats. The decisions the team makes during this step determine whether a given child receives services. However, many tests designed to assess young children are inadequate. When professionals participate in this aspect of the assessment process, they have a responsibility to become familiar with the attributes of good tests as well as to be knowledgeable about the limitations of specific tests. The following chapters provide an understanding of these important aspects.

There is a second pitfall related to assessment to qualify for services. Eligibility depends on whether a child meets the defined criteria according to IDEA and the amendments to IDEA. These criteria were established to ensure that children who really needed the services would be the ones to receive them. To account for the children being served, Congress needed to define the population. Thus, we use certain terms such as *autism, serious emotional disturbance,* and *developmental delay.* However, these terms can become labels that follow a child for many years and restrict future opportunities. Sometimes individuals working with children allow these terms to establish expectations of what children can and cannot do. This is not only unfair to each child, it is ethically inappropriate.

The only purpose of this step in the assessment process is to determine eligibility for services. Much of the information gathered in the next step will be much more useful in planning the child's program and developing realistic goals.

Step 3: Planning the Program

How Will We Start? The third step, program planning, helps the members of the team in developing the components of the program and in devising adaptations and modifications to assist children in being successful. Team members who are working with infants, toddlers, and preschoolers assist the families in identifying their concerns, resources, and priorities for services. Family members may accept or decline any early intervention service (Individuals with Disabilities Education Act Amendments, 1991, Sec. 17[3]). Program planning for children of all ages, including school-age children, includes assessing the individual's skill level and determining the point at which intervention should begin. The team members may use commercial criterion-referenced tests, checklists, observations, or informal curriculum-based assessments. Assessment that includes observations is a very important aspect this step. Through observation, the team members can gather information about the child's interests, interactions with other children and adults, and level of play, as well as information of other types that is difficult to acquire through more formal means.

Caveat. Program planning should not focus on the child alone. Factors within the home, the child care setting, and the school environment should also be examined to increase the child's chances for success in the program. In some instances environmental factors may be responsible, at least in part, for initiating or maintaining learning and behavioral problems that are of concern to the team (Wallace & Larsen, 1978, p. 100). An environmental assessment of a child care or early education setting may include reports on teacher and staff preparation for the arrival and departure of children, schedules, physical arrangement of the room, physical arrangement of materials, and degree of child–teacher interaction. Through environmental assessment, team members gather information that can be used in deciding what modifications or adaptations might be helpful.

Step 4: Monitoring Progress

The fourth step in the assessment process is monitoring. The family's set of priorities as well as the child's progress in the program should be assessed frequently. Information from this type of assessment allows the team members to modify the intervention, teaching procedures, or materials if the child is not progressing as expected.

Caveat.   Young children exhibit a wide range in the rate of growth and development. Frequency of monitoring should reflect a sensitivity to this factor in addition to following the general and statutory guidelines described for step 5.

Step 5: Evaluating the Program

Is the Program Effective?   This type of assessment may be used to make decisions about the effectiveness of the intervention program for individual children. Are the IFSP/IEP objectives being met? The IFSP must be reviewed every six months (or more frequently, if appropriate), and a full evaluation must be conducted annually. The IEP must be reviewed annually (or more frequently, if appropriate), and a full evaluation must be conducted every three years. Another way of evaluating the program is to look at the overall services to multiple children. For example, by combining information on the children in the program, one could answer two important questions: Are children receiving effective special education services? Do parents feel satisfied with the services? Such assessments are referred to as *program evaluation.*

Assessment should be viewed as an ongoing process, particularly in the areas of program planning, monitoring progress, and program evaluation. This ongoing process should include a variety of informal assessments such as checklists and observations as well as formal assessment. Figure 1.3 summarizes the steps in the cycle of information gathering and decision making that constitutes assessment. After step 5, the team will need to decide whether the program should be continued, and, if so, whether changes should be made. If the child will continue to receive special services, the team returns to step 3, planning the program.

Key Terms

Multidisciplinary Team. Professionals from different disciplines conduct separate assessments, plan in isolation, and independently implement the area of the written plan related to their own discipline.

Interdisciplinary Team. Professionals from different disciplines conduct separate assessments but share their separate plans and incorporate activities from other disciplines into their interactions with the child whenever possible.

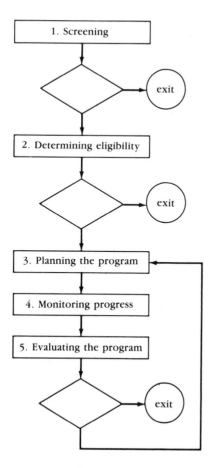

FIGURE 1.3 Steps in the assessment process

Transdisciplinary Team. Professionals from different disciplines and family members conduct assessment together and cooperatively plan services. Implementation is carried out by the primary service provider and family members.

Direct Assessment. A traditional model of assessment in which the evaluator works with the child, one on one.

Indirect Assessment. A flexible model of assessment in which information is gathered during routine or child-initiated activities.

Arena Assessment. A model of assessment in which a facilitator works with the child in assessment activities across disciplines. Other team members including·the parents sit away from the child–adult dyad to observe and record information during these activities. Arena assessment may also occur via videotape.

WORKING WITH OTHERS

Assessing young children involves working and sharing information with parents and other team members from different disciplines. IDEA mandates that assessments be conducted by individuals from more than one discipline. Some of these different disciplines might include early childhood special education, early intervention, speech and language pathology, occupational therapy, physical therapy, psychology, nutrition, and mobility specialty. The involvement of representatives of these different professions with one another and with the family may range from a minimal amount to a great deal of collaboration.

Some teams have a minimal amount of interaction during the assessment process. For example, members of different disciplines test the child in the area(s) related to their respective disciplines and report the results in a team meeting. Parents are asked to contribute information also. In this model, called *multidisciplinary assessment,* each individual member develops a section of the intervention plan and works directly with the child to implement it.

The trend in early intervention, however, places an emphasis on collaboration among professionals. In fact, the success of early intervention rests on our ability to work closely with parents and individuals from other disciplines.

In an *interdisciplinary assessment* model, team members conduct individual assessments of the child and then develop an intervention plan together. Parents contribute information during the development of the plan. The responsibility for carrying out the intervention falls to individual professional disciplines; however, this approach is characterized by cooperation and interaction in planning and implementing activities. During the intervention process, team members try to incorporate goals from other disciplines when possible. For example, an occupational therapist who is working on specific fine motor skills may use some of the language concepts defined and implemented by the speech therapist. This type of collaboration helps the child because skills are not taught in isolation nor limited to a particular therapy session.

In *transdisciplinary assessment* the team members assess and plan the child's program together. Implementation of the plan is carried out by one team member with consultation from the rest of the team. Thus only one person works with the child and family, but representatives of the different disciplines are responsible for helping the service provider carry out the plan. This usually involves teaching across disciplines. Table 1.2 presents these different philosophical models of assessment and summarizes the differences.

VARIOUS APPROACHES IN GATHERING INFORMATION

Traditional assessment has typically involved a *direct approach* in working with the child, one on one, in a quiet room. The evaluator presents the test items and records the score. Usually the evaluator looks for and notes additional descriptive information, such as how the child approaches a certain task. The test items are scored, and the additional information is synthesized into a report, which is shared with the family and other professionals at the team meeting. This approach has been used traditionally with school-age children and continues to be used with younger children, particularly in assessment to determine eligibility.

However, assessment of young children may be completed using less direct approaches. As early childhood assessment continues to evolve, assessments for the purposes of planning and monitoring the child's program are most likely to be conducted within the daily activities of the child. This *indirect approach* might include observing the preschooler playing "duck duck goose" within an early educa-

TABLE 1.2 Team approaches to assessment

	Multidisciplinary	**Interdisciplinary**	**Transdisciplinary**
Assessment	Separate assessments by team members	Separate assessments by team members	Team members and family conduct a comprehensive developmental assessment together
Parent participation	Parents meet with individual team members	Parents meet with team or team representative	Parents are full, active, and participating members of the team
Service plan development	Team members develop separate plans for their discipline	Team members share their separate plans with one another	Team members and the parents develop a service plan based upon family priorities, needs, and resources
Service plan responsibility	Team members are responsible for implementing their section of the plan	Team members are responsible for sharing information with one another as well as for implementing their section of the plan	Team members are responsible and accountable for how the primary service provider implements the plan
Service plan implementation	Team members implement the part of the service plan related to their discipline	Team members implement their section of the plan and incorporate other sections where possible	A primary service provider is assigned to implement the plan with the family
Lines of communication	Informal lines	Periodic case-specific team meetings	Regular team meeting where continuous transfer of information, knowledge, and skills is shared among team members
Guiding philosophy	Team members recognize the importance of contributions from other disciplines	Team members are willing and able to develop, share, and be responsible for providing services that are a part of the total service plan	Team members make a commitment to teach, learn, and work together across discipline boundaries to implement unified service plan
Staff development	Independent and within their discipline	Independent within as well as outside their discipline	An integral component of team meetings for learning across disciplines and team building

SOURCE: Woodruff, G., & McGonigel, M. J. (1988), p. 166. Reprinted by permission.

tion program, examining samples of the child's paintings and drawings, observing a toddler at home, or interviewing the caregiver.

Linder (1990) described a type of assessment called *transdisciplinary play-based assessment* (TPBA) which was developed for use with children from six months to six years of age. TPBA uses information from the parents to plan a play session during which members of the team use guidelines in the form of questions to observe the child's cognitive, social—emotional, communication and language, and sensorimotor development.

Another approach used by team members who are exploring a transdisciplinary approach to teaming is the *arena assessment.* In this type of assessment, individuals from various disciplines and the family gather in one room. One person has been designated to be the facilitator. This person may be a parent, or perhaps the team member who is most familiar with the child or has the most expertise in a particular area of development. As the facilitator presents items to the child, other team members record their observations. After the assessment has been completed, the team meets to share their individual observations and develop an intervention plan. Figure 1.4 illustrates the room arrangement and the different professional disciplines participating in a typical arena assessment.

The arena assessment has several distinct advantages for everyone—the child, the family, and the other team members:

The child does not have to go through several different assessment sessions on different occasions.

The family has all the members of the different disciplines available at one time.

Individuals from different areas may learn from one another.

This approach may be difficult for some families and team members, however, because:

Some professionals may feel threatened by the more "open" nature of the proceedings.

Individuals may find it difficult to yield turf that has been discipline specific.

The family may not wish to be so directly involved with the assessment process.

We have examined several different models for the assessment of young children. In addition, team members may develop special "hybrids" to fit unique situations. For example, in rural areas with scarce resources for travel and personnel, team members may conduct an arena assessment via videotape. Some rural states have developed interactive television systems that link remote sites in community schools or university campuses with other schools or campuses and a central location. Such a system allows a practitioner in a central location to "participate" in a live arena assessment being conducted in a remote location. Other modes of communication such as telephone conference calls and e-mail provide alternative ways for team members to keep in touch.

The special capabilities of technology hold much promise for teams who work in rural areas as well as for teams working with children under conditions of low

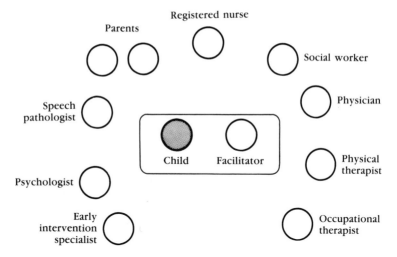

FIGURE 1.4 Team members conducting an arena assessment

incidence. Technology allows practitioners from a variety of disciplines to come together in ways other than sitting in the same room.

GENERAL CONSIDERATIONS FOR ASSESSING YOUNG CHILDREN

There are several important considerations for assessing young children (Bailey & Wolery, 1989; Peterson, 1987; Sattler, 1988).

About the Practitioner

The assessment of young children calls for a variety of skills on the part of the examiner or observer, plus preparation. Practitioners must develop good interpersonal skills in working with children and their families, as well as skills in various assessment procedures. Some of these skills will lie in areas a practitioner needs to develop; other skills may come more naturally for the practitioner because of experience and work with children. Some preparations must be completed before seeing the child. Some of the skills and considerations for practitioners are listed as follows.

Choice of an appropriate approach or instrument. Be sure that the approach or instrument chosen was developed for the purpose for which it will be used. Instruments designed for screening purposes should not be used for diagnostic work or program planning.

Training in assessment. Practitioners have a responsibility to the children and families with whom they work. Assessments must be administered by personnel who are trained in appropriate methods and procedures and are knowledgeable about the specific instruments they use. Be aware that the titles of some commercial tests may seem to indicate a purpose different from that for which the tests were developed. Training in assessment instruments should include a thorough review of the examiner's manual.

Practice in assessment. Conducting accurate observations takes skill and practice. Learning to use an assessment instrument involves giving the instrument many times. The student may wish to practice on children who are developing typically.

Organization of materials. Before the assessment session begins, be sure to have all the necessary materials assembled.

Review of all assessment items. When using an observation record form, review the purpose for the observation and know how the observation will be recorded. When using an assessment instrument, complete a review of all the test items to be given before the child arrives. Some examiners find it helpful to mark the different sections in the manual with a paper clip for easy reference.

Establish and maintain rapport. Plan to spend enough time in play or conversation to permit the child to feel comfortable before the assessment is begun. Sharing a small toy with the child may be a good way to begin to establish rapport.

Flexibility. Work with young children often involves adapting plans. When using an assessment instrument, the practitioner should remember that the child may need more time to explore test materials or to share an interesting thought that has nothing to do with the test items! A test "break" may be needed, or an additional session may have to be scheduled.

About the Child

There are a number of considerations to remember during the assessment.

Daily routine. Consideration should be given to time of day and the child's typical schedule. For example, assessments scheduled for early afternoon may interfere with normal naptime.

Motivation. The child may have little interest in the proceedings, or insufficient social awareness to complete the activity or to please the examiner (Peterson, 1987).

Health issues. A child who does not feel well may be unable to tell you so.

Fatigue. Young children tire easily, especially when working within a highly structured activity. This factor may be decreased by using a variety of high-interest materials. Another way to promote interest is to place the toys or other materials in a box or bag. Then, as each one is needed, reach into the bag and pull it out. Simple procedures such as these can help to make the session more enjoyable.

Response time. Some children respond more slowly than others. Be sensitive to the child's temperament, allowing enough time for a response.

Independence. Children who are beginning to assert their independence may refuse to complete an activity. Children may refuse to complete test items that require them to build a structure "just like mine." Children who have participated in child-centered programs may find that such test items run counter to the way other adults have encouraged them to design their own structure.

About Family Members

Family members may be very anxious about the assessment process. Here are some considerations that may be helpful as practitioners and the family work together.

Awareness of anxiety. Be aware that family members may be very anxious about their child's development, and be sensitive to this anxiety.

Adequate time for sharing information. Family members have much information about their child and may wish to share it. Valuable information can be gathered by talking with family members about the growth and development of the child as well as typical behaviors seen at home.

Appreciation of individual differences. One family may be comfortable with a minimal level of involvement, whereas another family will want to be fully involved with their child. Such individual differences should be recognized and appreciated.

About Other Team Members

Team members may differ in philosophy and in amount and type of training. Teams may be comprised of members from various agencies and programs with different job responsibilities and schedules. But the way in which team members work together has an impact on the success of the assessment process. Assessments should be coordinated as much as possible with other members of the team.

ASSESSING CHILDREN WHO COME FROM DIVERSE LINGUISTIC AND CULTURAL BACKGROUNDS

Children and families from diverse linguistic and cultural backgrounds bring with them various cultural perspectives and values, knowledge of languages other than English, and attitudes about the roles and responsibilities of the family, educators, therapists, and early intervention specialists. In working with these children and their families, we must respect and appreciate the richness of languages and cultures that may be unfamiliar to us. The perspectives and values these children bring to the assessment situation can affect their attitudes toward the testing environment, the examiner, and the purposes of the assessment (Sattler, 1988).

Insensitivity to a child's linguistic and cultural background can cause problems. One problem is that misperceptions, once created, can lead to misunderstandings between the examiner and the child about the benefits of testing and the behaviors expected of the child during testing. A second problem has to do with cultural stereotyping (Chamberlain & Medeiros-Landurand, 1991). Sattler (1988) correctly cautioned practitioners about making generalizations about individuals who have diverse backgrounds. Every child must be assessed individually, based on the family and subculture. Culturally diverse groups are not monolithic, and children within these groups bring their own personal experiences to the assessment situation.

Another problem related to insensitivity is miscommunication. If the examiner and the family do not share a particular culture or language, there may be misinformation and miscommunication. As you assist families in identifying their strengths, concerns, and resources, remember that family units will have different cultural histories and beliefs that must be recognized.

> Families may differ in their views of medical care, in the meaning of a disability, and in childrearing practices. They may also differ in their willingness to seek help, in their communication style, in the amount and type of their participation, in their goals and in the involvement of family members. (*Coalition Quarterly,* 1991, p. 3)

Finally, assessment bias may reflect the insensitivity of the examiner. When the examiner does not take into account the linguistic and cultural background of the child, bias can occur.

Avoiding Assessment Bias

Discrimination in assessment relating to the disability is prohibited. Table 1.3 highlights legislation and court cases relating to the cultural and linguistic diversity of individuals with disabilities. Failure to comply with applicable legislation and court rulings can result in serious penalties.

There are special considerations for children whose primary language is not English. Just because a test has been translated into another language, the content, difficulty, reliability, and validity may not be the same as for the English-language version. Words in one language can have a different meaning, a different frequency of

TABLE 1.3 Litigation and legislation relating to the assessment of culturally and linguistically diverse individuals

Case	Ruling
Diana v. State Board of California (1970)	A consent decree in education, in which the State of California agreed that: All children whose primary language is not English should be tested in their primary language and in English. All Mexican-American and Chinese students enrolled in classes for students who were educable mentally retarded (EMR) should be reevaluated in their primary language and in English to eliminate unfair verbal items.
Larry P. v. Riles (California, 1979)	Intelligence tests cannot be used in California to place African-American students in EMR classes. All African-American students who were in EMR classes must be reevaluated.
Parents in Action on Special Education (PASE) v. Hannon (Illinois, 1980)	Certain intelligence tests are not biased against African-American children.
PL 94-142 The Education for All Handicapped Children Act (1975)	Testing must be conducted in the child's native language.

use, or a different difficulty level in another language (American Educational Research Association, American Psychological Association, & National Council on Measurement in Education, 1985).

Few tests have been developed for use with children in U.S. schools who come from culturally and linguistically diverse backgrounds. This lack of appropriate instruments is especially acute for young children. Although standardized tests do have special limitations in the assessment of culturally and linguistically diverse children, they can still be used if these limitations are recognized. Sattler (1988) states: "Tests should be used if the potential exists for them to contribute to the development of the child. Obviously, tests should never be used when they would physically or emotionally harm any child" (p. 592).

The following standards (American Educational Research Association et al., 1985) have been developed for testing linguistically diverse individuals:

> For non-native English speakers of some dialects of English, testing should be designed to minimize threats to test reliability and validity that may arise from language differences.
>
> Linguistic modifications recommended by test publishers should be described in detail in the test manual.
>
> When a test is recommended for use with linguistically diverse test takers, test developers and publishers should provide the information necessary for appropriate test use and interpretation.
>
> When a test is translated from one language or dialect to another, its reliability and validity for the uses intended in the linguistic groups to be tested should be established.
>
> When it is intended that the two versions of dual-language tests be comparable, evidence of test comparability should be reported. (pp. 74–75)

Key Term

Family Educational Rights and Privacy Act (FERPA). The federal Family Educational Rights and Privacy Act, enacted in 1974 (PL 93–380), gives the family the rights to review all records kept on their child and to challenge any of the information in the records.

Confidentiality and Informed Consent

Professionals who are involved with the gathering of information about children and families have both a legal and an ethical responsibility to ensure that the information is used appropriately. All individuals who are working with a given child and family need to agree that the information being shared is for the purposes of enabling the family and assisting the child through early intervention and educational services. The same responsibilities apply to school-age children as well. One should discuss a particular child and family only with professionals who have a legitimate interest in the information and with whom the family has consented to share information. Identifying information should be used with caution in written reports other than those stamped CONFIDENTIAL.

The *Family Educational Rights and Privacy Act of 1974* (PL 93–380, commonly referred to as the "Buckley amendment" or FERPA) states that no educational agency may release student information without written consent from the child's parents. This consent specifies which records are to be released, to whom, and the reason(s) for such release. A copy of the records to be released must be sent to the student's parents.

A Family's Right to Inspect Records

The Family Educational Rights and Privacy Act also allows families to access and inspect any of their records held at any educational agency that accepts federal money. Parents also have the right to challenge and correct any information contained in these records. Professionals will want to ensure that only materials relevant to the target child have been filed in the folder for that child. Irrelevant information about the personal lives of families or information that is at best subjective and impressionistic has no place in a family's record.

PREFERRED PRACTICES

Examiners must carefully select assessment approaches. Assessment must not be limited to the use of assessment instruments. Because so few appropriate instruments are available, examiners should also plan to obtain information from informal testing, observations, interviews, and work samples.

Early childhood special education, as a relatively new field, continues to grow and develop. New partnerships of families and professionals are being formed to assess, develop, and provide appropriate services. New ways of assisting young children with disabilities to play and grow within their neighborhoods are being explored. The assessment process, too, continues to evolve as we add to our knowledge and understanding of services for young children and their families.

Thus, good assessment practices involve addressing a number of key considerations. The following list outlines some key questions and provides a framework from which we can evaluate our assessment practices.

A. Child and Family Considerations
   1. What is the purpose of this assessment?
   2. What types of information can be gathered?
   3. How does the instrument allow for parental input?
   4. Does this instrument meet cultural considerations?
   5. How long will the assessment take?
B. Test Instrument Considerations
   1. Was the instrument designed for the purpose for which it is intended to be used?
   2. Which team member or members should administer this instrument?
   3. Are the criteria for scoring clearly stated?
   4. Is the instrument easily scored?
   5. Can the instrument be administered in different modes of communication, if necessary?
   6. For standardized instruments:
      a. Did the norming population include children who are similar to the child who will be tested?
      b. How reliable is the instrument?
      c. How valid is the instrument?

C. Examiner Considerations
   1. Do you meet the qualifications of education and experience necessary to administer this instrument?
   2. Do you need additional training in administration and/or scoring of this instrument?
D. Program Considerations
   1. Is the use of this instrument consistent with the philosophy of the program?
   2. Will available funding cover the costs of the instrument, additional test materials, and staff training?

STUDY QUESTIONS AND SUGGESTED ACTIVITIES

1. Discuss the rationale for including families in the assessment process.
2. What are the steps in assessment, and how do they differ in purpose from one another?
3. Outline the critical issues and considerations in assessing young children.
4. What is the status of services to infants and toddlers with or at risk for disability in your state?
5. What are some of the advantages and disadvantages of the different models of teaming?
6. Contact your lead state agency for services to young children with special needs and your state department of education. What information resources do they provide on assessment of young children?
7. Contact an early intervention specialist or special educator, an occupational therapist, and a public health nurse who works with young children. How are they involved with the assessment process?

REFERENCES

American Educational Research Association, American Psychological Association, & National Council on Measurement in Education (1985). *Standards for educational and psychological testing.* Washington, DC: Author.

Bailey, D. B., & Wolery, M. (1989). *Assessing infants and preschoolers with handicaps.* Columbus, OH: Merrill.

Bennett, T., Lingerfelt, B. V., & Nelson, D. E. (1990). *Developing individualized family support plans.* Cambridge, MA: Brookline.

Chamberlain, P., & Medeiros-Landurand, P. (1991). Practical considerations for the assessment of IEP students with special needs. In E. V. Hamayan & J. S. Damico (Eds.), *Limiting bias in the assessment of bilingual students* (pp. 111–156). Austin, TX: Pro-Ed.

Coalition Quarterly (1991). Early Childhood Bulletin.

Cunningham, C., & Davis, H. (1985). *Working with parents: Frameworks for collaboration.* Philadelphia: Open University Press.

Education of the Handicapped Act Amendments (Report No. 99-860). (September 26, 1986). Washington, DC: U.S. Government Printing Office.

Federal Register (September 29, 1992). Vol. 57, No. 189, pp. 44794–44852. Washington, DC: U.S. Government Printing Office.

Individuals with Disabilities Education Act Amendments (October 7, 1991). Washington, DC: U.S. Government Printing Office.

Linder, T. W. (1990). *Transdisciplinary play-based assessment: A functional approach to working with young children*. Baltimore: Paul H. Brookes.

McLean, M., Smith, B. J., McCormick, K., Schakel, J., & McEvoy, M. (1991). *Developmental delay: Establishing parameters for a preschool category of exceptionality* (Division for Early Childhood Position Paper). Reston, VA: Council for Exceptional Children.

Meisels, S. J., & Provence, S. (1989). *Screening and assessment: Guidelines for identifying young disabled and developmentally vulnerable children and their families*. Washington, DC: National Center for Clinical Infant Programs.

Peterson, N. L. (1987). *Early intervention for handicapped and at-risk children*. Denver: Love.

Salvia, J., & Ysseldyke, J. E. (1991). *Assessment* (5th ed.). Boston: Houghton Mifflin.

Sattler, J. (1988). *Assessment of children*. San Diego, CA: Jerome M. Sattler, Publisher.

Wallace, G., & Larsen, S. C. (1978). *Educational assessment of learning problems: Testing for teaching*. Boston: Allyn & Bacon.

Woodruff, G., & McGonigel, M. J. (1988). Early intervention team approaches: The transdisciplinary model. In J. B. Jordan, J. J. Gallagher, P. L. Hutinger, & M. B. Karnes (Eds.), *Early childhood special education: Birth to three* (pp. 162-181). Reston, VA: Council for Exceptional Children.

CHAPTER 2

Measuring Performance

CHAPTER OBJECTIVES

This chapter describes the basic measurement concepts used in analyzing and interpreting the performance of children. These concepts are fundamental to the understanding and interpretation of informal and formal test instruments. Knowledge of the terms and conventions covered here will make you a better user and consumer of tests.

This chapter discusses key concepts relating to measurement. Upon completion of the chapter, you should be able to:

Describe different ways of presenting and interpreting test scores.

Understand ways in which errors in measurement can be taken into consideration.

Discuss the advantages and disadvantages of using test scores of different types when interpreting test performance.

Define the concept of correlation and show how this concept is closely related to reliability and validity.

Define reliability and describe the different types of reliability.

Define validity and describe the different types of validity.

Describe the application of the concepts of standard error of measurement, estimated true scores, and confidence intervals.

Differentiate between norm-referenced standardized assessment and criterion-referenced assessment.

Key Terms

Nominal Scale. The items on the scale represent names; the values assigned to the names do not have any innate meaning or value.

Ordinal Scale. The items on the scale are listed in rank order.

Interval Scale. The items on the scale are the same distance apart; the scale does not have an absolute zero.

Ratio Scale. The items on the scale are the same distance apart; the scale does have an absolute zero.

SCALES OF MEASUREMENT

The performance of children can be estimated using test scores, which are based on measurement scales of different types. The description of a child's performance depends on the measurement scale used. The four different scales used in measurement are nominal, ordinal, interval, and ratio.

Nominal Scale

A *nominal scale* represents the lowest level of measurement. It is a naming scale. Each value on the scale is a name, and the name does not have any innate or inherent value. Lists of hair color, children's names, and numbers on football jerseys are all examples of nominal scales. Although there are numerals on football uniforms, they have no inherent rank or value. The numeral is just associated with the name of the football player. A teacher may use a nominal scale to distinguish between three groups called 1, 2, and 3. The numbers 1, 2, and 3 have no intrinsic value; they simply label the groups. Nominal scales have limited usefulness because scale items cannot be added, subtracted, multiplied, or divided; they just represent names. These scales are rarely used in reporting test performance.

Ordinal Scale

An *ordinal scale,* which represents the next level of measurement, orders items on a scale or continuum. The ordering of students according to class rank is an example of an ordinal scale (Table 2.1). Suppose a teacher wants to rank the activity level of a group of young children from 1 to 10, with 1 being the most active and 10 the least active. The child who is the most active will be ranked 1, the next active 2, and so on. Ordinal scales do have one important limitation. The distance between the ranks— that is, the distance between children ranked 1, 2, 3, etc.—is not necessarily equal. The child who is ranked 1 may be somewhat more active than the child who is ranked 2, but child 2 may be a great deal more active than the child who is ranked 3. Because of this limitation, ordinal scale items cannot be added, subtracted, multiplied, or divided.

Interval Scale

Interval scales are similar to ordinal scales but have several important advantages. *Interval scales,* like ordinal scales, order items on a scale or continuum, but, unlike ordinal scales, the distance between the items is equal. In addition, interval scales have a zero. But the 0 is placed at an arbitrary point along the measurement scale; it is not an absolute zero. For example, the Fahrenheit scale is an equal-interval scale:

TABLE 2.1 Ordinal scale

Child	Rank
Seth	10
John	9
Sue	8
Phyllis	7
Juan	6
Megan	5
Mia	4
Xran	3
Roy	2
Paul	1

The distance between 50 and 51° F is equal to the distance between 211 and 212° F; but the 0 point was arbitrarily established by Daniel Fahrenheit when he developed the temperature scale. IQ scores are also based on equal-interval scales. Although there is an equal distance between, say, IQs of 104 and 105 and 115 and 116, an IQ of 0 cannot be measured. Another well-known measurement scale that uses an interval scale is the Scholastic Aptitude Test (SAT). SAT scores range from 200 to 800. There is no zero!

Ratio Scale

Ratio scales have all the characteristics of ordinal and interval scales and they have an absolute zero. Height and weight measurements are examples of ratio scales. Teacher-developed tests, such as classroom spelling or arithmetic tests, frequently are based on the ratio scale. The total number of test items answered correctly, or the raw score, is based on a ratio scale. Some observation and rating scales are also ratio scales. Because the ratio scale has an absolute zero, the scores can be used in mathematical operations. If we record the number of times the children in a group raise their hands, we may conclude on the basis of a ratio scale that one child exhibits this behavior two or three times more often than another child.

Key Terms

Frequency Distribution. A way of organizing test scores based on how often they occur.

Normal Curve. A symmetrical bell-shaped curve.

Skewed Distribution. An organization of test scores represented by a curve in which most of the scores are at the low end or the high end of the curve.

Leptokurtic Curve. A curve in which most of the scores occur in the middle.

Platykurtic Curve. A curve in which the scores occur in a broad, flat distribution.

FREQUENCY DISTRIBUTION

A *frequency distribution* helps us to understand test scores better by organizing them based on how often they occur. To create a frequency distribution, arrange the

TABLE 2.2 Frequency distribution

Score	Frequency
100	1
98	2
90	2
85	4
70	6
50	5
42	3
30	2
25	1

Total number of children 26

test scores in a column from high to low. Next to each test score, record the number of children who obtained that score. The frequencies are added to find the total number of students who took the test (Table 2.2). Next, a frequency polygon can be constructed (Figure 2.1).

Frequency distributions can have different shapes. The shape represents how students' scores are grouped. When scores are normally distributed, most fall in the middle and fewer scores occur at the ends of the curve obtained by plotting all the scores. The normal curve is a symmetrical bell-shaped curve (Figure 2.2). There has been considerable debate about whether human characteristics are distributed along a normal curve. While there is some evidence that physical characteristics such as height and weight are normally distributed, it has not been demonstrated that such other characteristics as intelligence, development, and achievement are normally distributed. While it is unlikely that the performance of small groups of children will be normally distributed on a specific characteristic, curves constructed from the test results from large norm samples tend to be more normal in appearance (Mehrens & Lehmann, 1991).

Some curves describe frequency distributions in which the scores are fast rising. These are called *leptokurtic* (Figure 2.3). Curves in which the scores occur in broad, flat distributions are called *platykurtic* (Figure 2.4).

FIGURE 2.1 Frequency polygon

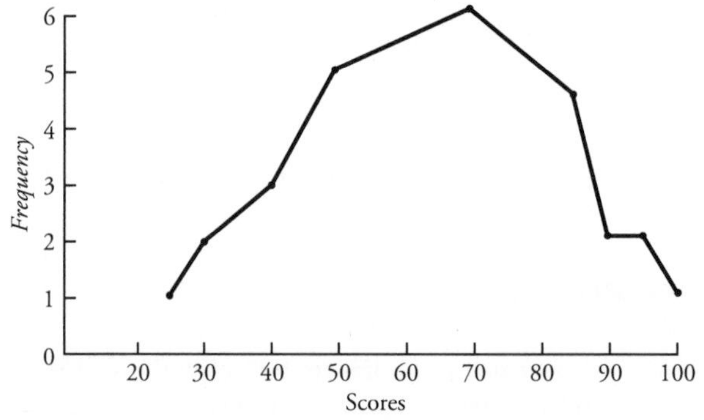

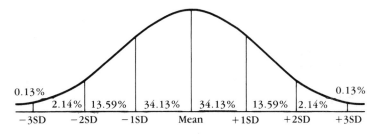

FIGURE 2.2 Normal distribution

Sometimes, the majority of scores lie at one end of the distribution. These scores are skewed. Positively skewed distributions contain only a few high scores, with the majority of scores occurring at the low end. Negatively skewed distributions have few scores at the low end and a majority of scores at the high end. When distributions are either positively or negatively skewed, the mean, median, and mode shift. Figure 2.5 shows the placement of the mean, median, and mode in skewed distributions.

Key Terms

Mean. Average score.

Median. The score that occurs in the middle of a group of scores when they are ranked from high to low.

Mode. The most common test score.

Standard Deviation (SD). A measure of the degree to which various scores deviate from the mean.

MEAN, MEDIAN, AND MODE

Measures of central tendency are used to describe typical test performance of a group of children using a single number. The number that results from the calcula-

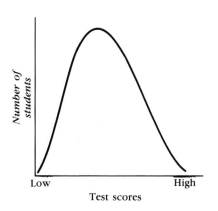

FIGURE 2.3 Leptokurtic curve

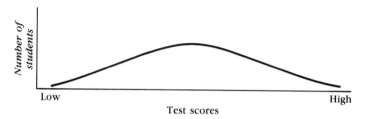

FIGURE 2.4   Platykurtic curve

tion of a measure of central tendency represents the typical score obtained by the group of children (Gay, 1985). Mean, mode, and median are measures of central tendency.

Mean

The *mean,* or the average score, is the most frequently used measure of central tendency. It is computed by adding all the scores and dividing by the total number of scores (Table 2.3). Because all the scores in a distribution are taken into account when the mean is calculated, the mean is affected by extreme scores.

Median

Another measure of central tendency is the *median,* which is the score that occurs in the middle of a group of scores when all the scores are arranged from high to low. The median is an excellent measure of central tendency when most of the scores cluster together but a few scores lie at the extreme ends of a distribution.

FIGURE 2.5   Relationship between the mode, median, and mean for skewed distributions

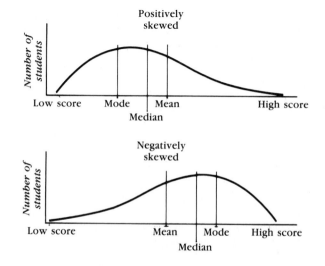

TABLE 2.3   Finding the average (mean)

Score	Frequency	Frequency × Score
100	1	100
98	2	196
90	2	180
85	4	340
70	6	420
50	5	250
42	3	126
30	2	60
25	1	25
	Number of scores 26	Sum of scores 1697

$$\frac{\text{sum of scores}}{\text{number of scores}} = \text{mean} \qquad \frac{1697}{26} = 65.26 \qquad \text{mean} = 65.26$$

Mode

Finally, the *mode* is the score that occurs most frequently in a list of scores. In a distribution of scores, the mode is the most common score. However, a distribution of test scores can have more than one mode. A teacher who wanted to know which test or test item has been answered correctly most frequently would use the mode. The mode is infrequently used because, however, it is not very helpful in describing the performance of an individual child or of a group of children. In a normal distribution, the mean, median, and mode all occur at the same point (Figure 2.2).

Standard Deviation

The *standard deviation* (*SD*) tells us the degree to which various scores deviate from the mean. It is a unit of measurement just as inches and feet are units of measurement. Scores can be expressed in terms of the number of standard deviation units by which they differ from the mean.

The standard deviation is useful when comparing several sets of scores. It can be helpful when interpreting the test performance of one child or a group of children. When comparing scores, the larger the standard deviation, the more variable is the performance; the smaller the standard deviation, the less variable is the performance of the children.

In a normal distribution, the percentages of scores that can be expected to fall within the first, second, and third standard deviations above or below the mean are shown in Figure 2.2. For example, when a group of scores is normally distributed, 34.13% can be expected to occur between the mean and +1 SD, and 34.13% also occurs between the mean and −1 SD. Approximately 14% of the scores fall between +1 SD and +2 SD, and 14% of the scores fall between −1 SD and −2 SD. Roughly 2% of the scores occur beyond +2 SD and 2% beyond −2 SD.

Most tests come with manuals that provide information about the mean and the standard deviation. You will not have to calculate the standard deviation. For example, the manual for the third edition of the Wechsler Intelligence Scale (WISC-III) reports that this test has a mean of 100 and a standard deviation of 15. This means that approximately 34.13% of children have intelligence quotients (IQs) between 100 and 115. Similarly, approximately 34.13% of children have IQs between 85 and 100.

Many states mandate specific guidelines for identification and placement of children. For example, some states define mental retardation of school-age children as represented by an IQ that is at least 2 standard deviations below the mean. Thus, in such states a child with an IQ of 65 would be labeled as mentally retarded because 65 is lower than the cutoff score of 70 ($100 - 30$ [2 SD] $= 70$).

Key Terms

Raw Scores. The number of items correct without adjustment for guessing.

Percentage Score. The percent of test items that were answered correctly.

Developmental Scores. Raw scores that have been transformed to reflect the average performance at age and grade levels.

Developmental Quotient. Estimate of the rate of development.

Percentile Rank. Point in a distribution at or below which the scores of a given percentage of persons fall.

Standard Scores. Raw scores that have been transformed so that they have the same mean and the same standard deviation.

Normal Curve Equivalent (NCE). A standard score with a mean of 50 and a standard deviation of 21.06.

Deviation IQ. A standard score with a mean of 100 and a standard deviation of 15 or 16.

Stanine. A type of standard score that has a mean of 5 and a standard deviation of 2; a distribution can be divided into 9 stanines.

Interpolation. The estimation of scores within the ages and grades that were tested.

Extrapolation. The estimation of the performance of children outside the normative sample.

TYPES OF SCORES

There are many ways of reporting test performance. Therefore, in interpreting children's test performance, it is important to understand the strengths and weaknesses of scores of these different types.

Raw Scores

The *raw score* is the number of items a child answers correctly without adjustment for guessing. For example, if there are 15 problems on an arithmetic test, and a student answers 11 correctly, the raw score is 11. Raw scores, however, do not provide enough information to permit us to describe student performance.

Percentage Scores

Percentage scores are also inadequate because they provide little information. A *percentage score* is the percent of test items that were answered correctly. However, percentage scores have a major disadvantage. We have no way of comparing the percentage correct on one test with the percentage correct on another test. Suppose a child earned a score of 85% correct on one test and 55% correct on another test. Although these scores should be interpreted in a way that reflects the difficulty level of the items, because the tests differ in level of difficulty, we have no common way to interpret these scores; there is no frame of reference (Anastasi, 1982).

To interpret raw scores and percentage correct scores, we must change the raw score to a different type of score before we can compare scores. Raw scores and percentage correct scores are rarely used when interpreting children's performance because it is difficult to compare one child's scores on several tests, or the performance of several children on several tests, when the performance is reported as a raw score or as a percentage score.

Derived Scores

Because of the disadvantages of raw scores and percentage correct scores, we are unable to compare these scores directly. *Derived scores* are a family of scores that allow us to make such comparisons. Derived scores are determined from raw scores. Developmental scores and scores of relative standing are two types of derived scores. Scores of relative standing include percentiles, standard scores, and stanines.

Developmental Scores.   Developmental scores are scores that have been transformed from raw scores and reflect the average performance at age and grade levels. Age and grade equivalents are developmental scores. Age equivalents are written with a hyphen between years and months (e.g., 2-4 means that the age equivalent is two years, four months old). In this book, the use of this convention is confined to tabular material. A decimal point is used between the grade and month in grade equivalents (e.g., 1.2 is the first grade, second month).

Both Sattler (1988) and Bailey and Wolery (1989) have pointed out that developmental scores can be useful. They are easily interpreted by parents and professionals, and the performance of children is placed in a context. Because these scores are easy to misinterpret, however, they should be used with extreme caution. They have been criticized for a number of reasons.

For a six-year-old child who is in the first grade, grade equivalents and age equivalents presume that for each month of first grade an equal amount of learning occurs. But, from our knowledge of child growth and development and from theories about learning, we know that neither growth nor learning occurs in equal monthly intervals. Age and grade equivalents do not take into consideration variations in individual growth and learning.

Teachers should not expect children to gain a grade equivalent or age equivalent of one year for each year they are in school. For example, suppose a child earned a grade equivalent of 1.5, first grade, fifth month, at the end of first grade. The teacher should not assume that at the end of second grade the child will or should obtain a grade equivalent of 2.5, second grade, fifth month. Such an assumption is incorrect for two reasons: (1) the grade and age equivalent norms should not be confused with performance standards; and (2) a gain of 1.0 grade equivalent is representative only of children who are in the average range for their grade. Children who are above average will gain more than 1.0 grade equivalent a year, and children who are below average will progress less than 1.0 grade equivalent a year (Gronlund & Linn, 1990).

A second criticism of developmental scores is that children who obtain the same score on a test will display the same thinking, behavior, and skill patterns. For example, a child who is in second grade earned a grade equivalent score of 4.6 on a test of reading achievement. This does not mean that the second grader understands the reading process as it is taught in the fourth grade. Rather, the child performed at a superior level for a second grader. It is incorrect to compare this second grade child to a fourth grader; the comparison should be made to other children who are in second grade (Anastasi, 1982; Sattler, 1988; Salvia & Ysseldyke, 1991).

A third criticism of developmental scores is that age and grade equivalents encourage the use of false standards. A second grade teacher should not expect all students in the class to perform at the second grade level on a reading test. Differences seen in children within a grade may mean that the range of achievement actually spans several grades. In addition, developmental scores are calculated so that half the scores fall below the median and half above. Age and grade equivalents are not standards of performance (Anastasi, 1982; Salvia & Ysseldyke, 1991).

A fourth criticism of age and grade equivalents is that they promote typological thinking. The use of age and grade equivalents causes us to think in terms of a typical kindergartner or a typical thirty-month-old child. But children vary in their abilities and levels of performance. Developmental scores do not take these variations into account (Salvia & Ysseldyke, 1991).

A fifth criticism is that most developmental scores are interpolated and extrapolated. When a test is normed, children of specific ages and grades are included in the norming sample. However, not all ages and grades are included. Sometimes we *interpolate*—that is, estimate scores within the ages and grades that were tested. Sometimes we *extrapolate,* or estimate the performance of children outside the normative sample (Salvia & Ysseldyke, 1991).

Developmental Quotient.   A developmental quotient is an estimate of the rate of development. If we know a child's developmental age and chronological age, it is possible to calculate a developmental quotient. For example, suppose a child had a developmental age of 80 months and a chronological age of 80 months. Using the following formula, we could arrive at a developmental quotient of 100.

$$\frac{\text{developmental age 80 months}}{\text{chronological age 80 months}} \times 100 = 100$$

But, suppose another child's chronological age was also 80 months, and that the developmental age was 60 months. Using the formula, this child would have a developmental quotient of 75.

$$\frac{\text{developmental age 60 months}}{\text{chronological age 80 months}} \times 100 = 75$$

Developmental quotients have all the drawbacks associated with age and grade equivalents. In addition, they may be misleading because developmental age does not always keep pace with chronological age. Consequently, there is likely to be a greater gap between developmental age and chronological age as the child gets older.

Percentile Ranks.   A percentile rank is the point in a distribution at or below which the scores of a given percentage of individuals fall. Percentage correct is not the same as percentile. Percentage correct refers to the percent of test items that were answered correctly. Percentiles provide information about the relative standing of children in comparison to the standardization sample. For example, if 47% of children in a standardization sample scored fewer than 25 test items correct, a raw score of 25 would coincide with the 47th percentile. These scores can be very useful. Percentiles can be used with a variety of tests. They are easy to calculate and easy to understand.

A percentile rank of 50 represents average performance. In a normal distribution, both the mean and the median fall at the 50th percentile. Half the children fall above the 50th percentile and half below. Percentiles can be divided into quartiles. A quartile contains 25 percentiles or 25% of the scores in a distribution. The 25th and the 75th percentiles are the first and the third quartiles. In addition, percentiles can be divided into groups of 10 known as deciles. Beginning at the bottom of a group of children, the first 10% are known as the first decile, the second 10% are known as the second decile, and so on.

The position of percentiles in a normal curve is shown in Figure 2.6. Despite their ease of interpretation, there are several problems associated with percentiles. First, the intervals they represent are unequal, especially at the lower and upper ends of the distribution. A difference of a few percentiles at the extreme ends of the

FIGURE 2.6   Relationships among scores of different types in a normal distribution

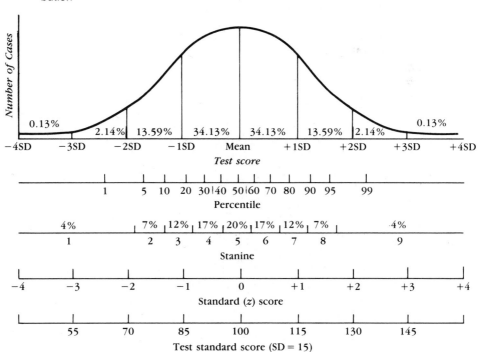

distribution should be taken more seriously than a difference of a few points in the middle of the distribution. Next, percentiles cannot be used in mathematical calculations (Gronlund & Linn, 1990). Finally, percentile scores are reported in one-hundredths. But, because of errors associated with measurement, they are only accurate to the nearest 0.06 (six one-hundredths) (Rudner, Conoley, & Plake, 1989). Because of these limitations, caution should be used when interpreting percentile ranks. Confidence intervals, which are discussed later in this chapter, should be used when interpreting percentile scores.

Standard Scores.   Another type of derived score is a standard score. *Standard score* is the name given to a group or category of scores. Each specific type of standard score within the group has the same mean and the same standard deviation. Because each type of standard score has the same mean and the same standard deviation, standard scores are an excellent way of representing a child's performance. Standard scores allow us to compare a child's performance on several tests and also to compare one child's performance to that of other children. Unlike percentile scores, standard scores can be used in mathematical operations. For instance, standard scores can be averaged.

Figure 2.6 compares standard or *z* scores with scores of the other types we have discussed. As can be seen, standard scores are equal-interval scores. The different types of standard scores, some of which are discussed individually in the subsections that follow, are:

1. *z* scores: have a mean of 0 and a standard deviation of 1
2. *T* scores: a mean of 50 and a standard deviation of 10
3. Normal curve equivalents: have a mean of 50 and a standard deviation of 21.06
4. Deviation IQs: have a mean of 100 and a standard deviation of 15 or 16
5. Stanines: standard score bands that divide a distribution of scores into nine parts

Normal Curve Equivalents.   Normal curve equivalents (NCEs) are a type of standard score with a mean of 50 and a standard deviation of 21.06. This means of scoring has been used in the evaluation of federally funded projects. When the baseline of the normal curve is divided into 99 equal units, the percentile ranks of 1, 50, and 99 are the same as NCE units (Lyman, 1986). Normal curve equivalents are not reported for some tests. One test that does report NCEs is the Battelle Developmental Inventory.

Deviation IQ Scores.   Deviation IQ scores are frequently used to report the performance of young children on norm-referenced, standardized tests. The deviation scores of the Wechsler Preschool and Primary Scale of Intelligence—Revised, the Wechsler Intelligence Scale for Children—III, and the Bayley Scales of Infant Development have a mean of 100 and a standard deviation of 15. The Stanford–Binet Intelligence Scale—IV has a mean of 100 and a standard deviation of 16.

Stanines.   Stanines are bands of standard scores that have a mean of 5 and a standard deviation of 2. As illustrated in Figure 2.6, stanines range from 1 to 9. Even though they are relatively easy to interpret, stanines have several disadvantages. A change in just a few raw score points can move a student from one stanine to another. Because stanines are a general way of interpreting test performance, caution should be used when making classification and placement decisions on the basis of this type of score. As an aid in interpreting stanines, descriptors can be associated with the numerical values:

9—very superior

8—superior

7—very good

6—good

5—average

4—below average

3—considerably below average

2—poor

1—very poor

Key Terms

Basal Level. The point below which the examiner assumes that the child could obtain all correct responses and at which the examiner begins testing.

Ceiling Level. The point above which the examiner assumes that the child would obtain all incorrect responses if the testing were to continue and at which the examiner stops testing.

Basal and Ceiling Levels

Because tests are constructed so that they can be used with children of differing abilities, many tests contain more items than are necessary when assessing a child. To determine the starting and stopping points for administering a test, test authors designate basal and ceiling levels. (Although really not score types, basal and ceiling levels sometimes are called rules or scores.) The *basal level* is the point below which the examiner assumes that the child could obtain all correct responses and at which the examiner begins testing. The *ceiling level* is the point above which the examiner assumes that the child would obtain all incorrect responses if the testing were to continue and at which the examiner stops testing.

Basal and ceiling rules differ from one test to another. The test manual will designate the point at which basal testing should begin. For example, a test manual may say, "Children who are four years old should begin with item 12." Or "Children who are in kindergarten should begin with item 3." Next, the test manual should be consulted to determine the basal and ceiling rules for each test to be used. With respect to the basal level, for example, a manual may state, "Continue testing when three items in a row have been answered correctly. If three items in a row are not answered correctly, the examiner should drop back a level." The instructions for determining the ceiling may read as follows: "Discontinue testing when three items in a row have been missed."

In individual tests, basal and ceiling rules generally match. For example, if the basal rule is to continue testing after three correct responses, the ceiling rule will be to stop after three incorrect responses. Once the basal level has been established, the examiner starts testing and continues until three incorrect responses have been made. This is the ceiling level, the point at which testing should stop.

If a child fails to obtain a basal score, the examiner must drop back a level on the test. Let's look at the example of the child who is four years old. Although the examiner begins testing at the four-year-old level according to the manual, the child fails to answer three items in a row correctly. Thus, the examiner has not established a basal level. Next, the manual may instruct the examiner to continue testing backward, dropping back one item at a time, until three correct responses have been obtained. Some test manuals instruct examiners to drop back a whole level—for instance, to age three—and begin testing again (Overton, 1992).

Key Terms

Correlation. The extent to which two or more scores vary together.

Correlation Coefficient. Quantifies the degree of relationship between scores.

CORRELATION

A *correlation* indicates the extent to which two or more scores vary together. It measures the extent to which a change in one score goes with a change in another score. A *correlation coefficient* quantifies the degree of relation between two or more scores. For example, in general, the higher a child's intelligence score, the higher will be the child's score on a vocabulary test. It follows that, in general, students with higher IQ scores will tend to have higher vocabulary scores, and students with lower IQ scores probably will have lower vocabulary test scores. We can say that IQ and vocabulary level are correlated. However, caution must be used when interpreting relationships; two scores may correlate, but this does not mean that one score causes a change in the other score.

A correlation coefficient quantifies a relationship and provides information about whether there is a relationship, the strength of the relationship, and the direction of the relationship. The value of a correlation coefficient can vary from +1.00 to −1.00. If there were a perfect relationship between IQ level and vocabulary achievement, the correlation would be expressed as either +1.00 or −1.00. (When positive correlation coefficients are written, the + is usually omitted.) For example, if for every increase in IQ there is a corresponding increase in vocabulary scores, it can be said that the relationship between IQ and vocabulary level is 1.00. But because there are so many other variables that influence both IQ and vocabulary achievement, this relationship will never be a perfect 1.00 (Figure 2.7). A perfect negative relationship is indicated by −1.00, and a coefficient of .00 expresses the absence of any relationship. The relationship between thumb sucking and the age of a child is a negative relationship (Figure 2.8). The relationship between visual acuity and linguistic ability approaches zero (Figure 2.9).

The strength of the correlation can be determined by how close the coefficient is to either 1.00 or to −1.00. The closer the correlation coefficient is to .00, the weaker the relationship. For example, a coefficient of −.73 is stronger than a coefficient of .32 because −.73 is closer to −1.00, just as a coefficient of .85 is stronger than a coefficient of .12 because .85 is closer to 1.00.

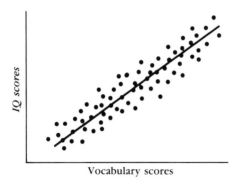

FIGURE 2.7 Scatterplot of a positive relationship

The direction of a correlation can be determined by inspection: A + sign indicates that a relationship is positive; a − sign indicates that a relationship is negative. When one test score increases as another test score increases, the relationship is positive. However, when one test score decreases while the other test score increases, the relationship is negative. In a positive relationship, the scores either increase together or decrease together. The relationship between IQ and vocabulary achievement is a positive relationship because both these variables usually increase together. The relationship between thumb sucking and age of the child is usually a negative relationship because this behavior tends to decrease as the child gets older.

Key Terms

Reliability. An indication of the consistency or stability of test performance.

True Score. The score an individual would obtain on a test if there were no measurement errors.

Test–retest Reliability. An estimate of the correlation between scores when the same test is administered twice.

Alternate Form Reliability. An estimate of the correlation of scores between two forms of the same test.

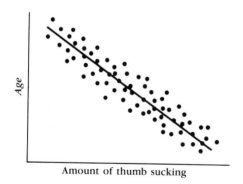

FIGURE 2.8 Scatterplot of a negative relationship

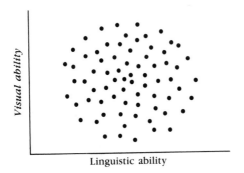

FIGURE 2.9   Scatterplot of no relationship

Split-half Reliability. An estimate of the correlation of scores between two halves of a test.

Internal Consistency Reliability. An estimate of the homogeneity or interrelatedness of responses to test items.

Interscorer/Interobserver/Interrater Reliability. An estimate of the extent to which two or more scorers, observers, or raters agree on how a test should be scored or behaviors should be observed.

RELIABILITY AND VALIDITY

Reliability and validity can be compared with quality control indicators of products. How do we know whether tests are useful? How do teachers know that the performance of children is consistent? How do we know that a test measures what the authors say it measures? Reliability and validity help us to determine the answers to these questions.

It is up to teachers to evaluate the reliability and validity that are reported in test manuals. While some books and journal articles report evaluations of tests, tests are not given "seals of approval." To be useful, they must meet certain standards.

Reliability

Reliability describes the consistency or stability of test performance. The teacher needs to know that a child's test performance is consistent over time and when measured by different test items that have similar content objectives. Suppose a test is administered to a child on one day. The teacher wants some assurance that if the same child were retested on the following day, the score would be about the same as the score obtained on the first test. Or suppose a child takes one form or version of a test. Again, the teacher needs to know that if the child were tested with a similar form of a test, the scores would be about the same. Of course, it is impractical and unnecessary for children to take tests every day. Reliability provides an estimate of the consistency of test results when a test is administered on multiple occasions under similar conditions. All types of reliability are expressed as the consistency or agreement between sets of test scores. This consistency or agreement is described by a correlation coefficient (Anastasi, 1982). A correlation coefficient is symbolized by r. Some test manuals use the term *reliability coefficient* in place of correlation coefficient. Reliability coefficients can range from 0.00 to 1.00.

In any testing situation, variability exists, and many sources of error can be associated with the testing situation. Errors in measurement can stem from the testing environment, the child, the test, and the examiner. Sources of error in the testing environment include noise distractions, poor lighting, and uncomfortable room temperature. The child may be hungry, tired, or ill, or the test instructions may be difficult to understand. The test administration directions may be unclear, the test items may be poorly worded, or scoring may be ambiguous. Finally, the examiner may not be prepared or may interpret administration or scoring guidelines incorrectly.

Reliability can also be thought of as consisting of the child's *true score* and an *error score.* The score a child gets on a test is the *obtained score.* This is the best estimate we have of a student's performance. If all testing conditions were perfect and there were no errors of measurement, we would be able to obtain a student's true score. But, since error is always present, we can never know the true score. We can, however, estimate an individual's true score by using the formula

$$X = T + E$$

where the child's obtained or observed score X equals the true score T plus the errors that are associated with measurement, represented by E.

Because of the possibility of error, it is important that the test publisher provide an estimate of reliability. Three professional organizations, the American Educational Research Association, the American Psychological Association, and the National Council on Measurement in Education, issued a guidebook, *Standards for Educational and Psychological Testing* (1985). These professional standards are very important. According to these standards:

> Reliability refers to the degree to which test scores are free from errors of measurement. A test taker may perform differently on one occasion than on another for reasons that may or may not be related to the purpose of measurement. A person may try harder, be more fatigued or anxious, have greater familiarity with the content of questions on one test form than another, or simply guess correctly on more questions on one occasion than on another. For these and other reasons, a person's score will not be perfectly consistent from one occasion to the next. Indeed, an individual's scores will rarely be the same on two forms of a test that are intended to be interchangeable. Even the most careful matching of item content and difficulty on two forms of a test cannot ensure that an individual who knows the answer to a particular question on Form A will know the answer to a matched counterpart on Form B. (p. 19)

A teacher who measures the performance of a child must have some confidence that the child's performance is as close as possible to the true performance of that child. The scores the child obtains should be an accurate estimate of that individual's ability. Because reliability is expressed by a correlation coefficient, the closer the coefficient is to 1.00, the higher the reliability of the test, and the more confidence the teacher can have that the test results reflect consistent performance.

It is incumbent on the test publisher to accurately report the results of reliability calculations. In a test manual, a lowercase r designates reliability. For example, if a test manual reports $r = .92$, we know that the reliability for this test is .92 and that because this value is close to 1.00, the teacher can have some confidence that the test measures performance with consistency.

It is important for teachers to judge the usefulness of correlation coefficients. Test publishers should tell how they obtained the samples of children, individuals, or observations on which their reliability coefficients are determined. For guidance in evaluating correlation coefficients, Salvia and Ysseldyke (1991) recommend that tests used for screening have a coefficient of at least .80. However, if the results of the testing are to be used for identification and placement purposes, a correlation coefficient of at least .90 is recommended. If test scores are to be reported for groups of children, not for individuals, a minimum reliability coefficient of .60 is considered to be sufficient.

Types of Reliability.   There are five types of reliability: test–retest, alternate form, internal consistency, split-half, and interobserver/interscorer/interrater reliability. For each type of reliability, there are several disadvantages, and it is up to the teacher to evaluate the usefulness of the reliability information. Thus it is very useful when test publishers provide information on more than one type of reliability.

Test–retest Reliability.   Test–retest reliability can be estimated when the same test is administered to the same child twice. The scores obtained on the first and second administrations can be correlated and a reliability coefficient obtained. This coefficient is an index of the stability of the test score. Because the same test is administered twice, it is very important to know the time interval between the two testings. Too short an interval will cause the reliability coefficient to be inflated. When the interval is too long, however, developmental changes may occur in the child, diminishing the validity of the reliability coefficient. Anastasi (1982) recommends the use of a short interval when estimating test–retest reliability, to avoid the influence of developmental changes. Salvia and Ysseldyke (1991) recommend an interval of two weeks.

There are several drawbacks to this measure of reliability. Having been exposed to the test items and to the directions for taking the test over two test administrations, the child may obtain a higher test score on the second testing. Also, as mentioned earlier, maturation, growth, and development of the child may artificially inflate the reliability coefficient.

Alternate Form Reliability.   Alternate form reliability is also known as equivalent form and parallel form reliability. Frequently, there is a need for two forms of a test that contain different test items but evaluate the same knowledge and skills. This procedure is especially useful when tests are used to pre- and post-test children. The two forms have different designations. For example, some forms are designated A and B; others may be labeled X and Y or L and M.

Like test–retest reliability, alternate form reliability has several disadvantages. For example, it is difficult to develop two parallel forms of a test. Like test–retest reliability, too, the reliability coefficient can be inflated by a shorter interval between test administrations, the effect of practice on similar test items, and the maturation, growth, and development of the child. When test publishers report alternate form reliability coefficients, the *Standards for Educational and Psychological Testing* (American Educational Research Association et al., 1985) recommends that test publishers state the order in which the alternate forms were administered, the time interval between the two administrations, and the reasons for choosing the particular time interval.

Split-half Reliability.   A split-half reliability coefficient is obtained by administering a test to a group of students, dividing the total number of test items in half to form two tests, and correlating the scores on the two halves of the test. For example, suppose a test has 20 items. We could administer the entire test to a group of children and then divide the test into two halves, each containing 10 items, which could then be correlated. Different methods may be used to break a test into halves: One can separate the first half from the second half or separate the even-numbered items from the odd-numbered items.

Dividing a test into a first and a second half can cause problems in determining the reliability. Fatigue, practice effect, failure to complete the test, and print quality can affect the reliability coefficient (DeVellis, 1991). Assuming random order of the test items, the test could be divided by odd—even items or by balancing the halves, as suggested above. Balancing halves could involve item length, response type, or other characteristic that is appropriate for the test. The most appropriate method of splitting the halves of a test will depend on the test and the testing situation (DeVellis, 1991).

With the split-half procedure, the test is administered only once. Therefore, reliability coefficients obtained through this procedure are a measure of internal consistency, not of the temporal stability of test performance.

Internal Consistency Reliability.   This type of reliability is similar to the split-half method. *Internal consistency reliability* is an estimate of the homogeneity or interrelatedness of responses to test items. The test is administered only once. Several formulas are used to obtain an estimate of internal consistency. Usually one of the Kuder—Richardson formulas is used to find the average coefficient obtained by calculating all the possible split-half coefficients. The more similar the test items are to each other, the higher will be the reliability coefficient. Like split-half reliability, internal consistency reliability does not provide an estimate of the stability of the test over time.

Interscorer/Interobserver/Interrater Reliability.   This type of reliability is a measure of the extent to which two or more scorers, observers, or raters agree on how a test should be scored. *Interscorer/interobserver/interrater reliability* is important when errors in scoring or differences in judgment can affect the test outcomes. Interscorer/interobserver/interrater reliability measures the agreement among examiners. This type of reliability should be reported when:

1. There is a possibility that errors can be made in computing the test score(s).
2. A test item can have more than one answer.
3. A response to a question can have more than one interpretation.
4. Observations are made about the behaviors of a child or children.
5. Interviews are used to collect information.

Factors That Influence Reliability.   Several factors can affect the reliability of a test (Mehrens & Lehmann, 1991; Salvia & Ysseldyke, 1991; Sattler, 1988):

1. *Test length.* Generally, the longer a test is, the more reliable it is.
2. *Speed.* When a test is a speed test, it is inappropriate to estimate reliability using internal consistency, test–retest, or alternate form methods. This is because not every child is able to complete all the items in a speed test. In contrast, a test in which every child is able to complete all the items is called a *power test.*
3. *Group homogeneity.* In general, the more heterogeneous the group of children who take the test, the more reliable the instrument will be.
4. *Item difficulty.* When there is little variability among test scores, the reliability will be low. Thus, reliability will be low if a test is so easy that every child gets most or all of the items correct or so difficult that every child gets most or all of the items wrong.
5. *Objectivity.* When tests are scored objectively, rather than subjectively, the reliability will be higher.
6. *Test–retest interval.* The shorter the interval between two administrations of a test, the less likely that changes will occur and the higher the reliability will be.
7. *Variation with the testing situation.* Errors in the testing situation (e.g., children misunderstanding or misreading test directions; noise level; distractions; sickness) can cause test scores to vary.

Key Terms

Validity. The extent to which a test measures what it says it measures.

Content Validity. The extent to which the test items reflect the instructional objectives.

Criterion-related Validity. The extent to which scores obtained on one test are related to scores obtained on a test measuring another outcome.

Concurrent Validity. The extent to which two different tests administered at about the same time correlate with each other.

Predictive Validity. The extent to which one measure predicts later performance or behavior.

Construct Validity. The extent to which a test measures a particular construct or concept.

Face Validity. The extent to which a test looks valid.

Validity

The *validity* of a test is the extent to which the test measures what it says it measures. Expressed in another way, a test is valid if it measures what it is intended to measure. According to *Standards for Educational and Psychological Testing* (American Educational Research Association et al., 1985): "Validity is the most important consideration in test evaluation. The concept refers to the appropriateness, meaningfulness, and usefulness of the specific inferences made from test scores" (p. 9).

Reliability is a prerequisite of validity. That is, reliability must be demonstrated before evidence of validity can be considered. A test that is reliable is not necessarily valid. There are several types of validity: content; criterion-related, which includes concurrent and predictive validity; construct; and face. A correlation coefficient is commonly used to report criterion-related and construct validity. The symbol r is used to represent validity coefficients. From our discussion of reliability, you will recall that r is also used to symbolize reliability.

Content Validity.   Content validity measures the extent to which the test items reflect the instructional objectives of a test; it is important for all educational and psychological tests (Salvia & Ysseldyke, 1991). Content validity is the most important type of validity for achievement tests, however. An estimate of the content validity of a test is obtained by thoroughly and systematically examining the test items to determine the extent to which they reflect the instructional objectives and the content that was intended to be tested. Content validity is usually evaluated by a panel composed of curriculum experts and specialists in tests and measurements, who determine the extent to which the test items reflect the test objectives. Cronbach (1971) has written that over time tests become unrepresentative of curriculum, with the result that users must determine the extent to which a given test retains content validity.

To facilitate the determination of content validity, it is important that the test developer document (1) the test objectives, (2) the items that are measured by specific objectives, (3) the number of items for each objective, (4) the format and response type of the test items, and (5) the role of the curriculum or content experts in the development of the test items.

Most norm-referenced tests are constructed to represent the curricula taught in various geographic regions of the United States. Because these tests are so broad, they inadequately represent the curricula taught in many schools. Thus, as a rule, the content validity of norm-referenced tests must be thoroughly assessed before a teacher can be confident that a particular test is appropriate in this respect.

Criterion-related Validity.   Criterion-related validity refers to the extent to which scores obtained on one test or other measure relate to scores obtained on a test measuring another outcome. Concurrent and predictive validity are two types of criterion-related validity. When determining criterion-related validity, test developers compare their test with another measure or criterion—another test, school grades, observations, or other measures.

The *Standards for Educational and Psychological Testing* (American Educational Research Association et al., 1985) states that test developers should include information on the sample and the statistics used when describing studies followed in establishing criterion-related validity. In addition, the criterion measures should be named and the justification for using them set forth. When assessing the criterion-related validity of a test, it is important to verify that the criterion measure itself is valid, as well.

Concurrent Validity.   Concurrent validity is the extent to which the results of two different tests administered at about the same time correlate with each other. To obtain concurrent validity, the two tests are administered within a brief interval and the correlation between the scores obtained on both tests is calculated. This method of estimating validity is especially useful when a new test has been constructed. Suppose we were developing a new way to test the hearing abilities of young children. We would administer our new test and also a standard hearing test. Next, we would establish concurrent validity by examining the relationship between the scores the children obtained on the two tests. The test author wants to know the extent to which a known instrument and a new test measure the same objectives. If the new hearing test correlates highly with the established instrument, we may conclude that the new test is valid and that it has an acceptable level of concurrent validity. Evidence of concurrent validity is important when tests are used for achievement, diagnostic, and certification purposes (American Educational Research Association et al., 1985).

Predictive Validity.   How accurately can current performance predict future performance or behavior? *Predictive validity* is used when a test score aids in making forecasts about student performance or behavior. Although predictive validity, like concurrent validity, uses a criterion measure, concurrent validity should never be substituted for predictive validity.

Be careful not to confuse concurrent validity with predictive validity. There are some important differences, which bear repeating. Concurrent validity is a measure of the extent to which two sets of test scores are related to each other, but predictive validity is an estimate of the accuracy with which one test describes future performance or behavior. It is critical that readiness and placement tests (e.g., preschool readiness, college entrance tests) have high predictive validity. For example, tests used to predict which students will be successful in kindergarten must have high validity in this area. The Gesell Developmental Schedules is an example of a test that has poor evidence of predictive validity. Despite this, the Gesell has been frequently used to make predictions about the future performance of young children.

Construct Validity.   Construct validity is the extent to which a test measures a particular trait, construct, or psychological characteristic. Reasoning ability, spatial visualization, reading comprehension, sociability, and introversion are "referred to as constructs because they are theoretical constructions about the nature of human behavior" (American Educational Research Association et al., 1985, p. 9). In determining construct validity, the test developer describes the construct, indicating how it differs from other constructs and how it relates to other variables. In addition to accommodating the conceptual nature of the construct, the test developer must take care when specifying the test format, test administration, and other facets of test construction (American Educational Research Association et al., 1985).

Construct validity is the most difficult type of validity to establish. It takes a long period of time and numerous research studies before a particular test can be said to have construct validity. Zeller (1988) compared the establishment of construct validity to a detective's search for clues. Evidence is accumulated bit by bit. The clues assist the test developer in determining the consistency of the evidence in the interpretation of construct validity. If the evidence falls into a systematic pattern, the test developer can have confidence in the validity of the construct.

Face Validity.   Face validity is the extent to which a test looks valid to its users and takers. Face validity has to do with the format and appearance of a test. Anastasi

(1982) has written that "face validity concerns rapport and public relations" (p. 136). Although some experts discount the importance of face validity, Anastasi (1982) believes that it is a useful feature. Face validity should never be substituted for other types of validity, however.

Factors Affecting Validity.   Since validity is a measure of the extent to which a test measures what it says it measures, validity is affected by a number of factors:

1. *Reliability.* Reliability is a prerequisite of validity. However, a test that is reliable is not necessarily valid.
2. *Item selection.* A test is valid to the extent that it measures a child's exposure to the content that is being tested. For example, when an achievement test is administered, it is assumed that the child has been exposed to the content relating to the test items. To the extent that the child was not exposed to the content, the validity of such a test is lower (Salvia & Ysseldyke, 1991).
3. *Norms.* When the norm sample is unrepresentative of the population for which the test was developed, the scores on the test are either incorrect or invalid (Salvia & Ysseldyke, 1991).

Key Terms

Standard Error of Measurement (SEM). The amount of error associated with individual test scores, test items, item samples, and test times.

Confidence Interval. The range within which the true score can be found.

STANDARD ERROR OF MEASUREMENT

The administration of a test is subject to many errors: Errors can occur in the testing environment; the examiner may make errors; the examinees may not exhibit their best performance; and the test itself may not elicit the best performance from the examinees. All these errors contribute to lowering the reliability of a test.

The standard error of measurement (SEM) is related to reliability and is very useful in the interpretation of test performance. The SEM is the amount of error associated with individual test scores, test items, item samples, and test times. Figure 2.10 shows the distribution of the SEM around the estimated true score.

If it is expected that the reliability or the standard error of measurement will differ for different populations, SEMs should be reported for each population for which the test will be used. The *Standards for Educational and Psychological Testing* (1985) cautions that because reliability coefficients obtained from a sample of students from several grades usually produce an inflated reliability coefficient, reliability coefficients and SEMs should be reported for each grade level.

When the SEM is small, we can be more confident in a score; when the SEM is large, there is less confidence in the score. Thus, it follows that the more reliable a test is, the smaller the SEM and the more confidence we can have. The less reliable a test, the larger the SEM, and the more uncertainty we have in a score.

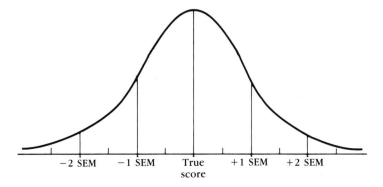

FIGURE 2.10   The standard error of measurement is the standard deviation of the error distribution around a true score for one subject. The formula for standard error of measurement is determined by subtracting the reliability *r* of a subject's scores from 1 and using a table or a pocket calculator to determine the square root of this fractional amount.

CONFIDENCE INTERVALS

Although we can never know a student's true score, we can use the concept of *confidence intervals* to give us a range within which the true score can be found. Because it is inadvisable to present a student's score as an exact point, the concept of confidence intervals is an important one to use when reporting a student's test score.

We can determine the probability that a child's score will fall within a particular range. The higher the probability level, the more confidence we can have that an individual's score will fall within a specific range. The lower the probability, the less confidence we have that a score falls within a particular range. The following list of the probabilities associated with z-scores indicates that different levels of probability can be used in the formula that determines the range in which a true score can be found. For instance, we can be 50, 68, 90, 95, 98, or 99% confident that a child's true score can be found within a range of scores.

z-Score	*Probability (%)*
0.67	50
1.00	68
1.64	90
1.96	95
2.33	98
2.57	99

Key Terms

Norm-referenced Test. A test that compares a child's test performance with that of similar children who have taken the same test.

Criterion-referenced Test. A test that measures a child's performance with respect to a well-defined content domain.

Norms. The scores obtained by the standardization sample. The scores to which children's results are compared when they have taken a test.

Sample. A subgroup that is representative of a larger group. The sample is the group that is actually tested.

Population. The larger group from which the sample is selected and to which individual comparisons are made regarding test performance.

Standardization Sample. A group of children who represent a larger group and are actually tested.

NORM-REFERENCED AND CRITERION-REFERENCED TESTS

There are several different ways of describing test performance. *Norm-referenced* and *criterion-referenced* are broad categories of tests that reflect different approaches to testing. Norm-referenced test performance compares a child's test results with those of a sample of similar children who have taken the same test. Criterion-referenced test performance compares a child's performance on a test to specific criteria or instructional objectives.

Norms

Norms are the average scores obtained by the norm or standardization sample. In developing or revising a test, the publisher administers it to a sample or group of children representative of a larger group known as the *population* (e.g., three-year-old children). This group of students who are actually tested constitutes the standardization or norm sample. The *raw scores* of the children in the standardization sample are obtained and then converted to one or more forms of derived scores. The test publisher includes these norms in the manual.

Standardization Sample

When a test is administered to an individual child, a teacher can compare the performance of that child with the norm sample. To be able to do this, however, it is very important to know the characteristics of the standardization sample. The sample should be representative of the population. Depending on the purpose of the test, it may be important to know the following characteristics about the sample: age, grade, number of females and number of males, parental occupation, socioeconomic status, and whether any children had special needs. It is also important to know when the test was standardized and the publication date of the test. For example, if a test designed to measure the cognitive development of children is intended to be administered to four- to six-year-olds, the standardization sample must include a representative group of children who are in this age range. The standardization sample should include, in the appropriate proportions, children from various geographic regions of the country, the appropriate numbers of male and females, and children who represent various racial, ethnic, and linguistic populations. In addition, some standardization samples are selected to ensure the inclusion of appropriate proportions of students from various socioeconomic levels. Some samples take into consideration the occupational and educational levels of the parents. The best way for a test publisher to determine what to include in the standardization sample is to refer to the most recent census data and base the selection of the standardization sample on those percentages.

Salvia and Ysseldyke (1991) believe that tests used to "identify students with particular problems should include such children in their standardization sample" (p. 112). Since specialized tests are frequently used to identify and classify students, the standardization samples of these tests should include children with similar problems. For example, the McCarthy Scales of Children's Abilities was designed to measure the cognitive abilities of children aged 2.5 to 8.5 years. The manual states that the test can be used to assess children for giftedness as well as for mental retardation, sensory deficits, speech difficulties, and learning disabilities. However, the standardization sample for this test did not include any of these special groups.

Norm-referenced Tests

A *norm-referenced test* compares a child's test performance with that of similar children who have taken the same test. Norm-referenced, standardized tests can be based on local, state, or national norms. That is, after a test has been constructed, the test developers administer it to all the students in a group using the same administration and scoring procedures for all the children. Then the administration and scoring are said to be "standardized." The test scores of this group are converted to norms, which include scores of a variety of types. Once a norm-referenced test has been standardized, it can be administered to children whose characteristics are similar to those of the norm group, and the scores of these children can be compared with those of the norm group. Because of the comparison of scores between a norm group and other groups of children, a norm-referenced test provides information on the relative standing of students. Norm-referenced tests can be administered both to individuals and to groups. Norm-referenced tests include the McCarthy Scales of Children's Abilities, the Kaufman Assessment Battery for Children, the Bayley Scales of Infant Development, and the Metropolitan Achievement Tests.

Criterion-referenced Tests

Instead of comparing a child's performance to a norm group, criterion-referenced tests measure a child's performance with respect to a well-defined domain (Anastasi, 1982; Berk, 1988). While norm-referenced tests are constructed to discriminate between the performance of individual children on specific test items, criterion-referenced tests provide a description of a child's knowledge, skills, or behavior in a specific range, called a *domain,* of test items. Test items on criterion-referenced tests are frequently tied to well-defined instructional objectives (Salvia & Ysseldyke, 1991). Since criterion-referenced tests provide information on the performance of a child with respect to specific test items, the results of such testing are not dependent on the performance of other students, as is the case in norm-referenced tests. An example of a criterion-referenced test is the Brigance® Diagnostic Inventory of Early Development.

Several characteristics distinguish criterion-referenced tests from norm-referenced tests. One of these is mastery. Performance on a criterion-referenced test indicates whether the child has attained a predetermined level of mastery. Sometimes, performance can be interpreted along a scale of mastery, nonmastery, or intermediate (Anastasi, 1982). While it is possible to construct a test that is both norm referenced and criterion referenced, caution must be used when interpreting the results of these tests because it is difficult to combine both types in one instrument.

Another distinction between norm-referenced and criterion-referenced tests is the breadth of the content domain that is covered by the test (Mehrens & Lehmann, 1991). Typical norm-referenced tests survey a broad domain, while criterion-referenced tests usually have fewer domains but more items in each domain. Criterion-referenced tests typically sample the domain more thoroughly than norm-referenced tests (Mehrens & Lehmann, 1991).

Criterion-referenced tests can also be very useful in helping to make instructional planning decisions. Since criterion-referenced tests frequently cover a more restricted range of content than norm-referenced tests, they can provide more information about a child's level of performance.

Do not confuse criterion-referenced assessment with curriculum-based assessment. This is another approach to assessment and is discussed in Chapter 11.

HOW SHOULD TESTS BE EVALUATED?

Many concepts have been discussed in this chapter. It is important for you to understand these concepts when using tests. The list below can be helpful when determining the technical adequacy of a test.

Reliability
Alternate form

Test–retest

Internal consistency

Split-half

Interrater/interscorer/interobserver
Validity
Content

Face

Concurrent

Predictive

Construct
Norms
Sample size

Representativeness
Scores
Age/grade equivalents

Developmental scores

Percentiles

Standard scores

Stanines

PREFERRED PRACTICES

This chapter has described different concepts relating to the measurement of student performance. While there are many different ways of reporting test scores, several are preferred. Standard scores, which can be transformed from raw scores to have the same mean and the same standard deviation, are an excellent way of reporting test performance. However, they have a major drawback. They may not be easily understood by professionals and parents. Percentile ranks, however, are fairly easily understood and should be used when reporting test performance. Age and grade equivalents should be used very cautiously, if at all. It is up to the teacher to judge the adequacy of the information presented in the test manual. To be able to evaluate the usefulness of particular tests, the teacher must be an educated consumer, aware of the characteristics of various instruments.

Teachers must determine whether consistent student performance is being measured and whether tests measure what the authors describe as the purpose of the tests. Test manuals provide information about reliability and validity, the concepts at the heart of such determinations. It is important that teachers, test examiners, and administrators review tests before using them and satisfy themselves that each test has acceptable levels of reliability and validity.

There are resources available that provide independent evaluations of tests. The *Mental Measurements Yearbooks* and *Tests in Print,* which are published by the Buros Institute of Mental Measurements at the University of Nebraska, Lincoln, are probably the best known sources of test reviews. *Test Critiques,* from the Pro-Ed Publishing Company, is another source. Frequently, journals also contain reviews of tests. Before selecting and using tests, professionals are urged to consult independent reviews of tests.

STUDY QUESTIONS AND SUGGESTED ACTIVITIES

1. The following test scores are available for Mary, a student in Mrs. Smith's class:

Key Math—Revised	87th percentile
Woodcock Reading Test—R	3.5 grade equivalent
Kaufman Assessment Battery for Children	110

   What are the advantages and disadvantages of using these scores to interpret Mary's performance?

2. Mr. Jones and Mrs. Smith both teach second grade. Mr. Jones believes that age and grade equivalents are helpful in determining student progress. Mrs. Smith disagrees. How can Mrs. Smith persuade Mr. Jones that age and grade equivalents are not very useful?

3. Jimmy has just received a score of 72 on an individual intelligence test. How could the examiner use the concept of confidence intervals to explain Jimmy's performance to his parents?

4. Maria, who recently moved to this country from Central America, is suspected of having a developmental delay. What must the examiner consider when deciding which tests to use to assess Maria?

5. What are the advantages of using norm-referenced tests? Of using criterion-referenced tests?

6. Imagine that you are the director of testing for a large metropolitan school district. What criteria should you use when selecting tests?

REFERENCES

American Educational Research Association, American Psychological Association, & National Council on Measurement in Education. (1985). *Standards for Educational and Psychological Testing.* Washington, DC: Author.

Anastasi, A. (1982). *Psychological testing.* New York: Macmillan.

Bailey, D. B., & Wolery, M. (1989). *Assessing infants and preschoolers with handicaps.* Columbus, OH: Merrill.

Berk, R. A. (1988). Criterion-referenced tests. In J. P. Keeves (Ed.), *Educational research, methodology, and measurement: An international handbook* (pp. 365–370). Oxford: Pergamon Press.

Cronbach, L. J. (1971). Test validation. In R. Thorndike (Ed.), *Educational measurement* (pp. 443–507). Washington, DC: American Council on Education.

DeVellis, R. F. (1991). *Scale development.* Newbury Park, CA: Sage.

Gay, L. R. (1985). *Educational evaluation and measurement.* Columbus, OH: Merrill.

Gronlund, N., & Linn, R. L. (1990). *Measurement and evaluation in teaching.* New York: Macmillan.

Lyman, H. (1986). *Test scores and what they mean.* Englewood Cliffs, NJ: Prentice-Hall.

Mehrens, W. A., & Lehmann, I. J. (1991). *Measurement and evaluation in education and psychology.* Fort Worth, TX: Holt, Rinehart & Winston.

Overton, T. (1992). *Assessment in special education.* New York: Merrill.

Rudner, L. M., Conoley, J. C., & Plake, B. S. (1989). *Understanding achievement tests: A guide for school administrators* (ERIC Document No. ED 314 426). Washington, DC: ERIC Clearinghouse on Tests, Measurement, and Evaluation.

Salvia, J., & Ysseldyke, J. (1991). *Assessment.* Boston: Houghton Mifflin.

Sattler, J. (1988). *Assessment of children.* San Diego, CA: Jerome M. Sattler, Publisher.

Zeller, R. A. (1988). Validity. In J. P. Keeves (Ed.), *Educational research, methodology, and measurement: An international handbook* (pp. 322–330). Oxford: Pergamon Press.

CHAPTER 3

Family Involvement

CHAPTER OBJECTIVES

Family involvement is the cornerstone of early intervention and early childhood special education services. Family–professional collaboration is essential for assisting and enhancing the child's growth and development. Furthermore, family members and practitioners bring different perspectives to the partnership. "While professionals can offer the expertise of their discipline and knowledge gained from working with a number of children, parents are the only ones who can contribute information on their particular child in all settings" (Shelton, Jeppson, & Johnson, 1987, pp. 2–3). In this chapter, we will explore some of the ways to build effective partnerships in the assessment process.

In addition, we will examine the area of family-directed assessment. As we saw in Chapter 1, the amendments to the Individuals with Disabilities Education Act (PL 102–119) provide for family-directed assessment. The focus is on an assessment process that assists families to identify needed services rather than assessing families to determine what services to deliver. Parents not only participate fully in the team process in identifying child-related strengths and needs, but also may exchange information with practitioners regarding their priorities of family-based needs and preferences for services. This chapter explores methods and selected instruments for assisting families in identifying their resources, priorities, and concerns with respect to the enhancement of the development of their child.

Upon completing this chapter, you should be able to:

Describe the philosophical framework of family-directed assessment.

Describe the three components of a family-directed assessment.

Describe the steps in conducting an interview with family members.

Discuss the use of "family stories."

Identify the advantages and disadvantages of self-report rating forms.

Key Terms

Family-focused Philosophy. An approach to working with families that enables family members to mobilize their resources to promote child and family functioning.

Family Systems Model. A model for understanding the special needs of the child within the broader context of family issues.

Family-directed Assessment. Information family members *choose* to share with other members of the early childhood team regarding family resources, priorities, and concerns.

Family Stories. Anecdotal descriptions of important experiences and significant life events in a family.

WORKING WITH PARENTS

Parents have been involved in the assessment process since the early days of special education services. Since 1975, with the passage of PL 94–142, parents have been asked to join the team that develops the individualized education program for their child with special needs. Parents have been asked to share information regarding their child's strengths and weaknesses, and parental input has been important in considerations of the services to be provided. The primary focus has been on the child.

Yet, the child does not function in isolation from the family. A change in the way practitioners think about providing services to children began to take place in the late 1980s. In this new way of thinking, called a *family-focused philosophy,* families are not just recipients of services; rather, they are instrumental in identifying priorities for the child. A family-focused philosophy demands that practitioners attempt to create opportunities for families to acquire the knowledge and skills necessary to strengthen family functioning (Dunst, Trivette, & Deal, 1988).

A CONCEPTUAL FOUNDATION

A family-focused philosophy in working with young children is strongly supported in the literature. McGonigel, Kaufmann, and Johnson (1991) have identified the underlying tenets in this process, which supports the role of families and their infants or toddlers. These principles include:

1. Infants and toddlers are uniquely dependent on their families for their survival and nurturance. This dependence necessitates a family-centered approach to early intervention.
2. States and programs should define "family" in a way that reflects the diversity of family patterns and structures.
3. Each family has its own structure, roles, values, beliefs, and coping styles. Respect for the acceptance of this diversity is a cornerstone of family-centered early intervention.
4. Early intervention systems and strategies must honor the racial, ethnic, cultural, and socioeconomic diversity of families.

5. Respect for family autonomy, independence, and decision making means that families must be able to choose the level and nature of early intervention's involvement in their lives. . . .

6. Early intervention services should be flexible, accessible, and responsive to family-identified needs.

7. Early intervention services should be provided according to the normalization principle—that is, families should have access to services [that are] provided in as normal a fashion and environment as possible and . . . promote the integration of the child and family within the community. (p. 9)

Turnbull and Turnbull (1990) describe the importance of recognizing family needs and priorities for preschoolers as well as school-age children.

Recognizing that parents are family members with myriad responsibilities and individual needs and preferences has a profound influence on parent–professional relationships in special education settings. The same concept of individualization that the field of special education embraces as pertinent to children and youth also applies to parents and other family members. (p. 19)

Turnbull and Turnbull (1990) developed a model for understanding the different aspects of a family and how these aspects affect a family's priorities during a particular point in time. Models such as this, which illustrate the complexity of interrelationships and the change process that is part of every family, are helpful in understanding our work with children and their families.

The model is composed of four major areas: family characteristics, family interaction, family functions, and family life cycle. The first area, family characteristics, includes the child's exceptionality. Other factors that contribute to the nature of family interactions include family size and cultural background; personal characteristics of family members, such as health and coping styles; and such special challenges as poverty, chronic illness, and unemployment.

Participants in family interaction may include members of the extended family. These relationships are responsive to the family's different needs, or family functions. During the family's life cycle, there will be changes in the characteristics of the family as well as in the kinds of needs the family may have.

CASE STUDY: THE BRACKETT FAMILY

The Brackett family includes the father, Dan, who is twenty-five years old and works as a school bus driver; the mother, Diana, who is twenty years old and is a homemaker; and their first child, Brittany, who is eighteen months old.

Brittany has a number of medical problems and must have oxygen available at all times. She is beginning to crawl and recognizes her name. The Bracketts live in a small, rural New England town. Dan's mother lives nearby, while Diana's parents live several hours away. The young couple have several close friends in the community, and both Dan and Diana are outgoing and energetic parents. Since the birth of their baby, however, Diana has used her energies primarily to take care of Brittany's needs. She is particularly concerned about exposing

Brittany to colds and illnesses, fearing that a sickness would lead to additional medical problems. Dan's mother, though, feels that it is important for Brittany to be taken out for walks and that this may build up her immune system. The family receives a number of services within the home. These include weekly visits from the public health nurse, the family service coordinator, and a teacher for children with visual impairments.

However, the primary concern (need) that Diana and Dan identified surprised all other members of the early childhood team (ECT). Both parents were very pleased with the services being provided and felt that they were coping with the additional care that Brittany required. They were proud of the progress that Brittany had made and felt good about their parenting skills. Dan's mother was an important support person and resource in helping to care for Brittany. Yet, Diana felt that her greatest concern was not addressed. How was the family going to pay the mounting bills? During the ECT meeting, the practitioners and parents briefly discussed Brittany's progress and then focused on discussing various options the Bracketts could investigate to alleviate Diana's concern about medical and service payments.

In many families, children are cared for by family members other than the parents. Grandmothers, aunts and uncles, siblings, or other individuals living in the home play a major role in the care and development of the child. Best practice suggests that practitioners view families as sources of strength—rather than focus solely on the problems a family may be having. All families are special, unique units. All families have the capability to grow and change. And no two families are the same.

Working with Culturally Diverse Families

Cultural diversity continues to have an impact on the changing population in the United States. In fact, in the not too distant future, "nearly 50% of all young children in many areas of the country will be from cultural and language groups that are different from those of most early intervention professionals" (Hanson, Lynch, & Wayman, 1990, p. 116).

In adopting a family-focused approach, the evaluator must be sensitive to the particular cultural orientation of the family. Different cultural heritages, values, and beliefs may dramatically influence the family's perception of and participation in the assessment process (Hanson et al., 1990). A number of factors have been identified that may differ across cultures (Hanson et al., 1990; Turnbull & Turnbull, 1990). Some of these cultural considerations include:

- *Children and child rearing.* Families may approach child rearing from very different perspectives. Some families view children as gifts to be treasured. There is much close physical contact between mother and child, and inter-action is characterized more by touch than by vocal stimulation. Other families, however, promote individualism rather than conformity; infants are talked to and played with; and young children are encouraged to be as-sertive, to meet their own needs, and to challenge authority as appropriate. On the other hand, some families consider that children's "bad" behaviors must be eliminated, and punitive methods of control are employed by the time the child is three years old (Hanson et al., 1990).

- *Children with disabilities.* Families differ widely in their attitudes toward a child's disability. Some come to believe that the disability contributes positively to the family; others view it as shameful. Most families go through a grieving process, moving back and forth between the various stages of denial, guilt, acceptance, and advocacy. The feelings some family members experience in one stage may last for a long time, leaving them emotionally immobile, whereas other family members may be able to become more active in advocacy work.

- *Involvement.* Some families may be comfortable working as equals with the practitioner; other families will wish to participate only minimally in a parent–professional partnership, however, for reasons including respect, fear, or intimidation.

- *Communication.* Communication between parents and practitioner may be misinterpreted. For example, among some Asian cultural groups, asking questions is sometimes seen as challenging the knowledge of the person queried. Thus, to avoid loss of face, an individual may smile and nod to mean assurance rather than understanding and agreement.

- *Assistance.* Seeking and receiving help may be relatively easy for the family; or the family may view its needs and problems as private matters to be addressed only by family members.

- *Medical practices.* Medical practices differ across cultures and may be the cause of misinterpretation when early childhood team members are working with families.

> One example of a traditional practice that has led to misunderstandings in the American culture is the use of coin rubbing. This massage treatment is utilized by the Vietnamese community to treat disorders such as headaches and colds. Coin treatment, or *Cao Gio,* literally translates to "scratching the (bad) wind out of the body." The treatment involves the massaging of chest and back with a medicated substance, like Ben-Gay, and the striking or scratching of the skin with a coin or spoon. This process leaves superficial bruises and, when spotted by professionals who are unaware of the techniques, has often resulted in a referral for child abuse. This practice provides a clear example of differences and also dramatically underscores the issues in diagnosis and interpretation when the various cultures meet. (Hanson et al., 1990, p. 122)

- *Achievement.* A family's aspirations for a child with special needs may range from elevated to depressed expectations. Some families may expect the child to conform to certain family or cultural expectations; other families will encourage independence, choices, and risk taking.

Bruder, Anderson, Schutz, and Caldera (1991) have described some considerations in working with Puerto Rican families. They found that the term "family" may include not only the extended family but also friends from the island who form the support network. This network is an important resource for many families.

Practitioners working with families should appreciate others' viewpoints and be willing to accept a perspective that may be very different from their own. Practitioners should also be aware that individual families will interpret the same culture differentially. In other words, *no general statements can apply to all families of any one cultural heritage.*

THE BEGINNING OF FAMILY-DIRECTED ASSESSMENT

In the early 1990s, the focus began to move from child and family to family-directed assessment for identifying services provided in an IFSP. The statements of outcomes and services for children and families written into the IFSP are based in part on family-directed assessment, or information provided by the family. As you will recall from Chapter 1, the Individuals with Educational Disabilities Act (IDEA) specified the requirements of the IFSP.

Assessment Information Requirements of the IFSP

1. A multidisciplinary assessment of the unique strengths and needs of the infant or toddler and the identification of services appropriate to meet such needs.
2. A family-directed assessment of the resources, priorities, and concerns of the family and the identification of the supports and services necessary to enhance the family's capacity to meet the developmental needs of their infant or toddler with a disability. (PL 99–457 amended by PL 101–476, Sec. 14)

This family-directed assessment should be based on information *volunteered* by the family. The federal law, however, does not provide further guidance about the types of information that could be gathered, how families might begin to identify or gather this information, or the role of the professional in this process. In this chapter, we will address these areas and some of the emerging issues in family-directed assessment.

BUILDING SKILLS IN FAMILY-DIRECTED ASSESSMENT

How does a family-focused approach affect the assessment process? As you begin to work with a family, you will need to meet them in their world (Schwab, 1991). For example, an early intervention practitioner working within a hospital setting could focus on "Welcome to the world of the Zucowsics, which now includes Anne, a preemie," or "Welcome to the world of preemies in the NICU, which now includes the Zucowsics." Although the difference between these two statements may appear minimal initially, the first example illustrates a professional orientation of meeting this family in *their* present circumstances. The second example focuses not on the family but on the Neonatal Intensive Care Unit (NICU), an environment that is unfamiliar to the family. The first focus is a good example of best practice.

Additional components of best practices in working with families have been identified by the Beach Center on Families and Disability at the University of Kansas:

- *Choices.* . . . Enabling families to act on their preferences allows them to build on their strengths.
- *Relationships.* . . . Family members need to be connected to each other and to friends in the community.
- *Inherent strengths.* Families have many natural capacities. Nevertheless, they may need support to affirm positive contributions, achieve great expectations, obtain full citizenship, act on their choices, and enjoy relationships. (Staff, *Families and Disability Newsletter,* 1989, p. 2)

Thus, family-directed assessment may begin with the recognition of the unique strengths a family has, even though these strengths and resources may not be clearly evident to the family members. In fact, family members may never have considered aspects of their family that are strengths and resources. Helping families to identify family resources and competencies as well as assisting families to identify needs and concerns is the basis for much of the work in family-directed assessment.

In your work with families you will probably be a visitor. Wayman, Lynch, and Hanson (1990) have developed a set of helpful guidelines for the home visitor. Questions that you may want to keep in mind when you visit a home include (Wayman, Lynch, & Hanson, 1990):

Family organization
Who are the family members?

How do friends help to support the family's needs?

Who are the primary caregivers?

How do the children interact with caregivers?

Child-raising practices
What are the daily routines for dressing, feeding, toileting, and bedtime?

How does the family respond to crying?

What are the procedures for discipline?

What activities does the family like to do together?

Perceptions of disability
What are the attitudes of the family toward the child's disability?

Do the family's cultural beliefs affect their attitude toward the child?

Intervention
How does the family meet routine medical needs?

What are attitudes toward seeking assistance?

What relationships does the family have with medical, social, and educational professionals?

Communication
To what extent is the home visitor knowledgeable about the family's native language and cultural beliefs?

What are ways in which the family prefers to communicate with professionals (telephone, letter, face-to-face)?

These guidelines are not to be used as a checklist but rather to provide a framework to assist you in understanding some of the important areas and issues.

Practitioners who are involved in family-directed assessment should carefully consider what families say about this process. Research studies (Summers et al., 1990) report that sensitivity to family issues was the single most important factor mentioned by families. These families wanted practitioners to:

1. Support family members who may be experiencing a wide range of emotions
2. Use nonjudgmental acceptance
3. Consider that casual comments or program expectations may have unintended consequences for the family
4. Offer an unhurried atmosphere in which to share interaction

FAMILY-DIRECTED ASSESSMENT AS PART OF THE ASSESSMENT PROCESS

In Chapter 1 we discussed the steps in the assessment process: (1) screening, (2) determining eligibility, (3) program planning, (4) monitoring progress, and (5) evaluating the program. Once the child's eligibility has been determined, assessment for program planning begins. For young children who receive services under an IFSP, program planning also entails *family-directed assessment;* the assessment steps of monitoring progress and evaluating the program include family-based assessment procedures as well.

ASSISTING IN FAMILY-DIRECTED ASSESSMENT

The three components of family-directed assessment are

Resources

Priorities

Concerns as they relate to enhancing the development of the child.

Dunst (1991) has identified the interdependence of family-identified strengths and needs. A family's resources and supports are additional important components that are identified during the assessment process and are included in the development of the IFSP. During intervention, families are assisted in meeting their needs, in learning new competencies, or in obtaining desired resources. As families grow and new needs and aspirations are identified, the process is repeated, as illustrated in Figure 3.1.

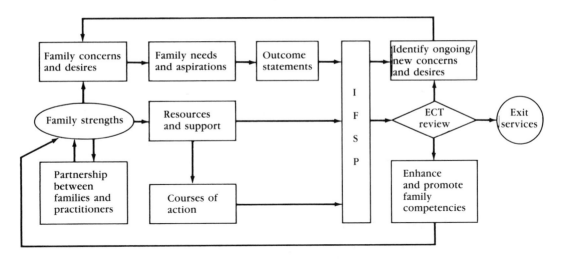

FIGURE 3.1 The process of identifying needs and supporting growth and well-being for children and their families

SOURCE: Adapted from Dunst (1991).

Identifying Resources

The resources that are available to a family are important in helping to meet needs. Yet for many families, identifying resources may be a new way of thinking. In the past, the family may have focused only on needed services or the skills the family wanted the child to acquire. But as the family begins to prioritize its needs and to participate in the development of an IFSP, the actual *process* of identifying family resources may increase the family's sense of strength.

> Knowledge of family strengths provides the necessary basis for promoting the acquisition of new competencies, as well as building upon existing capabilities. This is particularly the case when assessment information is used as part of the IFSP procedures designed to have families use their competencies to mobilize resources and supports to meet their needs. (Trivette, Dunst, Deal, Hamer, & Propst, 1990, p. 29)

Assisting families to identify strengths often gives families a sense of empowerment. Dunst et al. (1988) have described *empowerment* as the feeling of family members that they can change behavior or events and can acquire a sense of control necessary to manage the family. Some families may never have considered family *strengths.* For example, one family member may have taken for granted that the spouse will always bring the children home from child care. Yet, couples who undertake to share responsibilities in child care may come to identify this division of labor as a family strength. Research (Summers et al., 1990; Whitehead, Deiner, & Toccafondi, 1990) suggests that the identification of family strengths and needs offers such potential in helping families to learn about themselves that the *process* itself could be considered to be a goal.

Identifying Concerns and Priorities

Young children and their families may have a wide variety of needs. *Family* concerns and priorities may extend beyond the specific needs resulting from a child's disability. These concerns may be placed along a continuum ranging from basic needs such as food, money, and shelter to enrichment needs such as a job, adult education, and child-focused intervention (Dunst et al., 1988). Concerns at the beginning of the continuum will need to be met first, before a family can address others. During the assessment process, you will need to assist the family in identifying concerns "that a family considers important enough to devote its time and energy" to (Dunst et al., 1988, p. 55). Best practice suggests that *family members themselves should clearly identify the needs they wish to be documented* during family-based assessment and IFSP development.

CASE STUDY: MS. T. AND SARAH

Ms. T., age eighteen, is a single parent. She recently left her parents' home to move to a neighboring state with three-year-old Sarah. Prior to the move, Sarah had shown delays in motor development, and an IEP had been developed to allow the child to receive occupational therapy services in the community preschool program she attended each morning. In the new area, Ms. T. was able to find low cost housing and applied for federal assistance while she looked for a job. An early childhood special educator, Mrs. Ray, visited the Thompsons' home and invited Sarah to join the nursery school program sponsored by the local elementary school. Mrs. Ray explained that through this preschool program an occupational therapist could be engaged to provide the needed services to Sarah. Two weeks passed and Ms. T. did not enroll Sarah. Mrs. Ray contacted Ms. T. to arrange for a convenient time to visit. During the second visit Ms. T. explained that although she wanted her daughter to continue in preschool, she was unable to complete the arrangements while all her energy was devoted to finding a job.

OVERVIEW OF ASSESSMENT TECHNIQUES

The first step in working with families is to acknowledge that you want to hear what parents are saying. Three techniques may be used in the process of family-based assessment:

Interviews

Family stories

Family self-report instruments

An interview allows you to talk with each member of the family and to hear individual perspectives about unmet needs and priorities. By spending time with the family in their home, you may gain a better understanding of the situation. Family stories help you to understand the importance of life experiences and events from the perspective of the narrator. Self-report instruments include checklists and rating scales, which are completed by the family. Table 3.1 summarizes these techniques,

TABLE 3.1 Selected techniques and instruments for family-based assessment and program evaluation

Area	Technique/Instrument	Step in Assessment Process	Reference
Strengths and capabilities	Interview Observation Family Functioning Style Scale	Program planning Monitoring	Dunst, Trivette, & Deal (1988), pp. 179–184.
Needs and aspirations	Interview Observation	Screening Program planning Monitoring	
	Family Needs Scale		Dunst, Trivette, & Deal (1988), p. 151.
	Family Resource Scale		Dunst, Trivette, & Deal (1988), p. 141.
	Support Functions Scale		Dunst, Trivette, & Deal (1988), p. 145.
	Resource Scale for Teen-age Mothers		Dunst, Trivette, & Deal (1988), p. 148.
	Family Needs Survey		Bailey & Simeonsson (1988).
	Comprehensive Evaluation of Family Functioning Scale		McLinden (1988).
	Parent Needs Survey		McGonigel, Kaufmann, & Johnson (1991), pp. D7–D8.
	How Can We Help?		McGonigel, Kaufmann, & Johnson (1991), D9–D11.
Support and resources	Interview Observation Personal Network Matrix	Program planning Monitoring	Dunst, Trivette, & Deal (1988), pp. 171–174.
	Family Resource Scale		Dunst, Trivette, & Deal (1988), p. 141.
	Resource Scale for Teen-age Mothers		Dunst, Trivette, & Deal (1988), p. 148.
	Family Support Scale		Dunst, Trivette, & Deal (1988), p. 157.
	Inventory of Social Support		Dunst, Trivette, & Deal (1988), p. 161.

lists selected instruments, and also indicates where in the assessment process the techniques may be used.

Assisting the family in identifying the types of information they wish to volunteer is a complex skill that requires sensitivity and respect. As you begin working with families in family-based assessment, you may wish to refer to such additional resources as Bennett, Lingerfelt, and Nelson (1990) and McGonigel et al. (1991).

CASE STUDY: THE BROWN FAMILY

The Brown family consists of Mrs. Brenda Brown, the mother; Charlie Natch, Brenda's friend; and Brenda's children—Eric, age seven; Jess, age six; Tanya, age three; and Bradlee, age sixteen months. Charlie and Brenda are expecting a child. Mrs. B. was due to go to the hospital within a few days when John Daigles, the family services coordinator, arrived for a scheduled visit with the family. Mr. Daigles, Mrs. Brown, and Mr. Natch had planned to discuss the progress of the three older Brown children, who were currently receiving speech and language services, and the early intervention toddler play group that Bradlee and Mrs. B. attend.

During the visit, Mrs. B. happened to mention that she was worried about bringing the new baby home because there was no place for the new arrival to sleep. Mr. Daigles was able to provide the name and telephone number of the community group that had baby furniture to loan.

Some family needs and priorities may be unexpected (or unanticipated!) by the practitioner. Such needs may be more readily identified by informal means.

Interviews

The interview, which allows a face-to-face meeting, is usually much more conducive to sharing information than telephone conversations. Dunst et al. (1988) have described a series of helpful steps to use in planning and conducting an interview with a family.

1. Scheduling the Interview
   a. *State the purpose for your visit:* "I'd like to visit with you to talk about the concerns you have for Heather."
   b. *Plan a meeting place:* Visiting the family in a familiar setting helps to make everyone more relaxed and at ease. Some families may prefer you to come to their home. Other families may feel more comfortable in another setting, such as their child care center.
2. Beginning the Interview
   a. *Acknowledge each family member present:* Chat briefly with each person and thank him or her for taking the time to be there.
   b. *Establish rapport:* Show a genuine interest in what the family has to say.
   c. *Reiterate the purpose of the meeting:* "I know that you have some concerns about Heather. I hope that from our visit I can begin to better understand your family and Heather's needs."
3. Listening to the Family
   a. *Help identify needs and resources:* Encourage each family member to share aspirations and concerns. Open-ended questions such as "Tell me more about . . . " can be helpful. Written notes will be helpful to you, but the family may be intimidated by seeing you record them.
   b. *Help clarify priorities:* Ask questions and rephrase statements to help the family clarify the most important points and to define items they would like to address first.

c. *Summarize the discussion:* Conclude the interview by summarizing the needs that have been identified and review the order of priority.

Darling (1989) recommends a semistructured method in which each family receives a set of questions, thus allowing programs and agencies to ensure some consistency in their dealings with a given family. Structured interview questions that have been used (Able-Boone, Sandall, Loughry, & Frederick, 1990) include:

> What are some tasks you do for your child? How do these tasks fit in with your daily schedule?
>
> Who do you go to for help with these tasks?
>
> What types of activity do you like to do with your family? What would you like to be able to do?
>
> What do you want from the professionals working with your child?

Interviewing Precautions. Although the interview technique can be a valuable method in assessment, there are several sources of error. As you assist the family in defining priorities, for example, there may be a tendency to filter the information through your own belief system. It may be very difficult to really hear what the family is saying if your own value system is quite different or if you hold certain beliefs about the family. Figure 3.2 illustrates a common statement that is subject to misinterpretation.

Another potential source of error in interviewing is overlooking an important area. You may decrease errors due to failure of the discussion to tap one or more areas of potential concern or priority of the family by becoming familiar with the general categories that most families identify. Areas that families have identified as priorities for their children include: independence, personal happiness, feelings of accomplishment, respect, ability to communicate, good friends, understanding that their child is loved, employment, adaptive or self-help skills, and the experience of having a loving relationship. Priorities that families have established for their families involve: social outings, typical sibling relationships, relatives and friends that understand their child and the child's disability, and help with making adaptations at home (Hunt et al., 1990).

The quality of the communication process itself is critical to interviewing. Parents may wonder why you are asking certain questions. Communication can be improved by explaining why you want the information. However, you will need to be sensitive to the content and to parents' reactions. Respect parents' right to share *only* the information they feel comfortable imparting. Some parents are not ready to address certain areas initially or may not want to confront them at certain periods of time.

Something to Think About. If you were a parent, what questions would be most helpful for you in attempting to share your perspective in the assessment step for program planning? For monitoring progress? For evaluating the program? Are there any questions you would feel uncomfortable in answering?

Sharing "Family Stories"

Sharing a "family story" is perhaps the least intimidating approach. Turnbull and Turnbull (1990) suggest visiting with the family for the purpose of acquiring the valuable information family members can provide about the child with special needs

Parent: I didn't get any sleep last night.

There are at least three different ways the practitioner may interpret this comment. One needs to guard against hasty conclusions.

1. Too many late night TV shows?
2. Need for respite care?
3. Isolated incident, parent usually sleeps well?

FIGURE 3.2   A common situation in which one should not draw a hasty conclusion.

and how others in the household relate to the child. Family members know a great deal about their own cultural values and practices, attitudes, habits, and behaviors. Family strengths and resources as well as needs may be identified as the family shares some of their daily responsibilities.

Atkinson (1992) wrote that inside every person is a story—many stories—waiting to be told and enrich our lives. These family stories can be a rich contribution to our knowledge about children. The stories give us a good idea of how families see themselves and how they want others to see them. There may be no other way to capture important experiences and significant life events, and to understand how these experiences and events are connected in the lives of the family members.

You may choose to interview various family members to gain a better understanding of a life story. You will need to select a person who knows the child well and has spent considerable time with the child. Under certain circumstances, interviews with the child can be very helpful.

In preparing to conduct a life story interview, the following guidelines, based on work by Atkinson (1992), will be useful.

Take Time to Prepare.   Prepare your materials: principally a small tape recorder. Taking notes can be helpful but may hamper the flow of the conversation. Prepare your questions ahead of time. Be sure to conduct several practice interviews so that the interview will flow smoothly.

Use Photographs and Drawings.   Photographs, drawings, and other materials can be used to encourage family members to remember stories and events. These objects also help to provide insight into children's lives and experiences.

Choose the Appropriate Setting.   A setting that is comfortable and familiar may be the family's home, the child's school, or a child care agency. Make sure that the room is quiet and that the person being interviewed is comfortable.

Get the Story.   Explain the purpose at the beginning of the family story interview. Emphasize that the information to be shared is valuable and will help you to understand the child and to develop interventions. Take your time, and encourage the person to reveal experiences and events in all their richness. You should plan to spend at least an hour taping this material.

Use Open-Ended Interview Techniques.   You are encouraging another person to tell a story. Allow this to happen by using open-ended interview techniques to guide the story telling.

Be a Good Listener.   An effective interviewer is a good listener. By being a good listener, you help to build trust and show that you care about what is being revealed. When appropriate, ask follow-up questions, probe for details, and be responsive.

Look for Connections.   The family story interview can provide valuable information about the development of the child. Look for connections between experiences and events. How do family members relate to the child? What are the significant events in the growth and development of the child? Drawing a timeline of significant family events can be useful.

Be Grateful.   Thank the person who shared his or her story with you and say that the details revealed will be treated with care. Reassure the person that the information will be treated confidentially.

Transcribe the Interview.   Write an account of the interview as soon as possible. If you delay the transcription, you may forget such important details as nonverbal gestures, the reason for an interruption, or the content of pictures the person shared with you.

As indicated above, you should prepare your questions ahead of time. You may not need to use them all, however, because the family member may disclose the desired information spontaneously. The following questions can be useful in obtaining the family story interview (Atkinson, 1992):

Introduction
1. Explain the purpose of the family story interview.

Birth and Infancy
1. Was there anything unusual about the birth of your child?
2. What events do you remember about the first year of life?
3. How would you describe the baby's growth and development?
4. What do you think your child inherited from you?

Family Traditions
1. Was your family different from other families in your neighborhood?
2. What beliefs or ideals did you want to pass on to your child?
3. What cultural influences are important to your family?

Social Factors
1. Do the family members get along?
2. How much time do you spend with your child?
3. What were some difficult times?
4. What were some happy times?

Education
1. What do you hope your child will learn in school?
2. What was school like for you?

3. What did you learn about yourself when you were in school?

4. What role should education play in a person's life?

Closure

1. How do you feel about your family now?

2. How do you feel about your child's role in the family?

3. What gives you the most hope?

4. Have any significant events been omitted from this interview?

5. What are your feelings about this interview and all that we have covered?

Self-report Rating Scales

There are other ways of helping family members to identify resources, priorities, or concerns. In addition to using interviews and family stories, a practitioner may ask the family to complete a self-report scale. Trivette et al. (1990) have described several steps in assisting families to identify strengths by means of a self-report scale.

1. Be sure to state why you are asking the family to complete the information. ("Could you please help me get a better idea about your family's special capabilities?")

2. Be clear about how the results of this information will be used. ("After you finish, we'll talk about the strengths you feel are important. This will help me focus on the positive aspects about your child and family.")

3. Clarify and specify concrete ways of defining strengths. ("You indicated that members of your family help each other. Could you give me some examples of how this has happened?")

4. Emphasize the positive aspects of functioning. ("The fact that your husband assists with child care must really help in dealing with the concerns we talked about earlier.")

5. Prompt descriptions and encourage suggestions about how the family can use its strengths. ("Since you have already gathered information about feeding techniques, which procedures do you feel most comfortable using?")

6. Build on family strengths by enabling them to use their capabilities to mobilize resources to meet needs.

Some of the scales are designed to assist families in identifying strengths and resources. The Family Functioning Style Scale is one example.

Family Functioning Style Scale

The Family Functioning Style Scale was developed by Deal, Trivette, and Dunst in 1988 (see Dunst et al., 1988, pp. 179–184), for the purpose of assessing the extent of different strengths and capabilities that characterize an individual family. Participants in the reliability and validity studies included 105 parents of preschool-age children; there were 64 parents of children who were developing typically and 41 parents of children with delays or disabilities (Trivette et al., 1990). Figure 3.3 illustrates this scale.

Administration.   The instrument is designed to be completed by an individual family member or by two or more family members.

Scoring.   Twenty-six items are rated on a 5-point rating scale by noting the degree to which the statements are "Not at all like my family" to "Almost always like my family."

Standardization.   This rating scale is not a norm-referenced instrument.

Reliability.   Internal consistency is reported as at least .77 for the subscales and .92 for total number of items.

Validity.   Construct validity is reported as adequate for five factors (subscales): commitment to the family, family cohesion, communication among family members, family competence, and family coping strategies. Criterion validity was assessed using the family hardiness index. Of 30 comparisons, 28 were significant. Predictive validity was assessed using the psychological well-being index and the mastery and health subscale of the Family Inventory of Resources and Management; results indicated $r = .64$.

Summary.   The Family Functioning Style Scale may be used by one or more family members to assist in determining family strengths and resources. Both mothers and fathers were included in the development of this instrument. The scale has adequate reliability. The authors continue to gather data on diverse families to determine whether the results can be generalized to apply to other families.

Some instruments assist family members in identifying resources as well as concerns. The following instrument is illustrative.

Comprehensive Evaluation of Family Functioning (CEFF)

The Comprehensive Evaluation of Family Functioning Scale was developed by McLinden in 1988 for assessing "both the frequency with which various situations or feelings occur as well as the extent to which parents perceive these situations or feelings to be problematic" (McLinden, 1990, p. 250). The CEFF has 51 items, which are organized into seven areas: time demands, acceptance, coping, social relationships, financial, well-being, and sibling relationships. The parents who participated in the psychometric study were 48 mothers and 35 fathers of 48 children between 26 and 50 months of age in an urban area in the Midwest. The majority of the families were Caucasian and middle class, and the children attended an early intervention program.

Administration.   The CEFF is a self-report scale designed to be completed by the parent.

Family Functioning Style Scale
(Experimental Version)
Angela G. Deal, Carol M. Trivette, & Carl J. Dunst

Family Name _____   Date _____

INSTRUCTIONS
Every family has unique strengths and capabilities, although different families have different ways of using their abilities. This questionnaire asks you to indicate whether or not your family is characterized by 26 different qualities. The questionnaire is divided into three parts. Part 1 below asks you about all members of your immediate family (persons living in your household). Part 2 on the next page asks you to rate the extent to which different statements are true for your family. Part 3 on the last page asks you to write down the things you think are your family's most important strengths.

Please list all the members of your immediate family and fill in the information requested. When you are finished, turn to the next page.

FAMILY MEMBER	DATE OF BIRTH	AGE	RELATIONSHIP

FIGURE 3.3 The Family Functioning Style Scale

SOURCE: *Enabling and Empowering Families: Principles and Guidelines for Practice* by Carl Dunst, Carol Trivette, and Angela Deal. By permission of Brookline Books, Inc. Copyright 1988 by Brookline Books, Inc.

Listed below are 26 statements about families. Please read each statement and indicate the extent to which it is true for your family. There are not right or wrong answers. Please give your honest opinions and feelings. Remember that no one family will be like all the statements given.

To what extent is each of the following statements like your family:	Not At All Like My Family	A Little Like My Family	Sometimes Like My Family	Generally Like My Family	Almost Always Like My Family
1. It is worth making personal sacrifices if it benefits our family	0	1	2	3	4
2. We generally agree about how family members are expected to behave	0	1	2	3	4
3. We believe that something good comes out of the worst situations	0	1	2	3	4
4. We take pride in even the smallest accomplishments of family members	0	1	2	3	4
5. We are able to share our concerns and feelings in productive ways	0	1	2	3	4
6. No matter how difficult things get, our famiy sticks together	0	1	2	3	4
7. We generally ask for help from persons outside our family if we cannot do things ourselves	0	1	2	3	4
8. We generally agree about the things that are important to our family	0	1	2	3	4
9. In our family we are always willing to "pitch in" and help one another	0	1	2	3	4
10. If something beyond our control is constantly upsetting to our family, we find things to do that keep our minds off our worries	0	1	2	3	4
11. No matter what happens in our famliy, we try to look "at the bright side of things"	0	1	2	3	4

(continued)

To what extent is each of the following statements like your family:	Not At All Like My Family	A Little Like My Family	Sometimes Like My Family	Generally Like My Family	Almost Always Like My Family
12. Even in our busy schedules, we find time to be together	0	1	2	3	4
13. Everyone in our family understands the rules about acceptable ways to act	0	1	2	3	4
14. Friends and relatives are always willing to help whenever we have a problem or crisis	0	1	2	3	4
15. When we have a problem or concern, we are able to make decisions about what to do	0	1	2	3	4
16. We enjoy time together even if it is just doing household chores	0	1	2	3	4
17. If we have a problem or concern that seems overwhelming, we try to forget it for awhile	0	1	2	3	4
18. Whenever we have disagreements, family members listen to "both sides of the story"	0	1	2	3	4
19. In our family, we make time to get things done that we all agree are important	0	1	2	3	4
20. In our family, we can depend upon the support of one another whenever something goes wrong	0	1	2	3	4
21. We generally talk about the different ways we deal with problems or concerns	0	1	2	3	4
22. In our family, our relationships will outlast our material possessions	0	1	2	3	4
23. Decisions like moving or changing jobs are based on what is best for all family members	0	1	2	3	4

FIGURE 3.3 (*continued*)

To what extent is each of the following statements like your family:	Not At All Like My Family	A Little Like My Family	Sometimes Like My Family	Generally Like My Family	Almost Always Like My Family
24. We can depend upon one another to help out when something unexpected comes up	0	1	2	3	4
25. In our family, we try not to take one another for granted	0	1	2	3	4
26. We try to solve our problems first before asking others to help	0	1	2	3	4

Please write down all things that you consider to be the major strengths of your family. Don't overlook the little things that occur everyday which we often take for granted (e.g., sharing the responsibility of getting your child fed and to school).

Scoring. Each item is responded to in two different ways. First, the frequency of the item is rated on a 5-point continuum called a *Likert scale*. On Likert scales, which are used frequently in social research, the lowest rating (generally 1) indicates, for example, that the item never occurs, and the highest rating (in this case, 5) indicates that the item always occurs. In addition, the parent's perception of whether the item described is a problem is indicated by yes or no for each item.

Standardization Sample. This rating scale is not norm-referenced.

Reliability. Internal consistency was .92 (McLinden, 1990). Test–retest reliability was adequate at one month.

Validity. Criterion-related validity was reported as adequate.

Summary. The Comprehensive Evaluation of Family Functioning Scale is designed to provide information about the family's strengths and needs as perceived by mothers and fathers. There is some indication (McLinden, 1990) that this instrument identifies differences in the degree of stress in some areas between mothers and fathers. An instrument that is sensitive to these differences could be helpful in individualizing program planning for family members, especially for addressing the needs of fathers. Readministering this instrument at a later date may be helpful in monitoring progress and evaluating the program.

Family Needs Survey

The Family Needs Survey, developed by Bailey and Simeonsson, is designed "to facilitate the identification of family needs for the purpose of prioritizing early intervention services" (Bailey & Blasco, 1990). This survey consists of 35 items that assess the family's needs in six domains: information, support, financial needs, explaining to others, child care, and community services. An open-ended question at the end of the survey allows parents to identify the family's greatest current need.

Administration. One or both parents completes the survey by indicating "No," "Not sure," or "Yes" after each item.

Scoring. Items may be grouped (or rank ordered) according to priority.

Standardization. This rating scale is not a norm-referenced instrument.

Reliability. Test–retest reliability over a six-month period was .67 for mothers and .81 for fathers (Bailey & Blasco, 1990).

Validity. Four groups of mothers (Caucasian/middle income, $N = 73$; Caucasian/low income, $N = 17$; minority/middle income, $N = 25$; and minority/low income, $N = 32$) and one group of matched mothers and fathers gave the scale relatively equal ratings on usefulness. Means for the five groups ranged from 3.41 to 4.25 (possible high of 5.00). Based on parental feedback, some of the items are being revised.

Summary. The Family Needs Survey was designed to assist parents in identifying areas of need. The instrument has been field tested with both Caucasian and minority families from different socioeconomic backgrounds. Test–retest reliability is adequate. This instrument may be helpful for families to use in the family-based assessment process.

Family Support Scale

The Family Support Scale was developed by Dunst, Trivette, and Jenkins (Dunst et al., 1988) for the purpose of measuring the helpfulness of different sources of support to families. The scale includes 18 items and 2 additional "fill-in-the-blank" items that allow family members to write an item or two not found on the scale. The family member rates each item on a 5-point scale ranging from not helpful to extremely helpful.

Administration.   Individual family members may complete the scale independently, with their family service coordinator, or with another person.

Scoring.   A total scale score is obtained by summing all the items. The items also yield subscores including "informal kinship," such as friends or other parents; social organizations, such as social clubs, parent groups, and coworkers; relatives; immediate family, such as spouse or partner; and specialized services, such as early intervention programs, child care, or early education programs.

Standardization Sample.   This rating scale is not a norm-referenced instrument.

Reliability.   Two types of reliability were reported. Split-half reliability was reported as .75. The test–retest reliability for the total scale scores was .91 at 1 month and .47 at 18 months. One might expect the test–retest reliability to decrease over time because of the changing needs of families.

Validity.   Criterion-related validity was reported as adequate.

Summary.   The Family Support Scale was developed to assist family members in identifying sources of support currently in place. (Often a family member does not think of these resources as sources of support.) The authors feel not only that these sources of support are important but that the sources themselves may be a significant form of intervention.

As with rating scales in general, the value of the scores does not lie in comparison of the scores of different families but rather in the examination of an individual's own rating of the items. The practitioner and the parent use the responses as a basis for discussing why certain members of the parents' network might or might not be helpful in meeting current needs. An instrument such as this is a good example of how practitioners can assist family members in identifying and meeting their unique needs within their respective personal networks.

Precautions in Using Rating Scales

There are limitations in the use of rating scales and checklists. The content of the items or the context in which a parent completes the form may have an impact on the results. Whitehead et al. (1990) report a study in which parents who had completed a needs survey were later asked to summarize their five greatest needs. The results of the survey had indicated that information on how to teach the child was seen as the greatest need, with help in finding babysitters or respite providers second. When asked to summarize their needs, however, the families named child care as the greatest need, followed by financial and medical needs.

A DILEMMA

In your work with families, you should be sensitive to family expectations that surface as a result of needs identification. Once a family has provided information concerning needs, the members may develop specific expectations. As Bailey and

Blasco (1990) have observed, "asking about specific needs communicates the impression that help or service will be provided for those needs that parents identify" (p. 202).

What are some of the implications for families who do not receive services to meet their identified needs, or families who feel that services are not being provided in a timely fashion? How do fiscal resources of community agencies affect the identified needs and the prioritizing of these needs? The field of early intervention continues to have many challenges ahead!

PREFERRED PRACTICES

As the field of early intervention continues to grow and develop, families will be of great assistance in providing feedback to professionals. According to Shelton et al. (1987), "Parents can enhance the communication process by helping professionals to understand how best to ask questions—what is supportive and helpful, and what is intrusive" (p. 17). In a study that involved asking parents about their perception of family-based assessment, Summers et al. (1990) found that families clearly felt that the identification of strengths and needs recorded in the IFSP was their responsibility alone. Some parents felt that they should be able to share with practitioners some strengths and needs that would not be written into the IFSP.

Moreover, families apparently prefer informal methods for gathering information rather than the use of rating scales (Bailey & Blasco, 1990; Staff, 1991; Summers et al., 1990). Informal, open-ended conversations were preferred over structured interviews, and the desire to avoid standardized family assessment scales was frequently mentioned (Summers et al., 1990).

Herein lies a dilemma. Families have basic rights under the law with respect to the identification of their needs, strengths, and resources. To ensure the validity and reliability of such information, assessment instruments that have adequate psychometric properties are essential. Yet, families may prefer other, less formal, ways of relating information. These preferred methods may be difficult to quantify for accountability purposes, but procedures that allow for the gathering of information (i.e., the use of instruments with verified psychometric properties) may not be viewed favorably by the family.

Many families prefer to divulge information through informal conversations conducted in their native language. There is not universal agreement among family members, however. Some prefer the anonymity or the structure of a written instrument. In such cases, the readability level of the instrument is an important factor for you to consider. Practitioners may wish to discuss the different ways of assisting families to identify their strengths, needs, and resources and allow people to choose the method with which they are most comfortable.

Enhancing the process of early intervention will depend on continued development of collaborative activities, which include opportunities for parents to share information on practices and procedures that are helpful for their family. We feel that techniques such as the sharing of "family stories" hold much promise. Refining the assessment process of early intervention may include the use of tools and techniques still to be developed.

STUDY QUESTIONS AND SUGGESTED ACTIVITIES

1. What is family-directed assessment?

2. What are the three components of family-directed assessment, and what techniques might you use to assist family members?

3. Interview an early intervention specialist or early childhood special education teacher. How does this practitioner assist families in identifying resources, priorities, and concerns?

4. Contact a parent organization in your community or call the office of your state parent organization for children with disabilities. What information is available regarding family-directed assessment?

5. Think about your own family. What are your family resources? Strengths? Needs?

6. Choose three approaches to family assessment. Identify the advantages and disadvantages of each. What are some possible dilemmas that might occur in connection with each approach?

REFERENCES

Able-Boone, H., Sandall, S. R., Loughry, A., & Frederick, L. L. (1990). An informed, family-centered approach to Public Law 99–457: Parental views. *Topics in Early Childhood Special Education, 10*(1), 100–111.

Atkinson, R. (1992). *The life story book from autobiography to personal myth.* University of Southern Maine, Gorham, ME: Center for the Study of Lives.

Bailey, D. B., & Blasco, P. M. (1990). Parents' perspectives on a written survey of family needs. *Journal of Early Intervention, 14*(3), 196–203.

Bailey, D. B., & Simeonsson, R. (1988). *The family needs survey* (Report No. CB 8180). Chapel Hill, NC: University of North Carolina, Frank Porter Graham Child Development Center.

Bennett, T., Lingerfelt, B. V., & Nelson, D. E. (1990). *Developing individualized family support plans.* Cambridge, MA: Brookline.

Bruder, M. B., Anderson, R., Schutz, G., & Caldera, M. (1991). Project profile: Niños especiales program: A culturally sensitive early intervention model. *Journal of Early Intervention, 15*(3), 268–277.

Darling, R. B. (1989). Using the social system perspective in early intervention: The value of a sociological approach. *Journal of Early Intervention, 13*(1), 24–35.

Dunst, C. (1991, January). Symposium on family-centered care—from principles to practices. Paper presented at the Leadership Training Institute for Faculty Involved in the Preparation of Family-centered Early Interventionists sponsored by the Center for Developmental Disabilities, the University Affiliated Program of Vermont and Parent to Parent of Vermont, Burlington, VT.

Dunst, C., Trivette, C., & Deal, A. (1988). *Enabling and empowering families.* Cambridge, MA: Brookline.

Hanson, M. J., Lynch, E. W., & Wayman, K. I. (1990). Honoring the cultural diversity of families when gathering data. *Topics in Early Childhood Special Education, 10*(1), 112–131.

Hunt, M., Cornelius, P., Leventhal, P., Miller, P., Murray, T., & Stoner, G. (1990). *Into our lives.* Akron, OH: Children's Hospital Medical Center.

Lynch, E. W., & Hanson, M. J. (1992). *Developing cross-cultural competence.* Baltimore: Paul H. Brookes.

McGonigel, M. J., Kaufmann, R. K., & Johnson, B. H. (Eds.). (1991). *Guidelines and recom-*

mended practices for the individualized family service plan. Bethesda, MD: Association for the Care of Children's Health.

McLinden, S. E. (1988). *The comprehensive evaluation of family functioning scale.* Logan, UT: Early Intervention Research Institute.

McLinden, S. E. (1990). Mothers' and fathers' reports of the effects of a young child with special needs on the family. *Journal of Early Intervention, 14*(3), 249–259.

Schwab, W. E. (1991, January). Symposium on family-centered care—from principles to practices. Leadership Training Institute for Faculty Involved in the Preparation of Family-Centered Early Interventionists sponsored by the Center for Developmental Disabilities, the University Affiliated Program of Vermont and Parent to Parent of Vermont, Burlington, VT.

Shelton, T., Jeppson, E., & Johnson, B. (1987). *Family-centered care for children with special health care needs.* Bethesda, MD: Association for the Care of Children's Health.

Staff. (1989, Spring). A positive view. *Families and Disability Newsletter,* p. 2.

Staff. (1991, Fall). Infants, toddlers, and families. *Families and Disability Newsletter,* p. 8.

Summers, J. A., Dell'Oliver, C., Turnbull, A. P., Benson, H. A., Santelli, E., Campbell, M., & Siegel-Causey, E. (1990). Examining the individualized family service plan process: What are family and practitioner preferences? *Topics in Early Childhood Special Education, 10*(1), 78–99.

Trivette, C. M., Dunst, C. J., Deal, A. G., Hamer, W. A., & Propst, S. (1990). Assessing family strengths and family functioning style. *Topics in Early Childhood Special Education, 10*(1), 16–35.

Turnbull, A. P., & Turnbull, H. R., III (1990). *Families, professionals, and exceptionality: A special partnership.* Columbus, OH: Merrill.

Wayman, K. I., Lynch, E. W., & Hanson, M. J. (1990). Home-based early childhood services: Cultural sensitivity in a family systems approach. *Topics in Early Childhood Special Education, 10*(4), 65–66.

Whitehead, L. C., Deiner, P. L., & Toccafondi, S. (1990). Family assessment: Parent and professional evaluation. *Topics in Early Childhood Special Education, 10*(1), 63–77.

CHAPTER 4

Observing the Child and the Environment

CHAPTER OBJECTIVES

Observation is a valuable technique that can be used in conjunction with other measures during each step of the assessment process. Observations may focus on the child or on the environment; they often provide information not easily obtainable by other means. For example, through observation professionals may gather information regarding a child's interests, abilities, and interactions with other children and with adults. Observing a child's environment can elicit information that will help to increase opportunities for children with disabilities.

The tools used to record observations may be informal and flexible or structured and focused.

This chapter provides information on how to plan and design tools to use in conducting observations. Upon completion of this chapter, you should be able to:

Provide a rationale for conducting observations.

Delineate concerns relating to reliability and validity during the conduct of interviews and observations.

Describe the use of anecdotal records, running records, specimen records or specimen descriptions, interval recording, event recording, duration recording, latency recording, category recording, product evaluations, rating scales, and checklists.

Discuss guidelines for conducting observations.

Identify and describe several behavioral rating scales.

Key Terms

Observation. A systematic process of gathering information by looking at children and their environments.

Informant. An individual who knows the child well and provides information about the child.

WHY ARE OBSERVATIONS IMPORTANT?

Observations of children are valuable sources of information, powerful tools that can give us detailed information about children's growth, development, characteristics, and behaviors. Observation is the systematic process of gathering information by looking at children and recording their behaviors, responses, and characteristics, and the products of their play and work, as well as by examining the environment to record the extent to which the setting provides appropriate furnishings, conditions, and activities for the child's development.

Beaty (1986) cited eight reasons for conducting observations:

1. To make an initial assessment of the child's abilities.
2. To determine a child's areas of strength and which areas need strengthening.
3. To make individual plans based on observed needs.
4. To conduct an ongoing check on the child's progress.
5. To learn more about child development in particular areas.
6. To resolve a particular problem involving the child.
7. To use in reporting to parents or specialists in health, speech, mental health.
8. To gather information for the child's folder for use in ongoing guidance and placement. (p. 5)

Key Terms

Anecdotal Record. A brief narrative description recorded after the events have occurred.

Running Record. A description of the events that is written as the events occur.

Specimen Record or Specimen Description. A detailed account of a specific event.

Interval Recording. A recording of specific events or behaviors during a prespecified time interval.

Duration Recording. A measurement of the length of time a specific event or behavior persists.

Event Recording. The recording of a behavior each time it occurs during an observation period.

Intensity of Behavior. A measure of the strength of a behavior.

Latency Recording. A measure of the amount of time elapsed between a behavior or event (or request to begin the behavior) and the beginning of the prespecified behavior.

Category Recording. A system of recording behavior by categories.

Product Evaluation. An assessment of specific characteristics of the products of children's work or play.

Rating Scale. A measure of the degree to which a child exhibits a prespecified behavior.

Checklist. A list of characteristics or behaviors arranged in a consistent manner that allows the evaluator to record the presence or absence of individual characteristics or behaviors.

TECHNIQUES FOR CONDUCTING OBSERVATIONS

Conducting an observation is more than just watching a child and writing down your impressions. It is a systematic process that involves watching and recording what you have seen; sometimes the observer interacts with the child and records the child's responses to these interactions. Observations can be conducted on such products of children's play or work as block structures, finger paintings, and writings. Observations can be videotaped and audiotaped. They can be conducted with the child alone or in the company of parents, professionals, and other children. Observations can be used alone or they can supplement information collected with other assessment tools.

There are various ways of conducting observations. This chapter discusses the following methods: anecdotal records, running records, specimen records or specimen descriptions, event recording, duration recording, latency recording, interval recording, category recording, rating scales, product evaluations, and checklists.

Anecdotal Records

An *anecdotal record* is a brief narrative description of an event or events the observer felt to be important enough to record after the fact. Anecdotal records usually are written, although they can also be taped. The observer notes the date, time and place of the event and as accurately as possible records the circumstances. Verbal and nonverbal cues and direct quotations should be included. Since the function of the anecdotal record is to describe what has been observed rather than to interpret the observation, the examiner should be as objective as possible (Sattler, 1988). Interpretive comments should be recorded separately from the description of the episode. Figure 4.1 is an example of an anecdotal record.

There are several advantages to maintaining anecdotal records:

1. The observer requires little special training.
2. Unanticipated events can be recorded.
3. Actual behavior in a natural setting is described.
4. A check on other types of assessment is provided.

However, there are several disadvantages associated with the use of this technique:

1. The validity of anecdotal records depends on the memory of the observer.
2. Bias may occur if an observer selects only certain aspects or incidents to record.
3. The technique may not completely describe specific behaviors.
4. It is difficult to validate narrative recording.
5. The recording of the behavior may be time-consuming.

Child's name: S. C.	Date: 1/22 Time: 9:20 a.m.
Observer's name: L. G.	Location: preschool classroom

Anecdote	Comment
S. C. was playing with the small blocks. He was putting one block on top of another. He was having difficulty balancing the blocks on top of each other.	Need to find out why he was having difficulty balancing the blocks.
He attempted to build a tower of 3 blocks. His teacher approached him and he turned away. Just then, B. D., another child in the room, walked over to where S. C. was playing. S. C. picked up the blocks and started to take B. D.'s blocks. B. D. began to retrieve the blocks.	Why did S. C. turn away from his teacher?
The teacher noticed this incident and encouraged B. D. to move to another part of the room.	Need to observe S. C. in other settings

FIGURE 4.1   An anecdotal record

6. It may be difficult to summarize records of several anecdotal observations (Beaty, 1986; Gronlund & Linn, 1990; Sattler, 1988).

Gronlund and Linn (1990) provide the following suggestions for recording anecdotal records:

1. Before observing, decide what behaviors to observe.
2. When observing, watch out for any unusual behaviors that should also be recorded.
3. Observe and record the complete incident, including any precipitating behaviors as well as behaviors that occur as a consequence of the incident.
4. As soon as possible after the observation, record the incident.
5. Individual incidents should be recorded in separate anecdotal records.
6. The anecdote should just be a record of what was observed; any interpretations should be kept separate from the description of the behavior.
7. Be sure to record both positive and negative behaviors.
8. Before making inferences about a child's behavior, record a number of anecdotes. It is difficult to generalize from one or two observations.
9. Training and practice in writing anecdotes are important.

Running Records

A *running record* (Figure 4.2), sometimes called a continuous record, also can be used to describe events. Unlike the anecdotal record, in which the events are recorded *after* the fact, the running record describes events *while* they are occurring. A running record can provide a rich description of events and can be helpful in analyzing the behavior of children. Whereas the anecdotal record is selective, the running record is a comprehensive, detailed account of everything that is observed.

When recording, the observer must carefully describe the events. It is much

```
Child's name S. C.                              Date 3/19          Time 11:10

Observer's name P. T.                           Location Head Start

Time                    Observation                         Comment
11:10                   Watching block building
11:12                   Watching K. M. color                Switches hands
11:14                   Writing name
11:16                   Moves to block area
11:18                   Playing with blocks                 Switches from right hand
11:20                   Playing with blocks                   to left, right again
11:22                   Playing with blocks
```

FIGURE 4.2 Running record

better to provide a factual, detailed account than to be judgmental. Factual accounts are less likely to be influenced by observer bias.

The observer should carefully and precisely describe the events, striving to write accurate, detailed descriptions. Instead of simply recording that a "child moved away from the table," the observer could write:

Ran toward doorway

Skipped to greet teacher

Cautiously avoided toys on floor

Beaty (1986) described several disadvantages of running records:

1. Writing a running record can be time-consuming.
2. It is difficult to record all the events that are observed; some details may be overlooked.
3. The technique is useful when observing individual children but difficult to apply to groups.

Specimen Records

A *specimen record,* sometimes called a specimen description, is a detailed account of a specific event (Figure 4.3). It is similar to a running record in that the event is recorded by the observer in real time. However, this type of observation technique is selective. Only certain events are recorded. It is good practice to establish specific criteria for recording a specimen record. Because specimen records are similar to running records, they have the same disadvantages (Beaty, 1986).

Event Recording

The recording of a behavior each time it occurs during an observation period is called *event recording,* or *event sampling.* For example, if an observation lasts for 15

Narrative Observation

Child's Name: B. D. (male, age 5)
Date: 3/22
Setting: Head Start
Activity: Eating lunch
Time: 11:15–11:35 a.m.
Observer: T. M.

Reason for Observation: To determine if B. D. has an established preferred hand.

B. D. came very willingly to the lunch table. He waited for the other children to come to the table. He began to serve himself when everyone was seated. To pour milk, B. D. held the cup in his right hand and the small carton of milk in the left. He showed good control and did not spill. He used two hands simultaneously to open the carton. B. D. served himself food using his right hand (food was being passed from the right). B. D. began to eat with the left hand, picking up a fork that was located on his left. He ate with equal ease using right or left hand. B. D. showed good control with both hands but no clear preference was observed.

FIGURE 4.3 Specimen record

minutes, the observer must record *each* time the behavior occurs during the designated quarter-hour. With this procedure, the observer must pay close attention to the child and precisely tally the number of times the behavior occurs. Before beginning event recording, the observer must carefully define the target behavior. It is important to describe the *beginning* of a behavior and the *end* of the behavior, to avoid any ambiguity about whether the behavior occurred. Event recording is useful for behaviors that occur very frequently or very infrequently.

Several different procedures can be used for recording events. The simplest one is a tally. A line is drawn on the page each time the behavior occurs, the lines are counted, and the total is jotted down.

////   *////*   *//*   **12**

Figure 4.4 illustrates event recording, which permits the rate of occurrences of a behavior to be calculated. This information is helpful when more than one observation is conducted, when behaviors before and after an intervention are evaluated, or when the behaviors of various children are compared. For example, suppose an observer saw a child engaged in throwing objects 30 times during a 15-minute period. If we call the number of occurrences of the behavior N and the length of time of the observation T, the calculation can be done as follows:

$$\frac{N}{T} = \text{rate of occurrences}$$

$$\frac{30}{15 \text{ min}} = 2 \text{ times a minute}$$

Event recording has several advantages (Beaty, 1986; Sattler, 1988):

1. The behavior or event is kept intact, thus facilitating analysis.
2. Behaviors that occur infrequently can be monitored.
3. Changes in behavior over a period of time can be recorded.

Despite the advantages, event recording also has several disadvantages (Beaty, 1986; Sattler, 1988):

1. Because the event is taken out of context it may be difficult to analyze the events that preceded the target behavior.
2. Patterns of behavior may not be detected.
3. Behaviors that are not easily defined cannot be recorded.
4. Reliability between observers may be difficult to establish.
5. Unless the length of the observation periods across the sessions is constant, it may be difficult to make generalizations.

Duration Recording

Duration recording is a measure of the persistence of a specific event or behavior. For example, in developing instructional goals for a young child, it may be critical to know how long a tantrum lasts or how long a child plays independently. Duration recording can be used when it is important to know the length of time the behavior or event lasted rather than whether it occurred.

The duration of a behavior or event can be hard to measure, and therefore this method should be used only when information about duration is essential. Before the observer begins duration recording, precise definitions for the *beginning* and *ending* of the behaviors must be established. For example, independent play could

FIGURE 4.4 Example of event record with one-minute intervals. Top part shows event data for throwing out behaviors counted within each interval. Bottom part shows same data as scored by interval-only method. By comparison one can see that interval scoring is not as sensitive to the dynamics of the high rate of behavior as is the event within interval record. With the event (top) record one can see a sudden increase in rate of throwing out after minute 9; the interval record is insensitive to this change. Likewise, the discrepancy between the two children is greater as measured by the actual rate (event) measure, and underestimated by the interval (bottom) measure.

SOURCE: Adapted from Alessi & Kaye (1983).

BEHAVIORS	Total	Ch.	1	2	3	4	5	6	7	8	9	10	11	12	13	14	15
1. Objects thrown	30	R	1	3	1	1	2	2	1	1	1	3	3	3	2	3	3
by event	9	C	0	0	0	0	0	0	3	0	0	0	3	0	2	0	1
record		T															
2.		R															
		C															
		T															
3. Objects thrown	15	R	X	X	X	X	X	X	X	X	X	X	X	X	X	X	X
by interval	4	C	0	0	0	0	0	0	X	0	0	0	X	0	X	0	X
record		T															

be said to begin when the child begins to look at the object, when the child approaches the object, or when the child actually picks up the object. Once the observer has defined the beginning and ending of a behavior or event, a stopwatch can be used to time the length of the event.

Besides recording the duration or length of a behavior or event, there are two other methods of analyzing the data. The observer can (1) determine the *percentage* of time a behavior or event occurs or (2) calculate the *average* length of the behavior or event (Sattler, 1988). To calculate the percentage duration rate, which is the percent of time the behavior or event occurs, the observer divides *d,* the total duration of the behavior or event, by *t,* the total time of the observation, and multiplies by 100 to obtain a percentage.

$$\frac{d}{t} \times 100$$

For example, suppose the beginning and end of independent play have been defined as the moments at which the child picks up and drops the object, respectively. The observer, using a stopwatch, would watch the child for 15 minutes. Suppose that during this 15-minute interval, the child plays independently three times, for 2 minutes, 3 minutes, and 1 minute, for a total duration of 6 minutes. Using the formula, we have:

$$\frac{6}{15} \times 100 = 40\% \text{ of the observation period}$$

The observer also may find it useful to determine the *average duration,* or the average amount of time the child played independently. Since we know that the child played independently three times during the observation period, we can use the following formula to calculate the average duration of each play period.

$$\frac{d}{e} = \text{average duration of behavior or event}$$

where *d* is the total duration of the behavior or event and *e* is the number of events.

Using the observation information, we can calculate the average length of time the child played independently:

$$\frac{6 \text{ min}}{3 \text{ events}} = 2 \text{ minutes}$$

When reporting duration of behavior, the observer may use one or all three of the methods just described: length of the behavior or event, percentage of time the behavior or event occurred, and the average length of time the behavior or event occurred.

Intensity of behavior, a measure of the strength of a behavior, can also be recorded (Sattler, 1988). For example, to record the intensity of behavior associated with independent play, we could create three categories: (1) plays independently but needs much encouragement; (2) plays independently but needs some encouragement; and (3) plays independently without encouragement. Using these categories, we could refine our record of the child's play behavior.

Latency of Behavior

Latency of behavior is a measure of the amount of time between a behavior or event (or request to begin the behavior) and the beginning of the prespecified or target behavior. For example, a child who has been encouraged to play independently may not actually began independent play immediately. Using a stopwatch, the observer can determine the amount of time that elapses between the request itself and the child's commencement of the desired behavior. In a variation of latency recording, instead of recording the time before the requested behavior is *begun,* the observer records the time between the request and the *completion* of the behavior (Alessi & Kaye, 1983).

Like duration, the average latency period can be determined. Using the observation information, we can calculate the average length of time it took for the child to begin to play independently. For example, suppose a child is encouraged to begin independent play four times and that for each request to begin the behavior, the following latency periods were recorded: 2 minutes, 3 minutes, 1 minute, and 2 minutes. In this formula, l represents total latency and e is the number of events.

$$\frac{l}{e} = \text{average latency}$$

Substituting the numbers from our example, we have:

$$\frac{8 \text{ min}}{4 \text{ events}} = 2 \text{ minutes (average latency)}$$

Latency can be difficult to measure (Alessi & Kaye, 1983). The observer must carefully define the stimulus behavior (the behavior that signals the request to initiate behavior), the beginning of the target behavior, and the end of the target behavior.

Interval Recording

One of the major disadvantages of anecdotal records, running records, and specimen descriptions is their vulnerability to observer bias and judgment. And, while these techniques can provide rich descriptions about events, it is difficult to quantify behaviors. For this reason, recording systems of other types have been developed.

Interval recording is an observational method in which specific events or behaviors are recorded during a prespecified time interval. Interval recording is effective when behaviors that can be easily seen tend to occur at a moderate rate.

The period of observation is divided into equal segments, and in each time slot the observer records the presence or absence of the behavior. Generally, the length of the time segment ranges from 5 seconds to 30 seconds.

An easy way to set up interval recording is to use a ruler to draw time intervals on graph paper. For example, if 30 seconds has been chosen as the length of the time segment and the observer will be watching for 10 minutes, there will be twenty 30-second intervals; for a 20-minute observation period, there would be forty 30-second intervals (Alessi & Kaye, 1983).

Figure 4.5 illustrates interval recording. If the behavior occurs during an interval, an *X* is marked. If the behavior does not occur, an *O* is written. The observer

Behavior	Child	Total	Interval									
			1	2	3	4	5	6	7	8	9	10
Requests help	M. G.	8	X	X	X	X	X	X	O	X	X	O

FIGURE 4.5 An interval record using one-minute intervals. An X indicates that the behavior occurs during the interval; an O indicates that the behavior was not observed. Contrast this figure with Figure 4.4. The interval record is insensitive to the frequency of the occurrence of the behavior.

SOURCE: Adapted from Alessi & Kaye, 1983.

proceeds from one 60-second interval to the next, until the observation period has been completed (Alessi & Kaye, 1983). Practice may be necessary before using this procedure. An alternative to using graph paper is to take advantage of portable computers that run special software to record behaviors.

Different methods of interval recording include whole-interval sampling, partial-interval sampling, and momentary time sampling.

Whole-Interval Sampling. During whole-interval sampling, the observer watches for the entire interval, and the behavior must cover the entire interval. If the behavior does not last for the entire interval, the observer must mark an O in the interval segment. This type of interval recording is useful for hyperactivity, withdrawal, and other behaviors that occur continuously or without interruption (Sattler, 1988).

Partial-Interval Sampling. Here the behavior is recorded if it is observed for any *part* of the interval. However, a behavior that occurs more than once during an interval is recorded only *one* time. Partial-interval recording is useful for behaviors of short duration (Sattler, 1988).

Momentary Time Sampling. Momentary time sampling is a technique in which a target behavior or activity is recorded if it is observed only at the *end* of a specific time interval. For example, an observer would record an *X* if a target behavior is observed to occur at the end of a 10-second interval. If the target behavior occurs six times over a three-minute period (eighteen 10-second intervals), the behavior is said to have occurred $6/18$ or 30% of the observed time. This technique can be especially useful when a number of children are to be observed at the same time. Suppose there were six children in a group. Each child could be observed for 10 seconds every minute and the target behavior recorded for child A at the tenth second, for child B at the twentieth second, for child C at the thirtieth second, and so on. Thus, the entire group could be observed once every minute.

Usefulness of Interval Recording

Each type of the interval recording procedure—whole interval, partial interval, and momentary time sampling—can provide useful information about children's behavior. When deciding which type to use, it is important to consider:

1. The behavior(s) that will be observed
2. The duration of the behaviors
3. The frequency at which the behaviors typically occur
4. The length of the observation period
5. The number of times the child will be observed

If behaviors occur fleetingly, partial-interval recording should be used. Whole-interval or partial-interval recording can be used in observing behaviors that have a long duration. A disadvantage of whole-interval recording is the tendency to underestimate the occurrence of the behavior, whereas partial-interval recording can lead to overestimates. Momentary time sampling is an efficient procedure because more than one child can be observed during an observation period. However, for behaviors that are of short duration, momentary time sampling is less useful (Bailey & Wolery, 1989).

Sattler (1988) points out that while interval recording is an efficient method of observation, it does have several disadvantages:

1. Important behaviors may be omitted or neglected.
2. Information about the quality of the behaviors is lacking unless the recording procedure provides an appropriate code.
3. Since the behavior is recorded as occurring in separate time intervals, information about the actual frequency and duration of the behavior will not be provided.
4. Behaviors that occur frequently may be underestimated.
5. Behaviors that occur infrequently or are of low duration may be overestimated.

For each of these interval recording methods, the data can be reported as a percentage of occurrences of the behavior (Bailey & Wolery, 1989). For example, suppose a child was observed, using the partial-interval method, for twenty 10-second intervals. The behavior observed was thumb sucking. The observer marked an X in 17 of the boxes. Thus, to calculate the percentage of occurrences of thumb sucking, the observer would divide the total number of occurrences, O, by the total number of observation intervals, N:

$$\frac{O}{N} \times 100 = \text{percentage of occurrences}$$

In our example,

$$\frac{17}{20} \times 100 = 85\%$$

Recording Interval

When the observation interval is very brief, the behavior to be observed is complex, or a number of children are being observed simultaneously, it is difficult for the observer to continue to observe and record, proceeding from one interval to the next. To help alleviate this problem, the observer can establish a recording interval.

With this technique, the child is observed for a time interval, such as 5 seconds, and the observation is recorded during the next time interval, which could be 2 seconds. The observer then proceeds from one interval to the next, observing, recording, observing, etc.

Graphing Behavior

Alessi & Kaye (1983) described a method of automatically graphing data while the information is being recorded. This approach is convenient because the data can be automatically summarized, as illustrated in Figure 4.6.

Category Recording

Figure 4.7 shows two observation instruments that use *category recording,* a system that can be as simple as two categories (e.g., on-task and off-task) or complex enough to contain many categories (e.g., compliant, requests assistance, resists help, verbalizes need for assistance, on-task, off-task). As with other types of observation, the target behaviors must be discrete, they must be carefully defined, and they must have an observable beginning and end.

FIGURE 4.6   Automatic graphing data collection format used across days (here day 1 through day 30). A fixed number of intervals (here 1 through 19) are observed each day. The heavy line between days 4 and 5 indicates the beginning of an intervention plan. Intervals in which the target behavior occurred are scored with Xs, while other behaviors are scored with Os. Reading from left to right and focusing on the Xs reveals a clear downward trend in the number of intervals scored for the target behavior over the 30-day period (more Xs in the earlier columns and fewer Xs in the later columns). There is a swift drop in the number of intervals scored for the target behavior just after the intervention was implemented (day 5), suggesting the effectiveness of this procedure.

SOURCE: Adapted from Alessi & Kaye, 1983.

	1	2	3	4	5	6	7	8	9	10	11	12	13	14	15	16	17	18	19	20	21	22	23	24	25	26	27	28	29	30
19	0	0	0	0	0	0	0	0	0	0	0	0	0	0	0	0	0	0	0	0	0	0	0	0	0	0	0	0	0	0
18	0	0	0	0	0	0	0	0	0	0	0	0	0	0	0	0	0	0	0	0	0	0	0	0	0	0	0	0	0	0
17	0	0	0	0	0	0	0	0	0	0	0	0	0	0	0	0	0	0	0	0	0	0	0	0	0	0	0	0	0	0
16	0	0	0	0	0	0	0	0	0	0	0	0	0	0	0	0	0	0	0	0	0	0	0	0	0	0	0	0	0	0
15	0	0	0	0	0	0	0	0	0	0	0	0	0	0	0	0	0	0	0	0	0	0	0	0	0	0	0	0	0	0
14	0	0	X	0	0	0	0	0	0	0	0	0	0	0	0	0	0	0	0	0	0	0	0	0	0	0	0	0	0	0
13	X	0	X	X	0	0	0	0	0	0	0	0	0	0	0	0	0	0	0	0	0	0	0	0	0	0	0	0	0	0
12	X	X	X	X	0	0	0	0	0	0	0	0	0	0	0	0	0	0	0	0	0	0	0	0	0	0	0	0	0	0
11	X	X	X	X	0	0	0	0	0	0	0	0	0	0	0	0	0	0	0	0	0	0	0	0	0	0	0	0	0	0
10	X	X	X	X	0	0	0	0	0	0	0	0	0	0	0	0	0	0	0	0	0	0	0	0	0	0	0	0	0	0
9	X	X	X	X	0	0	0	0	0	0	0	0	0	0	0	0	0	0	0	0	0	0	0	0	0	0	0	0	0	0
8	X	X	X	X	0	0	0	0	0	0	0	0	0	0	0	0	0	0	0	0	0	0	0	0	0	0	0	0	0	0
7	X	X	X	X	X	X	X	0	0	0	0	0	0	0	0	0	0	0	0	0	0	0	0	0	0	0	0	0	0	0
6	X	X	X	X	X	X	X	X	0	0	0	X	0	0	0	0	0	0	0	0	0	0	0	0	0	0	0	0	0	0
5	X	X	X	X	X	X	X	X	0	0	0	X	0	0	0	0	0	0	0	0	0	0	0	0	0	0	0	0	0	0
4	X	X	X	X	X	X	X	X	X	X	0	X	0	0	0	0	0	0	0	0	0	0	0	0	0	0	0	0	0	0
3	X	X	X	X	X	X	X	X	X	X	X	X	X	0	0	0	0	X	0	0	0	0	0	0	0	0	0	0	0	0
2	X	X	X	X	X	X	X	X	X	X	X	X	X	X	X	0	0	X	0	X	0	0	0	0	0	0	0	0	0	0
1	X	X	X	X	X	X	X	X	X	X	X	X	X	X	X	X	X	X	X	X	X	X	X	0	X	X	0	X	0	0

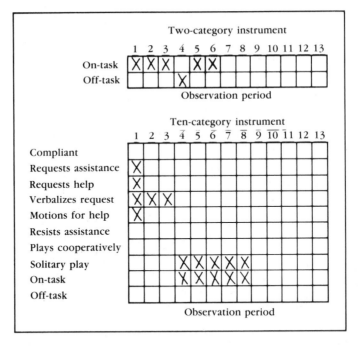

FIGURE 4.7   Category recording

Rating Scales

Rating scales are applied at the end of an observation period to measure the degree to which a child exhibits a prespecified behavior. There are different types of rating scale, including the semantic differential, the graphic rating scale, the visual analog scale, and the numerical scale. Rating scales are useful when they are combined with other types of assessment such as interval recording, event recording, and formal standardized testing. By supplementing the information obtained from observations, rating scales can help in the evaluation of the quality of the behavior of one child or many children. While rating scales can be useful, they have been criticized as being impressionistic, lacking interrater reliability, and being affected by the subjectivity of the observer (Sattler, 1988).

Semantic Differential Scale.   This kind of rating scale uses opposite adjectives, or *bipolar* adjectives, which are rated along a continuum. Figure 4.8 is an example of a semantic differential scale.

Graphic Rating Scale.   Figure 4.9 is an example of a graphic rating scale, which logs behaviors along a graduated continuum; points on the scale are separated by equal intervals (Gronlund & Linn, 1990; DeVellis, 1991).

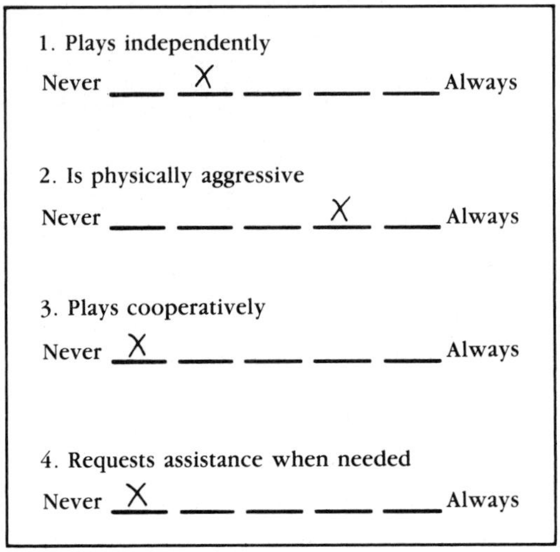

1. Plays independently
Never X Always
2. Is physically aggressive
Never X Always
3. Plays cooperatively
Never X Always
4. Requests assistance when needed
Never X Always

FIGURE 4.8 Semantic differential scale

Visual Analog Scale. A visual analog scale (Figure 4.10) is a continuous scale; the observer can make a mark at any point along the scale, which is simply a line (DeVellis, 1991).

Numerical Scale. A numerical scale indicates the extent to which a characteristic or behavior is present (Gronlund & Linn, 1990). This type of scale, sometimes called a Likert scale, is useful when the observer is able to define the behavior and each instance of behavior can be assigned a rating from the lowest number to the highest number (e.g., 1 to 5). Figure 4.11 shows an example.

FIGURE 4.9 Graphic rating scale

1. Dresses oneself
X
Never Seldom Occasionally Frequently Always
2. Requests assistance
X
Never Seldom Occasionally Frequently Always
3. Plays cooperatively
X
Never Seldom Occasionally Frequently Always

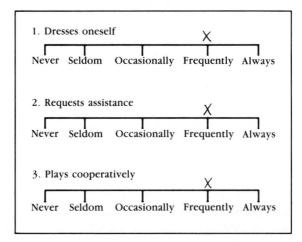

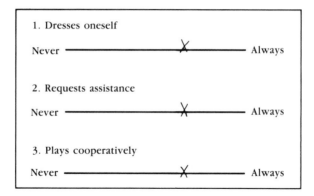

FIGURE 4.10 Visual analog scale

Product Evaluation

Product evaluation, an assessment of specific characteristics of the results of children's work or play, can be very useful. For example, drawings, structures made of building toys, paintings, clay figures, math manipulatives, and other objects can be evaluated. Ratings of products can supplement information obtained from observations of the child (Gronlund & Linn, 1990).

Product evaluations can be conducted using rating scales of various types. Three different scoring techniques can be used.

Analytic Scoring.   Analytic scoring calls for a scale or rubric that breaks down the product into various components. For example, a finger painting could be evaluated using the following criteria: color, creativity, and attention to detail. The scales

FIGURE 4.11 Numerical rating scale

Directions: Rate the degree to which the child engages in creative activities, with 1 representing very low creativity and 5 representing extremely creative behavior.

1. To what degree does the child play creatively?

    1   2   3   ④   5

2. To what extent are the child's drawings creative?

    1   2   3   ④   5

3. To what extent does the child use creative and inventive language?

    1   2   ③   4   5

4. To what degree is the child's fantasy play creative and inventive?

    1   2   3   ④   5

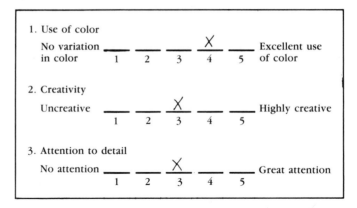

FIGURE 4.12 Analytic scoring

we have discussed—the semantic differential, the graphic rating scale, the visual analog scale, and the numerical scale—can be adapted for use in analytic scoring. Figure 4.12 presents an example of analytic scoring.

Holistic Scoring.   Here the evaluator assigns one score to the product, looking for a particular, previously identified characteristic. This technique is useful when a quick, superficial impression will suffice.

General Impression Scoring.   This technique can be used when the evaluator is able to define the characteristic that is to be evaluated by rating it from the highest score (say, 5) to the lowest number (say, 1).

Checklists

Checklists are similar to rating scales. While rating scales can help to evaluate the *degree* or *frequency* with which behavior occurs, checklists usually require just a simple *yes* or *no* response. A *checklist* is a consistent array of characteristics or behaviors that allows the evaluator to note the presence or absence of each characteristic or behavior. Checklists can be used to assess behaviors and products (e.g., drawings, journals, constructions) of one or more children. Checklists look like rating scales, but the items are usually checked off (Beaty, 1986; Gronlund & Linn, 1990), as illustrated in Figure 4.13, where the observer has indicated the presence of a behavior in several children and noted the evidence of each recorded instance.

Checklists are fairly easy to develop. The following guidelines can be used (Beaty, 1986; Gronlund & Linn, 1990):

1. The checklist items should be brief, yet detailed and easily understood.
2. Parallel construction should be used in drafting the items. That is, word order, subject, and verb tense should be the same for all items.
3. The items should be nonjudgmental.
4. The checklist should stress positive behavior. The emphasis should be on what the child *can do* as opposed to what the child cannot do.

Daily Observation			
Directions: Use this checklist as children first arrive in the morning. Check all that apply.			
	Child 1	Child 2	Child 3
1. Name and age	Y. G. 3	M. G. 4	G. B. 3
2. Child's entrance into room			
a. entered room willingly	✓		✓
b. clung to parent		✓	
c. entered room reluctantly			
d. other (specify)			
3. Reaction to the environment			
a. freely explored	✓		✓
b. curious but hesitant to move out		✓	
c. reluctant to explore			
4. Relationship to others			
a. sought contact with other children	✓		✓
b. sought contact with teacher			
c. remained apart from the group		✓	
d. rejected advances made by others			
e. aggressive toward others			
5. Response to materials			
a. chose materials freely (specify)	blocks		books
b. needed help in selecting materials		✓	
c. behaviors seemed to lack direction			

FIGURE 4.13   Observation checklist

5. Items should not be repeated in different parts of the checklist.
6. The items should be representative of children's behavior.
7. The items should be arranged in the order in which they are expected to appear.
8. A procedure should be provided for indicating each behavior as it occurs (e.g., checkmark, yes or no, plus or minus sign).

Checklists, like rating scales, are useful when they are combined with other types of assessment. By supplementing the information obtained from observations, checklists can help in the evaluation of children's behavior; they can be used with one or more children. Checklists have been criticized for lacking interrater reliability and for being affected by the subjectivity of the rater. In addition, behaviors not itemized may be missed. Moreover, being limited to the presence or absence of behaviors, checklists do not provide qualitative information (Beaty, 1986).

RELIABILITY OF DIRECT OBSERVATION

Reliability, the consistency or stability of the observations, is an important facet of direct observations. When conducting direct observations, determining interobserver reliability is very important. Repp, Nieminen, Olinger, and Brusca (1988) discussed several factors that can affect the accuracy of observers. These include reactivity, observer drift, recording procedure, location of the observer, reliability checks, observer expectancy, and characteristics of the child and the setting.

Reactivity refers to the changes observers make in their own behaviors in response to what they are observing. If, for example, observers alter their instructions, give additional prompts, or increase the amount of feedback during a recording period, by their change in behavior they offer a threat to the accuracy of the observations. The use of videotapes and audiotapes may also increase reactivity if they are intrusive and disrupt activities.

When the observer shifts away from the original objectives of the observation, usually without being aware of it, we say that *observer drift* has occurred. To prevent this phenomenon from occurring, the observer needs to periodically check the originally established purposes and criteria for conducting the observation.

The type of *recording procedure* that is used can affect the accuracy of the observation. In summarizing earlier research, Repp et al. (1988) found that (1) the use of partial intervals can result in the overestimation of continuous recording; (2) the use of whole intervals can lead to underestimation of the occurrence of the behavior; and (3) momentary time sampling is reliable. These authors recommend that small intervals be used but note that the interval size should allow for only one response per interval.

The *location* in which the behavior is observed may also affect the accuracy of the observations. Most observations are conducted in a natural setting. Although as indicated in this discussion, audio- and videotaping may be necessary, care should be taken that such potentially intrusive procedures do not disrupt activities.

The conduct of *reliability checks* can also affect the accuracy of the observations. An observer who is aware that the process is being monitored for accuracy may change his or her usual methods of conducting the observation. Reliability tends to increase when an observer knows that the observations are being checked.

Bias can occur if the observer comes to the task with a certain *expectation*. For example, if an observer knows that the child to be observed has been referred for aggressive behavior, the results may be influenced by the observer's expectation that such behavior will occur.

Certain *characteristics* associated with the *child* and the *setting* can also influence the accuracy of the observations. The child's sex, the complexity of the behaviors to be observed, the predictability of the child's behaviors, and the observer's familiarity with the setting can all affect accuracy.

Thus, reactivity, observer drift, recording procedure, location of the observer, reliability checks, observer expectancy, and the characteristics of the child and the setting can all affect the accuracy of observations. To minimize these threats, Repp et al. (1988) recommended that:

1. Observers be well trained.
2. Uncomplicated codes be used to record observations.
3. Observations be done by both male and female observers.
4. Interaction between observers be avoided.
5. Accuracy of observations be checked against a criterion.
6. Both observers and children be given a period of time in which to adapt to one another.
7. Observations be conducted as unobtrusively as possible.
8. Permanent products (audiotapes, videotapes, children's drawings, etc.) be used, whenever possible.
9. Observations be conducted frequently and systematically.

Calculating Interobserver Reliability

There are several ways of determining reliability of observations (Frick & Semmel, 1978; Alessi & Kaye, 1983). In calculating reliability, it is important that (1) all data be collected independently, (2) at least two observers conduct observations, and (3) the observers look at the same phenomenon. If it is not possible for two observers to be present at the same time, a videotape or audiotape can be used for the second observation (Alessi & Kaye, 1983).

Event Recording.   One way of determining interobserver reliability for event recording is to find the percentage of agreements between the observers (Alessi & Kaye, 1983). The following formula can be used:

$$r = \frac{a}{a + d} \times 100$$

where the number of times the observers agreed with each other (a) is divided by the sum of the number of times the observers agreed (a) and disagreed (d). This number is multiplied by 100 to give the percentage of agreements. For example, suppose two people were observing the number of times a child interrupted other children. This type of observation, known as event recording, was introduced earlier in this chapter. The observers agreed 10 times and disagreed 4 times. Using the formula, we write:

$$r = \frac{10}{10 + 4} \times 100$$

$$r = \frac{10}{14} \times 100$$

$$r = 71\%$$

Thus, the percentage of agreement between the observers is 71%.

Duration Recording. Computing interobserver reliability for duration recording is similar to calculating interobserver reliability for event recording (Sattler, 1988). The formula for duration recording is:

$$\% \ A_{dr} = \frac{t_1}{t_2} \times 100$$

where $\% \ A_{dr}$ = percentage agreement for duration recording

t_1 = time recorded by the observer with the smaller time duration

t_2 = time recorded by the observer with the larger time duration

For example, suppose two observers were recording the length of time a child played independently. One observer recorded 180 seconds; the other observer recorded 190 seconds. We apply the formula:

$$\% \ A_{dr} = \frac{180}{190} \times 100$$

$$\% \ A_{dr} = 95\%$$

Thus we have 95% agreement between these observers.

Rating Recording. When computing agreement between two raters or observers the following formula can be used (Sattler, 1988):

$$\% \ A_r = \frac{A_r}{A_r + D} \times 100$$

where $\% \ A_r$ = percentage agreement for rating recording

A_r = number of items for which observers agreed on the rating

D = number of items for which observers disagreed on the rating

For example, suppose two observers, using a 15-item rating scale, agreed on the ratings for 12 of the items. Using the formula, we have:

$$\% \ A_r = \frac{12}{12 + 3} \times 100$$

$$\% \ A_r = 80\%$$

In this example, there was 80% agreement between the two observers.

VALIDITY OF DIRECT OBSERVATION

Validity is the extent to which an instrument measures what it is intended to measure. Validity standards depend on the observability of behaviors, the objectivity of the instrument, observer variability, and the representativeness of the instrument items of the behaviors that are observed (Herbert & Attridge, 1975). While there is some evidence of validity for some observational instruments, the validity of many instruments is either unsubstantiated or questionable.

Hoge (1985), who had several suggestions for assuring validity, recommended that existing instruments be used when possible. Using existing instruments has several advantages: (1) time and effort are saved; (2) reliability and validity information may be available; and (3) information about the use of these instruments can lead to the development of sounder measures. In addition, Hoge (1985) pointed out the need for care in assuring instrument reliability. Finally, he felt that instruments that broadly define behavior (e.g., on-task, off-task) are more likely to be valid than instruments that categorize behaviors into numerous subskills and categories. Remember that although it may be more difficult to determine the validity of observational measures, validity is a very important area of concern.

DEVELOPING NORMS

Developing norms will help to evaluate the behavior that is to be observed. The behavior of one or more children in the group can serve as the norm or comparison for the child who is to be observed. In such a case, the other children in the group are known as the *norm* group and the child who is to be observed is referred to as the *target* child. In the absence of norms, it is difficult to determine whether the target child's behavior is atypical or abnormal (Alessi, 1980; Sattler, 1988).

There are three ways to develop norms. The first is to use several children or a group of children as the norm sample. This approach calls for the scan-check method, in which the observer scans the group of children for several seconds every few minutes and counts the number of children who are exhibiting the target behavior. For example, every 2 minutes, an observer scans a group of children for 5 seconds and counts the number of children who are on-task. After this scan-check, the observer can watch the target child and the comparison child for 5 seconds to determine whether they are on-task. Figure 4.14 is an example of the results of a scan-check observation. This technique can be used for interval or momentary time sampling recording.

The second way of establishing a norm sample is to ask the teacher to identify a child whose behavior is *representative* of or *typical* of the behavior of the children in the group. By watching the behavior of the *typical* child, the observer can use the scan-check method to compare the typical child's behavior with that of the target child.

The third way of developing a norm is to conduct several separate observations of the behavior of the target child and compare the findings. In this way, the behavior of the target child is evaluated with respect to the individual's behavior at different times (Alessi, 1980; Sattler, 1988).

THE OBSERVER

When conducting an observation it is important not to disrupt the normal activities and routine of the environment. In general, the observer should be able to gather information with a minimum of disruptions to children's play or activities. Teachers

Record of Preschool Observation

Child's name: P. A.	Observer: N. T.
Age: 4-2	Date: May 3, 19xx
School: Applegate	Teacher: L. S.

Reason for Observation: To determine the extent P.A.'s behavior differs from her peers.

Activity Observed: circle time

Observation Techiques Used (e.g., interval, time sample): 30-second interval for P. A.   1 minute interval for class scan.

Behavior Codes	**Grouping Codes**	**Teacher and Peer Reaction Codes**
T On-task	L Large group	AA Attention to all
O Off-task	S Small group	A+ Positive attention
P Passive	O One-to-one	A- Negative attention
M Motor activity	C Cooperative	NA No attention
	P Parallel	NT Neutral attention
	F Free-time	

Time	Child	Comp. Child	Class Scan	Anecdotal Notes	Group	Tchr	Peer
9:16	P	T		not attending to teacher	L	NT	NA
	M	T	80%	walks away	L	A-	NA
9:17	M	T			L	NA	NA
	M	O	83%	Walks to block area	L	NA	NA
9:18	M	T			L	NA	NA
	M	T	76%		L	NA	NA
9:19	T	O		attends to teacher	L	NA	NA
	T	T	80%		L	A+	NT
9:20	T	T			L	A+	NT
	P	T	80%		L	NA	NA
Summary	3/10 30%	8/10 80%	80%		L=10	NT=1 A-=1	NA=8 NT=2

FIGURE 4.14   Scan-check recording sheet

SOURCE: Adapted from Alessi & Kaye (1983).

and caregivers who are regularly present can conduct observations in a less obtrusive way than outsiders. Professionals who are not a regular part of the program, such as consultants, psychologists, or specialists, may influence the behaviors of the children no matter how careful they have been to be unobtrusive. A one-way window provides an unobtrusive way to observe children. If a one-way window is not available, the following guidelines can be helpful:

Enter the room quietly.

Sit in an area of the room that allows you to view all the children.

Before beginning the observation, allow the children to become comfortable with the presence of an observer.

If the children ask why you are there, be natural and warm. Tell them you are interested in their activities.

After conducting the observation, ask the teacher or caregiver if the behavior of the children was typical of their behavior.

When possible, conduct several observations on different days.

FORMAL BEHAVIOR CHECKLISTS, RATINGS, AND SCALES

While inappropriate behavior can be assessed using techniques of direct observation, a number of published rating scales and checklists are available as well. Some instruments are very specific in that they target unique conditions such as hyperactivity or aggression, whereas others assess a broad range of behaviors.

Typically, rating scales and checklists are written questionnaires. The person who completes the questionnaire, often a teacher or a caregiver, is called the informant. Informants provide information that is considered to be judgmental. Informants bring their own perspectives, experiences, attitudes, response styles, and biases to the task of completing a checklist, rating scale, or questionnaire. There is some evidence that ratings by informants overestimate the abilities of children (Fewell, Langley, & Roll, 1982). It may be helpful to ask more than one informant to complete an instrument or scale (Sattler, 1988).

Representative Behavior Scales

The checklists and rating scales commonly used to assess behavior are followed by descriptions of several representative behavior rating scales.

Behavior Rating Scales and Checklists (Adapted from Sattler, 1988)

Instrument	Age Range
Abbreviated Parent/Teacher Questionnaire (Conners, 1985)	Preschool, school age
AML Behavior Rating Scale—Revised, (Hightower, Spinell, & Lotyczewski, 1990)	School age
Behavioral Observation Form (Garwood & Fewell, 1983)	Preschool
Behavior Assessment System for Children (Reynolds & Kamphaus, 1992)	Preschool, school age
Behavior Evaluation Scale—2 (McCarney & Leigh, 1990)	School age
Behavior Rating Profile—2 (Brown & Hammill, 1990)	School age
Child Behavior Checklists (Achenbach, 1988, 1991a)	Preschool, school age

Child Behavior Scale (Lahey, Stempniak, Robinson, & Tyroler, 1978)	School age
Classroom Adjustment Ratings Scale (Lorion, Cowen, & Caldwell, 1975)	School age
Conners Parent Rating Scale (Conners, 1985)	Preschool, school age
Conners Teacher Rating Scale (Conners, 1985)	Preschool, school age
Devereux Child Behavior Rating Scale (Spivack & Spotts, 1966)	School age
Devereux Elementary School Behavior Rating Scale (Spivack & Swift, 1967)	School age
Health Resources Inventory (Gesten, 1976)	School age
Kohn Problem Checklist (Kohn, 1986a)	Preschool, school age
Kohn Social Competence Scale (Kohn, 1986b)	Preschool, school age
Preschool Behavior Questionnaire (Behar & Stringfield, 1974)	Preschool
Revised Behavior Problem Checklist (Quay & Peterson, 1983)	School age
Social Skills Rating System (Gresham & Elliott, 1990)	Preschool, school age
Teacher Behavioral Description Form (Seidman et al., 1979)	School age
Teacher's Report Form (Achenbach, 1991b)	School age
Test of Early Socioemotional Development (Hresko & Brown, 1984)	Preschool, school age
Walker–McConnell Scale of Social Competence and School Adjustment (Walker & McConnell, 1988)	School age

Behavioral Observation Form (Birth to Three Years) (Garwood & Fewell, 1983). A brief form serves as a guide to the observation of behaviors of young children. This informal guide can be a useful adjunct to formal assessment. Areas assessed include sensory intactness, gross motor, fine motor, cognition, communication, social, play, self-help, and learning preferences.

Behavior Evaluation Scale—2. The Behavior Evaluation Scale—2 (BES-2) (McCarney & Leigh, 1990), intended for children in grades kindergarten through 12, is a checklist that is completed by school personnel. The BES-2 has five subscales: learning problems, interpersonal difficulties, inappropriate behavior, unhappiness/depression, and physical symptoms/fears. The manual reports adequate reliability and validity.

Child Behavior Checklist/2–3 and Child Behavior Checklist/4–18.
These checklists (Achenbach, 1988, 1991a), along with the Teacher's Report Form
(Achenbach, 1991b), are completed by parents and teachers. The first is to be used
for children who are two to three years of age; the second is intended for older
children. The checklists have adequate technical characteristics.

Revised Behavior Problem Checklist.   The Revised Problem Behavior Checklist (Quay & Peterson, 1983, 1987) measures behavioral characteristics of children
in grades kindergarten through 12. The respondents can be a parent, teacher, or
other person who knows the child well. The 89 items in the checklist are classified
in six scales: conduct disorder, socialized aggression, attention problems, anxiety/
withdrawal, psychotic behavior, and motor excess. The reliability and validity are
acceptable.

Social Skills Rating System.   The Social Skills Rating System (SSRS) (Gresham
& Elliott, 1990) assesses problem behavior and social skills of children ages three to
eighteen years old. Three questionnaires are available: child, parent, and teacher.
Separate questionnaires are available for preschool, elementary, and secondary age
children. Depending on the age of the child, up to three questionnaires are completed for each child. For preschool age children, only the parent and teacher questionnaires are completed. The SSRS has good technical characteristics.

Test of Early Socioemotional Development.   The Test of Early Socioemotional Development (TOESD) (Hresko & Brown, 1984) is a tool for rating the behavior of children between the ages of three years and seven years, eleven months. The
TOESD has four components: student rating scale, parent rating scale, teacher rating
scale, and a sociogram (in which other children provide information about their
perceptions of their peers). The technical characteristics are acceptable.

AN INTRODUCTION TO ASSESSING ENVIRONMENTS

In addition to gathering specific information about the child, the observer will need
to examine aspects in the child's environment. Smith, Neisworth, and Greer (1978)
identified four major aspects of the environment for assessment purposes:

1. Physical
2. Methods and materials
3. Available services
4. Social

Physical Aspects

Physical aspects of the environment may affect how well the child functions. For
example, the arrangement of furnishings may encourage certain skills. A small table
with three or four chairs enables and supports small-group activities that promote
social skills. Storage shelves that are accessible to children promote independence
and responsibility in taking care of classroom materials. Differences in texture or

color of carpeting between centers enable children who are blind or have multiple disabilities to increase orientation and independent travel (mobility) skills.

The physical arrangement of furnishings may also decrease opportunities for inclusion. Lack of well-defined areas may lead to aimless wandering and impede the emergence of appropriate developmental skills. Large open spaces encourage running, an important gross motor skill but not necessarily appropriate for indoor spaces!

Materials in the Environment

The type and quantity of materials in the environment may support opportunities for increased interaction among children. By limiting the number of available materials, one expands their chances for learning how to share. Martin, Brady, and Williams (1991), who examined the influence of social and isolate toys on the social behavior of preschool children, found that the selection of toys is a valuable and nonintrusive method for promoting social interaction among children with and without disabilities.

Scheduling

Programmatic factors such as the scheduling of daily activities—or the lack of a schedule—may also affect children's functioning. When the environment is reorganized, there may be positive changes in both adults' and children's behavior. Nordquist, Twardosz, and McEvoy (1991) found that changes in room arrangement, additions of materials, and changes in scheduling resulted in increased adult smiling and use of affectionate words in the free play area, while children with autism showed an increase in use of play materials and compliance with adult instructions.

Social Aspects

Social aspects of the environments also must be considered. How do adults interact with the children? How are the children greeted when they arrive at the program? What is the quality of the interactions? How do adults support the learning and playing among children?

WHEN SHOULD AN ENVIRONMENTAL ASSESSMENT BE COMPLETED?

An environmental assessment may be completed during one or more of the steps in the assessment process depending on the kind of information being sought. Team members should make sure that the assessment incorporates all aspects of the child's environment, including home and child care settings, school and community programs, and family life. An assessment that reflects all these areas is referred to as *ecologically valid* (Benner, 1992).

1. *Screening.* During the screening procedure, an environmental assessment may provide information that results in changes to the environment,

sometimes eliminating the need for intervention or special educational services.

2. *Determining eligibility.* This step focuses on gathering in-depth information about the child. Information about environments and how the child functions in each of them is valuable.

3. *Planning the program.* When a team is considering different program options, an environmental assessment may provide helpful information for decision making. An environmental assessment of the least restrictive setting tells the extent to which a given setting provides appropriate furnishings, conditions, and activities for child development.

4. *Monitoring individual progress.* An environmental assessment may be included in monitoring the progress of a child with disabilities. Information gathered may result in further changes and adaptations to the environment to increase opportunities for interaction with children who are developing typically.

5. *Evaluating the program.* Environmental assessment can be an important aspect of program evaluation. Teachers and caregivers as well as supervisors and directors may use the results of an environmental assessment to improve their program.

A number of different instruments can be used to gather information about the environment. The instrument you choose should allow you to transcribe your observations into a useful format. Tools for recording observation data include:

Scaled drawings

Checklists

Rating scales

USING SCALED DRAWINGS OF THE ENVIRONMENT

After completing a drawing of the layout of the room, the observer will be able to analyze the setting to determine whether the physical arrangement is supporting certain behaviors. Representing the environment through a scaled drawing provides an opportunity for close analysis of the setting. This technique is best used to gather information to answer questions such as:

Does the environmental design encourage (or discourage) certain behaviors?

Are certain activity centers used more frequently than others?

What are the child's interests?

Drawings should be as close to scale as possible. The following case study illustrates why.

CASE STUDY: MRS. HALL'S CLASSROOM

Mrs. Hall, one of the coteachers in the classroom for four-year-old children at Brice Harbor Elementary School, is concerned about the fighting that sometimes erupts during free play time. She began to gather information, first completing a scaled drawing of the classroom and then analyzing the picture with her coteacher. Figure 4.15 depicts the room arrangement. What problems would an assessor identify with respect to the arrangement of the different centers? Notice the proximity of the gross motor area to the block area. What problems might arise?

As a result of their observations, the team, which included the teachers and one assistant teacher, decided to move the block area away from the gross motor area. This simple measure helped to decrease the number of aggressive outbursts. The teaching team decided to continue their observations using event recording.

FIGURE 4.15 Mrs. Hall's classroom

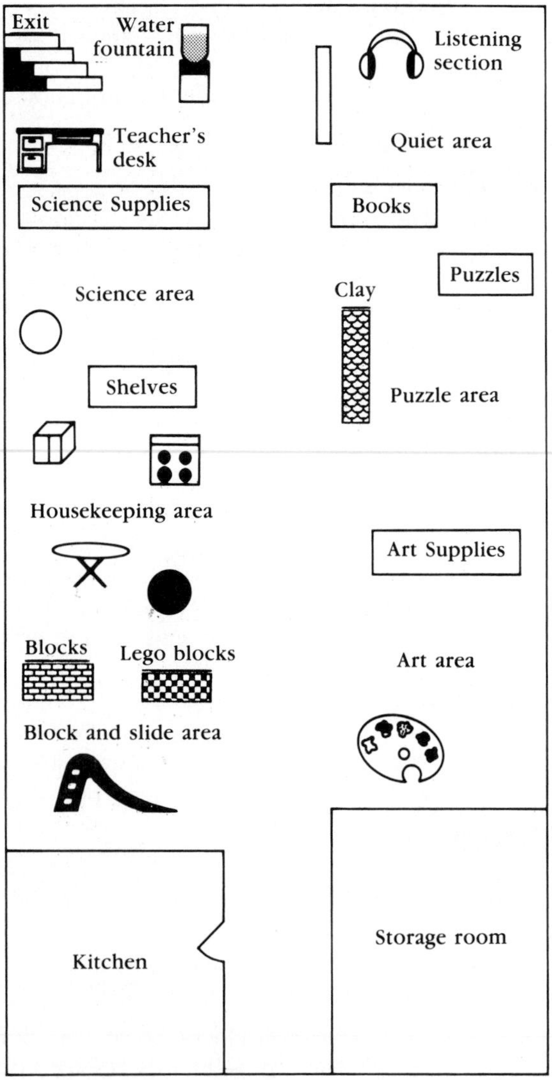

TRACING A CHILD'S PATH

Scaled drawings may be enhanced by tracing the child's travel route. This tracing provides a picture regarding a child's interests and travel pattern during a specific period of time. In the next case study, the kindergarten teacher is concerned about Rusty, a disruptive and overactive student. Is the classroom environment contributing to these difficulties?

CASE STUDY: MR. TAYLOR'S KINDERGARTEN

Mr. Taylor's classroom is a large room, which has been divided into several activity centers. Shelves and storage cabinets separate the centers from the large open space in the middle of the room.

Mr. Taylor feels that five-year-old Rusty is often disruptive to other children's play and notes that the boy cannot seem to "settle down" at any one center during free play. Mr. Taylor has asked the special educator to observe his classroom and make some suggestions. Figure 4.16 depicts Rusty's activity pattern during the 20-minute free play period. How could this information help Mr. Taylor? What centers seem to interest Rusty? Which areas might you examine more closely to determine Rusty's interaction with materials? What are some possible reasons that some centers were not visited?

FIGURE 4.16 Rusty's travel route

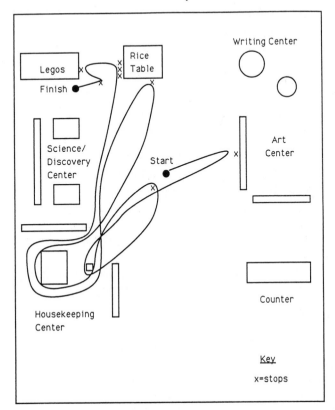

Upon inspecting Rusty's travel route, Mr. Taylor was surprised to find that Rusty spent a lot of time going in and out of the housekeeping center. The teacher decided to examine this space in more detail. The housekeeping center is a large area that may not encourage play ideas. In restructuring the center, Mr. Taylor planned to create smaller, more defined areas. The travel patterns indicated that Rusty entered the housekeeping center area several times, circled the area without stopping, and then left. The teacher planned to look more closely at the materials in this center. Are there enough choices? Does Rusty know how to use the materials? Mr. Taylor also decided to think about ways to more actively involve Rusty in the science and writing centers.

COMPLETING ENVIRONMENTAL CHECKLISTS

Checklists provide a more structured way of recording observations. A checklist may be organized in terms of specific categories that are important in the environment. For example, a category for furnishings might include several subitems. Or, if a checklist is organized according to the age of the children in the environment, the furnishings category might be divided into subcategories: one that has items related to infants and toddlers and another somewhat different set for preschoolers.

Checklists can be useful tools in program planning and program evaluation, particularly when the observer has questions of the following types:

What are the basic components needed to ensure a quality program?

Is this environment appropriate for the needs of the child?

How can I improve the environment?

COMPLETING ENVIRONMENTAL RATING SCALES

In using rating scales to assess environments for young children, a few prerequisites should be observed:

First: To be able to make accurate judgments, the observer must be familiar with early childhood programs in general.

Second: The observer must become familiar with all the test items and the criteria for judging and rating each one. As with any assessment instrument, the observer will need to practice giving a scale a few times to gain familiarity with the items.

Third: The accuracy of the ratings should be checked by comparing the scores with those of another observer.

Some rating scales allow the user not only to record observations but also to make determinations about degrees of quality of behaviors, interactions, and products. For example, an assessor who wants to rate the quality of interactions between adults and children may use an instrument which includes descriptive information about each of the numbers on a numeric scale, say from 1 to 5. Many rating scales, however, do not include enough information to allow the rater to make valid judgments about qualitative differences. Rating scales that use detailed descriptions of the differences between the numeric ratings of an item are the most useful because they maintain adequate reliability. Rating scales will help in answering questions such as:

What is the overall quality of this program?

Which areas of our program need attention first?

The rating scales commonly used to assess the environment are described in the following section. As discussed in Chapter 1, PL 101–476, the Individuals with Disabilities Education Act, requires that families be involved at all levels of assessment. Early childhood educators believe that it is very important to include family members in each step of the assessment process. Some families may choose to participate in assessing environments.

Home Observation for Measurement of the Environment (HOME)

The Home Observation for Measurement of the Environment (HOME) (Caldwell & Bradley, 1984) consists of a scale for infants and toddlers, one for preschoolers, and one for elementary age children. These scales gather information regarding the child's early developmental environment. In addition to making direct observations, the examiner interviews the parents. The categories of the three HOME scales are listed below.

The Three Scales of the HOME Inventory
The HOME Inventory for Families of Infants and Toddlers
1. Emotional and verbal responsivity of parent
2. Acceptance of child's behavior
3. Organization of physical and temporal environment
4. Provision of appropriate play materials
5. Parent involvement with child
6. Opportunities for variety in daily stimulation

The HOME Inventory for Families of Preschoolers
1. Learning stimulation
2. Language stimulation
3. Physical environment
4. Warmth and affection
5. Academic stimulation
6. Modeling
7. Variety in experience
8. Acceptance

The HOME Inventory for Families of Elementary Children
1. Emotional and verbal responsivity
2. Encouragement of maturity
3. Emotional climate
4. Growth-fostering materials and experiences
5. Provision for active stimulation
6. Family participation in developmentally stimulating experiences

7. Paternal involvement

8. Aspects of the physical environment

Long before the fields of early intervention and early childhood special education existed, the HOME was developed for work with families and children who do not have disabilities. Yet, some of the aspects of the HOME, with modifications, may be helpful to teachers and therapists today. In using this instrument, the examiner should keep in mind that families of children with disabilities are an integral part of the team, rather than just recipients of services. The use of an observation instrument to make judgments about the family's routine should be the result of a family's request for assistance in this area, and observations should focus on family-voiced priorities.

Early Childhood Environment Rating Scale

The Early Childhood Environment Rating Scale (ECERS), developed by Harms and Clifford (1980), was designed for use in a variety of settings, including Head Start programs, parent cooperative preschools, private preschools, play groups, and kindergarten programs. The scale examines the quality of the environment currently provided in a center or school and offers a background for planning improvements. The scale consists of 37 items, which are organized under the following categories:

Personal care routines of children

Furnishings and display for children

Language/reasoning experiences

Fine and gross motor activities

Creative activities

Social development

Adult needs

The subcategory for social development includes an item designed to rate provisions for children with special needs.

Administration.   This scale may be used by a trained observer. Each item is rated according to a 7-point Likert scale. A small amount of space after each item allows the observer to record additional information.

Scoring.   To aid the observer in assigning accurate ratings, each item includes descriptions of the possible numeric ratings. Information about the items is then tallied for a subtotal of each category. This instrument includes a profile sheet in which category subtotals are recorded. This profile allows the user to quickly identify areas, or subcategories, of strength and weakness, as seen in Figure 4.17.

Standardization.   This is not a norm-referenced instrument. The scale was field tested by the North Carolina Division of Social Services Day Care Consultants and County Day Care Coordinators. The final version was field tested in 25 classrooms in 17 child care centers in St. Louis.

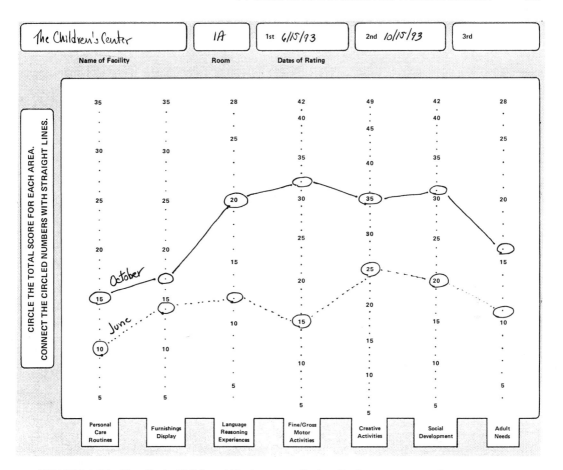

FIGURE 4.17 The Early Childhood Environment Rating Scale summary profile

SOURCE: From *Early Childhood Environment Rating Scale* by Thelma Harms and Richard M. Clifford. Reprinted by permission of the publisher. (New York: Teachers College Press, © 1980 by Thelma Harms and Richard M. Clifford. All rights reserved), p. 18(d).

Reliability.   The manual reports three measures of reliability: interrater reliability by item, interrater reliability by classroom, and internal consistency. Two evaluators participated in the interrater reliability by item study of the 25 classrooms, which yielded a correlation of .932; the correlations for interrater reliability by classroom were .790–.899 (Harms & Clifford, 1980). Internal consistency in some of the scales was weak.

Validity.   In validating this instrument, the authors asked seven "nationally recognized experts" to rate each item: 78% of the ratings given were of "high" importance; 1% were of "low" importance (Harms & Clifford, 1980, p. 38). The authors also compared the scale with the opinions of "trainers" and "expert observers" in being able to distinguish varying quality. This study yielded a correlation of .737.

Summary.   The ECERS may be used in a variety of programs serving young children from birth through age six. The information provided in describing each of the items is very helpful to the user in several steps of the assessment process including planning and evaluating the program. This scale is also very useful in understanding the quality of the environment. Given the philosophical differences among early childhood programs, the potential user should examine this scale in context to ensure that it will be valid for a given program.

Family Day Care Rating Scale

The Family Day Care Rating Scale (FDCRS) was developed by Harms and Clifford (1989). The format of the FDCRS is similar to that of the ECERS, although the content is different. The scale defines aspects of quality home-based child care for children from infancy through kindergarten. The 32 items organized under six categories are:

Space and furnishings
Basic care
Language and reasoning
Learning activities
Social development
Adult needs

A supplemental category, provisions for exceptional children, contains items that are rated when a child with special needs is enrolled in the facility. Figure 4.18 shows these items and the descriptions for rating.

Administration.   The scale may be used by a family child care provider as a self-assessment in program evaluation or by an observer who is assisting in program planning or monitoring. Each item is rated according to a 7-point Likert scale. A small amount of additional space after each item allows the user to record additional information. Figure 4.19 illustrates the recording sheet for the first category, which assesses space and furnishings for care and learning.

Scoring.   The manual includes descriptions of each item; assigning numerical ratings is similar to the ECERS. Information about the items is then tallied for a subtotal of each category, a total raw score, and an average item score. Unfortunately, this scale does not include a summary profile. The most useful information is gleaned by examining the ratings of individual items within each of the categories.

Standardization.   The FDCRS is not a norm-referenced instrument.

Reliability.   Interrater reliability studies have been conducted in a model program in Ann Arbor, Michigan, and in family child care homes in Los Angeles, California (Harms & Clifford, 1989). These studies have all reported high interrater reliability (at least .83). Internal consistency is also high (at least .83).

Validity.   There are limited studies concerning validity of this instrument. Content validity was found to correlate highly (.80) with home visitors' ratings of family child care settings.

FIGURE 4.18 Sample items from the Family Day Care Rating Scale

SOURCE: From *Family Day Care Rating Scale* by Thelma Harms and Richard M. Clifford. Reprinted by permission of the publisher. (New York: Teachers College Press, © 1989 by Thelma Harms and Richard M. Clifford. All rights reserved), pp. 36–39.

Items 33–40 are to be rated in addition to the preceding 32 items only when a child with special needs is included in the child care home. The terms *exceptional*, *special needs*, and *handicapped* are used interchangeably.

Since some handicapping conditions are not readily observable, it is necessary to know the nature of the child's handicap in order to correctly assign scores. While these items have been extensively field-tested and used in assessing programs that integrated children with special needs, they have not undergone the formal reliability testing given to the main body of the scale.

Supplementary Items: Provisions for Exceptional Children

Item	Inadequate 1	2	Minimal 3	4	Good 5	6	Excellent 7
33. Adaptations for basic care (physically handicapped)	• Adaptive equipment needed for basic care routines is lacking (eating, sleeping, toileting, grooming), or not clean and in good repair. • Child's special basic care needs not met consistently. • Caregiver does not perform special basic care procedures competently (Ex. child positioned inappropriately for feeding).		• Special adaptive equipment for basic care routines is clean and in good repair. • Caregiver consistently and competently follows special basic care routines (Ex. catheterization, turning bedridden child).		• Care provider does not allow child's need for adaptive equipment and special procedures to isolate him from the group during routines (Ex. child eats at table with or very near other children). • Care provider is gentle and respectful in the performance of the special basic care and health routines (Ex. respects child's need for privacy, handles special equipment with care).		• Caregiver plans and provides learning activities to develop higher levels of child's self-help skills. (Ex. gradually introduces more advanced forms of solid food to child with chewing problems, encourages child to do as much as he can by himself). • Caregiver responds sensitively to child's special basic care needs (Ex. anticipates when nonambulatory child feels tired of sitting and changes his position).
34. Adaptations for activities (physically handicapped)	• Barriers limit child's use of space and materials and caregiver doesn't compensate (Ex. toys out of reach, steps prevent easy movement). • Needed adaptive equipment not present or used,		• Barriers may be present but caregiver helps child gain access to activities when needed (Ex. moves nonwalker to area where other children are playing). • Some adaptive equipment		• Needed adaptive equipment available for self-help, learning, and play activities, both indoors and out. • Environment permits child free use of space and materials (Ex. toys put within		• Caregiver encourages independent use of adaptive equipment. • Care provider plans activities for child to learn to use adaptive equipment, where needed. • Caregiver helps other children

(continued)

FIGURE 4.18 (continued)

Item	Inadequate 1	2	Minimal 3	4	Good 5	6	Excellent 7
	thus preventing child from joining learning and social activities.		present, clean, safe, and in good repair. • Adequate space for adaptive equipment.		child's reach, barriers to movement indoors managed effectively).		dren accept adaptive equipment (Ex. by telling what it is for, answering questions, quieting fears, letting children try out equipment and help handicapped child).
35. Adaptations for other special needs	• No adjustments made in space, furnishings, and/or schedule to meet special emotional, behavioral, or mental needs of child.		• Some adjustments in space, furnishings, and/or schedule made to prevent the problems that could be caused by the special emotional, behavioral, or mental needs of child (Ex. removes breakable object, watches child carefully, simplifies cluttered area).		• Many adjustments of space, furnishings, and/or schedule made to meet the needs of child (Ex. quiet work and play areas with appropriate toys for child who is easily distracted, time provided for one-to-one work on special needs skill development).		• Caregiver encourages child to use space, furnishings, and time constructively and independently. • Caregiver changes space, schedule, and/or furnishings as child's needs change.
36. Communication (exceptional)	• Caregiver communicates less with special-needs child than with other children. • Caregiver does not adjust speech to child's level of understanding; speaks in same fashion to all children. • Caregiver does not provide communication options required by child's handicap (Ex. does not face hard-of-hearing child, does not provide alternatives to speech such as		• Care provider communicates equally with special-needs child and other children. • Caregiver attempts to adjust speech to child's level of understanding, but may use sentences that are too long or talk baby talk to child who can understand more. • Communication options exist, where needed, but are not routinely used throughout the day (Ex. communication board		• Caregiver communicates frequently with the special-needs child. • Caregiver actively encourages child to communicate with caregiver. • Caregiver encourages children to communicate with each other. • Caregiver appropriately adjusts speech to child's level of understanding. • When needed, use of communication options encouraged all day.		• Care provider praises or reinforces child's attempts to communicate. • Caregiver extends language interaction with special-needs children. • Caregiver plans activities to teach more advanced use of communication options as needed (Ex. teaches other children to sign, adds new communication board symbols or signs).

	Inadequate	Minimal	Good	Excellent
37. Language/reasoning (exceptional)	manual signing or communication boards where needed). • No attempt to adapt language/reasoning materials or provide special materials to meet the needs of exceptional child (Ex. no large-print books, textured books, or high-contrast pictures).	used only during language lessons, hearing aid only used occasionally). • Caregiver adapts regular materials for use by exceptional child.	• Language and reasoning goals for special-needs child are specified and worked on. • When needed, caregiver provides specialized language/reasoning materials for exceptional child.	• Caregiver uses routines and activities throughout the day to reach specified language/reasoning goals for the child. • Specialized materials used as part of planned activities to reach specified language/reasoning goals.
38. Learning and play activities (exceptional)	• Special-needs child excluded from play and learning activities available to other children (Ex. child in wheelchair not allowed to participate in messy activities, hearing-impaired child excluded from music, mentally handicapped child not given appropriate activities).	• Special-needs child present during activities but not actively involved (Ex. child in wheelchair present as observer near dramatic play but not helped to participate). • Some substitute activities available for exceptional child (Ex. child allowed to use free-play toys while others are involved in learning activities).	• Developmentally appropriate activities provided for exceptional child. • Activities adapted to help special-needs child participate (Ex. reduces size of group for aggressive child, uses table for activity usually done on floor). • Care provider participates in activities with the exceptional child to provide model. • Caregiver provides additional directions and makes limits explicit as required to motivate and make special-needs child successful. • Care provider praises and reinforces child for play and learning using newly developed skills.	• Caregiver helps child develop skills needed to participate in a variety of regularly available learning activities. • Specialized learning activities provided to help child reach specific developmental goals (Ex. activities used to teach self-help skills like buttoning, feeding self).

(continued)

FIGURE 4.18 (continued)

Item	Inadequate 1	2	Minimal 3	4	Good 5	6	Excellent 7
39. Social development (exceptional)	• Few opportunities provided for social interaction involving all children, including handicapped and nonhandicapped children.		• Schedule provides ample opportunities for social interaction involving all children, handicapped and nonhandicapped. • Caregiver shows acceptance of handicapped child (Ex. hugs child to show affection, makes eye contact when child speaks).		• Caregiver praises and reinforces child for learning social skills related to special needs. • Caregiver encourages and reinforces social interaction involving all children, including handicapped and nonhandicapped children, throughout the day. • Caregiver models appropriate social behavior and encourages children to imitate. • Handicapped child accepted as part of group by other children.		• Care provider identifies new social skills needed by the handicapped child and others, and provides learning activities to teach those skills (Ex. teaches handicapped child to respond when approached by others, encourages handicapped child to invite others to join him in play). • Some books, pictures, dolls showing handicapped persons available, if appropriate.
40. Caregiver preparation	• Caregiver does not seek additional information and skills required for care of handicapped child. • No specialists are involved in assessing the handicapped child's special needs or in planning an appropriate program of child care. • Caregiver and parents do not share information about child's special needs.		• Caregiver requests basic information from assessments by specialists. • Caregiver and parents share information about child's special needs (Ex. parents give caregiver information from professional assessments).		• Caregiver uses information from assessments and advice of specialists to plan an appropriate program for child throughout the day. • Caregiver works closely with parents to incorporate their goals and interests in daily activities.		• Caregiver participates in specialized training on working with handicapped children (Ex. takes one workshop a year on needs of special children, works closely with a professional consultant, joins special education training or support group). • Caregiver is sensitive to the special needs of parents of handicapped children (Ex. shares information with parents about parent groups, works appropriately with parents who have difficulty in recognizing child's special needs).

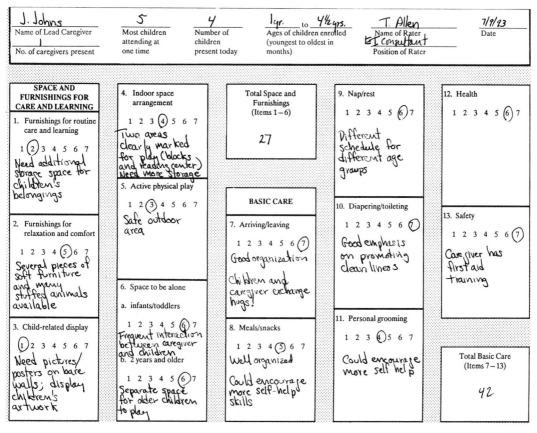

FIGURE 4.19 Family Day Care Rating Scale rating sheet

SOURCE: From *Family Day Care Rating Scale* by Thelma Harms and Richard M. Clifford. Reprinted by permission of the publisher. (New York: Teachers College Press, © 1989 by Thelma Harms and Richard M. Clifford. All rights reserved), p. 40.

Summary. This scale may be used in evaluating a family child care program. Interrater reliability is adequate, and content validity, although based on a limited number of studies, appears to be adequate. Similar to the ECERS, the descriptive information provided on each of the items is useful in understanding aspects of quality home-based child care.

Infant/Toddler Environment Rating Scale (ITERS)

The Infant/Toddler Environment Rating Scale (ITERS) of Harms, Cryer, and Clifford (1990) is similar in format to the ECERS and the FDCRS described above. This third scale defines aspects of quality center-based child care for children from birth through thirty months. Thirty-five items are organized under the following categories:

Furnishings and display for children

Personal care routines

Listening and talking

Learning activities

Interaction

Program structure

Adult needs

A subcategory entitled program structure includes an item related to provisions for children with special needs.

Administration.   This scale may be used by a trained observer. Each item is rated according to a 7-point Likert scale. A small amount of space after each item allows the observer to record additional information. Figure 4.20 shows a completed recording sheet of the first category, which assesses furnishings and display for children.

FIGURE 4.20   The Infant/Toddler Environment Rating Scale recording sheet

SOURCE: From *Infant/Toddler Environment Rating Scale* by Thelma Harms, Deborah Reid Cryer, and Richard M. Clifford. Reprinted by permission of the publisher. (New York: Teachers College Press, © 1990 by Thelma Harms, Deborah Reid Cryer, and Richard M. Clifford. All rights reserved).

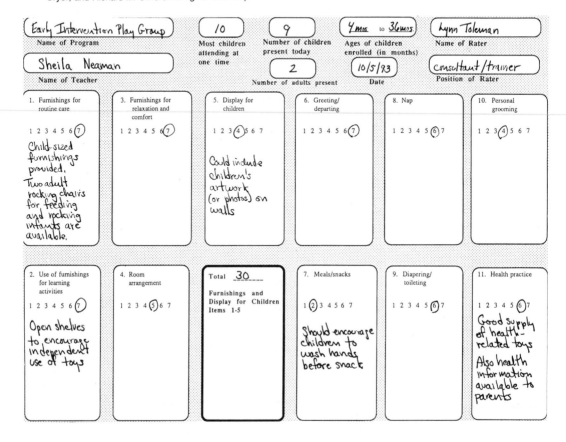

Scoring. Each item includes descriptions of various numerical points on the scale. Information about the items is then tallied for a subtotal for each category. The authors suggest that a total raw score and an average item score be computed. However, there are no guidelines for interpreting either of these scores. Moreover, the scale does not include a summary profile in which the subtotals of each category could be arrayed, to provide the user with an overall visual picture of the areas of strength and weakness in the environment.

Standardization. The ITERS is not a norm-referenced instrument.

Reliability. The manual reports three measures of reliability: interrater reliability, test–retest reliability, and internal consistency. Interrater and test–retest reliability studies were conducted at 30 child care centers located in central North Carolina representing "a wide variety of quality of environments" (Harms et al., 1990, p. 2). Two observers participated in the interrater reliability study, which yielded an overall correlation of .84. Eighteen of the centers were revisited by one of these observers to conduct the test–retest reliability study, which yielded an overall correlation of .79. Internal consistency on the overall scale was .83.

Validity. The manual reports three separate validity studies: one measure of criterion validity and two measures of content validity. Criterion validity was assessed by taking high and low scores from the ITERS and comparing them with expert evaluations for twelve programs. There was an overall agreement rate of 83%. Content validity was assessed in two studies. The first study examined the items contained in the ITERS with "seven other widely used instruments for assessing the quality of infant/toddler programs" (Harms et al., 1990, p. 2). An average of 82% of the ITERS items was also included in the other instruments. In the second study of content validity, "five nationally recognized experts rated the importance of each ITERS item . . . using a 1 (low) to 5 (high) scale" (Harms et al., 1990, p. 2). The scores on 86% of the items were rated as high (4 or 5).

Summary. This instrument provides the observer with descriptions of 35 items on which to rate center-based child care. These descriptions increase the accuracy of an observer's ratings, thus contributing to the reliability of the instrument. The descriptions are very helpful in using the scale for at least two steps in the assessment process: planning and evaluating the program. The ITERS is also very useful in understanding aspects of quality center-based child care environments. Information about the quality of each of the 35 items is perhaps the most valuable aspect of this instrument.

The Preschool Assessment of the Classroom Environment (PACE)

The Preschool Assessment of the Classroom Environment (PACE), developed by McWilliam and Dunst (1985), was designed for use in classrooms of children *functioning* from birth to six years of age. Thus the scale can be used for environments serving children chronologically older than six. The instrument assesses four areas of the classroom environment and gathers information that can be used to recommend changes "to improve provision of educational experiences to preschool-aged children" (Dunst, McWilliam, & Holbert, 1986, p. 213). There are four main areas:

Program organization
Environmental organization
Methods of instruction
Program outcomes

Each category includes several subcategories with five items each. For example, program organization is divided into management, integration of children with and without disabilities, and parent involvement. The subcategory of integration consists of five items on which to rate the program:

1. Activities are appropriate for an integrated population.
2. Children with disabilities participate in group activities with children who are developing typically.
3. Children with and without disabilities are encouraged to interact.
4. Equipment and furnishings are appropriate for children with disabilities.
5. Equipment and furnishings are appropriate for older children.

The total scale consists of 70 individual items.

Administration.   Administration of the PACE involves a classroom observation of 2 to 4 hours; an interview with the person responsible for the overall management of the classroom, covering program philosophy, policies, and procedures; and a review of written materials such as IFSPs or IEPs.

Scores.   The PACE consists of a 5-point Likert rating scale. The observer rates each item in terms of the extent to which it describes the program. Some of the items reference information that cannot be gathered through observation and are scored after the interview or after the review of written materials.

Standardization.   Twenty preschool programs from rural, western North Carolina constituted the sample. There were four programs each, representing different early childhood educational settings including private preschools, Head Start programs, parent cooperative preschools, developmental day centers, and parent–child play groups. Additional information concerning details of the programs would have been helpful.

Reliability.   Interrater reliability for five examiners was reported as 82 median percent.

Validity.   Construct validity was reported as adequate.

Summary.   The PACE scale was developed as a tool to assess preschool programs serving children who are developing typically as well as children with disabilities. The items included in this scale are good indicators of an effective program. However, the scale lacks a set of descriptions to help the rater in assigning a numerical score to each item. Absence of criteria on which to base a judgment may increase bias and is a major weakness of the scale. Users will need to ensure that their ratings are accurate by checking interobserver reliability. The scale does not include a profile or other means of synthesizing data. Thus, one needs to analyze the rating of each item to gain helpful information.

The Instructional Environment Scale (TIES)

The Instructional Environment Scale (TIES) was developed in 1987 by Ysseldyke and Christenson for use with school-age children. The purposes of this scale include "(a) to systematically *describe* the extent to which a student's academic or behavior problems are a function of factors in the instructional environment and (b) to identify starting points in *designing appropriate instructional interventions* for individual students" (Ysseldyke & Christenson, 1987, p. 3). Thus, this instrument may be used after the classroom teacher has made an initial referral. Information from the TIES can be used to assist in prereferral intervention, whereby the student is helped indirectly by modifying the learning environment. This scale also can be used for purposes of planning the program and monitoring individual progress.

The scale consists of 12 components that encompass not only the physical environment but the learning and teaching environment as well:

Instructional presentation

Classroom environment

Teacher expectations

Cognitive emphasis

Motivational strategies

Relevant practice

Academic engaged time

Informed feedback

Adaptive instruction

Progress evaluation

Instructional planning

Student understanding

Administration.   TIES uses information from a structured classroom observation of both teacher and students, student interviews, and classroom teacher interviews. Guidelines for the structured observation are included in the manual.

After observing the teacher and the student, the examiner interviews the student regarding the child's understanding of the learning activity and strategies the child employs during the teaching process.

The examiner also interviews the teacher regarding the activity observed as well as on general planning for student instruction.

Scores.   The 12 components are scored on a 4-point Likert scale according to the degree that each component is similar to that of the instruction of the student. This scale is then used to make decisions regarding intervention recommendations.

Suggestions for improving instructional environments that have received low scores are provided in the manual.

Standardization.   TIES is a rating scale that gathers qualitative information. There were no norms developed for this instrument.

Reliability.   The manual includes good descriptions of the 12 components. The examiner must clearly understand each of the constructs to be observed, however, to know what to look for as well as how to rate the degree of the component.

The test developers report only one type of reliability: interrater reliability scores. Interrater reliability was calculated on each of the 12 components. All components exceeded .80; all but two exceeded .90.

The manual states that the examiner must integrate information from three different sources in assigning a score of 1 to 4 to each component. Because this assignment process involves synthesizing and judging observations and interviews, there is much possibility for error. Examiner bias, or *intra*rater reliability, may also be a source of error. The test developers do not address this potential problem.

A confusing note appears in the last section of the booklet when the authors state that the examiner may use all or *parts* of the instrument, because it can be "adapted or abridged to fit the needs of the user" (Ysseldyke & Christenson, 1987, p. 38). Decreasing the sources of information will influence the type and amount of data, potentially affecting the scores you assign to the rating scale, thus affecting reliability.

Validity.   The test developers report only content validity. The authors discuss each of the 12 components and include adequate numbers of references to support each component as an important factor in effective instruction.

Summary.   The TIES measures 12 different aspects of the student's learning environment. All these aspects are fully defined, with many descriptors included for each one. Data are gathered through structured observations and interviews with the teacher and student. Because the examiner must synthesize these sources of information in assigning a numerical rating to the environment, the examiner must be very familiar with the constructs being rated. The examiner must take great care not to allow bias to interfere until all the information has been collected.

Working with classroom teachers regarding their instructional environment requires particular sensitivity to collaborative teamwork. The examiner must be not only a skilled observer of information but a skilled conveyer of information as well. In discussing the scores obtained, the assessor will need to be proficient in consulting skills. Care must be taken to focus on the child's needs rather than on weaknesses in the teacher's skills.

The information on the 12 components of the physical environment may be very helpful as stand-alone information for the beginning as well as the experienced teacher. The authors do not state the grades for which this scale is designed. Some of the constructs are less relevant (or inappropriate) for young children, such as lesson development as part of component 1, instructional presentation. Before using this instrument, team members will need to carefully examine all the constructs to determine content validity for use in an environment for a young child.

PREFERRED PRACTICES

Each of the techniques discussed in this chapter can provide very useful information. Observations, when carefully and systematically conducted, are powerful tools. When conducting observations it is important to remember that reliability and validity are important concerns and that it is important to follow the guidelines provided in this chapter.

Herbert and Attridge (1975) made the following recommendations for developers and users of observation instruments:

1. The title of the instrument should accurately describe the purpose of the instrument.
2. A statement of purpose should be included.
3. There should be a rationale or theoretical support.
4. The behaviors to be observed should be clearly described.
5. The uses of the instrument should be delineated.
6. Instances in which the instrument should not be used should be described.
7. All terms, especially those that relate to behaviors, should be clearly defined.
8. If an observation instrument is derived from theory, the use of the terms should be consistent.
9. The observation items should be comprehensive.
10. The items should be representative of the behaviors observed.
11. The items should be mutually exclusive. That is, items should not overlap.
12. Procedures for the use of the instrument should be described.
13. The degree of inference permitted the observer should be low. Although some degree of judgment is usually required, this should be minimized.
14. When the observer is required to make inferences, the circumstance should be described.
15. Guidelines for making inferences should be explicated.
16. The setting, or context, for the observations should be clearly described.
17. Procedures for use of the instrument in various settings must be described.
18. The effects of the observer and other personnel on the setting should be explicated.
19. The types of reliability should be described.
20. The procedures used to determine validity and the results should be delineated.

STUDY QUESTIONS AND SUGGESTED ACTIVITIES

1. What are the purposes of conducting observations?
2. Discuss the advantages and disadvantages of using the following techniques:
   Anecdotal record
   Running record
   Specimen record or specimen description

Interval recording
Duration recording
Event recording
Latency recording
Category recording
Product evaluation
Rating scale
Checklist

3. How can you assure that the observations you make are reliable and valid?

4. Describe several different ways of computing interobserver reliability.

5. What guidelines should be used when conducting observations?

6. You have been asked to assist your community child care center in making recommendations for redesigning the toddler room. What might you use to assist you in your observation of the current environment? What are some important components of an environment for toddlers?

7. Mr. Xi, the new kindergarten teacher, is concerned that six-year-old Sarah seems to interact only with the classroom aide. He feels that she spends little time with the other children. Mr. Xi would like to help Sarah learn how to play with others. However, first he must collect some information about Sarah's interactions with others. What procedure could he use to record his observations? Develop a form he could use.

8. Make arrangements to observe an early childhood environment. What guidelines should be used when conducting observations? How will you record the information you gather?

REFERENCES

Achenbach, T. M. (1988). *Child behavior checklist/2–3.* Burlington, VT: Center for Children, Youth, & Families.

Achenbach, T. M. (1991a). *Child behavior checklist/4–18.* Burlington, VT: Center for Children, Youth, & Families.

Achenbach, T. M. (1991b). *Teacher's report form.* Burlington, VT: Center for Children, Youth, & Families.

Alessi, G. J. (1980). Behavioral observation for the school psychologist: Responsive-discrepancy model. *School Psychology Review, 9,* 31–45.

Alessi, G. J., & Kaye, J. H. (1983). *Behavior assessment for school psychologists.* Kent, OH: National Association of School Psychologists.

Bailey, D. B., & Wolery, M. (1989). *Assessing infants and preschoolers with handicaps.* Columbus, OH: Merrill.

Bayley, N. (1969). *Bayley scales of infant development.* San Antonio, TX: Psychological Corporation.

Beaty, J. (1986). *Observing the development of the young child.* New York: Macmillan.

Behar, L., & Stringfield, S. (1974). A behavior rating scale for the preschool child. *Developmental Psychology, 10,* 601–610.

Benner, S. M. (1992). *Assessing young children with special needs.* New York: Longman.

Brown, L., & Hammill, D. (1990). *Behavior rating profile—2.* Austin, TX: Pro-Ed.

Caldwell, B. M., & Bradley, R. H. (1984). *Home observation for measurement of the environment.* Little Rock, AK: University of Arkansas.

Conners, C. K. (1985). *The Conners rating scales: Instruments for the assessment of childhood psychopathology.* Unpublished manuscript, Washington, DC: Children's Hospital National Medical Center.

DeVellis, R. F. (1991). *Scale development.* Newbury Park, CA: Sage.

Dunst, C. J., McWilliam, R. A., & Holbert, K. (1986). Assessment of preschool classroom environments. *Diagnostique, 3–4*(11), 212–232.

Fewell, R. (1983). Assessing handicapped infants. In S. G. Garwood & R. R. Fewell (Eds.), *Educating handicapped infants* (pp. 257–297). Rockville, MD: Aspen.

Fewell, R., Langley, M., & Roll, A. (1982). Informant versus direct screening: A preliminary comparative study. *Diagnostique, 7,* 163–167.

Frick, T., & Semmel, M. I. (1978). Observer agreement and reliabilities of classroom observational measures. *Review of Educational Research, 48,* 157–184.

Garwood, S. G., & Fewell, R. R. (Eds.). (1983). *Educating handicapped infants.* Rockville, MD: Aspen.

Gesten, E. L. (1976). A Health Resources Inventory: The development of a measure of the personal and social competence of primary-grade children. *Journal of Consulting and Clinical Psychology, 44,* 775–786.

Gresham, F. M., & Elliott, S. N. (1990). *Social skills rating system.* Circle Pines, MN: American Guidance Service.

Gronlund, N. E., & Linn, R. L. (1990). *Measurement and evaluation in teaching.* New York: Macmillan.

Harms, T., & Clifford, R. M. (1980). *Early Childhood Environment Rating Scale.* New York: Teachers College Press.

Harms, T., & Clifford, R. M. (1989). *Family day care rating scale.* New York: Teachers College Press.

Harms, T., Cryer, D., & Clifford, R. M. (1990). *Infant/Toddler environment rating scale.* New York: Teachers College Press.

Herbert, J., & Attridge, C. (1975). A guide for developers and users of observation systems and manuals. *American Educational Research Journal, 12,* 1–20.

Hightower, A. D., Spinell, A., & Lotyczewski, B. S. (1990). *AML behavior rating scale—Revised (AML-R) guidelines.* Rochester, NY: University of Rochester (Primary Mental Health Project, Inc.).

Hoge, R. D. (1985). The validity of direct observation. *Review of Educational Research, 55,* 469–483.

Hresko, W. P., & Brown, L. (1984). *Test of early socioemotional development.* Austin, TX: Pro-Ed.

Kohn, M. (1986a). *Kohn problem checklist.* San Antonio, TX: Psychological Corporation.

Kohn, M. (1986b). *Kohn social competence scale.* San Antonio, TX: Psychological Corporation.

Lahey, B. B., Stempniak, M., Robinson, E. J., & Tyroler, M. J. (1978). Hyperactivity and learning disabilities as independent dimensions of child behavior problems. *Journal of Abnormal Psychology, 87,* 333–340.

Lorion, R. P., Cowen, E. L., & Caldwell, R. (1975). Normative and parametric analyses of school maladjustment. *American Journal of Community Psychology, 3,* 291–301.

Martin, S. S., Brady, M. P., & Williams, R. E. (1991). Effects of toys on the social behavior of preschool children in integrated and nonintegrated groups: Investigation of a setting event. *Journal of Early Intervention. 15*(2), 153–161.

McCarney, S. B., & Leigh, J. E. (1990). *Behavior evaluation scale—2.* Austin, TX: Pro-Ed.

McWilliam, R. A., & Dunst, C. J. (1985). *Preschool assessment of the classroom environment.* Morganton, NC: Family, Infant and Preschool Program.

Nordquist, V. M., Twardosz, S., & McEvoy, M. A. (1991). Effects of environmental reorganization in classrooms for children with autism. *Journal of Early Intervention, 15*(2), 135–152.

Quay, H. C., & Peterson, D. R. (1983). *Revised behavior problem checklist.* Coral Gables, FL: Author (University of Miami).

Quay, H. C., & Peterson, D. R. (1987). *Manual for the revised behavior problem checklist.* Coral Gables, FL: Author (University of Miami).

Repp, A. C., Nieminen, G. S., Olinger, E., & Brusca, R. (1988). Direct observation: Factors affecting the accuracy of observers. *Exceptional Children, 55,* 29–36.

Reynolds, C. R., & Kamphaus, R. (1992). *Behavior assessment system for children.* Circle Pines, MN: American Guidance Service.

Sattler, J. (1988). *Assessment of children.* San Diego, CA: Jerome M. Sattler, Publisher.

Seidman, R., Linney, J. A., Rappaport, J., Herzberger, S., Kramer, J., & Alden, L. (1979). Assessment of classroom behavior: A multiattribute, multisource approach to instrument development and validation. *Journal of Educational Psychology, 71,* 451–464.

Smith, R. M., Neisworth, J. T., & Greer, J. B. (1978). *Evaluating educational environments.* Columbus, OH: Merrill.

Spivack, G., & Spotts, J. (1966). *Devereux child behavior rating scale manual.* Devon, PA: Devereux Foundation.

Spivack, G., & Swift, M. (1967). *Devereux elementary school behavior rating scale manual.* Devon, PA: Devereux Foundation.

Walker, H. M., & McConnell, S. R. (1988). *Walker–McConnell scale of social competence and school adjustment.* Austin, TX: Pro-Ed.

Ysseldyke, J. E., & Christenson, S. L. (1987). *The instructional environment scale.* Austin, TX: Pro-Ed.

CHAPTER 5

Using Screening Instruments

CHAPTER OBJECTIVES

Children born in hospitals in this country receive one or more screening tests soon after birth. Medical screenings are successful in identifying babies who need immediate special care. Older infants and young children may attend a community screening clinic. These screenings are designed to locate children who should be evaluated further to determine eligibility for early intervention or special education services. Screening *does not identify children for services* but rather *finds children who need to be further evaluated;* based on these assessments, some children may be identified for services. Often before a child participates in the screening process, the family must be alerted to the benefits of early intervention and the purpose for screening. These awareness activities are known as Child Find.

After completing this chapter, you should be able to:

Discuss the Child Find system.

Identify and discuss the major factors in evaluating and using screening instruments.

Describe medical reasons for screening newborns.

Describe several screening instruments.

CHILD FIND

Through Child Find activities, parents and caregivers become aware of screening activities, the first step in the process of identifying young children who may be eligible for special services. Professionals involved with Child Find spend hours attempting to *locate* children with whom they will eventually work. Once children reach school age, there are daily opportunities for teachers to observe performance and "find" children, whom they will refer for further assessment. Infants, toddlers, and preschoolers, however, may not come in contact with professionals on a routine basis.

Early childhood special educators and early intervention specialists are not the only professionals involved with Child Find. Peterson (1987) stated:

> Canvassing neighborhoods to locate preschoolers and infants who should be referred for screening is a major task. It requires the cooperation of individuals who are in continuous contact with young children and can act as casefinders and referral agents (e.g., parents, caregivers, relatives, or professionals in service roles such as public health nurses, social workers, physicians, or clergy). (p. 286)

In addition, practitioners who already have established a relationship with the family may continue to be of assistance during screening and the other steps of the assessment process, if appropriate.

The process of locating children, also known as *case finding*, involves a variety of activities at both local and state levels. Child Find activities may begin by educating families and caregivers about the questions they should ask about the child. Examples might include: Do I have any concerns about the overall development of Jessica? Am I concerned that she is not talking or walking as I think she should? Would I like suggestions in how to manage certain behavior difficulties?

Child Find activities include providing to families and other caregivers such information as pamphlets giving the ages at which children typically crawl, walk, or begin to say two-word phrases. Child Find activities also entail the promotion of early intervention. Peterson (1987) identified a number of case finding activities that may be carried out by local communities. Parent, religious, or civic groups may sponsor speakers to discuss the importance of early identification and intervention. Local newspapers may feature articles about screening clinics and early intervention programs. Brochures and newsletters may be distributed to physicians' offices. In rural communities, informal networks and "word of mouth" are important resources in case finding. In urban areas, certain community agencies may take the lead in case finding activities.

At the state level, personnel from the lead state agency responsible for implementing PL 101–476 and the amendments are involved in Child Find activities. Projects may include developing and distributing information packets about screening and early intervention services to various other state agencies. Brochures may be developed for families as well. The brochure shown in Figure 5.1 was developed by a state interagency coordinating council to help families become more aware of available services.

The lead agency at the state level also works to coordinate activities and share information among professionals from other disciplines involved with case finding such as mental health workers, public health nurses, and social service caseworkers. This agency may be the Department of Education, or it may be located in a different department such as health or human services or welfare. Practitioners should be familiar with the lead agency in their state.

Key Terms

False Positive. Designates a child who has been referred by the screening but does not need special services.

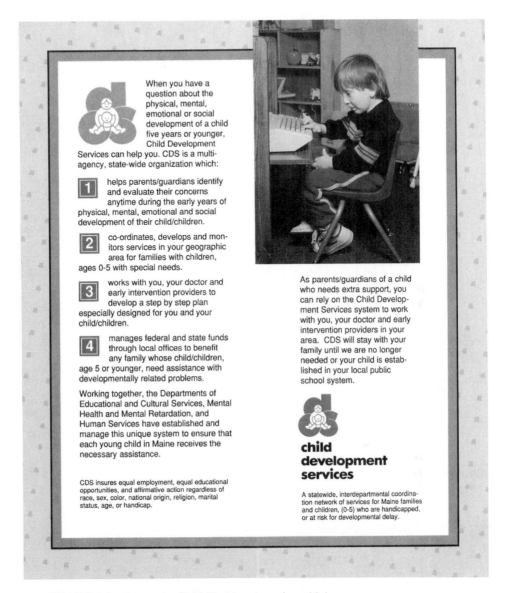

When you have a question about the physical, mental, emotional or social development of a child five years or younger, Child Development Services can help you. CDS is a multi-agency, state-wide organization which:

1 helps parents/guardians identify and evaluate their concerns anytime during the early years of physical, mental, emotional and social development of their child/children.

2 co-ordinates, develops and monitors services in your geographic area for families with children, ages 0-5 with special needs.

3 works with you, your doctor and early intervention providers to develop a step by step plan especially designed for you and your child/children.

4 manages federal and state funds through local offices to benefit any family whose child/children, age 5 or younger, need assistance with developmentally related problems.

Working together, the Departments of Educational and Cultural Services, Mental Health and Mental Retardation, and Human Services have established and manage this unique system to ensure that each young child in Maine receives the necessary assistance.

CDS insures equal employment, equal educational opportunities, and affirmative action regardless of race, sex, color, national origin, religion, marital status, age, or handicap.

As parents/guardians of a child who needs extra support, you can rely on the Child Development Services system to work with you, your doctor and early intervention providers in your area. CDS will stay with your family until we are no longer needed or your child is established in your local public school system.

child development services

A statewide, interdepartmental coordination network of services for Maine families and children, (0-5) who are handicapped, or at risk for developmental delay.

FIGURE 5.1   A sample Child Find brochure from Maine

SOURCE: Child Development Services, Maine State Department of Education, Division of Special Education, State House Station #23, Augusta, ME 04330.

False Negative. Designates a child who needs special services but was *not* referred by the screening.

Sensitivity. Refers to a screening instrument's ability to identify children who should be identified.

Specificity. Refers to the capacity of a screening procedure to accurately select out children who should not be identified.

CHOOSING APPROPRIATE SCREENING INSTRUMENTS

Certain criteria are important for judging the usefulness of screening instruments. According to Meisels and Wasik (1990), developmental screening tests "should be brief, norm-referenced, inexpensive, standardized in administration, objectively scored, broadly focused across all areas of development, reliable, and valid" (p. 613). These authors include two additional criteria for screening tests. The tests should be sensitive and specific. These criteria are discussed in the sections that follow.

Brevity

Screening tests are generally given to large numbers of children to determine whether further assessment is necessary. For this reason, screening tests should be brief. Additional time and money can be devoted to conducting comprehensive assessments on children who are identified by the screening.

Norm Referenced

Norm-referenced tests compare a child's performance with the performance of other children who have taken the same test. In addition, the norm or standardization sample provides a basis on which to determine the reliability and validity of the test scores. It is very important that a test used for screening be a norm-referenced instrument. For example, if a child is identified as needing further evaluation on the Developmental Indicators for the Assessment of Learning—Revised (DIAL-R), the norm sample of the DIAL-R should include children who are similar in background and characteristics to the target child and have also been identified as needing further evaluation.

Inexpensive

Screening tests should be inexpensive to use. This also means that they should be *efficient* and relatively *easy* to use. Because of the amount of time that must be devoted to screening large numbers of children, the screening materials must be low in cost and inexpensive to administer. It must be possible for many different professionals and paraprofessionals to administer the tests quickly, and with a minimum of training and supervision.

Standardized Administration

To assure that the administration of the screening test is standardized and that the outcomes will be consistent no matter who administers the test, the directions, items, and scoring must be the same for all children.

Objective Scoring

Many different professionals and paraprofessionals administer and score screening tests. As in the case of the standardized administration of screening tests, the scoring of screening instruments must be objective. This means that the directions, calculation of scores, and determination of outcomes must be clearly explained and must be the same for all children who are screened. The outcomes of screening should not be subject to the judgment and biases of the many individual test examiners.

Broad Focus

Screening tests merely indicate whether further assessment should be conducted. Because of this, they should be broadly focused. To ensure that a broad picture and general information are obtained, screening tests should include items from many different developmental areas. Too narrow a focus could mean that important aspects about some children will be missed.

Reliability

Reliability has to do with the consistency or stability of test performance. Because some children are screened only once, the test examiner should be able to have confidence that each child would obtain similar scores if tested the next day or the next week. However, no test has perfect reliability. The reliability of screening tests should be carefully examined, and appropriate safeguards instituted, to assure that children who should be identified will be identified and those who should not be identified will not be identified. Several types of reliability should be considered, including internal consistency, split-half, test–retest, alternate form, and interrater or interscorer reliability; these are discussed in detail in Chapter 2.

Validity

Validity is a concept that covers whether a test measures what it claims to measure and whether it meets the purposes for which it was developed. Thus, the crucial questions are:

Do screening tests actually screen children in specific areas?

Do screening tests identify children who need further evaluation and/or intervention?

Because these questions are so important, screening tests must be carefully examined for validity.

There are several types of validity, and these are discussed in detail in Chapter 2. The *content* validity of a screening test refers to the extent that the content, consisting of the test items, measures specific areas. For developmental screening tests, the content is the sequence of development of infants and young children. For academic screening tests, the content is academic skills. The *concurrent* validity of a screening test has to do with the extent to which the results of one screening test coincide with the results of another instrument. For example, Meisels (1988) correlated the test scores of children on the Early Screening Inventory (ESI) with the test scores obtained by the same children on the McCarthy Scales of Children's Abilities (MSCA). Meisels concluded that the ESI and the MSCA generally measured the same abilities. The *predictive* validity of a screening test refers to the extent to which the scores on the screening test foretell later performance (e.g., need for special services; report card grades). *Construct* validity refers to whether the test measures a particular construct or trait (e.g., adaptive skills, cognitive ability, motor ability).

Lichtenstein (1984) states that the goal in making screening decisions is to have a high correspondence between the group of children that is referred and the group of children that actually have a problem. The *hit rate model* can be used to describe this relationship. When considering the screening outcomes for a child, there are four possibilities:

1. The child who is referred by the screening does need special services—accurate decision.
2. The child who is *not* referred by the screening does *not* need special services—accurate decision.
3. The child who is referred by the screening does *not* need special services—*false-positive* decision.
4. The child who is *not* referred by the screening does need special services—*false-negative* decision.

The consequences of making false-positive or false-negative decisions can be serious. Obviously, to miss a child (false negative) who should be referred can have profound consequences for the child and the family. The benefits of early intervention may be minimized or lost when a false-negative error is made. While false positives are not considered to be as serious as false negatives, the referral of a child who should not have been selected can affect the child's self-esteem, as well as how the family and professionals interact with the child.

The hit rate model does have a problem, however. The "hits" are dependent on the accuracy of the screening instrument. Children who need special services are only a small proportion of all the children who are screened.

> The smaller the base rate, the more likely that a referral screening outcome will be incorrect and a nonreferral outcome will be correct. As a result, the screening procedure that makes the fewest referrals typically yields the highest overall hit rate. Consider an extreme example: if only 5 percent of the children in a population have special needs while a screening procedure refers no children at all, this screening procedure will have a 95 percent overall hit rate. (Not bad for a worthless device!) (Lichtenstein, 1984, p. 199)

For a screening instrument to be valid, it must fulfill two criteria: (1) refer children who should be referred (minimize underreferrals); and (2) not refer children who should not be referred (minimize overreferrals). Thus, the hit rate method is not very useful because the screening instrument can fail on the first criterion, but be successful on the second criterion (Lichtenstein, 1984).

The *sensitivity* of a screening test refers to the instrument's ability to identify children who should be identified. A screening test with a high sensitivity will yield few false negatives and will minimize underreferrals. The *specificity* of a screening test is the capacity of the instrument to accurately select out children who should not be identified. A screening test with a high specificity rate will minimize false positives and overreferrals (Lichtenstein, 1984; Meisels, 1989). Sensitivity and specificity of screening instruments are simple statistics that must be considered when using screening instruments. To learn more about sensitivity and specificity, you are encouraged to read Lichtenstein's book *Preschool Screening: Identifying Young Children with Developmental and Educational Problems* (1984).

SCREENING NEWBORNS IN HOSPITAL SETTINGS

Hospital screening of all newborn babies has become common practice in the United States as well as in many other countries. Some of these screening procedures begin immediately following birth.

Apgar Test

The Apgar test is probably the most common screening test given to newborn babies. This test (Apgar, 1953) measures five areas of physiological functioning— heart rate, respiration, reflex response, muscle tone, and color— immediately following birth and then again 5 minutes later. Each area is rated 0 (not present), 1 (some response), or 2 (good response) with a maximum possible total of 10 points. Infants who are considered healthy score between 8 and 10, while infants who are considered to be at risk score 6 or less. The results of this screening procedure identify babies in need of special care and services, but Apgar scores do not appear to be good predictors of later difficulties in development (Widerstrom, Mowder, & Sandall, 1991).

Other Procedures

Other hospital screening procedures include tests to determine whether the newborn is vulnerable to disorders that could result in a disability. Some of these conditions may be treated successfully if discovered at once. For example, some newborns lack an essential enzyme for metabolizing the protein phenylalanine; the condition is known as *phenylketonuria* (PKU). When PKU is left untreated, the protein builds up to toxic levels in the blood and results in progressive damage to the brain, causing severe retardation. If the condition is identified before toxic levels are reached, however, dietary treatment can prevent brain damage. Most hospitals routinely use a urine or blood test to screen newborns for PKU.

Although *most* states require newborns to be tested for PKU, only a *few* states screen for other metabolic disorders (Thurman & Widerstrom, 1990). Yet, other metabolic disorders may also cause mental retardation and other difficulties if not discovered early. For example, newborns who are unable to metabolize lactose in milk build up toxic substances that damage the brain and liver. If this condition, known as *galactosemia,* is discovered and treated early, damage can be prevented. The American Academy of Pediatrics (1989) has identified 10 major conditions that can be identified through newborn screening. As the field of early intervention continues to evolve, more comprehensive medical screenings may become more commonplace.

Screening newborn babies is a procedure of critical importance. Identifying infants at risk for disorders is one of the cornerstones of early intervention. Even though some disorders may be untreatable, early identification of a disability or at-risk condition can result in linking families to necessary support groups and services.

When a family leaves the hospital to return home, community service providers will assist them in obtaining services and in monitoring the infant's development.

The results of hospital screenings may also provide important historical information. When questions arise later regarding a young child's development, practitioners can obtain a developmental history from the parents and from the hospital. Very early data such as infant weight, length, and gestation, along with Apgar results, presence of asphyxia, and complications of the birth process may be noted. Meisels and Provence (1989) note the importance of also including a history of parental lifestyle, including the use of drugs, alcohol, and cigarettes. Any use of these substances during pregnancy should be recorded.

Older infants and young children typically attend community clinics, many of which offer a comprehensive screening program.

PLANNING A COMPREHENSIVE SCREENING PROGRAM

The purpose of a comprehensive screening program is to locate children who, because they may be eligible for early intervention or special education services, should receive further assessment. Practitioners plan comprehensive screening programs to assess large numbers of children in a cost-effective manner. A comprehensive screening program is designed to be a relatively quick procedure. Under the federal law (PL 101–476), public schools are *required* to locate children from birth (and older), residing in the jurisdiction of the public school, who may have disabilities.

WHAT SHOULD A COMPREHENSIVE COMMUNITY SCREENING PROGRAM INCLUDE?

Peterson (1987) has suggested that a screening program might include the following:

1. Pediatric examination.
2. Developmental history obtained through interview of the parent(s) or primary caregiver and possible use of a checklist or questionnaire to gather specific facts about the developmental history.
3. Parental or primary caregiver input regarding special problems or concerns about the child.
4. Evaluation of the child's general developmental status using a screening instrument.
5. Specialized developmental reviews (as determined by the services available, the child population, and the individual subject) in four domains: (a) physical status, (b) psychological–developmental reviews, (c) family status, and (d) environmental, social–cultural status. The psychological–developmental domain may include a review of cognitive development, emotional development, speech and language development, auditory perception, visual perception, self-help and adaptive skills, and motor development. (p. 291)

These components help to illustrate several important features of the screening procedure: (1) screenings should involve more than one source of information; (2) screenings should include information regarding hearing and vision as well as general overall development; (3) screenings should include information from parents or caregivers; (4) screenings should include clinical judgments of the practitioner(s); and (5) screenings should include information gathered through observation.

As a result of Child Find activities, parents and caregivers of young children who may be eligible for special services are located and encouraged to have their children participate in screening. Children may be screened in a variety of settings. Mobile vans may come to the family's neighborhood, or screening centers may be set up in community halls, churches, or other easily accessible places. Families who live in rural areas or are unable to reach the neighborhood settings may have the screening completed in their own home by a visiting examiner.

Screening in Home-based Settings

When a family is unable to bring a child to a community screening, the screener may go to the child's home. Screenings in the home have several advantages for the child, including functioning in familiar settings and playing with familiar toys; however, limited time and additional cost may prevent several different professionals from traveling to the child's home.

Screening in Mobile Units

Some communities sponsor a mobile unit that visits different neighborhoods. Advantages of this type of setting include increased control over the environment, to ensure good testing conditions and freedom from unexpected disruptions; availability of specialized equipment and personnel, for a more comprehensive screening procedure; and easy accessibility for families in the neighborhoods served. Disadvantages include limited space for testing and talking with parents as well as cost to operate and maintain the mobile unit.

Screening in Center-based and Preschool Settings

Head Start programs conduct regular screening programs for the children they serve. Public school districts typically conduct screening clinics that may be open to infants, toddlers, and preschool children. For children who will be entering kindergarten in the fall, public schools set up screening clinics preceding the school entrance date, usually in the spring or summer.

MODELS USED IN THE SCREENING PROCEDURE

A Unidisciplinary Approach

In the unidisciplinary approach to screening, one evaluator works with the family. This professional may have a background in education, allied health (including occupational and physical therapy), nursing, speech and language, or social services, but training in screening and identification of special needs is essential. The evaluator discusses the child's development with the parents, responds to any questions or concerns, and then surveys the child's level in each of the developmental domains. Although this approach may be cost effective, it has its disadvantages. For example, when only one professional completes the screening assessment, the results may not be as strong and significant as they tend to be when the process involves several different practitioners representing different areas of expertise.

A Team Approach

Sometimes several evaluators from different disciplines work with the child in specific areas such as cognitive development, physical development (including vision and hearing), language, speech, and adaptive development. Parents are an important part of the team approach; in addition to airing questions and concerns, they provide information about the child's development. There are many different ways of designing a team screening procedure. The following case study illustrates one approach.

CASE STUDY: A VISIT TO A SCREENING CLINIC

The small city of Brownville holds monthly screening clinics in four sections of the city. One of the clinics is held in the Northend Community Hall. Figure 5.2 diagrams the large room on the first floor, which has been set up for today's clinic.

A separate area is designed to welcome the child and to collect basic information from the parent(s) or primary caregiver. A member of the staff answers any questions the parents have about the screening procedure and gives the child a name tag. Not only does the tag allow the evaluators to see the child's name but, when a station has been completed, the child receives a balloon sticker representing that station. This simple convention streamlines the screening process and allows the different evaluators to know what stations the child has completed. A sample tag is shown in Figure 5.3.

The family then moves into the waiting area, where there are a number of different toys. By informally observing children in this area, a practitioner such

FIGURE 5.2 A community screening program with five separate stations

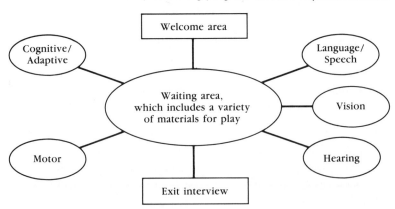

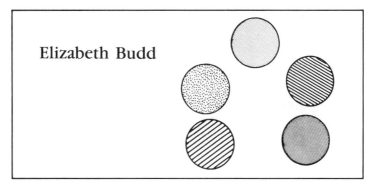

FIGURE 5.3   A screening clinic name tag: Balloon stickers indicate the stations the child has completed.

as an early intervention specialist or early childhood special educator may gather important information. How does the child approach the toys? Other children? How does the child interact with the materials? How does the child communicate with adults? With other children? The practitioner who makes observations in this informal setting must identify the types of information to be gathered and will need to choose a method for recording observational data as discussed in Chapter 4.

The clinic includes five separate screening stations. A speech and language pathologist evaluates children coming to the first station. Trained paraprofessionals in the next two stations screen for vision and hearing difficulties. Motor development is checked by a physical therapist and/or an occupational therapist in the fourth station. An educator or early intervention specialist screens children in the areas of cognitive and adaptive development at the fifth station. Notice that Figure 5.2 shows an exit area. Some parents may have questions about particular aspects of their child's development or may want to clarify something they have been told. An exit interview provides an opportunity for parents to talk further with the professional staff. Children who exhibit a problem or developmental delay will be referred for additional assessment. The exit area also provides the occasion to refer a family to other agencies in the community that may be able to help.

SELECTING SCREENING INSTRUMENTS

There are a number of screening instruments currently available. We will examine some of these instruments in detail in the following section. Table 5.1 lists these selected instruments and summarizes important areas of information.

AGS Early Screening Profiles

The AGS Early Screening Profiles (Harrison et al., 1990) is intended for use with children between the ages of two years and six years, eleven months. This screening battery, published by the American Guidance Service (AGS), measures development

TABLE 5.1 Selected screening instruments

Instrument	Purpose	Age Range	Reliability	Validity	Norms	Time to Administer
AGS Early Screening Profiles (Harrison et al., 1990)	To identify children who have disabilities or other problems that can affect development; has seven parts: cognitive/language; self-help/social; articulation survey; behavior survey; motor profile; home survey; health history survey	2 years to 6 years, 11 months	Internal consistency mean = .85; test–retest range = .78–.89; inter-rater mean = .92	Numerous studies support concurrent, predictive, and construct validity	1,149 children from 26 states and the District of Columbia stratified by geographic region, race, age, gender, socioeconomic status, and enrollment of school district	15–30 minutes for children; 10–15 minutes for teacher and parent questionnaires.
Battelle Developmental Screening Test (1984; norm recalibration, Newborg, Stock, Wnek, Guidubaldi, & Sviniski, 1988)	To determine areas of development that require further assessment; has five domains: personal–social; adaptive; motor; communication; and cognitive	Birth to 8 years, 6 months	None reported	Limited information reported	800 children, aged birth to 95 months, stratified by age, race, and gender	10–30 minutes
Brigance® Preschool Screen (Brigance, 1985)	To identify children who should be referred for further evaluation; this criterion-referenced instrument compares a child's performance in various skill areas	2 years, 9 months to 5 years	None reported	None reported	None reported	12–15 minutes

Instrument	Purpose	Age range	Reliability	Validity	Standardization sample	Time
Denver II (Frankenburg & Dodds, 1990)	To identify potential developmental problems	Birth to 6 years	Limited information reported	Limited information reported	2,096 children stratified by maternal education, residence, and ethnicity	20–30 minutes
Developmental Activities Screening Inventory—II (DASI-II) (Fewell & Langley, 1984)	To screen children	1 month to 60 months	None reported	None reported	None reported	25–30 minutes
Developmental Indicators for the Assessment of Learning—Revised (DIAL-R) (Mardell-Czudnowski & Goldenberg, 1990)	To identify children who need diagnostic evaluation or curricular modification in three areas: motor skills, conceptual abilities, and language skills	2 years to 5 years, 11 months	Test–retest reliability is based on 1983 edition; median internal consistency coefficients range from .70 to .87	Validity data reported on 1983 edition; limited validity data reported for 1990 edition	Reanalysis of 1983 standardization; sample was stratified by age and gender; minority sample is overrepresented	20–30 minutes
Early Screening Inventory (ESI) (Meisels & Wiske, 1988)	To identify children who need further evaluation; to determine if they are at risk; has three sections: visual–motor/adaptive; language and cognition; gross motor/body awareness	4 years to 6 years	Interscorer reliability = .91; test–retest = .82	Evidence of validity is adequate	465 Caucasian children from low to lower-middle-class urban communities	15–20 minutes

through individual testing of children and questionnaires that are completed by parents, teachers or child care providers, and examiners. The battery serves to identify children who may be disabled, children who have problems, and gifted children. Since this is only a screening instrument, further assessment must be conducted before a diagnosis can be made.

The AGS Early Screening Profiles are based, in part, on the Kaufman Assessment Battery for Children (K-ABC), the Bruininks–Oseretsky Test of Motor Proficiency, and the Vineland Adaptive Behavior Scales. In fact, the authors of all three of these instruments participated in the development of the AGS Early Screening Profiles. The battery has seven components, any of which can be administered individually: cognitive/language profile, motor profile, articulation survey, self-help/social profile, home survey, health history survey, and the behavior survey.

Administration.   The authors suggest that a screening examiner be responsible for coordinating the screening and supervising the interdisciplinary team of professionals, administrators, and parents, which is responsible for planning the screening, establishing screening guidelines, developing criteria for referral, and making postscreening decisions about children.

Three of the components, cognitive/language profile, motor profile, and articulation survey, are administered to the child individually. Parents, teachers, or day care providers respond to questionnaires for the self-help/social profile, the home survey, and the health history survey. The behavior survey is completed by the examiner after the cognitive/language and motor profiles have been administered.

The battery is designed to be administered to large numbers of children. Because not all the components need to be administered to every child, the administration time will vary. In general, the total administration time for each child is between 15 and 30 minutes. It takes 10 to 15 minutes for the teacher and parent questionnaires to be completed.

A large room, free of distractions, should be used for the screening. The manual provides guidance in setting up the various screening stations and the waiting area.

Scoring.   The AGS Early Screening Profiles provide a choice of two types of scoring. Level I scoring provides information about six categories of performance, which the authors call the *screening index;* Level II scoring provides standard scores, normal curve equivalents, percentiles, stanines, and age equivalents. Norm-referenced scores are available for the cognitive/language, motor, and self-help profiles, and for total screening. For the articulation, home, and behavior surveys, descriptive information (above average, average, and below average) is provided.

The screening index, which is central to the scoring and interpretation of Level I performance, is a score that was developed by the authors. It is designed to provide a quick estimate of general development and to identify children who may be disabled or gifted and need further assessment. Depending on the profile, the screening index was derived either from normalized standard scores (cognitive/language profile) or from frequency distributions transformed to percentile ranks (motor profile, self-help profile). Interpolation was used in constructing the screening indexes.

The screening indexes for the profiles correspond to the following standard score and percentile rank ranges:

Screening Index	Standard Score Range	Percentile Rank Range
1	70 and below	2 and below
2	71–85	3–16
3	86–100	17–50
4	101–115	51–84
5	116–130	85–98
6	131 and above	99 and above

For the surveys, only three broad categories were developed that correspond to the screening index:

Category	Corresponding Screening Indexes	Corresponding Percentile Ranks
Below average	1 and 2	16 and below
Average	3 and 4	17–84
Above average	5 and 6	85 and above

Level I uses the screening index. When using Level I interpretation, the screening team should consider the referral rate, that is, the percentage of children who will be referred for additional evaluation. The manual provides some guidance in establishing the referral rate.

Level II scoring does not use the screening index; it is based on standard scores or percentile ranks. Level II allows the examiner to determine patterns in performance and to compare the child's score to a national norm.

Standardization.   The standardization occurred between October 1987 and December 1988 in 26 states and the District of Columbia. The sample contained 1,149 children, ages two years to six years, eleven months, and was stratified according to age, gender, geographic region, total enrollment of the school district, socioeconomic status (measured by parental education level), and race or ethnic group. For the self-help/social profile, 366 teachers or child care providers composed the standardization sample.

Reliability.   Reliability is the consistency or stability of test performance. The manual reports three types of reliability: internal consistency, test–retest, and interrater. The median internal consistency reliability coefficients for each of the components of the AGS Early Screening Profiles ranged from .41 to .95.

When establishing test–retest reliability, the entire battery, except the self-help/social profile, was administered in an immediate retest and in a delayed retest. For the immediate retest, data were collected on 74 children. Reliability coefficients ranged from .66 to .91. In the delayed retest, the battery was readministered to 42 children between 22 and 75 days after the initial testing. Reliability coefficients ranged from .55 to .91.

Interrater reliability, or the reliability of scoring by different examiners, was conducted for the motor profile. Two different examiners rated 63 children. When their ratings were correlated, the interrater reliability coefficients ranged from .83 to .99.

Validity.   Validity is the extent to which a test measures what it was intended to measure. The content validity of the test is an estimate of the extent to which the test measures the content it was designed to measure. The only evidence of content validity that is provided is the authors' statement that because each of the components was extensively developed and because the test is reliable, it has content validity.

The authors provide considerable evidence of concurrent validity, citing numerous studies, which included comparisons with the Kaufman Assessment Battery for Children, the Stanford–Binet, the Peabody Picture Vocabulary Test–Revised, the Metropolitan Achievement Test, the Vineland Adaptive Behavior Scales, and other instruments. Evidence of predictive validity is also furnished. While predictive validity appears to be adequate, because this instrument was published so recently, the time interval between the administration of the AGS Early Screening Profiles and criterion instruments is less than two years. Additional predictive validity studies will have to be undertaken.

Construct validity is the extent to which a test measures a particular construct or trait; the authors provide several types of evidence. Of interest are a number of studies demonstrating that the AGS Early Screening Profiles effectively identified both at-risk and gifted children. In general, this instrument appears to have adequate validity. Additional studies by independent researchers should be conducted in this area.

Summary.   The AGS Early Screening Profiles is an individually administered norm-referenced screening battery. There is considerable evidence relating to the reliability and validity of this instrument. While additional studies by independent researchers are necessary, this instrument appears to be very useful.

Battelle Developmental Inventory Screening Test

The Battelle Developmental Inventory Screening Test (BDI Screening Test) (Newborg, Stock, Wnek, Guidubaldi, & Sviniski, 1988) is intended to identify children from birth to eight years who may be disabled or delayed in development. It can also be used to evaluate the strengths and weaknesses of typically developing children, as well as children who are above average or gifted. The authors list the following applications of the BDI Screening Test:

- Assessment of children, particularly infants, who are considered to be "at risk" in any developmental area
- General screening for developmental strengths and weaknesses
- General screening of preschool and kindergarten children
- Monitoring student progress on a short- and long-term basis (Newborg et al., 1988, p. 2)

The BDI Screening Test consists of 96 items taken from the 341 items of the Battelle Developmental Inventory. Information about children is gathered in five domains: personal–social, adaptive, motor, communication, and cognitive.

Administration.   The BDI Screening Test uses three different procedures for collecting information about children: structured administration of items; observations; and interviews with parents, caregivers, or teachers to collect information about children in each of the five domains. A total of 96 items is included in the domains. All the domains must be administered. Depending on the age of the child, this instrument takes between 10 and 30 minutes to administer. A variety of professionals can administer the BDI Screening Test, including teachers, special educators, speech pathologists, psychologists, adaptive physical education teachers, and clinical diagnosticians. The manual provides specific adaptations for modifying the test for use with children who are disabled. For some items, more than one type of administration procedure may be appropriate. Examiners are instructed to "use the procedure that will yield the most valid data" (p. 7). There are no additional directions to guide the examiner in deciding which administration procedure to use.

The BDI Screening Test should be administered in a quiet location with a minimum of distractions. Unlike several other screening tests, a parent, teacher, or caregiver may be present during the administration of the structured items. Informal observations can be conducted separately from the structured observations over a period of several weeks in the child's normal environment. If this is not possible, the examiner can interview a parent, caregiver, or teacher. For most items, the interviewee is asked to respond yes or no; for some items, the interviewee may be asked to provide an example of the behavior.

Scoring.   The BDI Screening Test uses basal and ceiling rules to determine where to begin and end the administration of each of the five domains. Items are scored 2 points if the child typically (90% success) exhibits the behavior; 1 point for sometimes (50% success); and 0 points for rarely or never.

The points a child earns for each domain and for the entire test are totaled. These raw scores are converted to percentile ranks, standard scores, developmental quotients, and normal curve equivalents. For states that require standard deviation cutoffs to identify children, cutoffs of 1.0, 1.5, and 2.0 standard deviations are provided.

The norms for the 1984 edition of the BDI Screening Test were inaccurate, which was a major drawback. For the 1988 edition, the authors recalibrated the original norms and used medians instead of mean performance. When using the BDI Screening Test, be sure not to use the 1984 standardization.

The authors provide little guidance in interpreting the results of the screening test. They do state that recommendations should be based on the pattern of domain weakness and on the results of the individual sections.

Standardization.   Stratified quota sampling was used to select the standardization sample. Eight hundred children were selected on the basis of geographical region, urban or rural residence, race, and gender. Forty-two test administrators, who had various levels of training, were selected in 24 states. The test administrators selected children to meet the sampling requirements. The test administrators were also asked to select children from a wide range of socioeconomic levels, but primarily children from middle-class backgrounds.

A second sample, called the clinical sample, also took the BDI Screening Test. The manual provides little information about this sample, which consisted of children with various disabilities.

Reliability.   There is no reliability information for the BDI Screening Test. While the authors report reliability data for the complete BDI, no reliability data are presented in the manual for the BDI Screening Test. Sheenan and Snyder (1989–1990) have pointed out that reliability of a test is heavily dependent on the total number of items in a test. Thus, the reliability of the BDI Screening Test should be much lower than the BDI. Of particular concern would be demonstration of internal consistency, test–retest, and interrater reliability. Studies should be undertaken to demonstrate the reliability of this instrument.

Validity.   The important validity questions of the BDI Screening Test relate to the original purpose of the test. The authors present only one validity study to support the validity of this instrument: 164 children, from the norming and clinical samples, were administered both the BDI and the BDI Screening Test. Correlations between the two instruments ranged from .92 to .99 for the five domains and the total score. The authors conclude that scores on the BDI Screening Test predict scores on the BDI. However, no information is given about the composition of the samples, the length of time between the two tests, or the qualifications of the examiners. Sheenan and Snyder (1989–1990) wrote that "the efforts made by the authors to validate the Screening Test, a 96-item subset of the complete instrument, were of greatest concern from a psychometric standpoint" (p. 27).

Summary.   The BDI Screening Test is an individually administered, norm-referenced screening test. While the authors claim that the BDI Screening Test has multiple uses, no validity data are presented to support these additional applications. Moreover, although it is crucial for a screening test to present data about the validity of cutoff scores as well as support for grouping the items into separate domains, no such evidence is provided.

Bayley Infant Neurodevelopmental Screen

The Bayley Infant Neurodevelopmental Screen (BINS), developed by Glen Aylward (in press), is designed to assess neuropsychological development in infants from 3 to 24 months of age. The BINS is administered by a practitioner, but caregiver reports may be utilized on some items. Six hundred children comprised the standardization sample, which is stratified according to age, race, sex, parent education level, and geographic region.

Brigance® Early Preschool Screen

The Brigance® Early Preschool Screen for Two-Year-Old and Two-and-a-Half-Year-Old Children was developed in 1990 for the purpose of identifying children "who should be referred for a more comprehensive evaluation of diagnostic assessment" (Brigance, 1990, p. v). This instrument consists of two sections: one designed for children between 21 and 30 months of age; and one for children between 27 and 36 months of age. The section for children 21 to 30 months of age includes eight skills, which represent typical developmental areas:

Fine motor (two skills: Builds Tower with Blocks and Visual Motor Skills)

Receptive language (three skills: Identifies Body Parts, Identifies People in Picture by Naming, Identifies Objects According to Use)

Gross motor (one skill: Gross Motor Skills)

Expressive language (two skills: Picture Vocabulary and Verbal Fluency)

Each skill area contains two to six items. For example, Picture Vocabulary consists of pictures of a cat, a dog, and a key, which the child is asked to name.

The section for children 27 to 36 months of age includes the same skills as the first section and an additional one, quantitative concepts. Within each of the nine skill areas, there are two to seven items. Figures 5.4 and 5.5 illustrate some language items assessed. The child's page is a good example of a culturally diverse test item.

The manual also includes a section of supplemental assessments designed "to assess additional, and in most cases, more advanced skills" (Brigance, 1990, p. 20). An additional section includes screening information forms which, the manual states, may be completed by the examiner, the teacher, and the parents (Brigance, 1990, p. 30).

Administration.   This test may be used by a teacher or by a paraprofessional. The manual suggests that vision and hearing screening be included; if this is not possible, however, the manual includes a list of suggestions for observing possible vision and hearing problems.

FIGURE 5.4 Examiner's page for assessing receptive language

SOURCE: *Brigance® Early Preschool Screen for Two-Year-Old and Two-and-a-Half-Year-Old Children* by Albert H. Brigance. North Billerica, MA: Curriculum Associates, Inc., 1990. Reprinted by permission.

Identifies People in Picture by Pointing

Skill:
Identifies people in picture by pointing to when requested.
1. man   2. girl   3. woman   4. boy

Data Sheet:
Two-Year-Old Child.

Assessment Method:
Child performance—identifies by pointing to when requested.

Material:
C-6.

Discontinue:
After the child fails to identify two consecutive pictures.

Time:
Your discretion; however, approximately ten seconds per picture is recommended.

Accuracy:
Give credit for each picture correctly identified. If the child self-corrects, give credit.

Point Value:
3 points for each picture.

Notes:
1. **Possible Observations:** As the child looks at the picture and responds to the items, you may wish to observe and make note of the following:
   a. *Physical Handicaps:* Does the child have a handicap that makes him or her unable to perform the skill?
   b. *Use of Eyes:* Do the child's eyes appear to move and focus on details without difficulty?
   c. *Attention to Task:* Does the child consistently attend to your requests, or does he or she have difficulty attending for reasons such as a short attention span or distractions?
   d. *Language Comprehension:* Which verbal direction does the child appear to comprehend best?
   • "Show me the . . ."
   • "Put your finger on the . . ."
   • "Where is the . . ."
   • "Point to the . . ."
   • "Touch the . . ."
   • (handing the child a block) "Put the block on the . . ."
   Use the direction which the child comprehends best as you continue the assessment.

Directions:
This assessment is made by asking the child to identify each person in the picture on C-6 by pointing to him or her as you request each person. Pause after each request for the child's response. If the child does **not** respond, rephrase the request. If helpful, give encouragement. Use the verbal direction which the child comprehends best. (*See* **Note** 1d.)

Point to the picture on C-6 and

Say: **Look at this picture. Where is the man?**
       Show me the man.

Pause for the child's response. Allow time for the child to study the picture. If needed, give encouragement and rephrase the request.

Say: **Put your finger on the man.**
   or **Point to the man.**

Follow the same procedure for the picture of the girl, the woman, and the boy.

   e. *Interest Level:* Does the child appear to have an interest in the picture? Does he or she volunteer additional information?
   f. *Confidence Level:* Does the child appear relaxed, or is he or she anxious about responding? Does he or she respond with confidence and assurance?
   g. *Assurance of Response:* Does the child respond automatically or hesitantly?

2. **Supplemental Assessments:**
   a. *Higher-Level Skill:* If the child is successful in identifying people by pointing to them as you request them, you may wish to assess the higher-level skill of "identifying by naming." This can be done by pointing to people in the picture one at a time and asking, "Who is this?"
   b. *Sentence Completion:* You may wish to say incomplete sentences such as those listed below and see if the child can complete the sentences.
      1. The girl will grow up to be a _____ .
      2. The boy will grow up to be a _____ .

FIGURE 5.5   Child's page for assessing receptive language

Scoring.   In the first section (21 to 30 months of age), each skill completed correctly receives points, which are added for a total score. Some skills are assigned more points than others. For example, the four skills within Identifies People in Pictures are worth 3 points each; the three skills within Identifies Objects According to Use are worth 4 points each. There is a possible total score of 100 points.

Scoring for the second section (27 to 36 months of age) is similar. Some of the test items in the two sections are identical, but more points are given for successful completion at an earlier age. For example, to complete the first item, Builds Tower with Blocks, the child must make a single-column tower with two blocks. For the younger age group, this item is worth 3 points; for the older age group, the task is worth 2 points.

To promote consistency among examiners, the manual includes specific information regarding each skill area. Examiners are encouraged to record informal observations of the child. A section of the data sheet allows for the following observations: handedness, grasp, hearing, vision, and other.

The author recommends that a child who scores 60 or below be referred, although another section of the manual encourages each screening program to establish its own cutoff score for referral. The manual states that referrals should not be based solely on the screening score; the use of observations and other information from parents and teachers is recommended.

Standardization.   The Brigance® Early Preschool Screen is a criterion-referenced test, not a norm-referenced instrument. The author suggests that a child's score be compared with the group of children of approximately the same age who are being screened. The manual offers suggestions for dividing the children's scores into three groups (high, average, and low), but no specific information is given to assist the examiner in distinguishing a high score from a medium score or a medium score from a low score.

Reliability.   There is no information concerning reliability data. A chart illustrating how the Brigance® Early Preschool Screen is correlated with the Brigance® Inventory of Early Development is included, apparently because the same items are contained in both instruments.

Validity.   Test items were found to be appropriate (content validity) based on a literature review. These references are included in the manual. The items were field tested by participants in nine different states, and the manual lists their names and job titles. The manual states that several changes were made as a result of the field testing: including additional information in assessing skill areas, eliminating a confusing item, and adjusting point values. Many of the differences between items for the two age groups seem small, and no data are given to substantiate the rationale for arriving at the differences between point values for the two age groups.

Summary.   The Brigance® Early Preschool Screen is a criterion-referenced test; no norms are reported. This developmental screening test is designed to identify children who need a more comprehensive assessment. The group of young children for whom this test was designed is typically referred to as toddlers; yet, the name of the instrument suggests that the test is for preschoolers, typically thought of as children ages three to five years. Such differences in terminology may increase confusion for potential users. The test items do include clear directions for the practitioner, but additional information is needed concerning their reliability and validity. Lack of norms limits use of this instrument in screening procedures.

Brigance® Preschool Screen

The Brigance® Preschool Screen for Three- and Four-Year-Old Children was developed by Albert Brigance (1985). The purpose of this measure is to identify children who should be referred for further evaluation. Unlike many of the other screening instruments, this measure is a criterion-referenced screening inventory. It determines whether children can perform specific skills rather than comparing each one to a norm or standardization sample. The instrument is intended for use with children who are three and four years old. The author considers the age range for a three-year-old to be 2 years, 9 months to 4 years; the age range for a four-year-old is 3 years, 9 months to 5 years. This inventory is similar in format to others developed by the same author, including the Early Preschool Screen, described above, and the K & 1 Screen—Revised, which is to be used with children in kindergarten and the first grade.

The Brigance® Preschool Screen for Three- and Four-Year-Old Children contains four components: (1) a list of skills to which the child is asked to respond orally or in written form, (2) a screening observation form, (3) a teacher's rating form, and (4) a parent's rating form. An example of the parent rating form is illustrated in Figure 5.6. In addition to the basic assessments, supplemental assessments provide for the testing of more advanced skills.

Three-Year-Old Children.   Three-year-old children are asked to demonstrate the following sets of skills:

1. Personal Data Response: recites first name, last name, age
2. Identifies Body Parts: ears, head, legs, arms, fingers, thumbs, toes, neck, stomach
3. Performs Gross Motor Skills: (a) stands on one foot for one second; (b) walks tiptoe three steps; and (c) walks forward heel-and-toe three steps
4. Identifies Objects According to Their Use: stove, coat, car
5. Repeats Sentences: 3 syllables, 4 syllables, and 5 syllables
6. Visual Motor Skills: copies circle, horizontal line, vertical line
7. Demonstrates Number Concepts: one, one more, two
8. Builds Tower with Blocks
9. Matches Colors
10. Picture Vocabulary: tree, bird, apple, pencil, sock
11. Understands the Use of Plurals and -ing

Four-Year-Old Children.   Four-year-old children are asked to demonstrate the following skills:

1. Personal Data Response: recites first name, last name, middle name, age
2. Identifies Body Parts: thumbs, toes, neck, stomach, chest, back, knees, chin, fingernails
3. Performs Gross Motor Skills: (a) stands on one foot for one second; (b) walks tiptoe four steps; and (c) walks forward heel-and-toe four steps
4. Tells Use of Objects: stove, coat, car
5. Repeats Sentences: 4 syllables, 6 syllables, 8 syllables
6. Visual Motor Skills: horizontal line, vertical line, cross
7. Demonstrates Number Concepts: two, three, five
8. Builds Tower with Blocks
9. Points to Colors as They Are Named
10. Picture Vocabulary: boat, kite, wagon, ladder, scissors, leaf
11. Understands the Use of Prepositions and Irregular Plural Nouns

Administration.   A single examiner or several examiners can conduct the screening. If several examiners are used, the author recommends that four stations be established and various skills be assessed at each station. Other arrangements are also permissible. Professionals and paraprofessionals can conduct the screening. The screening should be conducted in a quiet, comfortable room that is free of distractions.

Scoring.   Points can be earned for each skill area, with a total of 100 possible points. The author recommends that cutoff scores for referral be established by each

PARENT'S RATING FORM—THREE-YEAR-OLD CHILD

PRESCHOOL ADMISSION INFORMATION

DIRECTIONS: Read each question and check the appropriate answer column.

Child's Name _____

Child's Age _____ Date _____

Parent's Name _____

Can this child tell others his or her

1. first name? ....
2. full name? ....
3. age? ....

Personal/Speech

Does this child

4. count by rote to five? ....
5. demonstrate the concepts of giving one, one more, two? ....
6. point to and name pictures in books? ....
7. understand action pictures in books? ....
8. understand stories read to him or her? ....
9. try to read books from memory? ....
10. recognize his or her name in print? ....

Academic Readiness

11. consistently use the same hand for performing?
12. draw recognizable pictures? ....
13. try to color pictures within the lines? ....
14. use scissors to cut paper? ....
15. assemble inset puzzles of 5 to 10 pieces? ......

Visual/Fine Motor Skills

16. wash and dry his or her hands without help? ..
17. undress without help? ....
18. dress without help? ....
19. button clothing? ....
20. totally care for toileting needs? ....
21. hold glass with one hand while drinking? ......
22. control spoon when eating? ....
23. hold spoon in fingers, not fist? ....
24. usually take care of personal belongings? .....

Self-Help Skills

Does this child

25. greet others in an appropriate manner? ....
26. usually play with at least one child? ....
27. show concern for safe and appropriate use of materials and equipment? ....
28. engage in new activities willingly? ....
29. usually make an effort to solve problems before seeking help? ....
30. usually continue an activity without seeking attention or encouragement? ....
31. usually accept limits set by adults? ....
32. usually reflect a happy disposition? ....

Emotional/Social Skills

33. orally express needs and make requests? .....
34. speak clearly? ....

Speech

35. pedal and steer a tricycle a distance of ten feet?
36. usually go up and down stairs without difficulty? ....
*37. appear to have stamina and be in good health?
*38. appear free of handicaps or problems that may require special services? ....

Health/Physical

*If the answer to this question is "No" or "Uncertain," please explain on the back of this form.

FIGURE 5.6 Parent's Rating Form. Brigance® Preschool Screen for Three- and Four-Year-Old Children.

SOURCE: *Brigance® Preschool Screen for Three- and Four-Year-Old Children* by Albert H. Brigance. North Billerica, MA: Curriculum Associates, Inc., 1985. Reprinted/adapted by permission.

screening program. A sample of 25 children was tested by the author, and higher than average, average score, and lower than average scores were determined. The manual does not report how these scores were derived. The manual recommends the reevaluation of children who receive scores of 60 or below.

There are three forms (screening observations form, teacher's rating form, and parent's rating form) in addition to the screening instrument, but the author does not provide any way of integrating the information collected from the various sources. Although the manual does state that referrals for further assessment should not be based on the total score alone, no guidance is provided on how to incorporate the information collected on the three forms with the results of the screening.

Standardization. The Brigance® Preschool Screen for Three- and Four-Year-Old Children is a criterion-referenced test and as such is not required to be norm referenced.

Reliability.   Reliability data are not reported. It would be helpful to have information relating to test–retest and interrater reliability.

Validity.   When developing this measure, the author reviewed literature relating to the development of children and consulted with professionals. No other data about validity are provided. It would be helpful to have information about concurrent, predictive, and construct validity of this measure. Of special interest would be information relating to specificity, sensitivity, and development of cutoff scores.

Summary.   The Brigance® Preschool Screen for Three- and Four-Year-Old Children is an individually administered, criterion-referenced screening instrument based on a literature search and consultation with professionals in the field. There are no studies that report the reliability or validity of this instrument. There are questions relating to the specificity and sensitivity. The test has limited usefulness.

Developmental Activities Screening Inventory—II (DASI-II)

The Developmental Activities Screening Inventory—II (DASI-II) (Fewell & Langley, 1984) is a revised edition of the DASI. The DASI-II includes two additional levels, extending the test downward to birth, and is appropriate for children functioning between 1 to 60 months. The revision also includes three replacement test items. The test is nonverbal and thus does not penalize children with suspected hearing or language disorders. The manual specifies adaptations for children with visual impairments. The test includes several skill categories, including fine motor coordination, cause–effect, association, number concept, size discrimination, memory, spatial relationships, object function, and seriation.

Administration.   Screening is conducted by an examiner working directly with the child. The examiner's manual includes a listing of materials needed and a description of the procedure for each test item, as well as a description of the scoring criteria. The DASI-II is not a timed test; estimated administration is between 25 and 30 minutes.

Scoring.   Test items are scored as either plus or minus. A child receives one raw score point for each correct answer. The manual provides a table for transforming raw scores to developmental age scores, which are used to obtain developmental quotients (DQs).

Standardization.   The DASI-II has not been standardized. The test manual has limited information regarding children who participated in some studies for the original DASI.

Reliability.   No information on the reliability of the DASI-II is included in the manual.

Validity.   The manual reports several studies concerning the extent to which test scores on the original DASI relate to scores on other tests (criterion-related validity); however, no studies have been done on the DASI-II.

Summary.   The DASI-II is a screening instrument designed for children functioning between 1 and 60 months of age. The test is nonverbal and includes good descriptions of testing procedures. The materials required are those typically found in early childhood settings. The lack of standardization and the lack of studies concerning reliability and validity of this instrument are significant problems, however. Until further research is completed, this instrument should be used with extreme caution.

Denver II

The Denver II (Frankenburg & Dodds, 1990) is a revision of the Denver Developmental Screening Test (DDST) of Frankenburg, Dodds, Fandal, Kazuk, and Cohrs (1975). According to the authors, the Denver II is to be used with children between birth and six years old who are "apparently well" (p. 1). The authors state that "the test is valuable in screening asymptomatic children for possible problems, in confirming intuitive suspicions with an objective measure, and in monitoring children at risk for developmental problems, such as those who have experienced perinatal difficulties" (p. 1).

The authors stress that the Denver II is neither a measure of intelligence nor a predictor of future ability. It is designed to compare a child's performance on a number of tasks with the performance of children who are the same age.

Of the 125 items on the Denver II, 34 are new, 18 were changed, and 18 omitted. The items are grouped into four categories: personal–social, fine motor–adaptive, language, and gross motor. In addition, the examiner completes five items that rate the behavior of the child during the screening.

Administration.   The Denver II can be administered several times to the same child. The individual's test form can be reused when screening is repeated; the authors suggest using different colored pencils to distinguish one screening from another. The manual for the Denver II includes general instructions for administration of the screening instrument as well as specific instructions for specific test items.

Examiners should be carefully trained and should pass a proficiency test before using the Denver II. Training materials are available from: William K. Frankenburg, M.D., M.S.P.H., Professor of Pediatrics and Preventive Medicine, University of Colorado Health Sciences Center, Box C-223, 4200 East Ninth Avenue, Denver, CO 80262.

The instrument is administered in the presence of the child's parent or caregiver. The examiner is strongly encouraged to spend time obtaining rapport with the child and the parent or caregiver. Clothes that may hamper movement by the child should be removed before the screening begins. The child may sit on the caregiver's lap or alone on a chair. The child's arms should rest on a table top.

The administration of the test items is flexible and can be altered according to the individual needs of the child. Although the authors encourage flexibility, the following guidelines are provided:

1. Items that require less active involvement by the child should be administered first.
2. Easy items should be administered before the more difficult ones.

3. Items that use the same or similar materials (e.g., blocks) can be administered one after the other.
4. Only materials for the specific item being tested should be placed in front of the child.
5. When testing infants, all the items that require the infant to lie down should be administered consecutively.
6. Testing should begin with items that are below the child's age and should progress to more difficult items.

The number of items administered to each child varies according to the time allotted to the testing and the age and ability of the child. Guidelines for determining whether the child is at risk developmentally and for assessing the relative strengths of the child are provided separately.

A small section on the Denver II test form allows the examiner to rate the test behavior of the child. The child's behavior can be rated on a scale from 1 to 3 in the following areas: typical, compliance, interest in surroundings, fearfulness, and attention span. Figure 5.7 illustrates the profile sheet for the Denver II.

Scoring.   Four possible scores can be given for each item: pass, fail, no opportunity (the child has not had an opportunity to demonstrate the item because of various restrictions), and refusal (the child refuses to try the item).

When interpreting test performance, the authors recommend that individual items be interpreted first, then the complete test. Individual items can be interpreted as advanced, normal, caution, delayed, or no opportunity. There are four interpretations when looking at the performance on the entire test: normal, abnormal, questionable, and untestable. While the manual provides several guidelines and a few examples for interpreting test performance, it is unclear how these guidelines were developed and whether they are based on the standardization sample.

Standardization.   The standardization sample consisted of 2,096 children in Colorado stratified according to maternal education, residence, and ethnic group. The sample was divided into 10 age groups between the ages of 2 weeks and 78 months. The data from the standardization sample was used to determine when 25, 50, 75, and 90% of the children had passed specific items.

Reliability.   Reliability information is limited. Interrater reliability and test–retest reliability were calculated based on a sample of 38 children. Calculated on this small sample, interrater reliability had a mean of .99, with a range from .95 to 1.00; test–retest reliability had a mean of .90, with a range of .50 to 1.00.

Validity.   Little information about validity is provided. The authors state:

Content validity of the original DDST items has been recognized through the test's acceptance all over the world. The new items were written and selected by professionals specializing in child development and pediatric screening. The validity of the test rests upon its standardization, not on its correlation with other tests, since all tests are constructed slightly differently. (p. 4)

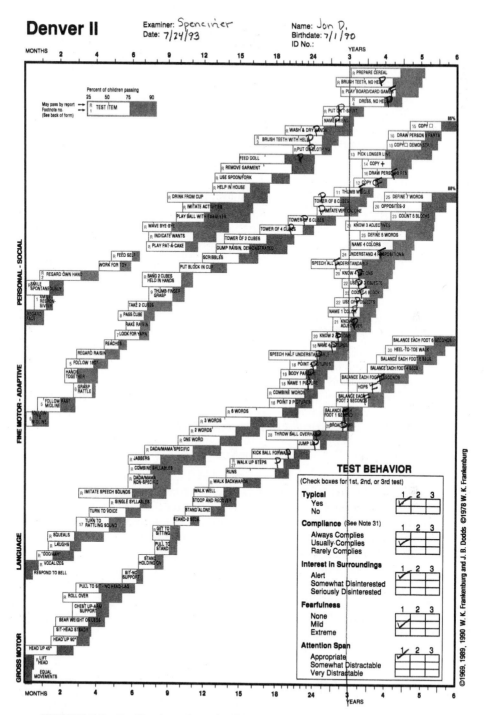

FIGURE 5.7 Profile sheet from the Denver II

SOURCE: Adapted in part from *The Denver II: A Major Revision and Restandardization of the Denver Developmental Screening Test* by W. K. Frankenburg et al. (1992). *Pediatrics, 89,* p. 93. Adapted by permission.

Summary.   The Denver II, a revision of the Denver Developmental Screening Test, is designed to identify potential problems in young children in four areas: personal–social, fine motor adaptive, language, and gross motor. Limited information about reliability and the standardization sample is presented. Additional information about validity is needed.

Developmental Indicators for the Assessment of Learning—Revised

The Developmental Indicators for the Assessment of Learning—Revised (DIAL-R) (Mardell-Czudnowski & Goldenberg, 1990) was originally published in 1975 as the Developmental Indicators for the Assessment of Learning (DIAL). In 1983 it was revised, restandardized, and published by Childcraft Education Corporation as the Developmental Indicators for the Assessment of Learning—Revised. The 1990 American Guidance Service (AGS) edition of the Developmental Indicators of Learning—Revised is a modification of the 1983 revision of the DIAL-R in which the 1983 norms were reanalyzed. The 1990 edition also includes a broader range of cutoff points, an expanded explanation of the norm sample, and additional information on reliability and validity. In developing the 1983 DIAL-R from the DIAL, 18 items were revised, 3 were introduced, and 8 were deleted.

The DIAL-R is intended for use with children between the ages of 2 years, 0 months and 5 years, 11 months. The DIAL-R is a screening test used to identify young children who need diagnostic evaluation or curricular modification. The test screens children in three areas: motor skills, conceptual abilities, and language abilities. Each area contains eight items; each item contains tasks that sample typical developmental behaviors. Each area also contains a checklist of social–emotional behaviors.

Administration.   Although children are screened individually, the instrument is administered by a team of four adults: a coordinator and three examiners, whom the authors refer to as "operators," administer the three different sections of the test. Total administration time for each child is approximately 20 to 30 minutes. The instrument is designed to screen a large number of children in a short period of time. Because each operator or examiner administers only one area, three children can be screened concurrently. The authors suggest that in addition to the professional coordinator and the operators, volunteers may be used to assist with the nontesting activities, which could include helping the child to feel comfortable, taking the child's photograph, or guiding the child from one area to the next. The authors recommend that vision and hearing screening be conducted along with the administration of the DIAL-R.

According to the authors, the screening should be conducted in a large, open room. The manual contains a floor plan indicating the arrangement of tables and chairs into the following sections: registration–play, photo, screening (this includes areas for motor, concepts, and language), parent observation, parent conference, and computer scoring.

Scoring.   A child's verbal response is marked with a circle; a motor response is underlined. For each item, a raw score is obtained. Raw scores are converted to scaled scores. For example, a raw score for item 4, Naming Nouns, on the language area, ranges from 1 to 15. This is converted to a scaled score of 1. However, as Salvia and Ysseldyke (1991) have pointed out, the scaled scores are not really scaled scores that have the same mean and the same standard deviation. They correspond to one-year age intervals. Thus, a scaled score of 1 is assigned to two to three years; a scaled score of 2 is assigned to three to four years, etc. A total score for the three areas is arrived at by adding up all the scaled scores. Then, each area scaled score and the total score are converted to a scale that has three labels: potential problem, OK, potential advanced.

Each area examiner is also expected to complete an eight-item behavioral checklist by placing a check mark next to each item that describes the child. The score is the sum of all of the items checked. These raw scores are not converted to scores of any other type.

The decision to use one of the labels (potential problem, OK, potential advanced) is based on cutoff scores. Standard deviation cutoffs of 1.0, 1.5, and 2.0 can be used, as well as percentile cutoffs of 10 and 90% and 5 and 95%. These have been computed for three norm samples: census, Caucasian, and minority. These cutoffs seem to have been arbitrarily determined; there is no documentation of how they were established.

The authors recommend that before determining which cutoff to use, coordinators examine the implications of using the various cutoffs. Despite this caution, the authors provide little guidance in making such determinations. In boldface type, the authors write:

> Although the DIAL-R offers many alternatives in terms of norm samples, types of cutoffs, and methods for obtaining an overall screening decision, the coordinator or other school or program officials must establish specific program-wide guidelines for the interpretation of screening test results and the subsequent decisions related to these results. (Mardell-Czudnowski & Goldenberg, 1990, p. 29)

The interpretation of performance on individual items is also left to the test administrator. Similarly, little guidance is provided on the interpretation of the behavioral checklist.

Cutoff scores for children who are "OK" or "potential problem" are provided. These are based on data from the 1983 standardization sample, not on the 1990 reanalysis. The authors do write that as the total score increases, the number of behavioral observations decreases. The cutoffs for the behavioral observations appear to have been arbitrarily established. In the absence of additional interpretive guidelines, however, it is left to test administrators to determine which cutoffs to use, how to interpret performance on individual sections and items, and how to interpret the performance on the behavioral scale. The authors provide little assistance.

Standardization. The 1990 version of the DIAL-R is based on the standardization that occurred between 1981 and 1983. This version is a reanalysis of the 1981–1983 standardization sample. Eight standardization testing sites were selected in the spring of 1981. Each site coordinator was in charge of selecting the children. Children were not excluded if they had a disability, but it is unknown what percentage of the sample was disabled or what the disabilities were. The test was standardized between September 1981 and March 1983. The sample consisted of 2,447 children.

For the 1990 reanalysis, data from 2,227 of these children were used: 220 cases were omitted from the original sample (2,447 children) because certain demographic information was missing. The authors report that the 1990 reanalysis incorporated information from the 1990 census.

The following variables were used in selecting the sample: chronological age, gender, geographic region, community size, and race. Information about educational level of the parents and language spoken in the home was collected on some of the children. The sample was weighted so that projections of the 1990 census could be approximated. For several variables, these approximations leave much to be desired. For example, the minority sample is overrepresented (45.2% of the total sample, versus a projected 1990 census of 30.6%). Racial and ethnic groups are clustered together, and the proportions of the various racial and ethnic groups constituting the minority sample are unknown. Eight age groups of children, spaced at 6-month intervals, beginning at age 2 years, 0 months to 5 years, 11 months, were selected. Eight communities, two in each region, were selected to represent four geographical regions in the United States. Both of the communities representing the South are in Florida. Similarly, the North Central region is represented by two communities in Illinois. The West is represented by communities in Hawaii and Washington; the Northeast is represented by communities in New York and Delaware.

Stratification of the sample, aside from age and gender, did not occur in each community. No information is given on how the sites were selected, the training of the coordinators, or how the individual children were recruited for the standardization sample. Children with disabilities were included in the sample, but as noted earlier, the proportions and the natures of the disabilities are not given. Parents were not stratified by socioeconomic status.

Reliability.   Test–retest and internal consistency reliabilities are reported. Information on test–retest reliability is based on the 1983 standardization. Correlation coefficients are reported for motor (.76), concepts (.90), language (.77) and total score (.87) for a sample of 65 children, stratified by age and gender. The testing interval ranged from 3 days to 175 days. The authors cite five other studies conducted by themselves and by other researchers after the publication of the 1983 DIAL-R that investigate test–retest reliability. Information on the composition of the samples as well as the test–retest interval is extremely limited. The correlation coefficients range from .13 to .98 for each of the three areas and the total score. Information on internal consistency reliability is based on the 1990 reanalysis. Median coefficients are reported for each of the three area scores and the total score for the census, Caucasian, and minority samples. These coefficients range from .70 to .87. The area scores had lower coefficients because each area has fewer items than the total score.

Validity.   Content validity is based on the DIAL. Eight experts reviewed the development, test items, instructions, and criteria for scoring of the DIAL. These experts judged the DIAL to have content validity.

The authors define criterion-related validity as "the relationship of a test to meaningful criteria" (Mardell-Czudnowski & Goldenberg, 1990, p. 65). They cite a number of studies that demonstrate both concurrent and predictive validity. In boldface type the authors caution that since these studies were conducted prior to the 1990 AGS edition, "any conclusions drawn from these studies must be made with care" (Mardell-Czudnowski & Goldenberg, 1990, p. 65).

Construct validity was demonstrated by showing that as children get older, their DIAL-R scores will increase. The authors also summarize data from other studies to demonstrate construct validity.

Summary.   The Developmental Indicators for the Assessment of Learning—Revised is an individually administered, norm-referenced screening instrument. Reliability and validity are based on the 1983 edition. While the DIAL-R is a useful instrument, examiners should carefully consider the results of screening because of the limitations relating to reliability and validity.

Early Screening Inventory—3

The Early Screening Inventory—3 (ESI-3) (Meisels, Henderson, Marsden, Browning, & Olson, 1991) is a developmental screening instrument designed for use with children who are three and four years old. It is a downward extension of the Early Screening Inventory (ESI). However, according to the manual, all the items in the ESI-3 were modified. The ESI-3 was designed to identify children who may require special education services.

The instrument has three main sections: visual-motor/adaptive, language and cognition, and gross motor/body awareness. None of these sections is intended to be used alone. Rather, the sections are to be combined with other information obtained from parents and professionals to provide an assessment of a child's relative strengths and weaknesses. In addition to these three sections, there are three other components: the Draw a Person task (DAP), formation of letters, and a parent questionnaire.

Administration.   The ESI-3 should be administered by professionals who have some formal background in early childhood development. It takes approximately 30 minutes to administer the ESI-3 to a three-year-old child. The parent questionnaire can be completed in about 15 minutes.

Scoring.   Each item on the score sheet is scored pass, fail, or refuse. In addition, there is a space for the examiner to note comments. The examiner calculates the total points. Only a total ESI score can be calculated, since individual components do not have total scores. The parent questionnaire is not scored. It is intended to provide an overview of the child's development.

A child's raw score is compared with cutoff scores. There are three possible choices: OK, rescreen, and refer. Children who are labeled OK are judged not to be at risk. Those in the rescreen group should be rescreened within 8 to 10 weeks; children in the refer group should be referred for further evaluation. The cutoffs, which were established by analyzing the performance of the standardization sample, should be viewed with caution because of limitations associated with the selection of the standardization sample. The manual states that the authors welcome feedback.

Standardization.   The standardization sample consisted of 614 children between the ages of 3 years and 3 years, 11 months, 15 days. Although the manual provides information about the characteristics of the sample, it says little about how the sample was selected or how it was stratified.

Reliability. Reliability data for the ESI-3 are very limited. Only two studies are reported in the manual.

One study reports interscorer reliability between one tester and one observer for 115 tests. The coefficient is .98. In the second study, reporting test–retest reliability, eight examiners screened 33 children one week apart. The reliability coefficients ranged from .68 to .94.

Validity. The manual does not provide evidence of validity.

Summary. The Early Screening Inventory—3 is an individually administered, norm-referenced screening instrument. Information on reliability and validity is lacking. Additional studies need to be conducted before the usefulness of this instrument can be determined.

Early Screening Inventory

The Early Screening Inventory (ESI) (Meisels & Wiske, 1988) is a developmental screening instrument intended for use with four- to six-year-olds who may need special educational services. The ESI was designed to measure a child's ability to acquire new skills rather than to assess current level of achievement. The ESI was developed from the Eliot–Pearson Screening Inventory (EPSI), which was developed in 1975. Like other screening instruments, the ESI identifies children who may need additional assessment. It is available in English and Spanish versions.

The instrument has three main sections: visual–motor/adaptive, language and cognition, and gross motor/body awareness. The score sheet can be found in Figure 5.8. Like the ESI-3, none of the sections is intended to be used alone. In addition to these three sections, there are three other components: the Draw a Person task (DAP), letter formation, and a parent questionnaire. The parent questionnaire was revised as part of the restandardization of the ESI.

Administration. The ESI should be administered by professionals who have some formal background in early childhood development. Unlike several other screening instruments, no special instructions are given for setting up separate stations for the administration of the various sections. Several screeners can work simultaneously, however. It takes approximately 15 to 20 minutes to administer the ESI to a four- to six-year-old child. The parent questionnaire takes about 15 minutes to complete.

There are no special instructions for room arrangement, although a quiet area, free from distractions, is recommended. If several screeners work in the same room, partitions can be set up.

Scoring. Each item on the score sheet is scored pass, fail, or refuse. In addition, there is a space for the examiner to note comments. The examiner calculates the total points. Only a total ESI score can be calculated, since individual components do not have total scores. The parent questionnaire is not scored. It is intended to provide an overview of the child's development.

A child's raw score is compared with cutoff scores. There are three possible choices: OK, rescreen, and refer. Children who are labeled OK are judged not to be at risk. Those in the rescreen group should be rescreened within 8 to 10 weeks; children in the refer group should be referred for further evaluation. The cutoffs, which were established by analyzing the performance of the standardization sample, should be viewed with caution because of limitations associated with the selection of the standardization sample.

Standardization. The manual accompanying the ESI states that the standardization sample consisted of 465 children, between the ages of four and six years. The children were primarily Caucasian and came from urban families in the low to lower-middle socioeconomic range. The sample is biased and is not representative of four- to six-year-old children in the United States.

A restandardization of the ESI was conducted by Meisels, Henderson, Liaw, Browning, and Have (n.d.) from 1986 to 1990. Based on the 1980 census, 2,746 children from 11 states were tested. The children were divided into four subgroups according to age at half-year intervals ranging from 4 years to 5 years, 11 months.

Reliability. Reliability data for the ESI are very limited. Only two studies are reported in the manual.

One study reports interscorer reliability for three examiners who screened 18 children. The manual states that the percent of agreement between examiners was higher than .80.

A second study reports test–retest reliability. In this study, six examiners screened 57 children one week apart. The correlation for the subscales was below .80, and the correlation for the total ESI score was .82. Reliability information from the restandardization of the ESI (Meisels et al., n.d.) showed stronger, but fluctuating correlations among examiners.

Additional reliability studies need to be conducted. It is important for independent researchers to investigate the reliability of the ESI. Information about the characteristics of the sample, the qualifications of the examiners, and the specific outcomes (OK, rescreen, refer) should be described.

Validity. For an instrument to be valid, it must also be reliable. Given the limited information on reliability, the authors' discussion on validity should be viewed with caution.

The authors conducted an item analysis to determine whether the items on the ESI discriminate between children who pass the screening and those who are referred. Limited information on this item analysis is provided. The authors conclude that the items do discriminate between these two groups. No mention is made about the group that is labeled rescreen.

A concurrent validity study was conducted using the McCarthy Scales of Children's Abilities (MSCA) as the criterion. The ESI and the MSCA were administered to 102 children from six school systems in the Boston area. The children were primarily Caucasian. A correlation of .73 was obtained.

Two types of predictive validity study were conducted. A short-term predictive validity study was conducted with the Metropolitan Readiness Test. The two tests were administered between 7 months and 1 year apart to 472 children. The correlation between the two instruments was significant and ranged from .44 to .49. In a

Early Screening Inventory

S.J Meisels and M.S. Wiske

Score Sheet For Four To Six Year Olds

Child's name __James Doelittle__

Date of screening	82 /	4 /	12
	year	month	day

Date of birth	78 /	3 /	5
	year	month	day

Current age	4 /	1
	years	months

School __Adams__

Teacher __Jefferson__

Screener __Wiske__

Sex: male _✓_ female ___   Parent questionnaire completed? yes _✓_ no ___

Complete all columns that apply

	Pass	Fail	Refuse	Total Points Possible	Total Points Received	Comments
I. Initial Screening Items						
A. Draw a Person (DAP) Let's play some drawing games. Draw a picture of a person — a boy, girl, man, or woman. (When the child seems finished:) Are you finished? (Ask child to write his/her name or other letters he/she knows. Note pencil grasp and hand preference in comments.)						switched hands
Draw a Person (5 or more parts)	✓			1	1	overhand grip
II. Visual-Motor/Adaptive						"Hi Lady"- wearing a cowboy hat,
A. Copy Forms						very outgoing, warms up easily,
Draw one just like this on your paper. (Repeat up to three times.)						seems confident.
1. Copy ○	✓			1	1	
2. Copy +	✓			1	1	
3. Copy □		✓		1	0	rounded corner
4. Copy △		✓		1	0	big gap at apex

Complete all columns that apply

	Pass	Fail	Refuse	Total Points Possible	Total Points Received	Comments
B. Visual Sequential Memory Now we're going to play a hiding game with these pictures. I'm going to hide this one (○) here and this one (+) here. (Lay down cards, from child's left to right, as shown below.) Look at them carefully and remember where they are — this one here (pointing) and this one here (pointing). Now I'll turn them over. Point to where this one is hiding. (Hold up cards, one at a time, as shown in instruction manual.) (If second trials are needed:) Now let's try it a different way. (Repeat instructions.) (Put a check by correctly remembered figures.)						
1. Child +✓ ○✓ (Repeat once, if necessary) Examiner	✓			0	0	
2. Child ○ +✓ □ or, if fails +✓ □✓ ○✓ Examiner Examiner	✓			1	1	wanted to peek after cards were turned over
C. Block Building Gate (screen)						
Now we're going to build with blocks. First, I'm going to make a gate and when I finish I want to see if you can make one just like it. (Make gate behind screen. Remove screen.) Now you make one just like mine. (Give child 5 blocks.) (When child seems finished:) Is this just like the one I made?						
Gate (screen)		✓		3		
or, if fails — Gate (imitate)						
Watch how I make this one. (Construct gate.) Now you make one just like mine. (Give child 5 blocks.) (When child seems finished:) Is that just like the one I made?						
Gate (imitate)	✓			or 2	2	barely, not trying very hard

FIGURE 5.8 Early Screening Inventory Score Sheet for Four- to Six-Year-Olds

SOURCE: *Early Screening Inventory Test and Manual*, 2nd Edition, by Samuel J. Meisels and Martha Stone Wiske. Reprinted by permission of the publisher. (New York: Teachers College Press, © 1988 by Teachers College, Columbia University. All rights reserved), Figure 4.1: pp 26–29.

II. C. Block Building (continued)

bridge

	Pass	Fail	Refuse	Total Points Possible	Total Points Received	Comments
Complete all columns that apply

or, if fails — Bridge (screen)

Now I'm going to make a bridge. (Make bridge behind screen.)
Take a good look at this one. (Remove screen.)
Now you make one just like mine. (Give child 3 blocks.)
(When child seems finished:) Is this just like the one I made?

Bridge (screen)				or 1	—	

III. Language and Cognition

A. Number Concept

1. Counting
Count these blocks. Point to each one
and count out loud so that I can hear you.
(Put 10 blocks in random order on an
8 1/2" by 11" piece of paper.)

	Pass	Fail		Total Pts Possible	Total Pts Received	Comments
10 blocks		✓		2	0	pointed, but counted several
or, if fails – 5 blocks	✓			or 1	1	blocks twice,

2. Altogether
How many are there altogether?
(If child begins counting:)
See if you can tell me without counting.

was more organized with
fewer blocks

		Fail		Total	Received	
10 blocks	or, if fails – 5 blocks	✓		1	0	started to count again

B. Verbal Expression

Now I have some things I want you to tell me about.
Tell me all about this. (Give child object.)
Tell me more about it. (Say no more than once for each object.)
(If child demonstrates without using words:) Tell me with your words.
(If child has not responded to four categories, ask, as needed:)

What do we call it? or What is it?
What color is it?
What shape is it? (except car)
What can you do with it?

(Score 2 points for each unsolicited correct response.
1 point for each response elicited with a specific question.)

(Maximum score)	Name (2)	Color (2)	Shape (2)	Use (6)	Other (6)	Total Points Received
Ball	2	2	1	2,2,2	2	
Button	2	1	2	2	2,2,2	
Block	2	2	1	2	2	
Car	2	1		2	2,2	

Total score: **44**

Points received (0-3): **3**

0 - 5 = 0 pts.
6 - 20 = 1 pt.
21 - 35 = 2 pts.
36+ = 3 pts.

Child's Spontaneous Responses (2 pts.)	Response Elicited by Screener (1 pt.)
Ball: ball, red, you can bounce it, roll it, throw it. You can play games with it.	Ball: round
Button: button, round, sew it on your clothes, it got two holes.	Button: blue
Block: block, green build with it, it got corners	Block: square
Car: car, a steering wheel, tires, you can drive it	Car: yellow

(continued)

	Pass	Fail	Refuse	Total Points Possible	Total Points Received	Comments
C. Verbal Reasoning						
Now we are going to play some talking games. Listen carefully and finish what I want to say.						
1. Brother is a boy; sister is a ____.	✓			1	1	<u>girl</u> blurts out answers,
2. A horse is big; a mouse is ____.	✓			1	1	doesn't take time
3. A table is made of wood; a window of ____.		✓		1	0	<u>tiny</u> to think much
4. A bird flies; a fish ____.		✓		1	0	<u>wood</u>
D. Auditory Sequential Memory						<u>is a fish</u>
I'm going to say some numbers. Listen carefully and when I'm all through, say them right after me. (Say the digits one second apart.)						
1. 9,3 ✓✓ or, if fails – 2,6	✓			0	0	<u>9 – 3</u>
2. 5,1,6 ✓ or, if fails – 6,7,8 ✓✓✓	✓			1	1	<u>"6... what you say ?"</u>
3. 2,7,4,9 ✓✓✓ or, if fails – 5,9,6,3		✓		2	0	<u>"I don't know." "I can't ."</u>

IV. Gross Motor/Body Awareness

	Pass	Fail	Refuse	Total Points Possible	Total Points Received	Comments
A. Balance (2 of 3 attempts, on either foot)						
Now we're going to play some standing up games. I want to see how long you can balance on one foot like this. (Demonstrate.) See if you can do it while I count to ten. (Count at one second intervals.) (Try second foot if unsuccessful with first.)						
10 seconds		✓		2	0	<u>could only balance a few</u>
or 5 seconds		✓		or 1	0	<u>seconds on either foot</u>

B. Imitate Movements

Watch me carefully and make your arms do what mine do.

	Pass	Fail	Refuse	Total Points Possible	Total Points Received	Comments
Smooth: 2 or less corrected errors	✓			2	2	
or Hesitant: more than 2 corrected errors and/or 2 less uncorrected errors				or 1		
or More than 2 uncorrected errors				or 0		
C. Hop						
I want to see you hop five times on one foot like this. (Demonstrate. Repeat for the other foot. No more than three trials on each foot.)						
Five times on each foot		✓		2		
or, Twice on either foot	✓			or 1	1	
D. Skip						
Let me see you skip. (Demonstrate.)						
Skip: On both feet		✓		2	0	<u>sort of walk/gallop – "I</u>
or, Skip: On one foot				or 1	0	<u>can't do that."</u>

TOTAL SCREENING SCORE: __16__

FIGURE 5.8 (*continued*)

Other Information: (Not scored)

A. Color-matching problems: no _____ yes _____   Describe: _____

_____

(If child doesn't know the names of the colors, test for color blindness.)

B. Consonant errors: __s = th___ "We got a ticky cat" = kitty cat_____

Vocal errors: __no_____

Is speech intelligible? no _____

only in context _____

with articulation errors __✓__

yes __✓__

C. Uses complete sentences: yes __✓__ no _____

Uses incomplete sentences: yes _____ no _____

Uses sentences with language errors: yes __✓__ no _____   "it gots" – no big problems, though

Screening Decision: Refer _____ Rescreen _____ OK __✓__

ESI Cutoff Scores

Age range	Refer	Rescreen	OK
4-0 to 4-5	<11	11-15	>15
4-6 to 4-11	<13	13-17	>17
5-0 to 5-5	<16	16-20	>20
5-6 to 5-11	<18	18-22	>22

Comments: __charming little boy, happy to play games,_____

_____not eager to work hard_____

_____

_____

further analysis of the performance of these children, the ESI failed to identify 44 of them.

In a longitudinal predictive validity study, the authors correlated ESI scores with various outcome measures in grades kindergarten through four. Statistically significant correlation coefficients between the ESI and report card grades ranged from .31 (third grade) to .70 (kindergarten).

An additional predictive validity study was conducted using test scores derived from restandardization of the ESI. The results showed that the ESI moderately predicted MSCA scores. However, the correlation was lower for minority children and for children in the western part of the United States (Meisels et al., n.d.).

Summary.   The Early Screening Inventory is an individually administered, norm-referenced developmental screening test intended for four- to six-year-olds. Additional information concerning reliability is needed. Because of the limited amount of information about validity, results of this test should be carefully used.

SCREENING SPECIFIC DEVELOPMENTAL AREAS

The selected instruments previously described are designed to screen several developmental domains. However, sometimes there may be questions regarding only one specific area. For example, you may wonder whether a child who appears to be developing typically in every other respect is experiencing a language delay. Or perhaps you are concerned about a child's motor development. Screening instruments such as the Fluharty Preschool Speech and Language Screening Test or the Milani–Comparetti Motor Development Screening Test have been designed to screen specific areas and, as such, give more information about their respective domains than a general screening instrument. Specific screening instruments, however, should not be used in isolation; rather, these instruments should be made available, when needed, to supplement the comprehensive screening process.

PROFESSIONAL CONSIDERATIONS IN SCREENING YOUNG CHILDREN

Members of a screening team should keep in mind the following considerations.

- *Sensitivity to parent concerns.* Some parents are very anxious about the screening test. "Will this person find something wrong with my child?" may be a question that parents ask—or don't ask, although it is a matter of primary concern. Be sure that parents fully understand the reason for screening their child. An important component of any screening procedure is a period for answering parents' questions, either before or after the testing.

- *Surroundings.* The screening should be conducted in a setting that is quiet and free of distractions.

- *Familiarity of examiner.* Results will be more accurate if the practitioner allows time for the child to become familiar with the situation. Many children take time to "warm up" to strangers. If the child does not feel comfortable, the responses given may not reflect true ability.

- *Environmental influences.* The infant is subject to environmental influences that either support or impede development. The single most important aspect in the environment is the nurturing quality provided by the caregiver(s) (Meisels & Provence, 1989). Screening procedures should include systematic observations of the interaction between the infant and the primary caregiver.

- *Physical state.* The child's current health status should also be observed. Young children frequently have colds leading to middle ear infections (which may result in a temporary decrease in hearing). Does the child appear to be tired? If so, consider screening at another time. Don't forget that young children have a limited attention span. A child's attention may wander or be lost if the screen has too many test items.

- *Areas of development.* Although separate areas of development can be defined (motor, communication, cognition, etc.), these areas are not independent but interact in complex ways. Screening procedures should be comprehensive in coverage and should not focus on one or two developmental areas alone.

LIMITATIONS OF SCREENING

A screening is only a "snapshot" of a child's development at one point in time. Children should not be given a single screening test during the early childhood years; rather, screening procedures should be administered on a regular basis.

Some children who, in fact, do have a disability may pass through the screening without being identified for further assessment. The causes for such false-negative results may include lack of sensitivity of the screening instrument, lack of training or clinical knowledge of the evaluators, or any number of other factors.

Caveat

When children are given periodic screening tests, the same standardized instrument is often used. The many advantages of this practice include the ease and usefulness of comparing the child's development on subsequent administrations. Yet the effectiveness of the instrument is reduced by the cumulative effect of repeating items on periodic screenings and by the tendency of some caregivers to "practice" the items with the child.

The use of observations and the careful recording of data should be an integral aspect of periodic screening procedures. The members of the screening team may want to develop their own recording sheets, as described in Chapter 4.

FUTURE DIRECTIONS IN SCREENING

Historically, hospitals have been the primary environment for the medical screening of newborns. Infants with medical disorders, such as Down syndrome or spina bifida, were identified, too. Yet, the evolution of early intervention has necessitated the development of instruments and other methods to screen children in their early years. Screening methodologies and more refined instruments will continue to emerge. Screening tools designed to assess infants and toddlers must be developed with an adequate norming sample of representative children. Screening tools must also be developed which are accurate and consistent in the skill areas they are designed to measure.

Other screening methodologies may evolve as alternatives to screening instruments. Observations of infant behavior may hold promise in identifying children who may be at risk. For example, unusual infant cries may be related to the ability of the infant's nervous system to process and inhibit stimulation (Meisels & Wasik, 1990).

Screening will continue to evolve as the field of early intervention develops. As Meisels and Wasik (1990) have stated, "Identifying infants and toddlers at risk for developmental problems remains a task in which more is known about what doesn't work than what does" (p. 624).

PREFERRED PRACTICES

Developmental screening is a brief initial procedure in the identification of children who may be disabled, developmentally delayed, or gifted. Criteria for judging the usefulness of screening tests have been established and should be used in making judgments regarding the use of a screening instrument. It is important to use norm-referenced screening measures that are standardized in administration and scoring, reliable, and valid. Two additional criteria for screening tests are critical. The tests should be sensitive and specific. To minimize underreferrals, screening tests should yield few false negatives and should have high sensitivity. A screening test with a high specificity rate will minimize both false positives and overreferrals. The consequences of false negatives and false positives are considerable. Examiners must select and use screening tests with care.

A periodic screening process allows families and community service providers opportunities to request that a child be surveyed whenever questions or concerns arise or a family's situation changes. Parents' observations and concerns should be given highest priority.

Practitioners who are part of a screening team should consider the model of screening being implemented in their community. Some communities give a full evaluation to every infant referred by a parent or by a service provider who is sufficiently concerned to make the referral. Other communities use a multistep process in which a child who had elicited some concern during the first screening is rescreened. This second stage in a screening procedure is usually held 2 to 4 weeks later.

Some communities conduct screenings in a quick and careless manner. Practitioners in these communities should advocate changes and work to ensure the implementation of comprehensive screening procedures.

STUDY QUESTIONS AND SUGGESTED ACTIVITIES

1. What precautions should be made to avoid making false-positive and false-negative errors?
2. Why are specificity and sensitivity important concerns?
3. Suppose you were the coordinator of a screening program. What criteria would you use when setting up the program?
4. Why should planners of community screening never use screening procedures for which validation of outcomes is not available?
5. Conduct a comprehensive review of several screening instruments. Compare how they are administered, standardized, and scored. What do the manuals state about reliability and validity?
6. Visit a screening program in your community. Describe the procedures and instrument(s) used.

REFERENCES

Aylward, G. P. (in press). *Bayley infant neurodevelopmental screen*. San Antonio, TX: Psychological Corp.

American Academy of Pediatrics, Committee on Genetics. (1989). Newborn screening fact sheets. *Pediatrics, 83,* 449–464.

Apgar, V. (1953). A proposal for a new method of evaluation of the newborn infant. *Anesthesia and Analgesia, 32,* 260–267.

Brigance, A. H. (1985). *Brigance® preschool screen for three- and four-year-old children.* North Billerica, MA: Curriculum Associates.

Brigance, A. H. (1990). *Brigance® early preschool screen for two-year-old and two-and-one-half-year-old children.* North Billerica, MA: Curriculum Associates.

Fewell, R. R., & Langley, M. B. (1984). *Developmental activities screening inventory (DASI-II).* Austin, TX: Pro-Ed.

Frankenburg, W. K., & Dodds, J. B. (1990). *Denver II screening manual.* Denver: Denver Developmental Materials.

Frankenburg, W. K., Dodds, J., Fandal, A., Kazuk, E., & Cohrs, M. (1975). *Denver developmental screening test.* Denver: LA-DOCA Project and Publishing Foundation.

Harrison, P. L., Kaufman, A. S., Kaufman, N. L., Bruininks, R. H., Rynders, J., Ilmer, S., Sparrow, S. S., & Cicchetti, D. V. (1990). *AGS early screening profiles.* Circle Pines, MN: American Guidance Service.

Lichtenstein, R. (1984). *Preschool screening: Identifying young children with developmental and educational problems.* Orlando, FL: Grune & Stratton.

Mardell-Czudnowski, C., & Goldenberg, D. S. (1990). *Developmental indicators for the assessment of learning—Revised (DIAL-R).* Circle Pines, MN: American Guidance Service.

Meisels, S. J. (1988). Developmental screening in early childhood: The interaction of research and social policy. *American Review of Public Health, 9,* 527–550.

Meisels, S. J. (1989). Can developmental screening tests identify children who are developmentally at risk? *Pediatrics, 83,* 578–585.

Meisels, S. J., Henderson, L. W., Liaw, F., Browning, K., & Have, T. T. (n.d.). *New evidence for the effectiveness of the Early Screening Inventory—3.* (Available from S. J. Meisels, Center for Human Growth and Development, University of Michigan, Ann Arbor, MI 48109.)

Meisels, S. J., Henderson, L. W., Marsden, D. B., Browning, K. G., & Olson, K. A. (1991). *Early screening inventory—3.* Ann Arbor, MI: University of Michigan, Center for Human Growth and Development.

Meisels, S. J., & Provence, S. (1989). *Screening and assessment: Guidelines for identifying young disabled and developmentally vulnerable children and their families.* Washington, DC: National Center for Clinical Infant Programs.

Meisels, S. J., & Wasik, B. A. (1990). Who should be served? Identifying children in need of early intervention. In S. J. Meisels & J. P. Shonkoff (Eds.), *Handbook of early childhood intervention* (pp. 605–632). Cambridge: Cambridge University Press.

Meisels, S. J., & Wiske, M. S. (1988). *Early Screening Inventory.* New York: Teachers College Press.

Newborg, J., Stock, J. R., Wnek, L., Guidubaldi, J., & Sviniski, J. (1988). *Battelle developmental inventory screening test.* Allen, TX: DLM.

Peterson, N. (1987). *Early intervention for handicapped and at-risk children with special needs.* Denver: Love.

Salvia, J., & Ysseldyke, J. (1991). *Assessment.* Boston: Houghton Mifflin.

Sheenan, R. & Snyder, S. (1989–1990). Battelle Developmental Inventory and the Battelle Developmental Inventory Screening Test. *Diagnostique, 15,* 16–30.

Shepard, L. A. (1990). Readiness testing in local school districts: An analysis of backdoor policies. *Journal of Education Policy, 5,* 159–179.

Thurman, S. K., & Widerstrom, A. H. (1990). *Infants and young children with special needs.* Baltimore: Paul Brookes.

Widerstrom, A. H., Mowder, B. A., & Sandall, S. R. (1991). *At-risk and handicapped newborns and infants development, assessment, and intervention.* Englewood Cliffs, NJ: Prentice-Hall.

CHAPTER 6

Assessing Development

CHAPTER OBJECTIVES

This chapter focuses on assessing the child's general development and on the instruments used to gather comprehensive information about several different areas or developmental domains. Early childhood team members need to assess development for one of three reasons: (1) to determine the child's eligibility for services; (2) to assist the team in program planning; or (3) to monitor the child's progress.

Upon completing this chapter, you should be able to:

Differentiate various perspectives on development (including developmental, functional, and biological) as they relate to assessment.

Discuss the relationship between theory and practice in test design and selection.

Describe several commonly used tests for assessing development.

Key Terms

Developmental Approach. Development is conceptualized as the process of progressing through regular stages that may be qualitatively different, depending on individual differences.

Maturational Theory. A developmental theory that emphasizes the importance of the internal (to the child) features that are responsible for the child being "ready" to learn.

Developmental Milestones. The significant points in the child's development.

Cognitive Stages of Development. A developmental theory proposed by Jean Piaget that describes the progression (stages) of cognitive development in young children.

Schema. A term used by Piaget to describe an infant's organized response sequence.

Functional (Behavioral) Approach. An approach that emphasizes the importance of external (to the child) factors in assisting skill development.

Task Analysis. The process of assisting a child to acquire a certain skill or behavior by breaking it into a series of substeps.

Biological Approach. A medical approach that focuses on the infant's physical status and the relationship between this status and the physical and social aspects of the environment.

Adaptive–Transactive Perspective. A perspective that centers on the importance of the interaction between the infant, the social environment, and the physical environment.

THEORIES OF DEVELOPMENT

Everyone who works with young children should have a broad background not only in theories of learning but in knowledge of early childhood development. This background provides a basis for understanding some of the differences in assessment instruments. The differences are due, in part, to the way that different approaches, or theoretical models, are interpreted by the test developer.

Many theories of how children learn and develop were constructed by philosophers and psychologists during the first half of the twentieth century. These theories were later applied to education for different purposes and for different groups of children—some for children who were developing typically; others for children with disabilities, including those with substantial developmental delays. Generally speaking, these approaches can be said to represent three strands: developmental, functional, and biological orientations. Although these strands are discussed separately here, they are not mutually exclusive; in fact, there may be considerable overlap among them. As the field of early childhood special education continues to evolve, and new ways of gathering information about a child's development emerge, authors of tests may blend further these orientations. Currently, however, there are many well-known and frequently used instruments based on a specific theoretical approach.

Developmental Theory

Theorists who have focused on a *developmental approach* to understanding the growth of young children describe development of *all* children as the process of progressing through regular stages or periods. However, individual differences affect the amount of time a given child remains at a certain stage. Qualitative differences within stages may also be observed, depending on individual differences.

Emphasis on Maturation.   Early developmental theorists believed that maturation alone governed the child's development; in other words, a specific behavior matures through regular stages regardless of intervention practice. For example, an infant aged four to six months who is developing typically will begin exploring weight shifting while resting on her elbows and reaching for objects; between six and eight months she will acquire greater trunk rotation and weight shifting for rolling over from back to stomach and begin to crawl forward; between eight and ten months, increased skills in weight shifting and trunk rotation will assist her to come to a sitting position. The progress of maturation is measured in *developmental milestones.* These milestones, such as "first sits independently" or "takes her first step," were identified by gathering data about children who were developing typically. Arnold Gesell (1925), one of the early developmentalists, conducted extensive observations of young children and identified the ages at which children typically reach these milestones.

Optimum Periods for Development. The theory of optimum periods for development states that during the early years, a child is more responsive to certain experiences at some times than at other times. In some areas of development, these optimum periods may be *critical periods*—that is, the interval of time in which the child is most responsive to learning a skill.

Examples of skills developed during critical periods include visual or auditory discrimination skills; the ability to form attachments; and the ability to babble, to learn to crawl, and to walk (Peterson, 1987). For example, there may be a period in which an infant is most sensitive to receiving feedback of speech sounds. If the infant has no opportunity to obtain reactions to babbling, the production of these sounds may decrease.

Language acquisition is a highly complex and abstract process. Some contemporary linguistic theorists believe that an infant is innately endowed with a small set of linguistic universals. Chomsky (1972) believes that language (from this set of universals) develops with maturation.

Yet the importance of critical periods has been debated as well as the construct. Pellegrini and Dresden (1991) use the term *sensitive periods* for development to suggest that many of these conditions can be remedied through intervention.

Regulatory, Family, and Interactive Factors Model. A developmental model for working with children with emotional and developmental disorders proposed by Greenspan (1992) includes maturation factors as well as such environmental factors as family, community, and culture. According to Greenspan (1992), the child's social–emotional growth is organized within six developmental levels, which describe the child's ability to:

1. Attend to multisensory affective experience and at the same time organize a calm, regulated state and experience pleasure.
2. Engage with and evidence affective preference and pleasure for a caregiver.
3. Initiate and respond to two-way presymbolic, gestural communication.
4. Organize chains of two-way communication (opening and closing many circles of communication in a row), maintain communication across space, integrate affect polarities, and synthesize an emerging prerepresentational organization of self and other.
5. Represent (symbolize) affective experience (e.g., pretend play, function use of language).
6. Create representational (symbolic) categories and gradually build conceptual bridges between these categories. (pp. 5–6)

This model may be very helpful for practitioners in working with young children. The interested reader should refer to Greenspan's book *Infancy and Early Child-*

hood (1992) for in-depth information regarding the process of clinical assessment and therapeutic intervention.

Effect on Assessment Practices.   Assessment from the maturationist perspective is viewed as gathering information about the sequence of skills the child has mastered. Developmental assessment may include informal scales and checklists or commercial scales. Test instruments developed from this perspective usually include the following areas, or domains:

1. Motor: may be subdivided into fine and gross motor
2. Communication: usually subdivided into expressive and receptive language
3. Cognitive
4. Social/emotional
5. Adaptive

An early instrument, the Gesell Developmental Tests (now called the Gesell School Readiness Test), was based on the philosophy that readiness is a matter of maturation. Many school programs used these tests to place children in school programs or to prevent children from entering kindergarten until they were "ready." The prevailing philosophy was that the number of children experiencing school failure could be decreased by placing children in appropriate programs or by waiting a year in the hope that the child would reach the specified skill level.

Today, most preschool and public school programs embrace a different philosophy. Among educators there is a growing belief that *teachers and schools* must be prepared for all children rather than testing children to determine who is "ready." Thus, assessment is focused on locating the children who may have a disability (screening) and determining eligibility for early intervention or special education services. There are several norm-referenced developmental instruments that may be used to assist in determining eligibility for services. For example, the Bayley Scales of Infant Development—II or the Battelle Developmental Inventory, discussed later in this chapter, may be used for this purpose. Other developmental assessments examined in this chapter include numerous criterion-based instruments, which may be used for program planning and monitoring.

Cognitive Stages of Development

Piaget (1951, 1954, 1968) was one of the most influential developmental theorists in history. He emphasized the critical importance of the child's early years of development and described the interaction of early motor abilities with developing cognitive abilities. According to Piaget, there is a specific sequence in which behaviors occur and cognition develops as a child interacts with the environment. Thus, the child's early neural and motoric development affects later cognitive development. Early experiences are critical as the child moves from one stage to the next.

For Piaget, the *schema* according to which an infant's response sequence is organized is basic to early development. Thus, an infant responds in one way to certain stimuli. As the child receives more opportunities to respond to these stimuli, the schema become more stable and refined. When the child has continued opportunities to respond, the schema become infused into the response repertoire.

According to Piaget, children may differ with respect to the chronological age at which they pass through individual stages, but the specific order of the stages does not vary. Depending on the stages, the child's level of cognition varies widely. The four main stages are as follows.

- *Sensorimotor intelligence.* This stage is the first period of intellectual development in which schemas, or patterns of movement, become increasingly complex and refined. Certain reflexes present in newborns, such as sucking and grasping, are the basis for schemas. As reflexes elaborate into more refined responses, they will aid cognitive development. For example, as the child grows older, refined movements of the thumb and fingers make it possible to pick up an object and to explore the article not only by touch but by sight and taste. Refined motor movements allow the infant to explore various attributes of objects in the environment and to gain new knowledge. Children who are developing typically are found in this stage between the ages of birth and two years of age.

- *Preoperational thought.* During this stage, the child becomes capable of symbolic representations. For example, the child comes to understand that a certain symbol represents a real object. The child also begins to think and talk about objects and people not physically present. This stage typically is observed in children between the ages of two and seven years.

- *Concrete operations.* In this stage, the child begins to form complex and well-organized cognitive processes. The child can start with a concrete idea and mentally put one or more concepts together or make hierarchical classifications of concepts. This period usually begins at age seven and lasts through age eleven.

- *Formal operations.* In the final stage, which characteristically begins after eleven years of age, the child no longer requires a concrete reference to think in terms of what is possible. Thinking involves abstractions, hypothetical ideas, or theoretical concepts.

Effect on Assessment Practices.   Several assessment instruments have been based on Piaget's theory of cognitive stages of development. The items in these instruments are arranged in an ordinal progression through the various cognitive stages. Perhaps the most frequently used instrument is the Infant Psychological Development Scales by Uzgiris and Hunt (1975) and adapted by Dunst (1980). This instrument, which focuses on the sensorimotor intelligence stage, is discussed in more detail later in this chapter.

Much has been written regarding the usefulness of Piagetian instruments. Since many of these assessment tools lack adequate technical information regarding norming population, reliability, and validity, they are not appropriate for determining a child's eligibility for services. However, the use of these instruments for purposes of program planning and monitoring may be valuable for practitioners and programs that incorporate a Piagetian philosophy.

Other instruments have been developed to measure cognitive growth in children. One of the early instruments, the Griffiths Mental Development Scales, published in 1954, gave an overall mental age and an intelligence quotient.

The Developmental Perspective Today

Today, most developmental theorists hold that nature, or the genetic influence, and nurture, or the influence of the environment, are interdependent and that both the child's biological inheritance and the natural environment are important to development. For example, Anya, a three-month-old infant, is much more active than Jessica who is the same age. The level of activity may be due to biological factors, including level of hormones, or to such prenatal environmental factors as mother's consumption of alcohol or use of tobacco, or it may be influenced by social expectations and care. Most probably, according to many developmental theorists, two or more of these factors interact.

Some authors (Meltzoff & Kuhl, 1989; Notari, Cole, & Mills, 1992; Zelazo & Barr, 1989) have expressed concern over a continued emphasis on theories of development, which may not represent current clinical assumptions and practice. For example, an infant's ability to "recognize" visual stimuli has long been thought to begin with black and white inanimate patterns. Facial imitation was thought to emerge later. However, current infant research challenges theories of early development regarding an infant's ability to process visual stimuli. Meltzoff and Kuhl (1989) have found that newborns, in the first hours and days, can duplicate an adult experimenter's facial gestures. These authors also report support for their findings in the work of other independent researchers. The new findings suggest to some that neonates have the ability to recognize similarities in body changes they see and ones they make themselves (Meltzoff & Kuhl, 1989).

Findings such as these both enhance our understanding of the beginnings of psychological development and directly affect assessment practices. Infant research is a large and growing field, which will serve to increase our knowledge and assist in strengthening theory and practice in the years to come. Readers interested in further reading are encouraged to investigate the following:

> Bredekamp, S. (Ed.). (1987). *Developmentally appropriate practice in early childhood programs serving children from birth through age 8.* Washington, DC: National Association for the Education of Young Children.
>
> Carta, J. J., Schwartz, I. S., Atwater, J. B., & McConnell, S. R. (1991). Developmentally appropriate practice: Appraising its usefulness for young children with disabilities. *Topics in Early Childhood Special Education, 11*(1), 1–20.
>
> National Association for the Education of Young Children and the National Association of Early Childhood Specialists in State Departments of Education. (1991). *Position statement: Guidelines for appropriate curriculum content and assessment in programs serving children ages 3 through 8* (NAEYC No. 725). Washington, DC: National Association for the Education of Young Children.
>
> Zelazo, P. R., & Barr, R. G. (Eds.). (1989). *Challenges to developmental paradigms: Implications for theory, assessment, and treatment.* Hillsdale, NJ: Lawrence Erlbaum Associates.

Functional (Behavioral) Approach

The *functional approach* emphasizes the importance of factors *external* to the child for assisting skill development. Behaviors are learned; skills do not just appear.

The functional approach is sometimes referred to as the *behavioral approach* because it is based on operant learning theory from the field of psychology.

Among the principal contributors to *behaviorist–associationist* theories were John Watson, who became one of the early leading researchers, and Thorndike, Pavlov, Gutherie, Hull, and Skinner. One of the most important principles associated with this approach, the *law of reinforcement,* states that a reinforcing event that follows a behavior will strengthen that behavior and serve to increase the chance that the behavior will occur again. A second important principle is that an *antecedent,* or event that precedes a behavior, will increase the likelihood of the behavior reoccurring if the behavior is reinforced when it occurs and not reinforced when it does not (Skinner, 1953).

Some contemporary theorists have focused on *learning theory* and its relation to improving instruction. Robert Gagné (1985) has been concerned with making traditional learning principles more applicable to contemporary learning situations. He developed a hierarchy of skills and rules for sequencing instruction.

Much of the work from the behavioral–associationist theorists has been adapted by practitioners in the field of special education and has provided a framework for the development of teaching strategies. Many of these strategies have been applied most successfully to children with severe developmental delays or significant behavior problems as well as children with moderate disabilities. These teaching strategies assist children in acquiring critical skills to improve functioning in normalized settings. Some useful ideas in this area are as follows.

1. Describing the goals of an educational program in concrete behavioral terms so that target skills can be measured and the child's progress evaluated.
2. Analyzing the target skill into small, discrete, sequential steps (task analysis).
3. Planning teaching and learning activities that focus on the simplest components of the target skill.
4. Linking the learned component(s), or subskills, from the task analysis to achieve the more complex target skill (chaining).
5. Encouraging active responding.
6. Carefully watching for the effect on the individual child to determine what is reinforcing and what is not.
7. Carefully arranging environments (settings) and events (antecedents) to elicit behaviors that one wishes to reinforce and thus increase.
8. Looking to the child's everyday routines, rather than to theory or to formal tests, to determine what skills should be taught.

The functional approach emphasizes the skills children will need to live and play in their natural environment—skills in the areas of home, community, leisure/recreation, and (later) vocational (Snell, 1987). Data collection and monitoring are an important aspect of the learning process. Strain et al. (1992) state that behaviorism has been the conceptual foundation for many current "best practices" in early childhood special education.

Effect on Assessment Practices.   The principles of behavioral associationism provide a framework for gathering information regarding factors that cause or sustain certain inappropriate behaviors in young children. Chapter 11 describes the application of these principles and useful tools at greater length.

Commercial instruments are also available. Typically these tests are divided into areas of functioning that incorporate skills the child needs to be able to participate more fully within the natural environment. Test items are typically grouped in the following areas:

Eating

Toileting

Dressing

Receptive language

Expressive language

Motor skills

Attention span

Some of these categories focus on communication; some areas focus on self-help or adaptive behavior skills. (What is the difference between self-help and adaptive areas? Assessment instruments developed prior to 1992 generally classified items such as feeding, toileting, and dressing under "self-help skills." However, the 1991 amendments to the Individuals with Disabilities Education Act, reauthorizing Part H (PL 102–119), uses new terminology. For example, the term "self-help" has been replaced by "adaptive development.")

Generally each skill is subdivided into several component steps. Some commercial tests include areas that may be very helpful for certain children. For example, Help for Special Preschoolers, which was developed by staff members of the Santa Cruz County Office of Education (1987), includes the area "sign language skills." Figure 6.1 illustrates the items from this category. Instruments such as this checklist are helpful in program planning, monitoring, or evaluating the child's progress.

Readers interested in the functional approach are encouraged to investigate the following resources:

Neisworth, J. (1985). A behaviorist approach to early childhood education. In D. Peters, J. Neisworth, & T. Yawkey, *Early childhood education: From theory to practice* (pp. 85–213). Monterey, CA: Brooks/Cole.

Snell, M. E. (Ed.) (1987). *Systematic instruction for persons with severe handicaps* (3rd ed.). Columbus, OH: Merrill.

Biological Approach

The *biological approach* focuses on the physical state of the child and originates within the fields of neurology and pediatrics. Historically, this approach has been used in hospitals and neonatal intensive care units to assess preterm and at-risk infants. Today, treatment and care of high-risk infants is a rapidly growing area. Early intervention and pediatric practitioners with backgrounds from education, medicine, occupational therapy, psychology, and social work are working increasingly in clinics or hospital settings to evaluate the status of the child and to plan treatment

AGE	ID#	SKILL/BEHAVIOR	DATE	DATE	COMMENT
		16. SIGN LANGUAGE skills			
2.0-3.0	16.01	Watches face and body of speaker to get clues as to meaning of signed communication			
2.6-3.2	16.02	Responds to single signs pertaining to own wants or needs when signed by another			
2.6-3.4	16.03	Imitates single signs expressing own wants or needs when signed by another			
3.0-3.6	16.04	Produces single signs expressing own wants without a model			
3.0-3.8	16.05	Uses 1 sign for many related things or for similarly formed signs			
3.0-4.0	16.06	Uses face and body to give clues to meaning of signs			
3.0-4.0	16.07	Smiles/frowns for clue to meaning of signed communication			
3.0-4.2	16.08	Uses hands, arms, feet, shoulders to add expression of signs			
3.0-3.6	16.09	Responds to sign for own name when signed by another			
3.2-3.6	16.10	Imitates sign for own name when signed by another			

FIGURE 6.1 Sign language skills in Help for Special Preschoolers

SOURCE: Reprinted by permission of VORT Corporation from *Help for Special Preschoolers Assessment Checklist* © 1987 Santa Cruz County Office of Education.

and/or intervention strategies. In this rapidly expanding field, early intervention specialists often assist in assessing the interaction between the child and the child's environment. This approach, known as an *adaptive–transactive perspective,* emphasizes the importance of the reciprocity between the child's temperament and behavior and the caregiver's response.

Temperament.   A visit to a newborn nursery reveals many individual differences in babies: Some infants appear to be irritable and cry frequently, while others cry but are easily soothed by the soft voice of the nurse. The general features of temperament were first described by Thomas, Chess, and Birch (1970; see also Thomas & Chess, 1977). The features that comprise the construct of temperament are:

- Rhythmicity
- Mood
- Activity
- Adaptability
- Distractibility
- Persistence
- Threshold
- Intensity
- Approach

Differences in temperament appear to be open to experiential influences (Kagan, Snidman, Reznick, Gibbons, & Johnson, 1989; Lewis, 1989; Thomas & Chess, 1977).

A comprehensive assessment of a newborn at risk usually involves examination of temperament as part of a neurobehavioral workup. O'Donnell and Oehler (1989) described this approach to gather information concerning:

1. Neurological integrity and developmental status of the nervous system (to plan a supportive social and physical environment for the preterm infant)
2. Behavioral organization and needs (to evaluate the effects of a biomedical event or to assess the effects of medical or environmental intervention strategies)
3. Temperament (to evaluate how the infant will contribute to the establishment of a relationship with the parents and other primary caregivers)

The primary focus in the biological approach is to assess the functioning level of the child's central nervous system and the reciprocal effects of the central nervous system and the child's environment in overall development. Two aspects of the environment are examined:

1. Physical aspects (such as intensity of light, decibel level of noise, quality and type of sounds, or type of visual stimuli present)
2. Social aspects (such as amount of touching or handling, amount of time holding or carrying the infant, soft talking, or degree of eye contact between caregiver and infant)

Effect on Assessment Practices.   There appears to be some evidence that assessment within this framework can be used across cultures. Barr (1989) reports that "the pattern of early infant crying may well be a behavioral universal of early infancy, while the overall quantity (bout length) of infant crying is sensitive to variations in infant caretaking practice" (p. 58).

HIGH-RISK NEWBORN AND INFANT ASSESSMENT INSTRUMENTS

Assessment of high-risk newborns and infants provides critical knowledge about the functioning of infant biological systems as well as providing information about individual children that is helpful to parents and caregivers. For example, preterm and high-risk infants, who may be affected by the positioning, handling, or movements of the caregiver, require special care. The Neonatal Behavioral Assessment Scale and the Assessment of Preterm Infant Behavior may serve as teaching tools for parents while being used for their primary purpose, which is to gather medical information about the infant.

Neonatal Behavioral Assessment Scale

The Neonatal Behavioral Assessment Scale (NBAS), developed by Brazelton (1984), is designed for newborns whose gestation period exceeded 37 weeks. The Brazelton scale can be used from birth through one month of age to diagnose neurological disabilities and to determine early individual differences (Tronick & Brazelton, 1975). The test items include observations of the presence of reflexes, behavior responses, predominant states of the infant during the assessment, and self-quieting activities used by the infant during this period. The Brazelton scale is a commonly used tool to assess an infant's best performance regarding neurological and behavioral responses. Reliability and validity information are included in the test manual.

Some examiners prefer to use this instrument in the presence of the child's parents so that they can readily observe the infant's skills and sensitivity to the social environment. Parents learn how to handle and position the baby in addition to acquiring strategies to facilitate certain behaviors. For families who are learning to cope with an infant who is very disabled, this information may prove to be invaluable. "This relatively simple treatment may help parents learn that their babies are skillful and may also promote significant changes in parenting skills and knowledge of child development" (Widerstrom, Mowder, & Sandall, 1991, p. 139). However, Wolff (1989) urges caution in the use of this diagnostic tool as an intervention procedure without further research into the effectiveness of the strategy.

Assessment of Preterm Infant Behavior

The Assessment of Preterm Infant Behavior (APIB) (Als, Lester, Tronick, & Brazelton, 1982a, 1982b) includes many items from the Neonatal Behavioral Assessment Scale and was designed to enhance and extend the Brazelton scale to preterm and high-risk infants. For example, a very-high-risk infant may display various communicative signals that do not include the use of sound. Communication may be visceral (coming from the infant's body), such as facial color changes that may indicate stress, motor signals such as postural changes, state-related signals such as hyperalert, or neurological changes such as tremors or startles. The APIB assists in interpreting these signals. Once familiar with these signs, caregivers are able to optimize the infant's current level of development within activities of daily routine.

INSTRUMENTS FOR ASSESSING INFANTS AND TODDLERS

Most of the tools for assessing infants include the evaluation of early social–emotional development, or temperament and early motor skills, including reflexes. An infant's reflexes are important precursors to early motor skills. A few reflexes are typically present just before or at birth. A good example is the *Moro reflex:* an extension of the arms outward, followed by a return movement of the arms in a flexed position close to the body. This response is important because it encourages the infant in a new motor pattern from the flexed position in utero. The Moro reflex typically disappears at about six months. However, if it persists for too long, it interferes with balance and movement.

Many reflexes gradually disappear in infants who are developing typically. Other reflexes usually appear and persist, such as the palmar hand grasp. Table 6.1 describes reflex development, indicating reflexes that typically persist and those that typically disappear.

Many of the instruments designed for children from birth through two years measure the existence of reflexes. Applicable test items might include "held standing—lifts foot" from the Early Learning Assessment Profile (Glover, Preminger, & Sanford, 1978) or "makes stepping movement," from the Brigance® Diagnostic Inventory of Early Development—Revised (Brigance, 1991). Assessment of the young child's reflexes provides important information about neuromotor development. Persistence of some responses such as the asymmetric tonic neck reflex (ATNR) results in the head turned persistently in a lateral position as shown in Figure 6.2. As the child attempts to bring a desired object closer to view, the abnormal

TABLE 6.1   Reflex development in infants

Behavior	Description	Emergence	Outcome
Moro reflex	Infant first extends arms with hands open and then brings them back to a flexed position.	Birth	Disappears between 3 and 5 months
Asymmetrical tonic neck reflex (ATNR)	When an infant's head is turned to one side, the arm and leg on the same side are extended; the opposite arm and leg remain in a flexed position.	First weeks following birth	Disappears by 5 months
Stepping reflex	Infant makes stepping movements when held in an upright position with feet touching surface.	Birth	Continues for life
Palmar grasp	Infant's fingers grasp object when touched to palm.	Birth	Disappears at 3 to 4 months as a reflex; continues as a voluntary response
Parachute reflex	Infant extends arms and legs (as if to break a fall).	6–7 months	Persists throughout life

reflex turns the head away and inhibits the free movement of the head and affected shoulder and arm. As a consequence, when the baby is placed in the prone position, reaching out, seeing, and manipulating objects in the environment will be difficult.

Other test items measure early motor control. These items are usually based on principles of growth and development. One such principle is *cephalocaudal development,* according to which infants develop motor control from the head downward; another principle is *proximal–distal development,* namely, that infants develop motorically from the center outward to the limbs. These principles are reflected on the first three items of the gross motor section of the Carolina Curriculum for Infants and Toddlers with Special Needs by Johnson-Martin, Jens, Attermeier, and Hacker (1991):

a. Lifts head, freeing nose; arms and legs flexed
b. Lifts head to 45 degree angle; arms and legs partially flexed
c. Extends head, arms, trunk, and legs in prone position (p. 15)

FIGURE 6.2   Asymmetrical tonic neck reflex in the supine position

SOURCE: *Program Guide for Infants and Toddlers* by Frances P. Connor, G. Gordan Williamson, and John M. Siepp. Reprinted by permission of the publisher. (Public Domain after 1983.) (New York: Teachers College Press, © 1978 by Teachers College, Columbia University. All rights reserved), p. 105.

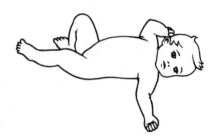

Adjusting for Prematurity

Infants who are born at full term have a gestational period of approximately 38 to 40 weeks. Infants born prematurely have a shorter (or much shorter, depending on the degree of prematurity) gestational period. In assessing infants and young children, some practitioners wonder whether to adjust the chronological age of premature infants. Should they, for example, give to a child who is 12 weeks old but was born 8 weeks prematurely an adjusted chronological age of 4 weeks? Some practitioners feel that this is a reasonable procedure (Rossetti, 1990), and some instruments allow the evaluator to compute an adjusted age.

A rationale for the use of age adjustment can be made (Wilson, 1987); yet little research has been done to support the technique. Siegel (1983) studied two different groups of demographically matched infants. The first group of 80 preterm infants and 58 full-term infants was followed for 5 years; the second group of 81 preterm infants and 63 full-term infants was followed for 3 years. The children were administered the Bayley Scales at 4, 8, 12, 18, and 24 months, and at 5 years were given several other standardized assessments that measure cognitive, language, and motor abilities. He found that the uncorrected scores of the infants born prematurely were significantly lower than those of the infants born full term (with the exception of some language measures at 5 years). A second finding was that the corrected scores were significantly lower in the younger children but were not lower at 5 years. Siegel concluded that adjusting for prematurity appears to be appropriate in the first few months; in older infants, slightly more accurate predictions are obtained by using the uncorrected scores. Siegel notes that the test scores of very young infants are influenced by the degree of biological maturity, but older infants are influenced by the environment.

Aylward (1986) conducted a study of 302 infants (236 infants who were developing typically and 66 infants who had a neurological dysfunction). The children had different degrees of prematurity. He found that the use of an adjusted age did not appear to "cover up" dysfunction in babies at 9 and 18 months.

Additional studies in the use of age adjustment and prematurity are needed. Caution is suggested in using this procedure in the assessment process until further research has been completed.

PRECAUTIONS IN ASSESSING INFANTS AND TODDLERS

One of the problems in assessing very young children is the low predictive validity of many of the assessment tools in use today. Much research remains to be completed regarding the assessment of very young children, and the ability of various measures to predict later performance needs to be evaluated. Predictive validity may be influenced by the nature of certain traumas. For example, dysfunction observed in certain infants may present only minor difficulties by the time they have reached toddler age because of the nature of the trauma and the eventual decrease of the initial neurologic dysfunction. Children who have experienced *birth asphyxia* (an unconscious condition of suffocation due to lack of oxygen and a buildup of carbon dioxide) or *intracranial hemorrhage* (bleeding within the skull area) display neurologic dysfunction as infants (Rossetti, 1990). Practitioners must be aware of the limitations of the information gathered and should monitor the child's progress over a period of the first three years.

Predictive validity is also influenced by environmental factors. Lack of good nurturing can affect the child in a negative way; early intervention services can affect the child's development in a positive way.

Many traditional instruments require the cooperation of the child on tasks presented by the practitioner. Unlike older children, very young children who are capable of performing the task at hand may have little motivation to complete it.

Young children with neuromotor or language delays may be unable to complete test items that rely on movement or expressive language. Temperament and behavioral issues may also interfere with obtaining an accurate picture of the very young child's development.

The familiarity of the practitioner and of the environment can also affect the cooperation and motivation of the very young child. Any and all of these factors may depress the child's performance and result in an underestimation of the child's ability. Such errors can have long-lasting effects for the child, parents, and caregivers.

CORE BATTERIES

Infants and toddlers with suspected or known disabilities are often referred for a battery of standardized developmental tests. Common instruments employed are Brazelton's Neonatal Behavioral Assessment Scale, the Assessment of Preterm Infant Behavior, and the Uzgiris–Hunt Scales of Infant Psychological Development. Other common batteries that extend beyond the birth through two years range include the Bayley Scales of Infant Development—II and the Battelle Developmental Inventory. The core battery is supplemented with more detailed examinations in the area(s) of concern by specialists in that discipline. For example, vision and hearing are also assessed. This additional testing could include domain-specific instruments and/or observation and informal assessment by a specialist depending on the infant's responses to the core assessment.

Many of the commonly used instruments in home- and center-based programs for infants and toddlers include a combination of test instrument and curriculum suggestions to assist in planning activities to promote skill development. Examples of these instruments include the Assessment, Evaluation, and Programming System, the Carolina Curriculum for Infants and Toddlers with Special Needs, the Early Intervention Developmental Profile, and the Hawaii Early Learning Profile. Many of the instruments are criterion referenced and include items in several different developmental domains.

When you review an instrument, be sure to examine the developmental areas covered. Does the instrument cover the domains you may need to address in accordance with the federal definition of developmental delay?

What is a development delay? A delay in one or more of the following:

- Cognitive development
- Physical development (which includes fine and gross motor)
- Communication development

- Social/emotional development
- Adaptive development

Assessment, Evaluation, and Programming System for Infants and Children (AEPS)

Volume 1 of the Assessment, Evaluation, and Programming System (AEPS) (Bricker, 1992) is a system for linking assessment, program planning, and monitoring of progress of children from birth to three years. The system includes (1) the AEPS Test, a criterion-referenced test for children; (2) the AEPS Family Report, a questionnaire, which may be completed by a family member to report the child's abilities; (3) the AEPS Family Survey, another questionnaire, which may be completed by a family member to help identify interests and concerns; (4) the AEPS Assessment Activity Plans, a collection of suggestions for assessing children (or individual children) during group activities; (5) the AEPS Curriculum for Birth to Three Years, Vol. 2 (Cripe, Slentz, & Bricker, 1992), a separate book containing programming steps and suggested activities; and (6) the AEPS Child Progress Record, a report used to record the child's current abilities, intervention plan, and progress.

The AEPS Test measures the developmental period from one month to three years of age. According to Bricker (1992), most of the items are appropriate for a child whose chronological age is from birth to six years but who is functioning within the range of 1 to 36 months. The AEPS Test covers six domains: fine motor, gross motor, adaptive, cognitive, social–communication, and social.

Test items are sequenced and grouped by skill (Figure 6.3). The items are stated in general, functional terms so that the practitioner may use the actual test item for an individualized outcome or objective on the child's IFSP. In addition, Appendix B of the AEPS contains a list of goals (or outcomes) and objectives from each of the domains for the IEP or IFSP:

Gross Motor Domain
Strand A: Movement and Locomotion in Supine and Prone Position

G1 When on back, the child will turn head, move arms, and kick legs independently of each other.

1.1 When on back, the child will turn head to the right and the left, at least 45° from midline position.

1.2 When on back, the child will alternately kick one leg and then the other.

1.3 When on back, the child will wave arms.

G2 The child will roll from stomach to back and from back to stomach by shifting weight to one side of the body, leading with head, shoulder, or hip.

2.1 The child will roll from back to stomach by shifting weight to one side of the body, leading with head, shoulder, or hip.

2.2 The child will roll from stomach to back by shifting weight to one side of the body, leading with head, shoulder, or hip.

G3 The child will creep forward at least 6 feet bearing weight on hands and knees using alternating arm and leg movements (i.e., moving one arm

Gross Motor Domain

S = Scoring Key	Q = Qualifying Notes
2 = Pass consistently	A = Assistance provided
1 = Inconsistent	B = Behavior interfered
performance	R = Reported assessment
0 = Does not pass	M = Modification/adaptation
	D = Direct test

Name: _____

Test Period: ____ ____ ____ ____
Test Date: __/__ __/__ __/__ __/__
Examiner: ____ ____ ____ ____

	IEP	S	Q	S	Q	S	Q	S	Q
A. Movement and locomotion in supine and prone position									
1. Moves body parts independently of each other									
1.1 Turns head past 45°									
1.2 Kicks legs									
1.3 Waves arms									
2. Rolls by turning segmentally									
2.1 Rolls: back to stomach									
2.2 Rolls: stomach to back									
3. Creeps forward using alternating arm and leg movements									
3.1 Rocks in creeping position									
3.2 Assumes creeping position									
3.3 Crawls forward on stomach									
3.4 Pivots on stomach									
3.5 Bears weight while reaching									
3.6 Lifts head/chest off surface									
B. Balance in sitting									
1. Assumes balanced sitting position									
1.1 Assumes hands and knees position from sitting									
1.2 Regains balanced sitting after reaching									
1.3 Regains balanced sitting after leaning									

FIGURE 6.3 Items from the AEPS assessment log for the gross motor domain

SOURCE: AEPS *Measurement for Birth to Three Years* by Diane Bricker (Ed.). Baltimore, MD: Paul H. Brookes Publishing Co., 1992, p. 267. Reprinted by permission.

and opposite leg, then other arm and opposite leg); stomach remains lifted off surface.

3.1 The child will rock back and forth at least two consecutive times while on hands and knees in a creeping position; stomach remains lifted off surface.

3.2 The child will assume a creeping position on hands and knees with stomach lifted off surface.

3.3 The child will crawl forward at least 2 feet with stomach touching the surface, pulling with both arms and supporting weight on hands and/or arms; legs alternately bend and straighten.

3.4 When on stomach, the child will pivot 180° in each direction in a semicircle.

3.5 When on stomach, the child will reach with each hand by supporting weight on one hand and/or arm while reaching toward object with the opposite hand.

3.6 The child will lift head and chest off surface with weight on bent or straight arms; head is in midline.

Strand B: Balance in Sitting

G1 The child will move to a sitting position on the floor from any position (e.g., creeping, lying down, standing).

1.1 From a sitting position, the child will move to a hands and knees position by using rotation (i.e., reaching across the body with either arm and shifting weight to knees).

1.2 The child will move back to a balanced, upright sitting position after reaching across the body to the right and to the left.

1.3 The child will move back to a balanced, upright sitting position after leaning to the left, to the right, and forward.

1.4 The child will sit in an upright position with back straight and hands not touching the floor for balance for at least 30 seconds.

1.5 When placed in sitting position, the child will use hands for balance and hold head in midline for at least 60 seconds.

1.6 When sitting in a supported position (e.g., supported by adult's hands), the child will hold head in midline for at least 30 seconds.

G2 The child will sit down in and get out of child-size chair.

2.1 The child will sit down in child-size chair.

2.2 The child will maintain sitting position in child-size chair without support.

Strand C: Balance and Mobility in Standing and Walking

G1 When walking unsupported, the child will move to avoid obstacles (e.g., toys, furniture, people).

1.1 The child will walk without support for at least 6 feet.

1.2 The child will walk when holding onto support with one hand for at least 15 feet.

1.3 The child will walk when holding onto support with two hands for at least 15 feet.

1.4 The child will stand alone for at least 30 seconds with back straight and head in midline.

1.5 The child will cruise (i.e., side-step to the left and to the right) while holding onto a stable support (e.g., couch, coffee table, wall) for at least 3 feet.

G2 The child will stoop by bending at waist or squat by bending knees to reach an object and will stand back up without support.

2.1 From a sitting position on the floor, the child will stand up without support.

2.2 From a sitting, kneeling, and/or creeping position, the child will pull to a standing position using a support (e.g., low table, chair).

2.3 From a sitting and/or creeping position, the child will pull to a kneeling position using a support (e.g., low table, chair).

G3 The child will walk up and down stairs. (The child may or may not use one-hand support and may or may not alternate feet.)

3.1 The child will walk up and down stairs using two-hand support (e.g., railings, adult's hands). (Child may or may not alternate feet.)

3.2 The child will move up and down stairs by creeping, crawling, and/or scooting on buttocks.

3.3 The child will climb onto and off of a low, stable structure (e.g., low step, raised platform).

Strand D: Play Skills

G1 The child will jump forward with feet together.

1.1 The child will jump up with feet together.

1.2 The child will jump from a low, stable structure (e.g., low step, raised platform, curb). (Bricker, 1993, pp. 89–90)

Administration.   The AEPS test was designed to be used by teachers and therapists working directly with the child. The AEPS Family Report and the AEPS Family Interest Survey may be completed by family members. The Family Report (Figure 6.4) contains items that correspond to the six domains in the AEPS Test (only the more detailed items in each strand are eliminated). Items in the fine and gross motor areas are also illustrated. At the end of each section, there is an area for the family member to fill in priority goals.

The AEPS Family Interest Survey consists of questions in three main areas around the child, the family, and the community. This information may be helpful to the family and practitioner in identifying interests and concerns to address in the IFSP.

Scoring.   Items on the AEPS Test may be assessed by observation, direct test, or by report. The possible scores are pass consistently (2), inconsistent performance (1), and fail consistently (0). The recording sheets allow the examiner to record additional information about each item, such as whether assistance was provided or the item was modified (qualifying notes A and M in Figure 6.4). Item scores are totaled for each domain, and a percent score is calculated. A summary page lists each of the domains with space for recording information on four separate occasions.

Gross Motor Domain

1. Does your child move arms, legs, and head separately while lying on his or her back? For example, your child waves both arms without kicking, or turns his or her head to the side without waving arms or kicking legs.

2. Does your child roll over from back to stomach *and* stomach to back, getting both arms out from under the body?

3. Does your child crawl forward at least 2 feet by alternating arms and legs? For example, your child will move one arm and opposite leg, then the other arm and opposite leg.

4. Does your child get to a sitting position on the floor from any position (e.g., standing, lying down, hands and knees) without help?

5. Does your child get into and out of a child-size chair without help?

6. Without help, does your child *walk* around large toys, furniture, or people without bumping into them?

7. Does your child bend over at the waist or bend at the knees to reach an object on the floor, and then stand back up without sitting down or leaning on something?

8. Does your child walk up and down stairs without help? He or she may walk with one or two feet on each stair and may or may not hold onto the railing with one hand.

9. Does your child jump forward with feet together?

(continued)

FIGURE 6.4 Items from the AEPS Family Report, gross motor domain

SOURCE: *AEPS Measurement for Birth to Three Years* by Diane Bricker (Ed.). Baltimore, MD: Paul H. Brookes Publishing Co., 1992, pp. 299–300. Reprinted by permission.

10. Does your child pedal with both feet while steer-
    ing a tricycle forward at least 5 feet?

11. Without help, does your child *run* around large toys,
    furniture, or people without bumping into them?

Y = Yes; S = Sometimes; N = Not Yet.

FIGURE 6.4   (*continued*)

Items on the AEPS Family Report are scored as Y (yes), S (sometimes), and N (not
yet).

Standardization.   The AEPS is a criterion-referenced instrument and is not
norm referenced. Children who participated in the reliability and validity studies
ranged in age from two months to six years and were involved in early intervention
programs in Oregon, Washington, Arkansas, and Idaho.

Reliability.   Two types of reliability are reported in the manual (Bricker, 1992).
Interrater reliability on total test scores of 122 children was .966. Test–retest reliability on 58 children ranged from .77 (social domain) to .95 (gross motor).

Validity.   Two types of validity are reported in the manual (Bricker, 1992).
Concurrent validity was completed by comparing AEPS test scores of 155 children
with their performance on either the Gesell Developmental Schedules or the Bayley
Scales of Infant Development. Correlation between the Bayley Mental Age and AEPS
was .93; correlation between the Bayley Motor Age and AEPS was .88. Correlation
between the Gesell and the AEPS was .51.

Content validity was reported to be very high in a study that examined protocols of 155 children. A second study examined the hierarchical arrangement of
items (from simple to more complex). Scores of 77 children who were not disabled
were examined, and 80 to 90% of the items were found to be arranged hierarchically. In a third study, which surveyed 23 practitioners regarding the content of
the AEPS, 76% of the respondents indicated that the test included the "most important behaviors" for assessing children.

In a controlled study with 48 early interventionists, researchers investigated the
usefulness of the AEPS Test to develop sound IEP/IFSP goals. The experimental
groups that used the AEPS Test wrote significantly better goals and objectives than
the practitioners who used other tools (Bricker, 1992).

Summary.   The Assessment, Evaluation, and Programming System represents
not just a single instrument but a system for program planning and monitoring and
evaluating child progress. Studies of the AEPS Test indicate high interobserver and
test–retest reliability. Content and concurrent validity are adequate.

In addition to the AEPS Test, the system includes a Family Report and a Family
Interest Survey, which allow family members to contribute important information
during team meetings. This system has many fine features that can assist practi-

tioners in assessments for the purposes of program planning and monitoring child progress. The second volume of the AEPS Curriculum for Birth to Three Years (Cripe, Slentz, & Bricker, 1992) contains a wealth of information regarding teaching strategies within the child's daily routines at home or in an early education setting, environmental arrangements, and instructional sequence. In addition, the AEPS Assessment Activity Plans provide suggestions for assessing children during group play activities and ideas for gathering information in the least intrusive manner. Assessment strategies such as these hold exciting promise.

Carolina Curriculum for Infants and Toddlers with Special Needs

The Carolina Curriculum for Infants and Toddlers with Special Needs (CCITSN) (Johnson-Martin, Jens, Attermeier, & Hacker, 1991) is a criterion-referenced instrument designed to assess developmental abilities of the child for the purpose of planning or monitoring the child's intervention program. The instrument, called the Assessment Log, includes 24 areas of development within the traditional six developmental domains (cognition, communication, social, adaptive, and fine and gross motor skills).

Individual items are arranged in logical sequences for teaching skills. In addition, many individual items include suggested adaptations for children with visual, hearing, or motor disabilities. The authors state that although the CCITSN was developed for children birth through 24 months, some older individuals were included in the field testing. Thus, use of this instrument may be considered if age-appropriate adaptations are made to the items and materials.

The strength of this instrument lies in the direct link between assessment and learning activities. In addition to describing the Assessment Log, the bulk of the manual includes suggestions for teacher- or therapist-directed activities as well as suggestions for incorporating activities into routine care or playtime.

Administration.   The manual suggests that much of the information be gathered by observing parent–child interactions for 15 to 20 minutes. Remaining information may be completed by asking the parent to attempt the item with the child or having the examiner do so. The parent report may also be solicited, or items that the child passed on other instruments may be recorded. If this more informal way of gathering information is used, the examiner must be very familiar with the test items.

Scoring.   Items are scored as passed ($+$), failed ($-$), or emerging ($+/-$). The Assessment Log includes columns for recording information on several different dates, which is helpful in monitoring progress.

Standardization.   This criterion-referenced test is also norm referenced. However, the norms were *not* developed through administration of the instrument but rather from a review of the literature.

Reliability.   No reliability data are provided. Information regarding interrater agreement would be most valuable. It is unfortunate that this instrument has only one form: Alternate form reliability data would be useful for practitioners who use the CCITSN for monitoring progress.

Validity.   The current edition (2nd ed., 1991) has no validity data. The authors addressed construct validity by reviewing and selecting items from a variety of norm-referenced tests; many of these tests were standardized on children who were developing typically (Bayley Scales of Infant Development, Cattell, Peabody Developmental Motor Scales, Gesell Developmental Schedules) as well as the Uzgiris–Hunt Scales, the Callier–Azusa Scale, and the Communicative Intention Inventory.

The manual includes general information regarding the content validity of the earlier edition. The data were gathered by asking interventionists to complete a questionnaire regarding their perceptions of the usefulness of the curriculum. The practitioners indicated that they could "use the curriculum as intended and found it to be useful both for assessing infants with disabilities and for developing their intervention programs" (p. 4). However, some respondents expressed reservations regarding the usefulness of the CCITSN for children with severe and profound disabilities.

Summary.   The CCITSN is a criterion-referenced assessment instrument designed to assess developmental abilities in young children, birth through 24 months. The instrument is directly linked to intervention strategies, and suggestions included in the manual may be very valuable for the practitioner in planning intervention activities. In addition, adaptations for children with visual, hearing, or motor disabilities are included in many of the assessment items. The norms should be used with caution, however, since they were not developed from this instrument. The manual reports no reliability data. Limited validity data suggest the usefulness of this instrument only for young children with mild to moderate delays; additional field testing is needed to determine its applicability to children with severe or profound involvement.

Early Intervention Developmental Profile

The Early Intervention Developmental Profile (Rogers et al., 1981) was designed to assist in planning programs for children who are functioning in the birth to 36-month developmental range. This criterion-referenced checklist and profile assesses functioning in six main areas: perceptual–fine motor, cognition, language, social–emotional, self-care, and gross motor.

The Early Intervention Developmental Profile is one of a set of five materials in a series originally developed by the Early Intervention Project for Handicapped Infants and Young Children at the Institute for the Study of Mental Retardation and Related Disabilities, University of Michigan. In addition to the instrument, there is a manual, *Assessment and Application* (Rogers & D'Eugenio, 1981), and a booklet of activities, *Stimulation Activities* (Brown & Donovan, 1981). Other materials include the Preschool Developmental Profile and accompanying booklet for preschoolers. These materials are now in the public domain.

Administration.   The manual suggests that a multidisciplinary team administer the Early Intervention Developmental Profile. Administration may be in the child's home or in the program setting.

Scoring. Items are scored as pass (P), fail (F), emerging skill (PF), or omitted (O). Raw scores from the six scales may be totaled and plotted on the profile graph. Age norms are also available.

Standardization. The Early Intervention Developmental Profile is a criterion-referenced instrument and has not been normed. Test items were selected from other norm-referenced instruments. Age norms from the Piagetian cognitive items are based on suggestions from Jean Piaget's book, *The Construction of Reality in the Child* (1954).

Reliability. Two types of reliability are described by the test authors. Interrater reliability is reported as good (percent of agreement ranged from 80 to 97%, with an average of 89%). Test–retest reliability correlations were high, ranging from .93 to .98.

Validity. The only type of validity the test authors describe is construct validity, the extent to which a test measures a particular trait or construct. In developing the test, the authors chose test items in two ways: according to whether an item appeared in at least two recognized scales, and according to whether an original item developed by the authors was based on current developmental theory.

Summary. The Early Intervention Developmental Profile is a criterion-referenced test for young children who are functioning in the birth through 36-month age range. The instrument includes six scales; the cognitive scale is based on Piagetian constructs. The instrument consists of three booklets: an assessment checklist with profile, an administration manual, and a set of activities to build skills. Thus, the Early Intervention Developmental Profile is closely linked to planning and monitoring a child's program. The accompanying booklet, *Stimulation Activities,* contains suggestions for building skills within daily routines, and some items offer specific suggestions by disability.

Reliability of this instrument is adequate; much validity information is lacking, however. Caution should be employed when using age norms because of the lack of standardization of this instrument. Since the Early Intervention Developmental Profile is in the public domain, the instrument as well as the activity suggestions may be freely shared by programs.

Early Learning Accomplishment Profile

The Early Learning Accomplishment Profile (Early LAP) (Glover, Preminger, & Sanford, 1978) is a criterion-referenced test for children from birth to 36 months of age. This instrument was designed for assessment in program planning. Items are included in the following domains: gross motor, fine motor, cognitive, language, adaptive (self-help), and social–emotional.

Administration. This instrument should be administered by teachers or other professionals who will be working with the child. The authors note that to address specific needs and to optimize the child's response, care should be taken to maintain flexibility in the selection of test materials and procedures. The record booklet includes a description of each of the test item procedures as well as criteria on which to assign credit.

Scoring.   Items are scored as plus, to indicate presence of the behavior, or minus, to indicate that the skill was not demonstrated. Raw scores from each of the domains may be entered into the profile, which provides space for both pre- and post-testing data.

Standardization.   This criterion-referenced test is also norm referenced. Norms were not developed through administration of this instrument, however; rather, they were drawn from the literature. The test booklet lists these references in the bibliography.

Reliability.   No information is reported. Interrater and test–retest reliability would be helpful in the use of this instrument for program planning and monitoring progress.

Validity.   No information is reported. Validity information would be helpful to those who are considering the use of the Early LAP.

Summary.   The Early LAP is a criterion-referenced instrument for assessing young children from birth through 36 months. The test is easily administered and scored. Caution is urged in the use of norms. Some assurances of content validity and interrater reliability would be helpful.

Hawaii Early Learning Profile

The Hawaii Early Learning Profile (HELP) (Furuno et al., 1988) is intended for children from birth through 36 months for the purposes of program planning and progress monitoring. This criterion-referenced instrument consists of the HELP checklist, HELP charts (profile sheets), and accompanying manual, *Help . . . At Home* (Parks, 1988), which includes activity suggestions for parents and caregivers.

The checklist covers 685 skills in six main developmental areas: cognitive, language, gross motor, fine motor, social–emotional, and adaptive (self-help) skills. Each of the skills includes cross-references to the activity sheets in the manual. These activity sheets may be reproduced and shared with parents.

Administration.   The manual states that much information may be gathered through observation, "unobtrusive" play, and interviews with parents.

Scoring.   The checklist provides columns for recording assessment data on more than one occasion, which facilitates monitoring progress. Items are scored by noting a plus (+) if the skill is observed or appropriately absent, an R if the skill is reported by parent, a minus (−) if the skill is assessed but not observed or reported, or an E, if the skill appears to be emerging. An age range is listed for each of the skills. A child's profile may be recorded on the HELP charts.

Standardization.   This criterion-referenced instrument is also norm referenced. The manual contains little information concerning the standardization except to note that the age ranges were based on "a synthesis of research and project data" (p. vi).

Reliability.   No information was reported.

Validity.   No information was reported.

Summary.   The Hawaii Early Learning Profile includes 685 individual skills for children from birth through 36 months. The instrument lists an expected age range for each individual skill yet gives no information about standardization procedures. Caution is urged in the use of age norms. Information concerning reliability and validity of this instrument would be helpful. The strength in this instrument lies in the cross-reference to the HELP . . . At Home activity sheets. These information sheets are written from the child's perspective and include many excellent suggestions for incorporating activities into the natural environment and daily routine. A feature is that a special copyrighted policy allows the user to share specific sheets with parents and caregivers.

Minnesota Infant Development Inventory

The Minnesota Infant Development Inventory (MIDI) (Ireton & Thwing, 1980) is a parent questionnaire for measuring development in infants 1 to 16 months old. The instrument includes five areas of development: gross motor, fine motor, language, comprehension, and personal–social. Statements about each of these areas may be answered by either the mother or the practitioner. A comment section offers the mother an opportunity to describe the child or state concerns about development.

Administration.   The child's mother answers the questions. The authors suggest that completing the instrument is in itself helpful in increasing the mother's awareness of her baby's development. A professional may also complete the instrument as part of a developmental assessment.

Scoring.   Items observed in the infant are marked. The infant's chronological age is then compared to the number of items passed. A chart indicates the number of items that place the infant 30% below or 30% above chronological age. The authors consider 30% below age expectations to indicate delayed development.

Standardization.   The MIDI has not been standardized. Test items were drawn from earlier research with another instrument developed by the authors, the Minnesota Child Development Inventory.

Reliability.   No information is reported.

Validity.   In a criterion-related validity study with the Bayley Scales of Infant Development Mental Scale, overall agreement ranged from 81 to 90%. The MIDI demonstrated sensitivity (85%) in identifying delay and specificity (77%) in identifying normal development (Ireton, undated).

Summary.   The Minnesota Infant Development Inventory is to be completed by the mother. Items cover five areas of development for infants from 1 to 16 months of age. The instrument may be scored by calculating the percentage of items passed. However, additional research with this instrument is needed in the use of age norms. The MIDI may be more useful as a tool in assisting parents to become more aware of infant development than as an instrument of assessment.

Uzgiris–Hunt Scales of Infant Psychological Development

The Uzgiris–Hunt Scales of Infant Psychological Development were developed in 1975 and updated in 1980 (Dunst, 1980). Dunst believes that the scales are useful for "identifying the particular types of experiences that would be most conducive to fostering cognitive growth. . ." (Dunst, 1980, p. 1) and in planning program activities. The Uzgiris–Hunt Scales assess sensorimotor development in various related branches:

1. Visual Pursuit and the Permanence of Object
2. Means for Obtaining Desired Environmental Events
3a. The Development of Vocal Imitation
3b. The Development of Gestural Imitation
4. The Development of Operational Causality
5. The Construction of Object Relations in Space
6. The Development of Schemes for Relating to Objects

The scales differ from other traditional tests in two main ways: (1) the scales are ordinal, and (2) the acquisition of lower level skills is considered to be essential for successive levels of achievement.

Administration.   The administration of the scales is very flexible with respect to both materials used and procedures followed. Because the purpose is to assess the child's optimal performance in each branch, the examiner may use varied materials and situations to elicit responses.

Scoring.   A child's developmental status is obtained by noting the highest item passed on each of the sensorimotor scales. This item indicates the point the child has reached on the developmental continuum. The child's scores determine the placement on each of the different branches of development, which can be represented in a profile. The record forms include an observation section to note responses or behaviors of interest. In addition, an estimated developmental age (EDA) may also be obtained.

Standardization.   This instrument was not normed. Rather, the estimated developmental ages were determined from the literature. The manual includes specific reference citations.

Reliability.   Interobserver reliability was reported to be between .85 and .99. Two separate studies examined test–retest reliability and reported coefficients ranging from .88 to .96.

Validity.   The original scales were based on Piagetian theory; that is, they were based on data from children who were developing typically. If a Piagetian-type instrument is used to plan a program for a child with or at risk for disability, there must be evidence that Piagetian theory holds for children with disabilities. To address construct validity, Dunst (1980) reviewed a number of studies and reported the general conclusion that children with differing abilities acquire behaviors in the stage sequence postulated by Piaget. However, children with physical disabilities and/or social–emotional needs may score lower on these scales (Heffernan & Black, 1984).

Concurrent validity with the Griffiths Mental Development Scales was reported between .67 and .98, with most of the correlations between .83 to .96 (Dunst, 1980).

Summary.   The Uzgiris–Hunt instrument consists of six ordinal scales designed to address the progress in the level of organization of central neural processes based on Piaget's theory of cognitive development. The manual and record forms developed by Dunst (1980) may be useful in the planning of programs for infants or toddlers. This instrument could complement programs based on a Piagetian philosophy. Additional data concerning reliability and validity issues would be helpful for practitioners.

Issues and Considerations in Assessment of Infants and Toddlers

In establishing an infant's eligibility for early intervention services, as well as in assessing the infant's developmental level for program planning and monitoring, there are several aspects to consider.

- What types of information can be gathered through observation in the natural environment rather than through more intrusive formal testing?
- How can the handling, positioning, and movement of high-risk infants during the assessment process be conducted as part of the sharing of an intervention plan to caregivers?
- Do the items in the instrument used in program planning reflect developmentally appropriate practice for infants? For toddlers?

Remember that the criteria for child care and programming for infants and toddlers are *distinctly different* from early childhood programs of all other types. Programming for birth through two is *not* an adjusted version of a good preschool program (Bredekamp, 1987).

INSTRUMENTS THAT SPAN INFANCY AND EARLY CHILDHOOD

A number of commonly used instruments are designed for a broad age range of children. These tests include children from birth through two as well as children who are older. Some of these instruments are standardized, such as the Bayley Scales of Infant Development—II, which may be used for children 1 to 42 months of age, and the Battelle Developmental Inventory (1988), for children birth to eight years. Other instruments include criterion-referenced tests and checklists that provide age range expectations.

Arizona Basic Assessment and Curriculum Utilization System (ABACUS)

The Arizona Basic Assessment and Curriculum Utilization System (ABACUS) (McCarthy, Lund, & Bos, 1986) is a system approach to assessment for the purposes of program planning, monitoring, and evaluating a child's progress. The ABACUS includes assessment forms for the screening and assessment that precede program planning and intervention activities. The system is designed for children functioning in the developmental age range of 2 to 5.5 years. The *ABACUS* consists of 10 books, which cover assessment for instruction and monitoring progress and include activity books on adaptive behavior, communication, socioemotional, and preacademic issues. There is also a book for parent involvement. The use of task analysis and charting behaviors is emphasized.

Battelle Developmental Inventory

The Battelle Developmental Inventory (BDI) is a standardized assessment battery developed by Newborg, Stock, and Wnek (1988) to facilitate the making of eligibility decisions in children from birth through eight years of age. This instrument includes a screening test (described in Chapter 5) as well as a full battery. Test items on both instruments are grouped in the following domains: personal–social, adaptive, motor, communication, and cognitive. Each domain is divided into several subdomains. Test items include descriptions of the testing procedure and criteria for scoring. A set of toys and other test materials may be purchased separately to ensure consistency of results.

The BDI allows for direct assessment of skills as well as observations and interviews for the evaluation of skills that are difficult to assess in a structured setting. For example, the adaptive domain includes items such as moving independently around the house or yard. Many of the test items include suggestions for adapting procedures when assessing children with disabilities.

The authors suggest that the BDI may also be used in planning and monitoring a child's program. However, test items are organized by subdomain rather than by developmental level within the general domain. Thus, between items in a subdomain, there may be a large developmental skill level gap. Care must be taken *not* to develop objectives for the child's program directly from this instrument. Several of the case studies are contained in the manual to illustrate the development of long-term goals and short-term objectives based on the test data. Several of these examples represent good ways of *generalizing* test information to practical, functional goals and objectives for children. *In examining these examples, however, care should be taken that one does not err in creating objectives that will focus on "teaching to the test."*

Administration.   The BDI was designed to be used by teachers of young children as well as by practitioners of other disciplines, including speech pathologists, psychologists, adaptive physical education specialists, and other diagnosticians. Testing time is approximately 1 hour for infants and toddlers; 1.5 to 2 hours is necessary for preschoolers. Practitioners may wish to consider testing over several days.

Scoring.   Test items are scored on a 3-point system (0, 1, or 2). Skills are scored as present "rarely or never," "sometimes" (emerging), or "typical" (present a high percentage of the time). Raw scores are totaled within each subdomain and summed to obtain a total domain score. These raw scores are then converted to percentile rank through tables in the test manual. Tables for conversion to various standard scores permit the construction of a profile for determining eligibility for services and age equivalent scores.

Standardization.   The BDI has undergone several pilot tests; final standardization was conducted in 1982–1983. In all, 800 children participated in the standardization process. The sample was gathered to represent the greater U.S. population in terms of gender, urban or rural communities, and minority status. Socioeconomic level was considered to be widely distributed. Children with disabilities were not included. In 1987 data were reanalyzed, accuracy of the norms was checked, and some adjustments were made in the age norms.

Reliability.   One type of reliability is reported. Test–retest data for a 4-week time period ranged from .71 to .99 across the test domains.

Validity.   Content validity of the BDI is based on expert opinion. The BDI test items were drawn from a pool of 4,000 items used in other instruments as well as in programming for young children.

Construct validity is represented by high positive intercorrelations between domains and within subdomains. Thus it is assumed that children who are developing typically will display a common rate of development. The test manual also reports data indicating that the BDI is able to discriminate between a sample of 160 children with disabilities and the norming sample of children who are developing typically. This type of information is important for examiners who are considering use of the instrument for the purposes of determining eligibility.

Criterion-related validity is reported in moderately high correlations between the BDI and the Vineland Adaptive Behavior Scale as well as the Developmental Activities Screening Inventory. Moderate correlations are reported with the Stanford–Binet, the revised Wechsler Intelligence Scale (WISC-R), and the Peabody Picture Vocabulary Test.

Summary.   The BDI contains a full assessment battery as well as a screening instrument. The test is designed to provide standard scores and may be used as part of a multidisciplinary assessment in determining eligibility for early intervention and special education services. Reliability and validity are adequate.

Bayley Scales of Infant Development II

The Bayley Scales of Infant Development II, the 1993 revision of the original Bayley Scales of Infant Development (Bayley, 1969), is a comprehensive battery designed to assess development in children ages 1 through 42 months. This instrument includes:

(1) a mental scale that assesses perceptual acuity, discriminations, object constancy and memory, learning and problem solving, verbal ability, generalization, and classification; (2) a motor scale that assesses muscle control and coordination; and (3) a behavior rating scale that allows comparisons of the child's behavior across testings as well as overall comparisons to other children of the same age. The behavior rating scale contains a total score as well as four subscales: orientation/engagement, attention, motor quality, and emotional regulation.

Administration.   This battery takes approximately an hour to administer. Practitioners must have advanced training in the administration, scoring, and interpretation of these scales.

Scoring.   The Bayley II uses standard scores and includes a two-tiered level of scoring. In addition to the mental and motor scale score, practitioners may derive a developmental age equivalent for cognition, language, personal/social, and motor. The behavior rating scale score provides classification of children in three categories: within normal limits, questionable, and atypical.

Standardization.   Seventeen hundred children between the ages of 1 and 42 months participated in the standardization sample, which was stratified by race (Caucasian, African American, Hispanic, and other), gender, parent education level, and geographic region. Although only children who were developing typically were included in the standardization sample, an additional clinical sample of children was assessed. This sample was used to examine group differences between the normative sample and children with disabilities. There were eight subgroups in the clinical sample including children who were: 1) premature; 2) HIV+; 3) prenatal drug exposed; 4) asphyxiated at birth; 5) Down syndrome; 6) autism; 7) developmental delay; and 8) otitis media.

Reliability.   Data from three types of reliability (internal consistency, test-retest, and interrater reliability) meet acceptable criteria.

Validity.   Extensive concurrent validity studies were completed. In addition, construct and content validity have been addressed.

Summary.   The Bayley Scales of Infant Development II is a comprehensive standardized battery for assessing the development of children 1 to 42 months of age. Practitioners must be trained in the administration, scoring, and interpretation of the Bayley II. The second edition has been restandardized and has undergone extensive reliability and validity studies. The Bayley Scales of Infant Development II should be considered a very useful instrument to team members.

Brigance® Diagnostic Inventory of Early Development—Revised

The Brigance® Diagnostic Inventory of Early Development—Revised (Brigance, 1991) is a criterion-referenced instrument designed for children from birth to seven years of age. The instrument includes items in 11 areas: preambulatory, gross motor, fine motor, adaptive (self-help), speech and language, general knowledge and comprehension, social–emotional, reading readiness, basic reading, writing, and math. A subset of play skills is included in the social–emotional area. The child's responses are recorded in an individual record book, and there is a procedure for recording successive assessments over a period of time.

Administration.   If the results of the test are going to be used in planning the child's program, the teacher or other professional who will be working with the child should conduct the assessment.

Scoring.   Test items are scored in the child's individual record book. Items that have been mastered are circled.

Standardization.   This criterion-referenced test is also norm referenced. However, the norms were *not* developed through administering of the instrument; rather, they were drawn from the literature. The literature references used are listed in the bibliography of the examiner's manual. Some of the norms given are widely disputed.

Reliability.   No information is reported.

Validity.   No information is reported.

Summary.   The Brigance® Diagnostic Inventory of Early Development—Revised is a criterion-referenced test that may be used with children from birth to seven years of age. The test is easy to use and score. Despite the term *diagnostic* in the title, the test is not designed to assist in determining a child's eligibility for early intervention or special education services. Because the instrument is criterion referenced, it could be very helpful in planning and monitoring a child's progress. Use of the norms should be done with caution because they were not developed specifically for this test but were drawn from the literature. Additional information concerning test–retest reliability and validity would be helpful.

Child Development Inventory

The Child Development Inventory (CDI) (Ireton, 1992) replaces the original Minnesota Child Development Inventory and is designed for children 15 to 72 months of age. According to the manual, older children who are functioning in the one- to six-year age range may also be assessed with this instrument. The CDI is different from other instruments in that it consists of a questionnaire to be completed by a parent. This instrument measures development in eight areas:

Social
Self-help
Gross motor
Fine motor
Expressive language
Language comprehension

Letters

Numbers

Some of these areas are covered by items in a ninth, or general development, scale. In addition, the instrument includes questions about the child's vision, hearing, behavior, and health. This parent-completed questionnaire was designed to be used in combination with other information as part of the assessment process.

Administration.   The CDI includes a booklet of statements that describe typical behaviors and an answer sheet. The parent completes the answer sheet by indicating a *yes* or *no* to the statements that apply to the child.

Scoring.   Raw scores (*yes* answers) are tabulated in each of the nine scales and recorded on a profile sheet. Separate profiles and norms are provided for each gender. The profile sheet allows a comparison of the child's performance to the mean number of items answered *yes* for the children in the norming sample. These scores are interpreted by drawing guidelines across the profile at different intervals: at age level, 25% below age level, and at 30% below age level. A child is identified as developing below age expectation if

> any of the scores are lower than the 30 percent below age line, or fall within the 25–30 percent below age range. . . . The 30 percent below age cutoff is equivalent to two Standard Deviations below the mean (-2 SD). A 25 percent below age cutoff (-1.5 SD) was defined to help identify those children whose development was "borderline" or "mildly delayed." (p. 21)

Standardization.   The norming sample consisted of 281 males and 287 females from one to six years, three months old. The children lived in South Saint Paul, Minnesota, and 95% of them were Caucasian. Mother's mean level of education was 13 years; father's mean level of education was 13.5 years. The author states that the CDI norms should not be generalized to children of families who are significantly different from the norm group.

Reliability.   Internal consistency for each scale was reported by specific age groups. Generally, scores in the range of 1 to 4.5 years were more reliable than in the older age groups. Coefficients in this range lay mainly between .70 and .89.

Validity.   Content validity was determined by selecting areas identified in the child development literature, psychological tests, and early childhood special education eligibility guidelines (Ireton, 1992). A study of kindergarten children in the norming sample compared their scores on the CDI and the results of reading and math tests. For these children, ages five and six, the study found correlations of .69 with the general development scale, .56 with the scale for letters, and .65 with the scale for numbers.

Summary.   The CDI is a parent-completed questionnaire designed to collect information from parents about their child. Because the responses depend solely on parent report, the correctness of the scores will depend on how accurately and completely the respondent is able to recall information and past observations of the child. The test manual includes information regarding reliability (internal consistency) that appears to be adequate. The information in this questionnaire could be helpful to parents as a means of recording information about the child's growth and development. A completed questionnaire would give team members valuable information concerning the child's areas of strength as well as need. However, care should be taken in comparing a child's scores to the norming sample because of the lack of broad representation by race or geographic region.

Learning Accomplishment Profile

The Learning Accomplishment Profile (LAP) (Sanford & Zelman, 1981) is a criterion-referenced test designed to be used with children from 36 to 72 months of age for the purposes of program planning and monitoring. Test items cover seven areas of development: gross motor, fine motor, prewriting, cognitive, language, adaptive (self-help), and personal–social. A child's responses are recorded in an individual record book. A profile sheet is also included, as seen in Figure 6.5.

Administration.   A teacher or other professional who is working with the child should administer this instrument.

Scoring.   Test items are scored as either plus or minus. Additional comments may be recorded. Items that are passed are colored on the profile sheet, thus indicating areas of strength and need as well as areas of splinter skills.

Standardization.   This criterion-referenced test is also norm referenced. However, the age norms were drawn from the literature. A reference code is included to indicate the sources from which the developmental ages of the test items were obtained.

Summary.   The Learning Accomplishment Profile is a criterion-referenced test for children 36 to 72 months of age. This instrument also includes age norms. Caution is advised in the use of these norms. The instrument may be useful in planning and evaluating a child's program. The profile sheet may be of particular value in identifying areas of strength and need. In addition, it may be helpful to share the sheet with parents in discussing their child's progress. Information about reliability and validity issues would be helpful.

System to Plan Early Childhood Services (SPECS)

The System to Plan Early Childhood Services (SPECS) was developed by Bagnato and Neisworth (1990) as a system, rather than an individual instrument, for children between the ages of two and six years. This system, which is comprised of three steps, links team assessment for program planning, the development of a plan for service delivery in the IFSP or IEP, and evaluation of child progress. During the first of the three steps, parents and practitioners use the instrument to rate the child's developmental and behavioral status in 19 areas based on observation, interview, or testing. The system then provides an organizational structure or chart, called Team SPECS, on which team members transfer their individual ratings. The second phase is designed to assist teams to reach a consensus on the child's needs and to create a

FIGURE 6.5 LAP Profile Sheet

SOURCE: The Learning Accomplishment Profile (Revised Edition) by Anne R. Sanford and Janet G. Zelman and published by Kaplan Press, 1981. Reprinted with permission.

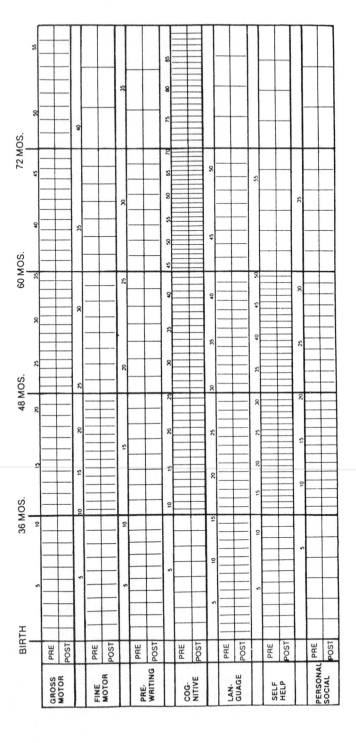

plan for service delivery. The final step involves the completion of the Program SPECS, which detail the scope and intensity of the child's program in 10 different option areas. Later, the initial scope and intensity ratings are used to monitor improvements in evaluating a child's progress.

Administration.   All members of the team complete a rating of the child in 19 developmental dimensions by assigning a rating of 1 (lowest) to 5 (typical) to describe the child. An additional space allows the respondent to comment on the following areas: communication, sensorimotor, physical, self-regulation, cognition, and self/social. The ratings can then be transferred to the individual rater profile, which gives a visual picture of the child's functional status. Likert ratings are labeled as follows: 5 (typical), 4 (at risk), 3 (mild), 2 (moderate), and 1 (severe).

Scoring.   Team members rate each dimension according to their observations, interviews, or the results of other testing of the child. Two potential problems exist in assigning a score. First, instructions on the front of each Developmental SPECS booklet state that rating numbers range from 1 (lowest) to 5 (typical). However, when the rater summarizes this information on the profile, the ratings carry a different focus.

The numbers on the profile sheet do not use "lowest" (1) to "typical" (5), but are equated with a different terminology. Furthermore, this terminology carries specific connotations within the field of special education. For example, a rating of 3 indicates a mild limitation in functioning, a 2 indicates a moderate functioning limitation, and a 1 indicates severe functioning limitations. These terms, *mild, moderate,* and *severe,* refer to limitations in cognitive functioning in special education and their use could be not only confusing but misleading.

A second potential problem exists in the use of these rating scales. A rating of 5 indicates that the target child typically performs as well as or better than other children of the same age. Thus, the evaluator needs not only a good knowledge of the target child but also a good understanding of typical child development.

Standardization.   SPECS is not a norm-referenced instrument.

Reliability.   Test–retest reliability coefficients are reported for early childhood educators and paraprofessional aides. For both groups, correlation coefficients exceed .70 with the exception of self-esteem (.62, educator) and vision and temperament (.60 and .67 respectively, paraprofessional).

Validity.   Construct validity is the extent to which a test measures a particular characteristic. As a judgment-based rating scale, SPECS requires the user to judge the child's functioning on certain characteristics or dimensions. The administration manual points out that this approach requires raters to use their internal sense of what is typical for each dimension, thereby eliminating the need to provide external age-related norms for score interpretation. The manual lists percentages of correct classification ("normal" or "handicapped") for six different disciplines ranging from psychologist (66%) to early childhood special educator (90%).

Concurrent validity studies indicate generally high levels of agreement between instruments that measure the same or similar dimensions and SPECS.

Summary.   The System to Plan Early Childhood Services (SPECS) is a system for (1) collecting and organizing information about a child's needs, (2) combining information from all members of the team to elicit a consensus regarding the child's needs and the types of service to be provided, and (3) making decisions regarding the extent and intensity of services and the monitoring of progress. One of the strengths of the design of this system is the support for full and active parent involvement throughout the program planning and monitoring process.

SPECS provides a valuable structure with Team SPECS for teams whose members may be finding collaboration difficult. The structure may also be useful for teams whose members do not typically work together in a program setting or with the same children across program settings.

The Program SPECS include a comprehensive list of services and program options that may be useful to practitioners and family members who are new to early intervention and early childhood special education services. However, for more experienced team members, completion of this step may be tedious. Although Program SPECS also are designed to assist in monitoring a child's progress, less formal and more useful information may be recorded in other ways (see Chapter 13).

The potential user should be aware that there are at least two potential difficulties with the SPECS rating scores. The rating scale presupposes that the evaluator has a strong knowledge of typical early childhood development; in reality, this is not always the case. A second problem is the lack of clear directions in rating the items. The criteria that are to be used in making judgments should be stated fully in the instructions on the Developmental SPECS.

The Developmental SPECS cover six domains. Some of the terms are used consistently with those included in the applicable federal legislation; however, others are not. For example, one of the SPECS domains is called "self/social." The items are a combination of two domains, social–emotional and adaptive development. Another SPECS domain is listed as "sensorimotor"; it assesses physical development. The SPECS domain called "physical" consists of health issues. *Test developers could greatly decrease confusion in the field of assessment of young children by using terms consistent with those recognized nationally by practitioners in the field.*

INSTRUMENTS FOR ASSESSING PRESCHOOLERS AND YOUNG SCHOOL-AGE CHILDREN

Instruments that focus on assessment of preschoolers typically include the following developmental domains: cognitive, expressive and receptive language, fine and gross motor, and adaptive (self-help) skills. Many commonly used instruments do not include the social–emotional domain. Yet this is perhaps one of the most critical areas in increasing opportunities for young children of differing abilities to play and work together.

Instruments designed for the preschool and primary age child typically include "preacademic" domains, and many commonly used instruments for the primary age child focus on one or two areas outside the cognitive domain. In describing appropriate practice in the primary grades serving 5 through 8 year olds, the National Association for the Education of Young Children (NAEYC) describes the importance of viewing domains of development (physical, social, emotional, and cognitive) as integrated.

Development in one dimension influences and is influenced by development in other dimensions. This premise is violated when schools place a great emphasis on the cognitive domain while minimizing other aspects of children's development. Because development cannot be neatly separated into parts, failure to attend to all aspects of an individual child's development is often the root cause of a child's failure in school. For example, when a child lacks social skills and is neglected or rejected by peers, her or his ability to work cooperatively in a school setting is impaired. (Bredekamp, 1987, p. 63)

Carolina Curriculum for Preschoolers with Special Needs

The Carolina Curriculum for Preschoolers with Special Needs (CCPSN) (Johnson-Martin, Attermeier, & Hacker, 1990), like the Carolina Curriculum for Infants and Toddlers with Special Needs described earlier, is designed to assess the child's current developmental abilities for the purpose of planning or monitoring an intervention program. The assessment log is similar to the Carolina Curriculum for Infants and Toddlers, and the areas of development within the traditional developmental domains are congruent with the sequences for infants and toddlers.

The strength of this instrument is the direct link between assessment and learning activities. In addition to describing the Assessment Log, the bulk of the manual includes suggestions for organizing and grouping preschool children and tips to better understand children with certain special needs. The manual also includes teacher- or therapist-directed activities and specific suggestions for incorporating activities into routine classroom activities.

Administration.   Much of the information in the assessment log may be gathered through observing the child in the natural environment.

Scoring.   Items may be scored as pass/fail, or additional information helpful to the evaluator, such as emerging skills, may be included. The log format provides columns to allow follow-up testing for monitoring the child's progress.

Standardization.   The Carolina Curriculum for Preschoolers with Special Needs is a criterion-referenced test.

Reliability.   No information is reported.

Validity.   No information is reported.

Summary.   The CCPSN is a criterion-referenced assessment instrument designed to assess developmental abilities in preschool children. The instrument is directly linked to intervention strategies, and programming suggestions are included in the manual. Teaching and learning activities focus on daily routines typically found in the natural environment. Helpful information regarding differential skills for children with visual, hearing, or motor disabilities is included. Future revisions should include information regarding reliability and validity of this instrument.

Gesell Preschool Test

The Gesell Preschool Test (Haines, Ames, & Gillespie, 1980), one of several Gesell tests, is an adaptation of the Gesell Developmental Schedules. The Preschool Test is designed to assess the rate of development of children two to six years of age. In addition, the test follows the philosophy that educational placement should be made on the basis of current developmental level of performance, rather than chronological age. For example, a child would not begin kindergarten on the basis of chronological age but would enter when the skills needed to be successful in kindergarten had been achieved.

Four primary areas are assessed: motor, adaptive, language, and personal–social. The adaptive area is really an assessment of the cognitive domain. The test items in the adaptive area minimize language skills.

Administration.   The Gesell tests should be administered by a trained practitioner.

Scoring.   Items are scored as "succeeds," "performs above age expectation," "questionable," or "failure." Items are scored solely on the basis of the norms. The practitioner may find some of the items very difficult to score accurately. This instrument yields a developmental age.

Standardization.   The norming sample, which consisted of 320 girls and 320 boys, was stratified by parent occupation. All the children resided in Connecticut and almost all were Caucasian.

Reliability.   No information is reported.

Validity.   No information is reported.

Summary.   The Gesell Preschool Test is designed to indicate a child's current level of development. The standardization of this instrument is inadequate, and important information is lacking regarding reliability and validity. This instrument should be used only with extreme caution.

HELP for Special Preschoolers

HELP for Special Preschoolers (Santa Cruz County Office of Education, 1987) was developed for use with children ages three through six for the purpose of program planning and monitoring. The instrument was designed to continue beyond the age range of birth to three years covered by the HELP (Hawaii Early Learning Profile described above). The HELP for Special Preschoolers consists of an assessment checklist and the accompanying manual, which includes activity suggestions and instructional strategies. Each of the skills is cross-referenced to the activity sheets in the manual. The checklist covers 625 skills in five main developmental areas: self-help, motor development, communication, social skills, and learning–cognitive. Within these areas, there are several components seldom included in criterion-referenced tests: the motor area contains a section on swimming skills as well as wheelchair skills; the communication area contains sections on sign language and speech/reading skills. Each of the 625 skills is cross-referenced to the activities and teaching strategies in the manual.

Administration.   The checklist is to be used by practitioners and parents. All the skills in any one area should be reviewed because they are arranged by age rather than by function. The manual suggests that much of the information can be gathered by observation, "unobtrusive" play, and parent interviews.

Scoring.   Skills are scored as "mastered," "not observed," or "emerging." The checklist includes additional columns for retesting and comments.

Standardization.   The HELP for Special Preschoolers is a criterion-referenced test.

Reliability.   No information is reported.

Validity.   The manual states: "To create this checklist, over 600 of the 2,400 BCP [Behavioral Characteristics Progression] skills were selected for age appropriateness (three to six years), compared against existing instruments and literature, and edited by field reviewers" (p. 1). No further information is provided regarding the instruments that were compared, the applicable literature references, or the qualifications of the field reviewers. The BCP, which is published by the same publisher, was not described.

Summary.   HELP for Special Preschoolers is a criterion-referenced instrument and therefore may be helpful in planning and monitoring a child's program. Since individual skill items are not clustered necessarily in a developmental sequence and the order in which individual skills are listed may not reflect their relation to each other, the user must be cautious in developing a plan for intervention or education plan on the basis of this instrument. Because of the lack of psychometric information, caution is urged in the use of age ranges, as well. However, practitioners and parents may find the suggestions and teaching strategies in the notebook most helpful in planning activities for a broad range of children.

WORKING WITH FAMILIES

Some of the instruments described in this chapter may be helpful in determining a child's eligibility for services. Some parents may be surprised to learn that their child has a disability; but for other parents, the finding may come as a relief. These parents may have had questions and concerns for some time regarding their child's development. Some general tips for sharing assessment information with family members include:

- Provide family members with an opportunity to receive the assessment report in a one-to-one setting rather than at a large IFSP or IEP team meeting. This premeeting allows family time to ask questions with an empathetic practitioner and to process the information in relative privacy.

- Share information with both parents (or major caregivers) at the same time.
- Be honest and straightforward regarding the disability.
- Be willing to say when you don't know.
- Allow time for families to express their feelings.
- Be sensitive to families if they are not ready to hear details.
- Offer to provide additional information.
- Suggest additional resources.
- Be available to the family.

In sharing knowledge and information, respect the sensibilities of the family, and realize that these may change from one period of time to another. One strategy is to offer choices. For example, in discussing the inconclusive results of a diagnostic assessment, the practitioner might ask, "Do you want to know the range of options or just the ones that are more likely?"

Be honest. Say "I don't know" when you don't. But also follow up with "I'll find out," or "We just don't know at this point."

SUGGESTIONS FOR BEST PRACTICE

Many of these instruments are used frequently in programs for young children. They are relatively inexpensive, and many of them are accompanied by good curriculum materials and activity suggestions. However, the practitioner should heed certain precautions. When developers design criterion-referenced tests, specific test items are grouped by the age at which children who are developing typically acquire each skill. Much work remains regarding skill acquisition of children with special needs and the impact of specific disabilities on a child's development. For example, children who are blind may lag behind their peers in gross motor development. In addition, acquisition of certain skills may not follow the same sequence observed for children with vision. In planning and monitoring progress, team members will want to supplement criterion-referenced assessment information with observations and other alternative assessment practices (described in Chapter 11).

Practitioners may wish to select instruments that address language as a broader, more encompassing area, such as *communication.* Communication involves not only the receiving but the sending of information. And the information may not be confined to oral language. Young children may employ a variety of communication modes including verbal (oral), the use of eye gaze, gestures, signs, and synthesized speech. With the new advances in assistive technology, young children may use simple switches or augmentative communication equipment to make choices in program activities and to communicate with their friends.

CAVEATS

Many developmental batteries and criterion-referenced tests group test items by age. This format is helpful in that it allows the practitioner to have all the skills of a certain age displayed together. However, the skills necessary to complete a task may be scattered across several age levels. In addition, there may be no logical sequencing of items. Thus, any one section may fail to display a developmental sequence of skills, with the result that a picture of the "whole" child is not obtained. This arrangement may lead to a fragmentation of skills through developmentally inappropriate programming practice.

A second caveat involves the development of programming objectives based on the test. Items the child fails may be items identified by the team as needing to be "taught." Some test items are very specific: for example, "Child stacks 3 blocks." It would be inappropriate to teach a child who had failed this item to literally stack three blocks. As a more appropriate programming activity, the child might be presented with opportunities to manipulate a variety of materials in different ways, one of which involved stacking. Teaching to the test is a common error and one that can be avoided by careful practitioners.

SUMMARY

There is a wide variety of instruments designed for assessing development. The format of the instrument and the test items selected often reflects the theoretical orientation of the test developer. The intended use of developmental assessments varies: some of the instruments were designed to assist in determining eligibility for services; others were developed to help in planning the child's program. Some of the instruments include information about the consistency and the appropriateness of the instrument; but information for many instruments that purport to measure a young child's development is limited or lacking.

STUDY QUESTIONS AND SUGGESTED ACTIVITIES

1. Describe your philosophy of child development. What are some of the factors that have influenced the way you feel? What assessment tools and practices support your philosophy?

2. Examine one of the developmental assessment instruments described in this chapter. Does the instrument appear to support a certain theoretical model or philosophy?

3. Compare the test items of two or more different instruments for a particular age group. What are the similarities? How are the items different? If you are assessing for the purpose of planning the child's program, which test items would provide the most helpful information?

4. Examine the examiner's manuals of two or more standardized instruments. Do the manuals describe the children included in the standardization sample? Do they report information concerning the validity and reliability of the instruments? How do they compare?

5. What additional resources are useful in helping you to select an assessment instrument? Choose one of the assessment instruments available to you and review the content. Next, check the reference section in your library for books that may provide additional information about your instrument. Two valuable resources are the *Mental Measurement Yearbooks* (see Kramer & Conoley, 1992) and *Tests in Print* (see Mitchell, 1983).

REFERENCES

Als, H., Lester, B. M., Tronick, E. C., & Brazelton, T. B. (1982a). Towards a research instrument for the assessment of preterm infants' behavior (APIB). In H. E. Fitzgerald, B. M. Lester, & M.

W. Yogman (Eds.), *Theory and research in behavioral pediatrics: Vol. 1* (pp. 35–63). New York: Plenum.

Als, H., Lester, N. M., Tronick, E. C., & Brazelton, T. B. (1982b). Manual for the assessment of preterm infant behavior (APIB). In H. E. Fitzgerald, B. M. Lester, & M. W. Yogman (Eds.), *Theory and research in behavioral pediatrics: Vol. 1* (pp. 65–132). New York: Plenum.

Aylward, G. P. (1986). To correct or not to correct: Age adjustment for prematurity (ERIC Document Reproduction Service No. ED 280 609). Paper presented at the Annual Meeting of the American Psychological Association, Washington, DC.

Bagnato, S. J., & Neisworth, J. T. (1990). *System to plan early childhood services (SPECS)*. Circle Pines, MN: American Guidance Service.

Barr, R. G. (1989). Recasting a clinical enigma: The case of infant crying. In P. R. Zelazo & R. G. Barr (Eds.), *Challenges to developmental paradigms: Implications for theory, assessment, and treatment* (pp. 43–64). Hillsdale, NJ: Lawrence Erlbaum Associates.

Bayley, N. (1969). *Bayley scales of infant development*. San Antonio, TX: Psychological Corporation.

Bayley, N. (1993). *Bayley scales of infant development—II*. San Antonio, TX: Psychological Corporation.

Brazelton, T. (1984). *Neonatal behavioral assessment scale* (2nd ed.). Clinics in Developmental Medicine, No. 88. Philadelphia: Lippincott.

Bredekamp, S. (Ed.). (1987). *Developmentally appropriate practice in early childhood programs serving children from birth through age 8*. Washington, DC: National Association for the Education of Young Children.

Bricker, D. (Ed.). (1992). *Assessment, evaluation, and programming system (AEPS) for infants and children: Vol. 1. AEPS measurement for birth to three years*. Baltimore: Paul H. Brookes.

Bricker, D. (1993). *Assessment, evaluation, and programming system for infants and children: Vol. 2*. Baltimore: Paul H. Brookes.

Brigance, A. H. (1991). *Brigance® diagnostic inventory of early development—Revised*. North Billerica, MA: Curriculum Associates.

Brown, S. L., & Donovan, C. M. (1981). *Stimulation activities*. Ann Arbor, MI: University of Michigan Press.

Carta, J. J., Schwartz, I. S., Atwater, J. B., & McConnell, S. R. (1991). Developmentally appropriate practice: Appraising its usefulness for young children with disabilities. *Topics in Early Childhood Education, 11*(1), 1–20.

Chomsky, N. (1972). *Language and mind* (enlarged ed.). New York: Harcourt Brace Jovanovich (1st ed., 1968).

Connor, F. P., Williamson, G. G., & Siepp, J. M. (Eds.). (1978). *Program guide for infants and toddlers with neuromotor and other developmental disabilities*. New York: Teachers College Press.

Cripe, J., Slentz, K., & Bricker, D. (1992). *AEPS curriculum for birth to three years: Vol. 2*. Baltimore: Paul H. Brookes.

Dunst, C. J. (1980). *A clinical and educational manual for use with the Uzgiris and Hunt scales of infant psychological development*. Austin, TX: Pro-Ed.

Furuno, S., O'Reilly, K. A., Hosaka, C. M., Inatsuka, T. T., Zeisloft-Falbey, B., & Allman, T. (1988). *Hawaii early learning profile (HELP)*. Palo Alto, CA: VORT.

Gagné, R. M. (1985). *The conditions of learning* (4th ed.). New York: Holt, Rinehart and Winston.

Gesell, A. (1925). *The mental growth of the preschool child*. New York: Macmillan.

Glover, M. E., Preminger, J. L., & Sanford, A. R. (1978). *Early learning accomplishment profile for young children (Early LAP)*. Lewisville, NC: Kaplan Press.

Greenspan, S. I. (1992). *Infancy and early childhood: The practice of clinical assessment and intervention with emotional and developmental challenges.* Madison, CT: International Universities Press.

Haines, J., Ames, L. B., & Gillespie, C. (1980). *Gesell preschool test.* Rosemont, NJ: Programs for Education.

Heffernan, L., & Black, F. W. (1984). Use of the Uzgiris and Hunt scales with handicapped infants. Concurrent validity of the Dunst age norms. *Journal of Psychoeducational Assessment, 2,* 159–168.

Ireton, H. R. (1992). *Child development inventory.* Minneapolis, MN: Behavior Science Systems.

Ireton, H. R. (undated). *Child development inventories for involving parents in developmental assessment.* Minneapolis, MN: Behavior Science Systems.

Ireton, H. R., & Thwing, E. J. (1980). *Minnesota infant development inventory.* Minneapolis, MN: Behavior Science Systems.

Johnson-Martin, N. M., Attermeier, S. M., & Hacker, B. J. (1990). *The Carolina curriculum for preschoolers with special needs.* Baltimore: Paul H. Brookes.

Johnson-Martin, N. M., Jens, K. G., Attermeier, S. M., & Hacker, B. J. (1991). *The Carolina curriculum for infants and toddlers with special needs* (2nd ed.). Baltimore: Paul H. Brookes.

Kagan, J., Snidman, N., Reznick, J. S., Gibbons, J., & Johnson, M. (1989). Temperamental inhibition and childhood fears. In P. R. Zelazo & R. G. Barr (Eds.), *Challenges to developmental paradigms: Implications for theory, assessment, and treatment* (pp. 191–202). Hillsdale, NJ: Lawrence Erlbaum Associates.

Kramer, J. J., & Conoley, J. C. (Eds.). (1992). *The eleventh mental measurement yearbook.* Lincoln, NE: University of Nebraska Press.

Lewis, M. (1989). Culture and biology: The role of temperament. In P. R. Zelazo & R. G. Barr (Eds.), *Challenges to developmental paradigms* (pp. 203–223). Hillsdale, NJ: Lawrence Erlbaum Associates.

McCarthy, J. M., Lund, K. A., & Bos, C. S. (1986). *ABACUS system manual: Book One.* Denver: Love.

Meltzoff, A. N., & Kuhl, P. K. (1989). Infants' perception of faces and speech sounds: Challenges to developmental theory. In P. R. Zelazo & R. G. Barr (Eds.), *Challenges to developmental paradigms: Implications for theory, assessment, and treatment* (pp. 67–91). Hillsdale, NJ: Lawrence Erlbaum Associates.

Mitchell, J. V. (Ed.). (1983). *Tests in print III.* Lincoln, NE: University of Nebraska Press.

National Association for the Education of Young Children and the National Association of Early Childhood Specialists in State Departments of Education. (1991). *Position statement: Guidelines for appropriate curriculum content and assessment in programs serving children ages 3 through 8* (NAEYC No. 725). Washington, D.C.: Author.

Neisworth, J. (1985). A behaviorist approach to early childhood education. In D. Peters, J. Neisworth, & T. Yawkey, *Early childhood education: From theory to practice* (pp. 85–113). Monterey, CA: Brooks/Cole.

Newborg, J., Stock, J. R., & Wnek, L. (1988). *Battelle developmental inventory.* Allen, TX: DLM.

Notari, A. R., Cole, K. N., & Mills, P. E. (1992). Cognitive referencing: The (non)relationship between theory and application. *Topics in Early Childhood Special Education, 11*(4), 1–12.

O'Donnell, K. J., & Oehler, J. M. (1989). Neurobehavioral assessment of the newborn infant. In D. B. Bailey & M. Wolery (Eds.), *Assessing infants and preschoolers with handicaps* (pp. 166–201). Columbus, OH: Merrill.

Parks, S. (Ed.). (1988). *HELP . . . at home.* Palo Alto, CA: VORT.

Pellegrini, A. D., & Dresden, J. (1991). The concept of development in the early childhood curriculum. In B. Spodek & O. N. Saracho (Eds.), *Issues in early childhood curriculum* (pp. 46–63). New York: Teachers College Press.

Peterson, N. (1987). *Early intervention for handicapped and at-risk children.* Denver: Love.

Piaget, J. (1951). *Play, dreams, and imitation in childhood.* New York: Norton.

Piaget, J. (1954). *The construction of reality in the child.* New York: Basic Books.

Piaget, J. (1968). *Six psychological studies* (A. Tenzer, Trans.). New York: Vintage Books.

Rogers, S. J., & D'Eugenio, D. B. (1981). *Assessment and application.* Ann Arbor, MI: University of Michigan Press.

Rogers, S. J., Donovan, C. M., D'Eugenio, D. B., Brown, S. L., Lynch, E. W., Moersch, M. S., & Schafer, D. S. (1981). *Early intervention developmental profile.* Ann Arbor, MI: University of Michigan Press.

Rossetti, L. M. (1990). *Infant–toddler assessment: An interdisciplinary approach.* Boston: College Hill Press.

Sanford, A. R., & Zelman, J. G. (1981). *Learning accomplishment profile (LAP).* Lewisville, NC: Kaplan Press.

Santa Cruz County Office of Education (1987). *Help for special preschoolers.* Palo Alto, CA: VORT.

Siegel, L. (1983). Correction for prematurity and its consequences for the assessment of the very low birthweight infant. *Child Development 1*(54), 1176.

Skinner, B. F. (1953). *Science and human behavior.* New York: Macmillan.

Snell, M. E. (Ed.). (1987). *Systematic instruction for persons with severe handicaps* (3rd ed.). Columbus, OH: Merrill.

Strain, P. S., McConnell, S. R., Carta, J. J., Fowler, S. A., Neisworth, J. T., & Wolery, M. (1992). Behaviorism in early intervention. *Topics in Early Childhood Special Education, 12*(1), 121–141.

Thomas, A., & Chess, S. (1977). *Temperament and development.* New York: Brunner/Mazel.

Thomas, A., Chess, S., & Birch, H. G. (1970). The origin of personality. *Scientific American, 223,* 102–109.

Tronick, E., & Brazelton, T. (1975). Clinical use of the Brazelton neonatal behavioral assessment. In B. Friedlander, G. Sterrit, & G. Kirk (Eds.), *Exceptional infant: Vol. 3. Assessment and intervention.* New York: Brunner/Mazel.

Uzgiris, I. C., & Hunt, J. M. (1975). *Assessment in infancy.* Urbana, IL: University of Illinois Press.

Widerstrom, A. H., Mowder, B. A., & Sandall, S. R. (1991). *At-risk and handicapped newborns and infants.* Englewood Cliffs, NJ: Prentice-Hall.

Wilson, W. M. (1987). Age adjustment in psychological assessment of children born prematurely. *Journal of Pediatric Psychology, 12*(3), 445–450.

Wolff, P. H. (1989). The concept of development: How does it constrain assessment and therapy? In P. R. Zelazo & R. G. Barr, (Eds.), *Challenges to developmental paradigms: Implications for theory, assessment, and treatment* (pp. 13–28). Hillsdale, NJ: Lawrence Erlbaum Associates.

Zelazo, P. R., & Barr, R. G. (Eds.). (1989). *Challenges to developmental paradigms: Implications for theory, assessment, and treatment.* Hillsdale, NJ: Lawrence Erlbaum Associates.

CHAPTER 7

Assessing Cognitive Development

CHAPTER OBJECTIVES

What is intelligence? What makes us intelligent? The nature of intelligence has received a great deal of investigation. This chapter provides an overview of the development of the measurement of intelligence and discusses several prominent theories on which we base our current views of cognitive processing. Specific tests of cognitive development will be examined.

Upon completion of this chapter, you should be able to:

Describe several theories of intelligence, including those of Cattell, Binet, Spearman, Wechsler, Horn, Guilford, Das, Gardner, and Sternberg.

Explain the concept of intelligence tests as samples of behavior.

Discuss the stability of test performance in infants and young children.

Describe specific tests of intelligence.

Key Terms

Eugenics Movement. Advocated the improvement of intellectual characteristics of the human race through selective breeding.

g. The symbol for general intelligence; thought to be the common link among various mental abilities.

S. The symbol for a specific factor of intelligence that is in contrast to a general factor of intelligence (g).

Gc. The symbol for crystallized abilities, which are mental abilities influenced by acquired skills and knowledge.

Gf. The symbol for fluid intelligence, which consists of nonverbal comparatively culture-free mental abilities that are dependent on new learning.

Simultaneous Processing. A type of mental processing that is integrated or synthesized in order to obtain a solution.

Metacomponent. A cognitive process that helps in planning, monitoring, and evaluating an individual's performance of a task.

Successive Processing. A type of mental processing that requires that a problem be solved in sequential or serial order.

THEORETICAL PERSPECTIVES

Sir Francis Galton (1822–1911)

Sir Francis Galton, who lived in England, was very influential among early theorists because he discovered several statistics that helped to quantify measurements of behavior. Galton began the eugenics movement, which advocated the improvement

TABLE 7.1 Major intelligence theorists

Theorist	Theory
Nineteenth Century	
Sir Francis Galton	Developed statistics to aid in the analysis of mental traits.
James McKeen Cattell	Originated the term *mental test;* advocated that tests be developed to measure certain abilities.
Twentieth Century	
Alfred Binet	With Theodore Simon in 1905, developed an intelligence test that later became the Stanford–Binet.
Charles Spearman	Developed two-factor theory of intelligence; believed that all intellectual activities require the use of General Intelligence or "*g.*"
David Wechsler	Created an intelligence scale that consisted of verbal and nonverbal items arranged in subtests. Additional instruments were developed later.
Contemporary Theorists	
John Horn	Produced a model of intelligence that consists of fluid (*Gf*) and crystallized (*Gc*) abilities.
J. P. Guilford	Proposed a model of intelligence called the structure-of-the-intellect model. Hypothesized that intelligence can be organized into a system of factors.
Jafannath Das	Theorized that there are two approaches to cognitive processing: simultaneous and successive processing.
Howard Gardner	Developed the theory of multiple intelligences. According to Gardner, there are at least seven different intelligences: linguistic, logical-mathematical, spatial, musical, bodily-kinesthetic, interpersonal, and intrapersonal.
Robert Sternberg	Proposed a triarchic theory of intelligence. Hypothesized that intelligence consists of at least three components: componential, contextual, and experiential.

of intellectual characteristics of the human race through selective breeding. He is credited with putting into general use the words "nature and nurture," a phrase that still produces much controversy (Fancher, 1985). He believed that heredity determined a person's physical and mental characteristics, talent, and character and that environment played a negligible role in the development of these abilities (Kevles, 1985).

James McKeen Cattell (1860–1944)

James McKeen Cattell, an American, was an assistant to Galton who returned to the United States and set up a laboratory at Columbia University. His major contribution to intelligence testing was to introduce the term *mental test* in an article published in 1890. In this article, Cattell argued that instruments should be developed to measure certain characteristics. His proposed tests were mainly intended to assess sensory discrimination and sensorimotor abilities (Thorndike & Lohman, 1990). Cattell introduced the concept of standardization of test administration procedures (Reynolds & Kaufman, 1985).

Alfred Binet (1857–1911)

In France, Alfred Binet and Theodore Simon (1873–1961) were working to develop a series of tasks to use in the differentiation of children with mental disabilities and those identified as normal. In 1905 they published their first scale, and in 1908 a revised test for children ages three to thirteen years was published. In 1911 Binet, alone, extended the scale to include adults. Binet's breakthrough came when he realized that age was a factor in intelligence. When normal children were compared with children with mental disabilities, the normal children passed the test items at a younger age than the children who were disabled. Binet conceived of intelligence as composed of various abilities, such as attention, memory, discrimination, and imagination, that are heavily influenced by practical judgment (Fancher, 1985).

Lewis Terman, a professor at Stanford University, became interested in the Binet scale. In 1916, he published a revised, standardized version, which became known as the Stanford–Binet. With the publication of the Stanford–Binet, Terman introduced the term intelligence quotient (IQ) (French & Hale, 1990). Since 1916, the Stanford–Binet has been revised or updated four times: in 1937, 1960, 1972, and 1986.

Charles Spearman (1863–1945)

Charles Spearman developed a two-factor theory of intelligence. He postulated that there is a general intelligence, which he frequently abbreviated as *g*. General intelligence was thought to be the common link among the various abilities. Spearman believed that all intellectual activities require the use of *g* and, when estimating a person's intelligence, knowledge about *g* is very important.

Spearman believed that there was a second factor of intelligence, a specific factor that determined the ability for a specific type of intelligence. This factor was symbolized by the letter *s* (Fancher, 1985).

David Wechsler (1896–1981)

David Wechsler, while basically accepting Binet's definition of intelligence as a global ability, developed a test that substantially deviated from Binet's approach. Wechsler took many tasks from Binet, including Comprehension, Similarities, Vocabulary, Digit Span, and Picture Completion. Rather than administering a series of brief tasks that were arranged by age level, Wechsler developed a series of tasks to which all individuals were asked to respond. In addition, rather than limiting his items to primarily verbal ability, he added nonverbal items (Reynolds & Kaufman, 1985).

In 1939 Wechsler published the Wechsler–Bellevue Scale. Since then, additional instruments have been developed. These include the Wechsler Intelligence Scale for Children (WISC) in 1949, the Wechsler Preschool and Primary Scale of Intelligence (WPPSI) in 1967, the Wechsler Intelligence Scale for Children—Revised (WISC-R) in 1974, the Wechsler Preschool and Primary Scale of Intelligence—Revised (WPPSI-R) in 1989, the Wechsler Intelligence Scale for Children—III (WISC-III) in 1991, the Wechsler Adult Intelligence Scale (WAIS) in 1955, and the Wechsler Adult Intelligence Scale—Revised (WAIS-R) in 1981.

CONTEMPORARY THEORISTS

Horn-Cattell

Building on the work of Cattell, John L. Horn developed a model of intelligence called the *Gf–Gc* theory of intelligence (Horn, 1985). Horn used *Gf* to represent *fluid intelligence,* which involves nonverbal, comparatively culture-free mental activities. Fluid intelligence is dependent on new learning and involves mental operations and processes. The symbol *Gc* represents *crystallized intelligence,* which is heavily influenced by acquired skills and knowledge. Crystallized intelligence is dependent on an individual's culture and environment and is related to overlearning and achievement (Horn, 1985; Sattler, 1988).

Horn constructed a hierarchical model of intelligence consisting of *Gf* and *Gc,* as well as visual sensory detectors, auditory sensory detectors, short-term acquisition retrieval, long-term storage retrieval, correct decision speed, broad visualization, clerical speed, and broad auditory thinking. The forms of intelligence symbolized by *Gf* and *Gc* depend on the other eight abilities. Figure 7.1 illustrates the arrangement of these abilities in the hierarchy.

Guilford

J. P. Guilford (1967) proposed a model of intellectual functioning which he called the *structure-of-the-intellect model.* He hypothesized that the intellect was organized into a system composed of numerous factors. The factors were organized around three major categories: contents, products, and operations. *Content* refers to the knowledge and information on which mental operations are performed. *Product* is the result of the combination of content and mental operations. Guilford organized the structure-of-the-intellect model into a three-dimensional cube (Figure 7.2).

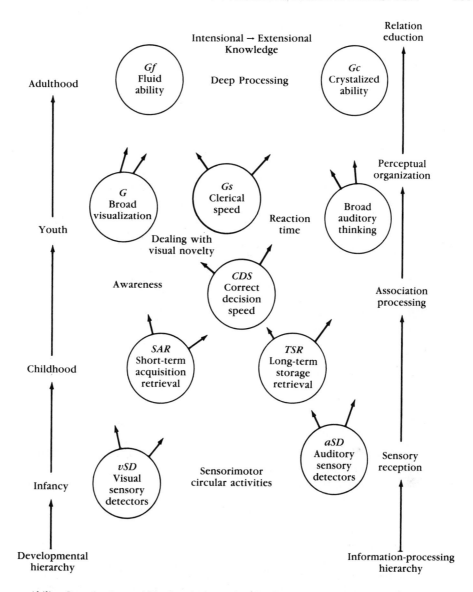

Ability Organizations within Developmental and Information-Processing Hierarchies.

FIGURE 7.1 *Gf-Gc* theory of intelligence

SOURCE: *Handbook of Intelligence* by Benjamin B. Wolman. Copyright © 1985 by John Wiley & Sons, Inc. Reprinted by permission.

Contents.   The first category, content, relates to knowledge and information and is composed of four factors:

1. *Figural:* meaning derived from figures and figural properties. Examples of figural information include shape, texture, color, and size.

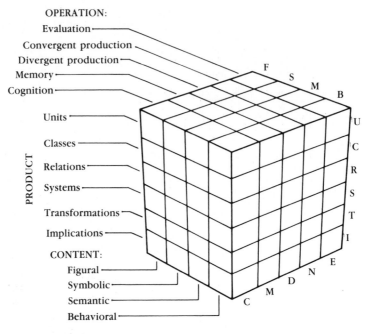

FIGURE 7.2   The structure-of-intellect model with three parameters.

SOURCE: *The Nature of Human Intelligence* by J. P. Guilford. Copyright © 1967 by McGraw-Hill, Inc. Reprinted by permission.

2. *Symbolic:* information that is derived from signs, letters, numbers, and musical notes.
3. *Semantic:* information relating to verbal thinking and verbal communication.
4. *Behavioral:* knowledge involved in perceiving, feeling, thinking, and intention.

Products.   The next category, products, involves the way "any information occurs" (Guilford, 1967, p. 63). It relates to how we know and how we understand. Guilford hypothesized that this category consists of six factors:

1. *Units:* separate or segregated pieces of information. Letters of the alphabet, vocabulary definitions, and numbers are examples of units.
2. *Classes:* sets of items of information that are clustered because they have similar characteristics. Examples include number classification and verbal classification.
3. *Relations:* connections between pieces of information relating to characteristics or variables they have in common. According to Guilford, this factor is closely related to Spearman's *g.* Analogies and trends are examples of relations.

4. *Systems:* complex, organized groups of items that have interrelated or interacting sections. Reasoning is an example of the use of this factor.
5. *Transformations:* changes in the characteristics, meaning, and use of information. Examples include solving mathematical equations and devising variations on a theme in music.
6. *Implications:* relate to predictions and anticipations.

Operations.   Finally, the category of operations refers to the mental operations that are performed. There are five factors in this category:

1. *Cognition:* refers to awareness and recognition of information in different forms.
2. *Memory:* involves the retention or storage of information, with some ability to retrieve the information in the same form in which it was retained.
3. *Divergent production:* pertains to the creation of information, with an emphasis on the variety and number of ideas produced.
4. *Convergent production:* like divergent production, convergent production involves the generation of information, but the output is more structured. Convergent production is related to deductive thinking.
5. *Evaluation:* involves using criteria to make a comparison between various products in order to assess them.

Jafannath Das

Jafannath Das and his associates (Das & Molloy, 1975; Das, Kirby & Jarman, 1975, 1979) proposed a model of cognitive processing based on the work of Alexander Luria. This model postulates that there are two approaches to cognitive processing: simultaneous processing and successive processing. In *simultaneous processing,* information is integrated or synthesized to obtain a solution. Examples of simultaneous processing include copying figures and completion of figures. *Successive processing* requires that problems be solved in a sequential or serial order. Color naming and reading words call for successive processing.

Howard Gardner

Howard Gardner (1991) has developed the theory of multiple intelligences (MI). According to Gardner, individuals

> are capable of at least seven different ways of knowing the world—ways that I have elsewhere labeled the *seven human intelligences.* According to this analysis, we are able to know the world through language, logical–mathematical analysis, spatial representation, musical thinking, the use of the body to solve problems or to make things, an understanding of other individuals, and an understanding of ourselves. (Gardner, 1991, p. 12)

According to MI theory, individuals have different profiles of strengths of the seven intelligences, and individuals differ in the ways they invoke and combine the various intelligences to carry out tasks and to solve problems. Gardner believes that school environments should be developed on the basis of these seven ways of knowing. Curriculum that is founded on these ways of knowing is worth assessing. According to Gardner, if the curriculum is not appropriately structured, assessment is useless.

MI theory may be used as an approach to assessment. Although there are no formal assessment tools based on MI theory, Gardner advocates the use of this approach to develop alternative and authentic forms of assessment. Assessment can take a variety of forms including observations, demonstrations, portfolios, and video-tapes.

Robert Sternberg

Robert Sternberg (1985) has described a theory of intelligence called the *triarchic theory,* which has three components: metacomponents, performance components, and knowledge-acquisition components. *Metacomponents* help to plan, monitor, and evaluate an individual's performance of a task. Sternberg (1985) listed 10 meta-components as important to intelligent functioning:

1. Recognition that a problem of some kind exists
2. Recognition of just what the nature of the problem is
3. Selection of a set of lower order, nonexecutive components for the performance of a task
4. Selection of a strategy for task performance, combining the lower order components
5. Selection of one or more mental representations for information
6. Decision on how to allocate attentional resources
7. Monitoring or keeping track of one's place in task performance and of what has been done and needs to be done
8. Understanding of internal and external feedback concerning the quality of task performance
9. Knowing how to act on the feedback that is received
10. Implementation of action as a result of the feedback (p. 62)

Performance components are employed to execute a variety of strategies for task performance. These are lower order processes. Performance components include:

1. Encoding the nature of a stimulus
2. Inferring the relations between two stimulus terms that are similar in some ways and different in others
3. Applying a previously inferred relation to a new situation (Sternberg, 1985, p. 62)

Knowledge-acquisition components are processes used to learn new information and to store it in memory. There are three knowledge-acquisition components:

1. Selective encoding involves selecting between relevant and irrelevant information
2. Selective combination involves combining what has been selectively encoded in order to maximize its coherence and connectedness

3. Selective comparison consists of relating the information that has been selectively encoded and combined with information already stored in memory in order to optimize the connectedness of the new knowledge (Sternberg, 1985, p. 62)

Intelligence Tests as Samples of Behavior

If we were able to directly measure intelligence, we would have to monitor the electrical activities, neurochemical changes, and neurobiological changes that occur during cognition. As educators, we rely on indirect measures or tests to estimate intelligence. Intelligence tests only sample behaviors that are associated with intelligence, like a knife cutting through a cake. The knife reveals a sample of the cake, and we assume that the texture and flavor of the cake are the same in the uncut or unsampled portion. This analogy can be applied to intelligence tests. While the tests sample behaviors, our assumption is that the sample provides information about the intellectual abilities of the child.

Although there are many intelligence tests, analysis shows that they sample similar behaviors. Salvia and Ysseldyke (1991) have described these behaviors.

1. *Discrimination.* Intelligence tests sample skills that relate to figural, symbolic, or semantic discrimination, usually by asking the child to find the item that is different from the other items.
2. *Generalization.* Skills relating to figural, symbolic, or semantic understanding are sampled. The child is asked to recognize the response that goes with the stimulus item.
3. *Motor behavior.* Young children are asked to demonstrate a motor response. For instance, they are asked to throw objects, construct block towers, and place subjects in certain places on a board. Older children are asked to draw geometric forms, solve mazes, or reproduce designs from memory. Many other test items evaluate motor abilities—that is, children are asked to point, imitate, or perform other motor activities to complete certain test items.
4. *General information.* These items are similar to items found on many achievement tests; they evaluate what the child has learned. Examples include: "What is the opposite of uncle?" and "How many eggs are in a dozen?"
5. *Vocabulary.* Intelligence tests assess knowledge of vocabulary in different ways. The child may be asked to point to a picture that has been named, to define words that are presented orally, or to identify a word that matches a definition.
6. *Induction.* Children are asked to induce or to infer a general principle after being presented with several stimuli. For example, after being shown a rock, a block of wood, a metal object, and a toothpick, the child is asked to describe the general rule governing why certain objects float.
7. *Comprehension.* The child is asked to demonstrate understanding or the nature of meaning of certain stimuli. The child may be asked to show that directions, certain materials, or societal customs are understood. Some tests ask how the child would respond to certain situations ("What

should you do if you see a young child playing with an electrical cord?").

8. *Sequencing.* The child is required to identify the correct sequences for a series of items. The items may consist of numbers, geometric figures, or abstract geometric designs.

9. *Detail recognition.* A few tests evaluate detail recognition. The child is asked to identify details that are missing from a picture or to draw a picture, which is evaluated on the basis of the number of details the child has included in the drawing.

10. *Analogies.* Items consist of a statement to which the child must give the appropriate response. The stimuli may be a series of words, geometric designs, or numbers. A sample item is as follows:
    parent:child::goose:_____.

11. *Abstract reasoning.* There are various ways to assess abstract reasoning. Children may be asked to identify the absurdity in a statement or picture, to state the meaning of a proverb, or to solve problems that call for arithmetic reasoning.

12. *Memory.* A variety of test items evaluate both long-term and short-term memory. Children may be asked to repeat sentences or a series of digits, to retell what they have read, or to reproduce a design from memory.

13. *Pattern completion.* Children are asked to complete a pattern or matrix from which a piece is missing.

There are many behaviors that intelligence tests do not sample. These behaviors include mechanical, motor, musical, artistic, motivational, emotional, and attitudinal behaviors (Anastasi, 1988). Recent research on the nature of intelligence has begun to explore the contribution of these behaviors to our understanding of intelligence.

Controversy over the Use of Intelligence Testing with Young Children

The value of intelligence testing has been debated over the years. Arguments against the use of intelligence testing include the contentions that testing limits children's opportunities, may be harmful to children from minority groups, and facilitates the placement of children into categories. Advocates of intelligence testing have argued that intelligence testing assists in the diagnosis of children, helps to identify children who need specialized instruction or therapy, and promotes educational opportunities (Sattler, 1988).

Neisworth and Bagnato (1992) wrote that intelligence testing of young children with disabilities and developmental delays must be rejected for several reasons. They pointed out that professionals do not agree on the definition of intelligence in infants and young children and emphasized the absence of a consensus on how to measure it.

The stability of performance on an intelligence measure is influenced by the age at which children are tested. In a review of the research on the predictive validity of infant and preschool tests, Anastasi (1988) concluded that infant tests of intelligence have no predictive validity and that preschool tests have moderate predictive validity.

There is some evidence, however, that for infants who are identified as disabled, the predictive validity coefficients are moderately accurate predictors of later intelligence. Clinical observations, coupled with the performance on an infant intelligence test, can improve the predictability of performance on the intelligence test. In addition, predictions about future performance can be enhanced by considering the results of repeated testings and examining trends over time (Anastasi, 1988).

Research on intelligence has confirmed that intelligence is not a unitary, stable ability during infancy. Correlations among various instruments of intelligence are very weak. In infants and young children, intelligence changes with age. By the ages of seven or eight, measured intelligence becomes much more stable. As the child gets older, it is likely that the performance on an IQ test will be a good predictor of later performance.

Intelligence tests provide just a part of what we want to know about a child. Intelligence tests are only one indicator. The assessment of children should never be dependent on the results of one test; rather, information should be gathered from the results of additional standardized tests and by means of observations, interviews, checklists, rating scales, samples of children's work, and other types of assessment.

In summary, it is important to remember that:

Intelligence tests do not measure innate ability.

Intelligence test scores change as a child gets older.

Intelligence test scores are just estimates of abilities.

Intelligence is just one of many abilities that children have.

Intelligence scores from various intelligence tests may not have the same meaning.

Multiple types of assessment should be used when assessing a child (National Association for the Education of Young Children, 1988; Sattler, 1988).

TESTS OF INTELLIGENCE

Cattell Infant Intelligence Scale

The Cattell Infant Intelligence Scale (Cattell, 1960, 1980), originally published in 1940, was designed to be a downward extension of Form L of the *Stanford–Binet Intelligence Scale.* The test has been changed very little since its original publication. It was intended to be administered individually to children with developmental ages of 2 to 30 months. The test was based, in part, on the Gesell tests. The Cattell is much more similar to developmental tests (Chapter 6) than to intelligence tests.

Administration. Approximately 20 to 30 minutes is needed to administer this test to a very young child; and 30 minutes is needed for a toddler.

Scoring. All items are scored either correct (+) or incorrect (−). Developmental scores are calculated and are reported in months.

Standardization. The Cattell manual (Cattell, 1980) has not been restandardized since its original publication in 1940. The standardization sample consisted of 274 children ages 3 to 36 months. The sample was neither stratified according to census proportions nor randomly selected. The sample consisted of children who were enrolled in a research project sponsored by Harvard University.

Reliability and Validity.   Specific data relating to reliability and validity are not reported in the manual.

Summary.   The Cattell Infant Intelligence Scale is an individually administered test for children ages 2 to 30 months. The items assess the development of young children. It is outdated and should be used very cautiously.

Cognitive Abilities Test

The Cognitive Abilities Test (CogAT) (Thorndike & Hagen, 1986) was developed from the Lorge–Thorndike Intelligence Tests and consists of a series of group-administered intelligence tests for grades kindergarten through 12. The description that follows is for the primary battery only, which is for children in kindergarten through grade 3. According to the manual, the CogAT assesses (1) ability to understand oral English; (2) ability to follow directions; (3) ability to hold material in short-term memory; (4) strategies for scanning pictorial and figural stimuli to obtain either specific or general information; (5) general information and verbal concepts; (6) ability to compare stimuli and detect similarities and differences in relative size, position, quantity, shape and time; (7) ability to classify, categorize, or order familiar objects; and (8) ability to use quantitative and spatial relationships and concepts.

The primary battery consists of three separate batteries covering verbal, quantitative, and nonverbal abilities. Each battery contains two subtests.

Verbal Battery

Oral Vocabulary.   The child fills in the oval next to the picture that illustrates a word that the examiner reads (e.g., pencil).

Verbal Classification.   The child marks the response that goes with the word that the examiner reads.

Quantitative Battery

Quantitative Concepts.   The child marks the object that illustrates a quantitative concept that the examiner reads (e.g., whole, how many more).

Relational Concepts.   The child fills in the oval next to an object that illustrates a relational concept (e.g., biggest, tallest).

Nonverbal Battery

Figure Classification.   The child marks the figure that goes with three figures that are shown.

Matrices.   The child chooses the response that correctly completes a figure.

Administration.   The teacher reads all the directions for the primary battery. The child is not required to read but must be able to follow the directions of the teacher. The child's responses are limited to identifying the one correct response by filling in an oval. Three sessions, each lasting from 35 to 40 minutes, are required to administer the primary battery.

Scoring.   Separate scores are obtained for the verbal, quantitative, and nonverbal batteries. There is no total score. Percentiles (fall, winter, spring) by age and by grade and stanines by age and by grade are available. IQ scores are standard scores with a mean of 100 and a standard deviation of 16.

Standardization.   The CogAT was normed at the same time as the Iowa Tests of Basic Skills. Public schools across the United States were stratified according to geographic region, enrollment, and socioeconomic status based on 1980 census data. Standardization took place during the fall of 1984 and the spring of 1985. Several hundred thousand children took part in the standardization of the CogAT for grades kindergarten through 12, with more than 13,000 in each grade level. In addition to the large public school sample, the CogAT was normed on children enrolled in parochial schools and private schools.

Reliability.   Internal consistency reliability is reported. In general, the coefficients are in the .80s and the low .90s. There is also some evidence of test–retest reliability for each of the three batteries. The reliability coefficients range from .64 to .92.

Validity.   Criterion-related validity is estimated by correlating the CogAT with the Iowa Tests of Basic Skills. Evidence of other types of validity is absent from the manual.

Summary.   The primary battery of the Cognitive Abilities Test is a group intelligence test that is intended for children in kindergarten through grade 3. While the standardization of this test is commendable, evidence of reliability and validity is lacking.

There is much hesitation on the part of early childhood educators to use group-administered tests with young children. It is much more difficult for the assessor to monitor a young child's performance on a group test. Because the CogAT is a group test, its results should be used for screening purposes only.

Detroit Tests of Learning Aptitude—Primary (Second Edition)

The Detroit Tests of Learning Aptitude—Primary (Second Edition) (DTLA-P:2) (Hammill & Bryant, 1991) is an instrument designed to measure the intellectual aptitudes or abilities of children ages 3 years, 0 months to 9 years, 11 months. According to the authors, the DTLA-P:2 has four uses: (1) to discover strengths and weaknesses among mental abilities, (2) to identify children who perform significantly below their peers, (3) to predict future performance, and (4) to aid as a research tool when investigating children's aptitude, intelligence, and cognitive ability. Depending on the child's age and abilities, the DTLA-P:2 takes between 15 and 45 minutes to administer.

The DTLA-P:2 consists of 100 items arranged in order from the easiest to the most difficult. The items yield six subtest scores and a general, overall mental ability score. The six subtests and the domains in which they are grouped are as follows.

Linguistic Domain
1. *Verbal quotient:* assesses the understanding, integration, and use of spoken language.
2. *Nonverbal quotient:* assesses abilities involved in spatial relationships and nonverbal symbolic reasoning.

Attentional Domain
3. *Attention—Enhanced quotient:* evaluates immediate recall, short-term memory, and ability to concentrate.
4. *Attention—Reduced quotient:* measures long-term memory, understanding, reasoning ability, and comprehension of abstract relationships.

Motoric Domain
6. *Motor—Enhanced quotient:* assesses complex motor abilities, especially fine motor abilities.
7. *Motor—Reduced quotient:* evaluates aptitude with reduced demands for motor activities. The child is asked to indicate the correct response by either pointing or speaking.

Administration. Examiners are expected to have some background in assessment. Directions for administration are on the test protocol. For some items, directions for administration are in the examiner's manual. The test is designed to be administered individually. Since the items are arranged from least to most difficult, the examiner begins testing at certain entry points. These entry points are determined by the child's chronological age. Testing continues until a ceiling is reached.

Scoring. The responses are scored either correct or incorrect. The scores for each item are used in the computation of the total score and the subtest scores. Raw scores can be converted to age equivalents, percentiles, and quotients, which are standard scores that have a mean of 100 and a standard deviation of 15.

Standardization. The standardization sample of the DTLA-P:2 consisted of 2,095 children in 36 states. In developing this instrument, the authors used data from the standardization sample (March–June 1985) of the DTLA-P and tested an additional 619 children between September 1989 and June 1990. These two samples were then combined to form the standardization sample for the DTLA-P:2. The additional sample population was assembled as follows: (1) professionals who had purchased the Detroit Tests of Learning Aptitude—2 were asked to administer the DTLA-P to 20 to 30 children in their area; (2) individuals who had helped to develop other tests published by Pro-Ed were asked to assist; (3) teams of examiners who had been trained by the examiners were asked to administer the DTLA-P in four census areas; and (4) a mailing list of examiners, purchased from a mail order company, served as another source of names of practitioners. Information on the percentage of children for each of the following variables is reported: gender, residence (urban, rural), race, geographic area (Northeast, North Central, South, West), ethnicity (Native American, Hispanic, Asian, other), and age.

Reliability.   Internal consistency reliability was estimated using a random sample of 350 protocols from the standardization sample. The average reliabilities for the total score and the six subtests ranged from .88 to .94. Test–retest reliability was also estimated. However, little information about the characteristics of the sample, the qualifications of the examiners, or the test–retest interval is provided.

Validity.   The authors maintain that the DTLA-P:2 has content validity because it measures behaviors that are found in a set of behaviors listed by Salvia and Ysseldyke (1988) in a taxonomy developed by three people, two of whom are the authors of this test. To demonstrate concurrent validity, the authors used evidence from four concurrent validity studies that were conducted with the DTLA-P. Scores from the DTLA-P were correlated with scores from selected aptitude and achievement tests. The size of the sample used in each of these correlations ranged from 28 to 81 children. The median reliability coefficient was .78. Three studies of concurrent validity are reported using the DTLA-P:2. As with the DTLA-P, scores from the DTLA-P:2 were correlated with scores from selected aptitude and achievement tests. The size of the sample used in each of these correlations ranged from 28 to 68 children. The reliability coefficients reported ranged from .31 to .87.

No evidence of predictive validity is contained in the DTLA-P:2 manual. While the authors present evidence of construct validity, additional validity studies need to be conducted.

Summary.   The Detroit Tests of Learning Aptitude—Primary (Second Edition) is an individually administered test for children ages 3 years, 0 months to 9 years, 11 months. It is designed to measure intellectual ability using six subtests and a general, overall score. Until questions about the appropriateness of the standardization sample, reliability, and validity have been answered satisfactorily, the DTLA-P:2 should be used with caution.

Differential Ability Scales

The Differential Ability Scales (DAS) (Elliot, 1990a) is a revision of the British Ability Scales. The DAS is designed to measure cognitive ability and achievement in children ages 2 years, 6 months to 17 years, 11 months. The test is not based on any one theory of mental ability. According to the manual, the test "is built on a collection of subtests that sample a range of human abilities thought to be useful in assessing children, particularly children with learning difficulties. The selection of the abilities sampled was influenced by a variety of theoretical approaches" (Elliot, 1990b, p. 14).

The DAS is organized into a hierarchical structure. The first level consists of the subtest scores; at the next level are the cluster scores; and at the general level the DAS yields a general cognitive ability (GCA) score. The test contains 17 cognitive subtests and 3 school achievement subtests. Not all the subtests are given to every child. Depending on the age of the child, selected subtests are administered. The following is a description of the subtests and clusters.

Preschool Core Subtests

Block Building (2 years, 6 months to 4 years, 11 months). Measures motor and perceptual abilities. The child is required to reproduce designs created by the examiner with wooden blocks.

Verbal Comprehension (2 years, 6 months to 6 years, 11 months). Measures receptive language ability. The child is asked to point to pictures that are named or to place objects and chips according to the examiner's instructions (e.g., *under* the bridge).

Picture Similarities (2 years, 6 months to 7 years, 11 months). Measures nonverbal reasoning ability. After being shown a row of four pictures or designs, the child must choose the picture or design that best goes with the ones shown.

Naming Vocabulary (2 years, 6 months to 8 years, 11 months). Measures expressive vocabulary. The child is asked to name several objects and pictures that are shown.

Pattern Construction (3 years to 17 years, 11 months). Measures visual–spatial problem solving. The child is asked to construct patterns using foam squares and plastic blocks.

Early Number Concepts (2 years, 6 months to 7 years, 11 months). Measures prenumerical and number concepts and skills. The child is asked to count chips and to answer questions about pictures. Many but not all of the subtests are nonverbal.

Copying (3 years, 6 months to 7 years, 11 months). Measures ability to copy, motor ability, and the ability to perceive similarities. After being shown a line drawing, the child is required to reproduce it.

School-Age Core Subtests

Recall of Designs (5 years to 17 years, 11 months). Assesses short-term recall, motor ability, and visual–spatial ability. After being shown a nonpictorial line drawing for 5 seconds, the child must draw it from memory.

Word Definitions (5 years to 17 years, 11 months). Measures verbal knowledge. The examiner says a word and the child must provide the meaning.

Pattern Construction (3 years to 17 years, 11 months). See the discussion of this subtest in the Preschool Core Subtests section.

Matrices (5 years to 17 years, 11 months). Measures nonverbal reasoning ability. The child is shown a series of matrices. For each one, the child is asked to choose the design that best completes the matrix.

Similarities (5 years to 17 years, 11 months). Measures verbal reasoning. The child must respond orally to a series of questions.

Sequential and Quantitative Reasoning (5 years to 17 years, 11 months). Assesses the ability to perceive sequential patterns or rules in numerical relationships. The items consist of abstract figures or numbers to which the child must respond.

Diagnostic Subtests

Matching Letterlike Forms (4 years to 7 years, 11 months). Measures the ability to visually discriminate among asymmetric letterlike figures. The child is asked to match similar figures that look like letters of either the Roman or Greek alphabet and are rotated on a page.

Recall of Digits (2 years, 6 months to 17 years, 11 months). Assesses short-term auditory–sequential recall of digits. The child must repeat a series of two to nine digits which have been presented rapidly.

Recall of Objects—Immediate and Delayed (4 years to 17 years, 11 months). Assesses short-term and delayed verbal memory. For three different trials the child recalls as many objects as possible after being shown a card with a number of objects on it.

Recognition of Pictures (2 years, 6 months to 17 years, 11 months). Assesses short-term visual recognition as opposed to visual memory. After being shown a card with one or more pictures for 5 or 10 seconds, the child is shown another set of pictures and must point to the items that were displayed in the first picture.

Speed of Information Processing (5 years to 17 years, 11 months). Assesses speed and accuracy of simple mental operations. After being shown a page consisting of figures or numbers, the child must mark, as quickly as possible, the circle containing the largest number of boxes or the highest number.

School Achievement Tests

Basic Number Skills (6 years to 17 years, 11 months). Assesses basic computational skills. The child is asked to solve problems involving printed numbers, basic operations, and word problems.

Spelling (6 years to 17 years, 11 months). Assesses ability to spell based on phonetically regular and irregular words. Children ages 6 years to 8 years, 11 months are also asked to write their names. The examiner says the word, uses the word in a sentence, and repeats the word.

Word Reading (5 years to 17 years, 11 months). Assesses ability to decode words in isolation. The child is asked to read a series of words that are shown on a card.

Clusters of the Preschool Level of the Cognitive Battery (3 years, 6 months to 5 years, 11 months)

Verbal Ability. Assesses learned verbal concepts and knowledge. The subtests that form this cluster are Verbal Comprehension and Naming Vocabulary; both present pictures and objects visually.

Nonverbal Ability. Assesses complex, nonverbal mental processing. The subtests in this cluster are Picture Similarities, Pattern Construction, and Copying, which use simple verbal instructions and do not involve any verbal responses.

Clusters of the School-Age Level of the Cognitive Battery (6 years to 17 years, 11 months)

Verbal Ability. Assesses verbal mental processing and acquired knowledge. The subtests that form this cluster are Word Definitions and Similarities.

Nonverbal Reasoning Ability. Assesses nonverbal inductive reasoning and mental processing. The subtests in this cluster are Matrices and Sequential and Quantitative Reasoning.

Spatial Ability. Assesses complex visual–spatial processing. The subtests that form this cluster are Recall of Designs and Pattern Construction.

Administration.   The DAS should be administered by an examiner who has a background in the principles of assessment. For children ages 2 years, 6 months to 3 years, 5 months, the total time to administer the DAS is approximately 35 minutes. Approximately 65 minutes should be allowed for administration to children ages 3 years, 6 months to 5 years, 11 months. It takes between 65 and 85 minutes to administer the DAS to children older than six. Separate directions for administering each subtest are provided in the manual.

The administration of the DAS has several unique features, notably decision points, alternative stopping points, teaching a failed item, extended selection of subtests, and out-of-level testing. While the starting points for each subtest are based on the child's age, the administration of items continues until the child reaches a *decision point,* whereupon the examiner must decide whether to stop, to continue to administer the difficult items, or to drop back and administer easier items. *Alternative stopping points* are provided to permit the examiner to halt the test administration if the items are too difficult or if rapport has not been obtained. In addition to these features, some subtests allow the examiner to *teach* the child an item that the child has failed.

Extended selection of subtests refers to the option of allowing the examiner to administer additional subtests that measure similar abilities. This option is useful with young children when it begins to appear that further assessment is necessary. *Out-of-level testing* refers to the administration of additional subtests to children whose abilities are unusually low or high. These subtests may not be appropriate for children of average ability.

For children with hearing impairments or speech or language problems, nonverbal subtests can be administered (e.g., Block Building and Picture Similarities). The scores from these subtests form a special nonverbal composite which, according to the manual, can be used in place of the GCA. However, separate norms for special populations are not included.

Scoring.   Raw scores are compared to ability scores, which are unique to the DAS and provide an estimate of the child's performance on specific subtests. However, ability scores of different subtests have an important limitation. They cannot be compared. Another transformation is required to convert ability scores to T scores (mean = 50, standard deviation = 10), percentiles, and standard scores (mean = 100, standard deviation = 15). Age and grade equivalents are provided for the achievement tests. Separate guidelines are provided for scoring each of the subtests.

Standardization.   The standardization sample consisted of 3,475 children, evenly divided by gender; there were 175 children representing each six-month interval for ages 2 years, 6 months to 4 years, 11 months, and 200 children at one-year intervals for ages 5 years, 0 months to 17 years, 11 months. Other stratification variables were race/ethnicity (African American, Hispanic, Caucasian, and other, including Asian, Pacific Islander, Native American, Eskimo, Aleut), parent education, geographic region, and educational preschool enrollment. The enrollment of young children in preschool is an important consideration, since performance on the DAS may be affected by their participation in the learning environment. In addition, information about community size, school dropouts, and special education status was monitored.

Children who were identified as learning disabled, speech impaired, emotionally disturbed, physically impaired, mentally retarded, and gifted were included in the standardization sample in approximate proportion to their presence in the U.S. population. Children with severe disabilities were excluded. Separate norms are not provided. According to the manual:

> The mere inclusion of exceptional children in a norm sample does not make the instrument appropriate for use with such children, nor does their exclusion make the test inappropriate. During item and subtest development, the DAS team sought to create tasks that would be suitable in content, format, and difficulty for many exceptional children. The success of these efforts, like those of any other test development project, can be determined only through research that focuses on how the test works with such children. (Elliot, 1990b, p. 116)

Reliability.   Internal reliabilities for each of the subtests and for out-of-level testing were determined. For the most part, the reliabilities were within the moderate range.

Test–retest reliability was estimated by selecting 100 children from the standardization sample for each of the following age ranges: 3 years, 6 months to 4 years, 5 months; 5 years to 6 years, 11 months; and 12 years to 13 years, 11 months. The testing interval ranged from 2 to 7 weeks. The reliabilities were in the moderate range for the subtests. The reliabilities of the clusters and the general cognitive ability score, however, were higher than the reliabilities for the subtests.

Validity.   The manual does provide evidence of the separate factor structure for the subtests and the clusters. Concurrent validity with other ability tests and achievement tests is reported. In addition, studies of small samples of students labeled educable mentally retarded, learning disabled, reading disabled, and gifted are described. However, additional studies need to be conducted by independent researchers to confirm and extend our understanding of the validity of this relatively new instrument. Caution should be used when interpreting the performance of children with special needs.

Summary.   The DAS is an individually administered ability test for use with children ages 2 years, 6 months to 17 years, 11 months. The subtests are designed to measure cognitive ability and selected areas of achievement. Reliability is adequate.

However, additional evidence of validity is needed before the test can be confidently used with children with exceptional needs.

Kaufman Assessment Battery for Children

The Kaufman Assessment Battery for Children (K-ABC) (Kaufman & Kaufman, 1983) assesses the intelligence and achievement of children ages 2 years, 6 months to 12 years, 6 months. The test consists of 16 subtests that take from 35 minutes for young children to 75 minutes for children of elementary age. A maximum of 13 subtests is administered to each child. The subtests are arranged into three scales: the sequential processing scale, the simultaneous processing scale, and the achievement scale.

Intelligence is "defined in terms of an individual's style of solving problems and processing information" (Kaufman & Kaufman, 1983, p. 2). The intelligence scales are based on a theoretical model of mental processing developed by Das, Luria, and others that holds that information is primarily processed sequentially or simultaneously. The sequential processing scale requires that problems be solved in a sequential or serial order. The simultaneous processing scale requires that information be integrated or synthesized to obtain a solution.

The mental processing scale is a combination of the sequential and the simultaneous processing scales. It is a measure of total intelligence. The mental processing composite score has a mean of 100 and a standard deviation of 15.

The achievement scale assesses knowledge and skills gained through formal and informal experiences. The manual states that the achievement scale does not yield a diagnostic assessment of achievement skills; it does provide a global estimate of achievement in the areas of reading, arithmetic, general information, early language development, and language concepts.

The following is a description of the subtests on each of the scales:

Sequential Processing Scale
Hand Movements (ages 2-6 to 12-5). A series of hand movements is performed in the same sequence given by the examiner.

Number Recall (ages 2-6 to 12-5). A series of digits is repeated in the order in which the examiner says them.

Word Order (ages 4-0 to 12-5). A series of silhouettes of common objects is touched in the order in which the examiner identifies them.

Simultaneous Processing Scale
Magic Window (ages 2-6 to 4-11). A picture is slowly revealed as the examiner rotates it behind a narrow window.

Face Recognition (ages 2-6 to 12-5). Faces that were exposed on the preceding page are identified in a group photograph.

Gestalt Closure (ages 2-6 to 12-5). An object or scene that is depicted in an "inkblot" drawing is named.

Triangles (ages 4-0 to 12-5). Triangles are formed into a pattern that matches a design.

Matrix Analogies (ages 5-0 to 12-5). A picture or abstract design is identified that best completes a visual analogy.

Spatial Memory (ages 5-0 to 12-5). The position of pictures on a page that is briefly exposed are recalled.

Photo Series (ages 6-0 to 12-5). Photographs of an event are placed in chronological order.

Achievement Scale

Expressive Vocabulary (ages 2-6 to 4-11). An object pictured in a photograph is identified.

Faces & Places (ages 2-6 to 12-5). A famous person, fictional character, or geographic location is identified.

Arithmetic (ages 3-0 to 12-5). Knowledge of mathematical concepts is demonstrated.

Riddles (ages 3-0 to 12-5). The concept is named when a list of characteristics is presented.

Reading/Decoding (ages 5-0 to 12-5). Letters and words are read.

Reading/Understanding (ages 7-0 to 12-5). Reading comprehension is shown by following written commands.

Depending on the age of the child, various subtests can be combined to form the nonverbal scale. The nonverbal scale, which provides an estimate of intelligence for children who demonstrate communication problems, can be used with children who do not speak English or are deaf, hearing impaired, speech or language disabled, or autistic.

Administration. The manual gives comprehensive directions for the administration of the K-ABC. Instructions for administering the battery in Spanish are provided in a supplement. The starting point for each subtest is determined by the child's chronological age. Each subtest has a designated stopping point, to prevent the administration of too many items to any child. In addition, a discontinue rule can be invoked if a child misses a number of items in a row. The first item of each subtest is designated as the sample item, and the next two items are labeled teaching items. For the sample and teaching items, it is permissible for the examiner to teach the child how to respond to the type of item in question. Each item on the K-ABC is scored as correct or incorrect.

The K-ABC provides for out-of-level testing for four- and five-year-olds. This helps to provide flexibility in testing young children. At age five, the number and difficulty of the subtests that should be administered changes. The subtests of Matrix Analogies, Spatial Memory, and Reading/Decoding are introduced. Magic Window, Face Recognition, and Expressive Vocabulary are intended for children younger than five years. For children between the ages of 5 years, 0 months and 5 years, 11 months who are suspected of being mentally retarded or developmentally delayed, portions of the K-ABC normally intended for four-year-olds may be administered. Similarly, if children ages 4 years, 6 months to 4 years, 11 months are thought to be advanced or gifted, subtests for children age five and older may be administered. Separate norms are provided for children who have been tested out of level. The scores obtained from out-of-level testing, while helpful, should be used cautiously. The norms were extended upward and downward by estimating the performance of children. A nationally representative sample was not tested to obtain these extended norms.

For the nonverbal scale, the examiner can pantomime the instructions (although this is not required), and the child responds by gesturing, pointing, or demonstrating. The subtests for the nonverbal scale are:

Age 4

Face Recognition

Hand Movements

Triangles

Age 5

Hand Movements

Triangles

Matrix Analogies

Spatial Memory

Ages 6 to 12

Hand Movements

Triangles

Matrix Analogies

Spatial Memory

Photo Series

Standardization.   The standardization sample of the K-ABC consisted of 2,000 children between the ages of 2 years, 6 months and 12 years, 5 months. Based on the 1980 census, the children were stratified within each age group according to gender, geographic region, socioeconomic status, race or ethnicity (African American, Caucasian, Hispanic, other), community size, and educational placement of the child (regular or special classes).

To make the K-ABC sensitive to the needs of the diverse population in the United States, an attempt was made to develop sociocultural norms by testing an additional 469 African-American and 199 Caucasian children. However, African Americans were overrepresented in the higher education group and underrepresented in the lower education group.

Subtest scores for the mental processing scales are reported as scaled scores (mean = 10, standard deviation = 3) and percentiles. These subtest scores can be combined to yield standard scores (mean = 100, standard deviation = 15) for the sequential processing, simultaneous processing, and mental processing composite and nonverbal scales. Achievement subtests are reported as percentiles and standard scores. Age equivalents are provided for the mental processing scales and grade equivalents are reported for the achievement scale.

Reliability.   Split-half, internal consistency, and test–retest reliabilities are reported in the manual. For the most part, the reliability coefficients are acceptable. Many coefficients exceed .90 and, in general, the composite scores are more reliable than the individual subtest scores. Mean split-half reliability coefficients range from .71 (Gestalt Closure) to .91 (Reading/Understanding). Mean internal consistency coefficients for the global scales range from .89 (sequential processing) to .97 (achievement). Test–retest reliability coefficients extend from .77 (sequential processing) to .97 (achievement).

Standard errors of measurement (SEM) vary by age. For school-age children on the subtests, the SEM for the mental processing subtests ranged from 1.1 (Matrix Analogies) to 1.6 (Gestalt Closure); on the achievement scale SEM varied from 4.0 (Reading/Decoding) to 5.9 (Faces and Places). For the global scales, the SEM ranged from 2.7 (achievement) to 5.0 (sequential processing).

Validity.   The manual reports the results of many studies relating to the validity of the K-ABC. The test authors as well as numerous independent researchers have investigated the validity of the K-ABC. Reviewers have been mixed in their evaluation of the validity of the K-ABC (Anastasi, 1985; Coffman, 1985; Merz, 1984; Page, 1985; Salvia & Ysseldyke, 1991). Some reviewers have felt that the K-ABC is promising and that, at the least, it is a measure of general intelligence. Other reviewers criticize construct validity, doubting especially whether the test actually measures the theoretical abilities of simultaneous and sequential processing.

Merz (1984) has written that "on balance, it appears that the goals listed in the interpretive manual have been met and that this battery is a valuable addition to the assessment effort" (p. 404). In contrast, Page (1985) suggested that the mental processing composite was much more closely related to g, a general intelligence factor, than to separate simultaneous and sequential abilities.

Salvia and Ysseldyke (1991) concluded that there was little evidence that the K-ABC could "be substituted for more traditional measures of intelligence and achievement" (p. 499). They questioned whether the achievement scale is an appropriate measure of school achievement. Page (1985) stated that the achievement scale may, in fact, be a better measure of g than the mental processing composite. In practice, performance on the subtests of the achievement scale should not be interpreted in a diagnostic fashion. Rather, the achievement scale should be viewed as a global measure of achievement.

In an effort to substantiate the validity of the K-ABC, the manual presents educational implications and remedial strategies based on performance on the K-ABC. While the manual contains some evidence in support of these strategies, much more research is needed to justify their use. Coffman (1985) wrote that "the detailed suggestions for approaches to instruction are thus more in the nature of interesting hypotheses than acceptable recipes" (p. 773). Further research must be conducted in order to substantiate their usefulness.

Summary.   The Kaufman Assessment Battery for Children (K-ABC) (Kaufman & Kaufman, 1983) is designed to assess the intelligence and achievement of children ages 2 years, 6 months to 12 years, 6 months. According to the manual, the test measures sequential processing, simultaneous processing, mental processing composite, and achievement. The K-ABC was designed to be sensitive to the preschool population and to the U.S. society, which is becoming increasingly pluralistic. The manuals present extensive evidence for the reliability and validity of the test. Additional research is needed to confirm construct validity. There is some concern that the African-American sample is biased toward the upper education levels.

Kaufman Brief Intelligence Test

The Kaufman Brief Intelligence Test (K-BIT) (Kaufman & Kaufman, 1990) measures verbal and nonverbal intelligence in individuals ages four to ninety years old. Because it is a brief test, the authors explain that it should not be used as a substitute for a more comprehensive measure. The results of this test should be used for screening only; the instrument is not appropriate for diagnostic, placement, or neurological assessment purposes. In addition to use as a screening instrument with young children, the K-BIT was developed to provide an estimate of intelligence for persons who may have psychiatric disorders and for job applicants, people awaiting court hearings, and individuals whose intellectual status needs to be monitored periodically.

The K-BIT consists of two subtests, Vocabulary and Matrices. The Vocabulary subtest contains 82 items to which children are asked to respond verbally. Part A, Expressive Vocabulary, contains 45 items, which are administered to all persons who take this test. The individual is asked to name an object that is pictured (e.g., lamp, calendar). Part B, Definitions, contains 37 items and is administered only to persons older than eight years of age.

The second subtest, Matrices, consists of 48 items to which each child is asked to respond by pointing to the correct response or by saying the corresponding letter. The items on this subtest contain people, objects, abstract designs, and symbols and are arranged so that a child must understand the relation among the items. This subtest is designed to measure nonverbal reasoning ability.

Administration.   A wide variety of professionals can administer the test: psychologists, special education teachers, educational diagnosticians, remedial reading teachers, counselors, social workers, nurses, and speech and language therapists. In addition, under certain circumstances, technicians and paraprofessionals can administer the K-BIT. According to the manual, little training is required to administer the test, but the interpretation of the results should be done by a trained professional.

The administration of the K-BIT takes from 15 to 20 minutes for children between four and seven years of age. For persons older than seven years, test administration can take up to 30 minutes.

Scoring.   Items are scored either correct or incorrect. Raw scores are converted to standard scores and percentile ranks. Scores are obtained for each of the subtests, Vocabulary and Matrices, and a composite intellectual ability score can be computed. The standard score is similar to intellectual ability scores for other tests. It has a mean of 100 and a standard deviation of 15.

Some guidance is provided for interpreting test scores. There is evidence that discrepancies between results for specific subtests can provide helpful diagnostic information. Using the results of the K-BIT, discrepancies between the standard scores on the Vocabulary and Matrices subtests can be determined. Since this instrument contains only two subtests, the interpretation of discrepancies should be made cautiously and only after further extensive testing.

The authors reported that the mean K-BIT scores were 6 points lower than full-scale scores from the Wechsler Intelligence Scale for Children—Revised (WISC-R). This may be of little concern since the WISC-R has been revised. However, information is not available on how the K-BIT scores compare with scores from the Wechsler Intelligence Scale for Children—III (WISC-III).

Standardization.   The K-BIT was standardized on 2,022 individuals between the ages of four and ninety years at 60 locations. Most of the standardization sample was between the ages of four and nineteen; 568 children in the standardization sample were between the ages of four and eight. The sample was stratified according to gender, geographic region, socioeconomic status, and race or ethnic group. The minority groups included African-American, Hispanic, and other (Native Americans, Alaskan natives, Asians, Pacific Islanders). The test examiners were teachers, counselors, psychologists, and graduate students who had received training by watching a videotape and had practiced administering the test.

Reliability.   Split-half reliabilities were computed for the two subtests and for the composite score. For Vocabulary, the split-half reliability coefficients ranged from .89 to .97; for Matrices the split-half reliability coefficients ranged from .74 to .95. The composite split-half reliability varied from .88 to .98. Lower reliabilities occurred at young ages.

To obtain test–retest reliability, the authors administered the K-BIT twice to 232 individuals between the ages of five and eighty-nine. The interval between the two tests ranged from 12 to 145 days, with an average of 21 days. There were 53 children in the age range between 5 and 12 years. For this group, test–retest reliabilities ranged from .83 to .92.

Validity.   Concurrent validity studies of the K-BIT with the Test of Nonverbal Intelligence (TONI) and with the Slosson Intelligence Test (SIT) were reported. For the TONI, the validity coefficients ranged from $-.04$ (Vocabulary subtest) to .36 (Matrices). When the K-BIT composite score was correlated with the SIT scores of typical children, correlation coefficients ranged from .50 to .76. When the K-BIT composite score was correlated with SIT scores from a gifted sample, the validity coefficient was .44.

Concurrent validity was also reported for the Kaufman Test of Educational Achievement (KTEA) (comprehensive form) for normal samples. Using K-BIT composite scores, validity coefficients ranged from .33 to .78. When K-BIT scores were correlated with scores from the KTEA comprehensive form, for two samples of students with learning disabilities, validity coefficients ranged from .32 to .65.

Evidence of construct validity is based on five normal samples. K-BIT composite scores were correlated with scores from the Kaufman Assessment Battery for Children (K-ABC), the Wechsler Intelligence Scale for Children—Revised (WISC-R), and the Wechsler Adult Intelligence Scale—Revised (WAIS-R). Validity coefficients ranged from .41 to .80. Thus, while there is some evidence that the K-BIT is assessing abilities similar to those tapped in the K-ABC, the WISC-R, and the WAIS-R, it is apparent that it is also assessing some abilities not tested by the other instruments. Therefore it would be difficult to justify the substitution of the K-BIT for these other instruments. There is limited evidence with regard to the usefulness of the K-BIT with young children.

Summary.   The K-BIT is a brief intelligence test. It can be used when a quick screening is required. It should not be substituted for a more comprehensive intelligence test, however. Reliability appears to be adequate, and there is some evidence of validity, but evidence of validity with samples of young children is limited. The K-BIT should be used cautiously when testing young children.

Leiter International Performance Scale (Arthur Adaptation)

The *Arthur Adaptation: Leiter International Performance Scale* (AALIPS) (Arthur, 1950) is a nonverbal measure of intelligence for individuals ages two through twelve years. The test consists of placing blocks in a series of trays according to directions given by the examiner. In general, this test measures the ability of children to solve problems by manipulating blocks according to prespecified directions.

The Leiter International Performance Scale (LIPS) (Leiter, 1979), originally published in 1927 and revised in 1948, was intended for individuals ages two through adult. Grace Arthur revised and adapted the LIPS. However, the items on the AALIPS and the LIPS are the same through age twelve.

Administration.   The manual contains confusing directions for administering the AALIPS, and a key to the subtests is not included. The examiner must figure the answers out. The test is administered with a minimum of verbal communication by the examiner. The examiner is encouraged to pantomime the instructions. Administration takes approximately 30 to 45 minutes.

Scoring.   The AALIPS yields two types of score: mental age and ratio IQ. These scores are based on the concept of developmental scores and have significant limitations in describing a child's performance.

Standardization.   The AALIPS was standardized on 289 children in the Midwest.

Reliability and Validity.   No information about reliability and validity are provided in the manual.

Summary.   The AALIPS is a test that could be useful in the assessment of cognitive ability. However, it lacks an adequate standardization sample. Reliability and validity information are missing. Until the AALIPS is revised, examiners are urged to use this test cautiously.

Stanford–Binet Intelligence Scale: Fourth Edition

The Stanford–Binet Intelligence Scale: Fourth Edition (Thorndike, Hagen, & Sattler, 1986a) is a revised edition of the Stanford–Binet Intelligence Scale: Form L-M. As noted earlier, the test was developed by Alfred Binet and Theodore Simon in France in 1905. Lewis M. Terman, a professor at Stanford University, revised the Binet–Simon test and introduced it to the United States in 1916. In 1937 Terman, along with Maud A. Merrill, standardized it again and created two revised forms, L and M. In 1960, Form L-M was created from these two forms, but the test was not restandardized until 1972. The Fourth Edition has some similarities to its predecessors: (1) it spans the same age range; (2) many of the item types are the same; and (3) basal and ceiling levels are established.

The Fourth Edition of the Stanford–Binet assesses cognitive abilities in individuals ages two to twenty-three years. The test contains 15 subtests that evaluate four broad areas: verbal reasoning, abstract–visual reasoning, quantitative reasoning, and short-term memory. In addition, there is a composite score that estimates *g,* general intellectual ability. Administration of specific subtests depends on the age of the individual; not all subtests are administered to each examinee.

The test is based on a three-level hierarchical model of intelligence. At the first, or top level, there is *g,* general reasoning ability. General ability consists of "the cognitive assembly and control processes that an individual uses to organize adaptive strategies for solving novel problems. In other words, *g* is what an individual uses when faced with a problem that he or she has not been taught to solve" (Thorndike et al., 1986b, p. 3).

The second level consists of three broad factors: crystallized abilities, fluid–analytic abilities, and short-term memory. Crystallized abilities are defined as "the cognitive skills necessary for acquiring and using information about verbal and quantitative concepts to solve problems" (Thorndike et al., 1986b, p. 4). It is thought that crystallized abilities are affected by experiences in school and outside school. Fluid–analytic abilities are "the cognitive skills necessary for solving new problems that involve figural or other nonverbal stimuli (Thorndike et al., 1986c, p. 4). This factor is influenced by general experiences and is related to flexibility and the ability to deal with novel situations.

The third level is based on verbal reasoning, quantitative reasoning, and abstract/visual reasoning. These factors are included because "they have special meaning to clinicians and educators" (Thorndike et al., 1986b, p. 5). Performance on the subtests contributes to these three factors, which in turn contribute to the abilities in the second level.

It is hypothesized that the Fourth Edition measures inferred abilities and influences. Figure 7.3 charts the association between the inferred abilities and the subtests. The 15 subtests and the abilities they measure are (Delaney & Hopkins, 1987; Sattler, 1988):

Verbal Reasoning

Vocabulary. Measures recall of expressive word knowledge and verbal comprehension.

Comprehension. Reflects verbal comprehension, vocabulary development, verbal expression, social knowledge, and factual information.

Absurdities. Assesses visual perception, factual knowledge, discrimination, verbal expression, attention, and social knowledge.

Verbal Relations. Assesses vocabulary development, concept formation, discrimination, inductive reasoning, verbal expression, and discrimination of essential details.

Quantitative Reasoning

Quantitative. Reflects knowledge of number facts, computation skills, and knowledge of mathematics concepts and procedures.

Number Series. Assesses logical reasoning, concentration, mathematics concepts and computation, and inductive reasoning.

Equation Building. Reflects knowledge of mathematics concepts and procedures, inductive reasoning, logic, flexibility, and trial and error.

Inferred Abilities and Influences Chart for the Stanford-Binet: Fourth Edition

Name _____

Age _____

Personal SAS Mean _____

The Riverside Publishing Company

Copyright © 1987 by The Riverside Publishing Company.
All rights reserved.

	VERBAL REASONING AREA				ABSTRACT/VISUAL REASONING AREA				QUANTITATIVE REASONING AREA			SHORT-TERM MEMORY AREA				
	Vocabulary	Comprehension	Absurdities	Verbal Relations	Pattern Analysis	Copying	Matrices	Paper Folding & Cutting	Quantitative	Number Series	Equation Building	Bead Memory	Memory for Sentences	Memory for Digits	Memory for Objects	Strength (S) or Weakness (W)
1. Record the Standard Age Score.																
2. Record the personal SAS mean.																
3. Record the score difference.																
4. Record an S or W or + or −.*																
Vocabulary development																
Verbal expression																
Concept formation																
Verbal comprehension																
Knowledge of English syntax																
Part-to-whole synthesis																
Visual analysis																
Visual imagery																
Visual memory																
Spatial visualization																
Visual perception																
Numerical fluency																
Mathematical concepts/computation																
Ability to impose structure on randomly presented material																
Ability to analyze word problems																
Discrimination of essential details from nonessential details																
Planning ability																
Inductive reasoning																
Range of factual information																
Meaningful long-term memory																
Sequencing, chunking, or clustering strategies																
Short-term auditory memory																
Reorganized recalled material																
Verbal labeling/memory strategy																
Ability to use and relate general life experiences																
Visual-motor coordination																
Social knowledge																
Attention																
Flexibility																
Manual dexterity																
Time pressure																

*S: + 7 or more points   W: −7 or more points   +: 0 to +6 points   −: −1 to −6 points

FIGURE 7.3 Inferred abilities and influences chart for the Stanford–Binet: Fourth Edition.

SOURCE: Reproduced with permission of The Riverside Publishing Company.

Abstract–Visual Reasoning

Pattern Analysis. Measures visual–motor ability, spatial visualization, pattern analysis, and visual–motor coordination.

Copying. Measures visual imagery, visual perception, visual–motor ability, and eye–hand coordination.

Matrices. Evaluates attention, concentration, visual perception, visual analysis, spatial visualization, and inductive reasoning.

Paper Folding and Cutting. Reflects spatial ability, visual perception, visual analysis, and inductive reasoning.

Short-term Memory

Bead Memory. Assesses short-term memory of visual stimuli. Also measures form perception, visual imagery, visual memory, discrimination, and alertness to detail.

Memory for Sentences. Measures short-term auditory memory, verbal comprehension, concentration, and attention.

Memory for Digits. Evaluates short-term auditory memory and attention.

Memory for objects. Reflects visual comprehension, attention, concentration, and visual memory.

Administration.   No one child is tested on all 15 subtests. All examinees, however, take the Vocabulary test first. Performance on this so-called routing test, along with the individual's chronological age, determines the remaining subtests that will be used. Depending on the age of the child, 8 to 13 subtests are administered. This can take between 1 and 2 hours. Specific instructions for the administration of each subtest are provided.

The routing test is inappropriate for children who are mentally retarded or have other disabilities if the entry items are too difficult. Test examiners may need to adjust the entry level to make it appropriate for these children (Sattler, 1988).

Several short or abbreviated forms of the test can be administered for screening purposes. A quick screening battery consists of four subtests: Vocabulary, Bead Memory, Quantitative, and Pattern Analysis. Another abbreviated form consists of six subtests: Vocabulary, Bead Memory, Quantitative, Memory for Sentences, Pattern Analysis, and Comprehension. In addition, there is a recommended brief battery for children who may be gifted. Depending on the age of the child, seven or eight subtests can be administered. For children who may have problems in learning, seven or eight subtests are suggested.

The *Examiner's Handbook: An Expanded Guide for Fourth Edition Users* (Delaney & Hopkins, 1987) provides guidelines for modifying the test administration for children who may be mentally retarded, deaf, visually impaired, or blind, as well as children who have limited English proficiency or who have difficulty in the understanding or production of language. When making modifications in the test administration, examiners should keep in mind that all children possess unique abilities.

Scoring.   The manual provides clearly written directions for scoring, which varies from one subtest to another. Raw scores are converted to a *standard age score* (SAS), a normalized standard score with a mean of 50 and a standard deviation of 8.

The standard age scores are converted to area scores and to a composite SAS. These scores have a mean of 100 and a standard deviation of 16.

There is some evidence that scores on the Fourth Edition will be somewhat lower than scores on the Form L-M. In one study, 139 children, with an average age of 6 years, 11 months, were administered the Fourth Edition with the Form L-M edition. The average composite score on the Fourth Edition was 105.8 with a standard deviation of 13.8; the mean total score on the Form L-M was 108.1 with a standard deviation of 16.7.

Standardization.   The standardization sample was based on the 1980 census, and five variables were used to select participants: geographic region, community size, ethnic group (Caucasian, African American, Hispanic, Asian/Pacific Islander), age, and gender. A total of 5,013 individuals participated in the standardization. Because children in the upper socioeconomic categories were overrepresented, weighting procedures were used to adjust the final sample to the 1980 census data on the U.S. population.

Reliability.   Internal consistency coefficients for the individual subtests ranged from .73 (Memory for Objects) to .94 (Paper Folding and Cutting). In general, the reliabilities for subtests administered to older children were higher than the reliabilities for the subtests administered to younger children.

For all age groups, the internal consistency of the composite score ranged from .95 to .99. The internal consistency reliability of the area scores ranged from .82 (Quantitative Reasoning Area for two-year-olds) to .97 (Abstract–Visual Reasoning for eighteen- to twenty-three-year olds), with many of the reliability coefficients above .90.

To examine test–retest reliability, two groups of children were tested: 57 five-year-olds and 55 eight-year-olds were retested between 2 and 8 months apart. For the younger group, the subtest reliabilities ranged from .56 (Bead Memory) to .77 (Memory for Sentences). Area score reliabilities ranged from .71 (Quantitative Reasoning) to .88 (Verbal Reasoning). The composite score reliability was .91. For the older group, subtest reliabilities varied from .28 (Quantitative) to .86 (Comprehension). Area scores extended from .51 (Quantitative Reasoning) to .87 (Verbal Reasoning); composite score reliability was .90.

Validity.   Construct validity was investigated by conducting a factor analysis of the subtest scores across all ages in the standardization sample. The Stanford–Binet: Fourth Edition is based on the theory that the test measures *g*, general ability. Evidence of *g* was found across all ages, although the factor loadings on *g* were greater in the eighteen- to twenty-three-year-olds than in the younger ages.

Several studies examined concurrent validity. In one study, 139 children, with an average age of 6 years, 11 months, were administered the Fourth Edition and the Form L-M edition. The correlation between the composite score on the Fourth Edition and the total score on the Form L-M was .81. Another study, with a sample of 205 children having an average age of 9 years, 5 months, investigated the correlations between area scores and composite scores on the Fourth Edition and Verbal IQs, Performance IQs, and Full Scale IQs on the *Wechsler Intelligence Scale for Children—Revised* (WISC-R). Correlations of the four area scores with verbal IQ and performance IQ ranged from .60 to .72, and the correlation between the composite score on the Fourth Edition with full-scale IQ on the WISC-R was .83.

Another study examined the correlation between the scores on the Fourth Edition and scores on the Wechsler Preschool and Primary Scale of Intelligence (WPPSI). The sample consisted of 75 children with an average age of 5 years, 6 months. Correlations of the four area scores with Verbal IQ and Performance IQ ranged from .46 to .80, and the correlation between the composite score on the Fourth Edition with full-scale IQ on the WISC-R was .80. A final study investigated the concurrent validity of the Fourth Edition with the K-ABC. The sample consisted of 175 children with an average age of seven years. Correlations of the four area scores on the Fourth Edition with four K-ABC scales (sequential processing, simultaneous processing, mental processing composite, and achievement) ranged from .71 to .89. The correlation between the composite score on the Fourth Edition and the mental processing composite on the K-ABC was .89.

Two studies of gifted children were conducted. The Fourth Edition and the Form L-M were administered to 82 gifted children with a mean age of 7 years, 4 months. The composite score on the Fourth Edition was 121.8 and the total score on the Form L-M was 135.3. With respect to gifted children, Thorndike, Hagen, and Sattler (1986c) wrote that children who are highly verbal but average or slightly above average in other cognitive abilities will receive a bonus on the Form L-M but not on the Fourth Edition. The correlation between the composite score on the Fourth Edition and the total score on the Form L-M was .27.

In another sample, 19 gifted children with an average age of 12 years, 11 months were administered the WISC-R and the Fourth Edition. The correlation between the composite score on the Fourth Edition with the full-scale score on the WISC-R was .69.

Three studies were conducted using samples of children who were identified as learning disabled. The performance of a group of 14 children with an average age of 8 years, 4 months was compared on the Fourth Edition and the Form L-M. The correlation between the composite score on the Fourth Edition and the total score on the Form L-M was .79. Another study investigated the relationship between Fourth Edition scores and WISC-R scores of 90 students with learning disabilities. The average age of the sample was 11 years. The correlation between the composite scores and the full-scale scores was .87. A third study, consisting of 30 children with learning disabilities, compared scores on the Fourth Edition with scores on the K-ABC. The average age of the children was 8 years, 11 months. The correlation between the composite score on the Fourth Edition and the mental processing composite score on the K-ABC was .66.

Three studies were conducted using samples of children who were identified as mentally retarded. The performance of a group of 22 children with an average age of 11 years, 11 months was compared on the Fourth Edition and the Form L-M. The correlation between the composite score on the Fourth Edition and the total score on the Form L-M was .91. Another study investigated the relationship between Fourth Edition scores and WISC-R scores of 61 students. The average age of the sample was 13 years, 11 months. The correlation between the composite score and the full-scale scores was .66. Finally, a third study, consisting of 21 mentally retarded individuals, examined the scores on the Fourth Edition against scores on the Wechsler Adult Intelligence Scale—Revised (WAIS-R). The average age of the sample was 19 years, 6 months. The correlation between the composite score on the Fourth Edition and the full-scale score on the WAIS-R was .79.

While evidence of validity is presented by the authors, additional research must be conducted over time with varied populations.

Summary.   The Stanford–Binet Intelligence Scale: Fourth Edition is a well-normed, reliable instrument. Evidence of validity is adequate. However, additional studies must be undertaken to investigate construct validity. While one important strength of the instrument is that it can be administered to individuals over a broad age range, not all subtests are administered to all examinees. Thus, the comparisons of the performance of examinees over time is difficult. Another disadvantage is that the Fourth Edition can take more time to administer than other intelligence tests.

Test of Nonverbal Intelligence, Second Edition

The Test of Nonverbal Intelligence, Second Edition (TONI-2) (Brown, Sherbenou, & Johnsen, 1990) is a nonverbal measure of abstract–figural problem solving for use with individuals ages 5 years to 85 years, 11 months. It can be used when assessing the performance of individuals who have language or motor problems that may make it difficult for them to respond to more traditional tests. The authors state that it can be useful when assessing persons who have "aphasia, hearing impairments, lack of proficiency with spoken or written English, cerebral palsy, stroke, head trauma, and lack of familiarity with the culture of the United States" (Brown et al., 1990, p. 5). The test has two forms, each containing 55 items which are a series of abstract figures that require individuals to select the correct response by problem solving. Figure 7.4 is an example of one test item.

Administration.   The test items are displayed on an easel, and the examiner pantomimes the instructions. The examiner begins the testing by pointing to a blank square in a pattern of figures, making a broad gesture to indicate the possible responses, pointing to the blank square again, and then looking questioningly at the

FIGURE 7.4   In the TONI-2, the child must identify the figure that belongs in the blank square.

SOURCE: *Test of Nonverbal Intelligence,* Second Edition, by Linda Brown, Rita J. Sherbenou, and Susan K. Johnsen. Austin, TX: Pro-Ed, 1990. Reprinted by permission.

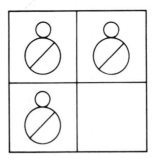

child. The child shows the correct response by pointing or by some other motor response. Throughout the administration of this instrument, neither the examiner nor the child speaks. This test is untimed, and the examiner is encouraged to allow the child sufficient time to respond to each test item. The total time to administer the TONI-2 is approximately 15 minutes. This nonverbal method of test administration has several advantages. The child is not required to listen to directions, speak, read, or write.

The test is designed to be administered individually. However, the manual does contain directions for administering the TONI-2 to groups of up to five children. Nonverbal administration is used, just as for individual administration. The examiner goes from one child to the next, giving each child a turn to respond to the same item. When administering the TONI-2 to a group, the examiner must use a separate answer booklet for each child.

The authors state that the TONI-2 can be administered by teachers, psychologists, psychological associates, and educational diagnosticians. It is expected that examiners will have sufficient training and knowledge in the area of assessment.

Scoring.   Items are scored as either correct or incorrect. Raw scores are converted to deviation quotients (standard scores with a mean of 100 and a standard deviation of 15) and percentile ranks. Since there are no subtests on the TONI-2, only the total score is reported.

Standardization.   The TONI-2 standardization sample consisted of 2,764 individuals, ranging in age from 5 years to 85 years, 11 months stratified by age, gender, race, ethnic group, geographic region, residence (rural, urban, suburban), and educational background. The stratification approximated the U.S. population, but some variables were either over- or underrepresented. For example, individuals who were classified as Caucasian were underrepresented while those from rural areas were overrepresented. There were 583 children between five and eight years old.

Reliability.   Reliability for the TONI-2 was calculated in several ways. Internal consistency reliability has a mean reliability coefficient of .95 for Form A and .96 for Form B.

Alternate form reliability was calculated. This was done by correlating the scores from forms A and B after they had been administered back to back to the same individuals. The mean reliability coefficient was .86. Alternate form reliability coefficients were reported for the various age groups in the sample. Reliability coefficients were computed for children ages 5 (.80), 6 (.86), 7 (.84), and 8 (.85).

The alternate forms were also used in a delayed retest design: Both forms of the TONI-2 were administered 7 days apart to 39 individuals ranging from 7 years, 9 months to 15 years, 9 months in age. The estimated reliability coefficient was .85.

Reliability coefficients are also reported for special populations, such as individuals who are mentally retarded, learning disabled, deaf, gifted, and Spanish speaking. The coefficients reported are in the moderate range. However, for the most part, the special population samples are small, and additional research must be undertaken in this area.

Validity.   Validity is concerned with determining whether a test measures what it purports to measure. The manual reports the results of studies conducted by the authors of the TONI-2 and by independent researchers. A number of validity studies were conducted, and validity coefficients range from low to moderate when the TONI-2 was correlated with measures of achievement and measures of intelligence.

Summary.   The TONI-2 is a nonverbal measure that assesses one aspect of intelligence, problem solving. Reliability and validity coefficients are low to moderate. This instrument should be used cautiously when assessing young children.

Wechsler Intelligence Scale for Children—Third Edition

Wechsler and Binet have greatly influenced the conceptualization and measurement of intelligence. Although their work has dominated intelligence testing in the United States, both men developed their instruments without a theoretical basis. The theories of Piaget, Horn and Cattell, Guilford, and others have, for the most part, been ignored by test publishers (Reynolds & Kaufman, 1985).

The Wechsler Intelligence Scale for Children—Third Edition (WISC-III) (Wechsler, 1991) is a revision of the Wechsler Intelligence Scale for Children—Revised and is the third version of the Wechsler Intelligence Scale for Children, which was originally published in 1949. It is an individually administered test designed to assess the intellectual ability of children ages 6 years through 16 years, 11 months. Wechsler conceptualized intelligence as a global ability, which is the "capacity of the individual to act purposefully, to think rationally, and to deal effectively with his or her environment" (Wechsler, 1944, p. 3, cited by Wechsler, 1991). According to the manual, the WISC-III can be used for a number of purposes including psychoeducational assessment, diagnosis of exceptional needs, and clinical and neuropsychological assessment.

The WISC-III consists of 10 subtests and 3 optional subtests grouped into two scales, Verbal and Performance. The sum of the scores on the verbal subtests results in a verbal IQ score; the total of the scores on the performance subtests results in a performance IQ score. The scores on both the verbal and performance subtests result in a full-scale IQ score.

Verbal Scale
Information. Questions testing common knowledge about events, objects, places, and people are presented orally by the examiner.

Similarities. The child explains the correspondence between pairs of words.

Arithmetic. Mathematical problems that the child solves mentally and responds to verbally are presented.

Vocabulary. Words are presented orally and the child defines them orally.

Comprehension. Questions that assess understanding of familiar problems and social concepts are presented orally by the examiner.

Digit Span. The child repeats a series of numbers forward in the Digits Forward section and a series of numbers in reverse order in the Digits Backward section.

Performance Scale
Picture Completion. A picture with a missing part is shown to the child, who must identify the missing piece.

Picture Arrangement. The child must correctly sequence a series of pictures.

Block Design. The child reproduces a pattern using blocks.

Object Assembly. The child assembles five jigsaw puzzles.

Coding. The child copies geometric symbols that are paired with either numbers or shapes.

Mazes. The child completes a series of mazes using a pencil.

Symbol Search. The child searches two groups of paired shapes to locate the target shape.

The WISC-III also contains four factor-based index scores: verbal comprehension, perceptual organization, freedom from distractibility, and processing speed. Twelve of the 13 subtests yield the four factors. The arrangement of the four factors and their subtests is as follows:

Factor	*Subtests*
I. Verbal comprehension	Information, Similarities, Vocabulary, Comprehension
II. Perceptual organization	Picture Completion, Picture Arrangement, Block Design, Object Assembly
III. Freedom from distractibility	Arithmetic, Digit Span
IV. Processing speed	Coding, Symbol Search

Administration.   The WISC-III is administered individually. The manual clearly explains the directions for administration and scoring for each of the subtests. The subtests have separate starting points, and the rules for stopping vary among the subtests. Administration time is approximately 60 to 90 minutes.

The WISC-III overlaps with the Wechsler Preschool and Primary Scale of Intelligence—Revised (WPPSI-R) for children who are 6 years to 7 years, 3 months. The manual recommends that the WPPSI-R be used for children who fall within this age range and are of low ability. The WISC-III is appropriate for children who have high ability or are gifted.

Scoring.   The manual provides clearly written directions for scoring. The scoring of the subtests varies from one subtest to another. Raw scores are converted to scaled scores, which are a form of standard score with a mean of 100 and a standard deviation of 15. The scaled scores are used to determine the verbal, performance, and full-scale IQ scores. The factor-based scores are optional and can be calculated from the scaled scores.

When children are retested using a revised instrument, there is usually some fluctuation in scores. When the WISC-III verbal, performance, and full-scale scores were compared with the scores from the WISC-R, it was found that the WISC-III scores were lower than WISC-R scores. In general, WISC-III full-scale scores were 5 to 9 points lower than WISC-R scores. Verbal and performance scale scores on the WISC-III ranged from 2 to 7 points lower than WISC-R scores. The average difference between WISC-III scores and WPPSI-R scores was about 4 points, with WPPSI-R scores generally being lower than WISC-III scores. However, this difference can be larger with children who fall at the upper or lower ends of the IQ range.

Standardization.   The WISC-III was standardized based on 1988 data ob-tained from the U.S. Bureau of the Census. The standardization sample consisted of 2,200 children in each of 11 age groups extending from 6 years to 16 years. The sample was stratified according to age, gender, race, ethnicity, geographic region, and parental education.

Children with exceptional needs were not systematically included in the WISC-III standardization sample, and separate norms are not provided for these children. However, the manual summarizes several studies conducted by independent re-searchers with special populations (including gifted, mentally retarded, learning disabled, attention deficit–hyperactivity disorder, behavior disorder, epilepsy, speech and language delays, and hearing impairment). These studies are few in number, and for the most part they used small samples. However, they are encourag-ing. Additional research is needed in this area.

Reliability.   Reliability refers to the consistency or stability of test performance. Split-half reliability coefficients are reported for each of the subtests, for the three IQ scales, and for the four factor-based scales. Because reliability is affected by the length of a test, the highest reliability coefficient reported was for full-scale IQ (.96). For the subtests, reliability coefficients ranged from .69 (Object Assembly) to .87 (Vocabulary and Block Design). Reliability coefficients for the factor-based scales ranged from .85 (processing speed) to .94 (verbal comprehension).

Test–retest reliability is an estimate of the stability of test scores over time. Test–retest reliability was assessed using a separate group of 353 children who were tested twice. The median interval between testings was 23 days. Separate reliability coefficients were calculated for various age groups. For ages six and seven, reliability coefficients for the subtests ranged from .60 (Mazes) to .82 (Vocabulary, Picture Completion). Because the reliabilities for the subtests are low, the results of individual subtests should be interpreted with caution. For the IQ scores, test–retest re-liabilities ranged from .86 (performance IQ) to .92 (full-scale IQ). The test–retest reliabilities for the factor-based scores ranged from .74 (freedom from distractibility) to .89 (verbal comprehension).

Like many tests, WISC-III scores show a slight increase when the testing interval is short. For children ages six and seven, when the median test–retest interval was 23 days, verbal IQ scores increased 1.7 points, performance IQ scores increased 11.5 points, and full-scale IQ scores increased 7 points.

Interscorer reliabilities were calculated for subtests that require more judgment in scoring. For each of four subtests (Similarities, Vocabulary, Comprehension, and Mazes), the interscorer reliability coefficients exceeded .90. The manual concludes that subtests that require some judgment in scoring can be reliably scored.

Validity.   According to the manual, because the WISC-R is valid, the WISC-III is also valid. While it is true that there is considerable evidence for the validity of the WISC-R, the WISC-III is a substantial revision of the WISC-R. Therefore, the state-ment about the validity of the WISC-III should be interpreted cautiously.

The manual does provide evidence for the separate factor structure of the subtests. In general, verbal subtests correlate more strongly with each other than with performance subtests; performance subtests correlate more strongly with each other than with verbal subtests. Factor analyses of the WISC-III scores confirm the likelihood of the four factors or abilities: verbal comprehension, perceptual organization, freedom from distractibility, and processing speed. However, Sattler (1992) has indicated that freedom from distractibility may be weak and that interpretations based on this factor should be made cautiously.

WISC-III scores were also correlated with scores from several other tests. This evidence supports the validity of the WISC-III. However, additional research must be conducted to add to our knowledge about the validity of the WISC-III.

Summary.   The WISC-III is an individually administered test of intelligence. For six- and seven-year-old children, reliabilities of the individual subtests are lower than for the full-scale IQ score. Validity appears to be adequate. This instrument is useful in the assessment of children, but additional research is needed to contribute to our understanding of it.

Wechsler Preschool and Primary Scale of Intelligence—Revised

The Wechsler Preschool and Primary Scale of Intelligence—Revised (WPPSI-R) (Wechsler, 1989) is a revision of the Wechsler Preschool and Primary Scale (WPPSI) (Wechsler, 1967). It is an individually administered test of intelligence for children ages three to seven years. The WPPSI-R is similar in format and content to the WISC-III. The WPPSI-R contains 12 subtests, 2 are optional, arranged in two scales: verbal and performance. Individual scores can be obtained for each of the subtests. Verbal, performance, and full-scale IQ scores are calculated from the subtest scores. The following list describes the subtests, which are organized as shown in Table 7.2.

Object Assembly. Pieces of a puzzle are arranged in front of the child in a standardized configuration. The child must put the pieces together within a certain time limit.

Information. The child is asked to respond to items that demonstrate knowledge about events or objects in the environment. Depending on the level of difficulty of the item, responses are expressed either verbally or by pointing to a picture of an item.

Geometric Design. This subtest includes items of two types. The first asks the child to match a visual stimulus with one of four choices that are presented. For the second type, the child is asked to copy a geometric figure.

Comprehension. The child is asked to express an understanding of the reasons for certains actions and consequences.

Block Design. The child must reproduce patterns constructed by the examiner from two-colored flat blocks.

Arithmetic. This subtest assesses the child's understanding of basic quantitative concepts. Pictures, counting tasks, and word problems are presented.

Mazes. Using paper and pencil, the child must solve, under specified time limits, printed mazes that increase in difficulty.

Vocabulary. Depending on the age of the child, the child is asked to name objects that are pictured or to give oral definitions of words presented verbally by the examiner.

Picture Completion. The child must identify what is missing from objects or events that are pictured.

TABLE 7.2 Organization of the subtests in the WPPSI-R

Performance	Verbal
1. Object Assembly	2. Information
3. Geometric Design	4. Comprehension
5. Block Design	6. Arithmetic
7. Mazes	8. Vocabulary
9. Picture Completion	10. Similarities
*11. Animal Pegs (formerly "Animal House")	*12. Sentences

*Animal Pegs and Sentences are optional subtests.
SOURCE: From the manual of the Wechsler Preschool and Primary Scale of Intelligence—Revised. Copyright © 1989 by The Psychological Corporation. Reproduced by permission. All rights reserved.

Similarities. The child's understanding of the concept of similarities is assessed in three ways: (1) the child points to one of several pictured objects that have a common attribute; (2) the child completes a sentence, presented verbally by the examiner, that contains an analogy or similarity; and (3) the child explains orally how two objects or events are similar.

Animal Pegs. The child must associate a colored peg with a corresponding animal according to a key at the top of the board. This optional subtest assesses speed and accuracy.

Sentences. The child repeats a sentence that the examiner has uttered. Like the Animal Pegs subtest, this subtest is optional.

Administration. Like the WISC-III, the WPPSI-R is administered individually. The directions for administration and scoring the subtests are clearly presented in the manual. The subtests are administered in a specified order. Each subtest has separate starting and stopping points. The WPPSI-R overlaps with the WISC-III for children between the ages of 6 years and 7 years, 3 months. The WPPSI-R manual recommends that if a child is suspected of having either average or below average ability, the WPPSI-R should be used. For children who may be gifted, the WISC-III should be administered.

Scoring. Directions for scoring are clearly explained in the manual. Raw scores are converted to scaled scores, which have a mean of 100 and a standard deviation of 15. These scaled scores are used to calculate the verbal, performance, and full-scale IQ scores.

Comparisons of WPPSI-R scores with other tests are reported in the manual. WPPSI full-scale IQ scores are approximately 8 points higher than full-scale IQ scores of the WPPSI-R. WPPSI performance scale IQ scores are approximately 9 points higher and verbal scale IQ scores are 5 points higher than WPPSI-R scores. The Stanford–Binet composite scores and the McCarthy Scales of Children's Abilities general cognitive index scores are approximately 2 points higher than WPPSI-R full-scale IQ scores. Similarly, the mental processing composite of the Kaufman

Assessment Battery for Children is 6 points higher than the WPPSI-R full-scale IQ score.

Standardization.   The standardization sample was selected based on 1986 data obtained from the Bureau of the Census. The sample consisted of 1,700 children, ages 3 to 7 years, 3 months. The sample was stratified according to age, gender, geographic region, ethnicity, parental education, and parental occupation. Four hundred additional minority group children were included to investigate item bias.

Children with exceptional needs were not systematically included in the standardization sample. However, several small studies were conducted with groups of children with exceptional needs. A sample of 16 gifted children who had been tested with the Stanford–Binet showed that some of these children would not be classified as gifted based on their performance on the WPPSI-R. Studies of children who are mentally retarded, learning disabled, and speech or language impaired showed that the WPPSI-R could be useful with these groups. However, the studies were limited and additional research is needed in this area.

Reliability.   Interscorer and test–retest reliabilities were determined. Interscorer reliability of the Comprehension, Vocabulary, Similarities, and Mazes subtests were calculated using a sample of 151 scorers. For the Geometric Design subtest, 188 scorers were used. The interscorer reliabilities were .96 for Comprehension, .94 for Vocabulary, .96 for Similarities, .94 for Mazes, and .88 for Geometric Design.

Test–retest reliability was determined based on a sample of 175 children who were randomly selected from the standardization sample. The test–retest interval ranged from 3 to 7 weeks. Corrected coefficients for the subtests ranged from .52 (Mazes) to .82 (Picture Completion). The correlation coefficients for the three scales were .90 for the verbal scale, .88 for the performance scale, and .91 for full-scale IQ. Because the coefficients on the subtests are relatively weak, less emphasis should be placed on their interpretation.

Validity.   Part of the manual's discussion of the validity of the WPPSI-R is based on research that was conducted earlier on the WPPSI. The WPPSI-R is a comprehensive revision, however, and much of the evidence presented for validity of the WPPSI is not applicable to the WPPSI-R.

Descriptions of concurrent validity studies with the WPPSI-R and other instruments are presented. In general, the WPPSI-R correlated higher with the WPPSI and the Wechsler Intelligence Scale for Children—Revised (WISC-R). Moderate correlations were obtained with the Stanford–Binet and the McCarthy scales. Relatively low coefficients resulted when WPPSI-R scores were correlated with K-ABC scores.

Summary.   The WPPSI-R is an individually administered test of intelligence for children ages three to seven years. The standardization is adequate. Information about reliability and validity is limited. The case study illustrates the use of the WPPSI-R.

CASE STUDY: PSYCHOLOGIST'S REPORT

Martin is a five-year-old who was referred by his preschool teacher because of aggressive behavior, which included kicking and punching. He came into state custody several years ago with the disclosure of sexual abuse by both biological parents. He has lived in two foster homes. Last year he was diagnosed as having post-traumatic stress syndrome brought on by the sexual abuse. He was also diagnosed as having attention deficit–hyperactivity disorder.

Information from Martin's records showed regressions in nearly all areas including preschool adjustment, self-help, language, social development, motor development, and cognitive development. Teachers and foster parents noted that his antisocial and aggressive behaviors increased in frequency before and after visits with his parents. After his mother was indicted on six counts of child neglect, she lost visitation rights.

As part of a comprehensive reevaluation of Martin's abilities, the Wechsler Preschool and Primary Scale of Intelligence—Revised (WPPSI-R) was administered. The boy obtained a full-scale IQ in the average range. The scores on the WPPSI-R were comparable to those obtained previously. The evaluation showed some attentional difficulties, which interfered with Martin's ability to respond to the test items. Greatest strengths were in visual–spatial ability. On the verbal measures, Martin generally performed in the low average to average range.

These results, combined with the results of other tests and observations of Martin in his preschool, show that Martin is a child with average intelligence who is experiencing significant learning difficulties. These results should be interpreted cautiously because of the attention deficit disorder, the significant emotional difficulties, and limited experiential opportunities.

Woodcock–Johnson Psychoeducational Battery—Revised

The Woodcock–Johnson Psychoeducational Battery—Revised (WJ-R) (Woodcock & Johnson, 1989) is an individually administered battery that assesses cognitive and academic abilities in individuals ages 24 months through adulthood. The battery consists of two tests, the Woodcock–Johnson Tests of Cognitive Ability (WJ-R COG) and the Woodcock–Johnson Tests of Achievement (WJ-R ACH). Each part contains a standard battery and a supplemental battery. The standard battery can be administered alone or with the supplemental battery. The WJ-R has the following purposes: diagnosis, determination of psychoeducational discrepancies, program placement, individual program planning, guidance, assessing growth, program evaluation, and research.

The WJ-COG is based on the Horn–Cattell theory of cognitive processing. The abilities measured by the WJ-COG are fluid reasoning, comprehension knowledge, visual processing, auditory processing, processing speed, long-term retrieval, and short-term memory. The subtests, which include at least two measures of each factor, form clusters for each of these abilities.

Cognitive Ability.   The standard battery of the WJ-COG consists of seven subtests, one for each hypothesized ability. For children who are younger than kindergarten age, five subtests (Memory for Names, Memory for Sentences, Incomplete Words, Visual Closure, and Picture Vocabulary) can be combined to form the early development scale. The seven subtests are:

Memory for Names. Assesses the ability to learn the names of nine drawings of space creatures after the examiner has said each name. This subtest is intended to measure long-term retrieval.

Memory for Sentences. Assesses the ability to repeat phrases and sentences that are either presented by the examiner or acquired by listening to an audiotape. This subtest is intended to measure short-term memory and attention.

Visual Matching. Assesses the ability to match numbers within a 3-minute time interval. This subtest is intended to measure processing speed.

Incomplete Words. Assesses the ability to repeat a word that has several phonemes missing. This subtest is intended to measure auditory processing.

Visual Closure. Assesses the ability to name a picture or drawing that has been distorted, has lines missing, or is partly obscured by a superimposed pattern. This subtest is intended to measure visual processing.

Picture Vocabulary. Assesses the ability to identify pictures of familiar and unfamiliar objects. This subtest measures comprehension–knowledge or crystallized knowledge.

Analysis–Synthesis. Assesses the ability to identify the missing pieces in a logic puzzle. This subtest measures reasoning or fluid intelligence.

There are an additional 14 subtests in the supplemental battery.

Visual–Auditory Learning. Measures the ability to associate abstract visual symbols with familiar words. This subtest measures long-term retrieval.

Memory for Words. Assesses the ability to repeat lists of unrelated words. This subtest measures short-term memory and attention.

Cross-out. Measures the ability to match 5 drawings in a row of 20 drawings within a 3-minute time interval. This subtest measures visual processing speed.

Sound Blending. Assesses the ability to say whole words after hearing the syllables. This subtest measures auditory processing.

Picture Recognition. Requires the ability to recognize a group of pictures that had been presented earlier with a group of distracting pictures. This subtest measures visual processing.

Oral Vocabulary. Measures the ability to provide synonyms or antonyms in response to words read by the examiner. This subtest measures comprehension–knowledge or crystallized intelligence.

Concept Formation. Assesses the ability to provide a concept when various stimuli are presented. This subtest measures reasoning or fluid intelligence.

Delayed Recall—Memory for Names. Measures the ability to recall the names of the space creatures that were presented in an earlier subtest, *Memory for Names,* after an interval of one to eight days. This subtest measures long-term retrieval.

Delayed Recall—Visual–Auditory Learning. Assesses the ability to recall the symbols presented in the subtest *Visual–Auditory Learning* after an interval of one to eight days. This subtest measures long-term retrieval.

Numbers Reversed. Assesses the ability to say a series of numbers backward. This subtest measures short-term memory and attention.

Sound Patterns. Measures the ability to identify whether certain sound patterns, presented on an audiotape, are the same or different. This subtest measures reasoning and auditory processing.

Spatial Relations. Assesses the ability to match shapes. This subtest measures fluid intelligence and visual processing.

Listening Comprehension. Measures the ability to provide the missing word after listening to a brief audiotaped passage. This subtest measures comprehension–knowledge or crystallized intelligence.

Verbal Analogies. Assesses the ability to complete phrases that contain analogies. This subtest measures comprehension–knowledge or crystallized intelligence.

Achievement. There are two parallel forms of the WJ-R ACH standard battery, each containing nine subtests. The subtests can be combined to form five clusters in reading, mathematics, written language, knowledge, and skills.

Letter–Word Identification. Assesses the ability to identify letters and words in isolation.

Passage Comprehension. Measures the ability to read a short passage and to identify the missing word.

Calculation. Assesses the ability to solve mathematical calculations using a booklet in which the child can record written answers.

Applied Problems. Measures the ability to solve practical mathematical problems.

Dictation. Assesses the ability to respond in writing to questions about letter forms, punctuation, spelling, capitalization, and word usage.

Writing Samples. Measures the ability to respond in writing to various response demands.

Science. Measures knowledge relating to biological and physical science.

Social Studies. Measures knowledge relating to history, geography, government, economics, and other areas.

Humanities. Assesses the ability to recall knowledge in art, music, and literature.

The WJ-R ACH supplemental battery consists of the following subtests.

Word Attack. Assesses the ability to apply the rules of phonic and structural analysis to read unfamiliar and nonsense words.

Reading Vocabulary. Assesses the ability to supply one-word synonyms and antonyms after reading words.

Quantitative Concepts. Measures knowledge of mathematical concepts and vocabulary.

Proofing. Measures the ability to identify a mistake in a passage and to indicate how to correct the error. The mistakes are in punctuation, capitalization, word usage, and spelling.

Writing Fluency. Assesses the ability to write simple sentences in 7 minutes.

Punctuation or Capitalization. Contains selected items from the Dictation and Proofing subtests.

Spelling. Contains selected items from the Dictation and Proofing subtests.

Usage. Selected items contained in the Dictation and Proofing subtests are used to obtain the score for this subtest.

Handwriting. The child's responses from the Writing Samples are compared against a ranked scale of handwriting. An informal checklist can be completed.

Administration.   The time to administer the WJ-R varies from 20 minutes to several hours depending on whether both the WJ-R COG and the WJ-R ACH are administered and whether the standard and supplemental batteries are used. Raw scores can be converted to age and grade equivalents, percentile ranks, and standard scores. The scoring can be cumbersome, and it is advisable to use a computer scoring program.

Norms.   The WJ-R was standardized on 6,359 individuals in more than 100 communities. The preschool sample consisted of 705 children who were two to five years of age and not enrolled in kindergarten. There were 3,245 individuals in the sample for kindergarten through grade 12. The rest of the standardization sample consisted of individuals who were in college or not in school. The sample was stratified according to region, community size, sex, race (Caucasian, African American, Hispanic, Native American, Asian Pacific, other), funding of college/university, type of college/university, occupational status of adults, and occupation of adults. The norms are continuous year (that is, collected throughout the year) norms.

Reliability.   For both WJ-R COG and the WJ-R ACH, only one type of reliability, internal consistency, is reported. It is of special interest that for young children, reliabilities are reported only for ages two, four, and six years. No reliability information is provided for ages three, five, seven, or eight. Users of this battery must be cautious in interpreting the reliability information.

For the WJ-R COG the internal consistency reliabilities for the subtests for ages two, four, and six range from .73 to .92. For the early development scale the reliabilities range from .91 (age six) to .95 (age two). For the WJ-R ACH standard battery, the internal consistency reliabilities for the subtests are reported by age and not by grade. The reliabilities for ages two, four, and six range from .74 to .93. For the clusters, the reliabilities range from .91 to .97.

Validity.   The manual reports a number of validity studies for both the cognitive and achievement batteries. In general, there is evidence to support content, concurrent, and construct validity. It should be remembered that the achievement portion of the battery reflects a skills-oriented approach to assessment and that the cognitive portion represents one theoretical perspective, the Horn–Cattell theory. The extent to which various subtests reflect children's abilities depends on the orientation of the team to assessment.

Summary.   The Woodcock–Johnson Psychoeducational Battery—Revised (WJ-R) (Woodcock & Johnson, 1989) is a norm-referenced, individually administered battery that assesses cognitive and academic abilities in individuals ages 24 months through adulthood. The battery consists of two parts, cognitive and achievement. Reliability information is lacking. Additional investigation of validity is warranted, especially regarding the use of the battery with young children.

Other Instruments

Our understanding of intelligence has developed and changed over the years. Besides the tests discussed in depth in this chapter, there are many other tests of intelligence:

Blind Learning Aptitude Test (Newland, 1969)	Uses a bas-relief format; assesses discrimination, generalization, sequencing, analogies, and matrix completion; ages 6 to 12
Columbia Mental Maturity Scale (Burgenmeister, Blum, & Lorge, 1972)	Nonverbal test; ages 3-6 to 9-11
Detroit Tests of Learning Aptitude—3 (Hammill, 1991)	Assesses verbal and nonverbal abilities; ages 6 to 17
Griffiths Mental Development Scales (Griffiths, 1979)	Useful with nonverbal children; ages birth to 8 years
McCarthy Scales of Children's Abilities (McCarthy, 1972)	Assesses general intellectual ability; ages 2-6 to 8-6
Nebraska Test of Learning Aptitude (Hiskey, 1966)	Assesses learning aptitude of children who are deaf or hearing impaired; ages 3 to 16 years
Perkins–Binet Tests of Intelligence for the Blind (Davis, 1980)	Assesses cognitive ability of children who are blind; ages 4 to 8 years
Pictorial Test of Intelligence (French, 1964)	Children respond either by pointing to the correct response or by movement of the eyes; ages 3 to 8 years

PREFERRED PRACTICES

Theorists have written about the nature of intelligence and how it should be measured. Although there are differing perspectives, we do know that intelligence is not a unitary construct. Beginning with Binet, researchers have conceptualized intelligence as being constructed of various abilities. However, they have disagreed about the exact nature of the abilities.

When interpreting a child's performance on an intelligence test, the following cautions should be kept in mind.

1. The interpretation of performance on an intelligence test depends on the skill of the examiner, the test environment, the child, and the demands of the test. The child's motivation, health, and emotional state can affect performance. Other factors include examiner bias, cultural and linguistic dif-

ferences between the child and the examiner, and rapport (Taylor, 1990).

2. Intelligence tests sample behaviors. Performance on a test helps us in our understanding of the child's approach to the demands of the tasks presented. There are many behaviors that intelligence tests do not sample, and our understanding of these is emerging.

3. Performance on an intelligence test should be regarded as helping to describe behavior rather than to explain it. Scores on an IQ test represent the child's performance at a given moment in time. We know that especially with young children, tested intelligence can change over time (Anastasi, 1988; Sattler, 1988).

STUDY QUESTIONS AND SUGGESTED ACTIVITIES

1. Explain how our concept of intelligence has evolved.

2. What special considerations should be made when measuring the intelligence of a child from another culture?

3. The results of intelligence tests should be used to describe rather than explain behavior. What does this statement mean?

4. Examine several different intelligence tests. How do they differ in form and content?

5. What do you think intelligence tests will be like 20 years from now?

REFERENCES

Anastasi, A. (1985). Review of the Kaufman Assessment Battery for Children. In G. Mitchell (Ed.), *Mental measurements yearbook: Vol. 1* (pp. 769–771). Lincoln, NE: University of Nebraska.

Anastasi, A. (1988). *Psychological testing.* New York: Macmillan.

Arthur, G. (1950). *Arthur Adaptation: Leiter International Performance Scale.* Wood Dale, IL: Stoelting Company.

Brown, L., Sherbenou, R. J., & Johnsen, S. K. (1990). *Test of nonverbal intelligence, second edition.* Austin, TX: Pro-Ed.

Burgenmeister, B., Blum, L., & Lorge, I. (1972). *Columbia mental maturity scale.* San Antonio, TX: Psychological Corporation.

Cattell, P. (1960). *Cattell infant intelligence scale.* San Antonio, TX: Psychological Corporation.

Cattell, P. (1980). *The measurement of intelligence of infants and young children.* San Antonio, TX: Psychological Corporation. (Fifth reprinting. Originally published in 1940.)

Coffman, W. E. (1985). Review of the Kaufman Assessment Battery for Children. In G. Mitchell (Ed.), *Mental measurements yearbook: Vol. 1* (pp. 771–773). Lincoln, NE: University of Nebraska.

Das, J. P., Kirby, J. R., & Jarman, R. F. (1975). Simultaneous and successive syntheses: An alternative model for cognitive abilities. *Psychological Bulletin, 82,* 87–103.

Das, J. P., Kirby, J. R., & Jarman, R. F. (1979). *Simultaneous and successive cognitive processes.* New York: Academic Press.

Das, J. P., & Molloy, G. N. (1975). Varieties of simultaneous and successive processing in children. *Journal of Educational Psychology, 67,* 213–220.

Davis, C. (1980). *Perkins–Binet test of intelligence for the blind.* Watertown, MA: Perkins School for the Blind.

Delaney, E. A., & Hopkins, T. F. (1987). *The Stanford–Binet Intelligence Scale: Fourth Edition, Examiner's Handbook.* Chicago: Riverside Publishing Company.

Elliot, C. D. (1990a). *Differential ability scales—Administration and scoring manual.* San Antonio, TX: Psychological Corporation.

Elliot, C. D. (1990b). *Differential ability scales—Introductory and technical handbook.* San Antonio, TX: Psychological Corporation.

Fancher, R. E. (1985). *The intelligence men.* New York: Norton.

French, J. L. (1964). *Pictorial test of intelligence.* Boston: Houghton Mifflin.

French, J. L., & Hale, R. L. (1990). A history of the development of psychological and educational testing. In C. R. Reynolds & R. W. Kamphaus (Eds.), *Handbook of psychological and educational assessment of children* (pp. 3–28). New York: Guilford Press.

Gardner, H. (1991). *The unschooled mind.* New York: Basic Books.

Griffiths, R. (1979). *The abilities of young children.* London: Child Development Research Center.

Guilford, J. P. (1967). *The nature of human intelligence.* New York: McGraw-Hill.

Hammill, D. D. (1991). *Detroit tests of learning aptitude—3.* Austin, TX: Pro-Ed.

Hammill, D. D., & Bryant, B. R. (1991). *Detroit tests of learning aptitude—Primary (second edition).* Austin, TX: Pro-Ed.

Hiskey, M. S. (1966). *Hiskey–Nebraska test of learning aptitude.* Lincoln, NE: Author.

Horn, J. L. (1985). Remodeling old models of intelligence. In B. B. Wolman (Ed.), *Handbook of intelligence* (pp. 267–300). New York: Wiley.

Kaufman, A. S., & Kaufman, N. L. (1983). *Kaufman assessment battery for children.* Circle Pines, MN: American Guidance Service.

Kaufman, A. S., & Kaufman, N. L. (1990). *Kaufman Brief Intelligence Test.* Circle Pines, MN: American Guidance Service.

Kevles, D. J. (1985). *In the name of eugenics.* New York: Knopf.

Leiter, R. G. (1979). *Leiter International Performance Scale* (rev. ed.). Wood Dale, IL: Stoelting Company.

McCarthy, D. (1972). *McCarthy scales of children's abilities.* San Antonio: Psychological Corporation.

Merz, W. R. (1984). Review of the Kaufman Assessment Battery for children. In K. Sweetland (Ed.), *Test critiques: Vol. 1* (pp. 393–404). Kansas City, MO: Test Corporation of America.

Neisworth, J. T., & Bagnato, S. J. (1992). The case against intelligence testing in early intervention. *Topics in Early Childhood Special Education, 12,* 1–20.

Newland, T. E. (1969). *Blind learning aptitude test.* Champaign, IL: Ernest Newland.

Page, E. B. (1985). Review of the Kaufman Assessment Battery for Children. In G. Mitchell (Ed.), *Mental measurements yearbook: Vol. 1* (pp. 773–777). Lincoln, NE: University of Nebraska.

Reynolds, C. R., & Kaufman, A. S. (1985). Clinical assessment of children's intelligence with the Wechsler scales. In B. B. Wolman (Ed.), *Handbook of intelligence* (pp. 601–661). New York: Wiley.

Salvia, J., & Ysseldyke, J. (1988). *Assessment in special and remedial education.* Boston: Houghton Mifflin.

Salvia, J., & Ysseldyke, J. (1991). *Assessment.* Boston: Houghton Mifflin.

Sattler, J. (1988). *Assessment of children.* San Diego, CA: Jerome M. Sattler, Publisher.

Sattler, J. (1992). *WISC-III and WPPSI-R supplement to assessment of children.* San Diego, CA: Jerome M. Sattler, Publisher.

Sternberg, R. (1985). Cognitive approaches to intelligence. In B. B. Wolman (Ed.), *Handbook of intelligence* (pp. 59–118). New York: Wiley.

Taylor, R. (1990). Intellectual assessment tips. *Diagnostique, 16,* 52–54.

Thorndike, R. L., & Hagen, E. (1986). *Cognitive abilities test.* Chicago: Riverside Publishing Company.

Thorndike, R. L., Hagen, E. P., & Sattler, J. M. (1986a). *Technical manual, Stanford–Binet intelligence scale: Fourth edition.* Chicago: Riverside Publishing Company.

Thorndike, R. L., Hagen, E. P., & Sattler, J. M. (1986b). *Guide for administering and scoring the fourth edition.* Chicago: Riverside Publishing Company.

Thorndike, R. L., Hagen, E. P., & Sattler, J. M. (1986c). *Stanford–Binet intelligence scale: Fourth edition.* Chicago: Riverside Publishing Company.

Thorndike, R. M., & Lohman, D. F. (1990). *A century of ability testing.* Chicago: Riverside Publishing Company.

Wechsler, D. (1944). *The measurement of adult intelligence* (3rd ed.). Baltimore: Williams & Wilkins.

Wechsler, D. (1967). *Manual of the Wechsler preschool and primary scale of intelligence.* San Antonio, TX: Psychological Corporation.

Wechsler, D. (1989). *WPPSI-R manual.* San Antonio, TX: Psychological Corporation.

Wechsler, D. (1991). *Wechsler intelligence scale for children—Third edition.* San Antonio, TX: Psychological Corporation.

Woodcock, R. W., & Johnson, M. B. (1989). *Woodcock–Johnson psychoeducational battery—Revised.* Allen, TX: DLM.

CHAPTER **8**

Assessing Adaptive Development

CHAPTER OBJECTIVES

The ways in which children perform tasks that are expected of their age group can broadly be conceptualized as *adaptive development*. The concept of adaptive development has been influenced by theory, professional practice, politics, and litigation. The assessment of adaptive development has also been affected by the push for inclusion of children with disabilities in schools and communities and the move toward more pluralistic assessment (Coulter & Morrow, 1978).

PL 102–119, known as the 1991 Amendments to the Individuals with Disabilities Act, uses the term *adaptive development* to refer to self-help skills in infants and toddlers. The older term, *adaptive behavior,* continues to be used to refer to "limitations to an individual's effectiveness in meeting the standards of maturation, learning, personal independence and/or social responsibility that are expected for his or her age level . . ." (Grossman, 1983, p. 11).

Identification of levels of adaptive development in young children is valuable for two reasons. Adaptive development is one of the five areas used to determine whether a child can be labeled developmentally delayed (the other areas are cognitive development, physical development, communication development, and social-emotional development). Chapter 1 includes an explanation of the term *developmental delay.* Second, identification of specific delays in adaptive development can assist in program planning.

Upon completion of this chapter, you should be able to:

Define and describe the concept of adaptive development.

Explain the changing nature of the concept of adaptive development.

Describe maladaptive behavior and problem behavior.

Describe specific tests of adaptive development and maladaptive behavior.

Key Terms

Adaptive Development. Limitations to an individual's effectiveness in meeting the standards of maturation, learning, personal independence and/or social responsibility that are expected for his or her age level.

Maladaptive Behaviors. Behaviors that are considered to be problem behaviors.

Informant. An individual who knows the child well and provides information about the child.

ADAPTIVE DEVELOPMENT

Two basic concepts are associated with adaptive behavior. The first is personal independence, which emphasizes self-help skills and the appropriate use of skills in the community. The second is social responsibility, which stresses behaviors related to early socialization and the demonstration of behaviors that correspond to community expectations (Bruininks, Thurlow, & Gilman, 1987). Table 8.1 summarizes adaptive behavior areas.

The definition of adaptive development and our assessment of it are influenced by several variables. Adaptive development is related to the age of the child. Deficits in adaptive development in infancy and early childhood can occur in the areas of sensorimotor skills, communication skills, self-help skills, and socialization. In childhood and early adolescence the emphasis is on academic skills, reasoning and judgment related to coping with the environment, and interpersonal skills. In late adolescence the focus is on vocational adjustment and social adjustment in the community (Bruininks et al., 1987).

Adaptive development may be influenced by the norms of racial, ethnic, or cultural groups, community expectations, and the life cycle. What may be adaptive in one environment may not be considered adaptive in another environment. The quality of adaptive development behaviors that are demonstrated may be different at various developmental levels. Thus, adaptive development is a dynamic concept (Horn & Fuchs, 1987).

There is some controversy over the meaningfulness and utility of the adaptive development concept. First, some theorists have argued that the term is too vague (Horn & Fuchs, 1987). Second, there is some overlap between the concepts of adaptive development and intelligence. In fact, correlations between intelligence tests and adaptive development scales are moderate. In addition, a stronger correlation exists between adaptive development and in-school achievement than with adaptive development and outside-school behavior. Next, questions have been raised about the usefulness of adaptive development scales to predict future behavior, although there is some evidence that adaptive behavior may be predictive of vocational performance (Harrison, 1987).

Because our views in this area have changed and will continue to change, there is considerable disagreement over what constitutes adaptive development. In general, instruments that assess adaptive development can be useful when determining eligibility, engaging in program planning, and monitoring progress. There is considerable overlap among instruments that assess adaptive development, behavior, functional skills, and development. In addition, the adaptive development instruments reviewed in this chapter are based on different theoretical orientations, and the

TABLE 8.1 Adaptive behavior areas

Clusters and Specific Adaptive Behavior Areas

Self-help, Personal Appearance
  Feeding, eating, drinking
  Dressing
  Toileting
  Grooming, hygiene
Physical Development
  Gross motor skills
  Fine motor skills

Communication
  Receptive language
  Expressive language

Personal, Social Skills
  Play skills
  Interaction skills
  Group participation
  Social amenities
  Sexual behavior
  Self-direction, responsibility
  Leisure activities
  Expression of emotions
Cognitive Functioning
  Preacademics (e.g., colors)
  Reading
  Writing
  Numeric functions
  Time
  Money
  Measurement

Health Care, Personal Welfare
  Treatment of injuries, health problems
  Prevention of health problems
  Personal safety
  Child care practices
Consumer Skills
  Money handling
  Purchasing
  Banking
  Budgeting
Domestic Skills
  Household cleaning
  Property maintenance, repair
  Clothing care
  Kitchen skills
  Household safety
Communicity Orientation
  Travel skills
  Utilization of community resources
  Telephone usage
  Community safety

Vocational Skills
  Work habits and attitudes
  Job search skills
  Work performance
  Social vocational behavior
  Work safety

SOURCE: Bruininks, R., Thurlow, M., & Gilman, C. (1987). Adaptive behavior and mental retardation. *Journal of Special Education, 21,* 74. Copyright 1987 by Pro-Ed, Inc. Reprinted by permission.

assessment of adaptive development will depend on the particular instrument that is used.

SCHOOL-AGE CHILDREN

In general, we use the term *adaptive behavior* instead of *adaptive development* in relation to school-age children. For school-age children, the measurement of adaptive development plays a large part in determining whether an individual is labeled mentally retarded. The identification of a child as mentally retarded is related to deficits in adaptive behavior when a child who is significantly below average in intellectual functioning is compared to other children of the same age group.

Knowledge about the adaptive behavior of a child can aid in program planning. Areas of strengths and needs can be identified and instructional goals can be developed.

MALADAPTIVE BEHAVIOR

Examples of *maladaptive* or problem *behaviors* include bed wetting; unusual physical aggressiveness; poor attention; impulsivity, self-injurious behaviors; rocking back and forth repeatedly; and poor eye contact. In general, a child's actions are considered to be a problem when they adversely affect the child, another child, or the environment (Bruininks et al., 1987). Problem behaviors can affect the extent to which young children can be integrated into social and community settings. Problem behaviors on the part of older children can have a negative impact on vocational and community placements (Bruininks et al., 1987).

The concept of maladaptive behavior, like the concept of adaptive behavior, is not without controversy. The assessment of maladaptive behavior is linked to expectations related to the child's age, family, culture, and community. For example, thumb sucking is not considered to be a maladaptive behavior for a two-year-old but may be so considered for a twenty-year-old. Read the case study of Anna, a child with below-average adaptive behavior. What would you include in Anna's IFSP? How would you evaluate the goals?

CASE STUDY: ANNA

Four-year-old Anna has been identified as developmentally delayed. She lives with her mother and three brothers. She attends the Community Child Care Agency, where she is enrolled in appropriate programs. Anna was born prematurely, and it was readily apparent at birth that she showed evidence of fetal alcohol syndrome. Her mother was a known abuser of alcohol and other drugs.

Observations indicate that Anna is hyperactive and has a short attention span. She is distractible and irritable. The caregiver and the parents reported that Anna has difficulty playing cooperatively with other children and they requested an assessment of Anna's adaptive behavior, as a first step in revising Anna's IFSP.

Using the survey form of the Vineland Adaptive Behavior Scales, the evaluator interviewed Anna's mother and the child's primary caregiver at the Community Child Care Agency. On the test, Anna scored well below average in adaptive development. Specifically, Anna had difficulty with the following:

Using a sentence of four or more words

Stating which of two objects is bigger

Understanding the words "behind," "between," and "around"

Feeding herself with a fork

Removing her coat or sweater by herself

Playing independently

Playing simple games with others

Jumping over a small object

Pedaling a tricycle

Hopping on one foot

The evaluation of Anna's maladaptive behavior shows evidence of the following behaviors:

Cries easily

Has poor concentration and attention

Is overly active

Is negativistic

Using the results of this test as well as information from other tests, observations, and interviews, the multidisciplinary team revised Anna's IFSP.

INFORMANTS

Instruments that assess adaptive development and maladaptive behavior usually rely on an *informant*—someone who knows the child well and provides information about the child. The informant responds to questions about the child either through an interview with the examiner or by completing a checklist or scale. Because the assessment of adaptive behavior relies on ratings provided by informants, the instruments can be administered frequently.

Informants may be child care providers, parents, teachers, aides, nurses, or social workers. Informants provide different information about children, although there may be considerable overlap in their reports. For instance, the child care provider may offer information about peer relationships, while the parent can supply information about sibling relationships and bedtime activities.

The information from informants is considered to be judgmental and may vary from one informant to the next. The input from informants reflects their own perspectives, experiences, attitudes, response styles, and biases. The child may behave differently depending on the environment or the situation. Because of these variables, it is important to evaluate the reliability and validity of the information that is provided. It may be helpful to ask more than one informant to complete an instrument or scale (Sattler, 1988).

ADAPTIVE BEHAVIOR INSTRUMENTS

The tests described in this chapter were developed specifically to evaluate the adaptive development of children. Many other tests, described in other chapters of this book, contain components that assess self-help skills. These tests are:

Battelle Developmental Inventory

Brigance® Inventory of Early Development

Carolina Curriculum for Infants and Toddlers with Special Needs

Carolina Curriculum for Preschoolers with Special Needs

Early Intervention Developmental Profile

Early Learning Accomplishment Profile

Hawaii Early Learning Profile (HELP)

Help for Special Preschoolers

Learning Accomplishment Profile

Portage Guide to Early Education

Preschool Development Profile

Adaptive Behavior Inventory

The Adaptive Behavior Inventory (ABI) (Brown & Leigh, 1986) is a norm-referenced measure of adaptive development intended for use with children who have disabilities, ages six to eighteen years, and for children who are not disabled, ages five to eighteen years. The ABI has five subscales: self-care skills, communication skills, social skills, academic skills, and occupational skills. Each subscale contains 30 items. A short form of the ABI, ABI—Short, has 50 items.

Administration. The ABI and the ABI—Short can be completed by the teacher or another professional in about 25 minutes.

Scoring. Standard scores and percentile ranks can be obtained for each of the subscales and the full scale.

Standardization. The ABI was standardized on 1,296 children with normal intelligence and 1,076 children who were mentally retarded. Although the characteristics of the sample are described, information about the selection of the sample is lacking.

Reliability. Information about internal consistency and test–retest reliability is provided. For the most part, the reliability coefficients are in the .80s and .90s.

Validity. Limited information about validity is presented. The manual provides information about concurrent validity. Additional information about the validity of the ABI should be provided.

Summary. The ABI and the ABI-Short are norm-referenced instruments that evaluate the adaptive development of school age children in five areas: self-care skills, communication skills, social skills, academic skills, and occupational skills. Additional information about the technical adequacy of this test is needed.

Adaptive Behavior Scales

There are two forms of the Adaptive Behavior Scale. Originally developed by the American Association on Mental Retardation, both scales have been revised. One scale, Adaptive Behavior Scales—Residential and Community Edition: 2 (ABS-RC:2) (Lambert, Leland, & Nihira, 1993a), is intended for individuals who may be living in institutional settings and in community settings. The other scale, *Adaptive Behavior Scales—School Edition: 2* (ABS-S:2) (Lambert, Leland, & Nihira, 1993b), is intended for use with school-age children. Only the ABS-S:2 will be described here.

The ABS-S:2 is divided into two parts. Part One assesses personal independence, coping skills and daily living skills. Part One is divided into nine domains:

Independent functioning. This domain assesses eating, toileting, maintaining a clean and neat appearance, dressing, and using transportation and other public facilities.

Physical development. This domain evaluates physical and motor abilities.

Economic activity. This domain assesses ability to manage money and to be a consumer.

Language development. This domain evaluates receptive and expressive language and behavior in social situations.

Numbers and time. This domain examines basic mathematical skills.

Prevocational/vocational activity. This domain assesses skills related to school and job performance.

Responsibility. This domain assesses the extent to which individuals can be held accountable for their actions, belongings, and duties.

Self-direction. This domain examines whether individuals choose to maintain an active or passive lifestyle.

Socialization. This domain assesses the ability to interact with others.

Part Two of the ABS-S:2 focuses on social maladaptation. The behaviors that are examined are divided into seven domains:

Violent and antisocial behavior. This domain examines behaviors that are physically or emotionally abusive.

Rebellious behavior. This domain assesses aspects of rebelliousness.

Untrustworthy behaviors. Behaviors that are related to stealing, lying, cheating, and showing disrespect for public and private property are examined.

Stereotyped and hyperactive behavior. This domain assesses behaviors that include making inappropriate physical contact, behaving in stereotypical ways, and being overactive.

Eccentric behavior. Behaviors that are considered to be very unusual are examined.

Withdrawal. This domain assesses the degree to which an individual withdraws or fails to respond to others.

Disturbed behavior. Bothersome types of behavior are examined.

Administration.   The ABS-S:2 is administered by an interviewer.

Scoring.   Raw scores are converted to standard scores with a mean of 10 and a standard deviation of 3. Scores are converted to quotients that have a mean of 100 and a standard deviation of 15. Percentiles are also available.

Standardization.   The ABS-S:2 was standardized in 31 states. The sample included both persons with disabilities and those who were not disabled.

Reliability and Validity.   According to the authors, the ABS-S:2 is a reliable and valid instrument. There is considerable research that documents the usefulness of this instrument.

Summary.   The Adaptive Behavior Scales—School Edition: 2 is an instrument that assesses the adaptive and maladaptive behavior of school-age children. It should be a useful tool.

Checklist of Adaptive Living Skills

The Checklist of Adaptive Living Skills (CALS) (Moreau & Bruininks, 1991) is a criterion-referenced checklist of approximately 800 items in the areas of self-care, personal independence, and adaptive functioning. It was developed to measure the adaptive behaviors of infants through adults and is individually administered, using an interview format, to a respondent who knows the examinee well.

The CALS is related, conceptually and statistically, to the Scales of Independent Behavior (SIB) (Bruininks, Woodcock, Weatherman, & Hill, 1984). The reason for this, according to the manual, is to allow users to predict scores on the SIB. The Adaptive Living Skills Curriculum (ALSC) (Bruininks, Moreau, Gilman, & Anderson, 1991), which is linked to the CALS, contains training objectives, strategies, and activities to facilitate program planning and intervention.

The CALS is divided into four domains: personal living skills, home living skills, community living skills, and employment skills. Each of these domains is organized into 24 specific skills modules. Each item covers a range of behaviors, which are arranged in order of difficulty.

Administration.   The respondent should know the child well. Persons with varied backgrounds, including parents, rehabilitation counselors, teachers, and aides, can serve as respondents. Depending on the needs of the child, some items may be omitted. Because the CALS is a criterion-referenced checklist, the items can be readministered periodically. It takes approximately 60 minutes to complete the CALS.

Scoring.   Items are checked if the child performs the skill independently.

Standardization.   This measure is criterion referenced and was not standardized. The manual states that the CALS was tried out with 627 individuals ranging in age from infancy to more than forty years old. The respondents were from eight states. Approximately half the sample were individuals who were disabled, and approximately equal numbers of females and males were selected. Little demographic information about the sample is provided.

Reliability.   Internal consistency and split-half reliabilities were calculated for two samples. A sample consisting of 213 individuals who were not disabled yielded reliability coefficients ranging from .67 to .99. For individuals with disabilities, the reliability coefficients ranged from .65 to .97. Little information is provided about the respondents. No other types of reliability are reported.

Validity.   Evidence of criterion-related validity is based on two studies. Correlations between the Scales of Independent Behavior and the Inventory for Client and Agency Planning (ICAP) for 213 individuals without disabilities ranged from .56 to .94. A sample of 150 persons who were mildly to moderately retarded yielded coefficients that ranged from .56 to .86.

Summary.   The CALS is a criterion-referenced instrument. Evidence of reliability and content and construct validity is limited. Additional information about the sample is needed. This instrument should be used cautiously. It may be most appropriate for program planning.

Pyramid Scales

The Pyramid Scales (Cone, 1984) is a criterion-referenced, rather than a norm-referenced, measure of adaptive development. The scales are intended to be used with persons from birth through adulthood. The scales consist of 20 subtests, which are organized into three skills clusters:

Sensory Skill Cluster
Tactile

Auditory

Visual responsiveness

Primary Skill Cluster
Gross motor

Eating

Fine motor

Toileting

Dressing

Social interaction

Washing and grooming

Receptive language

Expressive language

Secondary Skill Cluster
Recreation and leisure

Writing

Domestic behavior

Reading

Vocational

Time

Money

Numbers

Because this is a criterion-referenced test, comparisons to a norm group are not made. Rather, the rating reflects how well the child has demonstrated certain behaviors. The Pyramid Scales are useful for program planning.

Administration.   The Pyramid Scales can be administered in three different ways: (1) an interview can be conducted with an informant who is familiar with the child; (2) an informant can complete the items without the prompting of an interviewer; and (3) an evaluator can observe the child and complete the scales. It takes approximately 30 to 45 minutes to complete all the scales, although not every scale needs to be done: The evaluator may select the scales most appropriate for the child.

Scoring.   Each item is scored on a 4-point system. Raw scores are converted to percentage correct for each subscale. The percentage correct is plotted on a graph for each of the subscales.

Technical Characteristics.   This test is criterion referenced, not norm referenced. Because of this, there is no standardization or norm sample. The manual contains several reports of reliability and validity. For the most part, this test is technically adequate.

Summary.   The Pyramid Scales are a criterion-referenced measure of adaptive behavior from birth through adulthood. This test is useful for program planning.

Scales of Independent Behavior

The Scales of Independent Behavior (SIB) (Bruininks et al., 1984) is an individually administered, norm-referenced measure of the adaptive and maladaptive behavior of individuals of all ages (infant through adult). According to the authors, the SIB can be used for identification, placement, program planning, and monitoring progress. The SIB is composed of the broad independence scale and four maladaptive scales. The broad independence scale consists of 14 subscales arranged into four clusters: motor skills, social interaction and communication skills, personal living skills, and community living skills. The four scales of maladaptive behavior are general maladaptive behavior, internalized maladaptive behavior, asocial maladaptive behavior, and externalized maladaptive behavior. In addition, two short forms are part of the SIB: the short scale form and the early primary scale. The early development scale provides a developmental measure of adaptive behavior from infancy to three years. This scale also can be used with older individuals who are severely handicapped.

Administration.   The broad independence scale takes from 45 to 60 minutes to administer as a structured interview. Subscales may be administered rather than the entire scale.

Standardization.   The SIB was standardized on the same 1,700 subjects as the Woodcock–Johnson Psychoeducational Battery (Woodcock & Johnson, 1977). It can be administered independently of the other scales in the Woodcock–Johnson

Psychoeducational Battery. The SIB was standardized on individuals randomly selected from 40 communities regionally distributed across the United States. The sample included persons between the ages of three months and forty years; some were disabled and some were not.

Scoring. If a computer scoring program is unavailable, the scoring is time-consuming and cumbersome because several conversions are needed to obtain the final scores. Scores that can be obtained include age scores, percentile ranks, standard scores, stanines, normal curve equivalents, and expected scores. For the maladaptive scales, stanines, maladaptive behavior indexes, and levels of seriousness can be obtained.

Reliability. Split-half reliability coefficients are reported for each subscale and scale. The coefficients range from very low to high. Stability coefficients are moderate to high. Interrater and interinterviewer agreement reliability coefficients are in the .90s.

Validity. According to the authors, content validity for the SIB was established through item selection.

Criterion-related validity was established by correlating the SIB with other adaptive behavior scales and with the broad cognitive scales of the Woodcock–Johnson Psychoeducational Battery.

Evidence of construct validity was demonstrated by a developmental progression of scores over the age span. Several studies with special groups (e.g., individuals with moderate disabilities) were conducted. Information in the areas of content validity and criterion-related validity also supports the claims of construct validity.

Summary. The Scales of Independent Behavior is an individually administered, norm-referenced measure of the adaptive and maladaptive behavior of individuals from infancy through adulthood. Evidence of reliability and validity is acceptable.

Vineland Adaptive Behavior Scales

The Vineland Adaptive Behavior Scales (VABS) has three forms.

Expanded form. The expanded form (Sparrow, Balla, & Cicchetti, 1984a) contains 577 items, 297 of which can be found on the survey form. It provides a comprehensive assessment of adaptive behavior and, according to the manual, is useful for developing educational, habilitative, or treatment programs.

Survey form. The survey form (Sparrow, Balla, & Cicchetti, 1984b) consists of 297 items and is intended to be used to identify strengths and weaknesses.

Classroom edition. The classroom edition (Harrison, 1985) contains 244 items and yields an evaluation of adaptive behavior in the classroom. In addition to items from the survey form and the expanded form, the classroom edition contains items relating to school performance.

All three forms measure communication, daily living skills, socialization, and motor skills. The expanded form and the survey form assess maladaptive behavior.

The domains are divided into subdomains: receptive, expressive, written communication, personal, domestic, community daily living skills, interpersonal relationships, play and leisure time, coping skills for socialization, gross and fine motor skills.

Administration.   Both the expanded form and the survey form can be administered in a semistructured interview with a parent, caregiver, or an adult who is disabled. It takes approximately 60 to 90 minutes to administer the expanded form and approximately 20 to 60 minutes to administer the survey form. The classroom edition is administered as a questionnaire, which is completed by a teacher of a child who is between the ages of 3 years and 12 years, 11 months. Approximately 20 minutes is required to complete the questionnaire.

Scores.   Normalized standard scores are obtained for the domains and the adaptive behavior composite. Other scores provided are percentile ranks, stanines, age equivalents, and adaptive levels. Adaptive levels are based on ranges of standard scores and provide a qualitative label for performance (e.g., high, moderately high, adequate, moderately low, and low). Tables are given for determining significant and unusual differences.

Standardization.   The expanded form was not administered during the standardization. The expanded form was standardized by equating it to the survey form by using the common items of each. The survey form was standardized on 3,000 individuals, with about 100 individuals in each of 30 age groups between birth and 18 years, 11 months. The standardization sample was based on the 1980 census and was stratified according to sex, race or ethnic group, community size, region, and parents' level of education. Supplementary norms for both the survey form and the expanded form were also developed. The standardization sample included approximately 1,800 ambulatory and nonambulatory adults who were mentally retarded, eighteen or older, and clients in residential and nonresidential facilities; and individuals who were emotionally disturbed, hearing-impaired and visually impaired, ages six through fifteen years, and clients of residential facilities.

The standardization sample for the classroom edition consisted of 2,984 children ages 3 years to 12 years, 11 months. The children selected for the sample were randomly chosen by teachers. This resulted in a sample that is largely unrepresentative of the U.S. population.

Reliability.   For the survey form, split-half, test–retest, and interrater reliability are reported. Median split-half reliabilities, based on odd–even correlations, ranged from .83 (motor skills) to .90 (daily living skills). The coefficient for the adaptive behavior composite was .94. Maladaptive behavior coefficients ranged from .77 to .88.

Test–retest reliability for the survey form was determined by administering the survey form twice to parents and caregivers of 484 children and youth from the age of 6 months to 18 years, 11 months. The time interval between the two administrations was 2 to 4 weeks. Most of the coefficients were in the .80s and .90s. The average difference between the first administration and the second was very small.

Interrater reliability for the survey form was estimated by interviewing the parents or caregivers of 160 persons in the standardization sample who were from 6 months to 18 years, 11 months of age. The average time between the two interviews was 8 days. Coefficients were in the .90s.

The reliability of the expanded form was estimated on the basis of data obtained during the standardization of the survey form. For the expanded form, estimated median split-half reliability coefficients ranged from .91 (motor skills) to .95 (daily living skills). The coefficient for the adaptive behavior composite was .97. Maladaptive behavior coefficients ranged from .77 to .88.

Test—retest reliability and interrater reliability were not estimated for the expanded form.

For the classroom edition, only internal consistency reliability was estimated. Median reliability coefficients ranged from .80 (motor skills) to .95 (daily living skills). The median coefficient for the adaptive behavior composite was .98.

Validity. According to the authors, content validity for the survey form and the classroom edition was established through a review of the literature, an analysis of the test items, item tryout, and standardization. No independent evaluation of content validity is provided.

Criterion-related validity for the survey form and the classroom edition was established by correlating the VABS with other adaptive behavior scales and intelligence scales.

Evidence of construct validity for the survey form and the classroom edition is demonstrated by a developmental progression of scores over the age span, factor analysis, and profiles of scores for supplementary norm groups. Information relating to content validity and criterion-related validity also supports the claims of construct validity.

For the expanded form, independent validity studies were not conducted. The authors state that the validity of the expanded form was determined on the basis of data for the survey form.

Summary. The Vineland Adaptive Behavior Scales consist of three forms: expanded form, survey form, and the classroom edition. The VABS is a norm-referenced, individually administered measure of adaptive and maladaptive behavior. Reliability and validity are adequate. However, the reliability and validity of the expanded form are based on the reliability and validity of the survey form.

PREFERRED PRACTICES

Adaptive development refers to a child's ability to adapt to the personal and social demands of the environment. The assessment of adaptive development is not without controversy. Predictions based on the assessment of adaptive development are related to several concepts. The assessment of adaptive development is related to age and cultural norms. As children develop, cultural expectations will change. Thus certain types of adaptive development (e.g., thumb sucking) are more acceptable in younger children than in older children.

Frequently, the term *adaptive behavior* is used instead of *adaptive development* for school-age children. The identification of deficits in adaptive behavior along with significantly below-average intellectual functioning plays a large part in determining whether a school-age child will be identified as mentally retarded. The concept of adaptive development is a dynamic one, and our views of this construct change over time. Theoretical arguments about the definition of adaptive development and the usefulness of the construct will continue (McCarver & Campbell, 1987). However, the assessment of adaptive development will remain important for identification, eligibility determinations, and program planning, especially for young children who have severe disabilities.

STUDY QUESTIONS AND SUGGESTED ACTIVITIES

1. Keeping in mind that the concept of adaptive behavior is related to cultural norms, give an example of a behavior that might be considered to be adaptive in one context and not adaptive in another.
2. In what ways are instruments that assess development similar to adaptive behavior scales?
3. In what ways are instruments that assess functional skills similar to adaptive behavior scales?
4. How does the concept of adaptive behavior overlap with that of intelligence?

REFERENCES

Amendments to the Individuals with Disabilities Act, Sec. 12, Part H, PL 102–119, 105 *Stat.* 595 (1991).

Brown, L., & Leigh, J. E. (1986). *Adaptive behavior inventory.* Austin, TX: Pro-Ed.

Bruininks, R. H., Moreau, L. E., Gilman, C. J., & Anderson, J. L. (1991). *Manual for the adaptive living skills curriculum.* Allen, TX: DLM.

Bruininks, R. H., Thurlow, M., & Gilman, C. J. (1987). Adaptive behavior and mental retardation. *Journal of Special Education, 21*(1), 69–88.

Bruininks, R. H., Woodcock, R. W., Weatherman, R. F., & Hill, B. K. (1984). *Scales of independent behavior.* Allen, TX: DLM.

Cone, J. D. (1984). *Pyramid scales.* Austin, TX: Pro-Ed.

Coulter, W. A., & Morrow, H. W. (1978). *Adaptive behavior: Concepts and measurements.* New York: Grune & Stratton.

Grossman, H. (1983). *Classification in mental retardation.* Washington, DC: American Association on Mental Retardation.

Harrison, P. L. (1985). *Classroom edition manual, Vineland adaptive behavior scales.* Circle Pines, MN: American Guidance Service.

Harrison, P. L. (1987). Research with adaptive behavior scales. *Journal of Special Education, 21*(1), 37–68.

Holman, J., & Bruininks, R. (1985). Assessing and training adaptive behaviors. In K. C. Lakin & R. H. Bruininks (Eds.), *Strategies for achieving integration of developmentally disabled citizens* (pp. 73–104). Baltimore: Paul H. Brookes.

Horn, E., & Fuchs, D. (1987). Using adaptive behavior in assessment and intervention: An overview. *Journal of Special Education, 21*(1), 11–26.

Lambert, N., Leland, H., & Nihira, K. (1993a). *Adaptive behavior scales—Residential and community edition: 2.* Austin, TX: Pro-Ed.

Lambert, N., Leland, H., & Nihira, K. (1993b). *Adaptive behavior scales—School edition: 2.* Austin, TX: Pro-Ed.

McCarver, R. B., & Campbell, V. A. (1987). Future developments in the concept and application of adaptive behavior. *Journal of Special Education, 21*(1), 197–207.

Moreau, L. E., & Bruininks, R. H. (1991). *Checklist of adaptive living skills.* Allen, TX: DLM.

Sattler, J. (1988). *Assessment of children.* San Diego, CA: Jerome M. Sattler, Publisher.

Sparrow, S. S., Balla, D. A., & Cicchetti, D. V. (1984a). *Interview edition, expanded form manual, Vineland adaptive behavior scales.* Circle Pines, MN: American Guidance Service.

Sparrow, S. S., Balla, D. A., & Cicchetti, D. V. (1984b). *Interview edition, survey form manual, Vineland adaptive behavior scales.* Circle Pines, MN: American Guidance Service.

Woodcock, R. W., & Johnson, M. B. (1977). *Woodcock–Johnson psychoeducational battery.* Allen, TX: DLM.

CHAPTER 9

Assessing Play

CHAPTER OBJECTIVES

In this chapter, we will examine various assessment procedures to increase our understanding of the child's skills, growth, and development through play-based activities. Through play, children have occasions to engage in gross and fine motor activities, to communicate with other children and adults, and to explore and gain new knowledge about their surroundings. Play is a natural way for children to express themselves. In fact, play activities often involve smiling and vocalizations or speech. During play activities, the child's level of motivation is usually high.

Play is an activity in which all children, regardless of ability, can participate. Play activities may be observed across all cultural settings. To the trained observer, environments that promote play activities offer a rich resource of information about the child. In later years, play continues to contribute to the growing child's intellectual, physical, and socioemotional development. When children enter the primary grades, play activities continue to provide important opportunities to explore, experiment, and create (National Association for the Education of Young Children and National Association of Early Childhood Specialists in State Departments of Education, 1991).

Upon completing this chapter, you should be able to:

Define the terms *play* and *play assessment*.

Discuss a developmental sequence of play behaviors.

Describe skills that may be assessed through play.

Describe the role of play assessment in the assessment process.

Describe the various approaches to play assessment.

Discuss the issues of culture, gender, and disability and their effects on a child's play and play assessment.

CASE STUDY: THREE-YEAR-OLD ARNIE BAKER

In September the Bakers will enroll their son Arnie in a regular preschool program for three-year-olds. Arnie was diagnosed as having microcephaly at birth and low vision at 14 months. His visual acuity at present is not known. Although he has been receiving early intervention services since he was born, this will be Arnie's first experience in a center-based program with other children. To assist in planning Arnie's program, the team decided to use an assessment through play procedure. But the first obstacle was one of logistics! How could the members of the team gather for several assessment procedures when limited resources at several agencies threatened cutbacks of services?

During a discussion of this problem at one of the team meetings, Mr. Baker volunteered to video Arnie over the following month as he played in the living room with his favorite toys and with his younger sister. By using the video recordings, Arnie's dad was able to capture several play periods on different days. When the team reconvened, Mr. and Mrs. Baker described to the other members of the team the activities that were common to Arnie's play with toys as well as in his attempts to communicate with his sister.

The tape provided valuable information to the team for planning Arnie's school-based program for the fall and monitoring his present progress. The team wished they had made a tape of Arnie's play earlier as a means of evaluating his early intervention program. The team members agreed that much of the information gathered by video during the play sessions would have been difficult to obtain in more formal assessment procedures. Let's look at some of the information that the team felt was most valuable:

1. *Visual functioning.* Arnie's use of residual vision, as he played with his favorite spinner box, indicated to team members that his preferred method of viewing was with his left eye approximately 5 inches from the object. To assess visual functioning as accurately as possible, team members felt that it was important for Arnie to be motivated in the use of the material.

2. *Communication.* Arnie used vocalization as well as pointing gestures to communicate with his sister. The speech and language pathologist, Bill Barnes, felt that Arnie should be supported in his use of verbal language. Bill will continue to assess communication skills during play and use this information in consulting with the staff at the preschool center. He plans to recommend ways in which the teachers can support Arnie's communication. For example, the teachers can help the other children to interpret Arnie's communications and suggest some ways for them to respond to him.

3. *Cognitive–motor skills.* Arnie prefers toys that move and toys he can spin by brushing the moving parts with his hands. He is attracted to toys that produce sound. Staff members of the preschool center felt this information was valuable in planning and ordering materials for the upcoming year. The teachers wanted to ensure the availability of materials that accommodated all children's levels of play.

Key Term

Play. An activity that gives pleasure, is flexible to change, is nonliteral, and is intrinsically motivating.

EARLY THEORETICAL PERSPECTIVES

Early theoretical perspectives emphasized different aspects of play activities. Erik Erikson (1963) focused on the social–emotional aspect of play. He described play activities as important ego-building functions. Through play, according to Erikson, children begin to build many skills, physical and social as well as cognitive and emotional. The development of these skills serves to enhance self-esteem.

Jean Piaget (1951, 1954, 1968) emphasized the importance of play for facilitating cognitive growth. He viewed play as the process of incorporating new knowledge into material that has been learned. According to Piaget, knowledge is facilitated through play by learning how objects move and how they change. Play activities are important throughout the Piagetian stages of development.

According to Piaget, play in an early form may be observed in the sensorimotor stage, which is typically present in infants and in children up to age two. In this form of play, children repeat the same action over and over. The child may engage in a simple motoric action such as waving a hand to cause a toy to spin. Children explore materials through taste and touch and sound and repeat these actions again and again. Piaget described several substages of sensorimotor development that relate to cognitive development. Table 9.1 presents a description of the types of play that are typical of these substages.

In the next stage (preoperational), children begin to engage in symbolic play.

TABLE 9.1 Types of play associated with Piagetian sensorimotor development

Age Range	Types of Play	Stages of Sensorimotor Development
Birth to 1 month	Child's movements are controlled primarily by primitive reflexes. This period is a precursor to play.	
1 to 4 months	Child repeats an activity that focuses on the body and gives pleasure, such as sucking and grasping activities.	Primary circular reactions
4 to 8 months	Child begins to repeat an activity not specifically oriented to its own body, but having an effect on the environment, such as banging a spoon on the high chair.	Secondary circular reactions
8 to 12 months	Child often focuses on the means rather than the end. For example, the child moves a blanket to expose a toy. The activity of moving the blanket may become a game in itself.	
12 to 18 months	Child intentionally varies aspects of an activity in order to make the activity more interesting.	Tertiary circular reactions
Over 18 months	Child gradually begins to choose one thing to represent something else, replacing sensorimotor play with make-believe play.	Moves beyond sensorimotor development to symbolism

SOURCE: Adapted from Hughes (1991).

Around two years of age, children move from simple repetition to using materials to satisfy a purpose. They may use simple materials to construct and create things. Later in this stage, play begins to involve games with rules.

CONTEMPORARY PERSPECTIVES

Several contemporary theorists have built on the early work of Piaget and others. Vygotsky (1978) describes the link between symbolic play and early language and literacy skills. During play children begin to use abstract symbols to convey meaning. Thus, three blocks become a bridge through which a toy car may be propelled. Later, symbolic play becomes more abstract. The child begins to make marks on paper with a pencil to signify an object or idea. Eventually the symbolic process leads to writing individual words to convey meanings as defined by the child's culture. Thus, play allows children many opportunities to explore the use of a variety of abstract symbols.

HOW CAN WE DESCRIBE PLAY?

Children engage in a variety of activities throughout the day. But how do we know which behaviors should be described as "play"? How can we identify a child's activity as being play-based? There are several different ways of thinking about play behaviors. One schema conceptualizes play in a developmental sequence with certain characteristics common to certain age levels. Another schema regards "play" as comprising discrete, child-centered characteristics.

Play as a Developmental Progression of Skills

One way of examining play behavior is to conceptualize play activities along a developmental sequence. Competencies in play become more sophisticated and complex as a child grows and matures.

Developing Social Skills with Peers.   Parten (1932) categorized levels of play in a developmental sequence. She emphasized the child's development of interaction with other children, and this sequence (Table 9.2) is used to locate highest levels of functioning. Children (as well as adults) move back and forth through this sequence. In fact, solitary and parallel play may be the most desirable types of play at times.

Smilansky (1968) adapted these classifications to categorize four different types of play:

1. *Functional play.* Play involves simple motoric actions repeated over and over. For example, the child may pour water from container to container at the water table.
2. *Constructive play.* Play involves construction with objects or materials. For example, the child may use a rolling pin (object) and clay (material) in the housekeeping center.

TABLE 9.2 Parten's categories of play behavior

Type	Age Range	Description
Unoccupied		Child watches anything of interest; is content to play with own body.
Solitary	24–30 months	Child plays with own toys. No attempt to interact with others.
Onlooker		Child watches other children but makes no attempts to enter into play.
Parallel	30–42 months	Child plays beside, rather than with, other children.
Associative	42–54 months	Child plays with and shares toys with other children.
Cooperative		Child plays with one or more children in a goal-directed activity.

3. *Dramatic play.* Play involves assuming a role or making believe. For example, the child may use a chair as a truck seat (make believe) or pretend to be a baby.
4. *Games with rules.* Play involves the use of rules, which are usually specific and relatively arbitrary. Rules are based on agreement between children. For example, answers must be either "yes" or "no."

The relevance of play, especially dramatic play for school adjustment, has been studied extensively. Smilansky and Shefatya (1990) report a number of studies that address the relationship between this form of play and school-related variables of achievement. For example, one study found a very high relationship between sociodramatic play in kindergarten and achievement in second grade.

Based on Piagetian theory of cognitive development, Largo and Howard (1979) described the systematic development of play in children between 9 and 30 months of age. This developmental progression of skills is seen in the list below. We will describe their work in detail to promote a better understanding of a developmental approach to play.

The Developmental Progression of Play Behavior at Four Developmental Levels

1. Behaviors with Exploratory Characteristics
   a. Manipulation: fingering, banging, throwing, waving
   b. Visual exploration: watching, tracking
   c. Mouthing
2. Behaviors with Functional Characteristics
   a. Functional play: child brushes own hair
   b. Representational play 1: child brushes doll's hair
   c. Representational play 2: child helps doll to brush hair
   d. Symbolic play: child uses an object to represent a brush (such as a wooden dowel)
   e. Sequential play: child brushes the dolls' hair, answers the telephone, dresses the dolls, and feeds them breakfast

3. Behaviors with Spatial Characteristics
   a. Relational play: child places car beside pail
   b. Container play: child places car inside pail
   c. Stacking play: child stacks objects
   d. Grouping play: child puts all the cars together
   e. Spatial arrangement: child places objects appropriately (e.g., sets the table)
4. Behaviors That Are Nonspecific
   a. Other: Behaviors that cannot be categorized as above
   b. Nonplay behavior: child refuses to participate (Adapted from Largo & Howard, 1979)

Exploratory Play.   Early play behavior is exploratory. That is, children play with an object by fingering it, looking at and turning the object, or placing it in the mouth. Largo and Howard (1979) found that children typically engage in exploratory play before nine months of age; gradually this type of play is replaced by more functional behaviors. However, these early behaviors never completely disappear. Some characteristics of exploratory behavior stay with us for a lifetime!

Functional Play.   As children develop, play behavior acquires functionality. The child uses objects in activities related to the self. For example, the child may pour sand over her hand using a plastic shovel or use a spoon to "eat" the "soup." By 18 months of age these behaviors are replaced by more representational activities (Largo and Howard, 1979).

Representational Play.   These activities are also functional but engage another person or object (e.g., doll, stuffed animal). Play behaviors are directed to performing an activity on or with the object. Thus, a teddy bear may be put to sleep, a rubber duck may have a bath, or you may be served a cup of tea! These activities are referred to as representational play activities and are most common in children between 18 and 30 months of age (Largo & Howard, 1979).

By 21 months, children begin inventing more involvement for the other person, doll, or stuffed animal (Largo and Howard, 1979). Objects take on a more active role, with the result that the child may have rubber duck scrub its own bill or assist teddy bear in using its paws to pull up the covers. These activities are a second level of representational play or play 2 in the classification of Largo and Howard.

Symbolic Play.   Symbolic play involves the substitution of an object for the actual one. Children may use sugar cubes as blocks to build structures or stones and clay as ingredients for cookies. Largo and Howard (1979) found that symbolic play begins around 36 months.

Sequential Play.   Somewhere between 21 and 30 months children begin to string a series of related play activities together (Largo & Howard, 1979). For example, the child may create several different activities for teddy bear: cooking and eating pizza for supper, reading a bedtime story, helping him brush his teeth, and tucking him in to bed.

Play with Spatial Characteristics.   Play activities can be described by the use and position of materials in space. For example, Largo and Howard (1979) found that:

> Children around 15 months of age enjoy placing objects in containers.
>
> Children between 18 and 21 months enjoy stacking objects.
>
> By 24 months children can set a table with plates, spoons, and cups.

Although age ranges assigned by Largo and Howard (1979) have been included in this discussion, we stress that all children exhibit a *wide range* of behaviors. Figure 9.1 represents the progressive sequence of play behaviors on a continuum. The normal curve is superimposed to illustrate the time period characteristic of certain play behaviors. The ends of the normal curve extend across the typical age range to represent the wide variation among young children. In addition, individual children may move back and forth across a sequence on any one day. This figure illustrates the importance of conducting several observations during a play assessment to ensure an accurate, reliable observation.

Play as a Developmental Progression of Object Use

Another way of looking at play is to order the way children use materials from a developmental perspective. Neisworth and Bagnato (1987), who summarized levels of play that involves objects, have grouped the findings into six progressive levels:

The Development of Play Skills with Objects

Level	Description of Child's Play
1	Repeated motions with toy, mouthing of toy
2	Pounds or throws, pushes or pulls toy
3	Uses toy with self (places block on head)
4	Manipulates movable parts of toy
5	Separates parts of toy
6	Combines different play materials (Adapted from Neisworth & Bagnato, 1987)

Again, one should remember that children often move back and forth through these stages (or levels), and some play activities may involve more than one stage.

FIGURE 9.1   The progressive sequence of play behaviors

SOURCE: Adapted from ages described by Largo and Howard (1979).

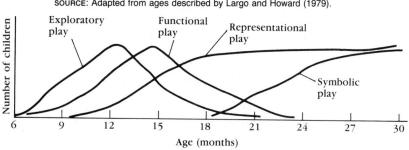

Generally, though, an earlier stage will recede in dominance as the child matures. Most theorists believe that children with or at risk for disability move through the same stages but at a slower rate. However, research on play and children with disabilities is limited and difficult to interpret (Hughes, 1991). Much remains to be learned about what happens when children with special needs are given opportunities to play with nondisabled peers in regular early childhood settings in their communities.

Play as an Activity with Specific Characteristics

A different way of conceptualizing play activities has been described by Rubin, Fein, and Vandenberg (1983), who describe several essential characteristics that distinguish play behaviors from the more random behaviors of children. These include:

Active engagement. A child who is actively engaged may be talking to self or to others, imaginary or real. The child evidences an unwillingness to be distracted.

Intrinsic Motivation. A child with intrinsic motivation displays a sincere desire to continue the activity.

Attention to means rather than ends. A child attends to the process, such as the combining of paint colors, rather than to the actual product.

Nonliteral behavior. A child engages in make-believe activities.

Freedom from external rules. Play does not entail rules imposed by others outside the play activity. In more advanced types of play, children may generate their own set of rules.

Adults may provide the setting and materials to enhance play activities. Adults may join play activities. However, Rubin et al. (1983) believe that an activity is no longer play when an adult structures or interferes with it inappropriately.

Key Term

Play Assessment. Observation of one or more children for the purpose of understanding their developmental, sensorimotor, cognitive, communicative, social, and emotional functioning.

PLAY ASSESSMENT

Play assessment is the observation of one or more children for the purpose of understanding their developmental, sensorimotor, cognitive, communicative, social, and emotional functioning. Some types of information, such as a child's strategies for joining a group or a child's skill in negotiating with other children, may be difficult to obtain by other procedures. The information gathered during play assessment can be integrated with the results of other assessment procedures. The assessment of play can be conducted in a variety of settings, from environments low in structure to highly structured conditions. The environments can be natural or arranged for the child (Figure 9.2). Participants, in addition to the child, can include one or more examiners (who may also be observers), one or more observers, parents, teachers,

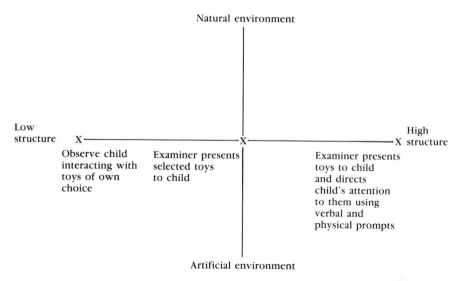

FIGURE 9.2 Continuum of play environments

and therapists. Play is a familiar area for children and allows them to demonstrate strengths and needs in a way that is less stressful than some of the assessment activities presented in earlier chapters (Schaefer, Gitlin, & Sandgrund, 1991).

BENEFITS OF PLAY ASSESSMENT

Formal testing is difficult to conduct with some children. For example, some children cannot respond to the demands of formal tests, perhaps because they are unable to attend to structured tasks or because they have behavior or other disabilities, such as autism, attention deficit disorder, or post–traumatic stress disorder, for which there are limited standardized tests. Play assessment provides a safe, comfortable, less threatening approach to the assessment of young children.

Play assessment, along with the results of formal testing, generates a wealth of information about a child's functioning. Because of the limitations associated with standardized testing, play assessment is another tool we can use to gather information about a child. Play assessment is a window on assessment and can provide information for program planning and monitoring. Play assessment can be used to support, contradict, elaborate, or complement the results of other approaches to assessment. Multiple sources of information help us to have confidence in the insights and conclusions we have about a child's functioning (Schaefer et al., 1991).

Play assessment must be conducted in a *natural environment*—that is, one in which the child is comfortable (Linder, 1990). In a natural environment, the child feels relaxed and less threatened. There are familiar toys as well as toys the child has not seen before. The child is able to explore the environment, sometimes interacting with the examiner, other professionals, and parents, and sometimes with other children. Artificiality is reduced. The format is close to the child's experiences. Linder, imagining how a child might respond to a play assessment setting, wrote:

Hey! This place is neat! Mommy is holding your hand, but you let go and run to the dollhouse area. It has a sink, refrigerator, and stove just like at home, only smaller. And it has dolls and beds and dishes and telephones. You look in the refrigerator. Suddenly you notice another lady next to you. She is telling you about what's in the refrigerator. She doesn't seem to mind that you just helped yourself to all these toys. In fact, when you pick up a doll and start to feed it, she does the same thing. She says her doll is hungry. You tell her yours is hungry too. Well, actually, all you say is "ungy," but she seems to understand. She pours more "milk" in your baby's cup. You and the lady play together in the doll house. Sometimes she does what you do, and sometimes you look at her and do what she does. You think she is a nice lady. (Linder, 1990, p. 14)

Rapport between the examiner and the child is another advantage of play assessment (Linder, 1990). It may be easier to obtain rapport with this type of assessment because the child is in a familiar environment. Artificiality is minimized. Play is a natural means of expression for the child. The child and the examiner are interacting using familiar objects and actions.

Flexibility is another advantage of play assessment (Linder, 1990). With standardized testing, the examiner must adhere to the directions for test administration. Adaptations can be made with play assessment. If the child is enjoying playing with a toy, a longer period of time can be spent with that toy. Or, if a child prefers a different toy, a change is permissible. The toys and the environment can be arranged to suit the needs and preferences of the child.

The language used during the assessment can also be adapted (Linder, 1990). The formal, scripted language of standardized tests is not used in play assessment. The language of the child can be used. Gestures, pointing, and other means of communication are acceptable.

Another advantage of play assessment is that the parents can be involved. By observing, participating, and contributing to the assessment (Linder, 1990), parents can gain a greater understanding of their child's capabilities and can offer interpretations of their child's play to other team members. They can see the link between the evaluation and the recommendations for intervention. The results of the assessment and the recommendations are relevant to the parents.

A final benefit of play assessment is that an unlimited number of observations can be conducted (Schaefer et al., 1991). In traditional testing, of course, this is not possible. For the purposes of play assessment, it does not matter if the toys or the situations are the same. In fact, frequent observations can be beneficial because they help to document progress and enhance our understanding of the child's play and the child's ability to interact with the environment. Frequent observations are not a compulsory component of play assessment. If changes in intervention strategies must be made, however, they can be made quickly if information obtained from frequent observations is available.

LIMITATIONS OF PLAY ASSESSMENT

In any testing situation, variability exists. This may be more true of play assessment, however, because variability is built into the assessment process. Unless the play assessment is conducted under structured conditions, there is variability in the toys and the environment. The flexibility and adaptability of the process also introduce variability. The assessment of play should be conducted with concern for reliability and validity (Schaefer et al., 1991).

Play assessment is accompanied by the same reliability and validity problems we have encountered with other types of assessment. Only recently have examiners started to consider standardized approaches to play assessment. Schaefer et al. (1991) have stated that much more research is needed to investigate the reliability and validity of play assessment instruments.

Reliability refers to the consistency or stability of performance. The methods used to gather information about the child must be reliable. That is, the rating scales, observation tools, and checklists must be consistent. If a child is observed one day, the examiner wants to have some assurance that the observations, if conducted on the next day, would be about the same. Or, if another examiner were to observe the play of the child, the reports of the two examiners would be about the same. Since it is impractical to conduct a play assessment every day or every week, we must have some assurance that the observations will be about the same even if conducted the next day or by a different examiner. Reliability can help in giving us this assurance.

There are a number of ways in which reliability can be increased, which were discussed in Chapter 4.

Validity is the extent to which the assessment procedure measures what it is intended to measure. Some forms of play assessment are intended to assess development; others assess cognition, affective development, social interactions, or language. In all cases, however, validity is an important consideration when conducting or evaluating a play assessment approach. Play assessment usually is valid if the child is observed in the natural environment and if the assessment questions refer to appropriate tasks.

Depending on the environment and the number of participants, play assessment can be intrusive. When observations are made in a child care setting, the presence of adults who are unfamiliar can be disturbing and distracting. The normal routine of the day may be disrupted. Children may respond differently when strange adults enter the room. Examiners should carefully consider the effects their presence may have on children and whether play activities have been disturbed because unfamiliar adults have entered the environment.

The skill levels of the examiner and the observer also can limit the effectiveness of play assessment. Examiners and observers need to have an extensive background in child development, both typical and atypical. They must be thoroughly grounded in understanding child's play and how it relates to cognitive, social, and emotional development. They must be skilled in relating to children and must know how to conduct reliable and valid observations. They must be able to integrate the observations of play assessment with the results of other forms of assessment.

A final limitation of play assessment is the need for additional forms of assessment to understand a child's strengths and needs (Linder, 1990). Norm-referenced, standardized tests are required by federal laws and by some states to identify a disability and to determine eligibility for services. Play assessment may not yield all the information called for in such cases. Play assessment may not provide information relating to many self-help skills (such as toileting, feeding, dressing, and undressing) or to academic skills. In addition to standardized tests, observations, interviews, and alternative assessment approaches may have to be used along with play assessment to obtain a comprehensive evaluation of the child.

MODELS OF PLAY ASSESSMENT

The three models of conducting play assessment—multidisciplinary, interdisciplinary, and transdisciplinary—were discussed in Chapter 1. Briefly, in the *multidisciplinary model* professionals from different disciplines conduct, plan, and implement the areas of the assessment related to their respective disciplines. For example, in a team composed of an educator, a speech therapist, an occupational therapist, and a physical therapist, the speech therapist would observe the child's play focusing on speech, language, and communication. From the results of this observation, the speech therapist would then develop an intervention plan and implement it; consultation with the other members of the team would be minimal.

In an *interdisciplinary model,* professionals from different disciplines conduct separate observations but share their plans and incorporate activities from other disciplines when possible. For example, a speech therapist who is part of an interdisciplinary team would observe the child's play, focusing on speech, language, and communication, but would share these observations with other members of the team and incorporate intervention activities that relate to the other disciplines.

In a *transdisciplinary model,* a facilitator engages in play with the child while the other team members, including the parents, record their observations of the activity. Each team member has an understanding of the other disciplines represented on the team. The team members collaborate in conducting the observations, sharing information, and developing the intervention plan. Linder (1990) has advocated a transdisciplinary approach to the assessment of play. In this model, the speech therapist would be knowledgeable about all the disciplines represented in the team and would collaborate with all the team members throughout the assessment process.

METHODS OF PLAY ASSESSMENT

Play assessment is a relatively new area. The techniques available range from highly structured, formal instruments to informal guidelines. Much more investigation is needed to identify appropriate techniques. There are many descriptions of play scales in the research literature. Many of these have developed out of informal procedures. Our understanding of these techniques has been greatly enhanced by the publication of the book *Play Diagnosis and Assessment* (Schaefer et al., 1991), which groups the techniques into categories. Our examination of the various techniques of play assessment follows several of the categories as described by Schaefer, Gitlin, and Sandgrund. While research has been conducted on some of the scales, practitioners are urged to use them cautiously. These instruments can be helpful when combined with other sources of information about the child. Representative scales are described in the list below:

Representative Play Assessment Instruments
Development
A Manual for Analyzing Free Play (McCune-Nicolich, 1980)

Developmental Progression in Play Behavior of Children between Nine and Thirty Months (Largo & Howard, 1979)

Developmental Scale of Infant Play (Belsky & Most, 1981)

Play Assessment of Infant Temperament (Matheny, 1991)

Play Assessment Scale (Fewell & Rich, 1987)

Play Observation Scale (Rubin, 1989)

Symbolic Play Test (Lowe & Costello, 1976; also described by Power & Radcliffe, 1991)

Transdisciplinary Play-Based Assessment (Linder, 1990)
Diagnosis
Goodman Lock Box (Goodman, 1991; Goodman & Field, 1991)

Mayes Hyperactivity Observation System (Mayes, 1991)

ETHOS Play Session (Siegel, 1991)

Structured Observation of Academic and Play Settings (Roberts, Milich, & Loney, 1985)
Parent–Child Scales
Interaction Rating Scales (Field, 1980)

Mother–Toddler Play Preferences Checklist (Roggman, 1991)

Parent–Child Interaction Play Assessment (Smith, 1991)

Marschak Interaction Method (Jernberg, 1991)

Peer Interaction Scale

Behavior Observation Record (Segal, Montie, & Iverson, 1991)

DEVELOPMENTAL PLAY SCALES

Play assessment is useful in monitoring the development of young children. As discussed in Chapter 6, a developmental approach assumes that children progress through regular stages or periods. Individual differences in children can affect the rate at which they traverse the stages. There may be qualitative differences between children while they are in a particular stage or period.

Analyzing Free Play

A Manual for Analyzing Free Play (McCune-Nicolich, 1980) describes a procedure for studying the symbolic play of toddlers and children. The mother and child are videotaped in the home, and the tape is analyzed using play episodes. A *play episode* is a single contact with an object or a continuous involvement with several objects. The episodes are then analyzed according to various symbolic schemes using specific codes.

Play Assessment Scale

The Play Assessment Scale (PAS) (Fewell & Rich, 1987) was developed to assess the cognition, language, and social behavior of children between 2 and 36 months. The PAS consists of 45 developmentally sequenced items. That is, based on the developmental age of the child, the examiner presents a set of toys, which are rearranged several times during the observation by the examiner. Observations are conducted under spontaneous and elicited conditions. A play age score can be obtained.

Play-based Assessment

Linder (1990), who advocates a transdisciplinary model for the assessment of play, has developed guidelines for assessing cognitive development, social–emotional development, communication and language, and sensorimotor development. Linder suggests that the play-based assessment be conducted in a large room that has distinct areas: house, block, art, sand/water, work, and gross motor. The assessment could also be conducted in the child's home or in any large room that has been arranged to permit the child to choose different toys and activities. Play-based assessment has the following general format:

Unstructured facilitation

Structured facilitation

Child–child interaction

Parent–child interaction
  Unstructured
  Separation
  Structured

Motor play
  Unstructured
  Structured

Snack

The total time for play-based assessment is approximately 60 to 90 minutes. Table 9.3 contains observation guidelines for transdisciplinary play-based assessment.

The Play Observation Scale

The Play Observation Scale (Rubin, 1989) is intended to assess the social and cognitive aspects of play and nonplay behaviors. The observer uses a coding sheet (Figure 9.3) to record the child's behaviors. Social play can be solitary, parallel, or group. Cognitive play is categorized as functional, constructive, dramatic, and games-with-rules. Nonplay behaviors are categorized as exploratory, reading, unoccupied, onlooker, transition, active conversation, aggression, and rough-and-tumble.

Symbolic Play Scale

The Symbolic Play Scale (Westby, 1980) is based on the work of Piaget. According to the author, symbolic skills are prerequisites for the development of meaningful communication. The development of symbolic play follows a consistent sequence and is a way in which a child mentally represents reality. The Symbolic Play Scale (Figure 9.4) posits that a child's symbolic skills develop in 10 stages beginning with Stage 1 at nine to twelve months and culminating at five years of age. The purposes of the scale are to identify children who may need language intervention and to assist in planning the type of intervention that is needed.

Using the Symbolic Play Scale as a basis for the observations, one child or as

TABLE 9.3 Guidelines for transdisciplinary play-based assessment

Cognitive Development	Social–Emotional Development	Communication and Language Development	Sensorimotor Development
Categories of play	Temperament	Communication modalities	General appearance of movement
Attention tone/span	Mastery motivation	Pragmatic stages	Muscle strength/endurance
Early object use	Social interactions with parent	Sound production patterns	Reactivity to sensory input
Symbolic/representational play	Social interactions with facilitator	Discourse skills	Stationary play positions
Imitation	Social interactions with peers	Comprehension of patterns	Mobility in play
Problem-solving approaches	Characteristics of dramatic play	Oral motor development	Other developmental achievements
Discrimination/differentiation	Humor and social convention	Observations related to hearing, voice quality, cognition, social–emotional development, sensorimotor development	Prehension and manipulation
One-to-one correspondence		Grammatic structure and meaning	Motor planning
Sequencing ability		Comprehension of language	
Drawing ability		Oral motor	

SOURCE: Adapted from Linder, T. (1990). *Transdisciplinary play-based assessment.* Baltimore, MD: Paul H. Brookes.

many as four children are brought into a room that has been arranged with five groups of toys:

1. *Infant stimulation area:* includes pull toys, windup toys, stuffed animals, and talking toys
2. *Household area:* includes dolls, doll furniture, kitchen area, child-sized furniture
3. *Store area:* includes cash register, play money, shopping cart, miniature food
4. *Creative play area:* includes sandbox, blocks, puppets, play animals
5. *Gross motor area:* includes slide, riding toys, bowling set, walking board

The children are permitted to explore the room freely and play within any of the areas. One or two adults interact with the children. Two observers, using the Symbolic Play Scale, record the children's activities. Interpretation is based on determining the child's stage of symbolic play and comparing the stage with the child's cognitive abilities.

THE PLAY OBSERVATION SCALE CODING SHEET

Child: _C.R._ School: _Main Street_

Date: _5/4/xx_ Sex: _F_ Minute: _1:10 – 2:10_

Transition	Unoccupied	Onlooker	Aggression	Teacher Conversation	Peer Conversation	Solitary						Parallel						Group						Affect (+ o −)	Names
						Functional	Exploratory	Reading	Constructive	Dramatic	Games	Functional	Exploratory	Reading	Constructive	Dramatic	Games	Functional	Exploratory	Reading	Constructive	Dramatic	Games		
T	U	O	AG	T/C	P/C	F	E	R	C	D	G	F	E	R	C	D	G	F	E	R	C	D	G	A	Names
								✓																+	
								✓																+	
								✓																+	
							✓																	+	
							✓																	+	

Anecdotal Notes and Comments:

Reading quietly in the block corner.

							Solitary						Parallel						Group						Affect			
T	T	U	O	AG	T/C	P/C	F	E	R	C	D	G	F	E	R	C	D	G	F	E	R	C	D	G	+	o	−	
O																													
T																													
A																													
L																													

FIGURE 9.3 Coding sheet for the Play Observation Scale

SOURCE: From *The Play Observation Scale* by Kenneth H. Rubin. Waterloo, Ontario: University of Waterloo, 1989. Reprinted by permission.

Symbolic Play Scale Check List

Play	Language
Stage I 9 to 12 months	

____ Awareness that objects exist when not seen; finds toy hidden under scarf
____ Means–end behavior—crawls or walks to get what he wants: pulls string toys
____ Does not mouth or bang all toys—some used appropriately
	____ No true language; may have performative words (words that are associated with actions or the total situation)
	
	Exhibits following communicative functions:
	    ____ Request (instrumental)
	    ____ Command (regulatory)

Stage II 13 to 17 months	
____ Purposeful exploration of toys: discovers operation of toys through trial and error: uses variety of motoric schemas ____ Hands toy to adult if unable to operate	____ Context-dependent single words, for example, child may use the word "car" when riding in a car, but not when he sees a car; words tend to come and go in child's vocabulary Exhibits following communicative functions: ____ Request ____ Protesting ____ Command ____ Label ____ Interactional ____ Response ____ Personal ____ Greeting
Stage III 17 to 19 months	
____ Autosymbolic play; for example, child pretends to go to sleep or pretends to drink from cup or eat from spoon ____ Uses most common objects and toys appropriately ____ Tool-use (uses stick to reach toy) ____ Finds toys invisibly hidden (when placed in box and box emptied under scarf)	Beginning of true verbal communication. Words have following functional and semantic relations: ____ Recurrence ____ Agent ____ Existence ____ Object ____ Nonexistence ____ Action or state ____ Rejection ____ Location ____ Denial ____ Object or person associated with object or location
Stage IV 19 to 22 months	
Symbolic play extends beyond the child's self: ____ Plays with dolls: brushes doll's hair, feeds doll a bottle, or covers doll with blanket ____ Child performs pretend activities on more than one person or object: for example, feeds self, a doll, mother, and another child ____ Combines two toys in pretend play, for example, puts spoon in pan or pours from pot into cup	____ Refers to objects and persons not present Beginning of word combinations with following semantic relations: ____ Agent-action ____ Action-locative ____ Action-object ____ Object-locative ____ Agent-object ____ Possessive ____ Attributive ____ Dative

(continued)

FIGURE 9.4   Symbolic Play Scale: Appendices A–C

SOURCE: From *Assessment of Cognitive and Language Abilities through Play* by C. E. Westby (1980). *Language, Speech, and Hearing Services in Schools, 11*, 154–168. Reprinted by permission of the American Speech-Language-Hearing Association.

Play	Language

Stage V 24 months

_____ Represents daily experiences; plays house—is the mommy, daddy, or baby; objects used are realistic and close to life size

_____ Events short and isolated; no true sequences; some self-limiting sequences—puts food in pan, stirs, and eats

_____ Block play consists of stacking and knocking down

_____ Sand and water play consist of filling, pouring, and dumping

_____ Uses earlier pragmatic functions and semantic relations in phrases and short sentences

The following morphological markers appear:

_____ Present progressive (ing) on verbs

_____ Plurals

_____ Possessives

Stage VI 2½ years

Represents events less frequently experienced or observed, particularly impressive or traumatic events

_____ Doctor–nurse–sick child

_____ Teacher–child

_____ Store shopping

Events still short and isolated. Realistic props still required. Roles shift quickly.

Responds appropriately to the following WH questions in context:

_____ What

_____ Who

_____ Whose

_____ Where

_____ What . . . do

_____ Asks WH questions—generally puts WH at beginning of sentence

_____ Responses to why questions inappropriate except for well-known routines, such as, "Why is the doctor here?" . . . "Baby sick."

_____ Asks why, but often inappropriate and does not attend to answer

---

Stage VII 3 years

_____ Continues pretend activities of Stages V and VI, but now the play has a sequence. Events are not isolated; for example, child mixes cake, bakes it, serves it, washes the dishes; or doctor checks patient, calls ambulance, takes patient to hospital, and operates. Sequence evolves . . . not planned.

_____ Compensatory toy . . . reenactment of experienced events with new outcomes

_____ Associative play

_____ Uses past tense, such as, "I ate the cake . . . I walked."

_____ Uses future aspect (particularly "gonna") forms, such as, "I'm gonna wash dishes."

Stage VIII 3 to 3½

_____ Carries out play activities of previous stages with a doll house and Fisher–Price toys (barn, garage, airport, village).

Descriptive vocabulary expands as child becomes more aware of perceptual attributes. Uses terms for the following concepts (not always

FIGURE 9.4 (_continued_)

APPENDIX A (*continued*)

Play	Language

_____ Uses blocks and sandbox for imaginative play. Blocks used primarily as enclosures (fences and houses) for animals and dolls
_____ Play not totally stimulus bound. Child uses one object to represent another.
_____ Uses doll or puppet as participant in play.
	correctly):
	    _____ shapes
	    _____ sizes
	    _____ colors
	    _____ texture
	    _____ spatial relationships
	_____ Gives dialogue to puppets and dolls.
	_____ Metalinguistic language use, such as, "He said . . ."
	_____ Uses indirect requests, such as, "Mommy lets me have cookies for breakfast."
	_____ Changes speech depending on listener.

Stage IX 3½ to 4 years	
_____ Begins to problem-solve events not experienced. Plans ahead. Hypothesizes "what would happen if . . ." _____ Uses dolls and puppets to act out scenes _____ Builds three-dimensional structures with blocks which are attempts at reproducing specific structures child has seen.	Verbalizes intentions and possible future events: _____ Uses modals (can, may, might, will, would, could) _____ Uses conjunctions (and, but, if, so, because) Note: Full competence for these modals and conjunctions does not develop until 10–12 years of age _____ Begins to respond appropriately to why and how questions that require reasoning about perception
Stage X 5 years	
_____ Plans a sequence of pretend events. Organizes what he needs—both objects and other children. _____ Coordinates more than one event occurring at a time _____ Highly imaginative. Sets the scene without realistic props. _____ Full cooperative play	_____ Uses relational terms (then, when, first, next, last, while, before, after) Note: Full competence does not develop until 10–12 years of age

(*continued*)

Symbolic Play Test

The Symbolic Play Test (SPT) (Lowe & Costello, 1976), as standardized and described by Power and Radcliffe (1991), evaluates the symbolic development of children who are functioning between the ages of 12 and 36 months. Four different groups of toys are introduced to the child (Figure 9.5) and the child is observed. Observations are conducted around four categories of play: tactile exploration, symbolic self-oriented usage, symbolic doll-related usage, and sequential symbolic repre-

FIGURE 9.4 *(continued)*

APPENDIX B

Observation Form

	Onlooking	Solitary	Parallel	Associative	Cooperative
Game					
Symbolic Spontaneous					
Symbolic Imitative					
Practice					

sentation. Figure 9.6 lists the specific play behaviors to be observed. The time to administer the SPT is approximately 15 to 20 minutes.

DIAGNOSTIC PLAY SCALES

Diagnosis of specific disabilities can be a complex and difficult process (Schaefer et al., 1991). Play assessment can assist in the identification of specific disabilities, especially in young children. Some young children are so disabled that it is difficult to use conventional published tests. Using a diagnostic approach, play assessment can be very useful in helping to identify and describe strengths and needs. Most of the presently available play assessment scales should be used cautiously because we lack information relating to standardization, reliability and validity.

Definition of play behaviors for the observation form

Practice	—	The child engages in gross motor activities such as running, riding on bikes or wagons, climbing, throwing balls. Child works puzzles, strings beads, stacks blocks and knocks them down, fills and empties containers, operates cause–effect toys such as music boxes, "busy" boxes, talking toys.
Symbolic/ Imitative	—	The child engages in pretend play, but it is initiated and guided by another child or an adult.
Symbolic/ Spontaneous	—	The child initiates the pretend activity.
Game	—	The child engages in rule-governed game behavior and exhibits some under-standing or appreciation of the rules.
Onlooking	—	The child observes but does not participate.
Solitary	—	The child plays without reference to other children.
Parallel	—	The child's play is of a companionable nature with similar materials, but with no personal interaction.
Associative	—	The children's play is loosely organized around a common activity, shared inter-ests, and materials.
Cooperative	—	The play includes different roles, common goals, usually with one or two lead-ers, and is of relatively long duration and complexity.

The observers using the forms record a description of the child's behavior within the appropriate box on the form. If a child engages in several different behaviors during a recording time, the behaviors are sequentially numbered.

FIGURE 9.5   Four groups of toys for Symbolic Play Test

SOURCE: From *Play Diagnosis and Assessment* by Charles E. Schaefer, Karen Gitlin, and Alice Sandgrund. Copyright © 1991 by John Wiley & Sons, Inc. Reprinted by permission.

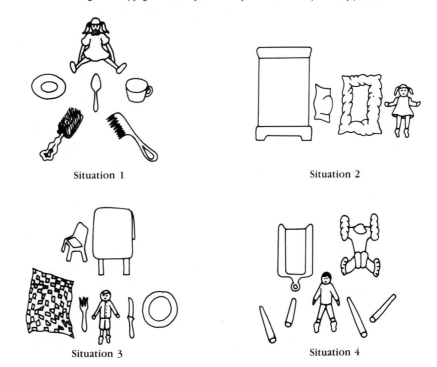

Situation 1

Situation 2

Situation 3

Situation 4

Situation I

1. Discriminate handling of the doll

+ Any indication that the child is aware of specific characteristics of doll (e.g., standing it up, making it jump, feeding it, naming it, pointing to eyes, mouth etc.). Liberal scoring.
− Bangs, puts doll in mouth, etc.

2. Relates spoon to cup or saucer

+ Places spoon in cup or on saucer, "picks up" food from saucer, "stirs" with spoon in cup.
− If cup or saucer are in upturned position or spoon applied with wrong end.

3. Feeds, combs, or brushes self or other person

+ "Drinks" from cup; "eats" from spoon, feeds or offers food to person present. + also if brush is clearly used as cloth − or toothbrush (e.g., dipped in the cup and moved to and fro in the mouth).
− Indiscriminate mouthing (e.g., if cup or spoon are in the wrong position; puts brush in mouth; puts brush in cup).
N.B. This item is scored + retrospectively if the child feeds, combs, or brushes doll in Situation I or feeds self in Situation III.

4. Feeds, combs, or brushes doll

+ Overt feeding (i.e., puts cup or spoon to doll's mouth) or implied feeding (e.g., places cup or spoon in doll's hand; places cup, spoon, saucer in front of doll in proper arrangement); bringing brush or comb to doll's hair, without actually combing it, also scores.
− Approaches doll with wrong end of spoon; applies spoon or cup to other areas of doll; applies spoon or cup to other areas of head (e.g., hair) unless there is an additional indication of intention (e.g., feeding noises, dipping the spoon first into the cup, etc.), brushes doll's clothes or teeth.
N.B. If child scores this item, he is also credited with item 3.

5. Places cup on saucer

+ Cup placed on saucer.
− Saucer placed on cup; cup or saucer upside down.

Situation II

6. Discriminate handling of doll

+ As in I/1. If the child handles the doll appropriately in Situation III, this is scored here in retrospect.

7. Relates doll to bed

+ Lays or seats doll on bed (head can be at foot-end).
− Stands doll on bed; puts doll casually across bed, unless there is additional evidence of intention (e.g., additional use of pillow or blanket).

FIGURE 9.6 Scoring guide for symbolic play test behavior

SOURCE: From *Symbolic Play Test* by C. M. Lowe and A. Costello, 1976. Reproduced by permission of NFER-Nelson Publishing Company, Windsor, England.

8. Relates blanket or pillow to doll

+   Lays doll on blanket or pillow; covers doll with blanket or pillow; seats doll on pillow; wraps doll into blanket; wipes doll's face with blanket.

9. Puts doll to bed

+   Involves use of doll, bed, blanket (or pillow); pillow need not be used specifically. Doll can lie on blanket (pillow), or be covered by it. Doll can sit on pillow.
−   Indiscriminate stacking.

10. Uses pillow correctly

+   Places doll's head on pillow. Pillow can be at either end of bed.
−   Seats doll on pillow. Covers pillow by blanket, before putting doll to bed.

Situation III

11. Relates knife or fork to plate

+   Places knife or fork on plate or clearly beside it; "picks up" or "cuts" food on plate
−   If plate is upside down.

12. Relates fork, knife, or plate to table

+   Child places either of these objects on the table, "picks up" food or "cuts" food on the table. Liberal scoring.
−   If table is upside down; sweeps knife or fork over table just once.

13. Relates tablecloth to other object

+   Wipes cutlery, table, or doll's face with tablecloth; uses cloth as feeder or blanket for doll; puts on table.
−   Wipes own face with cloth; covers plate, chair, etc. with cloth. Places any of the objects on the cloth unless there is additional evidence that it is being used as "lino," "carpet," or "tablecloth" [e.g. places both chair *and* table on cloth; puts plate *and* cutlery (while it is on the examination table) in correct arrangement on the cloth].

14. Places doll on chair

+   Seats, tries to seat, stands doll on chair.
−   Lies doll across chair; doll or chair upside down; doll faces back of chair.

15. Relates fork, knife, or plate to doll

+   Feeds doll; places fork or knife in doll's hand; places fork, knife, or plate clearly in front of doll (feeding need not be carried out). Because of the small size of the doll, fork need not be brought exactly to doll's mouth.
−   Fork applied to other parts of doll beyond area of head.

(*continued*)

FIGURE 9.6   *(continued)*

Scoring Guide

16. Relates chair to table

+   Correct position.
−   Chair with back against table; places chair on table.

17. Relates doll to table

+   Doll on chair, placed at table; doll standing at table.
−   Stands or lays doll on table (table used as "bed"); doll underneath table; table upside down.

18. Places tablecloth on table

+   Needs additional indication that the tablecloth is being used specifically (i.e., plate, knife, or fork must be put on it, or chair placed at table).
−   Places tablecloth on table without above additions, does not score here, but scores item III/13.

ETHOS Play Session

The ETHOS Play Session (Siegel, 1991) was developed to assist in the identification of children who are autistic. The play session consists of nine 2-minute episodes during which the child interacts with the examiner, a parent, or both. The episodes or situations are designed to introduce a variety of social situations that tend to elicit degrees of responsiveness and avoidance in young children. Three of the episodes are very intrusive, as the examiner and/or the parent directly attempts to engage the child in interactions. Three situations are moderately intrusive attempts to engage the child in play with a toy. In the three least intrusive episodes, the child is left alone to play. The situations change quickly; thus the child must adapt rapidly to each one. The examiner uses a prepared coding sheet to record the child's behaviors.

Goodman Lock Box

The Goodman Lock Box procedure (Goodman, 1991; Goodman & Field, 1991) is used to gather information relating to the mental organization and playfulness of children two through six years of age. According to Goodman and Field (1991), this technique can be used with a child who is suspected of having a developmental delay, hyperactivity, a specific learning problem, behavioral difficulties, or an emotional disorder. This procedure takes $6^{1}/_{2}$ minutes to complete.

The Goodman Lock Box is a large wooden box, $2^{1}/_{2}$ feet long, 11 inches high, and 6 inches deep; it has 10 different doors. Each door is closed with a different catch, and behind each door is a different toy. The Lock Box is presented to the child, and the examiner directs the child to open the doors and play with the toys. The child explores the box and its contents, and the examiner records these behaviors on a prepared protocol. The Goodman Lock Box procedure should be used with information gathered from multiple sources.

Mayes Hyperactivity Observation System

The Mayes Hyperactivity Observation System (MHOS) (Mayes, 1991) is intended to identify hyperactivity in preschool children during free play. The procedure takes approximately 10 minutes to complete.

A small area, approximately 12 feet by 12 feet, is arranged with seven manipulative toys: a wooden puzzle; a "busy" box with lids that pop up after being manipulated, to reveal familiar characters; a plastic car with wheels that move; a rubber doll dressed, wrapped in a blanket, and accompanied by a bottle; three sheets of paper and four crayons; alphabet blocks; and a small ball of modeling clay. The child enters the room and is directed to play with the toys. The observer remains in the room.

While the child is exploring the toys, the observer records the child's behavior. The coding form (Figure 9.7) has 10-second intervals and gives codes for noting the types of behaviors the child demonstrated. The score sheet assists in the interpretation of the behaviors that were observed. Practice is required to use the form.

FIGURE 9.7 Coding form for the Mayes Hyperactivity Observation System

SOURCE: From *Play Diagnosis and Assessment* by Charles E. Schaefer, Karen Gitlin, and Alice Sandgrund. Copyright © 1991 by John Wiley & Sons, Inc. Reprinted by permission.

Mayes Hyperactivity Observation System Protocol

Name _____ *J. B.* _____   Observation Date _____ *2/17/XX* _____

10-Second Intervals

Locomotion	✓	✓	✓	✓	✓	✓	✓			✓	✓	✓							✓		✓	✓						
Activity			R	R			R	R		R			R	S	S	S	S	S	R	R								
Material	P	P			C	C	J	J	J	J	D	D	D	BB					BB	BB	BB	BB						

Locomotion																												
Activity																												
Material																												

✓ if in locomotion

		Activity			Material
	A	adaptive play		P	puzzle
	I	sensory inspection		BB	busy box
	N	nonadaptive play		C	car
	S	social interaction		D	doll
	R	reaching for, arranging toys		PC	paper & crayons
	Blank, no material activity, holding			B	blocks
				Cl	clay
				O	other
				S	self
				X	several materials

Structured Observation of Academic and Play Settings

The Structured Observation of Academic and Play Settings (SOAPS) (Roberts, Milich, and Loney, 1985; Roberts, 1987) is an observation procedure that assesses hyperactivity. Initially developed for use with young boys, the SOAPS involves two 15-minute observations during free play and in academic settings. During the free play observation the child is permitted to play with any toys in the room. For the academic observations, the child is asked to complete worksheets and not to play with any toys.

DEVELOPING PLAY OBSERVATION INSTRUMENTS

Many of the observation techniques that were described in Chapter 4, "Observing the Child and the Environment," can be used when conducting an assessment of children's play. Interval recording, anecdotal recording, running record, specimen record, event recording, and category recording are techniques that can be used to observe play. Figures 9.8 and 9.9 are examples of instruments that have been developed by teachers.

PARENT–CHILD INTERACTIONS

Social play develops in the first months of infancy. It is usually initiated by a caregiver who uses facial expressions, vocalizations, and physical contact with the infant. The infant responds by smiling, laughing, and looking. As the child gets older, the social play becomes more complex. The child initiates play, and toys or objects may be incorporated into the activity. Changes in play reflect the social and cognitive abilities of the child (Roggman, 1991).

Parent–child interactions can be observed using several of the methods de-

FIGURE 9.8   A teacher-developed interval play scale

Child's name: *S. A.*   Observer: *C. L.*

Age: *4 years, 6 months*   Date: *3/19/XX*

Minute	Solitary	Parallel	Group	Cooperative	Uninvolved
1	X				
2	X				
3	X		X		
4			X		
5			X		
6					
7	X				
8					
9					
10					

Child's name:|*S. A.*	Observer:|*C. L.*
Age: *4 years, 6 months*	Date: *3/19/XX*

Onlooker	Solitary
11:10 S. A. watched M. T. and Y. G. playing with blocks. He was hesitant to join the group. M. T. and Y. G. did not invite S. A. to join in.	*11:15 S. A. picked up a block that had been dropped by M. T. He began to turn it over and over in his hands.*
Parallel	**Cooperative**

FIGURE 9.9 A teacher-developed narrative record

scribed in Chapter 4 including anecdotal record, running record, event recording, and interval recording. The following types of play situations can be used.

Free Play

The observer instructs the parent to play with the child. The parent and child are encouraged to engage in play without any restrictions or structure imposed by the observer.

Arranging the Toys

The observer may choose specific toys and ask the parent and child to play with these. For example, a ball, a pull toy, a toy telephone, a doll, or plastic shapes could be used. Specific toys could be selected to elicit certain types of behavior. For example, puzzles, building toys, or unusual toys could be used to demonstrate problem-solving skills and help-seeking behaviors (Roggman, 1991).

Instructing the Parent

The observer may give specific instructions to the parent. For example, the parent may be asked to not initiate play within the first few minutes of the play period. Or, the parent may be asked to read a magazine and wait for the child to initiate the play. In another situation, a parent may be asked to not pick up a toy when the child drops it. In each case, the observer is interested in the behaviors of the child and how the child responds to the parent's behaviors (Roggman, 1991).

Controlling the Child

Placing restrictions on the child may be difficult to do. Some observers, however, are interested in eliciting certain behaviors when restrictions are placed on the child.

For example, the amount of floor space may be restricted, or the child may be placed in a high-chair or other fixed seat (Roggman, 1991).

Checklist of Parent–Child Interactions.   Instead of conducting an observation of the parent–child play situation, the examiner may ask the parent to respond to a list of questions about the child's play (Roggman, 1991). Sample questions could ask about how much the child and the parent like to:

Play peekaboo

Bounce

Play hide-and-seek

Do action rhymes

Read books

Work with blocks and puzzles

Play pretending games (dolls, puppets, eating)

Strange-Situation Procedure.   Ainsworth, Blehar, Waters, and Wall (1978) believe that there are four phases of child–mother attachment that last beyond infancy into later childhood:

1. *The initial preattachment phase.* This phase lasts from birth through the first weeks of life. During this phase, the infant does not visually discriminate between other persons and the mother or principal caregiver.
2. *The phase of attachment-in-the-making.* During this phase, the infant distinguishes familiar from unfamiliar figures and is also able to differentiate one familiar figure from another.
3. *The phase of clear-cut attachment.* During this phase, the baby is actively exploring the environment and seeks out preferred figures. This phase continues through ages two and three.
4. *The phase of goal-directed partnership.* During this phase, the child is able to take the viewpoint of the caregiver and understand the caregiver's feelings and motives.

The Strange-Situation Procedure (Ainsworth et al., 1978) examines patterns of attachment between children one year old or younger and their mother or principal caregiver. The strange situation consists of eight episodes that are presented in a predetermined order ranging from least stressful to most stressful. Observations are conducted by trained observers for each of the eight episodes.

The eight episodes of the strange situation are:

1. The mother or caregiver and infant are alone in a room for 30 seconds.
2. The caregiver allows the baby to explore the room and the toys that have been arranged. The caregiver is instructed to read or to pretend to read a magazine. This session lasts for three minutes.
3. At the beginning of this episode, a stranger enters the room and says to the caregiver, "Hello! I'm the stranger" and begins to interact with her and the baby. After three minutes, the mother leaves the room.

4. The stranger tries to get the child to notice that the caregiver is absent. If the baby cries, the stranger will try to comfort the baby. This episode lasts for three minutes.
5. The mother returns to the room and comforts the child. When the child is comforted, the mother leaves the room again.
6. The baby is allowed to explore the room alone for three minutes.
7. The stranger reenters the room and interacts with the baby.
8. The mother returns, comforts the baby, and the stranger leaves.

INCREASING OPPORTUNITIES FOR PLAY

In planning the program, adults can create environments that enhance play opportunities for children. Some of the environmental rating scales described in Chapter 4 may be helpful. Or practitioners may consider creating an informal checklist. A number of different aspects should be considered, including the physical setup, choice of materials, selection of group games, and amount of time allotted to play activities.

Physical Space

The physical setup of the room and the amount of space available influence children's play behavior. Classrooms set up with different activity centers help promote certain play activities. For example, a center for housekeeping, a store, or a doctor's office promotes social interaction and the use of more complex language. A block area promotes fine motor skills and creativity. Water and sand areas tend to produce more functional play (Christie, 1991).

The amount of space also encourages certain activities. Rooms with wide-open spaces may encourage running; rooms with well-defined areas foster increased use of materials and social interaction.

Materials

The types of material also influence play activities. Toys typically found in table areas (puzzles, beads, clay, art materials, etc.) encourage independent activities. Limiting the number of materials available encourages sharing and turn taking. Thus, a teacher may decide to place five pair of scissors in the basket rather than to provide enough scissors for all the children.

By providing a variety of materials, the teacher can encourage children of various abilities to participate. For example, the teacher may provide several materials that can be used to stick two pieces of paper together, ranging from paste, which is applied with a brush and requires much fine motor control, to a glue stick, which needs only to be rubbed across the paper, as well as materials to pat down (double-sided tape) and push (stapler).

Selection of Group Games

The group games that are selected also have an impact on children's play. DeVries and Kohlberg (1987) have categorized group games into the following areas:

1. Aiming games
2. Races
3. Chasing games
4. Hiding games
5. Guessing games
6. Games involving verbal commands
7. Card games
8. Board games

These authors have developed several criteria a teacher may use to judge whether a group game is educationally useful. These are:

1. Is there something interesting and challenging for children to figure out how to do?
2. Can children judge success themselves?
3. Are there opportunities for all players to participate actively throughout the game?

Time Allotted for Play

The amount of time devoted to play activities in the daily schedule is crucial to the type of play that occurs. Christie (1991) describes the problems that spring up when play periods are too short for children to develop dramatic play. Short play periods foster less advanced types of play, and children resort to lower-level functional or construction activities, which can be completed within short periods of time.

IMPACT OF A CHILD'S DISABILITY ON PLAY

Young children with or at risk for disability are often viewed as having limited play skills. Hughes (1991) makes an important point in differentiating between children's observed play and their potential for play. He describes a number of studies addressing physical and social environments that may have limiting characteristics. Limiting factors may include lack of appropriate physical surroundings in which to play, lack of teacher (or child care provider) facilitation in assisting children to plan and carry out their choices of play activities, and lack of suitable playmates. In planning to gather information through play activities with young children, be aware of any of these limiting factors that may affect results. Figure 9.10 is a checklist for assessing whether an environment supports play for children of differing abilities.

In addition to making sure that the environment supports play for all children, there is another precaution. Some evidence (Kennedy, Sheridan, Radlinski, & Beeghly, 1991) suggests that children with or at risk for disability demonstrate more variability in performance over time than children who are developing typically. Practitioners should make repeated assessments of play activities to ensure an understanding of individual differences.

Yes/No

1. Are the activity centers within the building and playground accessible for children using crutches or wheelchairs?   _____

2. Is the play equipment accessible to children with physical disabilities?   _____

3. Are the activity centers and playground designed to support independent travel for children with visual impairments?   _____

4. Are there children who may provide positive role models?   _____

5. Are there toys/materials that support and promote different levels of play?   _____

6. Are the toys/materials appropriate for the age level(s) of all the children?   _____

7. Do teachers (or child care providers) assist children in planning and carrying out their choices of play activities?   _____

8. Do all children have access to a communication system that others can understand?   _____ .

9. Do teachers (or child care providers) encourage development of social skills by interpreting a child's attempts to communicate with others?   _____

FIGURE 9.10 Does the environment support play activities for all children?

ISSUES AND CONSIDERATIONS

Impact of Culture on Play

The cultural heritage of some children will have a direct effect on the materials considered appropriate for play or on types of interaction. In fact, play materials that are typical of children from Anglo-European backgrounds may differ significantly from the play materials considered to be appropriate by families of children from minority cultures. For example, some Native American groups consider certain animals and dolls to be bad luck; and touching the head (adult or child) is traditionally offensive to Native Hawaiians, Cambodians, Lao, and some Buddhists because of the spiritual belief that the head is the most sacred part of the body (Lynch & Hanson, 1992).

In one of the most well-known studies of cultural differences in sociodramatic play, Smilansky (1968) looked at two different groups of children ages three to six years who had been divided by social class. She found that among the lower class children there was significantly less sociodramatic play, which was defined as role playing, make-believe activities, social interaction, and verbal communication. Her suggested explanations included the idea that some parents provide less direct training in and encouragement of pretend play and that some child rearing techniques may inhibit the development of certain skills.

Impact of Gender on Play

A number of interesting studies have focused on the gender of the child and the role of gender in toy selections made by adults. Hughes (1991) reported several studies in which an infant was introduced to some adults as a baby girl and to other adults as a baby boy. Each adult was asked to offer a toy to the infant from a choice of gender-typed and neutral toys. Consistently, adults of both sexes more often offered female toys to the "girl" baby and male toys to the "boy" baby. Thus, a child's preference for certain toys, experiences with particular playthings, and even the ability to handle certain materials may be influenced early on.

A classic study by Rheingold and Cook (1975) examined gender differences in boys' and girls' toys. They found that although the *number* of toys was about the same, the *range* of toys for boys was considerably broader, and the boys had more toys that were *educationally oriented.*

More recently, research on computer usage and gender differences in children has raised further questions regarding equity issues. In a study of 114 primary grade students, Siann, MacLeod, Glissov, and Durndell (1990) found that boys were more likely to have a computer at home and that boys were significantly more likely to describe themselves as frequent users. Sutton (1991) found in a review of the literature that educational software was more gamelike and aggressive in content. Inherent biases of software material may limit what girls—and boys—will choose to do during free time. Teachers responsible for choosing software have a responsibility to carefully evaluate programs that will be available in the classroom. Some authors (Kirk, 1992; Sadker, Sadker, & Klein, 1990) suggest that gender inequalities have long existed within traditional curriculum areas and that content reflects the attitudes of the society in which it is embedded.

CONCLUSION

As assessment practices continue to evolve, the current difficulties with accountability in assessment through play may be overcome. The potential of this vast area of information was well stated by Monighan-Nourot, Scales, Van Hoorn, and Almy (1987):

> Although the quality of play cannot be measured by pupil outcomes on standardized tests, accountability demands adequate means of evaluation. Typical assessment instruments are too gross to measure play, which may be as ephemeral as "angel's hair." But it is just possible that as our research advances we will discover that play has a strength and resilience that reveals itself to the touch of those who respect its aims. (p. 152)

STUDY QUESTIONS AND SUGGESTED ACTIVITIES

1. Observe a child engaged in play. How would you describe the play activities according to Parten? Rubin et al.?
2. Describe a developmental progression of play activities. How might typical progression be affected by a child's disability?
3. Discuss six ways to increase reliability in play assessment.
4. Describe three issues in ensuring adequate validity measures.
5. Visit a local program for young children. Using the questions suggested in Figure 9.10, critique the program in terms of how it supports play activities for *all* children. Are there other questions you should include?

REFERENCES

Ainsworth, M. D. S., Blehar, M. C., Waters, E., & Wall, S. (1978). *Patterns of attachment.* Hillsdale, NJ: Lawrence Erlbaum Associates.

Belsky, J., & Most, R. K. (1981). From exploration to play: A cross-sectional study of infant free play behavior. *Developmental Psychology, 17,* 630–639.

Christie, J. F. (1991). Psychological research on play: Connections with early literacy development. In J. F. Christie (Ed.), *Play and early literacy development* (pp. 27–43). Albany, NY: State University of New York Press.

DeVries, R., & Kohlberg, L. (1987). *Constructivist early education: Overview and comparison with other programs.* Washington, DC: National Association for the Education of Young Children.

Erikson, E. H. (1963). *Childhood and society* (2nd ed.). New York: Norton.

Fewell, R., & Rich, J. S. (1987). Play assessment as a procedure for examining cognitive, communication, and social skills in multihandicapped children. *Journal of Psychoeducational Assessment, 5,* 107–118.

Field, T. (1980). Interactions of preterm infants born to lower SES teenage mothers. In T. Field, S. Goldberg, D. Stern, & A. Sostek (Eds.), *Interactions of high-risk infants and children.* New York: Academic Press.

Goodman, J. (1991). *The Goodman lock box.* Chicago: Stoelting.

Goodman, J. F., & Field, M. (1991). Assessing attentional problems in preschoolers with the Goodman Lock Box. In C. E. Schaefer, K. Gitlin, & A. Sandgrund (Eds.), *Play diagnosis and assessment* (pp. 219–247). New York: Wiley.

Hughes, F. P. (1991). *Children, play, and development.* Boston: Allyn & Bacon.

Jernberg, A. M. (1991). Assessing parent–child interactions with the Marschak Interaction Method. In C. E. Schaefer, K. Gitlin, & A. Sandgrund (Eds.), *Play diagnosis and assessment* (pp. 493–526). New York: Wiley.

Kennedy, M. D., Sheridan, M. K., Radlinski, S. H., & Beeghly, M. (1991). Play–language relationships in young children with developmental delays: Implication for assessment. *Journal of Speech and Hearing Research, 34,* 112–122.

Kirk, D. (1992). Gender issues in information technology as found in schools: Authentic/Synthetic/Fantastic? *Educational Technology, 32*(4), 28–31.

Largo, R. H., & Howard, J. A. (1979). Developmental progression in play behavior of children between nine and thirty months. I: Spontaneous play and imitation. *Developmental Medicine and Child Neurology, 21,* 299–310.

Linder, T. (1990). *Transdisciplinary play-based assessment.* Baltimore: Paul H. Brookes.

Lowe, M., & Costello, A. J. (1976). *Manual of the symbolic play test.* Berks., England: National Foundation for Educational Research.

Lynch, E. W., & Hanson, M. J. (1992). *Developing cross-cultural competence.* Baltimore: Paul H. Brookes.

Matheny, A. P., Jr. (1991). Play assessment of infant temperament. In C. E. Schaefer, K. Gitlin, & A. Sandgrund (Eds.), *Play diagnosis and assessment* (pp. 39–63). New York: Wiley.

Mayes, S. D. (1991). Play assessment of preschool hyperactivity. In C. E. Schaefer, K. Gitlin, & A. Sandgrund (Eds.), *Play diagnosis and assessment* (pp. 249–281). New York: Wiley.

McCune-Nicolich, L. (1980). *A manual for analyzing free play.* New Brunswick, NJ: Douglass College, Rutgers University.

Monighan-Nourot, P., Scales, B., Van Hoorn, J., & Almy, M. (1987). *Looking at children's play: A bridge between theory and practice.* New York: Teachers College Press.

National Association for the Education of Young Children and National Association of Early Childhood Specialists in State Departments of Education. (1991). Guidelines for appropriate curriculum content and assessment in programs serving children ages 3 through 8. *Young Children, 46*(3), 21–38.

Neisworth, J. T., & Bagnato, S. J. (1987). *The young exceptional child: Early development and education.* New York: Macmillan.

Parten, M. B. (1932). Social participation among preschool children. *Journal of Abnormal and Social Psychology, 27,* 243–269.

Piaget, J. (1951). *Play, dreams, and imitation in childhood.* New York: Norton.

Piaget, J. (1954). *The construction of reality in the child.* New York: Basic Books.

Piaget, J. (1968). *Six psychological studies* (A. Tenzer, Trans.). New York: Vintage Books.

Power, T. J., & Radcliffe, J. (1991). Cognitive assessment of preschool play using the symbolic play test. In C. E. Schaefer, K. Gitlin, & A. Sandgrund (Eds.), *Play diagnosis and assessment* (pp. 87–113). New York: Wiley.

Repp, A. C., Nieminen, G. S., Olinger, E., & Brusca, R. (1988). Direct observation: Factors affecting the accuracy of observers. *Exceptional Children, 55,* 29–36.

Rheingold, H. L., & Cook, K. V. (1975). The contents of boys' and girls' rooms as an index of parents' behavior. *Child Development, 46,* 459–463.

Roberts, M. (1987). How is playroom behavior observation used in the diagnosis of attention deficit disorder? In J. Loney (Ed.), *The young hyperactive child* (pp. 65–74). New York: Haworth Press.

Roberts, M., Milich, R., & Loney, J. (1985). *Structured observation of academic and play settings.* This manual can be obtained from Mary Ann Roberts, University Hospital School, University of Iowa, Iowa City, IA 52242.

Roggman, L. A. (1991). Assessing social interactions of mothers. In C. E. Schaefer, K. Gitlin, & A. Sandgrund (Eds.), *Play diagnosis and assessment* (pp. 427–462). New York: Wiley.

Rubin, K. H. (1989). *The play observation scale.* Waterloo, Ont., Canada: Author (University of Waterloo).

Rubin, K. H., Fein, G. C., & Vandenberg, B. (1983). Play. In E. M. Hetherington (Ed.), P. H. Mussen (Series Ed.), *Handbook of child psychology: Vol. 4. Socialization, personality, and social development* (pp. 693–774). New York: Wiley.

Sadker, M., Sadker, D., & Klein, S. (1990). The issue of gender in elementary and secondary education. *Review of Research in Education, 3,* 175–191.

Schaefer, C. E., Gitlin, K., & Sandgrund, A. (Eds.) (1991). *Play diagnosis and assessment.* New York: Wiley.

Segal, M., Montie, J., & Iverson, T. J. (1991). Observing for individual differences in the social interaction styles of preschool children. In C. E. Schaefer, K. Gitlin, & A. Sandgrund (Eds.), *Play diagnosis and assessment* (pp. 579–607). New York: Wiley.

Siann, G., MacLeod, H., Glissov, P., & Durndell, A. (1990). The effect of computer use on gender differences in attitudes to computers. *Computers in Education, 14*(2), 183–191.

Siegel, B. (1991). Play diagnosis of autism: The ETHOS play session. In C. E. Schaefer, K. Gitlin, & A. Sandgrund (Eds.), *Play diagnosis and assessment* (pp. 331–365). New York: Wiley.

Smilansky, S. (1968). *The effects of sociodramatic play on disadvantaged preschool children.* New York: Wiley.

Smilansky, S., & Shefatya, L. (1990). *Facilitating play: A medium for promoting cognitive, socio-emotional and academic development in young children.* Gaithersburg, MD: Psychosocial and Educational Publications.

Smith, D. T. (1991). Parent–child play assessment. In C. E. Schaefer, K. Gitlin, & A. Sandgrund (Eds.), *Play diagnosis and assessment* (pp. 463–492). New York: Wiley.

Sutton, R. (1991). Equity and computers in the schools: A decade of research. *Review of Educational Research, 61*(4), 475–503.

Vygotsky, L. (1978). *Mind in society.* Cambridge, MA: Harvard University Press.

Westby, C. E. (1980). Assessment of cognitive and language abilities through play. *Language, Speech, and Hearing Services in Schools, 11,* 154–168.

CHAPTER 10

Assessing Achievement

CHAPTER OBJECTIVES

Achievement testing is the assessment of past learning, which is usually the result of formal and informal educational experiences. As young children approach the age for entering school and during the early school years, attention is focused on assessing achievement. Assessment of achievement can include standardized tests as well as alternative forms of assessment such as systematic observations, anecdotal records, interviews with caregivers and children, samples of children's work, videotapes, audiotapes, and portfolios. This chapter examines the standardized tests that are used to assess the achievement in children ages three through eight. Chapter 11 describes alternative forms of assessing the achievement of young children.

Upon completion of this chapter, you should be able to:

Differentiate between readiness tests and developmental tests.

Discuss the appropriate use of standardized achievement tests with young children.

Describe the usefulness of several achievement tests.

Key Terms

Achievement Testing. The assessment of past learning.

High-stakes Testing. The use of readiness or achievement tests to make classification, retention, or promotion decisions about children.

Readiness Tests. Instruments that assess curriculum-related skills a child has already acquired.

Developmental Tests. Instruments that assess a child's developmental abilities.

SCHOOL READINESS

The concept of school readiness and the assessment of readiness trouble educators. Anastasi (1988) defined *school readiness* as "the attainment of prerequisite skills, knowledge, attitudes, and motivations, and other appropriate behavioral traits that enable the learner to profit maximally from school instruction" (pp. 441–442).

Readiness testing is distinct from developmental testing. According to Meisels (1989a), *readiness tests* focus on the acquisition of skills, while *developmental tests* concentrate on the ability to acquire skills. Developmental tests assess a child's current level of functioning. Developmental testing is related to the age of the child when tested. Developmental testing, which is discussed in Chapter 6, is used to identify children who may need individualized instruction and to assess a child's ability or potential to learn skills (Meisels, 1987).

Although academic readiness testing has been used since the 1930s, there has been a resurgence of popularity of this form of testing (Shepard, 1990). Tests of school readiness are usually administered before children enter school. Meisels (1987) wrote that readiness tests "are concerned with those curriculum-related skills a child has already acquired—skills that are typically prerequisite for specific instructional programs" (p. 4). Typically, readiness tests are derived from the behaviorist tradition, which holds that learning can be separated into constituent parts or subskills (Shepard, 1990).

Academic readiness tests are a form of high-stakes testing because they are frequently used to make decisions about children's entrance into school. *High-stakes testing* is the use of readiness or achievement tests to make classification, retention, or promotion decisions about children (Meisels, 1989b). A child's performance on a school readiness test can be used to determine whether the child will be (1) asked to delay entrance into school; (2) allowed to enter school with the child's age-mates; (3) identified as at risk and asked to participate in additional testing; or (4) asked to participate in a special class before entering kindergarten. The latter decision is viewed by many experts as a form of retention. Thus, a child can be retained before actually entering school!

Shepard (1990) believes that the research on readiness, especially on reading readiness, is "outmoded and seriously flawed" (p. 169) and inadequate. The tests rely on outdated theories in which learning is fragmented into skills and subskills. The child is supposed to somehow integrate these skills at a later time. Another criticism of school readiness tests is that they lack predictive validity. That is, for the most part, there are limited data on how accurately school readiness tests predict performance in school. In addition, these tests are inadequate as technical bases for such decisions about school placement as those involving special education placements, two-year kindergarten placements, and delays in school entry (Shepard, 1990). Finally, the use of readiness tests encourages teachers to adjust the curriculum so that they teach to the test. Thus, the kindergarten curriculum is heavily determined by the test content. The effect of this is to restrict the curriculum, emphasize basic skills, and limit the teacher's creativity (Meisels, 1989b).

REFORM

In 1990 the National Governors' Association set school readiness goals for the country (Figure 10.1) (Engel, 1991). This emphasis on school reform gave educators an opportunity to focus on the modification of readiness assessment practices.

The Division for Early Childhood of the Council for Exceptional Children (1992) adopted a position statement on the national readiness goal entitled *All Children Should Begin School Ready to Learn*. It included the following statements:

- Schools should be ready to accept and effectively educate all children. Schooling will succeed or fail, not children.

- When we say all children, we do mean all—including children with disabilities, children placed at risk for school failure, children of poverty, children who are non-English-speaking, and children with gifts and talents.

- Reaching Goal One (which refers to readiness) requires healthy and competent parents, wanted and healthy babies, decent housing, and adequate nutrition.

- Quality early education and child care should be a birth right for all children. These services must be comprehensive, coordinated, focused on individual family and child needs, and available to all families that need and choose to use them.

- It is not appropriate to screen children into or out of early education programs. All children must be given a legitimate opportunity to learn.

- Education in the twenty-first century must attend to children's social and emotional growth and development, not merely focus on academic outcomes.

- Early educators must be schooled in and encouraged to use a wide variety of developmentally appropriate curricula, materials, and procedures to maximize each child's growth and development.

- Achieving long-term academic goals does not imply that young children be drilled in English, science, and math. These academic goals are best achieved when young children are provided with environments that encourage their eager participation, exploration, and curiosity about the world.

FIGURE 10.1   National Goals for Education Readiness

SOURCE: National Governors' Association, Task Force on Education (1990). *Educating America: State strategies for achieving the national education goals.* Washington, DC: National Governors' Association (p. 10).

Readiness Goal 1: By the year 2000, all children in America will start school ready to learn.

Objectives:

- All disadvantaged and disabled children will have access to high-quality and developmentally appropriate preschool programs that help prepare children for school.

- Every parent in America will be a child's first teacher and devote time each day helping his or her preschool child learn; parents will have access to the training and support they need.

- Children will receive the nutrition and health care needed to arrive at school with healthy minds and bodies, and the number of low-birthweight babies will be significantly reduced through enhanced prenatal health systems.

- No important social aims are ever achieved by rhetoric. Reaching this goal will require strong and continuing leadership, a wise investment in human and related capital, and collaboration between families, service providers, government, and business (p. 4).

APPROPRIATE ASSESSMENT PRACTICES FOR CHILDREN AGES THREE THROUGH EIGHT

The National Association for the Education of Young Children (NAEYC) & National Association of Early Childhood Specialists in State Departments of Education, (1991) issued guidelines for the assessment of young children ages three through eight:

1. Curriculum and assessment are integrated throughout the program; assessment is congruent with and relevant to the goals, objectives, and content of the program.
2. Assessment results in benefits to the child such as needed adjustments in the curriculum or more individualized instruction and improvements in the program.
3. Children's development and learning in all the domains—physical, social, emotional, and cognitive—and their dispositions and feelings are informally and routinely assessed by teachers' observing children's activities and interactions, listening to them as they talk, and using children's constructive errors [sic] to understand their learning.
4. Assessment provides teachers with useful information to successfully fulfill their responsibilities: to support children's learning and development, to plan for individuals and groups, and to communicate with parents.
5. Assessment involves regular and periodic observation of the child in a wide variety of circumstances that are representative of the child's behavior in the program over time.
6. Assessment relies primarily on procedures that reflect the ongoing life of the classroom and typical activities of the children. Assessment avoids approaches that place children in artificial situations, impede the usual learning and developmental experiences in the classroom, or divert children from their natural learning processes.
7. Assessment relies on demonstrated performance, during real, not contrived activities, for example, real reading and writing activities rather than only skills testing (Engel, 1991; Teale, 1988).
8. Assessment utilizes an array of tools and a variety of processes including but not limited to collections of representative work by children (artwork, stories they write, tape recordings of their reading), records of systematic observations by teachers, records of conversations and interviews with children, teachers' summaries of children's progress as individuals and as groups (Chittenden & Courtney, 1989; Goodman, Goodman, & Hood, 1989).
9. Assessment recognizes individual diversity of learners and allows for differences in styles and rates of learning. Assessment takes into consideration children's ability in English, their stage of language acquisi-

tion, and whether they have been given the time and opportunity to develop proficiency in their native language as well as in English.

10. Assessment supports children's development and learning; it does not threaten children's psychological safety or feelings of self-esteem.

11. Assessment supports parents' relationships with their children and does not undermine parents' confidence in their children's or their own ability, nor does it devalue the language and culture of the family.

12. Assessment demonstrates children's overall strengths and progress, what children can do, not just their wrong answers or what they cannot do or do not know.

13. Assessment is an essential component of the teacher's role. Since teachers can make maximal use of assessment results, the teacher is the primary assessor.

14. Assessment is a collaborative process involving children and teachers, teachers and parents, school and community. Information from parents about each child's experiences at home is used in planning instruction and evaluating children's learning. Information obtained from assessment is shared with parents in language they can understand.

15. Assessment encourages children to participate in self-evaluation.

16. Assessment addresses what children can do independently and what they can demonstrate with assistance, since the latter shows the direction of their growth.

17. Information about each child's growth, development, and learning is systematically collected and recorded at regular intervals. Information such as samples of children's work, descriptions of their performance, and anecdotal records is used for planning instruction and communicating with parents.

18. A regular process exists for periodic information sharing between teachers and parents about children's growth and development and performance. The method of reporting to parents does not rely on letter or numerical grades, but rather provides more meaningful, descriptive information in narrative form.

In addition, NAEYC (1988) has issued guidelines for using and evaluating standardized tests with children ages three through eight:

National Association for the Education of Young Children Guidelines for Using Standardized Tests with Children Ages 3 through 8

1. All standardized tests used in early childhood programs must be reliable and valid according to the technical standards of test development (AERA, APA, & NCME, 1985).

2. Decisions that have a major impact on children such as enrollment, retention, or assignment to remedial or special classes should be based on multiple sources of information and should never be based on a single test score.

3. It is the professional responsibility of administrators and teachers to critically evaluate, carefully select, and use standardized tests only for the purposes for which they are intended and for which data exist

demonstrating the test's validity (the degree to which the test accurately measures what it purports to measure).

4. It is the professional responsibility of administrators and teachers to be knowledgeable about testing and to interpret test results accurately and cautiously to parents, school personnel, and the media.

5. Selection of standardized tests to assess achievement and/or evaluate how well a program is meeting its goals should be based on how well a given test matches the locally determined theory, philosophy, and objectives of the specific program.

6. Testing of young children must be conducted by individuals who are knowledgeable about and sensitive to the developmental needs of young children and who are qualified to administer tests.

7. Testing of young children must recognize and be sensitive to individual diversity. (National Association for the Educational of Young Children, 1988).

In issuing these guidelines, NAEYC recognized that standardized tests can have a role in objectively, accurately, and appropriately assessing the needs of young children and in providing information to help plan instruction. But standardized tests are just one of many different types of information that can be used when making decisions about young children. According to NAEYC, the most important criterion for using standardized tests is *utility;* that is, tests must be *useful* in helping to improve services and outcomes for young children.

ACHIEVEMENT TESTS

The assessment of achievement occurs regularly in the primary grades. Standardized achievement tests can assist in improving services and outcomes for young children. Depending on the test, achievement tests can be used for screening, determining eligibility, program planning, monitoring progress, and program evaluation.

Screening.   One frequent use of achievement tests is to identify children who perform below, at the same level, or above their peers. The use of an achievement test in the screening process assists in identifying children who need further assessment. Examples of achievement tests that can be used for screening are the Metropolitan Achievement Tests and the Peabody Individual Achievement Test—Revised.

Determining Eligibility.   Achievement tests, when used in conjunction with tests of other types, help to determine eligibility for services. For example, the Wechsler Individual Achievement Test, when used with a measure of cognitive ability, can help to determine eligibility for services.

Program Planning.   Achievement tests can aid in instructional planning and can be helpful in identifying what the child knows. While it is not necessary to use a norm-referenced test to plan a child's program, some norm-referenced tests are suitable. For example, the Brigance® Diagnostic Inventory of Basic Skills and the KeyMath—R may be useful for instructional planning. The teacher may also use informal methods, alternative methods of assessment, and observations to assist in program planning.

Monitoring Progress.   The progress a child makes in a particular academic area should be monitored. It is a good practice to monitor children's progress in literacy, mathematics, and academic content areas frequently. Norm-referenced tests, which are not always sensitive to small changes, may not be as useful in monitoring progress as in the other steps in the assessment process. Frequent monitoring can assist the teacher in modifying instruction to meet the needs of the child. As with program planning, the teacher may also use informal methods, alternative methods of assessment, and observations to assist in monitoring progress.

Program Evaluation.   When the school is interested in examining the progress of a class or grade over a period of time, a norm-referenced test can be used. Standardized achievement tests can assist in improving services and outcomes for young children. Achievement tests are also useful when evaluating the effectiveness of a curriculum or program. For program evaluation, a group achievement test is usually used.

Brigance® Diagnostic Inventory of Basic Skills

The Brigance® Diagnostic Inventory of Basic Skills (Brigance, 1977) is one of a series of tests that are similar in design. This criterion-referenced measure for children in grades kindergarten through 6 assesses a child's skills in 14 areas: readiness, word recognition, reading, word analysis, vocabulary, handwriting, grammar and mechanics, spelling, reference skills, math placement, numbers, operations, measurement, and geometry.

Administration.   It is not necessary to administer all items or all subtests to every child. The examiner uses professional judgment to determine the items and subtests to be administered. A record booklet is used for each child and follows the child through several years of school. Instructional objectives accompany the items, facilitating program planning. Because this is a criterion-referenced test, it can be used frequently to monitor progress.

Scoring.   The child's responses are color coded by skill area so that the teacher can see which skills have been mastered. There are no summary scores.

Standardization.   This test was not standardized. It was developed as a criterion-referenced test.

Reliability.   No reliability information is reported. Information on interscorer reliability would be helpful.

Validity.   The test was developed by examination of the literature and of children's textbooks and through field testing. The coverage of the items is comprehensive. As with all achievement tests, the teacher should determine the content validity.

Summary.   The Brigance® Diagnostic Inventory of Basic Skills is a criterion-referenced test of skills that are typically acquired in grades kindergarten through 6. Content validity should be determined by the user. This test can be useful in instructional planning and monitoring progress.

Kaufman Test of Educational Achievement

The Kaufman Test of Educational Achievement (K-TEA) (Kaufman & Kaufman, 1985) is an individually administered test of achievement for children in grades 1 through 12. It also has age-based norms that range from 6 years, 0 months to 18 years, 11 months. The K-TEA has two forms, the comprehensive form and the brief form. Although the forms are not interchangeable, they do have overlapping uses. The uses listed for the brief form are: contributing to a battery, screening, program planning, research, pre- and post-testing, making placement decisions, and student self-appraisal. Uses by government agencies, in personnel selection, and for measuring adaptive functioning also are cited. The comprehensive form has all these uses except screening. In addition, the comprehensive form is recommended for analyzing strengths and weaknesses and for examining errors. There is some overlap of items between the K-TEA and the items included in the Kaufman Assessment Battery for Children (K-ABC).

Description of the Subtests in the Comprehensive Form
Mathematics Applications. The examiner presents the items orally while using pictures and graphs as visual stimuli. The items assess the application of mathematical principles and reasoning.

Reading Decoding. The items assess the ability to identify letters and to pronounce words that are phonetic and nonphonetic.

Spelling. The examiner pronounces a word and uses it in a sentence. The child is asked to write the word. Children who are unable to write are allowed to spell the word orally.

Reading Comprehension. The child is asked to read a passage and to respond either gesturally or orally to the items that have been presented.

Mathematics Computation. The child is asked to use a paper and pencil to solve written mathematical problems.

Description of the Subtests in the Brief Form
Mathematics. This subtest measures basic computational skills and the application of mathematical principles and reasoning.

Reading. The items assess both decoding by asking the child to read words and reading comprehension by requiring the child to read statements.

Spelling. The items consist of words that are read by the examiner and used in a sentence. The child is asked to write the word or to spell it orally.

Administration.   The K-TEA may be administered by persons who have had training in educational and psychological testing as well as persons who have limited training. For children in grades 1 through 3, the comprehensive form takes 20 to 60 minutes to administer; the brief form requires 10 to 35 minutes.

Scoring. Raw scores can be converted to standard scores, with a mean of 100 and a standard deviation of 15. These scores are available for both fall and spring testing by grade level or by age. In addition, percentile ranks, stanines, normal curve equivalents, age equivalents, and grade equivalents can be obtained. The size of the difference and the significance of the difference between subtests and between composite scores are also available. Information is available to assist the user in analyzing strengths and weaknesses, identifying errors, and determining scatter. Figure 10.2 shows the front page of the K-TEA scoring record.

FIGURE 10.2 Front page of the K-TEA scoring record

SOURCE: Copyright © American Guidance Service, Inc., Circle Pines, MN 55014. Reprinted by permission.

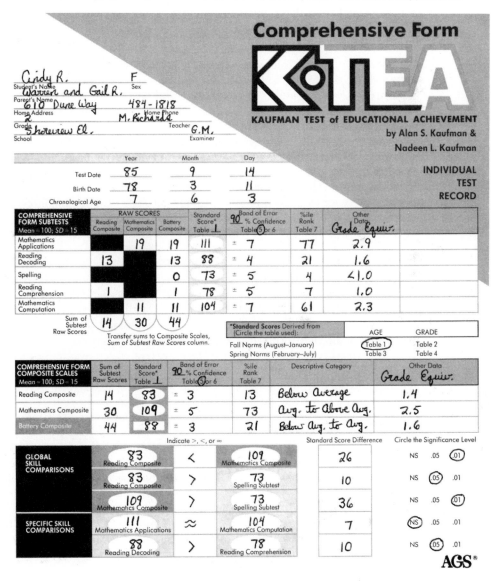

Standardization.   The comprehensive form was standardized during the spring and fall of 1983. The standardization samples for the spring and fall consisted of 1,409 and 1,067 children, respectively. The sample was based on census reports issued in 1983 and 1984 and was proportionally stratified according to grade, sex, geographic region, socioeconomic status (as determined by parental occupation), and race or ethnic group (Caucasian, African American, Hispanic, and other). The group that was designated "other" included Native Americans, Alaskan natives, Asians, Pacific Islanders, and all other groups that were not classified as Caucasian, African American, or Hispanic.

For the brief form, norms were developed by equating the brief form to the comprehensive form. The brief form standardization occurred during the fall of 1983, when both the comprehensive form and the brief form were administered to 589 children. The sample was stratified by grade, sex, geographic region, socio-economic status (as determined by parental occupation), and race or ethnic group (Caucasian, African American, Hispanic, and other).

Reliability.   With regard to the comprehensive form, average split-half re-liabilities for the spring and fall standardization samples were computed using the Spearman–Brown formula. The reliabilities of the five subtests ranged from .90 (Mathematics Computation) to .95 (Reading Decoding). The reliability of the com-posite scores was computed. For grade levels, the reliability of the battery composite ranged from .97 to .98; for age groups, the reliability ranged from .97 to .99. The reliability for the reading composite and mathematics composite extended from .93 to .98.

Test–retest reliability for the comprehensive form was estimated by administer-ing the test twice to 172 students in grades 1 through 12. The time interval between testings extended from 1 to 35 days. For grades 1 through 6, test–retest reliability coefficients ranged from .83 (Mathematics Computation) to .95 (Spelling and Read-ing Decoding).

With regard to the brief form, average split-half reliabilities for the standardiza-tion sample were computed using the Spearman–Brown formula. The reliabilities of the three subtests for all grades ranged from .85 (Mathematics) to .89 (Reading), and for all ages the reliabilities extended from .87 (Mathematics) to .91 (Reading). The reliability of the battery composite score was computed using Guilford's formula. For grades 1 through 6 the reliability of the battery composite was .94.

Test–retest reliability for the brief form was estimated by administering the test twice to 153 students who were in grades 1 through 12. The time interval between testings extended from 1 to 27 days. For grades 1 through 6, test–retest reliability coefficients ranged from .84 (Reading) to .90 (Spelling).

Although the comprehensive form and the brief form "are not alternate forms in the true sense" (Kaufman & Kaufman, 1985, p. 189), for the purpose of reliability testing, the two forms were treated as alternate forms. Alternate form reliability was estimated by administering both forms to 582 students in grades 1 through 12. The interval between the two test administrations ranged from 1 to 51 days. The average intercorrelations between the comprehensive form and the brief form by grade level were .84 (Mathematics), .80 (Reading), .88 (Spelling), and .92 (battery composite). The average intercorrelations between the comprehensive form and the brief form by age level were .85 (Mathematics), .83 (Reading), .90 (Spelling), and .93 (battery composite).

Validity. The validity of the comprehensive form and the brief form was estimated using similar procedures. Content validity was established through consultation with curriculum experts in each subject area. Three national tryouts were conducted during fall 1981 and spring 1982. From these tryouts the final selection of the items emerged.

Construct validity was estimated by showing that subtest and composite scores increased across age and grade levels. Criterion-related validity was demonstrated by correlating the results of the K-TEA with the results of other tests given to the same students. These tests included the Kaufman Assessment Battery for Children (K-ABC), Wide-Range Achievement Test (WRAT), the Peabody Individual Achievement Test (PIAT), and other tests.

Summary. The Kaufman Test of Educational Achievement is an individually administered test of achievement for children in grades 1 through 12 whose ages range from 6 years, 0 months to 18 years, 11 months. The K-TEA has two forms, the comprehensive form and the brief form. Although the forms overlap in content, they are not interchangeable. Evidence for the technical adequacy of the test is sufficient. Reliability and validity are adequate for both forms. As with all achievement tests, educators must evaluate the content validity to determine how well it measures what has been taught.

CASE STUDY: SPECIAL EDUCATION TEACHER'S COMMENTS

Anne L. is in second grade in a school in Texas. She had been referred for special education testing while in kindergarten because she seemed to have difficulty understanding directions. As a result, speech and language services were started and continued through first grade. Anne's first grade teacher raised concerns about the child's behavior in the classroom, and her parent had been asked to seek a medical opinion about the possibility that Anne had an attention deficit disorder. The parent did not follow this advice and the school did not follow up. When the second grade teacher reintroduced the earlier concerns, Anne was referred for further evaluation.

As part of the evaluation, I administered the Kaufman Test of Educational Achievement (K-TEA). Anne came willingly to the testing room. She seemed to listen carefully while I explained that some of the questions would be easy but that items would get harder, since this was a test that could also be given to older children. The test began with the Mathematics Applications subtest. Anne was given a pencil and paper but chose not to use it until item 27, when the directions stated that she had to use it. She did so reluctantly and did not use it again until another test item required her to do so. We proceeded through the subtest and the next one, Mathematics Computation.

The third subtest, Spelling, caused an immediate change in the child's behavior and attitude. As soon as I gave her the Spelling sheet and a pencil and told her to write the words I would pronounce, she became restless and silly. Her pencil grip seemed unsteady, and she wiggled in her seat. She repeated every word slowly and talked to herself throughout this subtest. She asked herself, "What's a *b?*" and "What's an *n?*" For the word blue, she wrote "bloo" and said, "That's not the way you spell *blue* . . . oh, well."

After the Spelling subtest we took a short break and then I proceeded to administer the remaining subtests in the K-TEA. The restlessness was still present but not to the degree exhibited during the Spelling subtest. When we were finished, I thanked Anne and walked her back to her classroom.

I returned to my room and scored the test. An analysis of Anne's performance showed that she had specific strengths and a number of weaknesses. I was very concerned about Anne's behavioral change when faced with tasks that involved writing. Her discomfort when given a writing task may have reflected feelings of inadequacy or uncertainty. Anne's literacy instruction is based on the whole-language approach, and a child exposed to a whole-language curriculum is usually more comfortable with writing tasks, even those requiring spelling unknown words, because of the nature of the curriculum. I wondered if Anne's behavior was an attempt to hide her perceived discomfort. I reported the test results and my observations at the team meeting.

KeyMath Revised: A Diagnostic Inventory of Essential Mathematics

KeyMath Revised: A Diagnostic Inventory of Essential Mathematics (KeyMath-R) (Connolly, 1988) is an individually administered test of mathematics concepts and skills. The KeyMath-R is intended for use with children in grades kindergarten through 9. There are two forms.

According to the author, the KeyMath-R has the following uses:

1. To guide general instructional planning
2. To develop remedial instruction
3. To assist in global assessment by making comparisons with the results of other instruments
4. To use as a pre- or post-test instrument when conducting research and program evaluation
5. To assist in assessing the usefulness of mathematics curriculum

When developing the scope and sequence of the test content, the author surveyed the basal mathematics textbooks of many publishers as well as materials that were published by the National Council of Teachers of Mathematics and other publishers. The resulting scope and sequence was organized into three areas: basic concepts, operations, and applications. These are divided into 13 strands, and the strands are subdivided into domains (Figure 10.3).

Administration.   The KeyMath-R can be administered by regular and special education teachers, aides, paraprofessionals, counselors, and school psychologists. Depending on the age of the child, it takes approximately 35 to 50 minutes to administer this test.

Scoring.   Raw scores can be converted to standard scores, percentile ranks, grade and age equivalents, stanines, and normal curve equivalents. In addition, for domain scores, using an optional scoring procedure, a child's scores can be rated as weak, average, or strong.

Standardization.   The standardization sample consisted of 1,798 children in kindergarten through grade 9. With the exception of grade 9, approximately 100 children were selected for each grade level. The standardization of the KeyMath-R took place during fall 1985 and spring 1986. The selection of the sample was based on census reports and was stratified according to geographic region, grade, sex, socioeconomic level, and race (Caucasian, African American, Hispanic, and other).

Reliability.   Alternate form reliability was determined by retesting approximately 70% of the children in grades kindergarten, 2, 4, 6, and 8 who took part in

FIGURE 10.3 Content specification of KeyMath-R: areas, strands, and domains

Areas:	BASIC CONCEPTS	OPERATIONS	APPLICATIONS
Strands and domains	Numeration	Addition	Measurement
	1. Numbers 0–9	1. Models and basic facts	1. Comparisons
	2. Numbers 0–99	2. Algorithms to add whole numbers	2. Using nonstandard units
	3. Numbers 0–999	3. Adding rational numbers	3. Using standard units—length, area
	4. Multidigit numbers and advanced numeration topics		4. Using standard units—weight, capacity
		Subtraction	
	Rational Numbers	1. Models and basic facts	Time and Money
	1. Fractions	2. Algorithms to subtract whole numbers	1. Identifying passage of time
	2. Decimals	3. Subtracting rational numbers	2. Using clocks and clock units
	3. Percents		3. Monetary amounts to one dollar
	Geometry	Multiplication	4. Monetary amounts to one hundred dollars and business transactions
	1. Spatial and attribute relations	1. Models and basic facts	
	2. Two-dimensional shapes and their relations	2. Algorithms to multiply whole numbers	Estimation
	3. Coordinate and transformational geometry	3. Multiplying rational numbers	1. Whole and rational numbers
	4. Three-dimensional shapes and their relations	Division	2. Measurement
		1. Models and basic facts	3. Computation
		2. Algorithms to divide whole numbers	Interpreting Data
		3. Dividing rational numbers	1. Charts and tables
		Mental Computation	2. Graphs
		1. Computation chains	3. Probability and statistics
		2. Whole numbers	Problem Solving
		3. Rational numbers	1. Solving routine problems
			2. Understanding nonroutine problems
			3. Solving nonroutine problems

the fall standardization. A time interval of between 2 and 4 weeks was used. The reliability coefficients reported are for the subtests, areas, and the total test score. Alternate form reliability is not reported for each grade. For the subtests, the reliability coefficients ranged from the .50s to the .70s; for the areas, the correlations were in the low .80s. The average alternate form correlation for the total test was .90.

Split-half reliabilities are reported by grade and were calculated by correlating the odd and even test items. For the subtests, most of the correlations were in the .70s and .80s; for the areas, the split-half reliability coefficients were in the .90s. The total test reliability coefficients were in the middle to high .90s.

A third method of estimating reliability, item response theory reliability, was used. Item response theory reliability is a method of achieving maximum correspondence between the knowledge, skill, or ability that is assessed by the item and the actual intention for that item as specified by the test developer. For this type of reliability, scores from the entire standardization sample were used to calculate reliability. Reliability coefficients are reported by grade. The reliability coefficients for the subtests were in the .70s and .80s. For the areas, the correlations were in the .90s; for the total test, the coefficients were in the middle to high .90s.

Validity.   When developing the KeyMath-R, the author devised a test blueprint that detailed the content of the test for the areas, strands, and domains. Next, items were developed according to the blueprint for the purpose of assessing mathematics achievement. When using achievement tests, educators must determine the content validity themselves. It is very important that the educator review the curriculum as it has been taught and determine the extent to which the test items measure the curriculum.

According to the manual, construct validity was determined in several ways. Evidence that is presented demonstrates that knowledge about mathematics increases with age and that the subtests intercorrelate with the areas, with the total test score and, by correlating scores on the KeyMath-R, with scores on other tests of mathematical achievement.

Summary.   KeyMath Revised: A Diagnostic Inventory of Essential Mathematics is an individually administered test of mathematics achievement. The reliabilities for the subtests and the areas are too low to make instructional decisions. Content validity should be determined by the educator by comparing the test items with the curriculum that has been taught.

Metropolitan Achievement Tests

The Metropolitan Achievement Tests 6 (MAT6) is composed of two sets of tests: the survey battery and the diagnostic battery. These tests are linked statistically and cover similar content areas.

The Metropolitan Achievement Tests 6: Survey Battery (Prescott, Balow, Hogan, & Farr, 1984) is a group-administered test that is both norm and criterion referenced. The survey battery of MAT6 assesses skill development in five areas: reading, mathematics, language, social studies, and science. The test can be used for screening, monitoring group performance, and program evaluation. The test has eight overlapping levels extending from kindergarten through grade 12.

There are three diagnostic batteries: the reading diagnostic tests (Farr, Prescott,

Balow, & Hogan, 1986), the mathematics diagnostic tests (Hogan, Farr, Prescott, & Balow, 1986), and the language diagnostic tests (Balow, Hogan, Farr, & Prescott, 1986). The diagnostic batteries are group administered and are both norm and criterion referenced. These tests are to be used for instructional planning and the evaluation of curriculum. The diagnostic batteries have six overlapping levels from kindergarten through grade 12.

The MAT6 reading diagnostic battery has 11 content areas: visual discrimination, letter recognition, auditory discrimination, sight vocabulary, consonant sounds, vowel sounds, vocabulary in context, word part clues, rate of comprehension, skimming and scanning, and reading comprehension.

The MAT6 mathematics diagnostic battery has subtests in six content areas: numeration, geometry and measurement, problem solving, computation with whole numbers, computation with decimals and fractions, and graphs and statistics.

The MAT6 language diagnostic battery assesses six content areas: listening comprehension, punctuation and capitalization, usage, written expression, spelling, and study skills.

The MAT6 writing test is optional. A writing prompt is presented to the child, and the child is asked to respond.

Administration.   The MAT6 is administered as a group test. Depending on the grade level used, the survey battery takes from 1 hour, 35 minutes to 4 hours, 15 minutes to administer. The administration of the diagnostic battery takes between 1 hour, 20 minutes and 3 hours, 45 minutes. Fewer subtests are administered to younger children.

Scores.   Raw scores are converted to derived scores. The derived scores that can be obtained are scaled scores, percentile ranks, grade equivalents, normal curve equivalents, and other scores that were developed for the MAT6.

Standardization.   The MAT6 was standardized during the fall and spring of the 1984–1985 school year. More than 200,000 children participated in the standardization. Variables used to select the sample included geographic region, school system enrollment, and socioeconomic status.

Reliability.   Internal consistency and alternate form reliabilities are reported. For grades 5 and over the reliabilities are acceptable. However, for children in grades kindergarten through 5, the reliabilities are moderate to low. Test–retest reliability is not discussed. While alternate form reliability is reported, the interval between the testings was too short to be useful.

Validity.   Although experts reviewed the content of the MAT6, the user should determine content validity. It is incumbent on professionals to examine the test items to determine the extent to which they correspond to the curriculum that has been taught.

Summary.   The Metropolitan Achievement Tests (MAT6) consist of two sets of tests: the survey battery and the diagnostic battery. An advantage of using the MAT6 is that the two tests are linked by a common standardization sample and by similar content. The MAT6 is a group-administered test that is both norm and criterion referenced. Reliabilities for the younger grades are moderate to low. Validity should be determined by the user.

Peabody Individual Achievement Test—Revised

The Peabody Individual Achievement Test—Revised (PIAT-R) (Markwardt, 1989) is an individually administered, norm-referenced test for children in grades kindergarten through 12 (5 years to 18 years, 11 months). The manual states that the PIAT-R has the following uses: individual evaluation, program planning, guidance and counseling, admissions and transfers, grouping students, follow-up evaluation, personnel selection, and research. The manual also describes the following limitations:

1. The PIAT-R is not a diagnostic test.
2. It does not provide a highly precise measurement of achievement.
3. It was not designed to sample curriculum of individual schools; rather, it represents a representative curriculum of schools in the United States.
4. The background and qualifications of the test administrator can influence the interpretation of the test.

The test assesses achievement in six areas:

General Information. This subtest measures general knowledge. The examiner reads the open-ended questions aloud and the child answers orally.

Reading Recognition. The initial test items consist of ability to recognize the sounds associated with letters. Later test items consist of isolated words. The child is asked to reproduce the sounds and to read the words orally.

Reading Comprehension. The child reads a sentence silently and then is asked to identify the one picture out of four that best depicts the sentence.

Mathematics. Using a multiple-choice format, knowledge of basic facts and applications is assessed. The examiner reads all the test items to the child. For the first 50 items, the child sees only the responses, not the test items. For items 50 to 100, the child sees the printed questions and the response choices.

Spelling. The format for the responses is multiple choice. The items at the beginning of this subtest measure the child's ability to identify a printed letter from an object and to recognize letters after hearing their names or sounds. Later items assess the child's ability to identify the one correctly spelled word out of four pronounced by the examiner.

Written Expression. This subtest has two levels. Level I can be administered to children in kindergarten or first grade and assesses copying and writing letters, words, and sentences that the examiner dictates. Level II is administered to children in grades 2 through 12. The child is asked to write a story in response to one of two picture prompts. A time limit of 20 minutes is allowed for a child to complete Level II.

Administration. The manual distinguishes between the qualifications of individuals who administer the PIAT-R and those who interpret the results. According to the manual, almost anyone can learn to administer the test. Persons who provide an interpretation are expected to have an understanding of psychometrics and curriculum. Depending on the number of items used, it takes between approximately 30 and 60 minutes to administer the total test.

Scoring.   For all the subtests except Written Expression, the test items are either correct or incorrect. Raw scores can be converted to standard scores, percentile ranks, grade and age equivalents, stanines, and normal curve equivalents. A separate scoring guide is in the manual for the Written Expression subtest.

Three composite scores can be obtained. The total reading composite is derived from the performance on the Reading Recognition and the Reading Comprehension subtests. The total test composite score is developed from the performance on the first five subtests. There is an optional written language composite, which is developed from the Written Expression and Spelling subtests.

Standardization.   Standardization of the PIAT-R took place in the spring of 1986 when 1,563 students, kindergarten through grade 12, were tested. In the fall of 1986 an additional 175 kindergarten children were tested to get a sample of children who were entering kindergarten. Children who were in special education classes were excluded from the standardization sample. The sample was based on census data and was stratified by geographic region, socioeconomic status, and race or ethnic group (Caucasian, African American, Hispanic, and other). The sample consisted of approximately the same number of females and males. Norms were developed based on the data from the spring standardization. Fall and winter grade-based norms were derived by interpolation of the spring standardization data.

Reliability.   Split-half reliability coefficients were calculated by age and grade for all the subtests except Written Expression. The coefficients range from .92 (Reading Comprehension) to .97 (Reading Recognition). The split-half reliability coefficients for the composites were .97 (total reading) and .98 (total test).

Internal consistency reliability coefficients were computed for all the subtests except Written Expression by grade and age. With few exceptions, almost all the coefficients were in the mid to high .90s. For Written Expression, internal consistency reliability was estimated. Reliability coefficients for Level I were .61 (kindergarten spring testing), .60 (kindergarten fall testing), and .69 (grade 1). Internal consistency reliability coefficients were calculated for Level II of the Written Expression subtest. For Prompt A the coefficient was .86; for Prompt B the coefficient was .88.

To estimate test–retest reliability, approximately 50 children from grades 2, 4, 6, 8, and 10 were randomly selected and retested within a 2- to 4-week interval. Median test–retest reliability coefficients for the subtests excluding Written Expression ranged from .84 (Mathematics) to .96 (Reading Recognition).

Item response theory reliability was estimated by grade and age for all the subtests excluding Written Expression. Median reliabilities ranged from .96 (General Information, Reading Comprehension, Mathematics, Spelling) to .98 (Reading Recognition).

Several interrater reliability studies were conducted on the scoring of the Level II Written Expression subtest. In one study, the median interrater reliabilities were .58 for Prompt A and .67 for Prompt B. In another study, intercorrelations between trained scorers and typical scorers ranged from .66 to .85.

Validity.   The manual reports that content validity was established through the development process. Content area experts, test reviewers, and others were consulted. As with any achievement test, however, the teacher should review the material to determine content validity.

Construct validity was estimated by showing that subtest and composite scores increased across age and grade levels. Concurrent related validity was demonstrated by correlating the results of the PIAT-R with the PIAT and the Peabody Picture Vocabulary Test—Revised (PPVT-R). Additional evidence is needed before construct validity can be said to have been demonstrated.

Summary.   The Peabody Individual Achievement Test—Revised is an individually administered, norm-referenced test that can be administered to children in kindergarten through grade 12. The test assesses achievement in six areas: General Information, Reading Recognition, Reading Comprehension, Mathematics, Spelling, and Written Expression. The standardization and the reliability are acceptable. As with all standardized achievement tests, the teacher should evaluate the content validity of this test.

Wechsler Individual Achievement Test

The Wechsler Individual Achievement Test (WIAT) (Psychological Corporation, 1992) is an individually administered achievement test for children who are in grades kindergarten through 12, ages 5 years, 0 months to 19 years, 11 months. One of the major purposes for the development of the WIAT was to make available a test that met the federal requirements in PL 94–142, the Education for All Handicapped Children Act, now known as PL 101–476, the Individuals with Disabilities in Education Act, for determining a learning disability. This law states that children with learning disabilities have a severe discrepancy between ability and achievement in one or more of the following areas: oral expression, listening comprehension, written expression, basic reading skill, reading comprehension, mathematics calculation or mathematics reasoning.

Three of the eight WIAT subtests, Basic Reading, Mathematics Reasoning, and Spelling, form the *Screener.* The eight subtests are described briefly as follows.

Basic Reading. This subtest assesses word-reading ability. The first series of items contain pictures and the child must point to the correct responses. Later items contain printed words and the child must respond orally to each word.

Mathematics Reasoning. Many items are presented with a visual stimulus. The examiner reads the problem orally and, for many problems, the child is able to read along on the child's page. Responses of a variety of types are required.

Spelling. Letters, sounds, and words are dictated. The child is required to write the responses.

Reading Comprehension. A series of brief printed passages is presented to the child. After reading a passage, the child must answer comprehension questions orally.

Numerical Operations. A series of problems assesses the ability to write dictated numbers and to solve basic arithmetic calculations (addition, subtraction, multiplication, and division). The child writes the responses in a response booklet.

Listening Comprehension. Early items assess the child's ability to point to one of four pictures that corresponds to a word the examiner presents. Later items assess the child's ability to answer questions that are presented after the examiner has read aloud a brief passage.

Oral Expression. The child must respond orally to the examiner's directions, which relate to a series of items that are presented.

Written Expression. This subtest is administered only to children who are in grades 3 through 12. One of two writing prompts is presented to the child, who is asked to write in response to the prompt.

Administration.   The WIAT is administered individually. For children in kindergarten through grade 2, it takes approximately 30 to 50 minutes to administer the WIAT. Approximately 15 minutes is required for the screener. The starting point for administration depends on the child's grade in school.

Scoring.   Items on the Basic Reading, Mathematics Reasoning, Spelling, and Numerical Operations subtests are scored either correct or incorrect. The items on the Reading Comprehension, Listening Comprehension, Oral Expression, and Written Expression subtests require some judgment by the examiner. The manual does provide general guidelines for scoring these subtests. The Written Expression subtest is scored both analytically and holistically. Raw scores are converted to grade-based standard scores. Percentiles, age and grade equivalents, and normal curve equivalents are also available. The discrepancy between WIAT standard scores and Wechsler Preschool and Primary Scale of Intelligence—Revised (WPPSI-R) standard scores or Wechsler Intelligence Scale for Children—III (WISC-III) standard scores can be determined.

Standardization.   The sample was stratified according to age, grade, gender, race/ethnicity (Caucasian, African American, Hispanic, Native American, Eskimo, Aleut, Asian, Pacific Islander, or other), geographic region, and the education of the parent(s) or guardian(s) based on 1988 data from the U.S. Bureau of the Census. The WIAT standardization sample was composed of 4,252 children, ages five to nineteen years, who were in grades kindergarten through 12. The standardization sample overrepresents children whose parents are in the higher education levels. In addition, children in the southern part of the United States are overrepresented. Weighting was used to adjust race/ethnicity proportions to those in the census. A subgroup of the WIAT standardization sample consisting of 1,284 children ages five to nineteen years was also administered the WPPSI-R, WISC-III, or the WAIS-R.

The manual states that children who were mainstreamed were not excluded from the standardization sample. Approximately 6% of the sample consisted of children who were categorized as learning disabled, speech or language impaired, emotionally disturbed, or physically disabled. Separate norms are not provided for these groups.

Several small studies were conducted with children in various disability groups including children with mental retardation, emotional disturbance, learning disabilities, attention deficit–hyperactivity disorder, and hearing impairments. According to the manual, one of the major purposes of the test is to aid in the identification of children with learning disabilities. However, the manual reports only one study of children who were learning disabled, and the sample size was 91. The publisher should be encouraged to conduct or sponsor additional studies so that more information can be gathered about the performance of children with disabilities on the WIAT.

Reliability.   Split-half reliability coefficients for the subtest and composite standard scores were computed at each grade. In general, the coefficients are in the .80s and .90s. Test–retest reliability was calculated for a separate group of 367 children in grades 1, 3, 5, 8, and 10. For first graders, the reliability coefficients for the subtest and the composite standard scores ranged from .80 (Oral Expression) to .95 (Spelling, Reading Composite, screener). Interscorer agreement was calculated for 50 test protocols, randomly selected from the standardization sample. Only 15 of these protocols were from children in kindergarten through grade 3. For the Reading Comprehension and Listening Comprehension subtests the average correlation was .98. For Oral Expression the average coefficient was .93; the average coefficients for Written Expression were .89 (Prompt 1) and .79 (Prompt 2).

Validity.   Content validity was assessed by a panel of reviewers. Criterion-related validity was determined by correlating the WIAT with individual and group administered tests of achievement and ability. There is some evidence of construct validity. However, as with all tests, independent validity studies should be conducted to obtain additional information about the construct validity of the WIAT.

Summary.   The WIAT is an individually administered achievement test that assesses achievement in children in kindergarten through grade 12. Additional studies investigating the validity of the WIAT and the use of this test with children with disabilities must be conducted. One of the major purposes of the WIAT is to assist in the identification of children who may be learning disabled. This may not be an appealing purpose to professionals who work with young children because of the extreme caution that should be used in identifying young children as learning disabled. Despite such hesitancy, this test can be a helpful means of assessing the achievement of young children. As with all achievement tests, caution must be used, and the test items should be examined to determine the degree to which they correspond with the curriculum the child has been taught.

PREFERRED PRACTICES

Considerations about developmentally appropriate practices are important when assessing young children. Achievement tests, when carefully chosen, can be important sources of information. But the achievement tests discussed in this chapter are only one of multiple sources of information that should be used when making decisions that improve instruction and outcomes for young children (NAEYC, 1988). Other sources of information include systematic observations, anecdotal records, interviews with caregivers and children, samples of children's work, videotapes, audiotapes, and portfolios. Alternatives to standardized testing are discussed in Chapter 11.

Any assessment of young children should inform and support the learning (Engel, 1991). Children should be helped to understand their mistakes. Finally, high-stakes testing should be avoided.

According to the National Association for the Education of Young Children (1988), assessment procedures should reflect ongoing activities in the classroom. Assessment activities should be natural, not contrived, and should rely on real activities in which children are engaged. For example, the assessment of reading and writing should involve real reading and writing activities rather than just the testing of skills. Parents, professionals, the school, the community, and children should collaborate during the assessment process. The activities should be used to support the relationships between parents and their children; they should not devalue any family or its culture.

STUDY QUESTIONS AND SUGGESTED ACTIVITIES

1. Differentiate between readiness tests and developmental tests.

2. Review NAEYC's guidelines for appropriate assessment of young children (pp. 330–331) and on standardized testing of young children (pp. 331–332). What are the implications for using achievement tests with young children?

3. What is high-stakes testing? Give some examples of the use of high-stakes tests.

4. Why should the assessment of the achievement of young children be undertaken cautiously?

5. Discuss several advantages of using norm-referenced tests to assess the achievement of young children.

REFERENCES

American Educational Research Association, American Psychological Association, & National Council on Measurement in Education. (1985). *Standards for educational and psychological testing.* Washington, DC: Author.

Anastasi, A. (1988). *Psychological testing.* New York: Macmillan.

Balow, I. H., Hogan, T. P., Farr, R. C., & Prescott, G. A. (1986). *Metropolitan Achievement Test 6: Language Diagnostic Tests.* San Antonio, TX: Psychological Corporation.

Brigance, A. (1977). *Brigance® diagnostic inventory of basic skills.* North Billerica, MA: Curriculum Associates.

Chittenden, E., & Courtney, R. (1989). Assessment of young children's reading: Documentation as an alternative to testing. In D. Strickland (Ed.), *Emerging literacy: Young children learn to read and write.* Newark, DE: International Reading Association.

Connolly, A. (1988). *KeyMath revised: A diagnostic inventory of essential mathematics.* Circle Pines, MN: American Guidance Service.

Division for Early Childhood of the Council for Exceptional Children. (1992). DEC position statement on goal one of America 2000: All children should begin school ready to learn. *DEC Communicator, 18*(3), 4.

Engel, B. (1991). An approach to assessment in early literacy. In C. Kamii (Ed.), *Achievement testing in the early grades* (pp. 119–134). Washington, DC: National Association for the Education of Young Children.

Farr, R. C., Prescott, G. A., Balow, I. H., & Hogan, T. P. (1986). *Metropolitan Achievement Test 6: Reading Diagnostic Tests.* San Antonio, TX: Psychological Corporation.

Goodman, K., Goodman, Y., & Hood, W. (1989). *The whole language evaluation book.* Portsmouth, NH: Heineman.

Hogan, T. P., Farr, R. C., Prescott, G. A., & Balow, I. H., (1986). *Metropolitan Achievement Test 6: Mathematics Diagnostic Tests.* San Antonio, TX: Psychological Corporation.

Kaufman, A. S., & Kaufman, N. L. (1985). *Kaufman test of educational achievement.* Circle Pines, MN: American Guidance Service.

Markwardt, F. C., Jr. (1989). *Peabody individual achievement test—Revised.* Circle Pines, MN: American Guidance Service.

Meisels, S. J. (1987). Uses and abuses of developmental screening and school readiness testing. *Young Children, 42*(2), 4–6, 68–73.

Meisels, S. J. (1989a). *Developmental screening in early childhood: A guide.* Washington, DC: National Association for the Education of Young Children.

Meisels, S. J. (1989b). High-stakes testing in kindergarten. *Educational Leadership, 46*(7), 16–22.

National Association for the Education of Young Children. (1988). NAEYC position statement on standardized testing of young children 3 through 8 years of age. *Young Children, 43*(3), 42–47.

National Association for the Education of Young Children & National Association of Early Childhood Specialists in State Departments of Education. (1991). Guidelines for appropriate curriculum content and assessment in programs serving children ages 3 through 8. *Young Children, 46*(3), 21–37.

National Governors' Association, Task Force on Education. (1990). *Educating America: State strategies for achieving the national education goals.* Washington, DC: National Governors' Association.

Prescott, G. A., Balow, I. H., Hogan, T. R., & Farr, R. C. (1984). *Metropolitan achievement tests 6: Survey battery.* San Antonio, TX: Psychological Corporation.

Psychological Corporation (1992). *Wechsler individual achievement test.* San Antonio, TX: Author.

Shepard, L. (1990). Readiness testing in local school districts: An analysis of backdoor policies. *Journal of Education Policy, 5*(5), 159–179.

Teale, W. H. (1988). Developmentally appropriate assessment of reading and writing in the early childhood classroom. *The Elementary School Journal, 89*(2), 173–184.

CHAPTER 11

Using Alternative Assessments

CHAPTER OBJECTIVES

The benefits and limitations of traditional norm-referenced assessment have been described in the preceding chapters. In this chapter we discuss alternatives to traditional assessment practices. The assessment of young children is evolving as we search for improved methods and strategies. Each of the alternative methods discussed in this chapter, curriculum-based assessment, task analysis, performance assessment, authentic assessment, dynamic assessment, and portfolio assessment, is developing. While norm-referenced tests have their place in the assessment process, alternatives to norm-referenced tests are a rich store of approaches that can be used to collect data of many types. This is an exciting area, and we encourage professionals to develop their own variations on the topics discussed.

Upon completion of this chapter, you should be able to:

Provide a rationale for the need for alternative assessment methods.

Describe curriculum-based assessment, dynamic assessment, performance assessment, authentic assessment, and portfolio assessment.

Key Terms

Authentic Assessment. Demonstration of a skill or behavior in a real-life context.

Curriculum-based Assessment (CBA). A broad approach to linking assessment to instruction.

Dynamic Assessment. An approach in which the assessor actively engages the learner in learning.

NOTE: Portions of this chapter were adapted from Cohen, L., & Spruill, J. (1990). *A practical guide to curriculum-based assessment for special educators.* Springfield, IL: Charles C. Thomas.

Performance Assessment. Demonstration of behavior that has been specified by the assessor.

Portfolio. A deliberate collection of the products of a child's play and work that demonstrates the child's efforts, progress, and achievement.

Task Analysis. The breaking down of a target behavior into small, isolated, sequential steps.

CRITICISMS OF NORM-REFERENCED TESTS

Requirement for Standardized Test Administration

Norm-referenced standardized tests have been criticized for a number of reasons. Because of the way they are constructed, norm-referenced tests require the examiner to follow strictly the instructions for test administration. The same procedures for test administration must be used, regardless of whether a child has a disability. Modifications to accommodate the individual needs of a child are not permitted (Bagnato, Neisworth, & Munson, 1989).

Bias

Depending on the composition of the standardization sample, norm-referenced tests may be biased against children who have developmental delays or disabilities, those who belong to certain cultural groups or minorities, and those to whom English is a second language (Galagan, 1985; Tindal & Marston, 1986; Webster, McInnis, & Carver, 1986).

Differences between Children Maximized

Norm-referenced tests are designed and constructed to provide assessment of individual children. The test items are selected to maximize the differences among children; individual performance is assessed by comparing one child with other children. Norm-referenced tests are intended to differentiate between children, and items are selected to foster this difference. Items on which most children would do well or poorly are not included because they do not enhance differences of the individuals tested.

May Lead to Retention and Tracking

The National Association for the Education of Young Children (NAEYC) (1988) has criticized the use of standardized tests because they may lead to tracking and may result in some children being denied admission to school. Based on the improper use of the results of a developmental or readiness test, a child may not be allowed to enter kindergarten or may be assigned to a "developmental kindergarten," retained in kindergarten, or placed in a "transitional" first grade. Retention and tracking of young children can have long-term negative effects on children's self-esteem and achievement in school. Research has shown that minority children may be disproportionately affected by these practices.

Negative Influence on the Curriculum

The NAEYC also believes that standardized tests can have a negative influence on the curriculum. The use of these tests in the early grades can lead to "teaching to the test" and the perpetuation of poor instructional methods and teaching strategies.

Norm-referenced tests may lack curriculum sensitivity (Airasian & Madaus, 1983; Fuchs & Deno, 1981; Fuchs, Fuchs, & Deno, 1982; Tindal & Marston, 1986). With regard to school-age children, some commercially published norm-referenced tests have been criticized because they do not adequately measure benefits of contemporary approaches to teaching literacy, mathematics, and problem solving. Many commercially published standardized tests focus on a skills approach to learning rather than on assessing development and the processes of learning. The instructional validity of these tests is low (Airasian & Madaus, 1983).

May Not Reflect Prior Learning Experiences

Another criticism of standardized tests is that test scores may not reflect the extent or manner in which performance is affected by prior learning experiences and do not identify the characteristic processes by which the individual children develop and learn (Meyers, Pfeffer, & Erlbaum, 1985). The tests may inadequately reflect the specific content and objectives of a program because the curriculum that has been taught is inadequately represented by the test items.

May Not Reflect Important Instructional Factors

Finally, commercially published standardized tests may not reflect important instructional factors such as time on task, timing of instruction, quality of instruction, reinforcement, and sequence of skills (Airasian & Madaus, 1983). They may not reflect individual child characteristics such as motivation, values, work habits, educational settings, and interpersonal relationships (Smith, 1980).

The National Governors' Association (1990) recognized the need for change in assessment practices in its report outlining strategies for achieving national education goals. Assessment was addressed as a specific strategy to achieve the goal: "By the Year 2000, All Children in America Will Start School Ready to Learn" (p. 12).

> *Improve student assessment and school entry policies.* Develop assessment systems for young children that reflect the ultimate goals of producing independent, creative, and critical thinkers. Train teachers to observe and assess children's work in different content areas, using methods such as portfolio systems, observational checklists, and cumulative sampling of children's work. Develop models to use teacher assessments of student proficiencies for reporting to parents and the public. Eliminate the use of screening or readiness tests that are inaccurate and unreliable. (p. 15)

THE LINK BETWEEN ASSESSMENT AND INSTRUCTION

Contemporary views of learning have influenced the development of alternative assessment approaches. From cognitive learning theory we know (Herman, Aschbacher, & Winters, 1992):

1. Knowledge is constructed from new information and prior learning.
   Implications for Assessment:
   Divergent thinking, rather than the search for one right answer, and multiple solutions should be encouraged.
   Multiple types of expression should be encouraged.
   Critical thinking skills should be fostered.
   New information is related to prior knowledge.

2. Children of all ages and abilities can solve problems. All learning is not developed in a linear progression of separate skills.
   Implications for Assessment:
   All children should be involved in problem solving.
   Problem solving and critical thinking do not have to be contingent on mastery of basic skills.

3. Children approach learning with a multiplicity of learning styles, attention spans, and developmental and cognitive differences.
   Implications for assessment:
   Choices in how to demonstrate what has been learned should be provided.
   Time should be provided to complete assessment tasks.
   Provide concrete tasks (manipulatives) and opportunities for demonstration of what has been learned.

4. Children do better when they know the goals and understand how their performance will be evaluated.
   Implications for assessment:
   Involve children in establishing goals.
   Discuss criteria for performance.
   Provide examples of acceptable levels of performance.

5. Children should know when to use knowledge and how to direct their own learning.
   Implications for assessment:
   Provide opportunities for children to monitor and evaluate their own learning.
   Provide authentic (real-world) opportunities for assessment.

6. Children's learning is affected by motivation, effort, and self-esteem.
   Implications for assessment:
   The design of assessment tasks should consider motivation, self-esteem, and promoting children's best efforts.

ALTERNATIVE ASSESSMENT

Alternative assessment holds the promise of directly linking instruction with assessment. While there are various alternative approaches to assessment, in general alternative assessment is characterized by tasks that require children to:

Demonstrate, produce, or create

Use critical thinking and problem-solving abilities

Use authentic, meaningful tasks (Herman et al., 1992)

When alternative assessment approaches are used, the teacher's role is changed. The teacher, who is so integrally related to instruction, has a direct influence on assessment. The link between instruction and assessment is closed. Assessment is no longer a stand-alone component of a child's program; it is directly tied to the child's formal and informal learning experiences. The teacher may be involved in designing, developing, setting criteria, scoring, and interpreting alternative assessment tools. Because of the close relationship between instruction and assessment, instructional goals, views of teaching, and theories of learning are articulated and aligned (Herman et al., 1992).

CURRICULUM-BASED ASSESSMENT

Curriculum-based assessment (CBA) is a broad approach to linking assessment to instruction. CBA has three purposes: to determine eligibility, to develop the goals for intervention, and to evaluate the child's progress in the curriculum. CBA can be very useful in assessing young children (Bagnato, Neisworth, & Capone, 1986) because instructional goals can be specified on the basis of performance on a CBA instrument. One important advantage is that a child's progress can be monitored regularly. Because assessment and instruction are so closely linked, it is very important to assess frequently to determine whether changes in the curriculum are necessary. Data collection, interpretation, and intervention are all integral parts of CBA. CBA is a test–teach–test approach (Bagnato et al., 1986). Children's performance in developmental, adaptive, social, preacademic, and academic areas is used as the basis for assessment and intervention. Other terms that may be used to describe CBA are *curriculum-referenced measurement, curriculum-embedded measurement, frequent measurement, continuous curriculum measurement, therapeutic measurement,* and *curriculum-based measurement.*

Bagnato and Murphy (1989) wrote that in an early intervention context, CBA entails the use of task analyses of developmental competencies within functional domains. The task analyses are hierarchically ordered, and preceding tasks are prerequisites for the ones that follow.

CBA directly links what has been taught with the assessment process. The educator knows the curriculum and what has been taught; the CBA instrument, developed by the teacher, provides a direct association with instruction. Based on the results of CBA, the teacher can modify instruction, assess again, determine the benefits of the instruction, and repeat the process.

Published Instruments

A number of published instruments reference or can be adapted to an existing curriculum (Bagnato & Neisworth, 1991). The tests listed below are examples.

Assessment of Basic Skills—Spanish Edition (Brigance, 1984).

Beginning Milestones (Sheridan, S., Murphy, D., Black, J., Puckett, M. & Allie, E. C., 1986).

Carolina Curriculum for Handicapped At-Risk Infants (Johnson-Martin, Jens, & Attermeier, 1986). Birth to 24 months.

Carolina Curriculum for Preschoolers with Special Needs (Johnson-Martin, Attermeier, & Hacker, 1990). 24 to 60 months.

Comprehensive Inventory of Basic Skills (Brigance, 1983). Prekindergarten to grade 9.

Diagnostic Inventory of Basic Skills (Brigance, 1977). Kindergarten to grade 6.

Diagnostic Inventory of Early Development—Revised (Brigance, 1991). Birth to age 7.

Early Learning Accomplishment Profile (E-LAP) (Glover, Preminger, Sanford, 1978). Birth to 36 months.

Hawaii Early Learning Profile (HELP) (Furuno, O'Reilly, Hosaka, Inatsuka, Allman, & Zeisloft-Falbey, 1979). Birth to 72 months.

HICOMP Preschool Curriculum (Willoughby-Herb & Neisworth, 1983). Birth to 5 years.

Learning Accomplishment Profile (LAP) (Sanford & Zelman, 1981). 36 to 72 months.

Portage Guide to Early Education Checklist (Bluma, Shearer, Frohman, & Hilliard, 1976). 2 to 6 years.

System to Plan Early Childhood Services (Bagnato & Neisworth, 1990). 2 to 6 years.

Development of Curriculum-based Assessment by Educators

While there are published CBA instruments, educators may want to develop their own. One important reason for this is that the curriculum may not correspond to the content of existing instruments. By constructing your own CBA instrument, you will be able to specify goals, build into the instrument any special adaptations for test administration, and help to ensure the instrument's validity. The steps in a model for developing a curriculum-based assessment instrument are discussed below.

Developing a Curriculum-based Assessment Instrument

Step 1: Purpose(s). The instrument may be used to determine eligibility or entry into a curriculum, to develop the goals for intervention, or to evaluate the child's progress in the curriculum. Sometimes, one instrument can serve multiple purposes. For example, the CBA instrument that is used to develop goals may also be able to be used to evaluate the child's progress.

Step 2: Analyze the Curriculum. Determine what is being taught. If you are using a developmental approach with young children, determine what specific tasks are being taught. Include social, adaptive, motor, communication, and play. You may wish to develop a CBA for one of these areas or for each of them. Some tasks require that prerequisite skills be taught first.

Step 3: Develop Performance Objectives.   Determine how you will know whether a child has demonstrated what has been taught. How will you know whether a child is able to share building blocks, take turns, or use free play materials appropriately? You will need to specify the behaviors the child must demonstrate to indicate that the curriculum has been learned.

One approach to specifying skills is to use a task analysis approach in which the elements of each facet of a skill are analyzed and broken down into simple components.

Step 4: Develop the Assessment Procedures.   In this step, you develop the specific test items that correspond to the performance objectives. Items of different types can be developed. For example, you can observe the child, ask the child to demonstrate a particular behavior, directly ask questions of the child, ask the child to perform specific actions or behaviors, or, for primary age children, ask them to perform specific academic tasks.

The scoring procedures must be delineated. You will have to specify how you will determine how well a child has performed.

Considerations about reliability and validity are important. You must be consistent each time you assess a child and when you compare the performance of one child to another. The CBA instrument must be valid. It must have a close correspondence to the curriculum.

Step 5: Implement the Assessment Procedures.   Once you have developed the assessment procedures, you can begin to use the CBA to collect information. How you decide to record and keep track of the information will be important. Frequently, recording sheets are helpful.

Piloting or trying out the CBA items before actual implementation is a good idea. Although you have put a great deal of thought into the development and construction of the items, it is always a good practice to try them out before you use them to assess a child.

You must be careful to administer the CBA items according to the methods you have developed. If you deviate from the procedures, you should explain and document what you have done. For instance, let's say that you have decided to assess whether Lisa L., a three-year-old, is able to engage in free play activities. But, when you go to assess Lisa, she is sitting by herself at the other side of the room from the free play materials. You decide to ask her if she would like to move to the side of the room where the free play materials are kept. She agrees, but does need encouragement. It is important to describe what your actions were in encouraging Lisa and what her responses were.

Step 6: Organize the Information.   Summarize the information you have collected. Tables, graphs, or charts can be useful.

Step 7: Interpret and Integrate the Results.   It is important to integrate the CBA information with information that has been collected from standardized tests, observations, anecdotal records, and other forms of assessment. This is the point in the assessment process where the link between instruction and assessment is made. The data are collected and integrated. The decision-making process continues as educators, along with the team, decide where, when, and how instruction should proceed.

TASK ANALYSIS

Task analysis is the breaking down of a target behavior into small, isolated, sequential steps. Some children can learn new skills and behaviors only after the target behaviors have been separated into their simplest components. For example, parents and caregivers have decided that it is important for three-year-old Rina to learn to wash her hands independently. To help Rina accomplish this, the target behavior, hand washing, must be broken down into small steps (going to the sink, turning on the water, adjusting the water temperature, etc.) (Sternberg & Adams, 1982). The number of steps in the task analysis will depend on the needs of the individual child.

Shaping

Some children who have severe disabilities are not able to learn a behavior the first time it is taught. For instance, Rina's parents and caregivers would like her to respond to the prompt or cue, "Rina, it's time to wash your hands now." The parents and caregivers reinforce Rina's behavior when she demonstrates successive approximations of the behavior: At first, when Rina looks toward the sink, she is reinforced; then, when she starts moving toward the sink she is reinforced. *Shaping* occurs when successive approximations of the behavior are reinforced.

Chaining

Chaining is the linking of the various steps in the task analysis to achieve the target behavior. With chaining, the parents and caregivers require that several steps be performed before reinforcement is given. Linking the various steps involved in hand washing is an example of chaining.

In *forward* chaining, the steps are taught from the first step to the last. In backward chaining the steps are taught in reverse order, from the last step to the first. *Reverse* chaining is similar to backward chaining. However, the child may be assisted with steps that cannot be performed independently.

Fading

Fading is the gradual withdrawal of a prompt or reinforcement. As the child responds independently, the parent or caregiver can gradually stop giving the cue that links one step in the task analysis to the next. To cue Rina to turn on the water in the hand washing example, the caregiver may have to move Rina's hand to the water taps. This can be faded to a light touch to Rina's hand and, finally, to no prompt at all. Similarly, if Rina had been rewarded with some type of reinforcement, the reinforcer could be gradually withdrawn as the steps were mastered.

Prompts

A *prompt* or cue helps the child to begin or to shape a behavior (Sternberg & Adams, 1982). "Rina, it's time to wash your hands," is an example of a prompt. Prompts can be verbal, physical, or gestural. An example of a physical prompt is a light touch. A gestural prompt would be pointing to the water taps.

Positive Reinforcement

A *positive reinforcement* is any reward that is used to strengthen a child's response. Reinforcers of various types can be used including food, hugs, and praise. Some types of positive reinforcement are more successful than others. When developing a task analysis, you may have to experiment with more than one type of reinforcement.

PERFORMANCE ASSESSMENT

Performance assessment is the elicitation of a demonstration of the behavior specified by the assessor (Diez & Moon, 1992). Performance assessment, an emerging area in early childhood education, may be looked at as the ultimate form of linking instruction with assessment. Grant Wiggins has been a strong proponent of performance assessment. He has urged that educators construct "tests worth taking" (Brandt, 1992, p. 35). Figure 11.1 illustrates important characteristics of tasks about which examiners should be aware.

FIGURE 11.1   Criteria for performance tasks

SOURCE: Reprinted with permission from *Mathematics Assessment,* copyright 1991 by the National Council of Teachers of Mathematics.

ESSENTIAL	• The task fits into the core of the curriculum.	vs.	TANGENTIAL
	• It represents a "big idea."		
AUTHENTIC	• The task uses processes appropriate to the discipline.	vs.	CONTRIVED
	• Students value the outcome of the task.		
RICH	• The task leads to other problems.	vs.	SUPERFICIAL
	• It raises other questions.		
	• It has many possibilities.		
ENGAGING	• The task is thought-provoking.	vs.	UNINTERESTING
	• It fosters persistence.		
ACTIVE	• The student is the worker and decision maker.	vs.	PASSIVE
	• Students interact with other students.		
	• Students are constructing meaning and deepening understanding.		
FEASIBLE	• The task can be done within school and homework time.	vs.	INFEASIBLE
	• It is developmentally appropriate for students.		
	• It is safe.		
EQUITABLE	• The task develops thinking in a variety of styles.	vs.	INEQUITABLE
	• It contributes to positive attitudes.		
OPEN	• The task has more than one right answer.	vs.	CLOSED
	• It has multiple avenues of approach, making it accessible to all students.		

Howard Gardner (1991) uses the term *performance-based assessment,* which he believes to be appropriate with young children as well as school-age children. Gardner has written that performance-based assessments can be described according to developmental levels. [Gardner's use of the term *developmental* differs somewhat from the way in which the term is used in this book. Gardner views children as learners who are at various points in their learning: (e.g., novice, expert).] For example, some children might be required to exhibit the performance of beginning learners while others would be asked to demonstrate the performance of experts. Evaluations do not need to focus on what children demonstrate about their own academic or cognitive abilities; they can determine as well the extent to which children work cooperatively, are sensitive to others, use computers, or use other resources.

Performance-based assessment can be used when children are working on long-term projects. In this way, they are able to use a variety of resources and to demonstrate mastery of certain concepts and principles. Performance-based assessments are related to the types of assessment the child will most likely encounter after leaving school (Gardner, 1991).

Four questions can guide us as we think about performance assessment (Diez & Moon, 1992). First, what is important for children to know and to be able to do? This question requires us to rethink curricula, standards, and approaches to teaching children. Is it important for a child to build a block construction, or is it important for a child to play cooperatively? There must be a consensus—the team must agree on what is important for a particular child.

Second, what is acceptable performance? The team must decide on the criteria, which in turn requires us to think about mastery. What does mastery of a specific skill or behavior look like? The criteria must be general enough to permit children to practice what they will be evaluated on. Acceptable performance may be difficult to define in young developing children.

How can expert judgments be made? This is the third question. In developing the criteria for acceptable performance, we must be able to specify them in advance. For example, suppose we want to know how well a child can retell a story. Criteria that could be prespecified might include the use of details, accuracy, vocabulary, and expression. When performance assessment is used, the educator gives the criteria in advance so that the child as well as the team is clear about the criteria to be used.

Finally, how can feedback be provided? The use of performance assessment is not to elicit only one solution or only one type of performance. Is the child using the skills in the preschool and at home? How can the family and the team provide feedback to the child? The criteria for making judgments become the goals for instruction and progress.

AUTHENTIC ASSESSMENT

Authentic assessment is similar to performance assessment, but the child completes or demonstrates the skill or behavior in a real-life context (C. A. Meyer, 1992). The conditions of the authentic assessment may be quite different from those of the performance assessment. In performance assessment, contrived or artificial conditions are permitted, while in authentic assessment the task complexity, motivation, standards, and stimuli must be true to life.

Just as with performance assessment, it is up to the educator to set the criteria for authentic assessment. Suppose, for example, that the educator asks Jiang to show how she puts on her coat as soon as the child has come inside. In a second example, the educator watches Suki as he gets materials ready for water play. The first example represents a contrived performance assessment: Jiang has just come inside the building; she does not need to put on her coat. In the second example, Suki is gathering toys he will use immediately. The observation of this behavior is an authentic assessment.

DYNAMIC ASSESSMENT

Dynamic assessment, as described by Carol Lidz (1991), is based on the work of Reuven Feuerstein (1979, 1980) and his associates. Dynamic assessment is an approach that actively engages the learner in learning. Using mediated learning experiences, which are at the center of dynamic assessment, this approach has a test–intervene–retest format. A *mediated learning experience* (*MLE*) is an interaction between the evaluator and the child that "'mediates' the world to the child by framing, selecting, focusing, and feeding back environmental experiences in such a way as to produce in [the child] appropriate learning sets and habits" (Feuerstein, 1979, p. 71, cited by Lidz, 1991). MLEs help to determine the child's potential to benefit from direct instruction. Dynamic assessment yields interventions based on the quality of the interactions between the assessor and the child.

This approach to assessment can be combined with other types of assessment. The actual tasks presented to the child can be taken directly from the curriculum, or they can be tasks that the evaluator develops. According to Lidz (1991), dynamic assessment has three components:

1. The assessor actively tries to facilitate learning and engage the learner in active participation in the learning task.
2. The assessment emphasizes the evaluation of the processes, especially the metacognitive processes (processes used to learn how to learn) the child uses in learning.
3. The results of the assessment include information about how change can be produced in the child and about the modifiability of the child.

Lidz (1991) developed the Mediated Learning Experience (MLE) Rating Scale and the Preschool Learning Assessment Device. These instruments are similar and are used to describe interactions between the child and a mediator. The MLE can consist of almost any interaction between a mediator and a child. Activities that can be evaluated using the MLE Rating Scale include making a salad, talking about emotions, and planning activities. The MLE Rating Scale assesses the child in the following areas, using an interactive format between the assessor and the child. Each area is rated from 0 (no evidence of the behavior) to 3 (strong evidence of the behavior):

Intentionality. Communication to the child of the purpose of the interaction and the intent to keep the child involved in the interaction.

Meaning. Communication to the child that the object of the interaction is important.

Transcendence. Facilitation of "cognitive bridges" (Lidz, 1991, p. 107) between the task and related experiences of the child.

Sharing (Joint Regard). Looking at an object from the child's point of view. Also includes commenting on an object that the child has or a task the child has performed.

Sharing (of Experience). Communication by the assessor or mediator to the child of a thought or experience that had not been shared with the child.

Competence (Task Regulation). Manipulation of the task to produce mastery by the child.

Competence (Praise/Encouragement). Verbal or nonverbal praise to the child for a specific accomplishment.

Competence (Challenge/Zone of Proximal Development). Assessment of the child's competence in maintaining a task within the zone of proximal development (i.e., the task is not too difficult or too easy for the child).

Psychological Differentiation. The emphasis of the learning experience is on the mediator facilitating learning by the child, not the creation of a final product.

Contingent Responsivity. Ability to understand cues and signals of the child and to respond to them appropriately.

Affective Involvement. A feeling of caring for the child by the mediator or parent should be evident.

Change. Communication to the child by the mediator that the learning experience has been positive and has been beneficial.

PORTFOLIO ASSESSMENT

A *portfolio* is a deliberate collection of the products of a child's play and work that demonstrates the child's efforts, progress, and achievement (Arter & Spandel, 1991; C. Meyer, Schuman, & Angello, 1990). A portfolio is like a story—it tells us about the child (Paulson & Paulson, 1991). Usually portfolios contain samples of children's artwork, self-portraits, and creative work, including drawings and paintings and photographs of block or other constructions. For school-age children, portfolios contain children's writings, including journal entries and stories (first drafts and final copies), as well as work samples in mathematics and reading, including audiotapes and videotapes. The teacher's and child's comments as well as interviews with parents and the child may also be included (Hills, 1992).

Like curriculum-based assessment, dynamic assessment, performance assessment, and authentic assessment, portfolio assessment is an emerging area that will continue to develop. The use of portfolios offers the potential to:

Provide a rich portrait of what children know and are able to do

Depict the processes children use when they work and play

Portray the products of children's work and play in a natural environment

Be a source of continuous information about children's work and play in order to depict development, give feedback, and plan interventions

Align assessment with the goals of instruction

Link assessment with intervention (Arter & Spandel, 1991)

Portfolio assessment is a type of performance-based assessment (Meyer et al. 1990). In general, experts (Arter & Spandel, 1991; Meyer et al., 1990) agree that a portfolio is a *purposeful* collection of the products of a child's work and play and must represent or include:

1. The participation of the child in the selection of the content of the portfolio
2. The criteria for selecting the contents of the portfolio
3. The criteria for evaluating the contents of the portfolio
4. An indication that the child has had an opportunity to reflect on the contents

Without a purpose, a portfolio is just a folder (Arter & Spandel, 1991); the educator must have a clear set of reasons for collecting the materials. There can be many purposes for developing and maintaining a portfolio.

Purposes of a Portfolio
1. To demonstrate growth
2. To show the processes used in work and play
3. To develop compilations of favorite or personally important works
4. To show the development of various works or products
5. To demonstrate achievement
6. To communicate to parents and teachers
7. To use in the evaluation of programs (Adapted from Arter and Spandel, 1991)

CASE STUDY: A PRESCHOOL TEACHER TALKS ABOUT ALTERNATIVE ASSESSMENT

At our preschool we had been using traditional norm-referenced tests until last year. Then, in September, our team attended a conference on using alternative assessment. After the conference, the team discussed the various types of assessments presented. Some of us were eager to try a new way of evaluating the children's performance, while several members of the team felt that the procedures we were currently using were fine.

We decided to try portfolio assessment, at least on a limited basis. The team met to plan the process we would use. We decided to involve the children in deciding the purpose of the portfolio, the contents, and the criteria for evaluating the portfolio. It was very exciting!

We explained the use of the portfolios to the parents at the open house. They offered suggestions and were eager for their children to participate in this new form of assessment.

At the end of the year, the team was pleased that we had tried this alternative assessment. We found that the portfolios were very helpful in showing the development of a child over the year. We were able to document the effectiveness of specific strategies and to show the pattern of growth and development. Next year, we will make some changes. But we found that our "experiment" gave us a great deal of useful information.

Organizing Portfolios

Portfolios for preschool and primary grade children can be organized according to the following categories (Meisels & Steele, 1991, cited by Grace & Shores, 1992):

Art Activities (fine motor development)
Drawings

Photographs of block constructions or projects

Samples of manuscript printing

Artwork using various media

Movement (gross motor development)
Teacher's comments or videotapes of classroom and playground activities

Photographs of the child participating in music activities

Observations of the child's play

Math and Science Activities (concept development)
Photographs and videotapes of the child working on math and science projects

Work samples

Language and Literacy
Audiotapes and videotapes of the child reading

Samples of the child's writings

Interviews with the child

Journal or log entries written by the child

Personal and Social Development
Teacher's comments and observations

Interviews with parents

Videotapes

Criteria for Selecting and Evaluating Contents

By clarifying the criteria for selecting and evaluating the contents of the portfolio, we decide what is important, what the instructional goals should be, and what we expect of the child. The criteria should parallel the goals of the curriculum as well as the daily expectations for the child's performance. Because the contents of the portfolio can be used to make judgments about the child's performance, the criteria must be explicit—parents, child, and caregivers should share in the development of the criteria. This may mean that we must teach the child how to engage in self-reflection and self-evaluation:

Fostering Self-Reflection
Ask the child:

1. To describe the process used while engaging in play or work.
2. What makes this piece so special?
3. How does this piece relate to previous ones or what you have learned?
4. How does a special piece differ from one that is not as special? (Adapted from Arter and Spandel, 1991)

Although the teacher can select the contents for the portfolio, value is added when the child has an opportunity to reflect on what should be included. The following products might be part of a child's portfolio: pictures, drawings, stories, photographs, and audio- and videotapes. We can gather information about the self-assessment and metacognition of a child who has had an opportunity to reflect on portfolio contents (Arter & Spandel, 1991). Figures 11.2 and 11.3 contain sample contents from two different portfolios.

FIGURE 11.2 Example of a page from a child's writing portfolio

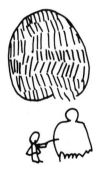

I was walking in the street. My hair is blonde. I
met a snake. The snake's scales were black and white.
The snake looked at me. I was scared. I've never
seen a snake before.

When I get home, I take a nap and have a dream. In
my dream the snake crawled out of the door into the
road. When I woke up he's still crawling around in
my room. My mom lets me keep him as a pet.

FIGURE 11.3   Excerpts from a child's writing portfolio

Scoring

There are several ways to evaluate the contents of a child's portfolio.

Narrative.   In a narrative, the teacher relates what the child knows or has
accomplished. Specific strengths and weaknesses can be delineated. Figure 11.4 is an
example of a narrative evaluation of a child's portfolio.

General Impression Scoring.   The teacher reviews the materials in the portfolio and gives it a score. This type of scoring, which can provide general feedback, is
useful when the teacher must score a great many portfolios. The teacher uses a scale
(e.g., 0–4) to score the collections.

FIRST GRADE PORTFOLIO
READING SUMMARY SHEET SAMPLE—EMERGENT READER

Student Name _____ JACOB _____ Teacher __ Hanson __ Date _____

School _____ Gastineau _____ Quarter 1 2 3 4 Year _____

I. Reading Strategies	Observations/Comments

1. Uses Visual Analysis
  • tells a story from pictures
  • focuses on print
  • uses knowledge of letters and sounds to read words
  • makes predictions based on letter shapes/letter sounds
2. Uses Meaning Cues
  • uses pictures to bring meaning to print
  • self-corrects when a word does not make sense
  • continues reading beyond unknown words
  • makes predictions based on what would make sense
  • rereads for sentence to make sense
3. Uses Sentence Structure Cues
  • uses knowledge of language patterns to predict words, phrases, events
  • self-corrects based on knowledge of sentence structure
4. When reading doesn't make sense, cross checks, using one or all of the strategies
  • rereads for sentence to sound right
	Jacob is an emerging reader. He is beginning to use his prior knowledge to bring meaning to what he's reading. He has been acomplishing this by pointing to words as he reads from left to right, and by using sounds to help decode unknown words. He's also beginning to use sentence structure cues with simple pattern stories.

II. Comprehension Strategies
 	
  • Remembers sequence of events
  • Summarizes major events of story
  • Predicts what will happen next
  • Backs up statements with proof from reading
  • Connects and builds to draw conclusions
  • Uses prior knowledge to form an opinion
  • Connects experiences with books
  • Evaluates/judges characters, authors, books
	Jacob is starting to connect events from the story with his own experiences. He tells what is happening in a story from the pictures, and predicts what will happen next.

III. Behavioral Aspects of Reading
 	
  • Is willing to read
  • Shows pleasure in reading
  • Selects books independently
  • Attends to reading independently
  • Chooses books of appropriate difficulty
	Recently he has been very positive about selecting and reading books, especially those with predictable patterns. One of his favorite books is *Chicka Chicka Boom Boom*.

(continued)

FIGURE 11.4 A sample for an *emergent* first grade reader, developed as a joint effort by reading specialists and first grade teachers

SOURCE: From *First Grade Portfolio*. Juneau, Alaska, School District. Reprinted by permission.

- Views self as reader
- Monitors by stopping reading when
  something is wrong

IV. Home/School Strategies for Reading Growth

Keep encouraging Jacob to read the books he brings home in the book bags. He may want to read the same book to more than one person. This will help him to read more fluently and increase his confidence.

It would also be beneficial for him to review letter names and sounds and learn some basic sight words. I will be sending a few home each night for him to practice.

FIGURE 11.4   (*continued*)

Focused Holistic Scoring.   This type of scoring is useful when a quick, superficial evaluation must be conducted. The teacher is looking for a particular, previously identified characteristic of the child's work. One score is produced in the evaluation.

Analytic Scoring.   This type of scoring is used to provide a detailed evaluation of the contents of a portfolio. The teacher uses a scale or *rubric* to assign points to different levels of performance. Several scores are produced. While this type of scoring can be very time-consuming, it can provide a great deal of information about a child's performance.

A portfolio is a natural link to instruction. The contents of the portfolio are developed in the child's natural environment. Many of the contents are developed directly from the child's work and play within the natural environment. The process of developing a portfolio helps us to determine what is important to the growth and development of the child.

Large-Scale Assessment

Some schools and some states use portfolios as a means of assessing groups of children. This is an appropriate use of portfolios, and the information obtained from aggregating the contents can be useful in curriculum planning and in informing policy decisions concerning young children. The purposes of using portfolios in assessing individual children and in assessing groups of children should not conflict. However, educators must carefully delineate the goals for the various types of portfolio and the criteria used to evaluate them.

Cautions When Using Portfolios

Careful design of portfolios is important to ensure that appropriate conclusions can be drawn. The usefulness of a portfolio can be diminished if we are unclear about our expectations. Several questions can guide us in designing portfolios:

Are the contents of the portfolio representative of the child's work? While a portfolio can include many items, we must consider whether the contents are representative of the child. For example, a portfolio might contain a number of beginning drawings but not a finished one. Videotapes might contain images of solitary play but not cooperative play.

Are the criteria for selection and evaluation clear? Have they changed over time? When designing a portfolio, the educator and parent may have said that all the drawings of a child should be included in the portfolio without specifying whether this meant all the finished drawings or all the drawings, regardless of state of completion.

Who evaluates the contents? Interpretations can vary depending on who evaluates the contents of a portfolio. Suppose that portfolios were maintained for all children in kindergarten to show their development over a year. Depending on their training, different educators may arrive at different conclusions (Arter & Spandel, 1991).

Who owns the portfolio? Children will feel a great deal of ownership and pride in the contents of the portfolio. Teachers may want to give some or all of the contents to the next year's teacher, or the school may want to use the contents in large-scale assessment. Parents and children may want to keep selected items. Ownership of the contents of the portfolio is an issue that deserves thoughtful consideration.

PREFERRED PRACTICES

The development of new assessment procedures is an exciting area, although not without its problems. New assessment procedures have the potential of helping us to develop valid and fair approaches to assessing young children. However, as this area continues to develop, we must proceed carefully (Hymes, Chafin, & Gonder, 1991).

Before assessment procedures are developed, standards should be in place which specify what children should know and be able to do. These standards should be developed through discussion with educators and parents. Unless there is consensus among the stakeholders, it is unlikely that valid assessment will result.

Assessment procedures should assist educators and policymakers to improve instruction and learning. If assessment is to be beneficial, the procedures must provide useful information about the capabilities of children. If the purposes of assessment are not beneficial, then the assessment procedures should not be used.

All assessment procedures should be fair to all children. Assessment procedures should be unbiased and should be attentive to differences in development and disabilities and to differences in culture, race, class, and gender. Children should be given multiple opportunities to demonstrate what they know. Educational decisions should not be based on a single test score.

The assessment tasks should be reliable and valid and should represent the standards children are expected to achieve. Multiple-choice tests give children inadequate opportunities to demonstrate what they know. Alternatives to traditional assessment, such as curriculum-based assessment, portfolios, and demonstrations, are rich sources of information.

Educators should be involved in the development and implementation of assessment procedures. Because assessment is closely linked to instruction, educators must participate in the development, administration, scoring, and interpretation of assessment procedures.

Finally, we should continuously evaluate the assessment procedures we use. We need to keep revising and improving on assessment procedures (Hymes et al. 1991).

STUDY QUESTIONS AND SUGGESTED ACTIVITIES

1. Why should early childhood educators consider alternatives to norm-referenced tests?

2. Think of your own work in early childhood. How could a portfolio be used to assess what you have learned?

3. Compare the advantages and disadvantages of using curriculum-based assessment.

4. Describe three advantages of alternative assessment.

5. Compare the various types of scoring of portfolios.

REFERENCES

Airasian, P. W., & Madaus, G. F. (1983). Linking testing and instruction: Policy issues. *Journal of Educational Measurement, 20*(2), 103–108.

Arter, J. A., & Spandel, V. (1991). *Using portfolios of student work in instruction and assessment.* Portland, OR: Northwest Regional Educational Laboratory.

Bagnato, S. J., & Murphy, J. P. (1989). Validity of curriculum-based scales with young neuro-developmentally disabled children: Implications for team assessment. *Early Education and Development, 1*(1), 50–63.

Bagnato, S. J., & Neisworth, J. T. (1990). *System to plan early childhood services.* Circle Pines, MN: American Guidance Service.

Bagnato, S. J., & Neisworth, J. T. (1991). *Assessment for early intervention: Best practices for professionals.* London: Guilford.

Bagnato, S. J., Neisworth, J. T., & Capone, A. (1986). Curriculum-based assessment for the young child: Rationale and review. *Topics in Early Childhood Special Education, 6,* 97–110.

Bagnato, S. J., Neisworth, J. T., & Munson, S. M. (1989). *Linking developmental assessment and early intervention: Curriculum-based prescriptions.* Rockville, MD: Aspen.

Bluma, S., Shearer, M., Frohman, A., & Hilliard, J. (1976). *Portage guide to early education checklist.* Portage, WI: Cooperative Educational Service Agency 12.

Brandt, R. (1992). On performance assessment: A conversation with Grant Wiggins. *Educational Leadership, 49*(8), 35–37.

Brigance, A. H. (1977). *Brigance® diagnostic inventory of basic skills.* North Billerica, MA: Curriculum Associates.

Brigance, A. H. (1983). *Brigance® comprehensive inventory of basic skills.* North Billerica, MA: Curriculum Associates.

Brigance, A. H. (1984). *Brigance® assessment of basic skills—Spanish edition.* North Billerica, MA: Curriculum Associates.

Brigance, A. H. (1991). *Brigance® diagnostic inventory of early development—revised.* North Billerica, MA: Curriculum Associates.

Cohen, L., & Spruill, J. (1990). *A practical guide to curriculum-based assessment for special educators.* Springfield, IL: Charles C. Thomas.

Diez, M. E., & Moon, C. J. (1992). What do we want students to know? . . . and other important questions. *Educational Leadership, 49*(8), 38–41.

Feuerstein, R. (1979). *Dynamic assessment of retarded performers.* Baltimore: University Park Press.

Feuerstein, R. (1980). *Instrumental enrichment.* Baltimore: University Park Press.

Fuchs, L., & Deno, S. (1981). *The relationship between curriculum-based mastery measures and standardized achievement tests in reading* (Research Report No. 57). Minneapolis: University of Minnesota, Institute for Research on Learning Disabilities. (ERIC Document Reproduction Service No. ED 212 662)

Fuchs, L. S., Fuchs, D., & Deno, S. L. (1982). Reliability and validity of curriculum-based informal reading inventories. *Reading Research Quarterly, 18,* 6–26.

Furano, S., O'Reilly, K. A., Hosaka, C. M., Inatsuka, T. T., Zeisloft-Falbey, B., & Allman, T. (1988). *Hawaii early learning profile.* Palo Alto, CA: VORT.

Galagan, J. E. (1985). Psychoeducational testing: Turn out the lights, the party's over. *Exceptional Children, 52*(3), 288–299.

Gardner, H. (1991). *The unschooled mind.* New York: Basic Books.

Glover, M. E., Preminger, J. L., & Sanford, A. R. (1978). *Early learning accomplishment profile for young children.* Lewisville, NC: Kaplan.

Grace, C., & Shores, E. F. (1992). *The portfolio and its use.* Little Rock, AR: Southern Association on Children Under Six.

Herman, J. L., Aschbacher, P. R., & Winters, L. (1992). *A practical guide to alternative assessment.* Alexandria: VA: Association for Supervision and Curriculum Development.

Hills, T. W. (1992). Reaching potentials through appropriate assessment. In S. Bredekamp & T. Rosegrant (Eds.), *Reaching potentials: Appropriate curriculum and assessment for young children* (pp. 43–63). Washington, DC: National Association for the Education of Young Children.

Hymes, D. L., Chafin, A. E., & Gonder, P. (1991). *The changing face of testing and assessment, problems and solutions.* Arlington, VA: American Association of School Administrators.

Johnson-Martin, N. M., Attermeier, S. M., & Hacker, B. J. (1990). *The Carolina curriculum for preschoolers with special needs.* Baltimore: Paul H. Brookes.

Johnson-Martin, N. M., Jens, K. G., & Attermeier, S. M. (1986). *The Carolina curriculum for handicapped at-risk infants.* Baltimore: Paul H. Brookes.

Lidz, C. S. (1991). *Practitioner's guide to dynamic assessment.* New York: Guilford Press.

Meisels, S. A., & Steele, D. (1991). *The early childhood portfolio collection process.* Ann Arbor, MI: University of Michigan Center for Human Growth and Potential.

Meyer, C., Schuman, S., & Angello, N. (1990). *Aggregating portfolio data.* Lake Oswego, OR: Northwest Evaluation Association.

Meyer, C. A. (1992). What's the difference between *authentic* and *performance* assessment? *Educational Leadership, 49*(8), 39–40.

Meyers, J., Pfeffer, J., & Erlbaum, V. (1985). Process assessment: A model for broadening assessment. *Journal of Special Education, 18*(2), 1–84.

National Association for the Education of Young Children. (1988). NAEYC position statement on standardized testing of young children 3 through 8 years of age. *Young Children, 43*(3), 42–47.

National Governors' Association, Task Force on Education. (1990). *Educating America: State strategies for achieving the national education goals.* Washington, DC: National Governors' Association.

Paulson, P., & Paulson, L. (1991). Portfolios: Stories of knowing. In P. H. Dreyer & M. Poplin (Eds.), *Claremont reading conference 55th yearbook 1991. Knowing the power of stories.* Claremont, CA: Center for Developmental Studies of the Claremont Graduate School.

Sanford, A. R., & Zelman, J. G. (1981). *Learning accomplishment profile.* Lewisville, NC: Kaplan.

Sheridan, S., Murphy, D., Black, J., Puckett, M., & Allie, E. C. (1986). *Beginning milestones.* Allen, TX: DLM.

Smith, C. R. (1980). Assessment alternatives: Nonstandardized procedures. *School Psychology Review, 1*(9), 46–56.

Stenmark, J. K. (1991). *Mathematics assessment.* Reston, VA: National Council of Teachers of Mathematics.

Sternberg, L., & Adams, G. L. (1982). *Educating severely and profoundly handicapped students.* Rockville, MD: Aspen.

Tindal, G., & Marston, D. (1986). *Approaches to assessment; Psychoeducational perspectives on learning disabilities.* New York: Academic Press.

Webster, R., McInnis, E., & Carver, L. (1986). Curriculum biasing effects in standardized and criterion-referenced reading achievement tests. *Psychology in the Schools, 23*(2), 205–213.

Willoughby-Herb, S. J., & Neisworth, J. T. (1983). *HICOMP preschool curriculum.* San Antonio: Psychological Corporation.

CHAPTER 12

Interpreting Specialized Testing

CHAPTER OBJECTIVES

This chapter is an introduction to the specialized assessment of children with specific needs in the areas of vision, hearing, motor, and communication. Through case studies, we will examine some of the common assessment procedures and instruments used by practitioners.

Upon completing Section 1, you should be able to:

Describe several warning signs that indicate the need for further assessment of vision.

Discuss key aspects in interpreting a vision report.

Describe the terms and procedures for assessing distance, near, and functional vision.

Discuss key aspects in an orientation and mobility assessment.

Upon completing Section 2, you should be able to:

Define the terms *deaf, hard of hearing,* and *hearing impairment.*

Identify early signs of hearing loss.

Describe methods used in the evaluation of hearing loss.

Describe standardized tests that can be used to assess development, cognition, communication, readiness, and achievement of children who are hearing impaired.

Upon completing Section 3, you should be able to:

Identify and define specialized terms used in assessing motor development.

Describe several warning signs of motor problems.

Discuss key models in the assessment and treatment of children with motor delays.

Upon completing Section 4, you should be able to:
Describe the various types of communication.
Discuss key terms in interpreting a communication assessment.
Describe informal ways of assessing language skills.

Section 1: Assessing Children
Who Have a Visual Impairment

Key Terms

Congenital Visual Impairments. Visual deficits caused by heredity or disease or other conditions present during the prenatal or perinatal period.

Adventitious Visual Impairments. Visual deficits acquired after birth as a result of heredity, accident, or disease.

COMMON VISUAL IMPAIRMENTS

Visual impairments differ among individuals in three ways: (1) in the type of impairment (condition), (2) in the age of onset, and (3) in the extent of the impairment (degree). Problem conditions that develop during the prenatal period or result from events during the birth process are referred to as *congenital blindness* or *visual impairment.* Conditions that develop during childhood as a result of heredity, accident, or disease are referred to as *adventitious blindness* or visual impairment.

Visual impairments that develop during the prenatal period include congenital anomalies and absence of all or part of the structures of the eye, as well as cataracts, glaucoma, and albinism (Ward, 1986). Infectious diseases such as toxoplasmosis and trachoma can result in damage to the eye, either before or during birth. Infants who are born prematurely are at a high risk for visual impairments including retinopathy of prematurity (ROP), amblyopia, strabismus, cortical blindness, or extreme near-sightedness.

In young children, injuries and diseases are the leading causes of visual disabilities. Table 12.1 lists and describes some of the common visual impairments seen in young children. Children with visual impairments may fluctuate in their ability to use their vision. A child who has difficulty with a visual task at times may experience no difficulty on other days.

Almost all children with visual impairments have *some* vision, albeit limited. In fact, most children who are legally blind have some usable vision. Oftentimes, children who are blind have enough vision to see hand or finger movement at a close distance. Children unable to see hand movement may have light perception. This ability will enable them to discern the shapes of large forms and to identify the direction of a light source (which may be important for independent travel). Few children who are blind have no sight at all. The challenge is to figure out what type

TABLE 12.1   Common visual impairments in young children

Condition	Effect	Prognosis
Amblyopia	Sometimes referred to as "lazy eye," this condition causes a double image.	Correctable by age six
Astigmatism	The image is seen out of focus.	Correctable
Cataracts	The image is clouded.	Correctable
Glaucoma	The image is hazy; field is constricted.	Controllable with medication
Myopia	The image is blurred.	Correctable
Achromatopsia	Sometimes referred to as *color blindness;* the child is unable to identify one or more primary colors.	Noncorrectable
Cortex damage	Child experiences loss of vision as a result of a lesion in the cortex area.	Noncorrectable
Nystagmus	The image is blurred because of involuntary eye movement.	Noncorrectable
Optic nerve damage	Child experiences loss of vision as a result of incomplete development or damage to the optic nerve.	Noncorrectable

and degree of vision is available for the child's use so that appropriate instruction can be provided.

WORKING WITH FAMILIES OF INFANTS WITH VISUAL IMPAIRMENTS

Families with infants with visual impairments often face unique challenges. For example, infants may not make eye contact or orient to the voices of family members—a lack of response that can be unsettling. Family members, in turn, may feel rejected or may question their ability to care for the infant. Feelings of rejection or inadequacy may lead to decreased interaction with the infant. To address some of the issues, Bradley-Johnson (1986) developed a series of questions to assist practitioners in gathering information that is particularly relevant to such families.

Questionnaire for Parents and Caregivers of Infants and Preschoolers with Visual Impairments
1. What are some of the ways your child uses to let you know that she is listening to your voice?
2. Are there special times during the day when your child chooses to reach out to others? To play with toys?
3. Is your child aware of hazards? How are they avoided?
4. How does your child search for lost or dropped objects?
5. How do you encourage your child to explore the surroundings? (Adapted from Bradley-Johnson, 1986)

These questions can provide helpful information in developing an intervention plan. A family might, for example, request assistance in becoming more aware of what behaviors indicate that the infant is responding to a voice. These indicators are often subtle but observable and may involve quieting responses or increasing activity such as arm waving.

SCREENING PROCEDURES AND TOOLS

Teachers and caregivers of young children are in the best position to make observations and to identify conditions that may indicate a visual problem. Several signs may indicate the need for a professional examination. A sample checklist is provided below. Lack of these signs should not be interpreted as an absence of problems, however; some impairments may not have visible symptoms. If there is any doubt, the practitioner should discuss the concern with the child's parents and encourage them to visit an eye specialist.

Signals that May Indicate Visual Problems in Young Children
A. Red Flags for Infants
   1. Infant does not track a moving object with eyes.
   2. Infant does not gaze at objects and people in the environment.
   3. Infant is extremely sensitive to light.
B. Red Flags for Toddlers and Preschoolers
   1. Child rubs eyes frequently.
   2. Child's eyes are frequently red or watery.
   3. Child's eyes do not focus properly.
   4. Child examines objects at very close range.
C. Red Flags for Primary School Children
   1. Child squints when attempting close work.
   2. Child experiences difficulty in judging distances.
   3. Child avoids close visual work.

Discovering Amblyopia

One of the most common visual impairments in young children is *amblyopia,* a condition that results when a muscle imbalance in one of the eyes causes the child to receive a double image. This dissonance prompts the brain to suppress the image from the problem eye. Left untreated, the suppressed eye will gradually lose the ability to function. However, if the condition is identified and treated by age six, there is no permanent loss of vision. A practitioner who notices that a child's eyes appear to be out of alignment should discuss this observation immediately with the family. Early intervention is extremely important. Treatment may include corrective surgery and/or a temporary patch over the dominant eye.

SCREENING INSTRUMENTS

There are several screening instruments available to assess visual functioning in young children. One common tool is the New York Lighthouse Symbol Flash Card Vision Test (Lighthouse Low Vision Services, 1970). This set of cards assesses distance acuity by depicting three symbols (an apple, a house, and an umbrella) in varying sizes.

First, the individual conducting the screening test verifies that the child can identify each of the symbols. Then the child is given the pack of cards and asked to name each card with both eyes open. Parents can be most helpful in assisting with this part of the test, interpreting the child's response if necessary. If the child answers correctly, the cards are shown at 5, 10, and 20 feet. At each distance, the examiner tests each eye separately, then both eyes together.

Another common screening device is the Snellen chart with symbols of *E* (National Society to Prevent Blindness, 1991). First, the adult shows the big letter *E* in various positions and makes sure that the child understands the directions by playing a pointing game. The child is asked to point the way the *E* points. During the actual screening test, the child is seated 10 feet from the eye chart and the adult begins with the largest *E*s on line one (Figure 12.1).

Key Terms

Distance Visual Acuity. A measurement of distance visual functioning, usually reported in terms of what a person with normal vision sees at 20 feet.

Near Visual Acuity. A measurement of near visual functioning, usually reported in inches, meters, or Jaeger chart numbers (which refer to type size).

Functional Vision. A measurement of visual functioning in the natural environment (as opposed to a clinical setting).

CASE STUDY: JOSE'S CHILD CARE PROGRAM

Malinda Teraz eased her compact car into the parking lot at Jose's Child Care Program. Yesterday afternoon, the center director had explained that a new child, Joshua, would be joining the children in Malinda's group. The director then introduced the itinerant teacher, Dan Jenkins, who would be visiting the center regularly to assist Malinda and the rest of the staff in planning for Joshua's needs. Dan explained that Joshua has low vision and that he hoped to complete a functional vision assessment within the first few weeks. Dan went on to explain that this assessment would give the staff members important information about how Joshua uses his remaining vision. Dan also talked about visual acuity and showed the staff a vision report from the ophthalmologist. This information was very helpful to the staff.

INTERPRETING A VISION REPORT

An eye examination report from an ophthalmologist or an optometrist provides much useful information regarding the child's eye condition. An eye report typically contains the following information.

History

Information about the child's history will be of critical importance in planning the child's early education program. Children who are born with some vision will be able to explore their surroundings by using visual as well as tactile examination.

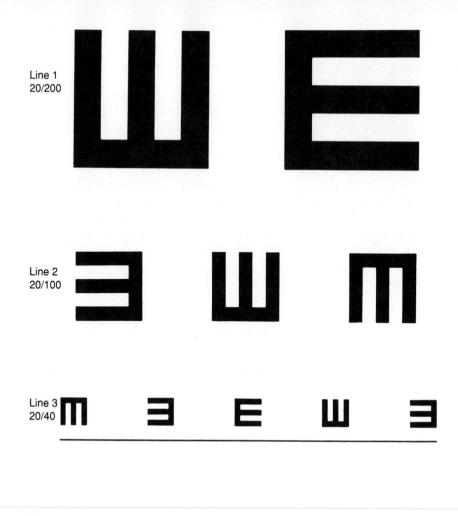

Line 1
20/200

Line 2
20/100

Line 3
20/40

Line 4
20/20

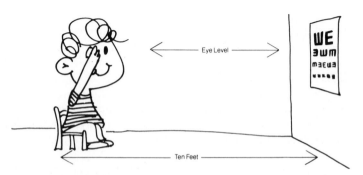

FIGURE 12.1   Preschool home eye test

376

Measurements

Measurement of the child's vision includes both distant and near vision. *Distance visual acuity* is, perhaps, the measurement most familiar to practitioners. The distance usually measured is 20 feet. Normal vision is described as 20/20 vision. A person with a visual impairment will have one of these numbers different from 20. For example, 20/200 indicates that the person must be only 20 feet away to be able to see what a person with normal vision can see at 200 feet. Some people, however, cannot see the target distance of 20 feet and need to have a figure at closer range. The eye specialist may then report the distance acuity at 10/200, which means that the individual recognized at 10 feet what a person with normal vision could identify at 200 feet.

Persons who have low distance visual acuity may not be able to see figures on the chart at any distance; however, they may be able to count fingers, identify hand movement, or recognize a light source. The following abbreviations may be used to note these acuities:

C.F.	Counts fingers (farthest distance)
H.M.	Hand movement (farthest distance)
L.P.	Light perception (ability to tell whether it is light or dark)
N.L.P.	No light perception

The most useful information in the measurement section of a vision report, however, is near vision. The use of *near vision* enables young children to explore their immediate environment and to learn by watching others. Measurements of near visual acuity are usually given in inches, meters, or Jaeger chart numbers, which refer to type size. The abbreviations used in reporting acuity in the left, right, and both eyes are:

O.D.	Right eye	(*oculus dexter*)
O.S.	Left eye	(*oculus sinister*)
O.U.	Both eyes	(*oculus uterque*)

The field of vision refers to central and peripheral vision. Some children have very good central visual acuity but limited peripheral vision. Some children have "islands" of vision in an otherwise restricted field. For these children, tilting the head or gazing indirectly at objects may be the only way to stimulate the usable field. The vision report provides an illustration to indicate field loss. This information is useful to confirm areas of visual functioning and to suggest intervention strategies such as positioning and direction of gaze. Information about field loss is also important in developing a technique for scanning the environment to take advantage of functional vision.

The last measurement in this section is one for color blindness. Color concepts are an integral part of most early childhood programs; however, some children experience difficulty in distinguishing colors because their retinal cone receptors lack the necessary pigments or are less sensitive in general to certain light waves.

Causes of Blindness or Visual Impairment

The next section of a vision report describes the type of condition that affects the eye, if known. Some types of impairment are due to hereditary factors, and this information will be important for family and other team members.

Prognosis and Recommendations

Is the reported condition stable or will the child's vision deteriorate? If the condition is not stable, then additional information should be requested from the ophthalmologist. Examples of questions you might ask include the following: Will the condition gradually deteriorate over time? Are there restrictions on certain activities of which you should be aware? Are problems likely to occur and what signs may warrant immediate action?

ASSESSMENT AREAS SPECIFIC FOR CHILDREN WITH VISUAL IMPAIRMENTS

In addition to the eye examination by an ophthalmologist, important areas for assessment include visual functioning in the environment, language and listening skills, and independent travel or orientation and mobility (O & M). For school-age children, assessment may also include braille and auditing skills. The list below summarizes areas that should be included in assessment of children with visual disabilities:

Functional vision assessment
How does the child use residual vision?
How does the child use other senses?

Language and listening
Does the child use turn-taking skills in communication?
Does the child understand important concepts (temporal, quantitative, positional, directional, sequential)?

Orientation and mobility skills
How does the child move from place to place?
Does the child move independently?
How does the child travel within the home? School? Neighborhood?

Academic skills
What is the child's achievement in braille reading and writing?
How is the child's use of auditing skills? (Adapted from Hall, Scholl, & Swallow, 1986; Division for the Visually Handicapped, 1991)

Functional Vision

Young children suspected of having a visual impairment may be difficult to assess as a result of the presence of one or more additional disabilities (e.g., a motor involvement, cognitive delay, or suspected hearing loss). Thus, an accurate vision assessment must ensure that the child's lack of response or difficulty with a vision task is not due to concomitant delays or disabilities.

In addition to the vision report completed by the ophthalmologist, a functional vision assessment should be completed in the child's home, with parental assistance, by a teacher trained to work with children with visual impairments. This assessment provides specific information regarding how the child is using vision during the daily routines and under various environmental conditions. Functional vision is measured in terms of visual efficiency; in other words, how well does the individual use residual vision?

Functional vision can be determined informally using toys and other materials in the home, child care, and education settings by a teacher trained in visual impairment. Or an assessment designed to assess visual efficiency may be used. One of the most well-known tools is the Program to Develop Efficiency in Visual Functioning (Barraga, 1980). This program includes two parts: a diagnostic assessment procedure and low vision observation checklist (to assess visual functioning) and a design for instruction and source book on low vision (to assist in program planning). This program was designed for children three years and up.

Orientation and Mobility (O&M) Skills

O&M skills are critical for persons who have a visual impairment. *Orientation* refers to the ability to determine one's position in the environment, to make possible directed movement from place to place. Different cues such as sounds, light, or pavement surface may assist an individual in orientation. *Mobility* refers to the ability to travel safely. Learning to use aids such as a seeing eye dog or a cane can increase a person's mobility.

The O&M instructor takes the lead role in assessing formal orientation and mobility skills in conjunction with the child's parents and other team members. Particular skill areas (Hill, 1992) that may be assessed include:

Ability to align the body to objects and sounds

Use of search patterns to explore the environment

Use of search patterns to recover a dropped object

Knowledge of how and when to ask for assistance

ASSESSING DEVELOPMENT OF CHILDREN WITH VISUAL IMPAIRMENTS

There are relatively few assessments specifically designed for children with visual impairments. The following instruments represent selected tools.

Informal Assessment of Developmental Skills for Younger Visually Handicapped and Multihandicapped Children

The Informal Assessment of Developmental Skills for Younger Visually Handicapped and Multihandicapped Children (Swallow, Mangold, & Mangold, 1978) is a series of checklists covering the following areas: self-help (adaptive), psychomotor, social–emotional, language, and cognition. The instrument is designed for infants and preschoolers for purposes of program planning. No information is provided concerning technical adequacy.

Oregon Project for Visually Impaired and Blind Preschoolers, 5th Edition

The Oregon Project for Visually Impaired and Blind Preschoolers, 5th Edition (Anderson, Davis, & Boigion, 1991) may be used with children birth through six years. This criterion-referenced inventory assesses the following areas: cognitive, language, self-help, socialization, and fine and gross motor movements. Some items indicate skills that are particularly helpful to a child with a visual impairment ("Locates dropped object up to 8 feet away with sound clue") or are appropriate for the child who will need orientation and mobility training ("Runs trailing a wall or rope"). This inventory is very helpful for planning the child's intervention or education program.

ISSUES IN ASSESSING VISUAL IMPAIRMENTS

In Chapter 6, we examined the process of assessing overall development and noted that common developmental scales were derived by observing children who were developing typically (i.e., children whose primary source of input is through vision). In fact, young children with normal vision learn much about the world around them by touching as well as by seeing. Yet, the experiences of children with visual impairments may be very different. Children with limited vision may interpret some concepts differently. For example, a tennis ball explored by touch and scanned visually presents different attributes. Ferrell (1986) raises some interesting questions regarding how this difference may (or may not) affect general concept development. Children who gather information by listening to and touching an object may have a concept of the object different from the concept of the child who examines the object visually.

Another issue involves the acquisition of developmental milestones. For many years, professionals believed that children who have visual impairments experience a delay in development. However, there is little empirical evidence to support this belief. Ferrell (1986) suggests that the "developmental lags" may in fact be the result of a self-fulfilling prophecy: "If blind infants are not expected to reach until late in the first year, for example, parents and teachers may not start looking for the child to reach until then, in effect decreasing the child's chances to learn to reach prior to that time simply because the opportunity has never been provided" (p. 124).

Thus, much remains to be learned about early developmental skills in young children with visual handicaps. Future research should address the development of skills and concepts in children whose primary mode of input is not vision. As early intervention practitioners continue to assist families in providing opportunities for children's growth and development, our beliefs may be further challenged.

PREFERRED PRACTICES

Today, many young children have multiple disabilities; vision may be only one area of need. Yet, early childhood teams should ensure that at least one team member has training and expertise in the field of visual impairment. Information about visual functioning provides the team with critical information regarding the child's use of residual vision. Ongoing functional vision assessment allows for programming adjustments as needed.

Increasingly, teachers with backgrounds in blindness/low vision have been very successful in designing their own functional vision assessments based on the individual child's natural environment (Pawelski, 1992). Information gathered through a functional vision assessment is important for supporting the child in home and community settings.

Knowledge of the child's visual efficiency will assist team members in assessing other areas of development. During the assessment process, the team will need to consider:

The types of accommodation the child may need

The flexibility of the assessment tool

Several of the developmental assessments discussed in Chapter 6 include specific adaptations or accommodations for children with sensory and other disabilities. However, caution should be used in attempting to use norm-referenced instruments such as the Battelle Developmental Inventory to determine the developmental level of children with visual handicaps. Many of these instruments do not include an adequate norming sample of this population of children.

Practitioners should consider criterion-referenced instruments that are consistent with the child's program and include accommodations as needed. By examining information collected over a period of time regarding the child's responses, the practitioner can obtain the most accurate account of the child's abilities and needs. Remember that multiple data points assure a more accurate, consistent picture. Furthermore, as a rule of thumb, all test items from formal and informal tests should be examined to ensure that they are fair for the children who will be assessed.

RESOURCES

1. Many states have an educational consultant for children with visual impairments. This person may be an important regional resource for early education programs and may assist staff in locating additional resources.

2. The American Foundation for the Blind (AFB), 15 West Sixteenth Street, New York, NY 10011, serves as a national clearinghouse for information about blindness. Educational consultants at AFB may assist practitioners in questions and issues regarding assessment.

3. The American Printing House for the Blind, 1839 Frankfort Avenue, Louisville, KY 40206, is a national organization that produces literature and distributes educational aids for children with visual impairments.

4. The Division on Visual Handicaps, Council for Exceptional Children, 1920 Association Drive, Reston, VA 22091-1589, is the professional organization for educators working with children with visual disabilities. The division is a good resource regarding "best practices."

5. The Lighthouse Low Vision Services, Low Vision Products, 36-02 Northern Boulevard, Long Island City, NY 11101, is a resource for low vision aids and equipment.

Section 2: Assessing Children Who Are Deaf or Have a Hearing Impairment

DEFINITIONS

Although there is some controversy about the negative connotations of the terms *deaf* and *hard of hearing,* the following definitions are generally used:

A *deaf* person is one whose hearing is disabled to an extent (usually 70 dB ISO[1] or greater) that precludes the understanding of speech through the ear alone, with or without the use of a hearing aid.

A *hard-of-hearing* person is one whose hearing is disabled to an extent (usually 35–69 dB ISO) that makes difficult, but does not preclude, the understanding of speech through the ear alone, without or with a hearing aid. (Moores, 1987, p. 9)

The federal definition states that *deafness* is:

a hearing loss so severe that with or without amplification the child is unable to process language through hearing. The condition adversely affects the child's educational performance. (*Federal Register,* 1992, Sec. 300.7)

Federal regulations define *hearing impairment* as a condition

whether permanent or fluctuating, that adversely affects the child's educational performance but that is not included under the definition of deafness. (*Federal Register,* 1992, Sec. 300.7)

There is some debate over the adequacy of these definitions. In general, the term *deaf* is used to describe individuals who cannot hear well enough to understand speech without visual cues, such as speech reading or signing. The term *hard of hearing* is generally used to describe persons who can understand speech through listening if other conditions (e.g., lighting, background noise, properly functioning hearing aid) are favorable. Children who are deaf have an absence of hearing in both ears. Children who have a hearing impairment have significant hearing loss in one or both ears.

EARLY SIGNS OF HEARING LOSS

Early identification of hearing loss is critical so that intervention can begin as soon as possible.

---

[1] An international standard for audiometers, called ISO-1964, was adopted by the International Organization for Standardization. An American standard, which is the same as the ISO standard, was published by the American National Standards Institute (ANSI).

Checklist of Symptoms for Early Detection of Hearing Loss

1. Does the child turn her or his head upon hearing a sound?

2. Does the child respond when her or his name is called?

3. Does the child startle when there is a loud noise or bang?

4. Does the child follow directions?

5. Does the child ask to have directions repeated?

6. Does the child speak clearly or demonstrate language difficulties?

7. Does the child have a history of earaches, colds, or allergies?

The Screening Instrument for Targeting Educational Risk (SIFTER) (Anderson, 1989) is a rating scale that is completed by a teacher of children in kindergarten through grade 5 who have been identified as having a hearing loss. The SIFTER helps to determine whether a child is experiencing problems in the areas of academics, attention, communication, class participation, and school behavior. Children suspected of having difficulty hearing should be referred for a hearing test. Referrals can be made to a physician, school nurse, speech–language pathologist, audiologist, otologist, or otolaryngologist. An *audiologist* is a specialist in testing hearing. An *otologist* or *otolaryngologist* is a physician who specializes in disorders of the ear (Frank, 1991).

TYPES OF HEARING LOSS

Hearing loss is classified according to the physiological basis for the hearing loss. A *conductive* hearing loss is due to some barrier to the sound waves that travel from the outer ear to the inner ear. Causes of conductive hearing loss include *otitis media* (inflammation in the middle ear), severe accumulation of wax, and poorly developed physiological structures in the ear (Bradley-Johnson & Evans, 1991; Ross, Brackett, & Maxon, 1991). Problems with the inner ear or auditory nerve can result in *sensorineural* hearing loss, which may be due to tumors in the ear, brain damage, developmental problems, genetic factors, pre- and postnatal infections, anoxia, and trauma (Bradley-Johnson & Evans, 1991; Ross et al., 1991). *Mixed* hearing loss is a combination of conductive and sensorineural hearing loss.

MEASURING HEARING LOSS

Early identification of hearing loss maximizes the child's opportunities to benefit from intervention. Early identification has a tremendous impact on the child's speech, personal, social, and academic skills (Garrity & Mengle, 1983).

Children who have hearing losses are not a homogeneous group, and it is important not to stereotype them. Many factors can influence a child's ability to hear. For example, it is important to know whether the hearing loss is congenital, the age at which the child acquired the hearing loss, the age at which the hearing loss was detected, and when intervention was begun, if in fact it has started. The ability of the child to acquire and use other modes of communication is another significant factor, as is the ability of the child and the family to deal with the hearing loss. It is also important to know whether the hearing loss occurred before the child developed language (prelingual) or after language had been developed (postlingual).

Pure-tone Audiometry

Hearing loss is assessed by an audiological evaluation, which establishes the type, configuration, laterality, and degree of hearing loss. The type of hearing loss can be sensorineural, conductive, or mixed. *Configuration* refers to the pattern of hearing acuity, which is depicted in an *audiogram,* or a graph that plots the intensity of sounds detected at five different frequencies. *Laterality* identifies the right ear/left ear difference; the configuration can be different for each ear.

Although hearing loss is measured in discrete levels, the determination of hearing impairment must include a functional assessment as well as the hearing loss reported on an audiogram.

Audiometers present tones at different levels of loudness (intensity) and pitch. Typically, headphones are placed on a child's head and the child is asked to respond to a series of tones by pointing or turning the head. Audiometers come in many different types, some more specialized than others. An audiometer produces a chart that describes the hearing loss (Figure 12.2). On the vertical side of the chart, hearing loss is measured in decibels (dB), units that indicate loudness or intensity. The range of normal hearing is between 0 and 90 dB. For example, at 0 dB a whisper is barely audible. The sound of an automobile 10 feet away might register as 50 dB.

Frequency of sound waves, expressed in hertz (Hz), is measured along the horizontal axis of an audiogram. Frequency is sometimes referred to as pitch. The human ear can detect very low pitch, at about 125 Hz, and very high pitch, at about 8000 Hz. The right and left ears are tested separately. On an audiogram an *O* indicates the right ear and an *X* the left ear.

FIGURE 12.2 Pure-tone audiogram. The audiogram shows that the child has difficulty hearing high-frequency sounds.

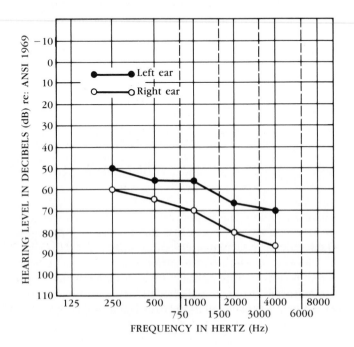

Although there is some disagreement in the literature, general categories for describing hearing loss have been established. Losses of 0 to 25 dB are classified as normal; 25 to 54 dB are considered mild; 55 to 69 dB are moderate; 70 to 89 dB are severe; and 90 dB or higher are profound. The term *deaf* is used to designate persons having severe or profound hearing losses (Bradley-Johnson & Evans, 1991; Brill, MacNeil, & Newman, 1986).

It is difficult to categorize children on the basis of an audiogram because so many factors can affect the ability to hear. In fact, it is misleading and inaccurate to describe a child's hearing loss based on an audiogram alone. Thus, eligibility for special services is based on whether or not the hearing impairment adversely affects the child's educational performance.

Air Conduction

Sounds are conducted by sound waves. Any loss of sensitivity at various frequencies can be detected by air conduction audiometry. In testing air conduction, headphones are placed over the top of the child's head and each ear is tested separately to determine the levels at which tones are heard (Martin, 1991).

Bone Conduction

Sensorineural loss is determined through bone conduction audiometry. The bones in the skull can be caused to vibrate by a bone conduction vibrator. This vibration can elicit electrochemical activity in the inner ear as well as changes in the inner and outer ear.

In testing bone conduction, the examiner tests each ear separately. A vibrator is placed on the mastoid bone behind the child's ear or on the child's forehead. Testing proceeds as in air conduction. The results are reported on an audiogram (Martin, 1991).

Speech Audiometry

Pure-tone audiometry and bone conduction audiometry provide limited information about a child's ability to hear. Speech audiometry provides information about a child's ability to use audition. How well a child is able to understand speech is more important than the ability to hear pure tones. In speech audiometry, a child wears earphones and the evaluator speaks into a microphone. (A tape recording can also be used.) Depending on the child's age and abilities, the child is asked to repeat the words, point to pictures, or write the words (Madell, 1990; Roeser & Price, 1981).

Immitance Screening

An audiological evaluation will not provide sufficient information about hearing loss in every child. Martin (1991) wrote that immitance screening should be conducted on almost all children who are suspected of having a hearing loss, especially if the loss is sensorineural, greater than 60 or 70 dB, or fluctuating, and if the child is inattentive or difficult to test, or does not understand the instructions.

Immitance screening is not the same as audiological screening. A child who had a middle ear disorder might pass the audiological evaluation. Immitance screening, also known as impedance audiometry, can be used to identify the presence of fluid in the middle ear and other abnormalities in the outer ear and middle ear (Ross et al. 1991; Salvia & Ysseldyke, 1991).

Immitance screening generally uses three measures: *tympanometry,* which evaluates how well the ear transmits energy as air pressure in the ear canal changes; *static immitance,* which measures the tympanic membrane and the middle ear cavity; and *acoustic reflex thresholds,* which are measures of the intensity of the contraction of the stapedius muscle in the middle ear. The results of immitance screening are plotted on a tympanogram (Ross et al., 1991).

One of the main disadvantages of using immitance screening with children is that the examinee must be almost motionless. Any speaking or crying will be detected by the probe microphone. Experienced examiners are frequently able to conduct immitance screening with few distractions. Some children may have to be sedated (Martin, 1991).

Hearing Screening

Generally, only the assessment of air conduction is made during hearing screening. Guidelines for hearing screening have been developed by the American Speech–Language–Hearing Association (ASHA) (1985). For children who function at a developmental level of three years through grade 3, ASHA recommends that screening be administered individually on an annual basis. The screening should consist of pure-tone air conduction screening. Immitance screening, for identifying children who have middle-ear disorders, should also be a component of this screening. Children whose hearing acuity may be in question as a result of the hearing screening should be rescreened. Any child who fails the rescreening should be referred for an audiological evaluation.

High-risk Register

A *high-risk register* is a list of infants who may be at risk of having a hearing loss. Shortly after birth, medical information relating to newborns is collected, and mothers are interviewed. Specialized audiological testing may be done shortly after birth. If risk indicators are discovered, the child's name is placed on the high-risk register and follow-up screenings are scheduled. This technique has been found to be very successful in the early identification of hearing loss (Amochaev, 1987; Fitch, Williams, & Etienne, 1982; Mahoney & Eichwald, 1987).

SPECIALIZED TESTING

It may be difficult to assess the hearing of very young children using pure-tone audiometry because young children do not always follow directions well. In addition, young children may object to the use of earphones. Specialized tests have been developed to assess the hearing of infants, toddlers, and children with developmental disabilities.

Evoked-Response Audiometry

Evoked-response audiometry is a procedure for measuring electrical activity in the brain as sounds are being presented. While this type of testing is very useful, the technique does not distinguish between sensorineural and conductive hearing losses. In addition, the evaluator must make certain that middle-ear problems have been ruled out as the cause of the hearing loss. The disadvantages to this procedure are several (Garrity & Mengle, 1983). For example, it is expensive and time-consuming, and because measurement entails placing electrodes on the child's head, some children may require sedation in order to be tested.

Cochleography

Cochleography is the measurement of the electrical impulses generated by the nerves in the cochlea, which is the hearing part of the inner ear. This technique is able to distinguish between sensorineural and conductive hearing losses. Because the electrical impulses to be measured are weak, the microphone must be surgically placed using anesthesia (Garrity & Mengle, 1983).

Crib-O-Gram

The Crib-O-Gram is a device that records on a graph the movements of a newborn before and after sounds are presented through a loudspeaker. A motion-sensitive pad is placed under the crib mattress. The movements of the newborn are recorded on a graph (McFarland, Simmons, & Jones, 1980).

Probe Microphone Evaluation

Probe microphone evaluation is used to measure the exact sound that reaches a child's eardrum after the sound has been changed or amplified by a hearing aid, ear mold, or the ear canal (Ross et al., 1991). A small microphone is inserted into the ear and measurements are made as sounds are presented. Probe microphone measurements can be made with and without a hearing aid in the ear.

USING STANDARDIZED TESTS

The use of standardized tests that assess developmental, cognitive, communication readiness, and academic areas with children who have a hearing loss can be problematic. Many commercially published standardized measures do not systematically include children who are deaf or hard of hearing in the standardization sample. When a child who has a hearing loss is given a test that has not been normed on children with hearing losses, the results obtained have limited usefulness. If the examiner does not know how to communicate with a child who has a hearing loss, the results also may be of little use. Frequently, examiners will modify administration and response procedures to accommodate the needs of the child. However, any modifications should be made carefully, and performance should be interpreted cautiously.

> Modification of tests to facilitate their use with the handicapped has both good and bad points. By modifying stimulus demands and/or response requirements, examiners are able to obtain samples of behavior. However, the test is no longer a "standardized" test, since the conditions under which it was normed have been altered. Consequently, it is no longer appropriate for test users to attempt to make norm-referenced interpretations of the "scores" handicapped students earn. The norms are no longer relevant. (Salvia & Ysseldyke, 1991, p. 37)

Tests that have been normed on children who are deaf or have a hearing impairment are listed in Table 12.2.

CASE STUDY: CHAD

Chad is a happy, well-adjusted four-year-old who is experiencing moderate to severe developmental delays. He was born after a normal pregnancy. Chad reached the childhood milestones at average ages. He was sitting alone at six months, crawling at eight months, and walking at one year. His speech and language development was typical.

When Chad was three years old he had a high temperature and a seizure that lasted for several hours, during which the blood oxygen supply to his brain was interrupted. After the seizure, there was a noticeable regression in Chad's development. He stopped using speech and stopping walking, choosing to crawl. This behavior was of great concern to Chad's mother and his pediatrician, and the child was referred for speech, language, and hearing testing. It was at this time that a moderate to severe bilateral hearing loss was discovered. Chad's audiogram resembled the sample shown in Figure 12.2. The child now uses two hearing aids and is receiving intervention services, which include language instruction and physical therapy.

RESOURCES

The following organizations can provide additional information:

Alexander Graham Bell Association
3417 Volta Place, NW
Washington, DC 20007
(202) 337-5220 voice/TDD

Gallaudet University Information Center
   on Deafness
800 Florida Avenue, NE
Washington, DC 20002
(800) 672-6720 voice/TDD

National Association of the Deaf
814 Thayer Avenue
Silver Spring, MD 20910
(301) 587-1788 voice/TDD

TABLE 12.2 Selected tests that have been standardized on children with hearing impairments

Test	Skills	Grade/Age
Achievement		
Kaufman Assessment Battery for Children (Kaufman & Kaufman, 1983)	Simultaneous processing, sequential processing, achievement	2 years, 6 months to 12 years, 5 months
Stanford Achievement Test (Gardner, Rudman, Karlsen, & Merwin, 1982)	Reading, vocabulary, arithmetic, spelling	Kindergarten to grade 12
Test of Early Reading Ability—Deaf or Hard of Hearing (Reid, Hresko, Hammill, & Wiltshire, 1991).	Reading	3 years to 13 years, 11 months
Uniform Performance Assessment System (White, Haring, Edgar, Affleck, & Hayden, 1981)	Preacademic communication, social, self-help, gross and fine motor development	Birth to 6 years
Cognition		
Nebraska Test of Learning Aptitude (Hiskey, 1966)	Intelligence	3 to 16 years
Communication		
Carolina Picture Vocabulary Test (Layton & Holmes, 1985)	Vocabulary	5 to 12 years
Grammatical Analysis of Elicited Language	Grammar	
Pre-Sentence Level (Moog, Kozak, & Geers, 1983)		3 to 6 years
Simple Sentence Level (Moog & Geers, 1985)		5 to 9 years
Complex Sentence Level (Moog & Geers, 1980)		8 to 12 years
Rhode Island Test of Language Structure (Engen & Engen, 1983)	Syntax	3 to 20 years
Test of Expressive Language Ability (Bunch, 1981a)	Expressive language	7 to 12 years
Test of Receptive Language Ability (Bunch, 1981b)	Receptive language	6 to 12 years
Total Communication Receptive Vocabulary Test (Scherer, 1981)	Receptive language	3 to 12 years
Adaptive Development		
Vineland Adaptive Behavior Scales (Sparrow, Balla, & Cicchetti, 1984) Expanded form Survey form	Adaptive development	Birth to 18 years

Section 3: Assessing Children with Physical Disabilities

Key Terms

Tone. The resting state of a muscle.

Hypertonicity. A condition in which the muscle is constantly tensed as a result of increased tone.

Hypotonicity. A condition in which the muscle cannot move or maintain good postural control because of lack of tone.

Tremors. Rapid, jerky, involuntary movement due to lack of muscle control.

Paresis. Weakness in movement.

-plegia. Inability to move; paralysis.

MOTOR DELAYS: WORKING WITH FAMILIES AND CHILDREN

Children with motor difficulties may experience problems in one or more areas including muscle development, bones or joints, and absence or malformation of structure. Families of children who are born with certain orthopedic/neurological disorders may receive prenatal and postnatal support as a result of early identification. However, many motor disabilities cannot be identified in utero or observed in the newborn. Family members and child care providers who see the day-to-day development of the child are in the best position to identify areas of concern in motor development. The most common types of difficulty that can be observed involve muscle deficits. These include:

- *Deficits in muscle tone.* Muscle tone refers to the amount of tension that is present in a resting muscle. Muscles that have too little tone appear limp, or *hypotonic,* whereas in *hypertonicity* the child has too much tension, and the muscles are constantly tensed or stretched.

- *Deficits in muscle control.* Problems in muscle control are seen as jerky, involuntary movements of the arms and legs, called *tremors.*

- *Deficits in muscle strength.* The child may differ noticeably in muscle strength on the right- and left-hand sides of the body or between the limbs. A muscle weakness is referred to as *paresis;* inability to move is denoted with the combining form *-plegia.* Thus hemiplegia is an inability to move one side of the body.

TABLE 12.3   Common disorders associated with motor disability

Disorder	Description	Prognosis
Cerebral palsy	Group of disorders resulting from intra-cranial lesions	Nonprogressive
Juvenile rheumatoid arthritis	Inflammation and swelling of the joints	Remission; possible recurrence
Muscular dystrophy	Degeneration of the voluntary muscles	Progressive
Spina bifida	Congenital malformation of the spinal cord	Nonprogressive, but spinal curvature may develop

Many disorders cause motor impairments; but cerebral palsy is one of the most common disorders of motor ability in young children. Table 12.3 lists and briefly describes the common motor disorders found in young children.

SIGNS AND SYMPTOMS

As children grow, caregivers may become increasingly concerned about their development. In some progressive disorders, children may experience a decrease in motor coordination. Or there may be concerns about equilibrium or posture. Several early signs that may indicate motor difficulties are:

1. Abnormal positioning of arms or legs during play or at rest
2. Tremor of hands or arms when performing an activity
3. Major difference in strength between the left and right sides of the body
4. Early hand preference (before 13 months)
5. Poor balance and equilibrium
6. Difficulty in visual tracking
7. Weakness and fatigue in gross motor activities
8. Poor coordination during gross and fine motor activities
9. Poor muscle control of lips and tongue
10. Jerking or twitching movements (Adapted from Cook, Tessier, & Klein, 1992, pp. 290–291)

THEORETICAL PERSPECTIVES ON MOTOR DEVELOPMENT

Common Assumptions

Common assumptions and beliefs about the development of all children provide the basis for assessing and working with children with motor delays and deficits. These assumptions include:

1. Motor development is one aspect in an integral picture of a child's development and should not be viewed in isolation. Motor, cognitive, and communication skills are interdependent. Delays in motor development may affect cognitive development or functioning in language or communication.
2. Learning begins with motor skill development. Infants first learn about the environment through innate reflex movement. Movements gradually become purposeful and more refined.
3. Typical motor development follows a predictable skill sequence; later skill development usually depends on mastery of earlier skills. Atypical motor development may show a pattern of prolonged stays at an immature stage or acquisition of partial skills that do not fit into any one particular stage.

Key Terms

Neurodevelopmental Treatment (NDT). The perspective according to which brain lesions (injuries to an area of the brain which affect the functioning of that part of the brain) interfere with normal development; emphasizes specific handling techniques that inhibit abnormal reflex activity and facilitate normal movement patterns.

Proprioceptive Neuromuscular Facilitation (PNF). The perspective according to which as voluntary movement becomes stronger, incoordination will fade.

Sensory Integration (SI). Theoretical perspective that focuses on the neurophysiological process in which sensory information is organized and interpreted.

Typical Motor Development

The development of motor skills typically follows a sequence of milestones, progressing from beginning skills such as rolling over, to creeping, then walking. Motor development is seen as a series of new skill acquisitions.

However, some practitioners take issue with this assumption. Katona (1989) describes the presence of elementary forms of crawling, creeping, walking, and sitting as developing simultaneously in the neonate. "We, however, believe that the basic patterns of human motor development are present in the neonate and the capabilities to control and to perfect them come later, simultaneously with the development of motor control in the central nervous system" (p. 173). If this theory proves to be true, it will be possible to diagnose many motor difficulties soon after birth.

Atypical Motor Development: Theoretical Perspectives

Several different theoretical perspectives form the basis of assessment and treatment procedures for children experiencing neuromuscular disorders. The most common approaches are the neurodevelopmental treatment approach (NDT), proprioceptive neuromuscular facilitation (PNF), sensorimotor approach (the Rood technique), and sensory integration (SI) programming. Each of these perspectives "concentrates on a limited range of the entire spectrum of need for training coordination" (Kottke, 1982, p. 413). Several of these perspectives were developed from work with a particular population of children; for example, the NDT approach was developed for use with children with cerebral palsy. In fact, certain child characteristics may render one approach more effective than another (Guess & Noonan, 1982). Usually practitioners will use a combination of approaches in their assessment and treatment procedures.

Neurodevelopmental Treatment (NDT). The basic principle behind the NDT approach is to facilitate the child's normal natural movement and to allow the child to experience that feeling through typical early childhood activities. NDT utilizes reflex facilitation to reinforce postural activities and works on inhibiting primitive reflexes to facilitate more mature responses. This approach, developed by Karel and Berta Bobath (1972), emphasizes the need to inhibit hypertonia before beginning therapy. Physical therapists often recommend neurodevelopmental therapy for children with cerebral palsy.

Proprioceptive Neuromuscular Facilitation (PNF). Methods such as *proprioceptive neuromuscular facilitation (PNF),* developed by Knott and Voss (1968) and the *Rood technique* (Tiffany & Huss, 1988) assume that as the voluntary activity becomes stronger, there will be a fading of incoordination (Kottke, 1982). Various techniques are used to induce muscle relaxation and to increase joint range of motion. PNF has been found to be successful in patients with ligament reconstruction and in other rehabilitative situations (Lutz, Stuart, & Sim 1990; Osternig, Robertson, Troxel, & Hansen, 1987).

Sensory Integration (SI).   The theory of sensory integration focuses on the importance of *organization* of sensory input, without which sensory information may be either lost or not fully utilized. During the learning process, the child receives information through the many sensory systems. The brain takes in, sorts, and organizes this knowledge, and integrates it with stored information from past experiences. Sensory input comes not only from the five common senses of vision, hearing, taste, smell, and touch but from several other sources as well. Young (no date) identified these sources as including:

1. Balance or vestibular functioning
2. Kinesthesia–proprioception—a conscious awareness of one's body position
3. Temperature
4. Pain
5. Chemical receptors in body organs
6. Vital receptors to pressure

The theory of sensory integration stresses the importance of the ability of the brain to accept some stimuli and reject others and then to send the information on to one or more processing centers for integration.

Sensory integration was originally developed in the early 1960s by Dr. A. Jean Ayres, who had been working with children with learning or behavior disabilities. This theoretical framework needs empirical research to evaluate its effectiveness.

For additional information, the reader should refer to the following resources:

Barnes, M. R., Crutchfield, C. A., Heriza, C. B., & Herdman, S. J. (1990). *Reflex and vestibular aspects of motor control, motor development, and motor learning.* Atlanta: Stokesville Publishing.

Hopkins, H. L., & Smith, H. D. (Eds.). (1988). *Willard and Spackman's occupational therapy* (7th ed.). Philadelphia: Lippincott.

Semmler, C. J., & Hunter, J. G. (1990). *Early occupational therapy intervention: Neonates to three years.* Gaithersburg, MD: Aspen.

Tecklin, J. S. (1989). *Pediatric physical therapy.* Philadelphia: Lippincott.

COMMON ASSESSMENT PROCEDURES AND TOOLS

Occupational and physical therapists are frequently the primary planners of assessments of motor development. Teachers and other team members may provide assistance.

Informal Assessment of Motor Development

The assessment of a young child's gross motor development typically covers several different areas of functioning. These areas include:

Elements of Development

What is the child's tone?

Are the child's arm and leg muscles too soft and floppy (hypotonia)?

Are the child's arm and leg muscles too resistant (hypertonia)?

What is the quality of the child's movement?

Are movements well coordinated?

Or are they disorganized?

How is the child's strength?

Basic Functions

Does the child have good coordination?

How is the child's balance?

Does the child display an appropriate level of coordination?

What is the child's reaction to touch?

Skills

What skills can the child perform?

Milestones

What milestones has the child achieved?

Jones (1978) identified several additional areas that should be addressed in examining an infant:

Assessment Areas of Infant Motor Development

1. The oropharyngeal area, including feeding difficulties, may provide the earliest indication of central nervous system damage.
2. Visual and auditory evaluations.
3. Behavior: observations of the infant's usual sleeping position, for example, may indicate abnormal positioning of the head, legs, feet, arms, or hands.
4. Family context: observations of feeding and soothing activities by family caregivers provide information regarding family members' awareness of and response to the infant's signals.
5. Milestones in development.
6. Hand use.
7. Locomotion.

Family members and practitioners may gather much important quantitative and qualitative information about a child's motor skills through observation. Neisworth and Bagnato (1987) suggest the following questions to keep in mind when observing and appraising patterns of neuromotor development:

1. How do the child's posture and muscle tone change under different conditions and in different positions?
2. Which parts of movement are absent, and which contribute to the child's delay in gaining motor milestones?
3. In which position is the child's postural tone most normal?

4. Which position helps the child to perform the greatest number of voluntary, self-initiated movements?

5. How does the child gather information from his or her surroundings? (p. 336)

Assessment of a child's fine motor skills may begin with informal observations regarding the child's level of self-sufficiency during feeding, dressing, toileting, and washing. Some of the fine motor skill areas that one might observe include:

Midline behaviors

Does the child bring hands together at midline?

Does the child transfer a toy from one hand to the other?

Does the child reach across midline to obtain a toy on the other side?

Hand grasp

Does the child reach for objects?

Does the child rake finger food such as Cheerios or raisins in an attempt to pick up the items?

Does the child use the whole hand (palmar grasp) to pick up a small (1-inch cube) block?

Does the child use the thumb and fingers to pick up a small (1-inch cube) block?

Can the child pick up a Cheerio or raisin using a pincer grasp (thumb and forefinger)?

Family members and practitioners may gather much helpful information about motor development by observation. More formal assessment may be completed by the occupational or physical therapist.

Instruments for Assessing Motor Development

Children suspected of having problems in motor development may be assessed by formal screening tools discussed in Chapter 5 such as the Denver Developmental Screening Test II or the Bayley Infant Neurodevelopmental Screen (BINS).

Common standardized assessment batteries that may be given to children with suspected motor delays include Brazelton's Neonatal Behavioral Assessment Scale and the Bayley Scales of Infant Development, 2nd Edition, discussed in Chapter 6.

To assist in program planning, criterion-referenced instruments may be used. For examples, motor sections from the Hawaii Early Learning Profile or the Learning Accomplishment Profile (discussed in Chapter 6) may be helpful.

Other instruments that have been designed to specifically assess motor development include the Peabody Developmental Motor Scales and the Bruininks–Oseretsky Test of Motor Proficiency.

Bruininks–Oseretsky Test of Motor Proficiency

The Bruininks–Oseretsky Test of Motor Proficiency (Bruininks, 1978) assesses motor functioning of children from 4 years, 6 months to 14 years, 6 months. The test comes in two forms: a short form, which consists of 14 items from the complete battery, and the complete battery, which consists of eight subtests with 46 items total. The subtests are:

1. Running speed and agility
2. Balance
3. Bilateral coordination
4. Strength
5. Upper-limb coordination
6. Response speed
7. Visual–motor control
8. Upper-limb speed and dexterity

The manual states that this instrument may be used for several different purposes: the short form may serve as a screening test, and the complete battery may be used for making decisions about educational placement (such as physical education programming), assessing gross and fine motor skills, and developing and evaluating motor training programs.

Administration. The manual states that the test may be given by physical education teachers, special education teachers, occupational therapists, and others with training in assessment practices.

Scoring. Test items are given a raw score, which is converted to a point score through a conversion scale. Point scores are then converted to derived scores, including standard scores, percentile ranks, stanines, and age equivalents.

Standardization. There were 765 children who participated in the standardization of this instrument. African American children and children from other races were included but not in the same proportion represented by the 1970 census. (For example, 6.9% of the children were African American while 13.7% of the U.S. population in the 1970 census were African American.) There were an equal number of boys and girls representing eight age groups (4 years, 6 months to 5 years, 5 months; 5 years, 6 months to 6 years, 5 months; etc.). Children coming from communities of different sizes were represented in approximately the same proportion as the U.S. population in the 1970 census. Fifty percent of the sample came from the North Central region of the United States. No children came from the Northeast region; children from Ontario, Canada, were substituted for this region. No students with severe physical disabilities were included.

Reliability. Two forms or reliability, test–retest and interrater, were reported for the complete battery and for the short form. Test–retest reliability was reported only for children in grades 2 and 6. Coefficients ranged from .56 (Balance subtest) to .86 (Upper-limb Speed and Dexterity subtest). Test–retest reliability correlation for the short form was .86.

Interrater reliability studies were conducted on one subtest (Visual–Motor control subtest) of the complete battery with coefficients ranging from .79 to .97.

Validity.   Evidence of construct validity is reported by comparing behaviors measured in the eight subtests with those judged to be significant in the research cited in the manual.

Tests that purport to be useful in making educational decisions must present data that support this use. The manual cites three studies that compared performance of children who were developing typically with (1) children with mental retardation (ages 5 years, 11 months to 14 years) and with (2) children with learning disabilities (ages 5 years, 8 months to 12 years, 10 months). These studies found that children who are developing typically perform significantly better on all subtests except one (Response speed for children with learning disabilities). However, the manual cautions: "The evidence presented here must be viewed as necessarily incomplete, since additional studies are needed to delineate further the usefulness of the test with children having different types of handicaps" (p. 28).

Summary.   The Bruininks–Oseretsky Test of Motor Proficiency was designed to assess motor development for the purposes of making decisions about educational placement (such as physical education programming), assessing gross and fine motor skills, and developing and evaluating motor training programs. According to the manual, the short form may be used as a screening test; however, the manual provides no information concerning the reliability or validity of the short form for screening purposes. The use of this instrument for screening purposes should be undertaken with caution.

This standardized instrument is norm referenced, and a child's raw score may be reported as a standard score, a percentile rank, or a stanine. The norms of this instrument are dated. Reliability and validity studies are limited. This instrument should be used cautiously by the practitioner who needs a standardized instrument for assessing fine and gross motor development.

Peabody Developmental Motor Scales

The Peabody Developmental Motor Scales (Folio & Fewell, 1983) includes both a standardized test and an instructional packet of activity cards. The test measures fine and gross motor skills in children 1 month to 83 months. According to the manual, this instrument may also be used with children with disabilities who are chronologically older than seven years if their motor development is in the developmental age range of birth to seven years. The Peabody Developmental Motor Scales includes the assessment of fine motor skills (112 items) grouped into four skill clusters: grasping, hand use, eye–hand coordination, and manual dexterity. Gross motor skills (170 items) are grouped into five skill clusters: reflexes, balance, nonlocomotor, locomotor, and receipt and propulsion.

The instructional packet of activity cards suggests intervention activities related to each test item.

Administration.   This instrument is designed to be administered by teachers and other practitioners who will be working directly with the child. There are no items scored by interview or caregiver report.

Scoring.   Raw scores may be transformed into a percentile rank, a motor age equivalent, or a developmental motor quotient. The response form includes space to make comments about the child's performance. A motor development profile form can provide team members with a picture of the child's motor performance across each of the skill clusters.

Standardization.   The norming sample, which was representative in terms of geographic region and race, consisted of 617 children. This is a relatively small sample size, especially for the proportion of children who are African American or Hispanic.

Reliability.   Two types of reliability are reported. Test–retest reliability was adequate based on the retesting of 38 children. Interrater reliability coefficients were .99 for both fine and gross motor scales.

Validity.   Both construct and criterion-related validity are reported. In the criterion-related study, this instrument was compared with the Bayley Scales of Infant Development and with the West Haverstraw Motor Development Test. The correlations for the fine motor scale with the Bayley Scales were .36 and with the West Haverstraw Test were .62. Additional studies are needed.

Summary.   The Peabody Developmental Motor Scales assess fine and gross motor skills of young children through seven years of age. The scales include activity cards with suggested intervention activities. The standard scores of this test should be used with caution, since the norms were developed on a relatively small sample of children, especially children who are African American or Hispanic. Additional research would be helpful in verifying some of the preliminary information regarding reliability and validity. However, the detailed information regarding a child's fine and gross motor development may be helpful to practitioners in program planning.

Other Methods for Assessing Motor Development

Observation recording sheets may be helpful in monitoring the child's daily progress (Hanson & Harris, 1986,). Figure 12.3 shows an observation data sheet for a period of 10 days. The target skill is crossing midline, and each of the child's successes is recorded as a plus; nonattempts are recorded as minuses. The total number of pluses for each day is circled. Thus the parent or practitioner can readily see a profile of the child's skills.

Inability to cross midline is one of the areas noted in the following case study. This account of a preschool child illustrates the type of information included in an assessment report, which in this case was completed by the occupational therapist to help the team in planning the child's program.

CASE STUDY: RICHIE

Richie is four and a half years old and attends a preschool program in his community. He has an extensive medical history, and partial chromosomal abnormality is suspected. An occupational therapist who consults for the pro-

GOAL:

Brings hands to midline when prompted (facilitated) to assume sitting position.

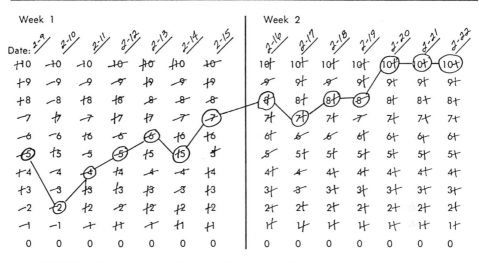

FIGURE 12.3 Data sheet for recording observations

SOURCE: From *Teaching the Young Child with Motor Delays* by Marci J. Hanson and Susan R. Harris. Austin, TX: Pro-Ed, Inc., 1986. Reprinted by permission.

gram recently completed the following assessment to help the team in planning Richie's program.

Sensorimotor Functioning. Richie does not cross midline during activities. During movement activities, he stiffens his body and lower trunk area (anterior tilt), which results in difficulties in balance and maintaining his body position in space. He compensates by protective extension (outstretched arms). Richie is also tactile defensive to soft materials.

Gross Motor. Richie can hop on two feet but has difficulty in walking along a taped line. He can catch a ball at 3 feet. Gross motor skills as measured by the Learning Accomplishment Profile are age appropriate.

Fine Motor. Richie shows a strong preference for using his right hand. He uses a palmar grasp when holding a crayon. He has some difficulty in applying a pincer grasp to small objects.

Adaptive. Mother reports that Richie is learning to dress himself but needs some assistance with buttons. He uses the toilet independently and can wash his hands with only an occasional reminder.

Summary

Richie's strengths are: gross motor skills within age-appropriate levels; learning to become independent in the areas of dressing, toileting, and washing.

Richie's needs are: fine motor difficulties; equilibrium reactions.

PREFERRED PRACTICES

Children with motor disabilities present special challenges in assessment. Information gathered through observation is an important addition to the use of formal instruments; home video recordings provide an important additional supplement.

In assessing cognitive and communication skills or overall development, practitioners must be alert to test items that require a motor response the child is unable to produce. Furthermore, if some test items have been omitted, the use of total scores will not accurately reflect the child's ability.

RESOURCES

The following organizations can provide additional information:

Association of Birth Defect Children
3526 Emerywood Lane
Orlando, FL 32812

Association of the Care of Children in
Hospitals
3615 Wisconsin Avenue
Washington, DC 20016

American Orthotic and Prosthetic Association
717 Pendelton Street
Alexandria, VA 22314

Child Amputee Prosthetic Project
University of California at Los Angeles
Los Angeles, CA 90032

Muscular Dystrophy Association
810 Seventh Avenue
New York, NY 10019

National Center for Therapeutic Riding
9244 East Mansfield Avenue
Denver, CO 80237

National Paraplegia Foundation
333 North Michigan Avenue
Chicago, IL 60601

United Cerebral Palsy Associations
66 East 34th Street
New York, NY 10016

Section 4: Assessing Children with Communication Needs

Key Terms

Communication. The transfer of information between two or more individuals.

Augmentative/Alternative Communication. The use of communication boards or synthesized speech systems for the purposes of communication.

Language. A system of symbols that are spoken, written, or expressed through manual signing to communicate meaning.

Expressive Language. Spoken language that must be verbalized if communication is to take place.

Receptive Language. Spoken language that must be understood if communication is to take place.

ASSESSING CHILDREN WITH COMMUNICATION DISABILITIES (INCLUDING SPEECH AND LANGUAGE IMPAIRMENTS)

What Is Communication?

Communication is the transfer of information between or among individuals; it may be verbal, such as the use of spoken language or a communication device that produces synthesized speech, or nonverbal, such as eye gaze or other physical movement, gestures, or signing. Young children with communication problems exhibit a wide range in ability levels: some experience only mild delays in language development, whereas others do not talk at all. Children with severe communication disabilities typically have other disabilities that affect their ability to communicate:

Categories of Impairment Frequently Accompanied by Severe Communication Disorders
Cognitive developmental delay

Sensory impairment

    Deaf

    Deaf–blind

Neurological impairment

    Cerebral palsy

    Aphasia

    Apraxia

    Learning disabilities

Emotional impairment

    Autism

    Childhood psychosis

Structural impairment (Adapted from Musselwhite & St. Louis, 1982)

Although children with developmental delays or other disabilities may share a common diagnostic classification, the degree of communication disability may vary widely. In fact, environmental influences play a major role in communication development. Kaiser, Alpert, and Warren (1988) stated, "Because individuals, even those with initially similar skills, experience widely varied environments, the specific characteristics of their communication skills may also vary" (p. 399).

Language and communication are sometimes used interchangeably; however, language is only one aspect of communication (Figure 12.4). Language is the use of symbols, which may be verbal (either spoken or produced through synthesized speech), manual (as in American Sign Language [ASL]; cued speech; or signed English), or written, to convey information. In this text, we will limit our discussion to the use of and assessment of verbal communication, that is, the expression of spoken or synthesized speech and the reception of spoken language.

Assessment of verbal communication focuses on a child's expressive language as well as receptive language. *Expressive language* refers to the child's ability to use

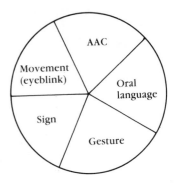

FIGURE 12.4 Various types of communication (AAC refers to alternative/augmentative communications)

words to communicate with others; *receptive language* refers to the child's understanding of the spoken language of others. Although spoken language is the primary mode of communication for persons without disabilities, many everyday interchanges involve a combination of other forms of communication. In fact, about 35% of our communication is verbal; 65% is nonverbal (Suddath & Susnik, 1991).

Individuals who are unable to produce spoken language may use equipment designed for *alternative/augmentative communications* (AAC). AAC refers to any method or device that assists communication. PL 101–476 (IDEA) defines the use of assistive technology as "any item, piece of equipment, or product system, whether acquired commercially off the shelf, modified, or customized, that is used to increase, maintain, or improve the functional capabilities of children" (*Federal Register,* 1992, Sec. 300.5). IDEA provides for the "functional evaluation" of a child with a disability and assistance in selecting, acquiring, and using an assistive technology device.

AAC may include simple homemade devices such as picture books or communications boards. These materials require the child to point to a picture symbol or spell letter by letter by using a finger, toe, or headstick.

In recent years, the use of synthesized speech in *voice output communication aids* (VOCA) has enabled children with severe communication disabilities to participate more fully with nondisabled peers. Children using VOCA may access the computer-based device in any number of ways: by pointing to pictures, by using a single switch, or by activating the device through eye gaze. These methods of access provide a wider range of input options than traditional communication books and boards. Frequently used messages may be stored in the communication device, which allows the user to access a prestored message with only one keystroke. Some systems have a word prediction feature for older children who are using written language. However, it is important to remember that VOCA is only a part of a child's communication system. VOCA users, as well as other people, use a variety of communication forms including gestures or eye gaze, eye blinks, and winks!

In the following section, we discuss some assumptions about communication and examine assessment of communication skills for children who use speech as well as children who will be using AAC and VOCA.

Assumptions about Communication

Kaiser, et al. (1988) described five basic assumptions regarding communication:

1. Communication is social in nature, and the purpose of the initiator's message is to affect the receiver's behavior.

2. Communication begins with the infant's nonverbal communicative interchanges with the caregiver.

   Typically, during the first 2 years of life, children progress from participating nonverbally in turn-taking interchanges with their caregivers, to signaling the caregiver by means of directed looking, gesture, vocalization, to using single words, and finally, to using linguistically complete multiword utterances. (p. 396)

3. Language is learned through the process of discrimination and generalization.

   Learning language depends on the ability to perceive, to organize, to associate, and to respond to complex visual and auditory stimuli. Thus, cognitive and perceptual processing skills are essential to language-learning. The efficiency and the breadth of learning will be influenced by the skills that the child brings to the social interaction in which language is learned and used. (p. 396)

4. More complex language skills are built upon early, simpler forms.

   The progression of communication moves from signals (e.g., cries) to the use of signs (e.g., systematic, consistent gesturing to indicate wants) to increasing complex linguistic forms. . . . Each step in this progression depends on the child's perceptual, cognitive, and social abilities at that point in time. A delay in any aspect of this triad may retard the language-learning process. (p. 396)

5. The reciprocal nature of language is an underlying factor, basic to language development. A child's responsiveness to communication attempts and conversely the response to the child of the caregiver, peer, or teacher alter the characteristics of the next interchange.

Key Terms

Phonology. The study of individual sounds that comprise words.

Morphology. The study of single units of letters, which comprise word meanings.

Syntax. The study of how words are combined to construct meaningful sentences.

Pragmatics. The study of the use of language in social situations.

General Types of Communication Disability

Communication disorders can be divided into three general types for assessment purposes: form, content, and use (Bloom & Lahey, 1978 cited by Kaiser et al., 1988).

Form.   Form relates to the structural properties of language. Children with articulation disorders often have difficulty in sound production. The term *phonology* describes the study of the system of sounds that comprise a language. The smallest units of sound that have meaning in a language are *phonemes*. The English language makes use of only about 45 different phonemes: The word "truck" is comprised of 4 phonemes (/T/R/U/K/). Substituting one phoneme for another and omitting phonemes are common characteristics of the speech of young children:

> Substitutions: wabbit for rabbit
>
> Omissions: car for cars

Morphology is the study of units of meaning in a language. The basic unit of meaning is a *morpheme*. Morphemes are basic words such as *house, car,* and *bracelet;* morphemes are also prefixes and suffixes, such as *re-, in-, -s,* and *-er*. Because morphemes are units of meaning, they are sometimes used to measure the level of a child's expressive language development. This is done by obtaining a sample of the child's language and counting the individual morphemes per speech utterance. The number of morphemes is totaled and divided by the number of speech utterances to obtain the average mean length of utterance (MLU). The following conversation was recorded during a 10-minute observation of free play.

> "My block . . ." (2 morphemes)
>
> "No, I want this." (4 morphemes)
>
> "You can be the driver." (6 morphemes [-er is a suffix])
>
> "Brrrr" (0 morphemes)

The MLU in the foregoing exchange is 12 divided by 4 or 3. Polloway and Smith (1992) state that although the MLU may be an oversimplification of the concept of spoken language, the unit is useful in comparing levels of linguistic development in children as well as measuring increases in individual mastery of expressive language. Other considerations that affect the MLU are the length of the observation needed to obtain an adequate language sample of speech utterances and the environment(s) to be observed.

Content.   Content relates to the meaning, or semantics, of language. *Semantics* refers to the system of the language that contains the rules of meaning. Development of semantics begins with association of single concrete morphemes—for example, the association of "mama" with a particular person. Development typically progresses to understanding complex utterances—for example, "Please get me the book." And later to understanding more complex language: "It's raining cats and dogs."

> Problems associated with the content dimension of language have been linked to limited learning about the perceptual and functional characteristics of objects, actions, and/or events and their relations, due to, for example, visual impairment, restrictions on mobility, and attentional and/or perceptual deficits and with more general deficits in learning abilities. (Kaiser et al., 1988, p. 400)

Furthermore, semantic ability is directly related to the experiences that children have in their everyday routines.

Use.   Use relates to pragmatics, or the ability to use language in a functional way. These skills include the ability to use language in taking turns, to enter into a conversation or discussion with other children (or adults), to continue the conversation, to interpret the meaning of the speaker, or to "read" the listener's nonverbal cues.

SCREENING LANGUAGE SKILLS

Informal assessment of language skills provides valuable information during the screening process as well as for program planning and monitoring. Polloway and Smith (1992) have identified the beginning skills in language acquisition that provide a framework for planning an informal assessment (Figure 12.5). Notice that gaining a child's attention and engaging in imitative behavior are considered to be initial steps in developing language skills.

Language probes are informal ways of measuring a child's language which take advantage of the natural environment. They are helpful in various stages of the assessment process and may be completed by several different members of the team, including parents. "Probes generally include a sampling of words, or sounds, that elicit specific information on a receptive or expressive skill" (Polloway & Smith, 1992, p. 133). Figure 12.6 illustrates language probes of several different types.

ASSESSMENT OF LANGUAGE SKILLS

The speech and language pathologist (SLP) does the primary planning of assessment of language skills, assisted by teachers and parents. Two factors should be considered in such planning. The first issue is the use of symbols. Many standardized tests use symbol recognition as a measure of the child's understanding of spoken or receptive language. A child's understanding of symbols moves from concrete to abstract. A test item that measures the child's understanding of common objects in the environment might include the task to "Point to the ball." The test developer must choose how to represent the object "ball," bearing in mind that some materials are more concrete than others. In the following list of possible test materials, how could the items be ordered from most concrete to most abstract?

Black and white line drawing of a ball

Actual ball

Photograph of a ball

In choosing an assessment instrument, the materials should be examined to determine whether they are developmentally appropriate for the children with whom they will be used.

A. Attention

  1. Remains seated for: 15 seconds _____
                             30 seconds _____
                             60 seconds _____
  2. Does not engage in interfering behavior during this time frame. _____
  3. Makes eye contact: "look at me" _____
                       name called _____

B. Imitation

  1. Motorically imitates clapping _____ (when told "do this") other movements _____
  2. Orally imitates: series of vowel sounds _____
  3. Orally imitates in response to commands: "Say this . . . ball (etc.)" for series of labels _____

C. Receptive Skills

  1. Responds to series of verbal commands calling for gross motor movements ("stand up") _____
  2. Responds to series of verbal commands calling for pointing ("point to ball") _____
  3. Responds to series of verbal commands pointing to pictures of agents, objects, and actions _____

D. Expressive Skills

  1. Responds to series of questions asking "What is this?"   object _____
                                   action _____
  2. Responds to series of questions about pictures asking "What is this?" with one-word response   object _____
                                   action _____
  3. Responds to series of questions about pictures asking "What is this?" with: "This is . . ."   two-word phrases _____
                       three-word phrases _____

E. Expansions

Shows receptive comprehension and expressive usage of:

  a. prepositional forms

in _____	to _____
on _____	into _____
under _____	with _____
by _____	from _____
for _____	

  b. adjective forms

big _____	numbers _____
little _____	other relevant
colors (list)	forms _____

  c. pronominal forms

I _____	himself _____
me _____	his _____
my _____	she _____
you _____	her _____
your _____	herself _____
he _____	they _____
him _____	them _____
other(s) _____	themselves _____

  d. alternative verb forms

past tense _____	subject–verb
future tense _____	agreement _____
to be verbs _____	
-ing verbs _____	other(s) _____

  e. negative forms

no _____	contractions
not _____	won't _____
none _____	don't _____
	other(s) _____

  f. interrogative forms

who _____	reversals:
what _____	is _____
when _____	does _____
where _____	will _____
why _____	did _____
how _____	tags _____

FIGURE 12.5 Initial language skills

SOURCE: From *Language Instruction for Students with Disabilities* (2nd ed., p. 132) by E. A. Polloway and T. E. C. Smith, 1992, Denver: Love Publishing. Reprinted by permission.

The second factor to consider is the response the child will use. Before the actual assessment begins, the practitioner will need to ensure that the child not only understands how to respond but is physically able to make such a response. Church and Glennen (1992) suggest that before the assessment begins, the examiner place a set of materials in front of the child, point to one of the objects, and ask the child to also point. This procedure assures that the child is able to make the response before

Sample Probes

1. Labeling—Select six common objects. Present each to the child three times and ask, "What is this?" Criteria: 2 of 3 for each object.

2. Imitation—Present a series of vowel sounds to child orally and use the directions, "Say _____." Criteria: 2 of 3 for each sound.

3. Receptive Vocabulary—Select six common objects and present each to the child three times with the directions, "Give me _____." Criteria: 2 of 3 for each object.

4. Two-Word Phrases—Present a series of pictures to the child and have him or her point to the correct one when given specific directions such as "Show me—boy run." Criteria: 2 of 3 for each item.

FIGURE 12.6   Sample language probes

SOURCE: From *Language Instruction for Students with Disabilities* (2nd ed., p. 136) by E. A. Polloway and T. E. C. Smith, 1992, Denver: Love Publishing. Reprinted by permission.

the actual assessment is begun. If the child is unable to make the response, Church and Glennen (1992) suggest several strategies:

1. Cut the stimulus items apart and spread them further or closer together as needed.
2. Using the cut stimulus pictures, see if eye gaze or another direct selection method can be used for responding.
3. Using the cut stimulus items, reduce the number of choices required for the pointing response. (p. 113)

Receptive language is best assessed by using standardized or nonstandardized tools in a multiple-choice format. The child uses a pointing response (or other response mode if unable to point) to indicate her choice. Children should be given ample time to make a response. For some children, response time may be very delayed; practitioners need to be sure that the child has adequate time to make a response.

The use of symbols on a test and the response mode the child uses to indicate a choice are two particularly salient factors in the assessment of receptive language skills. However, they are also important factors to remember in general assessment practices.

Assessment of expressive language involves determining the level of development of the child's use of verbal language. A common error in assessing expressive language is neglecting to consider the child's need or desire to communicate. A child must have a reason for using language as well as for wanting to respond. One useful method of collecting information is a language sample. Teachers and parents may collect samples of the child's language during the different daily routines and activities. Samples of the child's language may be tape-recorded or written on a chart. Since communication is a two-way activity, some of the information collected should include examples of dyadic interaction. In fact, the type of communication of the caregiver, teacher, or other child is very important in assessing the target child's utterances, requests, or responses.

This informal information can be used alone or in conjunction with the more formal assessment typically conducted by the speech and language pathologist. In the following section, we examine some of these common standardized instruments for assessing a children's language.

STANDARDIZED INSTRUMENTS FOR ASSESSING LANGUAGE DEVELOPMENT

Expressive One-Word Picture Vocabulary Test— Revised (EOWPVT-R)

The Expressive One-Word Picture Vocabulary Test—Revised (EOWPVT-R) (Gardner, 1990) was developed for the purpose of obtaining a basal estimate of the expressive language of children. The test may be used for children ages two through twelve years. According to the examiner's manual, the test also gives information regarding speech defects, learning disorders, a bilingual child's fluency in English, auditory processing, and auditory–visual–verbal association ability (Gardner, 1990). The test can be administered in Spanish to assess Spanish vocabulary; however, only the English version is addressed here. The test material consists of black line drawings on 7 inch by 8 inch test plates.

Administration.   The test may be administered by teachers, speech therapists, and other professionals. The test is individually administered and untimed. The amount of time to administer varies between children, of course, but ranges between 7 and 15 minutes. Children are allowed only one response for each item.

Scoring.   All responses, both right and wrong, are written down in the individual record form. This allows examiners to evaluate the child's speech and analyze incorrect responses. The basal level is eight consecutive correct responses. The ceiling level is the last item of six consecutive incorrect responses. The raw score is computed by adding the number of correct responses, including all responses below the basal level as correct. From the raw score several types of derived score may be obtained, including age equivalent, standard scores, scaled scores, percentile ranks, and stanines. The manual also includes helpful information regarding the use of derived scores.

Standardization.   The revised edition was normed on 1,118 children ages two to twelve years in the San Francisco Bay Area. There were about equal numbers of boys and girls represented in the sample. The examiner's manual does not provide information regarding sampling procedures except that children "were enrolled in parochial schools, private schools, public schools, and nursery schools. Some children who were too young to be in any school program were tested in their homes or in an office" (Gardner, 1990, p. 8). There was no further description of the sample such as parent's education level, socioeconomic status, or ethnicity.

Reliability.   Split-half reliability for each age level is reported and ranges from .84 to .92 with a median reliability of .90.

Validity.   Content validity was addressed by selecting all 110 items of the original Expressive One-Word Picture Vocabulary Test (1979) and adding 33 new items. Words were chosen that would "be considered common in the home and those that are usually learned through formal education" (Gardner, 1990, p. 8). No information is given about the individuals or group who chose the words.

Criterion-related validity was addressed by correlating scores of the EOWPVT-R with the vocabulary subtests of the Wechsler (WPPSI-R or WISC-R) and Peabody (PPVT-R) tests. Correlation with the PPVT-R was .59; correlations with the vocabulary subtests of both the Wechsler tests were slightly lower. In a 1991 study, correlations with the PPVT-R ranged from .54 to .79 across age groups, with an overall correlation of .69.

Summary.   The EOWPVT-R provides a measure of a child's basic expressive vocabulary that may be expressed in standard scores. The test may be used with children ages two through twelve and is relatively easy to administer and score. The test has been designed to be administered in a relatively short time (7 to 15 minutes, approximately); and children are asked to give only a one-word response to each of the items on the test plates. The black line drawings on these plates may not hold a young child's interest. The test results allow the examiner to compare the child's performance with the norming sample and to analyze the oral responses for articulation or other problems.

Caution is recommended in using the EOWPVT-R because of limited information about the norming sample as well as the limited geographic distribution of the sample itself. Some of the important variables that may affect language, such as the education, socioeconomic status, and first language of the parents, have not been addressed. In addition, since all the children came from one area of California, the scores from this sample may not be representative of children in other areas.

Peabody Picture Vocabulary Test—Revised

The Peabody Picture Vocabulary Test—Revised (Dunn & Dunn, 1981) is designed to measure receptive language (vocabulary) for children age 2 years, 6 months to 40 years. The test consists of a series of pictures or test plates. Each plate has four pictures, and children are asked to point to the one that best tells the meaning of the word. For example, the beginning items for children ages 2 years, 6 months through 3 years, 5 months are *bus, hand, bed, tractor,* and *closet.*

Administration.   This instrument has two forms, Form L and Form M. Instruments with alternate forms are important to examiners who are going to be using the same instrument with the child on subsequent occasions. For example, a child may be given the test before beginning a program and retested at the end of the year.

After choosing one of the forms, the examiner determines the starting point by finding the child's age band and beginning with the first item in that band.

Scoring.   The basal point is the highest of eight correct responses; the ceiling point is the lowest of eight consecutive responses containing six errors. Test items are marked as pass or fail. Raw scores may be converted to standard scores, percentile ranks, or stanines.

Standardization.   The norming sample consisted of 4,200 children ages 2 years, 6 months through 18 years, 11 months. The sample was stratified by geographic location, community size, occupation, and race.

Reliability.   Two types of reliability are reported: internal consistency and alternate form reliability. Internal consistency reliability coefficients are derived by comparing a person's performance on different parts of the test, such as odd versus even numbered test items. Internal consistency data were examined for all children who participated in the standardization sample. The coefficients ranged from .67 to .88 on Form L and from .61 to .86 on Form M.

Alternate form reliability was computed by administering both forms to more than 600 children in the norming sample. The reliabilities ranged from .71 to .89.

Validity.   The test manual provides evidence to support construct validity. No information is reported on criterion-related validity, although the test manual states that this issue will be addressed in future printings.

Summary.   The Peabody Picture Vocabulary Test—Revised is a standardized instrument for assessing receptive language skills in children, youth, and adults from age 2 years, 6 months to over 18 years of age. The instrument is well normed; however, the PPVT-R will need to be updated and restandardized in the near future. Future editions should provide additional information concerning validity.

Preschool Language Scale—3

The Preschool Language Scale—3 (PLS-3) (Zimmerman, Steiner, & Pond, 1992) is designed to measure language acquisition and prelanguage skills in children birth to 6 years, 11 months. The test includes two subscales: for auditory comprehension and for expressive communication (which includes preverbal communication skills). This revision is the first time the PLS has been standardized. The test also includes a Spanish-language version, based on research results on Spanish-speaking children in the United States.

Administration.   This instrument takes approximately 20 to 30 minutes to administer.

Scoring.   Scores are reported as standard scores and percentile ranks by age. Language age equivalents may also be calculated.

Standardization.   Approximately 1,200 children from ages 2 weeks to 6 years, 11 months participated in the standardization sample. The sample was stratified on race, parent education level, and geographic region. In terms of these variables (race, parent education level, and geographic representation) the sample approximated the census of 1980.

Reliability.   Three types of reliability are reported: internal consistency, test–retest, and interrater reliability. Internal consistency coefficients for the total language scores ranged from .74 (children birth to 2 months) to .94 (children 3 years, 6 months to 3 years, 11 months). The two subscales also generally fall within this range except for auditory comprehension in children birth to 2 months (.47).

Test–retest reliability coefficients were high for children ages three to five (total language score coefficients .91 to .94). No reliability studies were reported on younger children.

Interrater reliability was very high (.98).

Validity.   Three types of validity are reported: content, construct, and concurrent validity. The authors state that the language skills tested by the PLS-3 are well documented in the literature, and several references are cited.

Construct validity was assessed in two ways. First an attempt was made to determine whether the instrument differentiated between children ages three to five years with no language needs and children with language disorders. The PLS-3 correctly identified three-year-olds as language disordered or non-language disordered 66% of the time; four-year-olds 80% of the time; and five-year-olds 70% of the time. Concurrent validity studies compared the PLS-3 with several standardized instruments (Denver II, Preschool Language Scale—Revised, and Clinical Evaluation of Language Fundamentals—Revised). Correlations ranged from .66 to .88.

Summary.   The Preschool Language Scale—3 is a standardized instrument for measuring preverbal and language skills in young children ages birth to 6 years, 11 months. The norming sample represents the 1980 census on several important variables including race, parent education level, and geographic region of the country. Reliability studies report good internal consistency and high test–retest and interrater reliability coefficients. The authors also report several validity studies. Construct validity studies found the instrument to be moderately successful in identifying children who had been assessed as language disordered. The PLS-3 is a well-normed instrument, which the practitioner may use with a certain degree of confidence.

Receptive–Expressive Emergent Language Test

The Receptive–Expressive Emergent Language Test (REEL-2) (Bzoch & League, 1991) is a checklist designed to identify receptive and expressive language problems in children from birth through age two. The instrument consists of four different levels of language development: phonemic (birth to 3 months), morphemic (3 to 8 months), syntactic (9 to 18 months), and semantic (18 to 36 months). These levels are further subdivided by age: for example, 0 to 1 month; 1 to 2 months, and so on. Each subdivision includes three receptive language and three expressive language test items. According to the manual, the REEL-2 may be used to screen, to assist in clinical diagnosis, or to aid in planning an intervention program.

Administration.   The REEL-2 may be completed by the examiner during an interview with the child's parents.

Scoring.   Items are scored as a typical behavior (+), a behavior that is emerging (+ −), or a behavior that has not yet been observed (−). A receptive language age and an expressive language age are obtained by recording the highest interval in which two out three test items received a plus (+). These scores can be converted into a combined language age or language quotients (receptive quotient, expressive quotient, or combined language quotient).

Standardization.   According to the manual, the infants who participated in the normative sample group were "selected to represent the probable norm of environmentally language-advantaged Caucasian infants. The normative sample group was selected to be free from any known sensory or organic disabilities and to come from families with habitually rich linguistic stimulation patterns" (p. 7). The number of infants who participated was not stated.

Reliability.   Two types of reliability are reported. Internal consistency for both the receptive and expressive sections is high (.95). Two test–retest reliability studies were reported. In the first study of 28 infants, the retest was completed after a 3-week interval. The study defined agreement as within plus or minus one age interval. Using this criterion, agreement between administrators ranged from 90 to 100%.

A second study of 46 children conducted several days apart yielded a receptive quotient of .79, an expressive quotient of .76, and a language quotient of .80.

Validity.   Several types of validity are addressed. Content validity entails the issue of whether the test items cover a representational sample of the area. The manual reports that test items were selected by a search of the literature and reconfirmed through "laboratory tests." No further information is given. A study of concurrent validity is mentioned but the text does not include enough information to be helpful.

Summary.   The Receptive–Expressive Emergent Language Test (REEL-2) is designed for children from birth through two years old and uses parent report to assess the child's development of receptive and expressive language. The test lacks information regarding the sources used to establish the developmental ages of test items. This is important information to the potential user who may be considering this instrument for screening or diagnostic purposes. In addition, the characteristics of the normative sample are not representative of the general population. This circumstance deepens our concerns regarding the use of this instrument for screening or diagnostic purposes.

Sequenced Inventory of Communication Development (SICD)

The Sequenced Inventory of Communication Development (SICD) (Hedrick, Prather, & Tobin, 1984) assesses the child's expressive and receptive language including the semantic, syntactic, and pragmatic processes as defined by the behavioral and processing models of communication described in the manual. The SICD also includes parental report items. This instrument was designed for children ages 4 through 48 months. The test materials consist of a variety of small toys and other objects that may be of high interest to young children.

Some work has been completed using the SICD with children from other cultures. The earlier instrument (1975) has been translated into Spanish with revisions but has not been standardized on Spanish-speaking children. The earlier version has been modified and standardized on Yup'ik Eskimo children.

Administration.   This instrument may be administered by a teacher or speech and language pathologist. The instrument was standardized with one parent, usually the mother, present. A basal level is three consecutive correct responses; a ceiling is obtained when three consecutive responses are incorrect.

Scoring.   Test items are scored by circling *Yes* or *No* on the response sheet. Many items not passed on the first trial may be attempted again. Parent report items are scored as either *Yes* or *No* based on what the parent reports about the child's current behavior in the home. Scores yield a receptive communication age (RCA) and an expressive communication age (ECA), which are reported in months.

Standardization.   The original standardization sample consisted of 252 Caucasian children from the greater Seattle area. The sample included children from three social classes defined by education and occupation. A child was excluded if his language development was judged abnormal by his parents, if he came from a bilingual home, if his hearing was suspect or if there were known ear pathologies, or if he had any visible physical or developmental disabilities. The manual reports the results of another study by Allen and Bliss conducted with 609 children in Detroit. These children, ages 31 to 48 months, were divided by social class, and included both Caucasian ($n = 333$) and African American ($n = 276$) children. The manual includes separate norms based on the work by Allen and Bliss for use in evaluating African American children.

   The SICD was also standardized on 167 preschool Yup'ik Eskimo children. As a result, culturally appropriate test items were retained and other items were modified or substituted. The manual gives an interesting, detailed explanation of the changes.

Reliability.   Several indexes of reliability were reported. Interrater reliability by two examiners was .96. Test–retest reliability was conducted with 10 subjects and average agreement was 92.8 percent.

Validity.   Criterion-related validity with the Peabody Picture Vocabulary Test ranged from .75 to .80.

Summary.   The Sequenced Inventory of Communication Development is based on a model of communication in which behaviors other than oral speech alone are used to address receptive skills and communication is viewed in the context of interaction between the child and materials or other individuals. Parent (or caregiver) input is solicited. The test materials are toys and objects that may be interesting to most young children as well as children who are hard to test. The authors have attempted to address the concerns raised by the limited Seattle sample, which consisted entirely of Caucasian children, by including information regarding field testing with both Caucasian and African American children in Detroit. However, caution should be employed when using the norms with children who may differ from the sample group.

Test of Early Language Development—2 (TELD-2)

The Test of Early Language Development—2 (TELD-2) (Hresko, Reid, & Hammill, 1991) was designed to assess early language development including receptive and expressive language, syntax, and semantics in children 2 years, 0 months through 7 years, 11 months of age. According to the manual, the TELD-2 can be used to:

> Identify children who are significantly below other children of the same age in early language development

Identify a child's strengths and weaknesses

Document a child's progress

Aid in planning instruction

The TELD-2 consists of 136 items, which are divided into alternate forms (A and B) of 68 items each. Depending on the child's age and ability, test administration time ranges from 15 to 40 minutes. Young children may be given breaks or may be allowed to complete the test in more than one session. The test materials are found in a picture book (Form A or B), which contains black line drawings on 8½ inch by 11 inch pages.

Administration.   According to the manual, professionals who administer this test should have supervised practice in using language tests in addition to formal training in administering and interpreting assessment instruments. Suggested prompts are listed for the examiner, for use when appropriate. In addition, suggested changes are indicated to accommodate for dialect and/or regional variation.

Scoring.   Test items are scored as either correct (1 point) or incorrect (0 points). The basal level is the point at which the child passes five items in a row; the ceiling is the point at which the child misses five consecutive items. The correct responses are totaled, and the raw score may be converted into a language quotient (LQ), percentile rank, normal curve equivalent, or age equivalent.

Standardization.   The norming sample consisted of 1,329 children who lived in the Northeast, North Central, South, and West. The characteristics of the sample were similar to the characteristics of the U.S. population as reported in the 1990 census. These characteristics include gender, urban and rural residence, race, parental occupation, and ethnicity.

Reliability.   Several types of reliability are reported. Internal consistency reliability for the entire sample exceeded .90 for each of the age groups. Both alternate form and test–retest reliability coefficients were high (.97 to .98).

Validity.   The manual addresses content, criterion-related, and construct validity. With respect to content validity, the authors discuss the model underlying the development of this instrument. After the test items had been developed, an experimental edition and several revisions were given to samples of children in New Jersey and Texas.

The manual reports several criterion-related validity studies using scores from both forms (A and B) of the TELD-2. This instrument was compared with other tests including the Test of Language Development—2 Primary, the Receptive–Expressive Emergent Language, the Preschool Language Scale, and the Peabody Picture Vocabulary Test. Coefficients ranged from .47 to .66.

Construct validity studies compared scores on the TELD-2 to chronological age and experience, intelligence, and academic ability. These studies found that the TELD-2 means increase with age and that the scores correlate positively both with intelligence tests and with abilities related to academics.

Summary.   The Test of Early Language Development—2 assesses language development in children ages 2 years, 0 months through 7 years, 11 months. The test measures receptive, expressive, syntax, and semantic skills. The norming sample appears to adequately reflect the general U.S. population. Validity and reliability measures of several types are reported, and all are moderate to high. This test should be considered when selecting a formal instrument to assess language development in young children.

Assessment for AAC and VOCA

Children who are nonvocal may be assessed for AAC or VOCA. The assessment and selection of a specific communication device should be made by the team: family members and practitioners in the fields of communication and language, occupational/physical therapy, and education. The assessment of an individual child for an augmentative/alternative communication device depends on a number of factors (Beukelman & Yorkston, 1982), including chronological age, imitative ability, motor control, cognitive ability, and visual needs. The relevant components of motor control include:

1. *Range of motion:* What input areas of the communication device can the child easily reach?
2. *Type of response:* Can the child make a direct selection, or should the device scan the areas of choice?
3. *Accuracy of response:* Does the layout of the communication area permit the child to respond without making unnecessary errors?

There are a number of different factors to consider when assessing a child for AAC. Some of the key questions that are appropriate to young children are included in the following list.

Checklist for Assessment of an Augmentative/Alternative Communication Device for a Young Child

1. What are the different environments in which the child spends portions of each day?
2. What types of communication does the child presently use?
3. How well do others understand each of these types?
4. During a typical day:
   a. With whom *might* the child *interact?*
   b. What are some messages the child *might use?*
5. How could additional opportunities to communicate be provided:
   a. By modifying the present system?
   b. By using another device?

CAVEAT IN ASSESSING COMMUNICATION SKILLS

Children with autism or communication disabilities related to similar conditions present special challenges. One should be extremely cautious in assessing communication development and in identifying prerequisite skills, as well as in drawing any conclusions. Children with disabilities of these types are often difficult to reach; they may have poor—or excellent—receptive language skills but show little indication of such. These children may experience great difficulty with expressive language; in fact, many children are nonverbal. Recent reports concerning the use of a facilitated communication offer the possibility of increasing the assistance given to nonverbal children (Biklen, 1990; Goad, 1992; Saks, 1993; Staff, 1990). In *facilitated communication* a nonverbal individual works with a parent, teacher, or friend in accessing a communication aid such as a communication board or voice output communication aid.

CASE STUDY: JOHN

Up until this past spring, seven-year-old John did not communicate with anyone. "Even for me to touch him," [his mother recalls,] "I would have to tell him in advance 'I'm going to touch you now' or else he would start screaming." (Goad, 1992, p. 14A). John spent much of his time pacing or twiddling his fingers. Often he seemed to be spinning out of control.

But both John's mother and his teacher believed that occasionally they saw glimpses of potential in the little boy who usually tormented their home and classroom. This spring, two things happened. John was put on medication, and his teacher began using facilitated communication. In using this technique, the facilitator supports the child's hand. This enables the child to point to letters in order to communicate to others. The support is decreased gradually over time. Eventually, an individual may need only the facilitator's hand lightly placed on the shoulder for emotional support to assist in communicating thoughts and feelings.

FIGURE 12.7 John and his mother

SOURCE: Jack Milton, staff photographer. *Maine Sunday Telegram,* Portland, ME.

At first John did not appear to be interested in using this technique with his teacher. Then one day that changed. He had accidentally been given too much medication and was crying. He pulled his teacher to the computer. As she supported his hand, he typed, "CALL MOM CALL MOM JOHN GO HOME" (Goad, 1992, 14A). This first contact was the major turning point. John's mother and teacher soon learned that not only could he read, he had been absorbing much information from his environment.

RESOURCES

The following organizations can provide additional information:

American Speech–Language–Hearing
    Association
10801 Rockville Pike
Rockville, MD 20852

Division for Children with Communication Disorders
Council for Exceptional Children
1920 Association Drive
Reston, VA 22091

International Society for Augmentative
    and Alternative Communication
    (ISAAC)
P.O. Box 1762 Station R
Toronto, Ontario, M4G 4A3
Canada

John Tracy Clinic
806 West Adams Boulevard
Los Angeles, CA 90087

Ski-Hi Institute
Department of Communicative
    Disorders
Utah State University
Logan, UT 84322

REFERENCES

American Speech–Language–Hearing Association. (1985). Guidelines for identification audiometry. *ASHA, 27,* 49–53.

Amochaev, A. (1987). The infant hearing foundation—A unique approach to hearing screening of newborns. *Seminars of Hearing, 8,* 165–168.

Anderson, K. L. (1989). *Screening instrument for targeting educational risk.* Austin, TX: Pro-Ed.

Anderson, S., Davis, K., & Boigion, S. (1991). *The Oregon project for visually impaired and blind preschool children* (5th ed.). Medford, OR: Jackson Educational Service District.

Barnes, M. R., Crutchfield, C. A., Heriza, C. B., & Herdman, S. J. (1990). *Reflex and vestibular aspects of motor control.* Atlanta: Stokesville Publishing.

Barraga, N. C. (Ed.). (1980). *Program to develop efficiency in visual functioning: Diagnostic assessment procedure (DAP).* Louisville, KY: American Printing House for the Blind.

Beukelman, D. R., & Yorkston, K. M. (1982). Speech and language disorders. In F. J. Kottke, G. K. Stillwell, & J. F. Lehmann (Eds.), *Krusen's handbook of physical medicine and rehabilitation* (pp. 102–123). Philadelphia: Saunders.

Biklen, D. (1990). Communication unbound: Autism and praxis. *Harvard Educational Review, 60*(3), 291–314.

Bobath, K., & Bobath, B. (1972). Cerebral palsy. In P. H. Peterson & C. E. Williams (Eds.), *Physical therapy services in the developmental disabilities.* Springfield, IL: Charles C. Thomas.

Bradley-Johnson, S. (1986). *Psychoeducational assessment of visually impaired and blind students.* Austin, TX: Pro-Ed.

Bradley-Johnson, S., & Evans, L. D. (1991). *Psychoeducational assessment of hearing-impaired students.* Austin, TX: Pro-Ed.

Brill, R. G., MacNeil, B., & Newman, L. R. (1986). Framework for appropriate programs for deaf children: Conference of educational administrators serving the deaf. *American Annals of the Deaf, 131,* 65–77.

Bruininks, R. H. (1978). *Bruininks–Oseretsky test of motor proficiency.* Circle Pines, MN: American Guidance Service.

Bunch, G. O. (1981a). *Test of expressive language ability.* Weston, Ont., Canada: G. B. Services.

Bunch, G. O. (1981b). *Test of receptive language ability.* Weston, Ont., Canada: G. B. Services.

Bzoch, K. R., & League, R. (1991). *Receptive–expressive emergent language test—2.* Austin, TX: Pro-Ed.

Church, G., & Glennen, S. (1992). *The handbook of assistive technology.* San Diego, CA: Singular Publishing Group.

Connor, F. P., Williamson, G. G., & Siepp, J. M. (Eds.). (1978). *Program guide for infants and toddlers with neuromotor and other developmental disabilities.* New York: Teachers College Press.

Cook, R. E., Tessier, A., & Klein, M. D. (1992). *Adapting early childhood curricula for children with special needs.* New York: Merrill.

Division for the Visually Handicapped. (1991). *Statements of position.* Reston, VA: Council for Exceptional Children.

Dunn, L. M., & Dunn, L. (1981). *Peabody picture vocabulary test—Revised.* Circle Pines, MN: American Guidance Service.

Engen, E., & Engen, T. (1983). *Rhode Island test of language structure.* Austin, TX: Pro-Ed.

Federal Register (Vol. 57, No. 189, pp. 44794–44852). Washington, DC: Government Printing Office, September 29, 1992.

Ferrell, K. A. (1986). Infancy and early childhood. In G. T. Scholl (Ed.), *Foundations of education for blind and visually handicapped children* (pp. 119–135). New York: American Foundation for the Blind.

Fitch, J. L., Williams, T. F., & Etienne, J. E. (1982). A community-based high risk register for hearing loss. *Journal of Speech and Hearing Disorders, 47,* 373–375.

Folio, R., & Fewell, R. R. (1983). Peabody developmental motor scales and activity cards. Allen, TX: DLM Teaching Resources.

Frank, T. (1991). Assessment of hearing difficulties. In J. Salvia & J. E. Ysseldyke (Eds.), *Assessment* (pp. 240–261). Boston: Houghton Mifflin.

Gardner, E. F., Rudman, H. C., Karlsen, B., & Merwin, J. C. (1982). *Stanford achievement test* (7th ed.). San Antonio, TX: Psychological Corporation.

Gardner, M. F. (1990). *Expressive one-word picture vocabulary test—Revised.* Novato, CA: Academic Therapy.

Garrity, J., & Mengle, H. (1983). Early identification of hearing loss: Practices and procedures. *American Annals of the Deaf, 128*(2), 99–106.

Goad, M. (1992, July 12). Computer helps break silent wall surrounding autistic Lewiston boy. *The Maine Sunday Telegram,* pp. 1A, 14A.

Guess, D., & Noonan, M. J. (1982). *Evaluating neurodevelopmental theory and training with cerebral palsied, severely handicapped students. Final report.* Lawrence, KS: University of Kansas, Dept. of Special Education.

Hall, A., Scholl, G. T., & Swallow, R. (1986). Psychoeducational assessment. In G. T. Scholl (Ed.). *Foundations of education for blind and visually handicapped children* (pp. 187–214). New York: American Foundation for the Blind.

Hanson, M. J., & Harris, S. R. (1986). *Teaching the young child with motor delays.* Austin, TX: Pro-Ed.

Hedrick, D. L., Prather, E. M., & Tobin, A. R. (1984). *Sequenced inventory of communication development.* Seattle: University of Washington Press.

Hill, E. (1992). Instruction in orientation and mobility skills for students with visual handicaps. *DVH Quarterly, 37*(2), 25–26.

Hiskey, M. S. (1966). *Nebraska test of learning aptitude.* Lincoln, NE: M. S. Hiskey.

Hopkins, H. L., & Smith, H. D. (Eds.). (1988). *Willard and Spackman's occupational therapy* (7th ed.). Philadelphia: Lippincott.

Hresko, W. P., Reid, D. K., & Hammill, D. D. (1991). *Test of early language development.* Austin, TX: Pro-Ed.

Jones, M. H. (1978). Consideration in assessment. In F. P. Connor, G. G. Williamson, & J. M. Siepp (Eds.), *Program guide for infants and toddlers with neuromotor and other developmental disabilities.* New York: Teachers College Press.

Kaiser, A. P., Alpert, C. L., & Warren, S. F. (1988). Language and communication disorders. In V. B. Van Hasselt, P. S. Strain, and M. Hersen (Eds.), *Handbook of developmental and physical disabilities.* New York: Pergamon Press.

Katona, F. (1989). Clinical neuro-developmental diagnosis and treatment. In P. R. Zelazo and R. G. Barr (Eds.), *Challenges to developmental paradigms: Implications for theory, assessment, and treatment.* Hillsdale, NJ: Lawrence Erlbaum Associates.

Kaufman, A., & Kaufman, N. (1983). *Kaufman assessment battery for children.* Circle Pines, MN: American Guidance Service.

Knott, M., & Voss, D. E. (1968). *Proprioceptive neuromuscular facilitation: Patterns and techniques* (2nd ed.). New York: Harper & Row.

Kottke, F. J. (1982). Therapeutic exercise to develop neuromuscular coordination. In F. J. Kottke, G. K. Stillwell, & J. F. Lehmann (Eds.), *Krusen's handbook of physical medicine and rehabilitation* (pp. 403–426). Philadelphia: Saunders.

Layton, T. L., & Holmes, D. W. (1985). *Carolina picture vocabulary test.* Austin, TX; Pro-Ed.

Lighthouse Low Vision Services (1970). *New York Lighthouse symbol flash cards.* Available from the New York Lighthouse, 111 East 59th Street, New York, NY 10022.

Lutz, G. E., Stuart, M. J., & Sim, F. H. (1990). Rehabilitative techniques for athletes after reconstruction of the anterior cruciate ligament. *Mayo Clinic Proceedings, 65*: 1322–1329.

Madell, J. R. (1990). Audiological evaluation of the mainstreamed hearing-impaired child. In M. Ross (Ed.), *Hearing-impaired children in the mainstream* (pp. 27–44). Baltimore: York.

Mahoney, T. M., & Eichwald, J. G. (1987). The "ups" and "downs" of high-risk hearing screening: The Utah statewide program. *Seminars of Hearing, 8,* 155–163.

Martin, F. N. (1991). *Introduction to audiology* (4th ed.). Englewood Cliffs, NJ: Prentice-Hall.

McFarland, W. H., Simmons, F. B., & Jones, F. R. (1980). An automated hearing screening technique for newborns. *Journal of Speech and Hearing Disorders, 45,* 495–503.

Moog, J. S., & Geers, A. E. (1980). *Grammatical analysis of elicited language: Complex sentence level.* St. Louis, MO: Central Institute for the Deaf.

Moog, J. S., & Geers, A. E. (1985). *Grammatical analysis of elicited language: Simple sentence level.* St. Louis, MO: Central Institute for the Deaf.

Moog, J. S., Kozak, V. J., & Geers, A. E. (1983). *Grammatical analysis of elicited language: Pre-sentence level.* St. Louis, MO: Central Institute for the Deaf.

Moores, D. (1987). *Educating the deaf: Psychology, principles, and practices* (3rd ed.). Boston: Houghton Mifflin.

Musselwhite, C. R., & St. Louis, K. W. (1982). *Communication programming for the severely handicapped: Vocal and nonvocal strategies.* San Diego, CA: College-Hill Press.

National Society to Prevent Blindness (1991). *Snellen eye chart with "E".* Schaumburg, IL: National Society to Prevent Blindness, 500 East Remington Road.

Neisworth, J. T., & Bagnato, S. J. (1987). *The young exceptional child.* New York: Macmillan.

Osternig, L. R., Robertson, R., Troxel, R., & Hansen, P. (1987). Muscle activation during proprioceptive neuromuscular facilitation (PNF) stretching techniques. *American Journal of Physical Medicine, 66* (5), 298–307.

Pawelski, C. (June 1992). Personal communication with Christine Pawelski, Early Childhood Consultant, American Foundation for the Blind.

Polloway, E. A., & Smith, T. E. C. (1992). *Language instruction for students with disabilities.* Denver, CO: Love.

Reid, D. K., Hresko, W. P., Hammill, D. D., & Wiltshire, S. (1991). *Test of early reading ability– Deaf or hard of hearing.* Austin, TX: Pro-Ed.

Roeser, R. J., & Price, D. R. (1981). Audiometric and impedance measures: Principles and interpretation. In R. J. Roeser & M. P. Downs (Eds.), *Auditory disorders in school children* (pp. 71–101). New York: Thieme-Stratton.

Ross, M., Brackett, D., & Maxon, A. B. (1991). *Assessment and management of mainstreamed hearing-impaired children.* Austin, TX: Pro-Ed.

Saks, J. B. (1993, Spring). New approach stirs hope, controversy. *Counterpoint,* pp. 1, 7.

Salvia, J., & Ysseldyke, J. E. (1991). *Assessment.* Boston: Houghton Mifflin.

Scherer, P. (1981). *Total communication receptive vocabulary test.* Northbrook, IL: Mental Health and Deafness Resources.

Semmler, C. J., & Hunter, J. G. (1990). *Early occupational therapy intervention: Neonates to three years.* Gaithersburg, MD: Aspen.

Smith, A. J., & Johnson, R. E. (1977). *Smith–Johnson Nonverbal Performance Scale.* Los Angeles: Western Psychological Services.

Sparrow, S., Balla, D. A., & Cicchetti, D. V. (1984). *Vineland adaptive behavior scales.* Circle Pines, MN: American Guidance Service.

Staff. (1990). Surprising success reported with facilitated communication. *Autism Research Review International, 4*(4), 1–2.

Suddath, C., & Susnik, J. (1991). *Augmentative communication devices.* Reston, VA: Center for Special Education Technology (ERIC Document Reproduction Service No. ED 339 146).

Swallow, R. M., Mangold, S., & Mangold, P. (1978). *Informal assessment of developmental skills for visually handicapped students.* New York: American Foundation for the Blind.

Tecklin, J. S. (1989). *Pediatric physical therapy.* Philadelphia: Lippincott.

Tiffany, E. G., & Huss A. J. (1988). Frames of reference—Organizing systems for occupational therapy practice. In H. L. Hopkins & H. D. Smith (Eds.), *Willard and Spackman's occupational therapy* (7th ed.). Philadelphia: Lippincott.

Ward, M. E. (1986). The visual system. In G. T. Scholl (Ed.), *Foundations of education for blind and visually handicapped children and youth* (pp. 35–64). New York: American Foundation for the Blind.

White, O. R., Haring, N. G., Edgar, E. B., Affleck, J. Q., & Hayden, A. H. (1981). *Uniform performance assessment system.* San Antonio, TX: Psychological Corporation.

Young, M. H. (no date). Sensory integration programming. In P. H. Campbell (Ed.), *Topics in therapeutic programming for students with severe handicaps* (sensory integration programming instructional module). Akron, OH: Children's Hospital Medical Center of Akron.

Ysseldyke, J. E., & Algozinne, B. (1990). *Introduction to special education.* Boston: Houghton Mifflin.

Zimmerman, I. L., Steiner, V. G., & Pond R. E. (1992). *Preschool language scale—3.* San Antonio, TX: Psychological Corporation.

CHAPTER 13

Implementing Program Evaluation

CHAPTER OBJECTIVES

Do the Naleski family members feel that early intervention services are benefiting them? Is Brian demonstrating increased ability to interact with his peers? Is Tina making progress academically? Is the program at the Children's Center effective? These are some of the questions practitioners need to answer in evaluating programs. Reviewing progress and evaluating the child's program are the last steps in the assessment process. Evaluation of the overall program of a school or agency is also included in this phase. But, although they are the last steps, they are not final! In this chapter we examine ways of monitoring and evaluating a child's progress, as well as methods of evaluating overall program services. We will see that this type of assessment is an ongoing process.

Upon completing this chapter, you should be able to:

Define the term *evaluation*.

Describe the rationale for evaluation.

Compare and contrast different models of evaluation.

Contrast the process of review and evaluation of the IFSP and an IEP.

Discuss important areas to address in evaluating an overall center or school program.

Key Terms

Evaluation. The process of establishing a value judgment based on actual data.

Stakeholders. Individuals who have an interest in the results of an evaluation.

External Evaluator. An individual who is hired from the outside to assess the program.

Internal Evaluator. An employee of the program who is assigned the responsibility of assessing it.

Formative. Describes evaluations that occur in an ongoing program.

Summative. Describes evaluations made at the end of the program or unit or at the completion of a period of time.

WHAT IS EVALUATION?

Evaluation is a process we all undertake frequently, especially as students. We may compare instructors: "Dr. DiMatina is so much more interesting than Dr. Doyle." We may rate exams: "That exam was terrible—it didn't cover what I had studied." Or we may measure the classroom learning activities: "That small-group exercise in class really helped me understand the different group dynamics involved in teamwork."

Regarding an overall course evaluation, we could provide our instructor with several different types of information. We could provide feedback on lectures (Are they interesting? Are they delivered too quickly?). Or on the classroom climate—physical and social (Is it too cold? Is the seating comfortable? Is there a feeling of support and encouragement?). Or on the assignments (There are too many. They did not relate to the course objectives stated in the syllabus.). We would hope that the results of our evaluation will be helpful to our instructor. Perhaps some changes will be made before the next term!

There are many different ways of "evaluating." In fact, there are many different definitions of "evaluation." An early definition such as that included in PL 94–142 defined evaluation as "procedures used . . . to determine whether a child is handicapped and the nature and extent of the special education and related services that the child needs. The term means procedures used selectively with an individual child . . ." (Sec. 121a.500). Other definitions are more specific. We will use the definition developed by Smith and Glass (1987), which states that evaluation is the process of establishing a value judgment based on the collection of actual data.

In 1981 the Joint Committee on Standards for Education Evaluation, which represented the major educational organizations, published a list of standards. According to the Joint Committee (1981), a good evaluation should satisfy four important criteria:

- *Utility.* An evaluation should be informative and useful as well as timely.
- *Feasibility.* An evaluation should be appropriate to the setting and cost effective.
- *Propriety.* The rights of individuals affected by the evaluation must be protected.
- *Accuracy.* The evaluation instrument should be valid and reliable.

Evaluation is an important aspect of our work with children and their families. In this chapter, we consider the evaluation process at four different programmatic levels. First, we examine ways of gathering information about the child on an ongoing basis, while providing services to the child and family. We will need to evaluate and document advancement toward the outcomes or objectives developed in the

IFSP or IEP. As a result of this evaluation, we may decide to make changes in the services or in how they are being offered.

Next, at another level, we will want to evaluate the child's overall program after a period of time. Did the child make progress? Does the program meet family needs? If not, what are some areas that need to be improved? Are services no longer needed?

Third, we should evaluate the services our center, school, or agency offers. We may choose to gather information from several different perspectives. Information from the perspective of the staff provides administrators with a valuable slant on work conditions, equipment needs, or training priorities. Many programs that have a high staff turnover could gain valuable information by regular program evaluation. We will want to gather information from parents or other family members, too. Do they feel that staff listens to their concerns? Can they obtain information to help them make better decisions?

At a fourth level, administrators and policymakers may need to evaluate a program's effectiveness in terms of costs and benefits. If the program is funded by public monies, periodic evaluations must be conducted to demonstrate accountability for funds expended.

INDIVIDUALS INVOLVED

The field of evaluation has its own terms for the individuals who are involved in the evaluation process. For example, *stakeholders* are people who may be interested in the results of the evaluation. An evaluation of the effectiveness of the program at the Children's Center may affect several different groups, or stakeholders: The teachers, therapists, and other staff at the center will want to know the results of the evaluation, as will the parents, advisory board, and administrators of the program. An evaluation of the cost-effectiveness of the same program, on the other hand, may be of primary interest to the advisory board and administrators.

The evaluator should have a background in research design, measurement, and evaluation. The person may be an *outside evaluator,* hired specifically for the evaluation at hand. An evaluation may also be conducted by a staff member or administrator who is trained in these skills, that is, an *inside evaluator.* There are advantages as well as disadvantages in using outside and inside evaluators. Which of the following aspects are considered to be advantageous in hiring an outside evaluator? An inside evaluator?

Nonbiased

Knowledge of early childhood programs

Time to complete evaluation

Cost savings

Knowledge of questions to ask

Knowledge of effective strategies for evaluation

The evaluator is hired by the *client* who has requested the evaluation. The client may be one person, such as the administrator of the program, or a group, such as an advisory board, parent group, or state education department.

WHEN DOES EVALUATION HAPPEN?

Evaluations may occur during the time period in which services are offered, only at the completion of a time period (e.g., a program year), regularly after a certain period of time, or as a result of a special request or commission (Smith & Glass, 1987). We will examine the timing of evaluations and look at several illustrative case studies.

An evaluation that is planned as the program is being developed and is ongoing during the period of implementation is termed *formative*. Formative evaluation (Figure 13.1) is very useful to teachers and therapists who are providing direct services because by examining the data they can determine whether adjustments need to be made before the end of the program cycle. Suppose practitioners conduct an evaluation to monitor a child's progress. If the data indicate a need to make the program *substantially different* from the arrangements described in the intervention or education plan, a team meeting must be called and parents must approve the changes.

An evaluation that is completed at the end of the cycle (e.g., of an individual child's program plan) is called a *summative evaluation*. For example, a summative evaluation might be completed during the end of a period of the IFSP or IEP.

Summative evaluations may also be conducted on entire programs. Depending on the focus, these evaluations can provide administrators with a variety of information, including accountability and cost-effectiveness data, parent or staff satisfaction data, or information about the program's curriculum.

A MODEL FOR EVALUATING AN INDIVIDUAL CHILD'S PROGRAM

Among the best-known models for evaluating special education services is that developed by R. W. Tyler (1950), one of the founders of evaluation in education. This model has long been used by teachers and administrators in special education in several different ways: (1) to evaluate a child's progress toward the objectives described in the IEP/IFSP, (2) to evaluate the child's program at the end of a time period or unit, or (3) to evaluate the overall program of the school.

An objectives-based evaluation begins with the identification of a set of objec-

FIGURE 13.1   Evaluation as an ongoing process

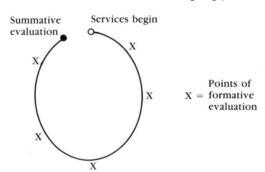

tives to be measured. Next the procedure or instrument to assess these objectives is chosen or developed. Teachers and therapists who are monitoring IEP/IFSP progress may collect products of the child's work, make periodic videotapes of the child, use criterion-referenced tests, or develop their own instruments for measuring progress. Products and test data are collected and analyzed to ascertain whether the objectives have been met. Tyler described this approach as a recurring sequence.

Dick and Carey (1985) have described a similar model, which stresses the identification of skills and the collection of data to revise instruction. The various steps in using this systems approach model are seen in Figure 13.2.

This approach is an example of an objectives-oriented model. We will return to this model later in our discussion of models for evaluating school and center programs.

PLANNING AN EVALUATION
OF A SPECIFIC CHILD'S PROGRAM

In early intervention and special education services, evaluations of the child (and family) service plan must be completed periodically. Early legislation, PL 94–142 and PL 99–457 (amended by PL 101–476), stated that the IFSP and IEP must be *evaluated* at least once a year. In addition, families receiving services under an IFSP must be provided a *review* of the plan at least every 6 months, or more often if

FIGURE 13.2 The Dick and Carey systems approach model for designing and evaluating instruction

SOURCE: From *Systematic Design of Instruction,* Second Edition, by Walter Dick and Lou Carey. Copyright © 1985, 1978 by Scott, Foresman and Company. Reprinted by permission of HarperCollins Publisher.

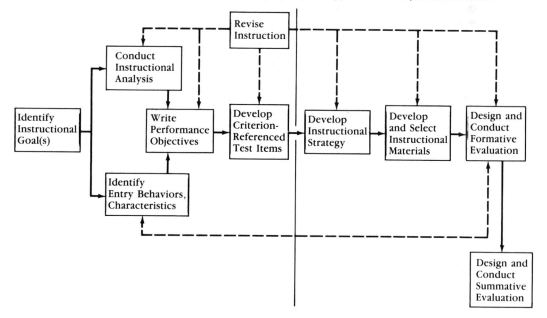

appropriate based on child or family needs. The review is important because services may need to be altered or adjusted frequently for young children or for the family members if the latter do not feel that the services are assisting them in meeting the priorities identified during the team meeting. (A note about terminology: We will be using the term *review* to indicate the process of examining IFSP outcomes and IEP objectives. The term *monitor* is used for the ongoing process evaluations undertaken by teachers and therapists to assess a child's daily or weekly progress.)

Steps in Reviewing and Evaluating the IFSP

Step 1: Identifying an Outcome.   During the early childhood team meeting, family concerns, priorities, and resources are identified. In Chapter 3, we saw that families have many different options in determining how these areas will be identified. Some families may choose a formal approach such as a written checklist or survey. Other families may choose more informal ways such as talking with one or more members of the team. No one approach is right for everyone.

Once these areas have been identified, an IFSP outcome statement is written to describe

> the changes family members want to see for their child or themselves. An outcome can focus on any area of child development or family life that a family feels is related to its ability to enhance the child's development. An outcome must be functionally stated in terms of what is to occur (process) and what is expected as a result of these actions (product). (Dunst, Trivette, & Deal, 1988, cited by Kramer, McGonigel, & Kaufman, 1991, p. 57)

One of the differences between an IFSP and an IEP is in the area of outcome statements. IFSP outcome statements are developed from family concerns and focus on the child's development or family life that is related to the developing child. The following list, adapted from Kramer et al. (1991), illustrates the difference in focus of outcomes statements used to describe the need Jennifer's family had voiced about feeding. Families may prefer to have different levels of involvement in early intervention services.

Focus	*Outcome Statement*
Child issues	Jennifer will increase her oral motor skills to permit her to eat more easily.
Family issues within the context of mealtime	Grandmother and dad will improve feeding methods so that Jennifer can learn how to eat more foods, be less fussy, and grow stronger.

Step 2: Agreeing on Evaluation Criteria.   The team will need to decide on the criteria for evaluating the outcome statements. How will we know if the outcome statement has been achieved? "Just as the family's agenda is the main determinant of outcome selection, so should the family's definition of success be the primary criteria for outcome evaluation" (Kramer et al., 1991, p. 65).

Step 3: Meeting Deadlines: IFSP Review and Evaluation.   The team member who is acting as service coordinator is responsible for ensuring that every 6 months the family receives a review of the IFSP. The review makes it possible to determine how much progress is being made and to decide whether modifications or revisions are necessary. Reviewing progress is especially crucial for very young children. Consider a 12-month-old child who has been receiving early intervention services for the past 9 months. If for the past 3 months the services have been inadequate, bear in mind that this 3-month period represents 25% of the child's lifetime. Kramer et al. (1991) suggest that a 6-month review and a 12-month evaluation will not suffice: "IFSP outcomes and strategies should be informally reviewed and evaluated for appropriateness and effectiveness at every contact between a family and staff" (p. 78). Practitioners working with a family might inquire, "How has it been going since the last time we met?"

Another way of providing opportunities to review services has been to include a review format within the IFSP. The State of Minnesota has developed an IFSP that includes an optional page to permit activities to be reviewed frequently by the family and facilitator or other team members. Figure 13.3 illustrates this IFSP form. Note that the ninth page of the form is an optional page, which may be used to provide an ongoing review of services. How would you complete this page for Brian and his family?

The family service coordinator is also responsible for ensuring that the IFSP is evaluated at least once a year. The purposes of the annual evaluation are:

- To review the outcomes and current information.
- To revise outcomes, if necessary.
- To write a new IFSP. (*Guidebook for Minnesota's Individualized Family Service Plan,* 1991)

An evaluation of an IFSP should also include, but not necessarily be limited to, the following questions:

- Has the child acquired additional skills?
- Do the strategies promote growth?

Kramer et al. (1991) suggest some additional questions:

- Were the services and activities flexible and responsive to family needs?
- Were the deadlines adhered to?
- Was the family satisfied?

The team will also be reviewing the decision regarding services.

- Should the child and family continue with the services described in the IFSP?
- Should services end?
- Should the child and family make a transition to other service areas? (*Guidebook for Minnesota's Individualized Family Service Plan,* 1991)

FIGURE 13.3

SOURCE: From *Guidebook for Minnesota's Individualized Family Service Plan (IFSP)*. Minneapolis, MN: Minnesota Interagency Early Childhood Intervention Project, a joint effort by the Minnesota Departments of Education, Health and Human Services, 1991. Reprinted by permission.

MINNESOTA INDIVIDUALIZED FAMILY SERVICE PLAN

Purpose: to "enhance the capacity of families to meet the special needs of their child with disabilities"

The IFSP must be done initially, anually, and be reviewed every six months or more frequently if conditions warrant or the family requests. It may also be helpful at times of major change (e.g. hospital discharge). The IFSP must include steps to support transition of the child upon reaching age three. IFSP Type: _____ interim _X_ initial _____ annual _____ other

Child's Name: __Brian Nelson__ Nickname: _____ Date of Birth: _3 – 29 – 89_

Sex: _M_ Resident School District: __School Administrative District #9__ CODE: _____

Child's presenting concerns and/or diagnosis: __Developmental Delay__

Parent/Guardian Information

Name __Margaret Nelson__   Parent/Guardian Information

Address __Box XX__   Name _____

__Farmington, ME__   County __Franklin__   Address _____

Telephone: day __778-XXX__   evening __same__   County _____

Primary Language at Home: __English__   Telephone: day _____ evening _____

Child's Primary Language: _____

DATE		
10 – 22 – 93	referral: made by __Doris Smith__ to: __Child Development Services__
	reason: __aggressive, non-compliant, hyperactive behavior__
10 – 27 – 93	assignment of Facilitator: name: __Jane Skinner__ position: __Early Intervention Specialist__
	agency: __CDS__ address: __200 Main St., Farmington, ME__ phone: __778-XXX__
10 – 30 – 93	initial family/facilitator collaboration: location: __Nelson home – 62 Sycamore St., Farmington, ME__
	persons present: __Mrs. Nelson, Jane Skinner__
	IFSP Team Meeting(s) to develop IFSP Date(s): __11 – 9 – 93__
11 – 9 – 93	IFSP Service Coordinator assigned: name: __Jane Skinner__ position: __Early Intervention Specialist__
	agency: __CDS__ address: __200 Main St., Farmington, ME__ phone: __778-XXX__
May, 1994	projected IFSP periodic review(s) (time/location if known): _____ projected annual review date: __Nov. 1994__
	date(s) reviewed (6 month): _____

On the following date(s), I received notice of my rights to request:
_10–30–93_   conciliation conference and/or due process hearing for special education services;
_____ conciliation conference and due process hearing for county developmental disability case management and related services;
_____ due process hearing for county social services and/or medical assistance.
I agree with and support the outcomes and services in this IFSP for my child.

Margaret Nelson   Date _Nov. 9, 1993_

Page 1

428

Family Considerations for the Individual Family Service Plan

1. Please describe how you see your child (what you most like, any concerns or needs).   Mom worried about Brian – she can't control him or get him to obey her, especially in public. He runs away from her and says "No" to a lot of what mom asks him to do. He doesn't play well with others, and he's destructive to other's toys, especially brother closest in age to him. Mom not sure if Brian understands when she asks him to do things, especially 2 or 3 step directions. Brian very good and gentle with elderly grandmother in nursing home – brings her wild flowers and will sit with his hand held in hers.

2. What type of help would you want for your child and family in the months or year ahead?
Mom would like suggestions on how to handle Brian's defiant behavior – especially in public.
Mom would like to talk with other parents who have children like Brian – If a support group, child care an important consideration.
Mom would like Brian to use words instead of pushing and taking things away from other children.

3. Which of the following do you or other family members feel are important concerns or areas about which you would like more information?

for your child   for your family...   notes:

___	getting around	X	meeting other families whose child has similar needs	X	child care
X	communicating	___	finding or working with doctors or other specialists	X	finding a support group
___	learning	___	coordinating, making appointments, dealing with agencies	___	finding or working with people who can help you in your home or care for your child so you can have a break
X	feeding, nutrition	___	coordinating your child's medical care	___	housing, clothing, jobs, food, telephone
X	having fun with other children	___	finding out more about how different services work or how they could work better for you	X	information or ideas for brothers, sisters, friends, relatives, others
X	challenging behaviors or emotions	___	planning or expectations for the future	X	information about the disability or diagnosis
___	equipment or supplies	X	more information about what resources might be available	___	money for extra costs of child's special needs
___	health or dental care	___	transportation	___	help with insurance
___	pain or discomfort			___	recreation
___	vision or hearing			___	other
___	other				

4. What else do you think would be helpful for others to know about your child?
That Brian does very well in a one-to-one situation with adults – especially grandmother even before she was ill.

2. ...about your family?
Margaret a single mom with three other children who do not exhibit any of the worrisome behaviors Brian does.

(continued)

FIGURE 13.3 (continued)

Child's Name: __Brian Nelson__

Agenda for the IFSP team meeting. (After reviewing the Family Considerations (page 2). The family and Facilitator create an agenda for the IFSP team meeting. (List the topics, questions and information to share; decide what sequence to follow and how much time will be needed.)

1. Brian's aggressive, non-compliant behavior:

   a: how can mom handle behavior in public and home

   b: how can we help Brian learn to respect others and their property

   c: who can mom talk to when she's really frustrated about these behaviors

2. Mom would like to know if Brian understands her 2 or 3 step directions

3. Mom would like information on respite care services

4. Assisting Brian with social/emotional/behavioral skills at preschool

5. Assisting Brian with body image, directional concepts and simple three-step directions

IFSP Team Membership Section – possibilities to consider for team members which will be helpful or supportive to child and family outcomes/issues/tasks

Family/Community:

* parents
- other family members, relatives, friends
- community, civic, disability or parent groups
- respite, child care providers
- advocates
- legal representation
- ministry, other support source
- other:

Social Services:

- developmental disabilities case worker
- income maintenance/economic assistance
- mental health
- child welfare
- social worker
- other private providers

Health Care:

- primary physician
- other physicians
- private home health care
- primary nurse

* must attend to meet IEP requirements

Health Care continued:

- other hospital staff
- public health nursing
- community health services
- habilitation providers (private therapy)
- Services for Children with Handicaps
- mental health providers
- personal care attendants
- other:

Education:

* administrator or designee
* Early Childhood Special Education
- school nurse
- Early Childhood Family Education
- Head Start
- Community Education
- early childhood programs (e.g., nursery school, child care)
- kindergarten – regular/special
- educators, related services
- occupational therapy
- physical therapy
- speech therapy
- other:

SCHEDULING IFSP MEETING

Settings and time convenient to family to ensure that they will be able to attend.

Nov. 16, 1993, 10:00 A.M. –
Mother Goose Preschool

Fill in details of team members on next page.

Page 3

IFSP Team Membership

Each agency or person who has a direct role in the provision of services responsible for making a good faith effort to assist each eligible child and their family in achieving the outcomes of the Child's IFSP.

Name	*	Position/Role	min/wk		start date	Duration	Agency and Address	Telephone/Availability
			indirect	direct				
Margaret Nelson		Mother						
Jane Skinner		Coordinator		✓	11/16/93	5/94	CDS, 200 Main St., Farmington, ME	778-XXXX
Doris Smith		Preschool Teacher		✓	11/17/93	5/20/94	Mother Goose Preschool, 8 Maple St., Farmington, ME	778-XXXX

Others Who May Be Helpful to the IFSP Team in planning and/or programming for the child.

Name	*	Position/Role	min/wk		start date	Duration	Agency and Address	Telephone/Availability
			indirect	direct				
Joe Lewis		MSW	✓		11/30/93		Area Mental Health Clinic, W. Farmington	673-XXXX

* Attendance at meeting: Y = yes, N = no

Page 4

(continued)

FIGURE 13.3 *(continued)*

Child's Name: **Brian Nelson**

DOB: **3 – 29 – 89**

Summary of Child's Present Levels of Performance (To be completed by the IFSP Team. Draw from description of the child, additional assessments and observations, for each category. Include needs and functioning in context of daily routine settings. Address all areas listed.)

1. Current health and medical status
2. Basic senses including hearing and vision
3. Communication: speech and language development
4. Social/emotional/behavioral development

5. Physical/motoric development
6. Cognitive development
7. Self-help skills
8. Academic Performance (when appropriate)

Present Levels of Performance	Child's Needs
1. Brian is a healthy child.	
2. Hearing and vision appear to be within a normal range.	
3. Brian shows appropriate language development for a child of his age.	
4. Brian needs assistance with his social/emotional development.	4. Brian is disrespectful of others and their property and he's non-compliant in public and at home.
5. Brian's physical/motoric development is at an age-appropriate level.	
6. Brian needs to increase body awareness.	6. Brian has difficulty identifying his chest, knee, chin, heel, elbow, and ankle.
7. Brian shows strength in the adaptive domain.	
8. Brian needs assistance with directional concepts and completing simple three-step directions.	8. Brian has difficulty following three-step directions and following directional concepts: above, below, in front of, behind, and beside.

Page 5

Initial Team List of IFSP Outcomes/Tasks/Issues

(An outcome is a statement of the changes family members want to see for their child, or for themselves, related to their ability to enhance their child's development.)

Priority #	Outcome/Issue/Task	People who can help with this outcome (to assess, plan, commit resources, and/or carry out the plan).	Additional Assessment Needed * INITIAL	FURTHER	NO ✓
1	Mrs. Nelson would like some help in managing Brian's behavior	Joe Lewis, MSW Behavior Consultant			
2	Mrs. Nelson would like to explore local respite care and family support services with accompanying child care	Jane Skinner CDS			
3	Brian will demonstrate increased ability to interact appropriately with his peers	Doris Smith, Mother Goose Preschool Teacher Joe Lewis, MSW Area Mental Health			
4	Brian will correctly follow simple three-step directions	Doris Smith Mother Goose Preschool Teacher			
5	Brian will improve his knowledge of body parts	Doris Smith Mother Goose Preschool Teacher			
6	Brian will improve his knowledge of directional concepts	Doris Smith Mother Goose Preschool Teacher			

* Attach assessment permits as needed

Page 6

(continued)

FIGURE 13.3 *(continued)*

Child's Name: _Brian Nelson_

Major Outcome to be achieved: Mrs. Nelson will have opportunity to explore behavior management strategies to use in public and at home

Current status: (include child and/or family resources, needs, concerns) Mom concerned about non-compliance in public and at home, also concerned about Brian's disrespect of others and property

Objective(s): (include criteria, procedures, and timelines used to determine progress)

Given specific behavior management strategies, Mrs. Nelson will implement these strategies obtaining the desired behaviors from Brian 100% of time as measured by mom's observation by May, 1994.

Activities/Services (describe type, amount, frequency, method)	Service available (Y or N) (comments)	Agency/Persons Responsible	Location	Payment arrangements
Joe Lewis, MSW, will observe in Nelson home 2 times a week for 2 weeks, and then consult with Mrs. Nelson regarding behavior management techniques useful to obtain desired behavior from Brian. After 2 weeks of implementing strategies, Joe Lewis will help Mrs. Nelson evaluate how they're working, making any necessary changes. Bi-monthly consultations thereafter until May, 1994 when plan is reviewed.	yes	Area Mental Health Clinic	home	CDS

Degree of Progress:
May, 1994

Date reviewed: _____

☐ Continue #s _____   ☐ Modify/revise #s _____   ☐ Discontinue #s _____

Page 7

Major Outcome to be achieved: __Brian will improve his knowledge of directional concepts__

Current status: (include child and/or family resources, needs, concerns) __Presently Brian has difficulty with directional concepts above, below, in front of, behind, beside__

Objective(s): (include criteria, procedures, and timelines used to determine progress)
__Given oral requests and/or pictures, Brian will correctly respond to and/or identify the directional concepts: above, below, in front of, behind and beside 9 out of 10 times as measured by teacher observation by Feb. 15, 1994__

Activities/Services (describe type, amount, frequency, method)	Service available (Y or N) (comments)	Agency/Persons Responsible	Location	Payment arrangements
Doris Smith will implement activities weekly in the preschool setting (Note: further evaluation by a speech language pathologist is recommended)	yes	Jane Skinner CDS		

Degree of Progress:
May, 1994

Date reviewed: _____

☐ Continue #s _____ ☐ Modify/revise #s _____ ☐ Discontinue #s _____

Page 7

(continued)

FIGURE 13.3 *(continued)*

Child's Name: Brian Nelson

Major Outcome to be achieved: Brian will improve his knowledge of body parts

Current status: (include child and/or family resources, needs, concerns) Presently, Brian has difficulty identifying the chest, knee, chin, heel, elbow and ankle

Objective(s): (include criteria, procedures, and timelines used to determine progress)
Given oral requests and/or pictures, Brian will correctly identify his chest, knees, chin, heel, elbow and ankle two out of three times as measured by teacher observation by Feb. 15, 1994

Activities/Services (describe type, amount, frequency, method)	Service available (Y or N) (comments)	Agency/Persons Responsible	Location	Payment arrangements
Doris Smith, Mother Goose Preschool, will implement weekly activities to foster this knowledge.	yes	Jane Skinner CDS		

Degree of Progress:
May, 1994

Date reviewed: _____

☐ Continue #s _____ ☐ Modify/revise #s _____ ☐ Discontinue #s _____

Page 7

Major Outcome to be achieved: __Brian will correctly follow simple three-step directions__

Current status: (include child and/or family resources, needs, concerns) __Currently Brian can only follow simple two-step directions, sometimes only one-step directions__

Objective(s): (include criteria, procedures, and timelines used to determine progress)
__Given simple three-step directions, Brian will correctly follow the request two out of three times as measured by teacher observation by Feb. 15, 1994__

Activities/Services (describe type, amount, frequency, method)	Service available (Y or N) (comments)	Agency/Persons Responsible	Location	Payment arrangements
Doris Smith will implement activities daily in the preschool setting (Note: further evaluation by a speech language pathologist is recommended)	yes	Jane Skinner CDS		

Degree of Progress: Date reviewed: _____
May, 1994

☐ Continue #s _____   ☐ Modify/revise #s _____   ☐ Discontinue #s _____

Page 7

(continued)

FIGURE 13.3 (continued)

Major Outcome to be achieved: Mrs. Nelson will have opportunity to explore local respite care and family support services with accompanying child care

Current status: (include child and/or family resources, needs, concerns) Currently Mrs. Nelson has no information at all

Objective(s): (include criteria, procedures, and timelines used to determine progress)
Given information on local respite care services and local family support services, Mrs. Nelson will utilize services she feels she needs by November 30, 1993

Activities/Services (describe type, amount, frequency, method)	Service available (Y or N) (comments)	Agency/Persons Responsible	Location	Payment arrangements
Jane will meet with Mrs. Nelson in her home to outline the available services and help Mrs. Nelson apply for services she feels she needs.	yes	Jane Skinner CDS	home	no payment necessary for respite care CDS will pay for any child care costs and transportation

Degree of Progress:
May, 1994

Date reviewed: _____

☐ Continue #s _____   ☐ Modify/revise #s _____   ☐ Discontinue #s _____

Page 7

Major Outcome to be achieved: Brian will demonstrate increased ability to interact in an age-appropriate way

Current status: (include child and/or family resources, needs, concerns) Currently Brian grabs toys from other children and pushes them, and has great difficulty sitting still and attending in small and large group activities

Objective(s): (include criteria, procedures, and timelines used to determine progress)

1. Given a situation when Brian wants a toy or material from another child, Brian will use words to obtain it 100% of the time as measured by teacher observation by Jan. 31, 1994
2. Given appropriate modeling and pre-arranged signal (thumbs up), Brian will sit still and attend to small and large group activities 8 out of 10 times as measured by teacher observation by Jan. 31, 1994
3. Upon discussion of classroom rules (with all children), Brian will follow rules 90% of the time as measured by teacher observation by Jan. 31, 1994

Activities/Services (describe type, amount, frequency, method)	Service available (Y or N) (comments)	Agency/Persons Responsible	Location	Payment arrangements
Joe Lewis, MSW, will observe in classroom 3 – 4 times during different time periods and consult with classroom staff members once a month from November 30, 1993 until May, 1994	yes	Mother Goose Preschool in consultation with Area Mental Health	Mother Goose Preschool	CDS

Degree of Progress:
May, 1994

Date reviewed: _____

☐ Continue #s _____   ☐ Modify/revise #s _____   ☐ Discontinue #s _____

FIGURE 13.3 *(continued)*

Early Intervention Settings/Least Restrictive Environment

"To the extent appropriate, early intervention services must be provided in the types of settings in which infants and toddlers without handicaps would participate." (Sect. 303. 12d)

Check all sites for early intervention:

[X]	child's home
[ ]	other family location
[ ]	family day care
[ ]	community-based program

[ ]	ECFE
[ ]	child care program
[X]	early childhood program
[ ]	Headstart
[ ]	hospital
[ ]	other:

[ ]	school district ECSE classroom
[ ]	other:

Explain why sites selected are appropriate and least restrictive and reasons others were considered and rejected.

Currently enrolled in early childhood program and mom will implement techniques learned through daily living at home

Describe opportunities to interact with peers not receiving special services and how interactions will be facilitated.

100% early childhood program activities daily

Indicate and describe below any changes necessary to permit successful accommodation of and programming for the child in the least restrictive alternative. (e.g. adaptations in rooms or environment, transportation, materials, equipment, technology, techniques or methods, curriculum, etc.)

Describe accommodations to be used in all sites to promote successful participation.

Describe additional accommodations – which are site-specific; indicate at which sites they are needed and why.

Page 8

Child's Name: Brian Nelson

Summary of Child/Family/Provider Activities:

to help look at the whole picture, organize, or cross check responsibilities and schedules, etc.

☐ Sample day   ☐ Sample week   ☐ Sample month   ☐ Other:

By IFSP Team or Family and Facilitator, as necessary

(optional) Page 9

441

How does all of this work? Let's sit in on the last few minutes of a meeting of the team planning services for Brian.

CASE STUDY: THE NELSON TEAM

The four members of the team were seated around the Nelsons' living room floor. Jane Skinner, the early intervention specialist and family service coordinator, was taking notes as Joe Lewis, the social worker skilled in behavior management, summarized the team members' observations. Margaret Nelson, Brian's mother, smiled as Doris Smith, the preschool teacher, described Brian's creative use of gestures and words.

As the outcomes for services were defined, Jane asked Ms. Nelson if she would be willing to assist in the review process. The team decided to review Brian's progress in one month.

Steps in Reviewing and Evaluating the IEP

Step 1: Identifying Annual Goals and Evaluation Criteria.   An IEP is written for children ages three through twenty-one; however, children ages three through five years may receive services provided by an IFSP if the IFSP contains all the information requested in an IEP developed by a multidisciplinary team. The IEP differs in style and content from the IFSP. The IEP document is less family focused and more child oriented. Rather than stating "outcomes," broad annual goals are developed along with specific objectives for the child.

An annual goal or goals are written for each area in which the child will receive services. These goals should be written to describe gains that could reasonably be achieved during the program year. How these goals will be evaluated should also be stated. Examples of an annual goal might be:

> *Motor:* Rachael will demonstrate good body movement during walking, running, and hopping activities by the end of the school year.
>
> *Adaptive:* Rachael will dress herself independently by the end of the program year.

Step 2: Identifying Behavioral Objectives and Evaluation Criteria. Specific objectives, designed to help the child meet the annual goal, are written. These objectives must be written in a way that will permit an observer to judge readily whether the objective is being met. Objectives written in this manner are called *behavioral objectives* because they describe a child's behavior and are not left to a chance interpretation.

Objectives must also state how an observer will decide whether the objective has been achieved. An IEP must also include the criteria and evaluation procedures that will determine whether the objectives of the plan are being achieved. Thus, behavioral objectives have three components:

1. A statement written in terms that can be observed
2. Criteria for successful performance
3. A method of evaluation

There are many different styles used in writing objectives, but in all cases the criteria used to determine whether the objectives have been met must be stated on the IEP as well as the time period for review. The following examples illustrate two different styles of writing goals and objectives with criteria for evaluation:

> Given a choice of primary colors, Robin will correctly identify each one with 100% accuracy as measured by teacher observation.

> Robin will correctly identify the primary colors over a period of 5 days as measured by the Brigance® Diagnostic Inventory of Early Development.

Step 3: Monitoring Progress. A child's progress should be monitored frequently. Some teachers and therapists will want to review objectives every 3 months, or more often, to monitor progress. Some of the questions that might be asked include:

> Is the child making progress toward this objective?

> Is this objective still appropriate, or have conditions changed?

Parents should be provided with a copy of the review, which represents an opportunity to make adjustments, if necessary.

Howell and McCollum-Gahley (1986) state that progress data should be reviewed every 2 weeks. Charting and graphing are excellent ways of monitoring progress, and there are many different types and formats. An easy method of monitoring progress is described by Essa (1990).

The chart shown in Figure 13.4 is used to record a child's frequency of interaction with peers before the beginning of the intervention (baseline) and during implementation of the program. Charts similar to this one allow continuous mon-

FIGURE 13.4 Charting a child's progress

SOURCE: From *A Practical Guide to Solving Preschool Behavior Problems* by Eva L. Essa, Ph.D. Delmar Publishers Inc., Albany, NY; Copyright 1990. Reproduced by permission.

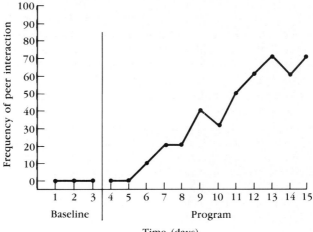

itoring and present a profile of progress over time (Figure 13.4 represents progress over a 2-week span). One of the disadvantages to charting is that the adult must find time to complete the recording.

Children may also take responsibility for charting their progress. In fact, children who are able to monitor their own behavior may grow in independence. Preschool children with disabilities have been shown to increase appropriate behaviors through self-monitoring (Sainato, Strain, Lefebvre, & Rapp, 1990). McGinnis and Goldstein (1990) have described a method for helping preschool and kindergarten children with behavior problems. This method is accompanied by various learning activities. Children use a self-scoring report sheet after each activity. Figure 13.5 illustrates a self-report after recess.

Older children may use self-monitoring techniques to increase opportunities for success in regular classroom settings. Dunlap, Dunlap, Koegel, and Koegel (1991) have described several examples of using self-monitoring for increasing on-task time, increasing responsivity to questions for a child with autism, and increasing accu-

FIGURE 13.5   A self-report for dealing with teasing

SOURCE: From *Skillstreaming in Early Childhood: Teaching Prosocial Skills to the Preschool and Kindergarten Child* by E. McGinnis and A. P. Goldstein. Champaign, IL: Research Press, 1990, p. 92. Copyright 1990 by the authors. Reprinted by permission.

1. Did I use a capital letter to begin each sentence?	Yes	No
2. Did I put a .? or ! at the end of the sentence?	Yes	No
3. Did I confer with my writing partner?	Yes	No

FIGURE 13.6   Becoming a writer: An example of a self-monitoring checklist

racy on subtraction problems. An example of the use of a self-monitoring checklist for academics is provided in Figure 13.6.

Step 4: Triennial Evaluation.   A complete evaluation (including psychological, physical, or adaptive behavior) must be conducted every 3 years or more frequently, if requested by the child's parents or teacher. During this evaluation, the team will consider whether the child continues to need services, whether changes are needed in the type of services, or whether the amount of service time should be changed. The federal regulations state that because children with speech impairments may not need a full battery of assessments, they may be excluded from this requirement.

We have examined the requirements of monitoring and evaluating an individual child's progress toward meeting the IFSP outcomes or goals of the IEP. Now we will examine methods of evaluating overall program services.

PLANNING AN EVALUATION OF YOUR PROGRAM

An evaluation of an overall program provides much useful information to advisory boards, administrators, staff, and parents. Borg and Gall (1983) identified four general categories that may be the focus in a program evaluation:

1. *Program goals.* What are the goals of the program? Does the program achieve the goals through the various services and activities? "A goal is the purpose, effect, or end-point that the program is attempting to achieve" (Borg & Gall, 1983, p. 743). Some programs have goals that are very specific; other programs have more general goals. However, goals are critical to the worth of the program.
2. *Program resources.* What are the program resources? Are they sufficient to meet our program goal(s)? Program resources may include a variety of areas such as personnel, volunteers, transportation, materials, equipment, and space.
3. *Program procedures.* What are the procedures used to achieve the program goal(s)? Procedures may include teaching techniques and strategies or arrangements of the environment.
4. *Program management.* How are resources and procedure monitored? Is the management as efficient as it can be?

One of the primary reasons for conducting an evaluation is to improve aspects of the program's resources and procedures. In planning an evaluation, there are several models to consider.

AN OVERVIEW OF MODELS FOR EVALUATING YOUR CENTER, SCHOOL, OR AGENCY

Over the years, theorists have proposed a number of different models of evaluation. Each approach has an underlying theory, discussions in the literature, a following of practitioners, and some critics. Listed below are various approaches to evaluation, as adapted from McMillan and Schumacher (1989, pp. 478–479).

Type	*Description*
Objectives-oriented	Focus is on specifying goals and objectives and determining the extent to which they have been attained.
Systems and cost-oriented	Focus is on identifying and meeting the informational needs of government funding agencies and policymakers.
Consumer-oriented	Focus is on educational products, to permit educational consumers to choose among competing services.
Expertise-oriented	Focus is on professional expertise to judge the quality of resources and products.
Decision-oriented	Emphasis is on describing and assessing an educational change process and resulting outcomes to provide information to a decision maker.
Adversary-oriented	Focus of the evaluation is on the pro and con views of different evaluators.
Naturalistic and participant-oriented	Focus is on naturalistic inquiry. Stakeholders are central in determining the values, criteria, needs, and data for the evaluation.

An Objectives-oriented Model

Educational evaluation has often been linked with an objectives-oriented approach (Borg & Gall, 1983). Early models of evaluation emphasized the objectives of the program and sought to determine how well these objectives were achieved. We examined this model earlier as an example of a useful approach to monitoring a child's progress or evaluating the child's program. An objectives-oriented model can be very useful in evaluating the overall program of a school, center, or agency, too.

One of the main advantages in using an objectives-oriented model is that the evaluation process itself is fairly simple and clear. By focusing on measurable objectives, the model encourages accountability and provides teachers with a clear method of demonstrating progress to parents and administrators (Johnson, 1988). However, Johnson (1988) cautions that this model has serious flaws: "Many of the most important educational outcomes are not amenable to behavioral statements. . . . outcomes not tied to objectives are not examined" (p. 185).

In using this evaluation model, consider: What are the aspects of the overall program I want to evaluate? Which of these aspects can be described in behavioral terms? Which aspects need to be included in a different type of evaluation? How might I gather this information?

A Systems and Cost-oriented Approach

The planning, programming, and budgeting system (PPBS) was first used by Robert McNamara in the 1960s to evaluate the efficiency of government programs. In this model, described by Smith and Glass (1987), the first step is to identify the goals and objectives of the program. Next the program is examined according to the various activities conducted. These activities are then related to the stated goals and objectives. The costs of the activities, including personnel and materials, are analyzed and alternative activities and their associated costs are identified.

This model encourages objectivity by focusing on the actual day-to-day activities of the program and relating these activities to a cost amount. Programs that need to demonstrate accountability to policymakers or local advisory boards may find this model helpful. The information collected enables the program director to make informed decisions and to allocate resources in the most effective way.

However, objectivity may prove to be a stumbling block, too. It may be difficult to assign a cost/benefit factor to some goals and objectives when working within a qualitative area. For example, the cost of weekly visits to a family in their home may be calculated, as opposed to the cost of transporting the family to a center once a week. But if the family strongly prefer one of these activities over the other, they may feel that the benefits far outweigh the cost.

A Decision-oriented Approach

The context, input, process, product (CIPP) model was developed by Stufflebeam et al. (1971) and Stufflebeam (1983). The CIPP model defines evaluation as an ongoing four-step process. The first two steps, context evaluation and input evaluation, are completed before the program begins.

1. *Context evaluation.* In this stage, the purpose is to identify the needs (which may be both met and unmet needs) of the individual(s) served by the program. Data from this *needs assessment* allow the current status of a program to be compared against unmet needs.
2. *Input evaluation.* During this stage, the team identifies ways to use resources to achieve goals.
3. *Process evaluation.* The focus is on identifying activities that are helpful and modifying activities that are not effective. This evaluation is conducted once the program has begun.
4. *Product evaluation.* This evaluation step, completed after the program year or ending date, serves to determine whether to continue, change, or terminate the program.

Johnson (1988) has described a modification of the CIPP model for evaluating early intervention programs. Evaluation is viewed as one process consisting of three interwoven phases: input, process, and product.

The Input Phase.   In the input phase we evaluate the needs of children and their families and develop a plan to meet those needs. This phase may be focused on specific children (and families). Whenever a child enters the program, needs are identified by the team and addressed by the IFSP or IEP. A key question for the team to consider is whether there are any discrepancies among three areas: what is identified, what ought to be identified, and what is proposed (Johnson, 1988). If there are discrepancies, the plan should be revised. This input phase is designed to ensure that needs are adequately identified and that the program will be able to carry out the proposed plan. This phase may be most helpful to programs that serve infants, toddlers, and their families, who may be clients of many different agencies and programs. The input phase offers an opportunity for service providers to coordinate and avoid duplication.

This phase is also important from a program's perspective. In fact, when additions to a program are developed or a new program is being proposed, an input evaluation should be conducted to provide information regarding the perceived needs of the program.

The Process Phase.   This phase ensures that teachers and therapists receive feedback on progress being made by individual children and their families as well as overall progress of the program. Monitoring the progress of each child permits modification of any inappropriate objectives to provide a more suitable program. Monitoring the overall program affords a means of evaluating such factors as personnel, materials, space, and costs: "How do these and other resources constrain or enhance the implementation of the program?" (Johnson, 1988, p. 200).

The Product Phase.   The final phase serves to determine the effect of the program on children, their families, and the community. Johnson (1988) suggests that some of the key questions might include:

> What impact did the support groups have on families that participated in the program?
>
> Do children make significant progress as measured by the Assessment, Evaluation, and Programming System for Infants and Children (AEPS)?
>
> Are parents satisfied with the program? (p. 205)

A Naturalistic and Participant-oriented Evaluation

Robert Stake (1975) was one of the first theorists to describe concerns for the emphasis on "mechanistic" approaches. His approach to evaluation embraces a holistic view of data collection in understanding different perspectives with a focus on the human element.

Evaluation is the process of completing various phases or events. McMillan and Schumacher (1989) have described these prominent phases as one might picture them on a clock face. In the first phase (noon to 4 o'clock) the evaluator talks with a variety of individuals to understand the different perspectives and values of the program. To obtain a better understanding of the operation and to conceptualize the issues and problems, the evaluator spends time observing the program.

In the second phase (4 to 8 o'clock), the evaluator identifies the data needs and selects collection methods. Observation is the primary method of data collection, although instruments may be utilized also. The data are organized as antecedents, transactions, and outcomes.

In the third phase (8 to 12 o'clock), the evaluator synthesizes the information, to be able to communicate the findings in natural ways. Portrayals, or descriptions of individuals, classrooms, or programs may take different forms such as descriptive case studies, artifacts, round-table discussions, or videotapes.

The advantages and disadvantages of these four approaches are summarized below.

Model	*Advantages*	*Disadvantages*
1. Tyler's model: focus is on the measurement of progress toward objectives	Focuses on measurable objectives, which encourages accountability; easy to understand and interpret; includes intervener as an integral member of the evaluation process.	Items not easily measured by objectives cannot be evaluated; many important educational outcomes cannot by described in behavioral statements.
2. PPBS model: focus is on the efficiency of the program	Identifies the most cost-efficient activities to meet program objectives; provides valuable information to programs with limited resources.	Overemphasis on quantitative information.
3. CIPP model: focus is on evaluation as a continuous cycle	Comprehensive; interrelationship between the different steps of the evaluation cycle.	Expensive; difficult to coordinate.
4. Naturalistic evaluation	Focuses on the "human element"; uses data from many sources.	Success depends on expertise of evaluator; "data" may not be accepted by scientific community.

The type of evaluation model practitioners and their colleagues choose will probably depend on a number of factors including philosophy and background as well as the purpose of the evaluation.

Borg and Gall (1983) noted that evaluation activities may be both beneficial and harmful. "It appears that people move truer and more certainly toward excellence to the extent that they clarify their purposes, measure the impact of their action, judge it, and move on—in a few words, evaluate their progress" (Glass, 1975, cited by Borg & Gall, 1983, p. 736). However, evaluation activities may use up scarce resources, which could be allocated to program development.

The following case (National Center for Clinical Infant Programs, 1987) illustrates many of the concepts we have just discussed.

When a Massachusetts early intervention program for disabled infants and toddlers was faced simultaneously with increasing demands for service, limited resources, and staff concern about the appropriate mix of services being delivered, program administrators engaged an independent evaluator to assess the program's service model and organizational structure. The evaluator conducted a relatively simple client satisfaction survey and a series of interviews with staff members. . . .

Virtually all parent respondents to the client questionnaire identified home-visiting as the most crucial element of the early intervention program. At a time when the high cost of home visits was generating pressure to curtail them, the unanimity of parental praise for this service format was a tremendous boost to staff morale.

The parent questionnaire also revealed that large numbers of previously uninvolved fathers were interested in participating in home visits if visits could be scheduled in the evening. . . . In response to this information, the program introduced flexible staff work schedules, and fathers did, in fact, become increasingly integrated into program activities. (pp. 15–16)

What model could best describe these evaluation activities? What were the benefits?

In planning a program evaluation, there are four basic questions to consider: (1) What do we wish to know? (2) Who will provide the information? (3) How shall we collect the information? and (4) What are the costs?

Key Terms

Quantitative Data. Descriptive information that consists of numbers.

Qualitative Data. Information that consists of words and text rather than numbers.

Focus Group. A gathering of a small group of informed stakeholders which is facilitated by the evaluator for the purpose of gathering information through the discussion of relevant issues.

Deciding What We Wish to Know

The first step in planning an evaluation is to identify the area in which to gather information. This may be done by the program director or through discussion in a staff meeting. Common concerns may have been voiced by an advisory board or staff members. More often than not, however, several different areas of concern or global questions regarding the program have been raised. Some of the program resources and procedure areas and questions that may be addressed in the evaluation follow. The questions are adapted from J. J. Carta, S. S. Ilene, J. B. Atwater, and S. R. McConnell (1991).

Sample Area	Possible Questions	Who Will Answer
Environment	Does the environment support the needs of all children? Is the room warm and inviting? Are the facilities accessible?	Expert evaluator, staff
Curriculum	Is the curriculum developmentally appropriate?	Expert evaluator, staff

Program effectiveness	Has the program made a difference (for children and their families)?	Expert evaluator, staff, and parent
	Do the program goals for the children focus on increasing the child's ability to function in home, school, and community?	
	Do the program goals assist children in making the transition to more integrated settings?	
	Do the program goals include the use of teaching strategies that increase the likelihood of effective functioning in normalized settings?	
	What are we doing well?	
	What can be improved?	
Satisfaction	Is the program meeting my child's needs?	Parent
	Is my job position satisfying?	Staff
	Is this a pleasant place to work?	Staff
	Do I feel valued and supported in my job?	Staff
Cost effectiveness	Are we providing services in the most cost-effective manner?	Expert evaluator, staff

Each of the areas yields different questions and distinct types of information. Sometimes programs need assistance in specifying an area for evaluation. An informal survey or needs assessment questionnaire is another excellent way of identifying the area(s) of greatest need.

Developing a Needs Assessment Questionnaire.   A questionnaire may be developed to provide information regarding program needs. Questionnaires should be fairly short and questions simply stated. Open-ended questions allow individuals to respond to areas that may have been overlooked. The design and development of questionnaires is beyond the scope of this book. The interested reader may want to refer to these additional resources:

Alreck, P. L., & Settle, R. B. (1985). *The survey research handbook.* Homewood, IL: Irwin.

Berdie, D. R., Anderson, J. F., & Niebuhr, M. A. (1986). *Questionnaires: Design and use* (2nd ed.). Metuchen, NJ: Scarecrow Press.

Fowler, F. J., Jr. (1988). *Survey research methods.* Newbury Park, CA: Sage.

Gorden, R. L. (1987). *Interviewing strategy, techniques, and tactics.* Chicago: Dorsey Press.

Yin, R. K. (1989). *Case study research.* Newbury Park, CA: Sage.

CASE STUDY: AN INFORMAL METHOD FOR IDENTIFYING NEEDS AT THE CHILDREN'S CENTER CHILD CARE PROGRAM

There are informal ways of identifying needs also. The staff at Children's Center Child Care used the following steps to come to identify and prioritize their needs. Anna Robles, director of the program, solicited input from each staff member, including the cook, by asking them to identify four areas they felt needed attention and to number them in order of priority. The papers were collected and priorities were assigned points numbering from 4 to 1. (The highest number was assigned to the first priority listed.) The total number of points was then calculated for each of the items listed and the top-priority item was identified. Through this informal needs assessment, Ms. Robles was able to utilize information solicited from her staff.

One of the most popular evaluation questions in early intervention and special education services was identified by the Children's Center staff: Has the program made a difference (for children and their families)? We will illustrate the process of program evaluation by indicating how this question may be approached.

Who Will Provide the Information?

The need for families to be a part of the evaluation process is critical, yet families may not be receiving the level of *family-focused* services contemplated by PL 102–119, the Individuals with Disabilities Education Act Amendments of 1991 (Sec. 12; 14–16). Mahoney, O'Sullivan, and Dennebaum (1990) found that a majority of the mothers they surveyed indicated that some components of family-focused intervention were not consistent features of the program and services they were receiving.

As we have seen, there are a number of individuals who may provide information. The reasons for the program evaluation should be considered in deciding whom to include in completing the evaluation.

Generally speaking, program evaluations should include information from the consumers of services. In our example, we will want to gather information about child progress as well as parent information.

How Shall We Collect the Information?

Information for the evaluation may be collected in a variety of ways. Best practice in program evaluations suggests the collection of both *quantitative* and *qualitative* data.

Quantitative data consist of numbers or scores. Program evaluations, for example, often include pre- and post-test scores. Data collection may also include the use of surveys or questionnaires on which respondents rate different statements. The rating forms the basis of quantitative data. Quantitative data are used to provide statistical information and analyses.

Qualitative data are gathered through interviews, discussions, or written answers. The information is descriptive rather than numeric. Qualitative data are more difficult to synthesize but often provide helpful and, sometimes, unexpected findings. In the following case study, we will assist the director of the Brownfield Early Education Program as she begins to plan a program evaluation.

CASE STUDY: EVALUATION OF THE BROWNFIELD EARLY EDUCATION PROGRAM

The director has decided to collect both quantitative and qualitative data. Since all the children who enter the program are given a standardized test at the beginning and end of the year, these test scores will be one quantitative measure. But we will need to decide how to measure change.

The Use of Gain Scores. The *gain score* (also referred to as the *change score* or the *difference score*) is the easiest method of interpreting change. The gain score is calculated by subtracting the first test score from the second test score. Table 13.1 illustrates the test scores of five of the children enrolled in the Brownfield early education program.

At first glance, it would seem that most of the children in the program have made good gains as measured by the test scores. However, one of the problems in the use of gain scores is their low reliability. In fact, even if the standardized test has a high test–retest reliability coefficient, the gain score will have a low reliability (Cronbach & Furby, 1970). This problem results from an increase in *measurement error* (also referred to as the *standard error of measurement*). Let's examine Annie's record in Table 13.1. Her fall test score was 52 and her spring test score was 59, a gain of 7 points. According to the testing manual, the test we are using has a fairly low measurement error, ± 3 points. Thus, Annie's true fall test score was between 49 and 55 and her true spring test score was between 56 and 62. Considering the measurement error, the difference between the fall and spring scores is still 7 but ± 6 points. Therefore, the true gain score is between 1 and 13 points. If the true gain is really 1 point, then Annie has shown little improvement in her test scores since the beginning of the year; if the true gain is really 13 points, however, then we would conclude that there has been a substantial change in Annie's performance since the beginning of the year.

There are other difficulties with gain scores. Children who have low scores on the pretest often demonstrate greater gains than children who score relatively well on the pretest (Hauser-Cram & Krauss, 1991). Thus, the initial status of the child appears to impact the observed gain.

Quantitative Measures for Evaluating Overall Progress of Children Participating in the Program

There are other ways to evaluate progress by using children's scores. Two of the most promising ways are the use of indexes of gain and residual change scores.

The Use of Indexes of Gain.   A number of different indexes of gain have been developed to address the problems associated with using gain scores. Generally

TABLE 13.1   Gain scores for children enrolled in the program

Child's Name	Fall Test Score	Spring Test Score	Gain Score
Tara	45	53	8
Jacob	38	41	3
Ian	52	59	7
Jill	40	36	−4
Annie	52	59	7

speaking, indexes of gain provide a way of expressing the gains children make in a program with respect to the amount of time they have been in the program. Two popular indexes of gain are the Intervention Efficiency Index, developed by Bagnato and Neisworth (1980), and the Proportional Change Index, developed by Wolery (1983). One major drawback of the use of these indexes has been the requirement to use them only with standardized assessments that yield developmental age scores.

The Use of Residual Change Scores.   One of the most promising ways to measure change in scores may be the use of *residual change scores,* obtained by calculating a predicted score for each individual based on the distribution of all the scores of the sample. "The distribution of the residual change scores alerts the evaluator to those individuals who changed more than predicted (a positive residual) and those who changed less than predicted (a negative residual) within the sample as a whole" (Hauser-Cram & Krauss, 1991, p. 293).

Quantitative Measures for Evaluating Family Satisfaction with the Program

Several instruments have been developed to assist families in evaluating programs and services. The following selected rating scales are tools to consider.

Family-Centered Program Rating Scale.   Developed at the Beach Center on Families and Disability at the University of Kansas, Lawrence, the Family-Centered Program Rating Scale (Murphy, Lee, Turbiville, Turnbull, & Summers, 1991) provides an opportunity for program evaluation by family members as well as service providers. The goal is to assist the program to become more family centered. The scale consists of questions around three main areas: the program, the staff, and families in the program. Respondents rate each question in terms of how well the program is doing and in terms of how important the item is to the individual. The scale, which is currently being standardized, also includes two open-ended questions. Figure 13.7 illustrates one of the pages from the scale.

The Parent Satisfaction Survey.   The Parent Satisfaction Survey was developed by Project Dakota Outreach in 1987 (McGonigel, Kaufman, & Johnson, 1991) to allow parents to evaluate the programs that serve their children. Family members rate five main areas: (1) program and staff responsiveness, (2) growth in knowledge and skills for helping your child, (3) growth in understanding normal behavior and problems, (4) utilization of community resources, and (5) building a support sys-

Page 2

	How well does your program do this? P = Poor, OK = Okay, G = Good, E = Excellent	How important is this to you? NI = Not Important, SI = Somewhat Important, I = Important, VI = Very Important
IN THIS PROGRAM...		
5. services are planned with families' transportation and scheduling needs in mind.	P OK G E	NI SI I VI
6. someone on the staff can help families communicate with all the other professionals serving them and their children.	P OK G E	NI SI I VI
7. the program administrator makes families feel comfortable when they have questions or complaints.	P OK G E	NI SI I VI
8. the IEP, or IFSP (Individualized Family Service Plan), is used as a "plan of action."	P OK G E	NI SI I VI
9. there is a comfortable way to work out disagreements between families and staff members.	P OK G E	NI SI I VI
B. THE PROGRAM...		
10. helps families when they want information about jobs, money, counseling, housing, or other basic family needs.	P OK G E	NI SI I VI
11. gives other children in families support and information about their brother's or sister's disability.	P OK G E	NI SI I VI
12. gives them information on how to meet other families of children with similar needs.	P OK G E	NI SI I VI
13. offers special times for fathers to talk with other fathers and with the staff.	P OK G E	NI SI I VI
14. offers information in a variety of ways (written, videotape, cassette tape, workshop, etc.).	P OK G E	NI SI I VI
15. helps families expect good things in the future for themselves and their children.	P OK G E	NI SI I VI

FIGURE 13.7 A page from the Family-Centered Program Rating Scale

SOURCE: From *Family-Centered Program Rating Scale: Provider's Scale* by D. L. Murphy, I. M. Lee, V. Turbiville, A. P. Turnbull, and J. A. Summers. Lawrence, KS: Beach Center on Families and Disability, 1991, pp. 1–2. Reprinted by permission.

Parent Satisfaction Survey
(Project Dakota Outreach)

Please indicate how satisfied you are with services you receive from your child's program. For each item put a check to show how strongly you agree or disagree with that statement. Your response to each statement is important -- any unanswered items have a negative effect on the final score.

Goal I - Program and Staff Responsiveness	Strongly Disagree	Disagree	Agree	Strongly Agree
The staff listen and respond to my concerns, questions, and ideas.	____	____	____	____
In my meetings with staff (for assessments, conferences, monthly updates, etc.), I feel I am an active member of the team and not just a listener.	____	____	____	____
Although one staff member mainly serves my child, I feel that we receive the expertise of other staff.	____	____	____	____
Staff give me information that is clear and useful to me.	____	____	____	____
I feel the program for my child includes what is important to me.	____	____	____	____
My child's program meets my child's needs.	____	____	____	____
The help my child is getting is based on his/her individual needs.	____	____	____	____
I am satisfied with my child's progress since beginning this program.	____	____	____	____
The help I get fits into our family routines and activities.	____	____	____	____
The staff respect the limits my family puts on our time and energy for our child's program.	____	____	____	____
I am informed of a variety of choices for how my child could be served.	____	____	____	____

FIGURE 13.8   A page from the Parent Satisfaction Survey

SOURCE: From *Parent Satisfaction Survey*. Project Dakota Outreach. Copyright 1987. Reprinted by permission.

tem. This survey includes space for additional comments. Figure 13.8 illustrates the questions from one area of this survey.

Family-Focused Intervention Scale.   The Family-Focused Intervention Scale (Mahoney, O'Sullivan, & Dennebaum, 1990) was developed to provide families with a tool for rating the degree of family-focused services they receive. The instrument contains 45 family service items to which the respondents indicate how often the intervention program provided each of the services: Never (1,2), Sometimes (3,4), or Always (5,6). The questionnaire also includes parents' perceptions of intervention program benefits. This instrument has undergone some reliability and validity studies. Internal consistency and construct validity were adequate (Mahoney et al., 1990).

The Use of Qualitative Data

In contrast, qualitative data have no numerical value. In evaluating specific children, a variety of sources for collecting qualitative information should be used. Materials children have produced from work and play activities, and video- and audiotape recordings, are all examples of qualitative data. Anecdotal and running records as well as specimen records are other excellent sources.

In overall program evaluation, interviews, surveys, and questionnaires with open-ended questions provide rich information. In Chapter 3, we saw some of the types of information that may be collected during an interview. Surveys and rating scales may be completed by family members as well as by staff. Products of the program including newsletters or monthly calendars of activities are other good sources.

Focus groups also provide an informal way of collecting information. Focus groups may be small gatherings of individuals from similar constituencies or from different backgrounds. The group may respond to specific questions or provide informal feedback to the group facilitator regarding the program. A parent focus group may involve several family units, and individual members may be mothers, fathers, grandparents, aunts, and so on. Some groups may include a deliberate mix of family members to encourage dialogue. The group leader may be a practitioner or a family member. Through group interaction, preferences are elicited, and satisfaction with programs and services is determined. Focus groups may be preferred by families because of their informal nature.

One of the difficulties associated with using qualitative data lies in synthesis and interpretation. In other words, how will the information be organized and how will it be evaluated? What standards will be used?

What Are the Costs?

Planning an evaluation should also include consideration of costs. Some typical cost items might include:

Consultant fees, mileage, lodging, and meals

Telephone, postage, computer time, graphics

Typing, copying, supplies

But not all costs are payable in money. Other cost considerations include:

Costs in time: How much staff time will be needed? Will additional costs of staffing substitutes be incurred?

Potential "costs" in terms of psychosocial issues: To the staff? To the children? To the parents and other family members?

Development of Local Instruments

In the absence of an appropriate nationally standardized instrument, program staff and administrators may develop a local instrument that asks key questions. The instrument may be as simple as a one-page questionnaire filled out by staff members or a three-question postcard given to family members to complete and return. Figure 13.9 illustrates an evaluation instrument developed by staff in an early intervention play group for children and their families.

Short evaluations that are easy to complete are much more likely to be filled in and returned than lengthy, complicated forms. Evaluations that allow the respondent to indicate a choice by checking an item are easier to complete than questions calling for written responses. Remember, a key issue in evaluation is obtaining as many responses as possible from all the stakeholders.

PARTICIPATING IN AN EVALUATION OF YOUR PROGRAM

Required Periodic Evaluations

Early legislation (PL 94–142) made provisions for the regular evaluation of various local educational agencies, such as public schools, which serve children with disabilities. In fact, each state Department of Education in the United States must submit an annual plan to Washington that includes a description of their plan for evaluation. This plan must assess the effectiveness of a sample of programs in the state that are serving individuals with disabilities. The state evaluation must address the effectiveness of the IEPs for individual children as well as the overall effectiveness of the program. The following case study illustrates how one state Department of Education organized such an evaluation.

FIGURE 13.9   An evaluation instrument developed by staff in an early intervention play group

Early Intervention Play Group

Please help us review the play group's activities this fall.
1. Our morning program consists of play time, a group activity, and a snack for the children. Would you like to see any changes?

2. Our play group also provides opportunities for parents and other family members to visit while at group. Would you suggest any changes?

3. Would you like to be involved:

    _____ by bringing a snack for the children once a month?

    _____ by doing an activity with the children from time to time?

    _____ by bringing recycled materials for art activities?

    _____ other _____

    _____ not now, but perhaps later.

CASE STUDY: EVALUATING SPECIAL EDUCATION
SERVICES AT SANDY BROOK PUBLIC SCHOOL

Three months ago Josh Leiberman, the director of Special Education Services at Sandy Brook Public School, received a form letter from the state Department of Education. The letter described the federal requirement that each local education agency receiving federal monies for the education of children with disabilities be evaluated periodically by members of the state education department team. Josh scanned the names of the individuals on the evaluation team. Four people would be arriving: two consultants from the state education department, a special education director from a nearby school district, and an administrator from a school district in the southern part of the state. The letter described a tentative schedule for the visit and the items the team would like to review.

The letter contained a clear description of what the team would need. They would want to review several different IEPs. They would also want to talk with several of the parents, as well as teachers in the building. Later, the team would send a report summarizing their findings and recommendations for improvement, if necessary.

Evaluating for a Special Purpose

An evaluation may be conducted for a special purpose. For example, members of a program advisory board, afraid of losing funding, may commission an evaluation in the hope of identifying the benefits and gains of the program to children and their families. A program director who observes some general problems may hire an evaluator in hopes of pinpointing areas of concern. In the following case study, the program director at the Ripley Preschool Center decides to hire an outside evaluator to assist her in gathering information and addressing some problems the center is experiencing.

CASE STUDY: RIPLEY PRESCHOOL CENTER

Anne Littlefoot, program director at the Ripley Preschool Center, was concerned. As November neared, many of the problems of the first few weeks of school seemed to persist. Transition times remained difficult. Some children frequently refused to move on to the next activity. Outdoor time had become very difficult. The collegial, supportive relationships of staff members, which had long characterized the program, seemed to be deteriorating.

Anne decided to bring these concerns up at the staff meeting that Monday afternoon. She began by asking the staff how they felt the day had gone. Then she moved into a general discussion about the program. The staff provided little feedback.

During the week, Anne wondered whether lack of staff input at the meeting had been due in part to the many "hats" she wore. As program director she assisted in curriculum development, made monthly reports to the advisory board, wrote the program newsletter, prepared the budget, and evaluated staff members, among other tasks. Perhaps an outside evaluator would be able to give an objective unbiased report. Such an individual might also be perceived as less threatening by the staff.

PREFERRED PRACTICES

Program evaluation is an important component in the assessment process, and its implementation should not be left to the chance that excess funding will be available at the end of a program cycle! Program evaluation should be a *routine* aspect of all programs. Evaluations should be addressed at different levels: from the perspective of the child (and family) and from the perspective of the overall program. The most useful program evaluations include both quantitative and qualitative data from a variety of sources. When conducting analyses of quantitative data, caution should be used in interpreting scores that reflect change.

As funding continues to be an issue in determining the types of service offered, programs will be under more and more pressure to demonstrate accountability. As our field continues to grow and develop, we must keep searching for adequate methods to measure the success of our work with children and their families.

STUDY QUESTIONS AND SUGGESTED ACTIVITIES

1. Describe the four levels of program evaluation.
2. What are the federal requirements for evaluating the IFSP? IEP?
3. Compare and contrast two models of evaluation.
4. Visit a program that serves infants and toddlers and arrange to meet with the program director. How do staff involve families in evaluating the program?
5. Evaluate your program with one of the suggested rating scales.

REFERENCES

Alreck, P. L., & Settle, R. B. (1985). *The survey research handbook.* Homewood, IL: Irwin.

Bagnato, S. J., & Neisworth, J. T. (1980). The intervention efficiency index: An approach to preschool program accountability. *Exceptional Children, 46,* 264–269.

Berdie, D. R., Anderson, J. F., & Niebuhr, M. A. (1986). *Questionnaires: Design and use* (2nd ed.). Metuchen, NJ: Scarecrow Press.

Borg, W. R., & Gall, M. D. (1983). *Educational research: An introduction.* New York: Longman.

Carta, J. J., Ilene, S. S., Atwater, J. B., & McConnell, S. R. (1991). Developmentally appropriate practice: Appraising its usefulness for young children with disabilities. *Topics in Early Childhood Special Education, 11*(1), 1–20.

Cronbach, L. J., & Furby, L. (1970). How should we measure "change"—Or should we? *Psychological Bulletin, 74,* 68–80.

Dick, W., & Carey, L. (1985). *The systematic design of instruction.* Glenview, IL: Scott Foresman.

Dunlap, L. K., Dunlap, G., Koegel, L. K., & Koegel, R. L. (1991). Using self-monitoring to increase independence. *Teaching Exceptional Children, 23*(3), 17–22.

Dunst, C. Trivette, C., & Deal, A. (1988). *Enabling and empowering families.* Cambridge, MA: Brookline.

Essa, E. L. (1990). *A practical guide to solving preschool behavior problems.* Albany, NY: Delmar Publications.

Federal Register (Vol. 57, No. 189, pp. 44794–44852). Washington, DC: U.S. Government Printing Office, September 19, 1992.

Fowler, F. J., Jr. (1988). *Survey research methods.* Newbury Park, CA: Sage.

Gorden, R. L. (1987). *Interviewing strategy, techniques, and tactics.* Chicago: Dorsey Press.

Guidebook for Minnesota's Individualized Family Service Plan (IFSP). (1991). Minneapolis, MN: Department of Health.

Hauser-Cram, P., & Krauss, M. W. (1991). Measuring change in children and families. *Journal of Early Intervention, 15,* 288–297.

Howell, K. W., & McCollum-Gahley, J. (1986). Monitoring instruction. *Teaching Exceptional Children, 19*(1), 47–49.

Individuals with Disabilities Education Act Amendments of 1991. Washington, DC: U.S. Government Printing Office, October 7, 1991.

Johnson, L. J. (1988). Program evaluation: The key to quality programming. In J. B. Jordan, J. J. Gallagher, P. L. Hutinger, & M. B. Karnes (Eds.), *Early childhood special education: Birth to three* (pp. 182–212). Reston, VA: Council for Exceptional Children.

Joint Committee on Standards for Educational Evaluation. (1981). *Standards for evaluation of educational programs, projects, and materials.* New York: McGraw-Hill.

Kramer, S., McGonigel, M. J., & Kaufman, R. K. (1991). Developing the IFSP: Outcomes, strategies, activities, and services. In M. J. McGonigel, R. K. Kaufman, & B. H. Johnson (Eds.), *Guidelines and recommended practices for the individualized family service plan* (pp. 57–66). Bethesda, MD: Association for the Care of Children's Health.

Mahoney, G., O'Sullivan, P., & Dennebaum, J. (1990). Maternal perceptions of early intervention services: A scale for assessing family-focused intervention. *Topics in Early Childhood Special Education, 10*(1), 1–15.

McGinnis, E., & Goldstein, A. P. (1990). *Skill-streaming in early childhood: Teaching prosocial skills to the preschool and kindergarten child.* Champaign, IL: Research Press.

McGonigel, M. J., Kaufman, R. K., & Johnson, B. H. (Eds.) (1991). *Guidelines and recommended practices for the individualized family service plan.* Bethesda, MD: Association for the Care of Children's Health.

McMillan, J. H., & Schumacher, S. (1989). *Research in education: A conceptual introduction.* Glenview, IL: Scott, Foresman.

Murphy, D. L., Lee, I. M., Turbiville, V., Turnbull, A. P., & Summers, J. A. (1991). *Family-centered program rating scale.* Lawrence, KS: Beach Center on Families and Disability.

National Center For Clinical Infant Programs (1987). *Charting change in infants, families, and services: A guide to program evaluation for administrators and practitioners.* Washington, DC: National Center for Clinical Infant Program.

Sainato, D. M., Strain, P. S., Lefebvre, D., & Rapp, N. (1990). Effects of self-evaluation on the independent work skills of preschool children with disabilities. *Exceptional Children, 56,* 540–549.

Smith, M. L., & Glass, G. V. (1987). *Research and evaluation in education and the social sciences.* Englewood Cliffs, NJ: Prentice-Hall.

Stake, R. (1975). *Evaluating the arts in education.* Columbus, OH: Merrill.

Stufflebeam, D. L. (1983). The CIPP model for program evaluation. In G. F. Madaus, M. Scriven, & D. L. Stufflebeam (Eds.), *Evaluation models: Viewpoints on educational and human services evaluation.* Boston: Kluwer-Nijhoff.

Stufflebeam, D. L., Foley, W. J., Gephart, W. J., Guba, E. E., Hammond, R. L., Merriman, H. O., & Provus, M. (1971). *Educational evaluation and decision-making.* Itasca, IL: Peacock.

Tyler, R. W. (1950). *Basic principles of curriculum and instruction.* Chicago: University of Chicago Press.

Wolery, M. (1983). Proportional change index: An alternative for comparing child change data. *Exceptional Children, 50,* 167–170.

Yin, R. K. (1989). *Case study research.* Newbury Park, CA: Sage.

CHAPTER 14

Interpreting and Reporting Assessment Information

CHAPTER OBJECTIVES

By the time an assessment report comes to be written, many hours have been spent conducting observations and interviews and administering formal and informal tests. The report is the culmination of the assessment process and should result in recommendations that can help to improve intervention services for the child. The report is an important tool that the examiner uses to communicate what has been learned about the child.

Upon completion of this chapter, you should be able to:

Describe the general principles that guide the development of assessment reports.

Describe the components of an assessment report.

Discuss the use of computers in testing and in generating reports.

TYPES OF ASSESSMENT REPORT

Assessment reports are written for a variety of purposes, and the information they contain varies accordingly.

Reports of Observations

A professional may write a report of the observations conducted on a child in a specific setting. To gather information about the full range of behaviors exhibited, it is often worthwhile to observe the child in different settings.

Monitoring Progress

It is valuable to have a summary of the progress a child makes during a specific time frame. The IFSP and the IEP require periodic reports of the child's progress.

Individual Test Reports

Summarizing the results of an individual test can be valuable. Individual reports of tests, however, may not be as useful as a comprehensive assessment report, because an individual report presents a restricted account of a child's performance.

An assessment report should be completed by each member of the unidisciplinary and multidisciplinary teams who conducted an assessment of the child. These reports become part of the child's records and document the procedures that have been tried and the team members' interpretations of the child's performance. Members of transdisciplinary or unidisciplinary teams contribute to team reports.

Comprehensive Assessment Report

One of the most frequent purposes of an assessment report is to integrate and interpret the results of assessment. This type of report is usually extensive. It summarizes what we know about the child and what we have learned based on the results of a thorough workup. Typically, a comprehensive report relies on multiple sources of information such as formal testing, observations, interviews, and alternative assessment.

Interpreting and reporting the results of a comprehensive assessment are important phases in the development of the intervention plan. In Chapter 1 you learned that there are five steps in the assessment process: screening, determining eligibility, program planning, monitoring progress, and program evaluation. To determine a child's eligibility for services and to develop a program or intervention plan, the team will have to review the results of assessment. A systematic organization of the results of the assessment can be very useful in helping the team to determine:

Whether the child is eligible for services

The current level of the child's performance in each domain

The outcome statements for the Individualized Family Service Plan (IFSP) or the annual goals and objectives for the Individualized Educational Plan (IEP)

The least restrictive environment in which the services will be delivered

GENERAL PRINCIPLES

The general principles that should guide the development of an assessment report are presented below.

Organize the Information Systematically

Write the sections separately and use headings throughout the report. Discuss conclusions and recommendations at the end of the report; do not insert them in the body of the document. In the following paragraph, the information is poorly organized. Discuss what the writer has done wrong, and suggest a way to reorganize the material.

Sasha, a 10-month-old child, was recently referred for screening. The screening team recommended that this child be monitored over the next few months because she may have a delay in developing speech and language. The vision screening reported normal development. The occupational therapist evaluated feeding skills. During the speech and language evaluation, Sasha did not babble. Her mother reported that she says "dada" but not "mama."

Relate Only the Facts

Report only factual information. Do not include hearsay or unsubstantiated information. When including information from other sources, such as other assessment reports, mention the date and name of the source. Identify the *unsubstantiated* information in the following example:

Eighteen-month-old Ricky was evaluated for delays in motor development. His mother reported that he rolls over and pulls himself to a sitting position. A neighbor was heard to say that Ricky liked to eat his sister's food. The occupational therapist, after evaluating Ricky, reported that he is able to feed himself.

Include Only Essential Information

Write about the facts, but avoid including extraneous information about the child or the family. Although your report should be comprehensive, some information may not be essential; you will need to make judgments about whether what you have learned is appropriate for inclusion. Use only information that contributes to the understanding of the child, the test results, and recommendations. In the following example, decide which information is essential and which information can be *disregarded:*

Heather had difficulty concentrating on the block building. She was distracted by noise in another part of the room and when the examiner handed her a block she immediately put it down. Her mother, who was neatly dressed, said that she had just bought Heather a toy at the new store around the corner. Her mother felt that Heather may have been distractible because she was thinking about her new toy.

Be Aware of Any Bias

Avoid generalizations that may bias the report. Be careful about stereotyping groups or cultures. Critically review your report for any systematic bias. Identify the *biasing* information in the following excerpts:

> The results of classroom observations and individual testing indicate that Jennifer does not make eye contact with adults. This is typical of other children in her sociocultural group.

> Juan was diagnosed as mentally retarded. Like other children who are mentally retarded, Juan will have difficulty getting along with the other children in his peer group.

Make Sure That the Information Is Accurate

Review the information to check for accuracy. When calculating test scores on the test form, be sure to double-check your work. Some tests require scores of several different types, and it is easy to make errors converting from one type of test score to another. The examiner should verify that the test scores were copied correctly from the test to the report. Be sure that the handwriting is legible and that there are no misinterpretations about performance due to illegibility, inaccurate calculations, or inaccurate copying.

Avoid Technical Jargon

Use clear, understandable language; technical jargon may make the report confusing or ambiguous. A discussion of formulas used to measure discrepancies or theoretical perspectives of various experts should be avoided. How could the language in the following excerpt be *simplified?*

> Tony has dual diagnostic deficits which include a developmental disorder affecting speech, language, articulation, motor coordination, cognition, and attention. A coexisting diagnosis can be made of Attention Deficit–Hyperactivity Disorder and mental retardation. This diagnosis is strongly suggested by biological maternal history of ethanol abuse, apparently during the gestational period, and Tony's striking physiognomy.

Write Clearly

Work to develop report writing skills. The following checklist may be useful:

- Use an outline.
- Reread and rewrite a rough draft.
- Check for grammatical mistakes.
- Check punctuation.
- Use a spell checker.
- Avoid ambiguous language.

WRITING THE REPORT

In general, an assessment report has the following sections:

1. Identifying data
2. Reason for referral
3. Background information
4. Family involvement
5. Behavioral observations
6. Observations of the environment
7. Tests and interviews
8. Discussion of results
9. Summary
10. Recommendations

Each of these sections is a separate area. Use appropriate subheadings to help organize the report as suggested by the lists in the sections that follow.

Identifying Data

Information in the first section of the report should identify the child, the parents, the school or agency, the test, and the examiner:

1. *About the child:* include the child's name, address, phone number, chronological age in years and months, birthdate, and sex.
2. *About the family:* include names and addresses of family members.
3. *About the school or agency:* include the placement (e.g., preschool, kindergarten, type of child care), address, phone number, director or principal's name, and teacher's name.
4. *About the testing:* include the name of the examiner, the date of testing, and the date the report was written.

Sources for this information include school or agency records, the referral form, interviews with family members or teachers, and records of tests administered earlier.

Reason for Referral

The second section contains a summary of the reasons for referral and the name of the person who initiated the referral. Throughout the report, be sure that the reasons for referral are directly addressed and that the conclusions and recommendations refer to them. As the report is developed, one theme will be the reasons for referral and the extent to which the testing addressed these reasons. This information can be obtained from the referral form and from interviews with family members, teachers, or child care providers.

Background Information

Information about the child's background relating to child care, education, family, medical care, and previous assessment results should be briefly summarized.

Medical history can include a description of any unusual medical problems, medical diagnoses, extended hospital stays, continuing medical care, general health, and results of vision and hearing testing. Young children who are referred for further assessment may have experienced early and prolonged medical interventions. Some of these children are survivors of neonatal intensive care units, having received extensive medical care for genetic abnormalities or other conditions. Their medical folders may be quite lengthy, and the examiner will need to judge which information is pertinent to the reason for referral. Extensive discussion of a child's medical history may bias the reader to think that the child is severely disabled or may be unusually difficult to manage.

A summary of the information about child care, preschool, or nursery school experiences is also important. Data about dates of attendance, regularity of attendance, type of placement or services provided, performance, interventions tried, and results of previous educational testing can be obtained from school/agency/center records, interviews, and home visits.

Information about familial and/or cultural background can be useful. This type of information should be used carefully and judiciously. Use it only when it is relevant and helps to explain the behavior of the child or the results of testing. McLoughlin and Lewis (1990) wrote that sociocultural aspects of a child's background may be important to consider.

> Factors that merit attention include size of the family, living and studying conditions, educational values, family status and crises, and the student's relations with parents and other family members. Information about favorite recreational activities and types of friendships may also contribute to a better understanding of the issues. (p. 460)

Knowledge about family and cultural background can be obtained from interviews with the child, family members, teachers, and other professionals, and through a home visit.

When summarizing background information before testing begins, it is important to review copies of the original documents. Frequently, these materials can be helpful in determining which tests, observations, or procedures to use when assessing the child. Sources of information include hospital and physician records, case histories, interviews (with physicians, family members, and caregivers), and school records.

Family Involvement

The Individuals with Disabilities Education Act Amendments of 1991 (PL 102–119) provide for family-directed assessment. Parents are full partners in the assessment process. As members of the assessment team, they can assist in identifying strengths and needs of their child. Also, they can advise the team regarding their priorities of family-based needs and preferences for services.

Behavioral Observations

The report includes a description of the child's behavior during formal and informal testing. The examiner will want to observe whether the child was cooperative, distractible, attentive, tired, or shy, or exhibited other types of behavior. What was the child's behavior at the beginning of the testing? During the testing? At the end? This section reports any observations conducted in the child care setting or in the school.

As discussed in Chapter 4, systematic observations can be an important source of data. Such observations help us to understand the child's behavior and learning strategies and may also inform us about intervention strategies. Observations about behavior that are gathered in the testing situation may not be generalizable to other settings. During testing, a narrow sample of behavior is assessed. To a certain extent, the testing situation is artificial, and this must be considered when drawing conclusions about a child's behavior (Sattler, 1988). A child's behavior may vary in different settings and with different examiners.

In writing the report, use the following list of behaviors as a starting point for discussion (Sattler, 1988, p. 728):

> Physical appearance
> Reactions to test session and to the examiner
> General behavior
> Typical mode of relating to the examiner
> Language style
> General response style
> Response to failures
> Response to successes
> Response to encouragement
> Activity level
> Attitude toward self
> Attitude toward the examiner and the testing process
> Visual–motor ability
> Unusual habits, mannerisms, or verbalizations
> The examiner's reaction to the child

Observations of the Environment

The description of the environment of the child covers the home and the child care center, preschool, or school. Approaches to assessing the environment were discussed in Chapter 4.

Tests and Interviews Used

The report includes a list of the tests, both formal and informal, and the interviews that were conducted to collect the assessment data. Interviews with family members, caregivers, teachers, and other professionals can provide useful information.

Discussion of Results

In listing the results of the assessment instruments, it is important to use scores of the same types throughout the section. Standard scores, percentiles, or stanines are preferred. It may be useful to report two or more types, such as standard scores and percentiles.

Hypothesis Generation.   When discussing the results of testing, we like the interpretive processes that are described by Kaufman (1979) and McGrew (1986). They use a technique known as hypothesis generation. When applied to test analysis, a hypothesis is an explanation of a child's performance and behavior based on the assessment data that have been collected.

As the report is developed, several hypotheses will emerge. One hypothesis will relate to the referral questions, which should be addressed as the report is developed. Other hypotheses may relate to levels of development, behavior, intelligence, functioning, achievement, communication, motor development, or sensory functioning.

The test data (here, we mean the results of formal and informal testing, observations, and interviews) will be used to support one or more hypotheses. For example, information obtained from interviews with caregivers, teachers, and family members can be integrated with information obtained from behavioral observations of the child to support the determination of attention deficit disorder.

Kaufman, in discussing his approach to test interpretation, cautioned that examiners should remember that hypotheses "are not facts and may indeed prove to be artifacts" (Kaufman, 1979, p. 177). Hypotheses are informed assumptions, and when hypotheses cannot be substantiated by evidence, further investigation is warranted. The test data may need to be reanalyzed, or additional data may have to be collected to generate new or modified hypotheses.

Each test should be analyzed separately, and then the results should be synthesized. The following steps for test interpretation are adapted from the works of Kaufman (1979) and McGrew (1986):

Step 1: Interpret overall performance. Describe the overall performance of the child on the tests, and supply an interpretation of the full-scale or total score performances.

Step 2: Determine relative strengths and needs in each area tested. Make a list of the subtests in each test that represent relative strengths and relative weaknesses. Determine the abilities that are represented by each of the subtests.

Step 3: Compare the subtests on all the tests. Consider each subtest and the abilities it measures. Compare the shared abilities across test data. If relative strengths and weaknesses do not emerge across the test data, then interpret unique abilities.

Step 4: Integrate the relative strengths and needs. Identify relative strengths and weaknesses by comparing all the test data including the results of formal and informal testing, interviews, and observations, and background information about the child.

Summary

The next-to-last section is a transition between the discussion of the results and the recommendations. Because the child's performance has already been analyzed, keep this section brief. Summarize the major points that have been discussed and synthesize the results. Report the current level of functioning, and indicate areas of relative strength and need. Answer the referral questions. Restate the themes that have emerged.

Recommendations

An assessment is conducted chiefly to answer the referral questions and to develop recommendations. The recommendations should logically be based on the information that is contained in the assessment report. Suggest realistic, practical recommendations that can be implemented. Recommendations can be developed for the child in a variety of settings and can include the home and the child care center. Specific goals and objectives should not be included in the assessment report. These should be written in the IFSP or IEP. Figure 14.1 contains an example of a case study.

EVALUATING THE REPORT

Writing an assessment report is an important way to communicate test results. A report helps you to systematically organize the results of testing, to analyze a child's performance, and to make recommendations. The checklist below can be used to review the adequacy of assessment reports.

Identifying Information
1. Is the information complete?
2. Is the information accurate?

Reason for Referral
1. Is the reason for referral clearly described?
2. Is the source of the referral included?
3. Does the reason for referral provide a reason for conducting the assessment?

Background Information
1. Is this section complete?
2. Are sources of information missing?
3. Can some information be omitted?

Behavioral Observations
1. Are the observations clearly described?
2. Are any of the descriptions vague?
3. Does this section help the reader to visualize the child's behavior?

Tests, Observations, and Interviews Used
1. Are the sources of information identified?

Discussion of Results
1. Does the discussion relate to the referral questions?
2. Is this section organized around themes?

Identifying Data

Name: Gina A.
Birth date: March 4, 19XX
Age: 5 years, 2 months
Sex: female
Address: 1 Hill Road
        Allen, _____
Foster parent: C. B.
Address: 1 Hill Road
        Allen, _____

Date: May 10, 19XX
Date of testing: May 6, 19XX
Examiner: L. A. Kahn
Teacher: M. Gordon

Phone: (XXX) XXX-XXXX

Reason for Referral

Gina was referred by her teacher because of problems of extreme activity within the classroom, developmental delay, and a history of physical abuse.

Background Information

Gina has been receiving early intervention services since infancy. Her caregivers have reported that her behavior is often oppositional, easily distractible, and passively aggressive. An evaluation by the E. C. Medical Center on 2/23/XX stated that Gina presented evidence of fetal alcohol syndrome. In at least four or five evaluations over the years, this child generally tests out as having a mild developmental delay. A recent psychological evaluation by Dr. Jones on 10/10/XX indicated a Stanford–Binet score of 62 and "functioning well below her chronological age in language, cognitive, and perceptual motor skill areas."

    Gina has been in foster care since the age of three when she was exposed to inappropriate sexual behaviors at home, neglect, and abuse. Her biological mother is reported to be an abuser of alcohol who has a history of physical and sexual abuse. Her brother, Paul, is living with a paternal grandmother. Her father has infrequent contact with the family. Her foster care family wants to help Gina, and the family has been very involved in the assessment process.

Family Involvement

Mr. and Mrs. B., Gina's foster family, have been in frequent contact with the assessment team. Several team members visited the home, where Mr. and Mrs. B. shared their concerns about Gina and volunteered to participate with the team in identifying Gina's strengths and needs.

Behavioral Observations

Informal testing and achievement testing were begun in a quiet corner of the preschool classroom so that Gina could get used to the examiner before going to the examiner's office for further testing. The child was very reluctant to participate in the testing, and her behavior was consistently negative. Testing sessions were very brief because Gina's attention span was short and because of her refusal to participate. She could attend to a task for a few seconds and then was distracted. She had to be coaxed to focus on the tasks. She was very distracted by all the test materials and touched everything throughout the session.

Observations of the Environment

Gina is currently in an inclusive setting. That is, the preschool classroom includes children who have disabilities and children who do not. Six children are in the classroom, with a teacher and an aide. In addition, an occupational therapist, a physical therapist, and a speech pathologist are available. The preschool room is divided into four centers: house, block, art, and reading. There is much

---

FIGURE 14.1 Case study

activity in the room as the children, teacher, aide, and related service personnel move about. Children's pictures and drawings cover the walls. The room appears to be stimulating and busy.

Tests and Interviews Used

The following tests were administered: Kaufman Assessment Battery for Children, Peabody Picture Vocabulary Test—R, and Boehm Test of Basic Concepts. Gina was observed three different times in her preschool class. Interviews were conducted with Gina's foster parent and with her teacher.

Discussion of Results

On the Kaufman Assessment Battery for Children Gina's mental processing composite score fell into the 2nd percentile; the achievement score fell into the 1st percentile. Relative strengths on the cognitive and achievement batteries were Hand Movements (motor planning, perceptual organization) and Gestalt Closure (recall, alertness to the environment). Significant weaknesses on the cognitive and achievement batteries were Number Recall (short-term auditory memory, reproduction of a model), Riddles (word knowledge/recall), Word Order (verbal/auditory comprehension), Photo Series (visual sequencing, visual perceptual organization), Arithmetic (quantitative concepts, applied school-related skills, reasoning, verbal comprehension), and Reading/Decoding (applied school-related skills, early language development, long-term memory, reasoning).

On the Peabody Picture Vocabulary Test—Revised, Gina had a standard score of 44 and a percentile rank of 1. Her performance remains consistent in terms of her overall standard score, indicating that her understanding of single words is commensurate with her cognitive ability.

On the Boehm Test of Basic Concepts Gina demonstrated mastery of 18 out of 25 concepts. She missed the following concepts: most, widest, over, starting, last, whole, and different. She is able to show that she understands many of these concepts in concrete situations, however.

Overall, it appears that Gina's short attention span and distractibility interfere with the formal testing. Observations confirmed that Gina performs somewhat better in the classroom than on the formal testing. However, when Gina's performance is compared with typical children in the preschool, she performs well below her age peers. Classroom observations also indicate that Gina is reluctant to comply with requests made by her teacher and that she rarely cooperates with other children. She has a constant need for limit setting.

Summary

Gina is a child who has been diagnosed as having fetal alcohol syndrome. The results of formal testing, observations, and interviews indicated that she has a developmental delay, has a short attention span, is distractible, and has many negative behaviors. Her concept and language development are well below that of her age peers.

Recommendations

Gina is certainly in need of continued intervention services to address her broad-based developmental delays. She will need intensive intervention services, consistent setting of limits, expectations for more age-appropriate behavior, and an environment with a great deal of structure.

Counseling and behavior management strategies should be offered to the foster family to help them deal with the negative behaviors, attention span, and distractibility.

3. Are the themes discussed separately, including references to appropriate tests and assessment procedures?

4. Are strengths and needs described?

Summary

1. Does this section restate the major themes and how the testing addressed the reasons for referral?

2. Is this section too long?

Recommendations

1. Do the recommendations logically follow from the rest of the report?

2. Can the recommendations be implemented?

3. Are recommendations for a variety of settings included?

4. Are the recommendations understandable?

General Evaluation

1. Is the writing clear?

2. Has the report been proofread?

3. Have the spelling, grammar, and punctuation been checked?

4. Are the sections of the report identifiable?

5. Has technical language been minimized?

6. Is there any bias?

USING COMPUTERS

Computer programs can be useful for record keeping, test scoring, writing reports, and test administration.

Record Keeping

Computer programs can be very effective in helping to store records. Professionals can enter information about a child directly into a computer file. With the use of a scanner, a child's records, including test records, can be conveniently stored for future use.

Test Scoring/Report Generation

Many test scoring computer programs are readily available and are easy to use. These programs not only compute test scores, they also generate reports. For most computer scoring programs, the examiner enters the identifying information and the raw scores. Within a few minutes the computer processes the information and produces a report. Computer scoring programs save valuable teacher time and also help to minimize scoring and computation errors. Many publishers offer test scoring programs. Computer scoring programs should be carefully selected and used. Figure 14.2 shows a sample computer printout for the Peabody Individual Achievement Test—Revised.

FIGURE 14.2 Sample computer printout for the Peabody Individual Achievement Test—Revised

SOURCE: Copyright © 1985 American Guidance Service, Inc., Circle Pines, MN 55014. Reprinted by permission.

Developmental Score Profiles

This one-page report provides either the Grade Equivalent Profile or Age Equivalent Profile for the student.

The Grade Equivalent profile gives a graphic representation of the subject's estimated grade equivalent range for each subtest and composite. The upper and lower limit for each grade equivalent is shown at the left of the page. On the body of the profile, this range is plotted using asterisks. The capital G in the profile indicates the subject's current grade placement.

The Age Equivalent profile provides the same information based on age equivalents. Here the capital A indicates the subject's actual age.

```
5/16/90      Peabody Individual Achievement Test - Revised
             By Frederick C. Markwardt, Jr

Student: Brown, Bill E                    Sex: Male

School/Agency: Golden Lake Elementary     Grade: 2

Teacher/Counselor: Ms M Perez             Examiner: Mr Paulson

             Year  Month  Day      Reasons for testing
             ----  -----  ---   -------------------------------
Test Date:    90     5    16    Bill is not achieving up to his ability.
Birth Date:   82     7    19
Chrono. Age:   7     8    27
Rounded Age:   7     9

                        SCORE SUMMARY
Standard scores were derived from Age norm tables.

Subtest or          68%       Raw   Grade   Age    Standard  %ile
Composite      Conf. Level   Score  Equiv.  Equiv.  Score    Rank   NCE

General        +1.00 SEM      57            10-0     135      99     99
Information    Obtained Score 54     4.4    9-8      131      98     94
Subtest        -1.00 SEM      51            9-4      127      96     88

Reading        +1.00 SEM      50            8-3      106      66     58
Recognition    Obtained Score 48     2.8    8-2      104      61     56
Subtest        -1.00 SEM      46            8-0      102      55     53

Reading        +1.00 SEM      55            9-0      111      77     65
Comprehension  Obtained Score 52     3.2    8-7      108      70     61
Subtest        -1.00 SEM      49            8-3      105      63     57

TOTAL          +1.00 SEM     104            8-7      108      70     61
READING        Obtained Score 100    3.0    8-5      106      66     58
               -1.00 SEM      96            8-2      104      61     56

Mathematics    +1.00 SEM      42            8-9      115      84     71
Subtest        Obtained Score 40     3.1    8-6      111      77     65
               -1.00 SEM      38            8-4      107      68     60

Spelling       +1.00 SEM      46            8-0      103      58     54
Subtest        Obtained Score 44     2.3    7-10     100      50     50
               -1.00 SEM      42            7-8      .97      42     46

TOTAL          +1.00 SEM     244            8-7      112      79     67
TEST           Obtained Score 238    3.1    8-5      110      75     64
               -1.00 SEM     232            8-4      108      70     61

Written Expression II (Prompt A)          Grade-based Stanine = 5
   Raw Score = 28  Developmental Scaled Score = 5

WRITTEN LANGUAGE
   Age Standard Score = 96 +/- 3  Scaled Score Sum = 3 + 5 = 8
                                  %ile Rank = 39  %ile Range = 32 - 47

COPYRIGHT 1990, AMERICAN GUIDANCE SERVICE, INC., CIRCLE PINES, MN 55014
```

```
5/16/90      Peabody Individual Achievement Test - Revised

             DEVELOPMENTAL SCORE PROFILES

Student: Brown, Bill E
Confidence Level: 68%          Age Equivalent Profile

Age
Equivalent Range: 4   5   6   7   8   9  10  11  12  13  14  15  16  17  18  19
=======================+===+===+===+===+===+===+===+===+===+===+===+===+===+===+
General Info.
  9-4 to 10-0                                   ****
-----------------------+===+===+===+===+===+===+===+===+===+===+===+===+===+===+
Reading Recog.
  3-0 to 8-3                          A       **
-----------------------+===+===+===+===+===+===+===+===+===+===+===+===+===+===+
Reading Comp.
  8-3 to 9-0                          A      ****
=======================+===+===+===+===+===+===+===+===+===+===+===+===+===+===+
TOTAL READING
  8-2 to 8-7                          A      ***
=======================+===+===+===+===+===+===+===+===+===+===+===+===+===+===+
Mathematics
  8-4 to 8-9                              A      ***
-----------------------+===+===+===+===+===+===+===+===+===+===+===+===+===+===+
Spelling
  7-8 to 8-0                             A    ***
=======================+===+===+===+===+===+===+===+===+===+===+===+===+===+===+
TOTAL TEST
  8-4 to 8-7                           A      ***
=======================+===+===+===+===+===+===+===+===+===+===+===+===+===+===+

COPYRIGHT 1990, AMERICAN GUIDANCE SERVICE, INC., CIRCLE PINES, MN 55014
```

(continued)

475

FIGURE 14.2 (continued)

5/16/90   Peabody Individual Achievement Test - Revised   Page 1
Brown, Bill E

PEABODY INDIVIDUAL ACHIEVEMENT TEST - REVISED

The Peabody Individual Achievement Test-Revised (PIAT-R) is an individually administered achievement test providing wide-range assessment in the content areas of: General Information, Reading Recognition, Reading Comprehension, Mathematics, Spelling, and Written Expression. In addition to these six subtests, the PIAT-R provides three composite scores: Total Reading, Total Test, and Written Language (optional).

Age Based Score Analysis Narrative Report for Bill Brown.

This report summarizes the PIAT-R performance of Bill Brown, who was tested on May 16, 1990. Bill is enrolled in Grade 2 at Golden Lake Elementary. At the time of testing, he was 7 years, 9 months. The examiner was Mr Paulson.

For each subtest and composite, Bill's score is reported as a grade or age equivalent, standard score, and percentile rank. Each is defined below.

1. The GRADE EQUIVALENT tells the grade level in the standardization sample for which that raw score was the mean, or typical performance. For example, a grade equivalent of 4.2 means that the obtained raw score was the average score for students in the second month of Grade 4.

2. The AGE EQUIVALENT is similar to the grade equivalent, except it tells the age in the standardization sample for which the obtained raw score was the mean.

3. The STANDARD SCORE relates a student's raw score to the performance of the corresponding standardization norm group, such as the grade level or age group. For all standard scores reported, the mean is 100 and the standard deviation is 15. A standard score of 115, for example, means that the obtained raw score was one standard deviation above the mean of the norm group.

4. PERCENTILE RANKS express an obtained raw score in terms of the percent of scores equal to or lower than the raw score when compared to the norm group. For example, a percentile rank of 50 means that the raw score was the same as or better than the raw scores of 50 percent of those in the norm sample.

I. General Information Subtest

General Information measures mastery of the general body of knowledge taught in school, including information from science, social studies, and fine arts. On this measure of general encyclopedic knowledge, Bill obtained an age equivalent of 9-8. Expressed another way, his performance yielded a standard score of 131 and percentile rank of 98. This means that he performed as well as or better than 98 percent of the seven-year-olds who took the subtest as part of the national standardization sample.

5/16/90   Peabody Individual Achievement Test - Revised   Page 2
Brown, Bill E

II. Reading Recognition Subtest

On the Reading Recognition subtest, which measures the ability to recognize sounds associated with printed letters and the ability to read words aloud, Bill obtained an age equivalent of 8-2. His performance yielded a standard score of 104 and percentile rank of 61, meaning that he performed as well as or better than 61 percent of the seven-year-olds who took the subtest as part of the national standardization sample.

III. Reading Comprehension Subtest

Reading Comprehension measures the ability to understand the meaning of written material. Bill obtained an age equivalent of 8-7. His performance yielded a standard score of 108 and percentile rank of 70, meaning that he performed as well as or better than 70 percent of the seven-year-olds who took the subtest as part of the national standardization sample.

IV. TOTAL READING

Bill's overall performance in reading ability is summarized by the Total Reading composite score, the combination of Reading Recognition and Reading Comprehension subtest scores. Bill obtained an age equivalent of 8-5. His performance yielded a standard score of 106 and percentile rank of 66, meaning that his Total Reading score is the same as or better than 66 percent of the seven-year-olds who took the reading subtests as part of the national standardization sample.

V. Mathematics Subtest

The Mathematics subtest measures the ability to understand mathematical concepts and procedures, to perform calculations, and to solve problems. Bill obtained an age equivalent of 8-6. His performance yielded a standard score of 111 and percentile rank of 77, meaning that he performed as well as or better than 77 percent of the seven-year-olds who took the subtest as part of the national standardization sample.

VI. Spelling Subtest

This subtest measures the ability to recognize letters from their names or sounds and to recognize the standard spelling of words. Bill obtained an age equivalent of 7-10. His performance yielded a standard score of 100 and percentile rank of 50, meaning that he performed as well as or better than 50 percent of the seven-year-olds who took the subtest as part of the national standardization sample.

VII. TOTAL TEST

The Total Test composite score is a measure of the overall level of achievement on the first five subtests: General Information, Reading Recognition, Reading Comprehension, Mathematics, and Spelling. Bill obtained an age equivalent of 8-5. His performance yielded a standard score of 110 and percentile rank of 75, meaning that his standard score of 131 was significantly greater than his Reading Comprehension subtest standard score of 108 at the .01 level of significance.

A comparison of Bill's subtest scores on General Information and Mathematics reveals that his General Information subtest standard score of 131 was significantly greater than his Mathematics subtest standard score of 111 at the .01 level of significance.

A comparison of Bill's subtest scores on General Information and Spelling reveals that his General Information subtest standard score of 131 was significantly greater than his Spelling subtest standard score of 100 at the .01 level of significance.

Total Test score is the same as or better than 75 percent of the seven-year-olds who took the five PIAT-R subtests as part of the national standardization sample.

VIII. Written Expression Subtest

On this assessment of written language skills, the Written Expression subtest, Level II, asks students to write a story to describe a picture shown to them. Bill received a Written Expression stanine score of 5, which is considered average in relation to the scores of other students in grade(s) 2 who took the subtest as part of the national standardization sample. Bill's performance on the Written Expression subtest can also be reported in terms of a Developmental Scaled Score that describes his performance in relation to the full range of scores of students in Grades 2 through 12 in the national standardization sample. On a 15-point standard score scale (mean of 8, standard deviation of approximately 3), Bill's Developmental Scaled Score was 5.

IX. WRITTEN LANGUAGE

This optional composite score, the combination of the Spelling and Written Expression subtests, assesses performance in written language. Bill obtained a standard score of 96, where the mean is 100 and the standard deviation is 15. His performance yielded a percentile rank of 39, meaning that his written language skills were the same as or better than 39 percent of the seven-year-olds who took the Spelling and Written Expression subtests as part of the national standardization sample.

SUBTEST COMPARISONS

Pairwise Comparisons			Age Based Standard Scores	Standard Score Difference	Significance Level
General Info.	vs.	Reading Recog.	131 > 104	27	.01
General Info.	vs.	Reading Comp.	131 > 108	23	.01
General Info.	vs.	Mathematics	131 > 111	20	.01
General Info.	vs.	Spelling	131 > 100	31	.01
Reading Recog.	vs.	Reading Comp.	104 < 108	4	NS
Reading Recog.	vs.	Mathematics	104 < 111	7	NS
Reading Recog.	vs.	Spelling	104 < 100	4	NS
Reading Comp.	vs.	Mathematics	108 < 111	3	NS
Reading Comp.	vs.	Spelling	108 > 100	8	NS
Mathematics	vs.	Spelling	111 > 100	11	NS

A comparison of Bill's subtest scores on General Information and Reading Recognition reveals that his General Information subtest standard score of 131 was significantly greater than his Reading Recognition subtest standard score of 104 at the .01 level of significance.

A comparison of Bill's subtest scores on General Information and Reading Comprehension reveals that his General Information subtest

(continued)

FIGURE 14.2 (continued)

Standard Score Profile and Subtest Comparisons

The Standard Score Profile, also one page, reports each standard score with its confidence interval and graphs them. In addition, for each pair of subtests comparisons, the Subtest Comparisons report gives the standard score difference and significance level of the difference.

```
5/16/90        Peabody Individual Achievement Test - Revised

                          STANDARD SCORE PROFILE

Student: Brown, Bill E
Confidence Level: 68%
Age Based

                        ------- STANDARD SCORE (Mean=100, SD=15) -------
Standard Score Range      60  70  80  90  100 110 120 130 140
========================
General Information                                 *****
  127 to 135

Reading Recognition                        ***
  102 to 106

Reading Comprehension                          *****
  105 to 111
========================
TOTAL READING                              ***
  104 to 108
========================
Mathematics                                  ******
  107 to 115

Spelling                               *****
  97 to 103
========================
TOTAL TEST                                 ***
  108 to 112
========================
WRITTEN LANGUAGE                       *****
  93 to 99
========================
Standard Score Range      --%--+--%--+--%--+--%--+--%--+--%--+--%--
                           1     5    25   50   75   95    99
                          ------ PERCENTILE RANK ------


                          SUBTEST COMPARISONS

                         Age Based
                         Standard  Standard Score  Significance
Pairwise Comparisons      Scores     Difference       Level
------------------------  -------   -------------   ------------
General Info.  vs.  Reading Recog.   131 > 104          27         .01
General Info.  vs.  Reading Comp.    131 > 108          23         .01
General Info.  vs.  Mathematics      131 > 111          20         .01
General Info.  vs.  Spelling         131 > 100          31         .01
Reading Recog. vs.  Reading Comp.    104 < 108           4         NS
Reading Recog. vs.  Mathematics      104 < 111           7         NS
Reading Recog. vs.  Spelling         104 > 100           4         NS
Reading Comp.  vs.  Mathematics      108 < 111           3         NS
Reading Comp.  vs.  Spelling         108 > 100           8         NS
Mathematics    vs.  Spelling         111 > 100          11         NS

COPYRIGHT 1990, AMERICAN GUIDANCE SERVICE, INC., CIRCLE PINES, MN 55014
```

Computer-administered Tests

A computer-administered test is one in which the child interacts directly with the computer and the computer scores and reports the performance of the child. There are few such tests suitable for young children; in fact, for very young children, their use should be discouraged.

For school-age children, Monitoring Basic Skills Progress (Fuchs, Hamlett, & Fuchs, 1990) is a computer-assisted measurement program that tests and reports on progress in three curriculum areas: reading, mathematics, and spelling. The computer graphs the child's progress. The Basic Reading program uses the cloze technique to evaluate progress in reading. Figure 14.3 shows a sample computer screen that is presented to a child and a sample graph of progress. Figure 14.4 lists useful criteria for selecting and evaluating software.

FIGURE 14.3   Sample printouts from Monitoring Basic Skills Progress: Basic Reading; and graphed record of child's progress

SOURCE: From *Monitoring Basic Skills Progress: Basic Reading* by L. Fuchs, C. Hamlett, and D. Fuchs. Austin, TX: Pro-Ed, Inc., 1990. Reprinted by permission.

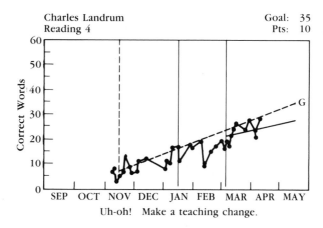

Charles Landrum

A TRIP TO THE FAIR

Mrs. Black decided that her students needed to go on a field trip to the farm. Mrs. Black and her students lived <u>in</u> a big city. They did not <u>have</u> a chance to go to the country often. The students were excited about _____ chance to go to a farm. _____ on a Monday morning, Mrs. Black ___ her students climbed onto the _____ bus, one by one. The driver ____ off and drove over the big bridge ____

Use ⟨SPACEBAR⟩, ⟨RETURN⟩, and ⟨ARROWS⟩

Sample computer screen showing student progress.

Charles Landrum   Goal: 35
Reading 4   Pts: 10

Uh-oh!   Make a teaching change.

Software Evaluation

Background Information

1. Name of program: Version:
2. Publisher: Copyright:
3. Publisher's address:

4. Publisher's telephone number: Hotline/support number:
5. Cost:

Hardware Requirements

6. Which computer system was used?
   _____ Macintosh
   _____ MS-DOS
   _____ Apple IIGS
   _____ Apple IIe/IIc
   _____ Other _____

7. For what other computers is this software available?

   _____ Macintosh
   _____ MS-DOS
   _____ Apple IIGS
   _____ Apple IIe/IIc
   _____ Other _____

8. What are the system requirements needed to run this software?

   _____ K required for memory   _____ Mouse   _____ Other _____

9. What type of monitor is required?

   _____ EGA   _____ VGA   _____ SVGA   _____ Apple   _____ Macintosh

10. What type of printer is required?

   _____ dot matrix   _____ ink jet   _____ laser printer   _____ daisy wheel

11. What assistive devices can be used?

   _____ Touch screen   _____ Speech synthesizer   _____ Switch
   _____ Adapted keyboard   _____ Other _____

Uses

12. For which applications can the program be used?
   _____ Record keeping
        a. Number of individual student records that can be stored _____
        b. Maximum number of scores that can be stored per child _____
        c. Does the program allow records to be entered by a scanner? _____
   _____ Test preparation
        a. Capacity (number of items) _____
        b. Does the program allow the teacher to enter items? _____
        c. Is the test generated by the computer? _____
        d. Does the program analyze test data? _____
   _____ Test scoring
   _____ Report writing

FIGURE 14.4 Evaluating computer software

_____ Test administration
   a. Does the program require teacher assistance? _____
   b. Can the program be adapted or customized? _____
   c. Does it use branching? _____

Overall Evaluation

	Very poor	Poor	Acceptable	Very good	Excellent
13. Comprehensiveness	_____	_____	_____	_____	_____
14. Appropriateness	_____	_____	_____	_____	_____
15. Ease of use	_____	_____	_____	_____	_____
16. Documentation	_____	_____	_____	_____	_____
17. Flexibility	_____	_____	_____	_____	_____
18. Screen displays	_____	_____	_____	_____	_____

PREFERRED PRACTICES

The writing of assessment reports takes patience, practice, and skill. Strive for a writing style that clearly communicates what has been learned about the child as well as your recommendations for intervention. The report should be free of grammatical, mechanical, and spelling errors.

Assessment reports can be useful in helping to make instructional decisions (Salvia & Ysseldyke, 1991). The results of assessment can assist in helping parents and professionals to develop goals and objectives for children. By determining what children know and what they have not yet learned, testing can help in determining the next steps in planning developmentally appropriate programs. The assessment of children can help us to decide _what_ to teach and how to plan to strengthen the abilities of children.

According to Salvia and Ysseldyke (1991), tests provide limited information on _how_ to teach; the best way to teach is "to rely on generally effective procedures" (p. 604). Decisions made about how to teach must reflect data gathered by professionals and represent strategies and interventions that have worked and hypotheses or informed guesses about what will work. These hypotheses are verified or discarded based on what we learn while working with the child.

The use of computers in testing will continue to develop in three areas: test administration, test scoring, and test reports. As computer programs proliferate, it will be important to be an informed consumer. The quality of computer programs will vary, and the professional will need to carefully evaluate the programs before using them to analyze, interpret, and develop recommendations about children.

STUDY QUESTIONS AND SUGGESTED ACTIVITIES

1. What are the purposes of assessment reports?
2. Discuss how the hypothesis generation approach can be useful in interpreting test performance.
3. Distinguish between deciding _what_ to teach and deciding _how_ to teach.
4. Obtain a computer program relating to testing. Using the criteria presented in this chapter, evaluate the usefulness of this program. What additional criteria would you add to our list?

5. Would young children have difficulty taking computer-administered tests? Under what conditions?

REFERENCES

Fuchs, L. S., Hamlett, C., & Fuchs, D. (1990). *Monitoring basic skills progress.* Austin, TX: Pro-Ed.

Kaufman, A. (1979). *Intelligent testing with the WISC-R.* New York: Wiley.

McGrew, K. S. (1986). *Clinical interpretation of the Woodcock–Johnson tests of cognitive ability.* Orlando, FL: Grune & Stratton.

McLoughlin, J. A., & Lewis, R. B. (1990). *Assessing special students.* Columbus, OH: Merrill.

Salvia, J., & Ysseldyke, J. (1991). *Assessment.* Boston, MA: Houghton Mifflin.

Sattler, J. (1988). *Assessment of children.* San Diego, CA: Jerome M. Sattler, Publisher.

Glossary

Achievement. Knowledge acquired as a result of instruction.

Achievement Tests. Tests that assess past learning.

Adaptive Behavior or Adaptive Development. Area of development that focuses on an individual's effectiveness in meeting the standards of maturation, learning, personal independence, and/or social responsibility expected for his or her age level.

Adaptive–Transactive Perspective. Emphasis on the importance of the interaction between the infant, the social environment, and the physical environment.

Adventitious Visual Impairments. Visual impairments acquired after birth as a result of heredity, accident, or disease.

Age Equivalent. A type of derived score; the average score for a particular age group. Age equivalents are stated in years and months (e.g., 4-2 means 4 years and 2 months).

Air Conduction Testing. The determination of loss of hearing at various frequencies.

Alternate Form Reliability. An estimate of the correlation of scores on two forms of the same test.

Alternate Forms. Equivalent forms of the same test.

Analytic Scoring. A type of scoring used to provide a detailed evaluation of a child's work.

Anecdotal Record. A brief narrative description recorded after the events have occurred.

Anoxia. An abnormally low amount of oxygen in the body.

Arena Assessment. A model of assessment in which a facilitator works with the child in assessment activities across disciplines. Other team members including the parents sit away from the child–adult dyad and observe and record information during these activities. Arena assessment may also occur via videotape.

Assessment. A global term for observing, gathering, and/or recording information for the purpose of decision making. The five steps in assessment are screening, determining eligibility, program planning, monitoring individual progress, and program evaluation.

Audiogram. A chart that measures hearing loss, produced by an instrument called an audiometer.

Augmentative/Alternative Communication. Communication used by nonverbal persons. Examples of augmentative/alternative communication devices include communication boards and synthesized speech systems.

Authentic Assessment. A type of assessment used to demonstrate a target skill or behavior in a real-life context.

Autism. A developmental disability, typically observed before age three, that significantly affects verbal and nonverbal communication, social interaction and the child's educational performance.

Basal Level. The point below which the examiner assumes that the child could obtain all correct responses and at which testing is begun.

Bimodal Distribution. A statistical distribution that has two modes.

Biological Approach. A medical approach that focuses on the infant's physical status and how it is related to the physical and social aspects of the environment.

Birth Asphyxia. A perinatal condition caused by a lack of oxygen and an excess of carbon dioxide in the blood.

Bone Conduction Testing. The determination of sensorineural hearing loss by vibrating bones.

Ceiling Level. The point above which the examiner assumes that the child would obtain all incorrect responses if the testing were to continue and at which testing is stopped.

Chaining. The linking of the various steps in a task analysis in order to achieve a target behavior.

Checklist. A list of characteristics or behaviors arranged in a consistent manner that allows the evaluator to check the presence or absence of the characteristic or behavior.

Child Find. One of the provisions of PL 101–476 (reauthorization of PL 94–142), Child Find is a series of activities that increase public awareness by providing information about screening, programs, and services.

Cloze Technique. A method of assessing reading level and comprehension by deleting every nth word from a 100- to 250-word paragraph and replacing each deletion with a blank line.

Cognitive Stages of Development. Described by Jean Piaget, these steps in the growth of human intelligence are successive, with each step building upon the previous one.

Communication. The transfer of information between two or more individuals.

Concurrent Validity. The extent to which two different tests administered at about the same time correlate with each other.

Conductive Hearing Loss. A hearing loss due to a barrier to the sound waves that travel from the outer ear to the inner ear. Causes include inflammation in the middle ear (otitis media), severe accumulation of wax, and poorly developed structures in the ear.

Confidence Interval. The range within which the true score can be found.

Congenital Visual Impairments. Visual impairments due to heredity, disease, or other conditions present during the prenatal or perinatal period.

Construct Validity. The extent to which a test measures a particular construct or concept.

Content Validity. The extent to which the test items reflect the instructional objectives.

Correlation. The quantification of the extent to which two or more scores vary together.

Correlation Coefficient. The quantification of the relationship between the scores. The letter r is used to represent the coefficient.

Criterion-referenced Test. A test that measures a child's performance with respect to a well-defined content domain.

Criterion-related Validity. The extent to which test scores obtained on one test or other measure relate to test scores obtained on the standardized test. There are two types of criterion-related validity: concurrent and predictive.

Curriculum-based Assessment (CBA). A broad approach to linking assessment to instruction, another test, or another outcome measure.

Deaf-blindness. A child with the disability of deaf-blindness exhibits concomitant visual and hearing impairments which together cause communication and other developmental and educational problems.

Deafness. A child who is deaf has a hearing loss so severe that with or without amplification the child is unable to process language through unaided hearing.

Decile. A measurement band that contains 10 percentiles.

Derived Score. The result of transforming a raw score to another type of score. Examples of derived scores include age and grade equivalents, standard scores, percentiles, and stanines.

Determining Eligibility. The establishment of whether a child meets the criteria for receiving services according to federal definitions. Professionals from various disciplines who have specific training on assessment approaches and on specialized instruments participate. Special educators and early intervention specialists may be involved in cognitive, readiness, adaptive development, or academic assessment. *Step 2* in the assessment process.

Developmental Approach. Development is conceptualized as a progression through regular stages, which may be qualitatively different, depending on individual differences.

Developmental Milestones. The significant points in a child's physical, mental, and emotional maturation.

Developmental Quotient. An estimate of the rate of development; a derived score.

Developmental Scores. Raw scores that have been transformed to reflect the average performance at age and grade levels.

Developmental Screening. A brief beginning procedure used to locate children who may be disabled, developmentally delayed, or gifted. Depending on the results of the screening, children may be referred for further assessment.

Developmental Tests. Instruments that assess a child's growth in one or more domains. These areas may include cognitive, motor, social-emotional, communication, or adaptive.

Deviation IQ. A standard score with a mean of 100 and a standard deviation of 15 or 16.

Diagnostic Test. A test that can be used to identify and describe a child's strengths and needs.

Direct Assessment. A traditional model of assessment in which the evaluator works with the child, one to one.

Direct Observation. A systematic process of gathering information by looking at children and their environments.

Distance Visual Acuity. A measurement of distance visual functioning, usually reported in terms of what a person with normal vision sees at 20 feet.

Due Process. A set of safeguards to be followed during the assessment process and the delivery of services described in PL 101–476. Due process ensures that the rights of children and their families are not violated.

Duration Recording. A recording that measures the length of time a specific event or behavior persists.

Dynamic Assessment. An approach to assessment in which the assessor actively engages the learner in learning.

Early Childhood Team (ECT). Parents, the family service coordinator, and representatives of various disciplines who assess and implement early intervention services.

Early Periodic Screening, Diagnosis, and Treatment (EPSDT) Program. Focuses on identifying health problems and developmental disabilities in preschool children whose families meet certain income requirements.

Equal-interval Scales. Scales constructed with an equal distance between points. The other scales of measurement are nominal, ordinal, and ratio.

Etiology. The cause or origin of a disease or disorder.

Eugenics Movement. The historical advocacy of improving the intellectual characteristics of the human race through selective breeding.

Evaluating the Program. The assessment of the effectiveness of the program; allows the team members to change or modify the program if needed. *Step 5* in the assessment process.

Evaluation. The process of establishing a value judgment based on actual data.

Event Recording. During an observation period, the recording of behavior each time it occurs.

Expressive Language. Spoken language that must be verbalized if communication is to take place.

External Evaluator. An individual who is hired to assess the effectiveness of a program.

Extrapolation. Estimates made of the performance of children outside of the normative sample.

Face Validity. The extent to which a test looks valid. Face validity is not considered to be a type of validity by all experts.

Facilitated Communication. A technique that allows the individual who is nonverbal to work with a facilitator in accessing a communication aid such as a communication board, computer, or voice output communication aid.

False Negative. The type of error that has been made when a child who is *not* referred for additional testing as a result of screening does need special services.

False Positive. The type of error that has been made when a child who is referred for additional assessment as a result of screening does *not* need special services.

Family-Directed Assessment. Information family members choose to share with other team members regarding family resources, priorities, and concerns.

Family Educational Rights and Privacy Act (FERPA). The Family Educational Rights and Privacy Act of 1974 (PL 93–380) gives families the right to review all records kept on their children as well as the right to challenge any of the information contained in such records.

Family-Focused Philosophy. An approach to working with families that enables family members to mobilize their resources in order to promote child and family functioning.

Family Stories. A family's stories about family background, important experiences, significant life events, interactions of family members, and family history.

Family Systems Model. A model for understanding the special needs of the child within the broader context of family issues.

Focus Group. A gathering of a small group of informed stakeholders, facilitated by an evaluator, for the purpose of gathering information through the discussion of relevant issues.

Focused Holistic Scoring. A type of scoring that focuses on a previously identified characteristic of a child's work.

Formative Evaluation. Evaluations that occur as the program is in progress.

Free Appropriate Public Education (FAPE). PL 101–476 (reauthorization of PL 94–142 and PL 99–457) specifies that every person with a disability, between the ages of three and twenty-one, must have an opportunity to attend public school and to receive services that address the individual's unique needs at no cost to the family.

Frequency Distribution. Way of organizing test scores that illustrates the range and number of scores.

Functional (Behavioral) Approach. Emphasis on the importance of external (to the child) factors for assisting skill development.

Functional Vision. A measurement of visual functioning in the natural environment (as opposed to a clinical setting).

g. The symbol for general intelligence; thought to be the common link among various mental abilities.

Galactosemia. A disorder in which the child is unable to metabolize lactose in milk. Left untreated, damage to the brain and liver can occur.

Gc. The symbol for crystallized abilities; that is, mental abilities that are influenced by acquired skills and knowledge.

General Impression Scoring. A type of scoring that provides general feedback on a child's work.

Gf. The symbol for fluid intelligence consisting of nonverbal comparatively culture-free mental abilities that are dependent on new learning.

Grade Equivalent. The average score of a particular grade; a type of derived score. Grade equivalents are always stated in grades and months (e.g., 1.2 means first grade, second month).

Hearing Impairment. A condition that adversely affects the child's educational performance but that is not included under the definition of deafness.

High-stakes Testing. The use of readiness or achievement tests to make classification, retention, or promotion decisions about children.

Hypertonicity. A condition in which the muscle is constantly tensed as a result of increased tone.

Hypotonicity. A condition in which the muscle cannot move or maintain good postural control because of lack of tone.

Immitance Screening. A type of screening for hearing loss which can be used to identify the presence of fluid in the middle ear and other abnormalities in the outer and middle ear. Immitance screening is also known as impedance audiometry.

Indirect Assessment. A flexible model of assessment in which information is gathered during routine or child-initiated activities.

Individualized Education Program (IEP). PL 101–476 mandates that all children and youth with disabilities (ages three to twenty-one) who require special education services have a written education plan, the IEP.

Individualized Family Service Plan (IFSP). PL 101–476 mandates that all eligible young children (birth through age two) and their families will have an IFSP. Children ages three to five may receive services provided by an IFSP or an IEP. The IFSP is a written document that specifies the plan for early intervention services and is guided by the family's concerns, priorities, and resources.

Informal Assessment. The assessment of performance that does not use a norm-referenced standardized test.

Informant. An individual who knows the child well and provides valuable information to the team.

Intelligence. A hypothesized construct used to describe cognitive abilities.

Intelligence Quotient (IQ). The score obtained on an intelligence test: IQ is usually expressed as a standardized score with a mean of 100 and a standard deviation of 15 or 16, depending on the test.

Intensity of Behavior. The strength of a behavior; a characteristic that can be measured.

Intercranial Hemorrhage. Bleeding within the skull.

Interdisciplinary Teams. Professionals from different disciplines, conducting separate assessments but sharing their plans and whenever possible incorporating activities from other disciplines into their interactions with the child.

Internal Consistency Reliability. The degree to which test items correlate with one another.

Internal Evaluator. An employee of the program who conducts a program evaluation.

Interpolation. The process of estimating scores within the ages and grades that were tested.

Interscorer/Interobserver/Interrater Reliability. An estimate of the extent to which two or more scorers, observers, or raters agree on how a test should be scored or behaviors should be observed.

Interval Recording. The recording of specific events or behaviors during a prespecified time interval.

Interval Scale. One of four scales of measurement (the others being nominal, ordinal, and ratio). The items on an interval scale are the same distance apart. The scale does not have an absolute zero.

Language. A system of symbols that are spoken, written, or expressed through manual signing to communicate meaning.

Latency Recording. A measurement of the amount of time that has elapsed between a behavior or event (or request to begin the behavior) and the beginning of the prespecified behavior.

Least Restrictive Environment (LRE). PL 101–476 (reauthorization of PL 94–142) specifies that to the maximum extent appropriate, children and youth with disabilities be educated with children who are nondisabled while also receiving special and related services as needed. PL 101–476 specifies that nonacademic and extracurricular services and activities be offered to maximize opportunities for interaction with nondisabled peers.

Leptokurtic Curve. A curve in which the scores are fast rising.

Maladaptive Behaviors. Behaviors considered to be problem behaviors.

Maturational Theory. A developmental theory emphasizing the importance of internal (to the child) features that are indicative of the child being "ready" to learn.

Mean. The average score.

Median. The score that occurs in the middle of a group of scores when they are ranked from high to low.

Mental Retardation. A child with mental retardation functions significantly below average in intellectual functioning and also exhibits deficits in adaptive behavior. Mental retardation is manifested during the developmental period.

Metacomponent. A cognitive process that helps in planning, monitoring, and evaluating an individual's performance of a task.

Microcephaly. A condition in which the head is abnormally small.

Mixed Hearing Loss. A combination of conductive and sensorineural hearing loss.

Mode. The most common or frequent test score in a distribution of scores.

Monitoring Individual Progress. The regular review of a child's work, accomplishments, and achievements by practitioners who are working directly with the child. *Step 4* in the assessment process.

Morphology. The study of single units of letters that comprise words.

Multidisciplinary Team. Professionals from different disciplines who conduct separate assessments, make plans, and independently implement the area of the written plan related to their respective disciplines. Family members also belong to this team.

Multiple Disabilities. A child has multiple disabilities (such as mental retardation and blindness, mental retardation and orthopedic impairment, etc.), the combination of which causes severe educational problems.

Near Visual Acuity. A measurement of near visual functioning, usually reported in inches, meters, or Jaeger chart numbers, which refer to type size.

Negatively Skewed Distribution. A distribution of scores in which the majority of scores are at the high end of the distribution.

Neurodevelopmental Treatment (NDT). A perspective that assumes that brain lesions interfere with normal development and emphasizes specific handling techniques that inhibit abnormal reflex activity and facilitate normal movement patterns.

Nominal Scale. Type of measurement scale in which the assigned values do not have any innate meaning. The other scales of measurement are ordinal, interval, and ratio.

Norm Group. A group of individuals to whom a child's performance can be compared.

Normal Curve. A symmetrical bell-shaped curve.

Normal Curve Equivalent (NCE). A standard score with a mean of 50 and a standard deviation of 21.06.

Norm-referenced Test. A test that compares a child's performance with those of similar children who have taken the same test.

Norms. Scores obtained by the standardization sample. The scores used for comparison when a norm-referenced test is administered to other children.

Observation. The process of systematically watching children or phenomena to gather information.

Obtained Score. The score the child gets on a test.

Ordinal Scale. Type of measurement scale in which the items are arranged in rank order. The other scales of measurement are nominal, interval, and ratio.

Orientation and Mobility. Orientation refers to the ability to determine one's position in the environment in order to move from place to place. Mobility refers to the ability to travel safely.

Orthopedic Impairment. This term includes disabilities caused by congenital anomaly (e.g., clubfoot, absence of an arm), disabilities caused by disease (e.g., poliomyelitis, bone tuberculosis), and disabilities from other causes (e.g., cerebral palsy, amputations, and fractures and burns that cause contractures).

Other Health Impairment. A child with a health impairment shows limited strength, vitality, or alertness due to chronic or acute health problems (e.g., heart condition, tuberculosis, rheumatic fever, epilepsy, etc.).

Otitis Media. Inflammation of the middle ear; a common condition among children.

Paresis. Weakness in movement.

Percentage Score. The percentage of test items that were answered correctly.

Percentile Rank. A derived score that expresses the percentage of children or scores that fall below a given raw score.

Performance Assessment. The demonstration of the same behavior that has been specified by the assessor.

Phenylketonuria (PKU). A condition in which the child lacks an essential enzyme for metabolizing the protein phenylaline. Left untreated, the protein builds up to toxic levels in the blood and eventually results in progressive damage to the brain causing severe retardation. Most hospitals routinely screen newborns for PKU using a urine or blood test.

Phonology. The study of individual sounds that comprise words.

PL 94–142. The Education for All Handicapped Children Act (amended in 1991 by PL 101–476, the Individuals with Disabilities Education Act) defines criteria for eligibility of school-age children with disabilities to receive special education or related services. In addition, this public law requires that all children from birth through twenty-one years of age who are suspected of having a disability be identified and evaluated.

PL 99–457. The Education for All Handicapped Children Act amendments (later included in PL 101–476) mandates the same provision of services to preschool children (ages three through five years). This law also requires that families be involved at all levels of identification, assessment, and intervention. In addition, these amendments offer incentives for states to provide interdisciplinary early intervention services to infants and toddlers.

PL 101–476. The Individuals with Disabilities Education Act (the reauthorization of PL 94–142 and PL 99–457) further defines eligibility criteria for children and youth with disabilities, ages three to twenty-one, to receive special education or related services. This law emphasizes "people first and then the disability" language.

PL 102–119. The Individuals with Disabilities Education Act amendments allow noncategorical definitions for eligibility for children three to five years under the term "developmental delay," according to a state's discretion. This law also permits local educational agencies to use IFSPs in lieu of IEPs for children ages three to five if consistent with state policy and if the parents concur.

Planning the Program. Deciding what to include in the IEP or IFSP. First the child's current level of functioning must be determined through assessment. Assessment of the child's environment is also an important aspect of planning. *Step 3* in the assessment process.

Platykurtic Curve. A curve in which the scores occur in a broad, flat distribution.

Play. An activity that gives pleasure, is flexible to change, is nonliteral, and is intrinsically motivating.

Play Assessment. The observation of a child or children for the purpose of understanding their developmental, sensorimotor, cognitive, communicative, social, and emotional functioning.

-plegia. Paralysis.

Population. The larger group from which a standardization sample is selected and to which individual comparisons are made regarding test performance.

Portfolio. A deliberate collection of the products of a child's play and work that demonstrates the individual's efforts, progress, and achievement.

Positively Skewed Distribution. A distribution of scores in which most of the scores are at the low end of the distribution.

Power Test. A test that is not timed.

Pragmatics. The study of the use of language in social situations.

Predictive Validity. The extent to which a given measure predicts later performance or behavior.

Product Evaluation. An assessment of specific characteristics of the products of children's work or play.

Proprioceptive Neuromuscular Facilitation (PNF). A perspective that assumes that as voluntary movement becomes stronger, incoordination will fade.

Qualitative Data. Descriptive information presented as words and text, not numbers.

Quantitative Data. Numerical descriptive information.

Quartile. A quartile contains 25% of the scores in a distribution or 25th percentile of scores.

Range. The distance between the highest and the lowest scores in a distribution of scores.

Rating Scale. Measurement of the degree to which a child exhibits a prespecified behavior.

Ratio Scale. A type of measurement scale in which the items are the same distance from each other; the scale has an absolute zero. The other scales of measurement are nominal, ordinal, and interval.

Raw Scores. The number of items correct without adjustment for guessing.

Readiness. The acquisition of prerequisite knowledge, skills, and behaviors that allow the child to benefit from instruction.

Readiness Tests. Tests that assess curriculum-related skills a child has already acquired.

Receptive Language. Spoken language that must be understood if communication is to take place.

Referral. A request for assistance; may be made by a parent or a professional who has concerns about the development and/or educational progress of a child.

Reliability. An indication of the consistency or stability of test performance.

Reliability Coefficient. A measure of the extent to which test scores are related.

Rubric. A scale used to assign points to different levels of performance.

Running Record. A description of events that is written as the events occur.

Sample. A subgroup of a larger group that represents the larger group. This is the group that is actually tested.

Scatter. The patterns or relationships among certain test items, tests, or subtests.

Scores of Relative Standing. A type of derived score that includes percentiles, standard scores, and stanines.

Screening. The identification of children who may be disabled or at risk for delay or disability and will be referred for further assessment. Screening typically involves testing large numbers of children, usually in a short amount of time. *Step 1* in the assessment process.

Semantics. The system of language that contains the rules for meaning.

Sensitivity. A screening instrument's ability to select children who should be referred for further assessment.

Sensorineural Hearing Loss. A hearing loss due to problems in the inner ear or auditory nerve. Examples of problems include tremors in the ear, brain damage, genetic problems, and infections.

Sensory Integration (SI). A theoretical perspective that focuses on the neurophysiological process in which sensory information is organized and interpreted.

Serious Emotional Disturbance. A child with a serious emotional disturbance exhibits one or more of the following characteristics over a long period of time and to a marked degree that adversely affects a child's educational performance: 1) an inability to learn that cannot be explained by intellectual, sensory, or health factors; 2) an inability to build or maintain satisfactory interpersonal relationships with peers and teachers; 3) inappropriate types of behavior or feelings under normal circumstances; 4) a general pervasive mood of unhappiness or depression; and 5) a tendency to develop physical symptoms or fears associated with personal or school problems.

Simultaneous Processing. A type of mental processing that is integrated or synthesized in order to obtain a solution.

Single-skill Test. A test that measures skills in one content area (e.g., mathematics).

Skewed Distribution. A curve in which most of the scores are at one end of the curve.

Specificity. The screening procedure's capacity to accurately select children who should not be identified.

Specific Learning Disability. A child with a specific learning disability exhibits a disorder in one or more of the basic psychological processes involved in understanding or in using language, spoken or written, that may manifest itself in an imperfect ability to listen, think, speak, read, write, spell, or do mathematical calculations. The term does not apply to children who have learning problems that are primarily the result of visual, hearing or motor disabilities, of mental retardation, of emotional disturbance, or of environmental, cultural, or economic disadvantage.

Specimen Records or Specimen Description. A detailed account of a specific event.

Speed Test. A test that is timed.

Split-half Reliability. An estimate of the correlation of scores between two halves of a test.

Stakeholders. Individuals who have an interest in the results of an evaluation.

Standard Deviation. A unit of measurement which indicates the amount of dispersion in a distribution. A measure of the degree to which a score deviates from the mean.

Standard Error of Measurement (SEM). The amount of error associated with individual test scores, test items, item samples, and test times.

Standardization Sample. A group of children who represent a larger group; the individuals who are actually tested.

Standard Scores. Raw scores that have been transformed so that they have the same mean and the same standard deviation.

Stanine. A type of standard score that has a mean of 5 and a standard deviation of 2; a distribution can be divided into nine stanines.

Successive Processing. A type of mental processing that requires that a problem be solved in sequential or serial order.

Summative Evaluations. Evaluations that occur at the end of the program or unit or at the completion of a period of time.

Syntax. The study of how words are combined to construct meaningful sentences.

Task Analysis. The process of breaking a certain skill or behavior into a series of substeps to assist the child in acquiring that skill.

Test. A series of questions, problems, or tasks designed to measure knowledge, skills, behavior, attitudes, development, or intelligence.

Test–Retest Reliability. An estimate of the correlation between scores when the same test is administered twice.

Tone. The resting state of a muscle.

Transdisciplinary Team. Professionals from different disciplines and family members who conduct assessment together and cooperatively plan services. Implementation is carried out by the primary service provider and the family members.

Traumatic Brain Injury. An acquired injury to the brain which was caused by an external force resulting in total or partial functional disability or psychosocial impairment, or both, that adversely affects a child's educational performance.

Tremors. Rapid, jerky, and involuntary movement due to lack of muscle control.

True Score. The score an individual would obtain on a test if there were no measurement errors.

T Scores. A type of standard score that has a mean of 50 and a standard deviation of 10.

Unidisciplinary Approach. An approach to assessment that involves one evaluator who works with the family and the child. This professional may have a background in education, allied health, nursing, speech and language, or social services.

Validity. The extent to which a test measures what it says it measures.

Validity Coefficient. The measure of the extent to which the performance is valid. The letter r is often used to represent a validity coefficient.

Visual Acuity, Test of. A measurement that provides information about how well a person can see.

Visual Impairment. An impairment in vision that, even with correction, adversely affects the child's educational performance. The term includes both partial sight and blindness.

z Scores. A type of standard score that has a mean of 0 and a standard score of ± 1.

Index